Eleventh Edition

STRATEGIC MANAGEMENT
and BUSINESS POLICY

CONCEPTS

Eleventh Edition

STRATEGIC MANAGEMENT
and BUSINESS POLICY

CONCEPTS

Thomas L. Wheelen
Wheelen Strategic Audits

J. David Hunger
Iowa State University
Saint John's University (MN)

PEARSON

Prentice
Hall

Upper Saddle River, NJ 07458

Library of Congress Cataloging-in-Publication Data
Wheelen, Thomas L.
   Strategic management and business policy. Concepts / Thomas L. Wheelen, J. David
Hunger. — Eleventh ed.
        p. cm.
   Includes bibliographical references and index.
   ISBN-13: 978-0-13-232319-2
   ISBN-10: 0-13-232319-2
1. Strategic planning.   I. Hunger, J. David, 1941-   II. Title.
   HD30.28.w43 2008
   658.4'012—dc22
A0   2007019807

Editor-in-Chief: David Parker
Acquisitions Editor: Bob Horan
Product Development Manager:
   Ashley Santora
Project Manager, Editorial:
   Claudia Fernandes
Assistant Editor: Denise Vaughn
Editorial Assistant: Kristen Varina
Media Project Manager: Ashley Lulling
Marketing Manager: Jodi Bassett
Marketing Assistant: Ian Gold
Associate Managing Editor: Renata Butera
Permissions Project Manager:
   Charles Morris

Senior Operations Supervisor: Arnold Vila
Operations Specialist: Michelle Klein
Art Director: Pat Smythe
Interior Design: Karen Quigley
Cover Design: Karen Quigley
Cover Illustration/Photo: Corbis/Jupiter
Composition: Aptara, Inc.
Full-Service Project Management:
   Aptara, Inc.
Printer/Binder: Courier/Kendallville
Typeface: 10/12 Times Roman

Pearson Education LTD.
Pearson Education Singapore, Pte. Ltd
Pearson Education, Canada, Ltd
Pearson Education-Japan

Pearson Education Australia PTY, Limited
Pearson Education North Asia Ltd
Pearson Educación de Mexico, S.A. de C.V.
Pearson Education Malaysia, Pte. Ltd.

10 9 8 7 6 5 4 3 2 1
ISBN-13: 978-0-13-232319-2
ISBN-10: 0-13-232319-2

Dedicated To

Kathy, Richard, and Tom

Betty, Kari and Jeff, Maddie and Megan, Suzi and Nick, Summer and Kacey, Lori and Dave, Merry and Dylan, and to Smokey the dog: Those for whom this book was written; and to Elizabeth Carey and Jackson S. Hunger—without whom there would be no book.

Special Dedication: *Thomas Wheelen expresses his admiration and indebtedness to* **Dr. Harry Page,** *Professor Emeritus of George Washington University. Dr. Page was a military leader, an excellent academic professor and administrator, a successful consultant and book author, and a true gentleman. Dr. Page was Tom Wheelen's dissertation chairman. Tom was his case grader for three years while in GW's doctoral program. Harry was an excellent role model for doctoral students. Tom ranks Harry among the top two or three men that he has had the honor to know.*

*This book is also dedicated to the following Prentice Hall sales representatives
who work so hard to promote this book:*

KEVIN AARON
DAVID ALEVY
GEORGE ALEXANDRIS
TARA ALGEO
KAY ALLEN
HECTOR AMAYA
PETER ANCONA
LAUREN ANDERSON
KATHY APOGEE
DAVID ARMSTRONG
RACHAEL AVERY
LINDA BABAT
NICK BAKER
BRAD BALABAN
HAL BALMER
ALICE BARR
SHERRY BARTEL
JESSICA BARTELT
JOHN BARTIZAL
KELLY BELL
KEITH BELLOFF
CATHY BENNETT
BILL BEVILLE
JOAN BLASCO-PAUL
JODI BOLOGNESE
JENNIFER BOYLE
CHARLENE BREWSTER
JULIE BROICH
JEANNE BRONSON
JARED BRUECKNER
ROSARIO BURGA-PINEYRUA
RUTH CARDIFF
MEREDITH CHANDLER
BEVERLY CHANNING
TARYLL CONNOLLY
DONNA CONROY
GEORGE COOK
CANDACE COONEY
JONATHAN COTTRELL
CYNDI CRIMMINS

KASEY CROCKETT
AMANDA CROTTS
DAN CURRIER
ERIN DAVIS
SHEILA DAVITT
SCOTT DAY
CHRISTOPHER DELANEY
IAN DESROSIERS
GEORGE DEVENNEY
WENDY DiLEONARDO
DANA DODGE
KATE DOLDER
BARBARA DONLON
AMY DUNKELBERGER
MATTHEW EARLY
TRISH EICHHOLD
CHRISTINE ELLINGTON
SUE FACKERT
TREY FEIGLE
DENNIS FERNANDES
MARY FERNANDEZ
KATIE FITCH
RACHEL FLANNERY
LINDSEY FLEISCHHAUER
CANDAS FLETCHER
JULIA FORD
BRAD FORRESTER
EVELYN FORTE
MARK GAFFNEY
JOSIE GALL
JESSICA GAMPER
AMBER GARDNER
ERIN GARDNER
CHERYL GEHRLICH
SYBIL GERAUD
CODY GILES
CHIP GILLIKIN
GINA GIMELLI
CAROLYN GOGOLIN
KERI GOLDBERG

ERIC GONZALES
LARRY GRANEC
JAY GUTHRIE
LOIS HAIGH
GREG HAITH
SANDI HAKANSON
GINNY HARBOLD
PAUL HARROLD
PHOENIX HARVEY
CARTER HASEGAWA
SARA HAUGEN
THOMAS HAYWARD
JESSICA HECTOR
JENNIFER HEILBRUNN
CHRISTINE HENRY
KATHERINE HEPBURN
LYNN HICKS
JULIE HILDEBRAND
DAUNNE HINGLE
KATIE HINKLE
KENT HUGHES
CHRISTINE HUMENIUK
CATHERINE HUTCHINSON
ANDREA IORIO
HEATHER JACKSON
MAIREAD JACOBY
PAM JEFFRIES
BETH JOHNSON
TOM JOHNSON
DAVID JURMAN
CHERYL KABB
KIMBERLY KANDEL
SUSAN KAPFF
GIA KAUL
LAUREN KEIBLER
ROCK KENDZIOR
MOLLY KETCHERSIDE
KIMBERLY KIEHLER
WALT KIRBY
EMILY KNIGHT

MARY-JO KOVACH
GREG KRAMP
EMILY KREIDER
MICHAEL KRISANDA
NICOLE KUNZMANN
DAVID KURZAWA
NILA LABORIEL
DAN LaCHAPELLE
GINA LaMANTIA
REBECCA LEIDY
APRIL LEMONS
ANDREA LINN
TRICIA LISCIO
JONATHAN LONGINO
DAVID LOPEZ
CARY LUNA
KELLY MANN
LAURA MANN
KIMBERLY MANZI
LISA MARCH
PATRICIA MARTINEZ
DEEDEE MARTINSON
SUSAN MATOS
CARRIE MATTAINI
BROOK MATTHEWS
JACK MAYLEBEN
KAREN McFADYEN
BRIAN McGARRY
IRENE McGUINNESS
RYAN McHENRY
KATE McKAIN
RAY MEDINA
MATT MESAROS
ANDREA MESSINEO
LAURA MIDDLETON
MAREN MILLER
CHRIS MILLIKAN
WHITNEY MONAHAN
KATE MOORE
JULIE MOREL
KATIE MORGAN
WYATT MORRIS

JENNIFER MOYERS
EARL MURPHY
BETSY NIXON
TOM NIXON
KIM NORBUTA
BRIAN NORMOYLE
CELESTE NOSSITER
DEBBIE OGILIVE
KATIE O'NEILL
SUE PALMER
TINA PANAGIOTOU
MATTHEW PASTIER
TONI PAYNE
MIKE PERMAN
CARRIE PIZZUTI
DAVID PLOSKONKA
BELEN POLTORAK
JIM PORTER HAMANN
JILL PROMESSO
STACEY PROPPS
JULIE RESLER
MARY RHODES
TELVIS RICH
TORIAN RICHARDSON
DAVID RINGLER
DAN ROBERTSON
CHRIS ROGERS
TESSA ROHDE
MICHAEL ROSEMAN
DOROTHY ROSENE
KELLY ROSS
RICH ROWE
GARY SACHECK
SUSAN SCHAUM
KRISTEN SCHMITT
CORRINA SCHULTZ
SCOTT SHAFER
KRISTINA SHUBEL
COLLETTE SIEVER
LEA SILVERMAN
PHYLLIS SIMON
ANGIE SMAJSTRLA

ROSS SMANIA
ELIZABETH SMITH
JANELL SMITH
KARA SMITH
KATE SPENCE
JEFF SPENCER
MATTHEW SPIEGEL
BEN STEPHEN
ANGELA STONE
BETH STONER
SUSAN STOUDT-SMITH
CINDY SULLIVAN
DAN SULLIVAN
LORI SULLIVAN
STEPHANIE SURFUS
KARIN SWANSON
LORI SYPHER
CHRISTINA TATE
DAVID THEISEN
SARAH THOMAS
NICHOLE THOMPSON
AMANDA TILLEY
FRANK TIMONEY
EMILY TRUMBOLD
JULIE TURLEY
HUNTER WAGNER
BALLARD WARD
MARY FRANCES WEATHERLY
LIZ WEIR
SHANNON WEIR
ERIC WEISS
DANIEL WELLS
TIFFANY WENDT
KIMBERLY WERNER
MARK WHEELER
LIZ WILDES
ERIN WILLIAMS
MONICA WOLFF
CRAIG WORTMANN
CINDY YATES
GEORGE YOUNG
SHARON YOUNG
ANDREW ZORICH

Brief Contents

Contents

Preface

Welcome to the 11th edition of *Concepts in Strategic Management and Business Policy*! This book contains the latest research and examples of well known and not-so-well-known companies dealing with complicated strategic issues. Enjoy!

How This Book Is Different from Other Strategy Textbooks

This book contains a **Strategic Management Model** that runs through the first 11 chapters and is made operational through the **Strategic Audit,** a complete case analysis methodology. The Strategic Audit provides a professional framework for case analysis in terms of external and internal factors and takes the student through the generation of strategic alternatives and implementation programs.

   To help the student synthesize the many factors in a complex strategy case, we developed three useful techniques:

- **External Factor Analysis (EFAS) Table in Chapter 4**
  This reduces the external Opportunities and Threats to the 8 to 10 most important external factors facing management.

- **Internal Factor Analysis (IFAS) Table in Chapter 5**
  This reduces the internal Strengths and Weaknesses to the 8 to 10 most important internal factors facing management.

- **Strategic Factor Analysis Summary (SFAS) Matrix in Chapter 6**
  This condenses the 16 to 20 factors generated in the EFAS and IFAS Tables into the 8 to 10 most important (strategic) factors facing the company. These strategic factors become the basis for generating alternatives and a recommendation for the company's future direction.

Suggestions for Case Analysis are provided in **Appendix 15.B (end of Chapter 15)** and contain step-by-step procedures for how to use the Strategic Audit in analyzing a case. This appendix includes an example of a student-written Strategic Audit. Thousands of students around the world have applied this methodology to case analysis with great success.

Time-Tested Features

This edition contains many of the same features and content that helped make previous editions successful. Some of the features are the following:

- A **strategic management model** runs throughout the first eleven chapters as a unifying concept. (Explained in *Chapter 1*)

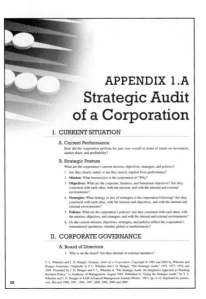

- The **strategic audit,** a way to operationalize the strategic decision-making process, serves as a checklist in case analysis. (***Chapter 1***) ▶

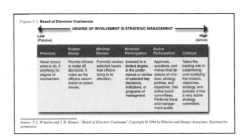

- **Corporate governance** is examined in terms of the roles, responsibilities, and interactions of top management and the board of directors and includes the impact of the Sarbanes-Oxley Act. (***Chapter 2***) ◀

- **Social responsibility and managerial ethics** are examined in detail in terms of how they affect strategic decision making. They include the process of stakeholder analysis and the concept of social capital. (***Chapter 3***) ▶

- Equal emphasis is placed on **environmental scanning** of the societal environment and on the task environment. Topics include forecasting and Miles and Snow's typology, in addition to competitive intelligence techniques and Porter's industry analysis. (***Chapter 4***) ◀

- **Core and distinctive competencies** are examined within the framework of the resource-based view of the firm. (***Chapter 5***)

- **Organizational analysis** includes material on business models, supply chain management, and corporate reputation. (***Chapter 5***)

- Internal and external strategic factors are emphasized through the use of specially designed **EFAS, IFAS**, and **SFAS tables.** (***Chapters 4, 5, and 6***)

- **Functional strategies** are examined in light of **outsourcing.** (***Chapter 8***)

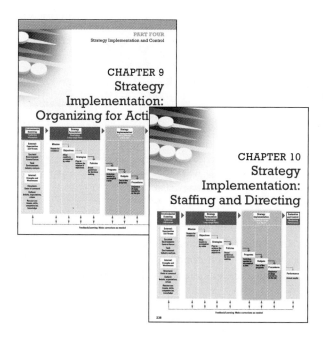

- Two chapters deal with issues in **strategy implementation,** such as organizational and job design plus strategy-manager fit, action planning, corporate culture, and international strategic alliances. (***Chapters 9 and 10***)

- A separate chapter on **evaluation and control** explains the importance of measurement and incentives to organizational performance. (***Chapter 11***)

- Special chapters deal with strategic issues in **managing technology and innovation, entrepreneurial ventures and small businesses,** and **not-for-profit organizations** (***Chapters 12, 13, and 14,*** respectively). These issues are often ignored by other strategy textbooks.

- **Suggestions for in-depth case analysis** provide a complete listing of financial ratios, recommendations for oral and written analysis, and ideas for further research. (***Chapter 15***)

- The **Strategic Audit Worksheet** is based on the time-tested strategic audit and is designed to help students organize and structure daily case preparation in a brief period of time. The worksheet works exceedingly well for checking the level of daily student case preparation—especially for open class discussions of cases. (**Chapter 15**) ▶

- An **experiential exercise** focusing on the material covered in each chapter helps the reader to apply strategic concepts to an actual situation. ◀

- A list of **key terms** and the pages in which they are discussed enable the reader to keep track of important concepts as they are introduced in each chapter.
- **Learning objectives** begin each chapter.
- **Strategy Bits** end each chapter with some interesting statistics.

The text has been class-tested in strategy courses and revised based on feedback from students and instructors. The first 11 chapters are organized around a strategic management model that begins each chapter and provides a structure for both content and case analysis. We emphasize those concepts that have proven to be most useful in understanding strategic decision making and in conducting case analysis. Our goal was to make the text as comprehensive as possible without getting bogged down in any one area. Endnote references are provided for those who wish to learn more about any particular topic.

Supplements

Supplemental materials are available to the instructor from the publisher. These include a *Concepts Instructor's Manual with Test Bank;* an *Instructor's Resource CD-ROM* containing testing software and PowerPoint files; videos; and a book-specific web site.

CONCEPTS INSTRUCTOR'S MANUAL

To aid in discussing the 15 chapters dealing with strategic management concepts, the *Concepts Instructor's Manual* includes:

1. *Suggestions for Teaching Strategic Management*—discusses various teaching methods and includes suggested course syllabi.

2. *Chapter Notes*—includes summaries of each chapter, suggested answers to discussion questions, and suggestions for using end-of-chapter cases/exercises, plus additional discussion questions (with answers) and lecture modules.

3. *Test questions*—contains more than 50 questions for each of the 15 chapters for a total of more than over 700 questions from which to choose. Questions include true/false, multiple choice, and essay.

INSTRUCTOR'S RESOURCE CD-ROM

The *Instructor's Resource CD-ROM* contains tools to facilitate the instructor's lectures and examinations. These include PowerPoint Electronic Transparency Masters containing figures and tables from the text. The instructor may customize these presentations and can present individual slides for student handouts. The CD also contains a computerized test bank of all the questions listed in the *Concepts Instructor's Manual*. Both Instructor's Manuals are included in the *Instructor's Resource CD-ROM,* as well as the video case notes for Newbury Comics.

VIDEO: NEWBURY COMICS

This video features part-ending segments shot at Newbury Comics, an exciting and current popular-culture retail chain. After beginning life as a store buying and selling used CDs, Newbury Comics has been expanding its product line and locations. Segments address key issues such as the company's basic model, mission and vision, and decision-making models. Accompanying case information can be found at the end of the parts in the concepts and full-volume text, and a video guide is included in the *Concepts Instructor's Manual*.

POWERPOINT SLIDES

PowerPoint slides, provided in a comprehensive package of text outlines and figures corresponding to the text, are designed to aid the educator and supplement in-class lectures. The PowerPoint slides can be found as ppt files on the Instructor's CD, as well as on the text web site, located at *www.prenhall.com/wheelen.*

COMPANION WEBSITE

The new Companion Website provides professors with a customized course. It features an online study guide for students that includes multiple choice, true/false, and essay questions. Instructors may download files from the Instructor's Manuals, PowerPoint slides, and test bank files from the Instructor's Resource Center link at the Companion Website. The site also includes additional min-cases for use in class. Point your browser to *www.prenhall.com/wheelen.*

Acknowledgments

We thank the many people at Prentice Hall who helped to make this edition possible. We thank our editor, David Parker. We are especially grateful to David's project manager, Claudia Fernandes, who managed to keep everything on an even keel. We also thank Renata Butera and Kelly Ricci who took the book through the production process.

In addition, we express our appreciation to Dr. Labh Hira, Dean, and Dr. Thomas Chacko, Management Department Chair, of Iowa State University's College of Business and to John Hasselberg, Management Department Chair of St. John's University, for their support and provision of the resources so necessary to produce a textbook. The University of South Florida provided no support for this book. Both of us acknowledge our debt to Dr. William Shenkir and Dr. Frank S. Kaulback, former Deans of the McIntire School of Commerce of the University of Virginia, for the provision of a work climate most supportive to the original development of this book.

Last to the many strategy instructors and students who have moaned to us about their problems with the strategy course: we have tried to respond to your problems and concerns as best we could by providing a comprehensive yet usable text. To you, the people who work hard in the strategy trenches, we acknowledge our debt. This book is yours.

T. L. W.
Tampa, Florida

J. D. H.
St. Joseph, Minnesota

Eleventh Edition

STRATEGIC MANAGEMENT
and BUSINESS POLICY

CONCEPTS

CHAPTER 1
Basic Concepts of Strategic Management

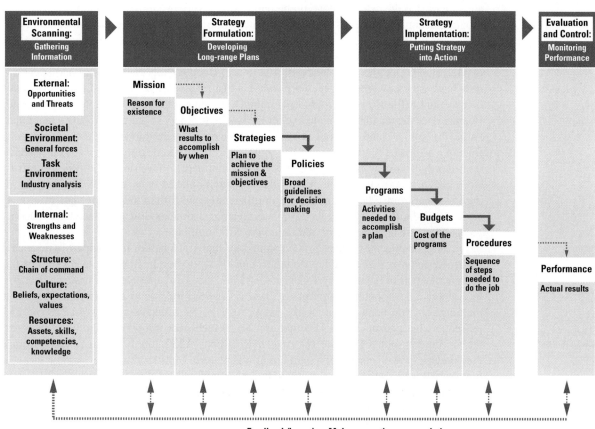

Environmental Scanning: Gathering Information	Strategy Formulation: Developing Long-range Plans	Strategy Implementation: Putting Strategy into Action	Evaluation and Control: Monitoring Performance

External: Opportunities and Threats

Societal Environment: General forces

Task Environment: Industry analysis

Internal: Strengths and Weaknesses

Structure: Chain of command

Culture: Beliefs, expectations, values

Resources: Assets, skills, competencies, knowledge

Mission
Reason for existence

Objectives
What results to accomplish by when

Strategies
Plan to achieve the mission & objectives

Policies
Broad guidelines for decision making

Programs
Activities needed to accomplish a plan

Budgets
Cost of the programs

Procedures
Sequence of steps needed to do the job

Performance
Actual results

Feedback/Learning: Make corrections as needed

Learning Objectives

After reading this chapter, you should be able to:

- Understand the benefits of strategic management
- Explain how globalization and electronic commerce influence strategic management
- Understand the basic model of strategic management
- Identify some common triggering events that act as stimuli for strategic change
- Understand strategic decision-making modes
- Use the strategic audit as a method of analyzing corporate functions and activities

HOW DOES A COMPANY BECOME SUCCESSFUL AND STAY SUCCESSFUL? CERTAINLY NOT BY playing it safe and following the traditional ways of doing business! This was the dilemma facing The Boeing Company, the well-known U.S.-based manufacturer of commercial and military aircraft, in 2004. Long the leader of the global airframe manufacturing industry, Boeing had been slowly losing market share since the 1990s to the European-based Airbus Industrie—a division of the European Aeronautic & Space Company (EADS). In December 2001, the EADS board of directors had committed the corporation to an objective it had never before achieved—taking from Boeing the leadership of the commercial aviation industry by building the largest commercial jet plane in the world, the Airbus 380. The A380 would carry 481 passengers in a normal multiple-class seating configuration compared to the 416 passengers carried by Boeing's 747-400 in a similar seating configuration. The A380 would not only fly 621 miles further than the 747, but it would cost airlines 15%–20% less per passenger to operate. With orders for 50 A380 aircraft in hand, the EADS board announced that the new plane would be ready for delivery during 2006. The proposed A380 program decimated the sales of Boeing's jumbo jet. Since 2000, airlines had ordered only 10 passenger Boeing 747s.

Boeing was clearly a company in difficulty in 2003. Distracted by the 1996 acquisitions of McDonnell Douglas and Rockwell Aerospace, Boeing's top management had spent the next few years strengthening the corporation's historically weak position in aerospace and defense and had allowed its traditional competency in commercial aviation to deteriorate. Boeing, once the manufacturing marvel of the world, was now spending 10%–20% more than Airbus to build a plane. The prices it asked for its planes were thus also higher. As a result, Boeing's estimated market share of the commercial market slid from nearly 70% in 1996 to less than half that by the end of 2003. Airbus claimed to have delivered 300 aircraft to Boeing's 285 and to have won 56% of the 396 orders placed by airlines in 2003—quite an improvement from 1994, when Airbus controlled only one-fifth of the market! This was quite an accomplishment, given that the A380 was so large that the modifications needed to accommodate it at airports would cost $80 million to $100 million.

Even though defense sales now accounted for more than half of the company's revenues, CEO Stonecifer realized that he needed to quickly act to regain Boeing's leadership of the commercial part of the industry. In December 2003, the board approved the strategic decision to promote a new commercial airplane, the Boeing 787, for sale to airlines. The 787 was a midrange aircraft, not a jumbo jet like the A380. The 787 would carry between 220 and 250 passengers but consume 20% less fuel and be 10% cheaper to operate than its competitor, Airbus' current midrange plane, the smaller wide-body A330-200. It was to be made from a graphite/epoxy resin instead of aluminum. It was planned to fly faster, higher, farther, cleaner, more quietly, and more efficiently than any other medium-sized jet. This was the first time since approving the 777 jet in 1990 that the company had launched an all-new plane program. Development costs were estimated at $8 billion over five years. Depending on the results of these sales efforts, the board would decide sometime during 2004 to either begin or cancel the 787 construction program. If the program was approved, the planes could be delivered in 2008—two years after the delivery of the A380.

The Boeing 787 decision was based on a completely different set of assumptions from those used by the EADS board to approve the A380. EADS' top management believed that the commercial market wanted even larger jumbo jets to travel long international routes. Airports in Asia, the Middle East, and Europe were becoming heavily congested. In these locations, the "hub-and-spoke" method of creating major airline hubs was flourishing. Using larger planes was a way of dealing with that congestion by flying more passengers per plane out of these hubs. EADS' management believed that over the next 20 years, airlines and freight carriers would need a minimum of 1,500 more aircraft at least as big as the B747. EADS' management had concluded that the key to controlling the future commercial market was by using larger, more expensive planes. The A380 was a very large bet on that future scenario. The A380 program would cost EADS almost $13 million before the first plane was delivered.

In contrast, Boeing's management believed in a very different future scenario. Noting the success of Southwest and JetBlue, among other airlines in North America, it concluded that no more than 320 extra-large planes would be sold in the future as the airline industry moved away from hub-and-spoke networks toward more direct flights between smaller airports. The fragmentation of the airline industry, with its emphasis on competing through lower costs, was the primary rationale for Boeing's fuel-efficient 787. A secondary reason was to deal with increasing passenger complaints about shrinking legroom and seat room on current planes flown by cost-conscious airlines. The 787 was designed with larger windows, seats, lavatories, and overhead bins. The plane was being designed in both short- and long-range versions. Boeing's management predicted a market for 2,000 to 3,000 such planes. Additional support for the midrange plane came from some industry analysts who predicted that the huge A380 would give new meaning to the term "cattle class." To reach necessary economies of scale, the A380 would likely devote a large portion of both of its decks to economy class, with passengers sitting three or four across, the same configuration as most of Boeing's 747s. "What's in it for me to sit on an airplane with 500 other people, wait for my bags with 500 other people, and check in with 500 other people?" asked Continental Airlines' chief, Gordon Bethune.

Which vision of the future was correct? The long-term fortunes of both Boeing and Airbus depended on two very different strategic decisions, based on two very different assessments of the market. If Airbus was correct, the market would continue to demand ever-larger airplanes. If Boeing was correct, the current wave of jumbo jets had crested, and a new wave of fuel-saving midrange jets would soon replace them. Which company's strategy had the best chance of succeeding?[1]

1.1 The Study of Strategic Management

Strategic management is that set of managerial decisions and actions that determines the long-run performance of a corporation. It includes environmental scanning (both external and internal), strategy formulation (strategic or long-range planning), strategy implementation, and evaluation and control. The study of strategic management, therefore, emphasizes the monitoring and evaluating of external opportunities and threats in light of a corporation's strengths and weaknesses. Originally called business policy, strategic management incorporates such topics as strategic planning, environmental scanning, and industry analysis.

Phases of Strategic Management

Many of the concepts and techniques that deal with strategic management have been developed and used successfully by business corporations such as General Electric and the Boston Consulting Group. Over time, business practitioners and academic researchers have expanded and refined these concepts. Initially, strategic management was of most use to large corporations operating in multiple industries. Increasing risks of error, costly mistakes, and even economic ruin are causing today's professional managers in all organizations to take strategic management seriously in order to keep their companies competitive in an increasingly volatile environment.

As managers attempt to better deal with their changing world, a firm generally evolves through the following four **phases of strategic management**[2]:

Phase 1—Basic financial planning: Managers initiate serious planning when they are requested to propose the following year's budget. Projects are proposed on the basis of very little analysis, with most information coming from within the firm. The sales force usually provides the small amount of environmental information. Such simplistic operational planning only pretends to be strategic management, yet it is quite time-consuming. Normal company activities are often suspended for weeks while managers try to cram ideas into the proposed budget. The time horizon is usually one year.

Phase 2—Forecast-based planning: As annual budgets become less useful at stimulating long-term planning, managers attempt to propose five-year plans. At this point, they consider projects that may take more than one year. In addition to internal information, managers gather any available environmental data—usually on an ad hoc basis—and extrapolate current trends five years into the future. This phase is also time-consuming, often involving a full month of managerial activity to make sure all the proposed budgets fit together. The process gets very political as managers compete for larger shares of funds. Endless meetings take place to evaluate proposals and justify assumptions. The time horizon is usually three to five years.

Phase 3—Externally oriented (strategic) planning: Frustrated with highly political yet ineffectual five-year plans, top management takes control of the planning process by initiating strategic planning. The company seeks to increase its responsiveness to changing markets and competition by thinking strategically. Planning is taken out of the hands of lower-level managers and concentrated in a planning staff whose task is to develop strategic plans for the corporation. Consultants often provide the sophisticated and innovative techniques that the planning staff uses to gather information and forecast future trends. Ex-military experts develop competitive intelligence units. Upper-level managers meet once a year at a resort "retreat" led by key members of the planning staff to evaluate and update the current strategic plan. Such top-down planning emphasizes formal strategy formulation and leaves the implementation issues to lower management levels. Top management typically develops five-year plans with help from consultants but minimal input from lower levels.

Phase 4—Strategic management: Realizing that even the best strategic plans are worthless without the input and commitment of lower-level managers, top management forms planning groups of managers and key employees at many levels, from various departments and workgroups. They develop and integrate a series of strategic plans aimed at achieving the company's primary objectives. Strategic plans at this point detail the implementation, evaluation, and control issues. Rather than attempting to perfectly forecast the future, the plans emphasize probable scenarios and contingency strategies. The sophisticated annual five-year strategic plan is replaced with strategic thinking at all levels of the organization throughout the year. Strategic information, previously available only centrally to top management, is available via local area networks and intranets to people throughout the organization. Instead of a large centralized planning staff, internal and external planning consultants are available to help guide group strategy discussions. Although top management may still initiate the strategic planning process, the resulting strategies may come from anywhere in the organization. Planning is typically interactive across levels and is no longer top down. People at all levels are now involved.

General Electric, one of the pioneers of strategic planning, led the transition from strategic planning to strategic management during the 1980s.[3] By the 1990s, most other corporations around the world had begun the conversion to strategic management.

Benefits of Strategic Management

Research has revealed that organizations that engage in strategic management generally outperform those that do not.[4] The attainment of an appropriate match, or "fit," between an organization's environment and its strategy, structure, and processes has positive effects on the organization's performance.[5] For example, studies of the impact of deregulation on the U.S. railroad and trucking industries found that companies that changed their strategies and structures as their environment changed outperformed companies that did not change.[6]

A survey of nearly 50 corporations in a variety of countries and industries found the three most highly rated benefits of strategic management to be:

- Clearer sense of strategic vision for the firm
- Sharper focus on what is strategically important
- Improved understanding of a rapidly changing environment[7]

To be effective, however, strategic management need not always be a formal process. It can begin with a few simple questions:

1. Where is the organization now? (Not where do we hope it is!)
2. If no changes are made, where will the organization be in 1 year? 2 years? 5 years? 10 years? Are the answers acceptable?
3. If the answers are not acceptable, what specific actions should management undertake? What are the risks and payoffs involved?

In 2003, Bain & Company's annual Management Tools Survey of senior executives at 708 companies on five continents revealed the most popular management tools to be strategic planning (used by 89% of firms) and developing mission and vision statements (used by 84%)—essential parts of strategic management.[8] Research into the planning practices of companies in the oil industry concludes that the real value of modern strategic planning is more in the *strategic thinking* and *organizational learning* that is part of a future-oriented planning process than in any resulting written strategic plan.[9] Small companies, in particular, may plan informally and irregularly. Nevertheless, studies of small and medium-sized businesses reveal that the greater the level of planning intensity, as measured by the presence of a formal strategic plan, the greater the level of financial performance, especially when measured in terms of sales increases.[10]

Planning the strategy of large, multidivisional corporations can be complex and time-consuming. It often takes slightly more than a year for a large company to move from situation assessment to a final decision agreement. For example, strategic plans in the global oil industry tend to cover four to five years. The planning horizon for oil exploration is even longer—up to 15 years.[11] Because of the relatively large number of people affected by a strategic decision in a large firm, a formalized, more sophisticated system is needed to ensure that strategic planning leads to successful performance. Otherwise, top management becomes isolated from developments in the business units, and lower-level managers lose sight of the corporate mission and objectives.

1.2 | **Globalization and Electronic Commerce: Challenges to Strategic Management**

Not too long ago, a business corporation could be successful by focusing only on making and selling goods and services within its national boundaries. International considerations were minimal. Profits earned from exporting products to foreign lands were considered frosting on the cake but not really essential to corporate success. During the 1960s, for example, most U.S. companies organized themselves around a number of product divisions that made and sold goods only in the United States. All manufacturing and sales outside the United States were typically managed through one international division. An international assignment was usually considered a message that the person was no longer promotable and should be looking for another job.

Similarly, until the mid-1990s, a business firm could be very successful without using the Internet for anything more than as a public relations web site. Most business was done through a sales force and a network of distributors, with the eventual sale to the consumer being made through retail outlets. Few executives used personal computers, let alone surfed the World Wide Web. The Internet may have been useful for research, but until recently it was not seriously viewed as a means to actually conduct normal business transactions.

Impact of Globalization

Today, everything has changed. **Globalization**, the internationalization of markets and corporations, has changed the way modern corporations do business. To reach the economies of scale necessary to achieve the low costs, and thus the low prices, needed to be competitive, companies are now thinking of a global (worldwide) market instead of a national market. Nike and Reebok, for example, manufacture their athletic shoes in various countries throughout Asia for sale on every continent. Like Nike and Reebok, many other companies in North America and Western Europe are outsourcing their manufacturing, software development, or customer service to companies in China, Eastern Europe, or India. Instead of using one international division to manage everything outside the home country, large corporations are now using matrix structures in which product units are interwoven with country or regional units. International assignments are now considered key for anyone interested in reaching top management.

As more industries become global, strategic management is becoming an increasingly important way to keep track of international developments and position a company for long-term competitive advantage. For example, General Electric moved a major research and development lab for its medical systems division from Japan to China in order to learn more about developing new products for developing economies. According to Wilbur Chung, a Wharton professor, "Whatever China develops is rolled out to the rest of the world. China may have a lower GDP per-capita than developed countries, but the Chinese have a strong sense of how products should be designed for their market."[12]

The formation of regional trade associations and agreements, such as the European Union, NAFTA, Mercosur, CAFTA, and ASEAN, is changing how international business is being conducted. See the GLOBAL ISSUE feature to learn how regional trade associations are forcing corporations to establish a manufacturing presence wherever they wish to market goods or else face significant tariffs. These associations have led to the increasing harmonization of standards so that products can more easily be sold and moved across national boundaries. International considerations have led to the strategic alliance between British Airways and American Airlines and to the merger between Daimler-Benz and Chrysler Corporation, among others.

GL🌐BAL ISSUE

Regional Trade Associations Replace National Trade Barriers

The **European Union (EU)** is the most significant trade association in the world. The goal of the EU is the complete economic integration of its 25 member countries so that goods made in one part of Europe can move freely, without ever stopping for a customs inspection. The EU includes Austria, Belgium, Denmark, Finland, France, Germany, Greece, Ireland, Italy, Luxembourg, The Netherlands, Portugal, Spain, Sweden, the United Kingdom plus the 10 countries admitted in 2004: Czech Republic, Estonia, Hungary, Latvia, Lithuania, Poland, Slovakia, Slovenia, Cyprus, and Malta. Romania and Bulgaria hope to join in 2007. Others, including Croatia, Macedonia, and Turkey, have either recently applied or are in the process of applying. One currency, the euro, is being used throughout the region as members integrate their monetary systems. The steady elimination of barriers to free trade is providing the impetus for a series of mergers, acquisitions, and joint ventures among business corporations. The requirement of at least 60% local content to avoid tariffs has forced many U.S. and Asian companies to abandon exporting in favor of having a strong local presence in Europe.

Canada, the United States, and Mexico are affiliated economically under the **North American Free Trade Agreement (NAFTA)**. The goal of NAFTA is improved trade among the three member countries rather than complete economic integration. Launched in 1994, the agreement requires all three members to remove all tariffs among themselves over 15 years, but they are allowed to have their own tariff arrangements with nonmember countries. Cars and trucks must have 62.5% North American content to qualify for duty-free status. Transportation restrictions and other regulations are being significantly reduced. Some Asian and European corporations are locating operations in one of the NAFTA countries to obtain access to the entire North American region. Vicente Fox, the President of Mexico, proposed that NAFTA become more like the European Union in that both people and goods should have unlimited access across borders from Mexico to Canada. A number of corporations, such as Sweden's Electrolux, are building manufacturing facilities in Mexico to take advantage of the country's lower wages and easy access to U.S. and Canadian markets.

South American countries are also working to harmonize their trading relationships with each other and to form

trade associations. The establishment of the **Mercosur** (**Mercosul**, in Portuguese) free-trade area among Argentina, Brazil, Uruguay, and Paraguay means that a manufacturing presence within these countries is becoming essential to avoid tariffs for nonmember countries. Claiming to be NAFTA's southern counterpart, Mercosur has extended free-trade agreements to Bolivia and Venezuela. With Chile and Argentina cooperating to build a tunnel through the Andes to connect the two countries, it is likely that Chile may also form an economic relationship with Mercosur.

In 2004, the five Central American countries of El Salvador, Guatemala, Honduras, Nicaragua, and Costa Rica, and the Dominican Republic, plus the United States signed the **Central American Free Trade Agreement (CAFTA)**. Previously, Central American textile manufacturers had to pay import duties of 18%–28% to sell their clothes in the United States unless they bought their raw material from U.S. companies. Under CAFTA, members can buy raw material from anywhere, and their exports are duty free. In addition, CAFTA eliminates import duties on 80% of all U.S. consumer and industrial goods exported to CAFTA countries and all duties on many U.S. farm exports. The agreement awaits ratification by the U.S. Congress before going into effect.

Asia has yet no comparable regional trade association to match the potential economic power of either NAFTA or the EU. Japan, South Korea, China, and India generally operate as independent economic powers. Nevertheless, the **Association of Southeast Asian Nations (ASEAN)**—composed of Brunei Darussalam, Indonesia, Malaysia, Philippines, Singapore, Thailand, Laos, Myanmar, Cambodia, and Vietnam—is attempting to link its members into a borderless economic zone. Increasingly referred to as ASEAN+3, it now includes China, Japan, and South Korea in its annual summit meetings. The ASEAN nations negotiated linkage of the ASEAN Free Trade Area (AFTA) with the existing free trade area of Australia and New Zealand. With the EU extending eastward and NAFTA extending southward to someday connect with CAFTA and Mercosur, pressure is already building on the independent Asian nations to form an expanded version of ASEAN.

Electronic Commerce

Electronic commerce refers to the use of the Internet to conduct business transactions. The Internet is reshaping the global marketplace, and it will continue to do so for many more years. Not only is the Internet changing the way customers, suppliers, and companies interact, it is changing the way companies work internally. Since its introduction, it has profoundly affected the basis of competition in many industries. Instead of the traditional focus on product features and costs, the Internet is shifting the basis for competition to a more strategic level in which the traditional value chain of an industry is drastically altered. A report by AMR Research indicated that industry leaders are in the process of moving 60%–100% of their business-to-business (B2B) transactions to the Internet. The net B2B marketplace includes (a) trading exchange platforms such as VerticalNet and i2 Technologies' TradeMatrix, which support trading communities in multiple markets; (b) industry-sponsored exchanges, such as the one being built by major automakers; and (c) net market makers, such as e-Steel, NECX, and BuildPoint, which focus on a specific industry's value chain or business processes to mediate multiple transactions among businesses.

The Internet either causes or accelerates seven current world-wide trends[13]:

1. The Internet is forcing companies to transform themselves. The concept of electronically networking customers, suppliers, and partners is now a reality.

2. New channels are changing market access and branding, causing the *disintermediation* (breaking down) of traditional distribution channels. By working directly with customers, companies are able to avoid the usual distributors—thus forming closer relationships with the end-users, improving service, and reducing costs.

3. The balance of power is shifting to the consumer. Now having unlimited access to information on the Internet, customers are much more demanding than their "non-wired" predecessors.

4. Competition is changing. New technology-driven firms plus older traditional competitors are exploiting the Internet to become more innovative and efficient.

5. The pace of business is increasing drastically. Planning horizons, information needs, and customer/supplier expectations are reflecting the immediacy of the Internet. Because of this turbulent environment, time is compressed into "dog years," in which one year feels like seven years.

6. The Internet is pushing corporations out of their traditional boundaries. The traditional separation between suppliers, manufacturers, and customers is becoming blurred with the development and expansion of extranets, in which cooperating firms have access to each other's internal operating plans and processes. For example, Lockheed Martin, the aerospace company, has an extranet that links Lockheed to Boeing, a project partner, and to the U.S. Department of Defense, a key customer.

7. Knowledge is becoming a key asset and a source of competitive advantage. For example, traditional accounting assets, such as cash and equipment, accounted for about 80% of the total market value of the Standard & Poor 500 firms in 1982, but they accounted for only about 25% in 2002. The remainder of the market value is composed of *intangible assets*, primarily powerful brands as well as intellectual capital, such as key relationships, proprietary processes, and skilled employees.[14]

1.3 | Theories of Organizational Adaptation

Globalization and electronic commerce present real challenges to the strategic management of business corporations. How can any one company keep track of all the changing technological, economic, political–legal, and sociocultural trends around the world and make the necessary adjustments? This is not an easy task. Various theories have been proposed to account for how organizations obtain fit with their environment. The theory of **population ecology**, for example, proposes that once an organization is successfully established in a particular environmental niche, it is unable to adapt to changing conditions. Inertia prevents the organization from changing. The company is thus replaced (is bought out or goes bankrupt) by other organizations more suited to the new environment. Although it is popular in sociology, research fails to support the arguments of population ecology.[15] **Institution theory**, in contrast, proposes that organizations can and do adapt to changing conditions by imitating other successful organizations. To its credit, many examples can be found of companies that have adapted to changing circumstances by imitating an admired firm's strategies and management techniques.[16] The theory does not, however, explain how or by whom successful new strategies are developed in the first place. The **strategic choice perspective** goes one step further by proposing that not only do organizations adapt to a changing environment, they also have the opportunity and power to reshape their environment. This perspective is supported by research indicating that the decisions of a firm's management have at least as great an impact on firm performance as overall industry factors.[17] Because of its emphasis on managers making rational strategic decisions, the strategic choice perspective is the dominant one taken in strategic management. Its argument that adaptation is a dynamic process fits with the view of **organizational learning theory**, which says that an organization adjusts defensively to a changing environment and uses knowledge offensively to improve the fit between itself and its environment. This perspective expands the strategic choice perspective to include people at all levels becoming involved in providing input into strategic decisions.[18]

In agreement with the concepts of organizational learning theory, an increasing number of companies are realizing that they must shift from a vertically organized, top-down type of organization to a more horizontally managed, interactive organization. They are attempting to adapt more quickly to changing conditions by becoming "learning organizations."

1.4 | Creating a Learning Organization

Strategic management has now evolved to the point that its primary value is in helping an organization operate successfully in a dynamic, complex environment. Inland Steel Company, for example, uses strategic planning as a tool to drive organizational change. Managers at all levels are expected to continually analyze the changing steel industry in order to create or modify strategic plans throughout the year.[19] To be competitive in dynamic environments, corporations are becoming less bureaucratic and more flexible. In stable environments such as those that existed in years past, a competitive strategy simply involved defining a competitive position and then defending it. As it takes less and less time for one product or technology to replace another, companies are finding that there is no such thing as a permanent competitive advantage. Many agree with Richard D'Aveni, who says in his book *Hypercompetition* that any sustainable competitive advantage lies not in doggedly following a centrally managed five-year plan but in stringing together a series of strategic short-term thrusts (as Intel does by cutting into the sales of its own offerings with periodic introductions of new products).[20] This means that corporations must develop *strategic flexibility*—the ability to shift from one dominant strategy to another.[21]

Strategic flexibility demands a long-term commitment to the development and nurturing of critical resources. It also demands that the company become a **learning organization**—an organization skilled at creating, acquiring, and transferring knowledge and at modifying its behavior to reflect new knowledge and insights. Organizational learning is a critical component of competitiveness in a dynamic environment. It is particularly important to innovation and new product development.[22] For example, Hewlett-Packard uses an extensive network of informal committees to transfer knowledge among its cross-functional teams and to help spread new sources of knowledge quickly.[23] Learning organizations are skilled at four main activities:

- Solving problems systematically
- Experimenting with new approaches

- Learning from their own experiences and past history as well as from the experiences of others

- Transferring knowledge quickly and efficiently throughout the organization[24]

Business historian Alfred Chandler proposes that high-technology industries are defined by "paths of learning" in which organizational strengths derive from learned capabilities.[25] According to Chandler, companies spring from an individual entrepreneur's knowledge, which then evolves into organizational knowledge. This organizational knowledge is composed of three basic strengths: technical skills, mainly in research; functional knowledge, such as production and marketing; and managerial expertise. This knowledge leads to new businesses where the company can succeed and creates an entry barrier to new competitors. Chandler points out that once a corporation has built its learning base to the point where it has become a core company in its industry, entrepreneurial startups are rarely able to successfully enter. Thus, organizational knowledge becomes a competitive advantage.

Strategic management is essential for learning organizations to avoid stagnation through continuous self-examination and experimentation. People at all levels, not just top management, participate in strategic management—helping to scan the environment for critical information, suggesting changes to strategies and programs to take advantage of environmental shifts, and working with others to continuously improve work methods, procedures, and evaluation techniques. For example, Motorola developed an action learning format in which people from marketing, product development, and manufacturing meet to argue and reach agreement about the needs of the market, the best new product, and the schedules of each group producing it. This action learning approach overcame the problems that arose previously when the three departments met and formally agreed on plans but continued with their work as if nothing had happened.[26] Research indicates that involving more people in the strategy process results in people not only viewing the process more positively but also acting in ways that make the process more effective.[27]

Organizations that are willing to experiment and are able to learn from their experiences are more successful than those that do not.[28] For example, in a study of U.S. manufacturers of diagnostic imaging equipment, the most successful firms were those that improved products sold in the United States by incorporating some of what they had learned from their manufacturing and sales experiences in other nations. The less successful firms used the foreign operations primarily as sales outlets, not as important sources of technical knowledge.[29]

1.5 | Basic Model of Strategic Management

Strategic management consists of four basic elements:

- **Environmental scanning**
- **Strategy formulation**
- **Strategy implementation**
- **Evaluation and control**

Figure 1–1 illustrates how these four elements interact; **Figure 1–2** expands each of these elements and serves as the model for this book.[30] The terms used in **Figure 1–2** are explained on the following pages.

Environmental Scanning

Environmental scanning is the monitoring, evaluating, and disseminating of information from the external and internal environments to key people within the corporation. Its purpose is to identify **strategic factors**—external and internal elements that will determine the future of the corporation. The simplest way to conduct environmental scanning is through **SWOT**

Figure 1–1
Basic Elements of the Strategic Management Process

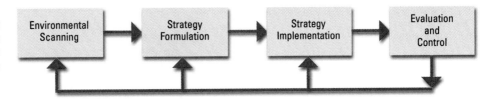

Analysis. SWOT is an acronym used to describe the particular strengths, weaknesses, opportunities, and threats that are strategic factors for a specific company. The **external environment** consists of variables (opportunities and threats) that are outside the organization and not typically within the short-run control of top management. These variables form the context within which the corporation exists. **Figure 1–3** depicts key environmental variables. They may be general forces and trends within the overall societal environment or specific factors that operate within an organization's specific task environment—often called its *industry*. (These external variables are defined and discussed in more detail in **Chapter 4**.)

The **internal environment** of a corporation consists of variables (Strengths and Weaknesses) that are within the organization itself and are not usually within the short-run control of top management. These variables form the context in which work is done. They include the corporation's structure, culture, and resources. Key strengths form a set of core

Figure 1–2 **Strategic Management Model**

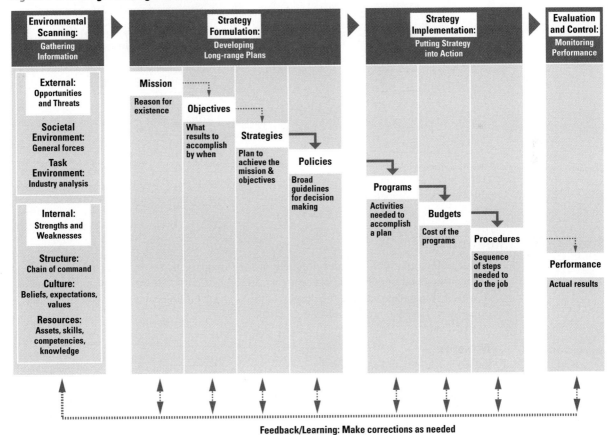

Feedback/Learning: Make corrections as needed

Source: T. L. Wheelen, "Strategic Management Model," adapted from "Concepts of Management," presented to Society for Advancement of Management (SAM), International Meeting, Richmond, VA, 1981. Copyright © 1981 by T. L. Wheelen and SAM. Copyright © 1982, 1985, 1988, and 2005 by T. L. Wheelen and J. D. Hunger. Revised 1989, 1995, 1998, 2000, and 2005. Reprinted by permission.

Figure 1–3
**Environmental
Variables**

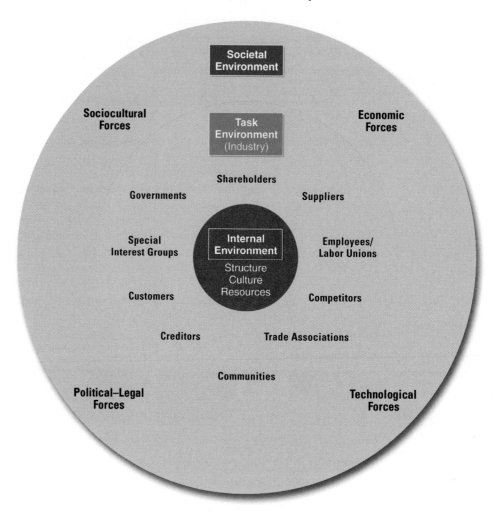

competencies that the corporation can use to gain competitive advantage. (These internal variables and core competencies are defined and discussed in more detail in **Chapter 5**.)

Strategy Formulation

Strategy formulation is the development of long-range plans for the effective management of environmental opportunities and threats, in light of corporate strengths and weaknesses (SWOT). It includes defining the corporate mission, specifying achievable objectives, developing strategies, and setting policy guidelines.

Mission

An organization's **mission** is the purpose or reason for the organization's existence. It tells what the company is providing to society—either a service such as housecleaning or a product such as automobiles. A well-conceived mission statement defines the fundamental, unique purpose that sets a company apart from other firms of its type and identifies the scope of the company's operations in terms of products (including services) offered and markets served. It may also include the firm's values and philosophy about how it does business and treats its employees. It puts into words not only what the company is now but what it wants to become—management's strategic vision of the firm's future. The mission statement promotes a sense of shared expectations in employees and communicates a public image to important stakeholder groups in the company's task environment. Some people like to consider vision and mission as two different concepts: A *mission statement* describes what the organization is now; a *vision statement* describes what the organization would like to become. We prefer to combine these ideas into a single mission statement.[31] Some companies prefer to list their values and philosophy of doing business in a separate publication called a *values statement*. For a listing of the many things that could go into a mission statement, see STRATEGY HIGHLIGHT 1.1.

One example of a mission statement is that of Maytag Corporation:

To improve the quality of home life by designing, building, marketing, and servicing the best appliances in the world.

Another classic example is that etched in bronze at Newport News Shipbuilding, unchanged since its founding in 1886:

We shall build good ships here—at a profit if we can—at a loss if we must—but always good ships.[32]

A mission may be defined narrowly or broadly in scope. An example of a *broad* mission statement is that used by many corporations: "Serve the best interests of shareowners, customers, and employees." A broadly defined mission statement such as this keeps the company from restricting itself to one field or product line, but it fails to clearly identify either what it makes or which products/markets it plans to emphasize. Because this broad statement is so general, a *narrow* mission statement, such as the preceding one by Maytag, which emphasizes appliances, is generally more useful. A narrow mission very clearly states the organization's primary busi-

STRATEGY HIGHLIGHT 1.1

Do You Have a Good Mission Statement?

Andrew Campbell, a director of the Ashridge Strategic Management Centre and a long-time contributor to *Long Range Planning*, proposes a means for evaluating a mission statement. Arguing that mission statements can be more than just an expression of a company's purpose and ambition, he suggests that they can also be a company flag to rally around, a signpost for all stakeholders, a guide to behavior, and a celebration of a company's culture. For a company trying to achieve all of the above, evaluate its mission statement using the following 10-question test. Score each question 0 for no, 1 for somewhat, or 2 for yes. According to Campbell, a score of over 15 is exceptional, and a score of less than 10 suggests that more work needs to be done.

1. Does the statement describe an inspiring purpose that avoids playing to the selfish interests of the stakeholders?

2. Does the statement describe the company's responsibility to its stakeholders?

3. Does the statement define a business domain and explain why it is attractive?

4. Does the statement describe the strategic positioning that the company prefers in a way that helps to identify the sort of competitive advantage it will look for?

5. Does the statement identify values that link with the organization's purpose and act as beliefs with which employees can feel proud?

6. Do the values resonate with and reinforce the organization's strategy?

7. Does the statement describe important behavior standards that serve as beacons of the strategy and the values?

8. Are the behavior standards described in a way that enables individual employees to judge whether they are behaving correctly?

9. Does the statement give a portrait of the company, capturing the culture of the organization?

10. Is the statement easy to read?

Source: Reprinted from *Long Range Planning*, Vol. 30, No. 6, 1997, Campbell, "Mission Statements," pp. 931–932. Copyright © 1997 with permission of Elsevier.

ness, but it may limit the scope of the firm's activities in terms of the product or service offered, the technology used, and the market served. Research indicates that a narrow mission statement may be best in a turbulent industry because it keeps the firm focused on what it does best; a broad mission statement may be best in a stable environment that lacks growth opportunities.[33]

Objectives

Objectives are the end results of planned activity. They should be stated as *action verbs* and tell what is to be accomplished by when and quantified if possible. The achievement of corporate objectives should result in the fulfillment of a corporation's mission. In effect, this is what society gives back to the corporation when the corporation does a good job of fulfilling its mission. For example, by providing society with office supplies of every kind for home and work at better quality, price, and location than its competitors, Staples has become one of the most successful retailers in the United States. Even though the office supplies market is maturing, Staples' management established the twin objectives of doubling sales to $20 billion from 2003 to 2008 while boosting net income more than 20% annually.[34]

The term *goal* is often used interchangeably with the term *objective*. In this book, we prefer to differentiate the two terms. In contrast to an objective, we consider a **goal** as an open-ended statement of what one wants to accomplish, with no quantification of what is to be achieved and no time criteria for completion. For example, a simple statement of "increased profitability" is thus a goal, not an objective, because it does not state how much profit the firm wants to make or when. A good objective should be action oriented and begin with the word *to*. An example of an objective is "to increase the firm's profitability in 2007 by 10% over 2006."

Some of the areas in which a corporation might establish its goals and objectives are:

- Profitability (net profits)
- Efficiency (low costs, etc.)
- Growth (increase in total assets, sales, etc.)
- Shareholder wealth (dividends plus stock price appreciation)
- Utilization of resources (ROE or ROI)
- Reputation (being considered a "top" firm)
- Contributions to employees (employment security, wages, diversity)
- Contributions to society (taxes paid, participation in charities, provision of a needed product or service)
- Market leadership (market share)
- Technological leadership (innovations, creativity)
- Survival (avoiding bankruptcy)
- Personal needs of top management (using the firm for personal purposes, such as providing jobs for relatives)

Strategies

A **strategy** of a corporation forms a comprehensive master plan that states how the corporation will achieve its mission and objectives. It maximizes competitive advantage and minimizes competitive disadvantage. For example, even though Staples is a major competitor in office supplies retailing, it is not likely to achieve its challenging growth objective of doubling sales within five years without making a major change in strategy. The North American and European markets for office supplies have been growing only 2% faster than their economies. Staples CEO Ronald Sargent decided to think "outside the box" by reducing new store openings and instead emphasizing delivering office supplies from warehouses directly to businesses. Sargent believed that the delivery business could equal revenue from Staples store sales.[35]

The typical business firm usually considers three types of strategy: corporate, business, and functional.

1. **Corporate strategy** describes a company's overall direction in terms of its general attitude toward growth and the management of its various businesses and product lines. Corporate strategies typically fit within the three main categories of stability, growth, and retrenchment. Staples, for example, was following a corporate strategy of growth by diversifying from its base in retailing into the delivery business.

2. **Business strategy** usually occurs at the business unit or product level, and it emphasizes improvement of the competitive position of a corporation's products or services in the specific industry or market segment served by that business unit. Business strategies are grouped into two overall categories, *competitive* and *cooperative* strategies. For example, Staples has used a competitive strategy to differentiate its retail stores from its competitors by adding services to its stores, such as copying, UPS shipping, and hiring mobile technicians who can fix computers and install networks. British Airways has followed a cooperative strategy by forming an alliance with American Airlines in order to provide global service. Cooperative strategy may thus be used to support a competitive strategy. Intel, a manufacturer of computer microprocessors, uses its alliance (cooperative strategy) with Microsoft to differentiate itself (competitive strategy) from AMD, its primary competitor.

3. **Functional strategy** is the approach taken by a functional area to achieve corporate and business unit objectives and strategies by maximizing resource productivity. It is concerned with developing and nurturing a distinctive competence to provide a company or business unit with a competitive advantage. Examples of research and development (R&D) functional strategies are technological followership (imitation of the products of other companies) and technological leadership (pioneering of an innovation). For years, Magic Chef had been a successful appliance maker by spending little on R&D but by quickly imitating the innovations of other competitors. This has helped the company to keep its costs lower than those of its competitors and consequently to compete with lower prices. In terms of marketing functional strategies, Procter & Gamble (P&G) is a master of marketing "pull"—the process of spending huge amounts on advertising in order to create customer demand. This supports P&G's competitive strategy of differentiating its products from those of its competitors.

Business firms use all three types of strategy simultaneously. A **hierarchy of strategy** is a grouping of strategy types by level in the organization. Hierarchy of strategy is a nesting of one strategy within another so that they complement and support one another. (See **Figure 1–4**.) Functional strategies support business strategies, which, in turn, support the corporate strategy(ies).

Just as many firms often have no formally stated objectives, many firms have unstated, incremental, or intuitive strategies that have never been articulated or analyzed. Often the only way to spot a corporation's implicit strategies is to look not at what management says but at what it does. Implicit strategies can be derived from corporate policies, programs approved (and disapproved), and authorized budgets. Programs and divisions favored by budget increases and staffed by managers who are considered to be on the fast promotion track reveal where the corporation is putting its money and its energy.

Policies

A **policy** is a broad guideline for decision making that links the formulation of a strategy with its implementation. Companies use policies to make sure that employees throughout the firm make decisions and take actions that support the corporation's mission, objectives, and strategies. For example, when Cisco decided on a strategy of growth through acquisitions, it estab-

Figure 1–4
**Hierarchy of
Strategy**

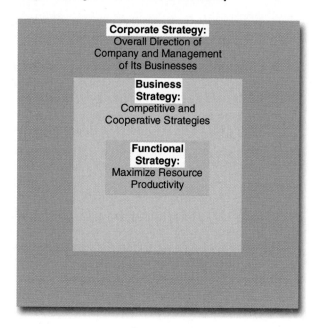

lished a policy to consider only companies with no more than 75 employees, 75% of whom were engineers.[36] Consider the following company policies:

- **Maytag Company:** Maytag will not approve any cost-reduction proposal if it reduces product quality in any way. (This policy supports Maytag's competitive strategy in which Maytag brands compete on quality rather than on price.)

- **3M:** 3M says researchers should spend 15% of their time working on something other than their primary project. (This supports 3M's strong product development strategy.)

- **Intel:** Intel cannibalizes its own product line (undercuts the sales of its current products) with better products before a competitor does so. (This supports Intel's objective of market leadership.)

- **General Electric:** GE must be number one or two wherever it competes. (This supports GE's objective to be number one in market capitalization.)

- **Southwest Airlines:** Southwest offers no meals or reserved seating on airplanes. (This supports Southwest's competitive strategy of having the lowest costs in the industry.)

Policies like these provide clear guidance to managers throughout the organization. (Strategy formulation is discussed in greater detail in **Chapters 6, 7**, and **8**.)

Strategy Implementation

Strategy implementation is a process by which strategies and policies are put into action through the development of programs, budgets, and procedures. This process might involve changes within the overall culture, structure, and/or management system of the entire organization. Except when such drastic corporatewide changes are needed, however, the implementation of strategy is typically conducted by middle and lower-level managers, with review by top management. Sometimes referred to as *operational planning*, strategy implementation often involves day-to-day decisions in resource allocation.

Programs

A **program** is a statement of the activities or steps needed to accomplish a single-use plan. It makes a strategy action oriented. It may involve restructuring the corporation, changing the company's internal culture, or beginning a new research effort. For example, Boeing's strategy to regain industry leadership with its proposed 787 airplane meant that the company had to increase its manufacturing efficiency in order to keep the price low. To significantly cut costs, management decided to implement a series of programs:

- Outsource approximately 70% of manufacturing.
- Reduce final assembly time to 3 days (compared to 20 for its 737 plane) by having suppliers build completed plane sections.
- Use new, lightweight composite materials in place of aluminum to reduce inspection time.
- Resolve poor relations with labor unions caused by downsizing and outsourcing.

Another example is discount retailer Dollar General's programs to double the amount of space in the company's distribution centers in order to reduce the number of truck deliveries and to redesign its stores to provide wider aisles and a brighter, cleaner appearance.[37]

Budgets

A **budget** is a statement of a corporation's programs in terms of dollars. Used in planning and control, a budget lists the detailed cost of each program. Many corporations demand a certain percentage return on investment, often called a "hurdle rate," before management will approve a new program. This ensures that the new program will significantly add to the corporation's profit performance and thus build shareholder value. The budget thus not only serves as a detailed plan of the new strategy in action, it also specifies through pro forma financial statements the expected impact on the firm's financial future.

For example, General Motors budgeted $4.3 billion during 2000 through 2004 to update and expand its Cadillac line of automobiles. With this money, the company was able to increase the number of models from five to nine and to offer more powerful engines, sportier handling, and edgier styling. The company reversed its declining market share by appealing to a younger market. (The average Cadillac buyer was 67 years old in 2000.[38]) Another example is the $8 billion budget that General Electric established to invest in new jet engine technology for regional-jet airplanes. Management decided that an anticipated growth in regional jets should be the company's target market. The program paid off in 2003 when GE won a $3 billion contract to provide jet engines for China's new fleet of 500 regional jets in time for the 2008 Beijing Olympics.[39]

Procedures

Procedures, sometimes termed Standard Operating Procedures (SOP), are a system of sequential steps or techniques that describe in detail how a particular task or job is to be done. They typically detail the various activities that must be carried out in order to complete the corporation's program. For example, when the home improvement retailer Home Depot noted that sales were lagging because its stores were full of clogged aisles, long checkout times, and too few sales people, management changed its procedures for restocking shelves and pricing the products. Instead of requiring its employees to do these activities at the same time they were working with customers, management moved these activities to when the stores were closed at night. Employees were then able to focus on increasing customer sales during the day. In order to repair poor labor relations, Boeing's CEO agreed to allow the machinists' union a greater voice in specifying manufacturing procedures. (Strategy implementation is discussed in more detail in **Chapters 9** and **10**.)

Evaluation and Control

Evaluation and control is a process in which corporate activities and performance results are monitored so that actual performance can be compared with desired performance. Managers at all levels use the resulting information to take corrective action and resolve problems.

Although evaluation and control is the final major element of strategic management, it can also pinpoint weaknesses in previously implemented strategic plans and thus stimulate the entire process to begin again.

Performance is the end result of activities.[40] It includes the actual outcomes of the strategic management process. The practice of strategic management is justified in terms of its ability to improve an organization's performance, typically measured in terms of profits and return on investment. For evaluation and control to be effective, managers must obtain clear, prompt, and unbiased information from the people below them in the corporation's hierarchy. Using this information, managers compare what is actually happening with what was originally planned in the formulation stage.

For example, when the Legend (renamed Lenovo) Group of China decided to diversify out of personal computers to increase its revenues from $3 to $10 billion over a five-year period, it monitored, among other things, the sales of its personal computers. When management noted that the Chinese market share of its PCs had dropped from 30% to 27% over three years, it realized that its strategy was flawed.

The evaluation and control of performance completes the strategic management model. Based on performance results, management may need to make adjustments in its strategy formulation, in implementation, or in both. (Evaluation and control is discussed in more detail in **Chapter 11**.)

Feedback/Learning Process

Note that the strategic management model depicted in **Figure 1–2** includes a feedback/learning process. Arrows are drawn coming out of each part of the model and taking information to each of the previous parts of the model. As a firm or business unit develops strategies, programs, and the like, it often must go back to revise or correct decisions made earlier in the process. For example, poor performance (as measured in evaluation and control) usually indicates that something has gone wrong with either strategy formulation or implementation. It could also mean that a key variable, such as a new competitor, was ignored during environmental scanning and assessment. In the case of the Legend (Lenovo) Group, falling market share in PCs meant that its diversification strategy was not performing as expected. According to Legend's Chairman Liu Chuanzhi: "In view of these developments, this year [2004] Legend carried out a thorough and careful review of our plans in the past three years. We have decided to retreat from diversification and refocus on the PC business."[41]

1.6 | Initiation of Strategy: Triggering Events

After much research, Henry Mintzberg discovered that strategy formulation is typically not a regular, continuous process: "It is most often an irregular, discontinuous process, proceeding in fits and starts. There are periods of stability in strategy development, but also there are periods of flux, of groping, of piecemeal change, and of global change."[42] This view of strategy formulation as an irregular process can be explained by the very human tendency to continue on a particular course of action until something goes wrong or a person is forced to question his or her actions. This period of strategic drift may result from inertia on the part of the organization, or it may reflect management's belief that the current strategy is still appropriate and needs only some fine-tuning.

Most large organizations tend to follow a particular strategic orientation for about 15 to 20 years before making a significant change in direction. This phenomenon, called **punctuated equilibrium**, describes corporations as evolving through relatively long periods of stability (equilibrium periods) punctuated by relatively short bursts of fundamental change (revolutionary periods).[43] After this rather long period of fine-tuning an existing strategy, some sort of shock to the system is needed to motivate management to seriously reassess the corporation's situation.

A **triggering event** is something that acts as a stimulus for a change in strategy. Some possible triggering events are[44]:

- **New CEO:** By asking a series of embarrassing questions, a new CEO cuts through the veil of complacency and forces people to question the very reason for the corporation's existence.

- **External intervention:** A firm's bank suddenly refuses to approve a new loan or suddenly demands payment in full on an old one. A customer complains about a serious product defect.

- **Threat of a change in ownership:** Another firm may initiate a takeover by buying a company's common stock.

- **Performance gap:** A **performance gap** exists when performance does not meet expectations. Sales and profits either are no longer increasing or may even be falling.

- **Strategic inflection point:** Coined by Andy Grove, past-CEO of Intel Corporation, a strategic inflection point is what happens to a business when a major change takes place due to the introduction of new technologies, a different regulatory environment, a change in customers' values, or a change in what customers prefer.[45]

Sun Microsystems is an example of one company in which a triggering event forced management to radically rethink what it was doing. See STRATEGY HIGHLIGHT 1.2 to learn how one phone call to Sun's president stimulated a change in strategy at Sun.

STRATEGY HIGHLIGHT 1.2

Triggering Event at Sun Microsystems

Sun Microsystems President Edward Zander received a personal phone call directly from Margaret Whitman, CEO of eBay, Inc., an Internet auction firm. After a string of small computer crashes, eBay had just suffered a 22-hour outage of its web site. Whitman called Zander to report that there was a bug in Sun's top-of-the-line server and that Sun had better fix it immediately or else lose eBay's business. A series of around-the-clock meetings at Sun revealed that the problem was that Sun's customers had no idea of how to maintain a $1 million-plus computer. eBay had failed to provide sufficient air conditioning to keep the machine cool. Even though Sun had issued a software patch to fix a problem many months earlier, eBay had neglected to install it. The list went on and on. Sun soon realized that the problem was bigger than just eBay. More than 40% of the servers that manage most web sites were made by Sun. As more firms were expanding their business to include the Internet, this market for Sun's servers was expected to boom. Nevertheless, many of these firms were too new and small to have the proper technology infrastructure. "It suddenly hit me," said Zander. "How many

future eBays are buying their first computer from us this very minute?" According to Scott McNealy, CEO of Sun, "That's when we realized that it wasn't eBay's fault. It was our fault."

Since that realization, Sun's management team has been rebuilding the company to make its servers as reliable as the telephone system. In a drastic strategic change, management decided to expand beyond simply selling servers to providing many of the technologies required to make Web servers completely reliable. It now provides storage products, e-business software, and consultants who not only supply the hardware but work directly with the customers to ensure that the servers are operated properly. Just as high-tech mainframe managers used to say that "No one gets fired for choosing IBM," Zander aims to have the same said of Sun Microsystems. "I want to be the safe bet for companies that need the most innovative technology," added Sun's president.

Source: Summarized from P. Burrows, "Sun's Bid to Rule the Web," *Business Week E.Biz* (July 24, 2000), pp. EB 31–42.

1.7 | Strategic Decision Making

The distinguishing characteristic of strategic management is its emphasis on strategic decision making. As organizations grow larger and more complex, with more uncertain environments, decisions become increasingly complicated and difficult to make. In agreement with the strategic choice perspective mentioned earlier, this book proposes a strategic decision-making framework that can help people make these decisions, regardless of their level and function in a corporation.

What Makes a Decision Strategic?

Unlike many other decisions, **strategic decisions** deal with the long-run future of an entire organization and have three characteristics:

1. **Rare:** Strategic decisions are unusual and typically have no precedent to follow.
2. **Consequential:** Strategic decisions commit substantial resources and demand a great deal of commitment from people at all levels.
3. **Directive:** Strategic decisions set precedents for lesser decisions and future actions throughout an organization.[46]

One example of a strategic decision was that made by Zippo Manufacturing, the maker of the Zippo cigarette lighter. The lighter's distinctive click, its windproof design, and its lifetime guarantee made it a favorite of smokers around the world. It was also popular with a worldwide community of Zippo "tricksters"—people who use Zippos not to light cigarettes but to perform sleight of hand. Realizing that tobacco products were a declining industry, in 2003 Zippo's management established the twin objectives of not only doubling current sales of $140 million but also deriving half the company's revenue from products unrelated to tobacco by 2010. The company began to think of itself as "selling flame" and no longer limiting itself to products that light tobacco. As a result, Zippo introduced a line of multipurpose lighters for candles, grills, and fireplaces. It also purchased the knifemaker Case Cutlery. Executives initiated discussions with manufacturers of grills, torches, space heaters, and fireplaces, among other fire-related products, for a series of Zippo-branded patio products. Management's decision to diversify was clearly a strategic one.[47]

Mintzberg's Modes of Strategic Decision Making

Some strategic decisions are made in a flash by one person (often an entrepreneur or a powerful chief executive officer) who has a brilliant insight and is quickly able to convince others to adopt his or her idea. Other strategic decisions seem to develop out of a series of small incremental choices that over time push an organization more in one direction than another. According to Mintzberg, the three most typical approaches, or modes, of strategic decision making are entrepreneurial, adaptive, and planning (a fourth mode, logical incrementalism, was added later by Quinn)[48]:

- **Entrepreneurial mode.** Strategy is made by one powerful individual. The focus is on opportunities; problems are secondary. Strategy is guided by the founder's own vision of direction and is exemplified by large, bold decisions. The dominant goal is growth of the corporation. Amazon.com, founded by Jeff Bezos, is an example of this mode of strategic decision making. The company reflected Bezos' vision of using the Internet to market books and more. Although Amazon's clear growth strategy was certainly an advantage of the entrepreneurial mode, Bezos' eccentric management style made it difficult to retain senior executives.[49]

- **Adaptive mode.** Sometimes referred to as "muddling through," this decision-making mode is characterized by reactive solutions to existing problems rather than a proactive search for new opportunities. Much bargaining goes on concerning priorities of objectives. Strategy is fragmented and is developed to move a corporation forward incrementally. This mode is typical of most universities, many large hospitals, a large number of governmental agencies, and a surprising number of large corporations. Encyclopaedia Britannica, Inc., operated successfully for many years in this mode, but it continued to rely on the door-to-door selling of its prestigious books long after dual-career couples made that marketing approach obsolete. Only after it was acquired in 1996 did the company change its door-to-door sales to television advertising and Internet marketing. The company now charges libraries and individual subscribers for complete access to Britannica.com and offers CD-ROMs in addition to a small number of its 32-volume print set.[50]

- **Planning mode.** This decision-making mode involves the systematic gathering of appropriate information for situation analysis, the generation of feasible alternative strategies, and the rational selection of the most appropriate strategy. It includes both the proactive search for new opportunities and the reactive solution of existing problems. IBM under CEO Louis Gerstner is an example of planning mode. When Gerstner accepted the position of CEO in 1993, he realized that IBM was in serious difficulty. Mainframe computers, the company's primary product line, were suffering a rapid decline in both sales and market share. One of Gerstner's first actions was to convene a two-day meeting on corporate strategy with senior executives. An in-depth analysis of IBM's product line revealed that the only part of the company that was growing was services, but it was a relatively small segment and not very profitable. Rather than focus on making and selling its own computer hardware, IBM made the strategic decision to invest in services that integrated information technology. IBM thus decided to provide a complete set of services, from building systems to defining architecture to actually running and managing the computers for the customer—regardless of who made the products. Because it was no longer important that the company be completely vertically integrated, it sold off its DRAM and disk-drive businesses and exited software application development. Since making this strategic decision in 1993, 80% of IBM's revenue growth has come from services.[51]

- **Logical incrementalism.** A fourth decision-making mode, which can be viewed as a synthesis of the planning, adaptive, and, to a lesser extent, the entrepreneurial modes. In this mode, top management has a reasonably clear idea of the corporation's mission and objectives, but, in its development of strategies, it chooses to use "an interactive process in which the organization probes the future, experiments and learns from a series of partial (incremental) commitments rather than through global formulations of total strategies."[52] Thus, although the mission and objectives are set, the strategy is allowed to emerge out of debate, discussion, and experimentation. This approach appears to be useful when the environment is changing rapidly and when it is important to build consensus and develop needed resources before committing an entire corporation to a specific strategy. In his analysis of the petroleum industry, Grant described strategic planning in this industry as "planned emergence." Corporate headquarters established the mission and objectives but allowed the business units to propose strategies to achieve them.[53]

Strategic Decision-Making Process: Aid to Better Decisions

Good arguments can be made for using either the entrepreneurial or adaptive modes (or logical incrementalism) in certain situations. This book proposes, however, that in most situations the planning mode, which includes the basic elements of the strategic management process, is a more rational and thus better way of making strategic decisions. Research indicates that the planning mode is not only more analytical and less political than are the other modes, but it is also more appropriate for dealing with complex, changing environments.[54] We therefore pro-

Figure 1–5
Strategic Decision-Making Process

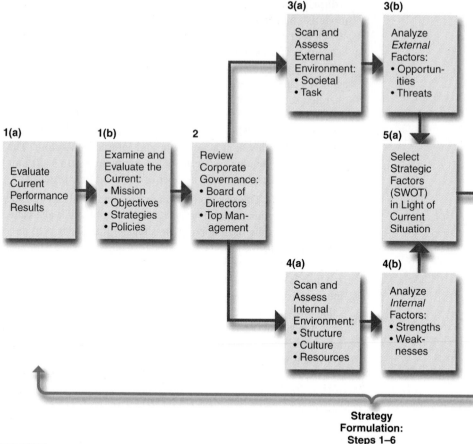

Source: T. L. Wheelen and J. D. Hunger, "Strategic Decision-Making Process." Copyright © 1994 and 1997 by Wheelen and Hunger Associates. Reprinted by permission.

pose the following eight-step **strategic decision-making process** to improve the making of strategic decisions (see **Figure 1–5**):

1. **Evaluate current performance results** in terms of (a) return on investment, profitability, and so forth, and (b) the current mission, objectives, strategies, and policies.

2. **Review corporate governance**—that is, the performance of the firm's board of directors and top management.

3. **Scan and assess the external environment** to determine the strategic factors that pose Opportunities and Threats.

4. **Scan and assess the internal corporate environment** to determine the strategic factors that are Strengths (especially core competencies) and Weaknesses.

5. **Analyze strategic (SWOT) factors** to (a) pinpoint problem areas and (b) review and revise the corporate mission and objectives, as necessary.

6. **Generate, evaluate, and select the best alternative strategy** in light of the analysis conducted in step 5.

7. **Implement selected strategies** via programs, budgets, and procedures.

8. **Evaluate implemented strategies** via feedback systems and the control of activities to ensure their minimum deviation from plans.

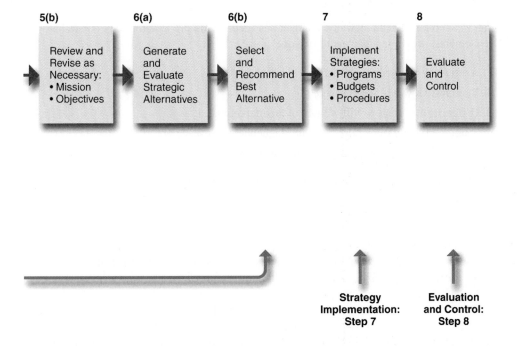

This rational approach to strategic decision making has been used successfully by corporations such as Warner-Lambert, Target, General Electric, IBM, Avon Products, Bechtel Group, Inc., and Taisei Corporation.

1.8 | The Strategic Audit: Aid to Strategic Decision Making

The strategic decision-making process is put into action through a technique known as the strategic audit. A **strategic audit** provides a checklist of questions, by area or issue, that enables a systematic analysis to be made of various corporate functions and activities. (See **Appendix 1.A** at the end of this chapter.) Note that the numbered primary headings in the audit are the same as the numbered blocks in the strategic decision-making process in **Figure 1–5**. Beginning with an evaluation of current performance, the audit continues with environmental scanning, strategy formulation, and strategy implementation. It concludes with evaluation and control. A strategic audit is a type of management audit and is extremely useful as a diagnostic tool to pinpoint corporatewide problem areas and to highlight organizational strengths and weaknesses.[55] A strategic audit can help determine why a certain area is creating problems for a corporation and help generate solutions to the problem.

A strategic audit is not an all-inclusive list, but it presents many of the critical questions needed for a detailed strategic analysis of any business corporation. Some questions or even some areas might be inappropriate for a particular company; in other cases, the questions may be insufficient for a complete analysis. However, each question in a particular area of a strategic audit can be broken down into an additional series of subquestions. A company can develop these subquestions when they are needed for a complete strategic analysis of the company.

1.9 | **Conclusion**

Strategy scholars Donald Hambrick and James Fredrickson propose that a good strategy has five elements, providing answers to five questions:

1. **Arenas:** Where will we be active?
2. **Vehicles:** How will we get there?
3. **Differentiators:** How will we win in the marketplace?
4. **Staging:** What will be our speed and sequence of moves?
5. **Economic logic:** How will we obtain our returns?[56]

This chapter introduces you to a well-accepted model of strategic management (**Figure 1–2**) in which environmental scanning leads to strategy formulation, strategy implementation, and evaluation and control. It further shows how that model can be put into action through the strategic decision-making process (**Figure 1–5**) and a strategic audit (**Appendix 1.A**). As pointed out by Hambrick and Fredrickson, "a strategy consists of an integrated set of choices."[57] The questions "Where will we be active?" and "How will we get there?" are dealt with by a company's mission, objectives, and corporate strategy. The question "How will we win in the marketplace?" is the concern of business strategy. The question "What will be our speed and sequence of moves?" is answered not only by business tactics but also by functional strategy and by implemented programs, budgets, and procedures. The question "How will we obtain our returns?" is the primary emphasis of the evaluation and control element of the strategic management model. Each of these questions and topics is dealt with in greater detail in the chapters to come. Welcome to the study of strategic management!

Strategy Bits

- From 1993 to 2002, U.S. trade with Canada and Mexico increased from 25% to 33% of total U.S. international trade.

- Average Gross Domestic Product (GDP) per person in the 10 countries joining the European Union in 2004 is only 46% of that of the original 15 member countries.

- Indonesia and Brazil have the fourth and fifth largest populations in the world after China (first), India (second), and the United States (third).[58]

Discussion Questions

1. Why has strategic management become so important to today's corporations?

2. How does strategic management typically evolve in a corporation?

3. What is a learning organization? Is this approach to strategic management better than the more traditional top-down approach in which strategic planning is primarily done by top management?

4. Why are strategic decisions different from other kinds of decisions?

5. When is the planning mode of strategic decision making superior to the entrepreneurial and adaptive modes?

Strategic Practice Exercises

Mission statements vary widely from one company to another. Why is one mission statement better than another? Using Campbell's questions in **STRATEGY HIGHLIGHT 1.1** as a starting point, develop criteria for evaluating any mission statement. Then do one or both of the following exercises:

1. Evaluate the following mission statement of Celestial Seasonings. How many points would Campbell give it?

   Our mission is to grow and dominate the U.S. specialty tea market by exceeding consumer expectations with the best tasting, 100% natural hot and iced teas, packaged with Celestial art and philoso-

phy, creating the most valued tea experience. Through leadership, innovation, focus, and teamwork, we are dedicated to continuously improving value to our consumers, customers, employees, and stakeholders with a quality-first organization.[59]

2. Using the Internet, find the mission statements of three different organizations, which can be business or not-for-profit. (Hint: Check annual reports and 10-K forms. They can often be found via a link on a company's Web page or through Hoovers.com.) Which mission statement is best? Why?

Key Terms

adaptive mode (p. 21)
Association of Southeast Asian
    Nations (ASEAN) (p. 7)
budget (p. 17)
business strategy (p. 15)
Central American Free Trade
    Agreement (CAFTA) (p. 7)
corporate strategy (p. 15)
electronic commerce (p. 7)
entrepreneurial mode (p. 20)
environmental scanning (p. 10)
European Union (EU) (p. 7)
evaluation and control (p. 17)
external environment (p. 11)
functional strategy (p. 15)
globalization (p. 6)
goal (p. 14)

hierarchy of strategy (p. 15)
institution theory (p. 9)
internal environment (p. 11)
learning organization (p. 9)
logical incrementalism (p. 21)
mission (p. 12)
Mercosur/Mercosul (p. 7)
North American Free Trade
    Agreement (NAFTA) (p. 7)
objective (p. 14)
organizational learning theory (p. 9)
performance (p. 18)
performance gap (p. 19)
phases of strategic management (p. 4)
planning mode (p. 21)
policy (p. 15)

population ecology (p. 8)
procedures (p. 17)
program (p. 16)
punctuated equilibrium (p. 18)
strategic audit (p. 23)
strategic choice perspective (p. 9)
strategic decision-making process
    (p. 22)
strategic decisions (p. 20)
strategic factors (p. 10)
strategic management (p. 3)
strategy (p. 14)
strategy formulation (p. 12)
strategy implementation (p. 16)
SWOT analysis (p. 11)
triggering event (p. 19)

APPENDIX 1.A
Strategic Audit of a Corporation

I. CURRENT SITUATION

A. Current Performance
How did the corporation perform the past year overall in terms of return on investment, market share, and profitability?

B. Strategic Posture
What are the corporation's current mission, objectives, strategies, and policies?
1. Are they clearly stated, or are they merely implied from performance?
2. **Mission:** What business(es) is the corporation in? Why?
3. **Objectives:** What are the corporate, business, and functional objectives? Are they consistent with each other, with the mission, and with the internal and external environments?
4. **Strategies:** What strategy or mix of strategies is the corporation following? Are they consistent with each other, with the mission and objectives, and with the internal and external environments?
5. **Policies:** What are the corporation's policies? Are they consistent with each other, with the mission, objectives, and strategies, and with the internal and external environments?
6. Do the current mission, objectives, strategies, and policies reflect the corporation's international operations, whether global or multidomestic?

II. CORPORATE GOVERNANCE

A. Board of Directors
1. Who is on the board? Are they internal or external members?

Source: T. L. Wheelen and J. D. Hunger, *Strategic Audit of a Corporation*, Copyright © 1982 and 2005 by Wheelen and Hunger Associates. Originally in T. L. Wheelen and J. D. Hunger, "The Strategic Audit," 1975, 1977, 1979, and 2005. Presented by J. D. Hunger and T. L. Wheelen in "The Strategic Audit: An Integrative Approach to Teaching Business Policy," to Academy of Management, August 1983. Published in "Using the Strategic Audit," by T. L. Wheelen and J. D. Hunger in *SAM Advanced Management Journal* (Winter, 1987), pp. 4–12. Reprinted by permission. Revised 1988, 1991, 1994, 1997, 2000, 2002, 2004 and 2005.

2. Do they own significant shares of stock?

3. Is the stock privately held or publicly traded? Are there different classes of stock with different voting rights?

4. What do the board members contribute to the corporation in terms of knowledge, skills, background, and connections? If the corporation has international operations, do board members have international experience?

5. How long have members served on the board?

6. What is their level of involvement in strategic management? Do they merely rubber-stamp top management's proposals, or do they actively participate and suggest future directions?

B. Top Management

1. What person or group constitutes top management?

2. What are top management's chief characteristics in terms of knowledge, skills, background, and style? If the corporation has international operations, does top management have international experience? Are executives from acquired companies considered part of the top management team?

3. Has top management been responsible for the corporation's performance over the past few years? How many managers have been in their current position for less than three years? Were they promoted internally or externally hired?

4. Has top management established a systematic approach to strategic management?

5. What is top management's level of involvement in the strategic management process?

6. How well does top management interact with lower-level managers and with the board of directors?

7. Are strategic decisions made ethically, in a socially responsible manner?

8. What role do stock options play in executive compensation?

9. Is top management sufficiently skilled to cope with likely future challenges?

III. EXTERNAL ENVIRONMENT: OPPORTUNITIES AND THREATS (SW**OT**)

A. Societal Environment

1. What general environmental forces are currently affecting both the corporation and the industries in which it competes? Which present current or future threats? Opportunities? (Refer to **Table 4–1**)

   a. Economic

   b. Technological

   c. Political–legal

   d. Sociocultural

2. Are these forces different in other regions of the world?

B. Task Environment

1. What forces drive industry competition? Are these forces the same globally, or do they vary from country to country? Rate each force as **high, medium,** or **low.**

   a. Threat of new entrants

   b. Bargaining power of buyers

    c. Threat of substitute products or services

    d. Bargaining power of suppliers

    e. Rivalry among competing firms

    f. Relative power of unions, governments, special interest groups, etc.

2. What key factors in the immediate environment (that is, customers, competitors, suppliers, creditors, labor unions, governments, trade associations, interest groups, local communities, and shareholders) are currently affecting the corporation? Which are current or future Threats? Opportunities?

C. Summary of External Factors *(List in the EFAS Table 4–5, p. 97)*

Which of these forces are the most important to the corporation and to the industries in which it competes at the present time? Which will be important in the future?

IV. INTERNAL ENVIRONMENT: STRENGTHS AND WEAKNESSES (**SW**OT)

A. Corporate Structure

1. How is the corporation structured at present?

    a. Is the decision-making authority centralized around one group or decentralized to many units?

    b. Is the corporation organized on the basis of functions, projects, geography, or some combination of these?

2. Is the structure clearly understood by everyone in the corporation?

3. Is the present structure consistent with current corporate objectives, strategies, policies, and programs, as well as with the firm's international operations?

4. In what ways does this structure compare with those of similar corporations?

B. Corporate Culture

1. Is there a well-defined or emerging culture composed of shared beliefs, expectations, and values?

2. Is the culture consistent with the current objectives, strategies, policies, and programs?

3. What is the culture's position on important issues facing the corporation (that is, on productivity, quality of performance, adaptability to changing conditions, and internationalization)?

4. Is the culture compatible with the employees' diversity of backgrounds?

5. Does the company take into consideration the values of the culture of each nation in which the firm operates?

C. Corporate Resources

1. **Marketing**

    a. What are the corporation's current marketing objectives, strategies, policies, and programs?

        i. Are they clearly stated or merely implied from performance and/or budgets?

        ii. Are they consistent with the corporation's mission, objectives, strategies, and policies and with internal and external environments?

b. How well is the corporation performing in terms of analysis of market position and marketing mix (that is, product, price, place, and promotion) in both domestic and international markets? What percentage of sales comes from foreign operations? Where are current products in the product life cycle?

  i. What trends emerge from this analysis?

  ii. What impact have these trends had on past performance and how might these trends affect future performance?

  iii. Does this analysis support the corporation's past and pending strategic decisions?

  iv. Does marketing provide the company with a competitive advantage?

c. How well does the corporation's marketing performance compare with that of similar corporations?

d. Are marketing managers using accepted marketing concepts and techniques to evaluate and improve product performance? (Consider product life cycle, market segmentation, market research, and product portfolios.)

e. Does marketing adjust to the conditions in each country in which it operates?

f. What is the role of the marketing manager in the strategic management process?

2. **Finance**

a. What are the corporation's current financial objectives, strategies, policies, and programs?

  i. Are they clearly stated or merely implied from performance and/or budgets?

  ii. Are they consistent with the corporation's mission, objectives, strategies, and policies and with internal and external environments?

b. How well is the corporation performing in terms of financial analysis? (Consider ratio analysis, common size statements, and capitalization structure.) How balanced, in terms of cash flow, is the company's portfolio of products and businesses?

  i. What trends emerge from this analysis?

  ii. Are there any significant differences when statements are calculated in constant versus reported dollars?

  iii. What impact have these trends had on past performance and how might these trends affect future performance?

  iv. Does this analysis support the corporation's past and pending strategic decisions?

  v. Does finance provide the company with a competitive advantage?

c. How well does the corporation's financial performance compare with that of similar corporations?

d. Are financial managers using accepted financial concepts and techniques to evaluate and improve current corporate and divisional performance? (Consider financial leverage, capital budgeting, ratio analysis, and managing foreign currencies.)

e. Does finance adjust to the conditions in each country in which the company operates?

f. What is the role of the financial manager in the strategic management process?

3. **Research and Development (R&D)**

a. What are the corporation's current R&D objectives, strategies, policies, and programs?

  i. Are they clearly stated or merely implied from performance or budgets?

  ii. Are they consistent with the corporation's mission, objectives, strategies, and policies and with internal and external environments?

  iii. What is the role of technology in corporate performance?

  iv. Is the mix of basic, applied, and engineering research appropriate, given the corporate mission and strategies?

  v. Does R&D provide the company with a competitive advantage?

b. What return is the corporation receiving from its investment in R&D?

c. Is the corporation competent in technology transfer? Does it use concurrent engineering and cross-functional work teams in product and process design?

d. What role does technological discontinuity play in the company's products?

e. How well does the corporation's investment in R&D compare with the investments of similar corporations? How much R&D is being outsourced?

f. Does R&D adjust to the conditions in each country in which the company operates?

g. What is the role of the R&D manager in the strategic management process?

4. **Operations and Logistics**

a. What are the corporation's current manufacturing/service objectives, strategies, policies, and programs?

   i. Are they clearly stated or merely implied from performance or budgets?

   ii. Are they consistent with the corporation's mission, objectives, strategies, and policies and with internal and external environments?

b. What are the type and extent of operations capabilities of the corporation? How much is done domestically versus internationally? Is the amount of outsourcing appropriate to be competitive? Is purchasing being handled appropriately?

   i. If the corporation is product oriented, consider plant facilities, type of manufacturing system (continuous mass production, intermittent job shop, or flexible manufacturing), age and type of equipment, degree and role of automation and/or robots, plant capacities and utilization, productivity ratings, and availability and type of transportation.

   ii. If the corporation is service oriented, consider service facilities (hospital, theater, or school buildings), type of operations systems (continuous service over time to same clientele or intermittent service over time to varied clientele), age and type of supporting equipment, degree and role of automation and use of mass communication devices (diagnostic machinery, videotape machines), facility capacities and utilization rates, efficiency ratings of professional and service personnel, and availability and type of transportation to bring service staff and clientele together.

c. Are manufacturing or service facilities vulnerable to natural disasters, local or national strikes, reduction or limitation of resources from suppliers, substantial cost increases of materials, or nationalization by governments?

d. Is there an appropriate mix of people and machines (in manufacturing firms) or of support staff and professionals (in service firms)?

e. How well does the corporation perform relative to the competition? Is it balancing inventory costs (warehousing) with logistical costs (just-in-time)? Consider costs per unit of labor, material, and overhead; downtime; inventory control management and scheduling of service staff; production ratings; facility utilization percentages; and number of clients successfully treated by category (if service firm) or percentage of orders shipped on time (if product firm).

   i. What trends emerge from this analysis?

   ii. What impact have these trends had on past performance and how might these trends affect future performance?

   iii. Does this analysis support the corporation's past and pending strategic decisions?

   iv. Does operations provide the company with a competitive advantage?

f. Are operations managers using appropriate concepts and techniques to evaluate and improve current performance? Consider cost systems, quality control and reliability systems, inventory control management, personnel scheduling, total quality management (TQM), learning curves, safety programs, and engineering programs that can improve efficiency of manufacturing or of service.

g. Does operations adjust to the conditions in each country in which it has facilities?

h. What is the role of outsourcing in the company's strategy for operations?

i. What is the role of the operations manager in the strategic management process?

5. **Human Resources Management (HRM)**

a. What are the corporation's current HRM objectives, strategies, policies, and programs?

  i. Are they clearly stated or merely implied from performance and/or budgets?

  ii. Are they consistent with the corporation's mission, objectives, strategies, and policies and with internal and external environments?

b. How well is the corporation's HRM performing in terms of improving the fit between the individual employee and the job? Consider turnover, grievances, strikes, layoffs, employee training, and quality of work life.

  i. What trends emerge from this analysis?

  ii. What impact have these trends had on past performance and how might these trends affect future performance?

  iii. Does this analysis support the corporation's past and pending strategic decisions?

  iv. Does HRM provide the company with a competitive advantage?

c. How does this corporation's HRM performance compare with that of similar corporations?

d. Are HRM managers using appropriate concepts and techniques to evaluate and improve corporate performance? Consider the job analysis program, performance appraisal system, up-to-date job descriptions, training and development programs, attitude surveys, job design programs, quality of relationships with unions, and use of autonomous work teams.

e. How well is the company managing the diversity of its workforce? What is the company's record on human rights?

f. Does HRM adjust to the conditions in each country in which the company operates? Does the company have a code of conduct for HRM in developing nations? Are employees receiving international assignments to prepare them for managerial positions?

g. What is the role of the HRM manager in the strategic management process?

6. **Information Systems (IS)**

a. What are the corporation's current IS objectives, strategies, policies, and programs?

  i. Are they clearly stated or merely implied from performance and/or budgets?

  ii. Are they consistent with the corporation's mission, objectives, strategies, and policies and with internal and external environments?

b. How well is the corporation's IS performing in terms of providing a useful database, automating routine clerical operations, assisting managers in making routine decisions, and providing information necessary for strategic decisions?

  i. What trends emerge from this analysis?

  ii. What impact have these trends had on past performance and how might these trends affect future performance?

  iii. Does this analysis support the corporation's past and pending strategic decisions?

  iv. Does IS provide the company with a competitive advantage?

c. How does this corporation's IS performance and stage of development compare with that of similar corporations? Is it appropriately using the Internet, intranet, and extranets?

d. Are IS managers using appropriate concepts and techniques to evaluate and improve corporate performance? Do they know how to build and manage a complex database, establish web sites with firewalls, conduct system analyses, and implement interactive decision-support systems?

    e. Does the company have a global IS and Internet presence? Does it have difficulty getting data across national boundaries?

    f. What is the role of the IS manager in the strategic management process?

D. Summary of Internal Factors *(List in the IFAS Table 5–2, p. 130)*

Which of these factors are core competencies? Which, if any, are distinctive competencies? Which of these factors are the most important to the corporation and to the industries in which it competes at the present time? Which might be important in the future? Which functions or activities are candidates for outsourcing?

V. ANALYSIS OF STRATEGIC FACTORS (SWOT)

A. Situational Analysis *(List in the SFAS Matrix, Figure 6–1, p. 141)*

Of the external (EFAS) and internal (IFAS) factors listed in III.C and IV.D, which are the strategic (most important) factors that strongly affect the corporation's present and future performance?

B. Review of Mission and Objectives

1. Are the current mission and objectives appropriate in light of the key strategic factors and problems?

2. Should the mission and objectives be changed? If so, how?

3. If they are changed, what will be the effects on the firm?

VI. STRATEGIC ALTERNATIVES AND RECOMMENDED STRATEGY

A. Strategic Alternatives *(See the TOWS Matrix, Figure 6–2, p. 144)*

1. Can the current or revised objectives be met through more careful implementation of those strategies presently in use (for example, fine-tuning the strategies)?

2. What are the major feasible alternative strategies available to the corporation? What are the pros and cons of each? Can corporate scenarios be developed and agreed upon? (Alternatives must fit societal environment, industry, and company for the next three to five years.)

    a. Consider *stability*, *growth*, and *retrenchment* as corporate strategies.

    b. Consider *cost leadership* and *differentiation* as business strategies.

    c. Consider any functional strategic alternatives that might be needed for reinforcement of an important corporate or business strategic alternative.

B. Recommended Strategy

1. Specify which of the strategic alternatives you are recommending for the corporate, business, and functional levels of the corporation. Do you recommend different business or functional strategies for different units of the corporation?

2. Justify your recommendation in terms of its ability to resolve both long- and short-term problems and effectively deal with the strategic factors.

3. What policies should be developed or revised to guide effective implementation?

4. What is the impact of your recommended strategy on the company's core and distinctive competencies?

VII. IMPLEMENTATION

A. What kinds of programs (for example, restructuring the corporation or instituting TQM) should be developed to implement the recommended strategy?

1. Who should develop these programs?

2. Who should be in charge of these programs?

B. Are the programs financially feasible? Can pro forma budgets be developed and agreed upon? Are priorities and timetables appropriate to individual programs?

C. Will new standard operating procedures need to be developed?

VIII. EVALUATION AND CONTROL

A. Is the current information system capable of providing sufficient feedback on implementation activities and performance? Can it measure strategic factors?

1. Can performance results be pinpointed by area, unit, project, or function?

2. Is the information timely?

3. Is the corporation using benchmarking to evaluate its functions and activities?

B. Are adequate control measures in place to ensure conformance with the recommended strategic plan?

1. Are appropriate standards and measures being used?

2. Are reward systems capable of recognizing and rewarding good performance?

CHAPTER 2
Corporate Governance

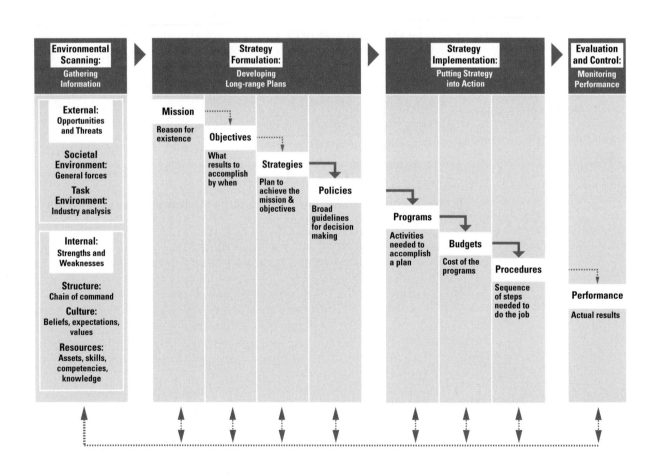

Environmental Scanning:	Strategy Formulation:	Strategy Implementation:	Evaluation and Control:
Gathering Information	Developing Long-range Plans	Putting Strategy into Action	Monitoring Performance

External:
Opportunities and Threats

Societal Environment:
General forces

Task Environment:
Industry analysis

Internal:
Strengths and Weaknesses

Structure:
Chain of command

Culture:
Beliefs, expectations, values

Resources:
Assets, skills, competencies, knowledge

Mission
Reason for existence

Objectives
What results to accomplish by when

Strategies
Plan to achieve the mission & objectives

Policies
Broad guidelines for decision making

Programs
Activities needed to accomplish a plan

Budgets
Cost of the programs

Procedures
Sequence of steps needed to do the job

Performance
Actual results

Learning Objectives

After reading this chapter, you should be able to:

- Describe the role and responsibilities of the board of directors in corporate governance
- Understand how the composition of a board can affect its operation
- Describe the impact of the Sarbanes-Oxley Act on corporate governance in the United States
- Discuss trends in corporate governance
- Explain how executive leadership is an important part of strategic management

TYCO INTERNATIONAL LTD. IS A DIVERSIFIED MANUFACTURING AND SERVICE COMPANY that operates in more than 100 countries and has annual revenues of over $36 billion. Taking over as CEO in 1992, Dennis Kozlowski transformed Tyco from an obscure U.S. manufacturer into the world's largest provider of undersea telecommunications systems, fire protection systems, and electronic security services. In doing so, Kozlowski treated Tyco as his own personal empire, lavishing hundreds of millions of dollars in unauthorized loans and exorbitant gifts on himself and his top managers. Even though his annual compensation jumped from $8.8 million in 1996 to $136.1 million in 1999, Kozlowski regularly took from the company loans worth hundreds of millions of dollars. Among his purchases were a $2.1 million birthday celebration for his wife plus a $6,000 shower curtain and a $15,000 dog umbrella stand for his $16.8 million New York apartment. By operating without a second in command and by handpicking top managers who were "smart, poor, and want-to-be-rich," he kept personal control of the corporation. He handpicked members of the board of directors and filtered all information, such as internal audits, that went to the board. Without board approval, Kozlowski gave $56 million in bonuses to 51 Tyco employees to effectively cancel loans they had earlier taken from the company.

In the wake of the Enron scandal, the U.S. Securities and Exchange Commission (SEC), the Internal Revenue Service, and the State of New Hampshire began investigating Tyco for accounting irregularities and its CPA firm for failing to report the questionable practices. Kozlowski resigned as CEO just before being indicted on tax evasion. Subsequent investigation revealed why the board of directors had been so silent during this period of top management excess. Of the company's 10 directors, 3 were Tyco executives who had serious conflicts of interest. Even though board member Joshua Berman had been serving as a Tyco executive since 1997, the company continued to pay millions of dollars in legal fees to his former law firm. John Fort, the Tyco executive who was named the company's interim CEO upon Kozlowski's resignation, had been an investor in a buyout fund that made an $810 million purchase of Tyco operations in 1999, while Fort served as a board member. Tyco's Chief Financial Officer, Mark Swartz, also served as a board member when he received $6.5 million in loans from the company.

In addition, the non-management, or "outside," directors had such deep ties to the company that it raised questions about the board's ability to oversee management. For example, Michael Ashcroft had previously worked for the company until 1997. Another board member, Stephen Foss, leased an airplane to Tyco. The lead director, Frank Walsh, Jr., received $20 million for his services in helping to arrange Tyco's disastrous 2001 acquisition of the commercial-finance company CIT Group.

In the first six months of 2002, the actions, inactions, and reversals of actions by the Tyco board cost stockholders about $88 billion in lost shareholder value, three times the $33 billion in equity losses at Enron and almost twice the equity losses at WorldCom. Tyco agreed to pay $5 million to the State of New Hampshire to reimburse shareholders and the public who had been hurt by the financial misconduct of its former officers. After pleading guilty of securities fraud, lead director Frank Walsh agreed to pay $22.5 million in fines and restitution to settle civil and criminal charges. In addition, Tyco's auditing firm was investigated for its failure to identify accounting irregularities. According to Lyn Turner, former Chief Accountant for the SEC, $41 million of a $96 million loan forgiveness scheme was charged to the balance sheet for "accrued federal income tax." Said Turner, "I can't understand how they missed that one."[1]

2.1 | Role of the Board of Directors

A **corporation** is a mechanism established to allow different parties to contribute capital, expertise, and labor for their mutual benefit. The investor/shareholder participates in the profits of the enterprise without taking responsibility for the operations. Management runs the company without being responsible for personally providing the funds. To make this possible, laws have been passed that give shareholders limited liability and, correspondingly, limited involvement in a corporation's activities. That involvement does include, however, the right to elect directors who have a legal duty to represent the shareholders and protect their interests. As representatives of the shareholders, directors have both the authority and the responsibility to establish basic corporate policies and to ensure that they are followed.[2]

The board of directors, therefore, has an obligation to approve all decisions that might affect the long-run performance of the corporation. This means that the corporation is fundamentally governed by the board of directors overseeing top management, with the concurrence of the shareholder. The term **corporate governance** refers to the relationship among these three groups in determining the direction and performance of the corporation.[3]

Over the past decade, shareholders and various interest groups have seriously questioned the role of the board of directors in corporations. They are concerned that inside board members may use their position to feather their own nests and that outside board members often lack sufficient knowledge, involvement, and enthusiasm to do an adequate job of monitoring and providing guidance to top management. Instances of widespread corruption and questionable accounting practices at Enron, Global Crossing, WorldCom, Tyco, and Qwest, among others, seem to justify their concerns. Tyco's board, for example, seemed more interested in keeping CEO Kozlowski happy than in safeguarding shareholder interests. The very passivity of the board (in addition to questionable financial dealings) was one reason why the Kozlowski-era directors were forced to resign in 2003.[4]

The general public has not only become more aware and more critical of many boards' apparent lack of responsibility for corporate activities, it has begun to push government to demand accountability. As a result, the board as a rubber stamp of the CEO or as a bastion of the "old-boy" selection system is being replaced by more active, more professional boards.

Responsibilities of the Board

Laws and standards defining the responsibilities of boards of directors vary from country to country. For example, board members in Ontario, Canada, face more than 100 provincial and federal laws governing director liability. The United States, however, has no clear national standards or federal laws. Specific requirements of directors vary, depending on the state in which the corporate charter is issued. There is, nevertheless, a developing worldwide consensus concerning the major responsibilities of a board. Interviews with 200 directors from eight countries (Canada, France, Germany, Finland, Switzerland, the Netherlands, the United Kingdom, and Venezuela) revealed strong agreement on the following five **board of director responsibilities**, listed in order of importance:

1. Setting corporate strategy, overall direction, mission, or vision
2. Hiring and firing the CEO and top management
3. Controlling, monitoring, or supervising top management

4. Reviewing and approving the use of resources

5. Caring for shareholder interests[5]

These results are in agreement with a recent survey by the National Association of Corporate Directors, in which CEOs reported that the four most important issues boards should address are corporate performance, CEO succession, strategic planning, and corporate governance.[6] Directors in the United States must make certain, in addition to the duties just listed, that the corporation is managed in accordance with the laws of the state in which it is incorporated. Because more than half of all publicly traded companies in the United States are incorporated in the state of Delaware, this state's laws and rulings have more impact than do those of any other state.[7] Directors must also ensure management's adherence to laws and regulations, such as those dealing with the issuance of securities, insider trading, and other conflict-of-interest situations. They must also be aware of the needs and demands of constituent groups so that they can achieve a judicious balance among the interests of these diverse groups while ensuring the continued functioning of the corporation.

In a legal sense, the board is required to direct the affairs of the corporation but not to manage them. It is charged by law to act with **due care**. If a director or the board as a whole fails to act with due care and, as a result, the corporation is in some way harmed, the careless director or directors can be held personally liable for the harm done. This is no small concern, given that one survey of outside directors revealed that more than 40% had been named as part of lawsuits against corporations.[8] For example, board members of Equitable Life in Britain were sued for up to $5.4 billion for failure to question the CEO's reckless policies.[9] For this reason, the percentage of U.S. boards purchasing directors' and officers' liability insurance had increased to 84% by 2003.[10]

Role of the Board in Strategic Management

How does a board of directors fulfill these many responsibilities? The **role of the board of directors in strategic management** is to carry out three basic tasks:

■ **Monitor:** By acting through its committees, a board can keep abreast of developments inside and outside the corporation, bringing to management's attention developments it might have overlooked. A board should at least carry out this task.

■ **Evaluate and influence:** A board can examine management's proposals, decisions, and actions; agree or disagree with them; give advice and offer suggestions; and outline alternatives. More active boards perform this task in addition to monitoring.

■ **Initiate and determine:** A board can delineate a corporation's mission and specify strategic options to its management. Only the most active boards take on this task in addition to the two previous ones.

Board of Directors Continuum

A board of directors is involved in strategic management to the extent that it carries out the three tasks of monitoring, evaluating and influencing, and initiating and determining. The **board of directors continuum** shown in **Figure 2–1** shows the possible degree of involvement (from low to high) in the strategic management process. Boards can range from being phantom boards with no real involvement to catalyst boards with a very high degree of involvement.[11] Research suggests that active board involvement in strategic management is positively related to a corporation's financial performance and its credit rating.[12]

Highly involved boards tend to be very active. They take their tasks of monitoring, evaluating, influencing, initiating, and determining very seriously; they provide advice when necessary and keep management alert. As depicted in **Figure 2–1**, their heavy involvement in the strategic management process places them in the active participation or even catalyst positions. For example, in a survey of directors of large U.S. corporations conducted by Korn/Ferry

Figure 2–1 **Board of Directors Continuum**

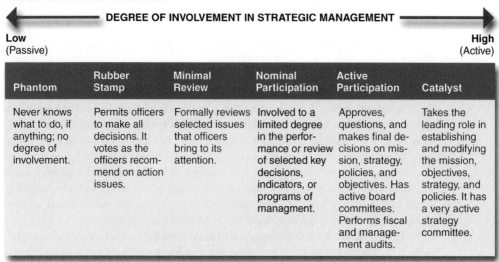

Source: T. L. Wheelen and J. D. Hunger, "Board of Directors Continuum," Copyright © 1994 by Wheelen and Hunger Associates. Reprinted by permission.

International, more than 60% indicated that they were deeply involved in the strategy-setting process. In the same survey, 54% of the respondents indicated that their boards participate in an annual retreat or special planning session to discuss company strategy. Nevertheless, only slightly more than 32% of the boards help develop the strategy. More than two-thirds of the boards review strategy only after it has first been developed by management. Another 1% admit playing no role at all in strategy.[13] This and other studies suggest that most large publicly owned corporations have boards that operate at some point between nominal and active participation. Nevertheless, the percentage of U.S. companies surveyed by Korn/Ferry International that have written corporate governance guidelines rose from 71% in 2002 to 88% in 2003.[14] Seventy-four percent now have periodic board meetings devoted primarily to the review of overall company strategy.[15] Some corporations with actively participating boards are Target, Medtronic, Best Western, Service Corporation International, Bank of Montreal, Mead Corporation, Rolm and Haas, Whirlpool, 3M, Apria Healthcare, General Electric, Pfizer, and Texas Instruments.[16] Target, a corporate governance leader, has a board that each year sets three top priorities, such as strategic direction, capital allocation, and succession planning. Each of these priority topics is placed at the top of the agenda for at least one meeting. Target's board also devotes one meeting a year to setting the strategic direction for each major operating division.[17]

As a board becomes less involved in the affairs of the corporation, it moves farther to the left on the continuum (see **Figure 2–1**). On the far left are passive phantom or rubber-stamp boards that typically never initiate or determine strategy (like Tyco) unless a crisis occurs. In these situations, the CEO also serves as Chairman of the Board, personally nominates all directors, and works to keep board members under his or her control by giving them the "mushroom treatment"—throw manure on them and keep them in the dark!

Generally, the smaller the corporation, the less active is its board of directors. In an entrepreneurial venture, for example, the privately held corporation may be 100% owned by the founders—who also manage the company. In this case, there is no need for an active board to protect the interests of the owner–manager shareholders—the interests of the owners and the managers are identical. In this instance, a board is really unnecessary and only meets to satisfy legal requirements. If stock is sold to outsiders to finance growth, however, the board becomes more active. Key investors want seats on the board so they can oversee their investment. To the extent that they still control most of the stock, however, the founders dominate the board. Friends, family members, and key shareholders usually become members, but the board acts primarily as a rubber stamp for any proposals put forward by the owner–managers. In this type of company, the founder tends to be both CEO and chairman of the board, and the board includes few people who are not affiliated with the firm or family.[18] This cozy relationship between the board and management should change, however, when the corporation goes public and stock is more widely dispersed. The founders, who are still acting as management, may sometimes make decisions that conflict with the needs of the other shareholders (especially if the founders own less than 50% of the common stock). In this instance, problems could occur if the board fails to become more active in terms of its roles and responsibilities.

Members of a Board of Directors

The boards of most publicly owned corporations are composed of both inside and outside directors. **Inside directors** (sometimes called management directors) are typically officers or executives employed by the corporation. **Outside directors** (sometimes called non-management directors) may be executives of other firms but are not employees of the board's corporation. Although there is yet no clear evidence indicating that a high proportion of outsiders on a board results in improved financial performance, as measured by return on equity,[19] there is a trend in the United States to increase the number of outsiders on boards. The typical large U.S. Fortune 1000 corporation has an average of 11 directors, 2 of whom are insiders.[20] Even though outsiders account for slightly over 80% of the board members in these large U.S. corporations (approximately the same as in Canada), they account for only about 42% of board membership in small U.S. companies.[21] Boards in the UK typically have 5 inside and 5 outside directors, whereas in France boards usually consist of 3 insiders and 8 outsiders. Japanese boards, in contrast, contain 2 outsiders and 12 insiders.[22] A survey of 1,376 *privately held* U.S. companies reveals that the average board consists of 4 members, but only 19% contain any outsiders.[23]

People who favor a high proportion of outsiders state that outside directors are less biased and more likely to evaluate management's performance objectively than are inside directors. This is the main reason why the U.S. Securities and Exchange Commission (SEC) in 2003 required that a majority of directors on the board be independent outsiders. The SEC also required that all listed companies staff their audit, compensation, and nominating/corporate governance committees entirely with independent, outside members. This view is in agreement with **agency theory**, which states that problems arise in corporations because the agents (top management) are not willing to bear responsibility for their decisions unless they own a substantial amount of stock in the corporation. The theory suggests that a majority of a board needs to be from outside the firm so that top management is prevented from acting selfishly to the detriment of the shareholders. For example, proponents of agency theory argue that management-controlled firms select less risky strategies with quick payoffs in order to keep their jobs. This view is supported by research revealing that manager-controlled firms are more likely to go into debt to diversify into unrelated markets (thus quickly boosting sales and assets)—resulting in poorer long-term performance—than owner-controlled firms.[24] Boards with a larger proportion of outside directors tend to favor growth through international expansion and innovative venturing activities than do boards with a smaller proportion of outsiders.[25] Outsiders tend to be more objective and critical of corporate activities. For example, research reveals that the likelihood of a firm engaging in illegal behavior or being sued declines with the addition of outsiders on the board.[26] Research on *privately owned* family businesses has found that boards with a larger number of outsiders tended to have better corporate governance than did boards with fewer outsiders.[27]

In contrast, those who prefer inside over outside directors contend that outside directors are less effective than are insiders because the outsiders are less likely to have the necessary interest, availability, or competency. **Stewardship theory** proposes that, because of their long tenure with the corporation, insiders (senior executives) tend to identify with the corporation and its success. Rather than use the firm for their own ends, these executives are thus most interested in guaranteeing the continued life and success of the corporation. (See STRATEGY HIGHLIGHT 2.1 for a discussion of Agency Theory contrasted with Stewardship Theory.) Excluding all insiders but the CEO reduces the opportunity for outside directors to see potential successors in action or to obtain alternate points of view of management decisions. Outside directors may sometimes serve on so many boards that they spread their time and interest too thin to actively fulfill their responsibilities. The average board member of a U.S. Fortune 500 firm serves on three boards. Research indicates that firm performance decreases as the number of directorships held by the average board member increases.[28] Only 10% of surveyed U.S. boards limit the number of directorships a board member may hold in other corporations.[29]

Those who question the value of having more outside board members point out that the term *outsider* is too simplistic because some outsiders are not truly objective and should be considered more as insiders than as outsiders. For example, there can be:

1. **Affiliated directors** who, though not really employed by the corporation, handle the legal or insurance work for the company or are important suppliers (thus dependent on the current management for a key part of their business). These outsiders face a conflict of interest and are not likely to be objective. The number of affiliated directors on Tyco's board was one of the reasons why the board was so strongly criticized. As a result of recent actions by the U.S. Congress, Securities and Exchange Commission, New York Stock Exchange, and NASDAQ, affiliated directors are being banned from corporate boardrooms. U.S. boards can no longer include representatives of major suppliers or customers or even professional organizations that might do business with the firm, even though these people could provide valuable knowledge and expertise.[30] The New York Stock Exchange decided in 2004 that anyone paid by the company during the previous three years could not be classified as an independent outside director.[31]

2. **Retired executive directors** who used to work for the company, such as the past CEO (who is partly responsible for much of the corporation's current strategy and who probably groomed the current CEO as his or her replacement). Many boards of large firms keep the firm's recently retired CEO on the board for a year or two after retirement as a courtesy, especially if he or she performed well as the CEO. It is almost certain, however, that this person will not be able to objectively evaluate the corporation's performance. Nevertheless, a survey by the Conference Board found that only 14% of U.S. boards surveyed require the former CEO to leave the board upon retirement.[32]

3. **Family directors** who are descendants of the founder and own significant blocks of stock (with personal agendas based on a family relationship with the current CEO). The Schlitz Brewing Company, for example, was unable to complete its turnaround strategy with a non-family CEO because family members serving on the board wanted their money out of the company, forcing it to be sold.[33]

The majority of outside directors are active or retired CEOs and COOs of other corporations. Others are major investors/shareholders, academicians, attorneys, consultants, former government officials, and bankers. Given that approximately 60% of the outstanding stock in the largest U.S. and UK corporations is now owned by institutional investors, such as mutual funds and pension plans, these investors are taking an increasingly active role in board membership and activities.[34] For example, TIAA-CREF's Corporate Governance team monitors governance practices of the 4,000 companies in which it invests its pension funds through its Corporate Assessment Program. If its analysis of a company reveals problems, TIAA-CREF first sends letters stating its concerns, followed up by visits, and it finally sponsors a share-

STRATEGY HIGHLIGHT 2.1

Agency Theory Versus Stewardship Theory in Corporate Governance

Managers of large, modern publicly held corporations are typically not the owners. In fact, most of today's top managers own only nominal amounts of stock in the corporation they manage. The real owners (shareholders) elect boards of directors who hire managers as their agents to run the firm's day-to-day activities. Once hired, how trustworthy are these executives? Do they put themselves or the firm first?

Agency Theory. As suggested in the classic study by Berle and Means, top managers are, in effect, "hired hands" who may very likely be more interested in their personal welfare than that of the shareholders. For example, management might emphasize strategies, such as acquisitions, that increase the size of the firm (to become more powerful and to demand increased pay and benefits) or that diversify the firm into unrelated businesses (to reduce short-term risk and to allow them to put less effort into a core product line that may be facing difficulty) but that result in a reduction of dividends and/or stock price.

Agency theory is concerned with analyzing and resolving two problems that occur in relationships between principals (owners/shareholders) and their agents (top management):

1. The agency problem that arises when (a) the desires or objectives of the owners and the agents conflict or (b) it is difficult or expensive for the owners to verify what the agent is actually doing. One example is when top management is more interested in raising its own salary than in increasing stock dividends.

2. The risk-sharing problem that arises when the owners and agents have different attitudes toward risk. Executives may not select risky strategies because they fear losing their jobs if the strategy fails.

According to agency theory, the likelihood that these problems will occur increases when stock is widely held (that is, when no one shareholder owns more than a small percentage of the total common stock), when the board of directors is composed of people who know little of the company or who are personal friends of top management, and when a high percentage of board members are inside (management) directors.

To better align the interests of the agents with those of the owners and to increase the corporation's overall perfor-

mance, agency theory suggests that top management have a significant degree of ownership in the firm and/or have a strong financial stake in its long-term performance. In support of this argument, research indicates a positive relationship between corporate performance and the amount of stock owned by directors.

Stewardship Theory. In contrast, stewardship theory suggests that executives tend to be more motivated to act in the best interests of the corporation than in their own self-interests. Whereas agency theory focuses on extrinsic rewards that serve the lower-level needs, such as pay and security, stewardship theory focuses on the higher-order needs, such as achievement and self-actualization. Stewardship theory argues that senior executives over time tend to view the corporation as an extension of themselves. Rather than use the firm for their own ends, these executives are most interested in guaranteeing the continued life and success of the corporation. The relationship between the board and top management is thus one of principal and steward, not principal and agent ("hired hand"). Stewardship theory notes that in a widely held corporation, the shareholder is free to sell her or his stock at any time. A diversified investor may care little about risk at the company level—preferring management to assume extraordinary risk so long as the return is adequate. Because executives in a firm cannot easily leave their jobs when in difficulty, they are more interested in a merely satisfactory return and put heavy emphasis on the firm's continued survival. Thus, stewardship theory argues that in many instances top management may care more about a company's long-term success than do more short-term–oriented shareholders.

For more information about agency theory and stewardship theory, see A. A. Berle and G. C. Means, *The Modern Corporation and Private Property* (New York: Macmillan, 1936); J. H. Davis, F. D. Schoorman, and L. Donaldson, "Toward a Stewardship Theory of Management," *Academy of Management Review* (January 1997), pp. 20–47; P. J. Lane, A. A. Cannella, Jr., and M. H. Lubatkin, "Agency Problems as Antecedents to Unrelated Mergers and Diversification: Amihud and Lev Reconsidered," *Strategic Management Journal* (June 1998), pp. 555–578; M. L. Hayward and D. C. Hambrick, "Explaining the Premiums Paid for Large Acquisitions: Evidence of CEO Hubris," *Administrative Science Quarterly* (March 1997), pp. 103–127.

holder resolution in opposition to management's actions.[35] Institutional investors are also powerful in many other countries. In Germany, bankers are represented on almost every board—primarily because they own large blocks of stock in German corporations. In Denmark, Sweden, Belgium, and Italy, however, investment companies assume this role. For example, the investment company Investor AB casts 42.5% of the Electrolux AB shareholder votes, thus guaranteeing itself positions on the Electrolux board.

Boards of directors have been working to increase the number of women and minorities serving on boards. Korn/Ferry International reports that of the Fortune 1000 largest U.S. firms, 80% had at least one woman director in 2003 (compared to 74% in 2000) for a total of 13.6% of all U.S. directors. In contrast, generally one-half of the boards in Australia, Canada, Japan, Norway, South Africa, Spain, and the United Kingdom included a female director. Korn/Ferry's survey also revealed that 75% of the U.S. boards had at least one ethnic minority in 2003 (African-American, 47%; Latino, 19%; Asian, 10%) as director compared to 65% in 2000.[36]

The globalization of business is having an impact on board membership. By 2003, according to the Spencer Stuart executive recruiting firm, 33% of U.S. boards had an international director, an increase of more than 50% over the previous five years.[37] Europe was the most "globalized" region of the world, with most companies reporting one or more non-national directors.[38] Asian and Latin American boards were still predominantly staffed by nationals, primarily because of travel requirements.[39] See the **GLOBAL ISSUE** feature to learn about a South Korean firm's addition of a non-Korean director.

Outside directors serving on the boards of large Fortune 1000 U.S. corporations annually earned on average $46,640. Most of the companies (71%) paid their outside directors an annual retainer plus a fee for every meeting attended. Almost 90% of these large U.S. corporations included stock options or grants in their compensation to board members.[40] Directors serving on the boards of small companies usually received much less compensation (around $10,000). One study found directors of a sample of large U.S. firms to hold on average 3% of their corporations' outstanding stock.[41]

The vast majority of inside directors are the chief executive officer and either the chief operating officer (if not also the CEO) or the chief financial officer. Presidents or vice presidents of key operating divisions or functional units sometimes serve on the board. Few, if any, inside directors receive any extra compensation for assuming this extra duty. Very rarely does a U.S. board include any lower-level operating employees.

Codetermination: Should Employees Serve on Boards?

Codetermination, the inclusion of a corporation's workers on its board, began only recently in the United States. Corporations such as Chrysler, Northwest Airlines, United Airlines (UAL), and Wheeling-Pittsburgh Steel have added representatives from employee associa-

GL🌐BAL ISSUE

POSCO Adds an International Director

In an attempt to make Korean businesses more attractive to foreign investors, the South Korean government recommended that companies listed on the stock exchange introduce a two-tiered structure. One structure was to consist entirely of non-executive (outside) directors. One of the few companies to immediately adopt this new system of governance was Pohang Iron & Steel Company, Ltd. (POSCO), the world's largest steelmaker. POSCO was listed on the New York Stock Exchange and had significant operations in the United States, plus a joint venture with U.S. Steel. According to Youn-Gil Ro, Corporate Information Team Manager, "We needed professional advice on international business practices as well as American practices."

Among the eight outside directors added to the board was Samuel Chevalier, an international financier from the United States. Chevalier previously sat on boards in Hong Kong and Brazil and had no problem traveling long distances to attend board meetings. In order to overcome language problems, Youn-Gil Ro explained, "There are simultaneous interpretations during the meetings, and agendas and other materials are written in English as well as Korean."

Source: Summarized from *Globalizing the Board of Directors: Trends and Strategies* (New York: Conference Board, 1999), p. 16. Reprinted by permission of the The Conference Board.

tions to their boards as part of union agreements or Employee Stock Ownership Plans (ESOPs). For example, United Airlines workers traded 15% in pay cuts for 55% of the company (through an ESOP) and 3 of the firm's 12 board seats. In this instance, workers represent themselves on the board not so much as employees but primarily as owners. At Chrysler, however, the United Auto Workers union obtained a temporary seat on the board as part of a union contract agreement in exchange for changes in work rules and reductions in benefits. This was at a time when Chrysler was facing bankruptcy in the late 1970s. In situations like this, when a director represents an internal stakeholder, critics raise the issue of conflict of interest. Can a member of the board, who is privy to confidential managerial information, function, for example, as a union leader whose primary duty is to fight for the best benefits for his or her members? Although the movement to place employees on the boards of directors of U.S. companies shows little likelihood of increasing (except through employee stock ownership), the European experience reveals an increasing acceptance of worker participation (without ownership) on corporate boards.

Germany pioneered codetermination during the 1950s with a two-tiered system: (1) a supervisory board elected by shareholders and employees to approve or decide corporate strategy and policy and (2) a management board (composed primarily of top management) appointed by the supervisory board to manage the company's activities. Most other Western European countries have either passed similar codetermination legislation (as in Sweden, Denmark, Norway, and Austria) or use worker councils to work closely with management (as in Belgium, Luxembourg, France, Italy, Ireland, and the Netherlands).

Interlocking Directorates

CEOs often nominate chief executives (as well as board members) from other firms to membership on their own boards in order to create an interlocking directorate. A *direct* **interlocking directorate** occurs when two firms share a director or when an executive of one firm sits on the board of a second firm. An *indirect* interlock occurs when two corporations have directors who also serve on the board of a third firm, such as a bank.

Although the Clayton Act and the Banking Act of 1933 prohibit interlocking directorates by U.S. companies competing in the same industry, interlocking continues to occur in almost all corporations, especially large ones. Interlocking occurs because large firms have a large impact on other corporations, and these other corporations, in turn, have some control over the firm's inputs and marketplace. For example, most large corporations in the United States, Japan, and Germany are interlocked either directly or indirectly with financial institutions.[42] Interlocking directorates are useful for gaining both inside information about an uncertain environment and objective expertise about potential strategies and tactics.[43] For example, Kleiner Perkins, a high-tech venture capital firm, not only has seats on the boards of the companies in which it invests, but it also has executives (which Kleiner Perkins hired) from one entrepreneurial venture who serve as directors on others. Kleiner Perkins refers to its network of interlocked firms as its *keiretsu*.[44] Family-owned corporations, however, are less likely to have interlocking directorates than are corporations with highly dispersed stock ownership, probably because family-owned corporations do not like to dilute their corporate control by adding outsiders to boardroom discussions.

There is some concern, however, when the chairs of separate corporations serve on each other's boards. Twenty-two such pairs of corporate chairs (who typically also served as their firm's CEO) existed in 2003. In one instance, the three chairs of Anheuser-Busch, SBC Communications, and Emerson Electric served on all three of the boards. Typically a CEO sits on only one board in addition to his or her own—down from two additional boards five years ago. Although such interlocks may provide valuable information, they are increasingly frowned upon because of the possibility of collusion.[45] Nevertheless, evidence indicates that well-interlocked corporations are better able to survive in a highly competitive environment.[46]

Nomination and Election of Board Members

Traditionally the CEO of a corporation decided whom to invite to board membership and merely asked the shareholders for approval in the annual proxy statement. All nominees were usually elected. There are some dangers, however, in allowing the CEO free rein in nominating directors. The CEO might select only board members who, in the CEO's opinion, will not disturb the company's policies and functioning. Given that the average length of service of a U.S. board member is for three 3-year terms (but can range up to 20 years for some boards), CEO-friendly, passive boards are likely to result. This is especially likely given that only 7% of surveyed directors indicated that their company had term limits for board members. (However, 60% of U.S. boards have a mandatory retirement around age 70.[47]) Research reveals that boards rated as least effective by the Corporate Library, a corporate governance research firm, tend to have members serving longer (an average of 9.7 years) than boards rated as most effective (7.5 years).[48] Directors selected by the CEO often feel that they should go along with any proposal the CEO makes. Thus board members find themselves accountable to the very management they are charged to oversee. Because this is likely to happen, more boards are using a nominating committee to nominate new outside board members for the shareholders to elect. Eighty-seven percent of large U.S. corporations now use nominating committees to identify potential directors. This practice is far less common in Europe, where only 60% of boards use nominating committees.[49]

Virtually every corporation whose directors serve terms of more than one year divides the board into classes and staggers elections so that only a portion of the board stands for election each year. This is called a **staggered board**. Sixty-three percent of U.S. boards currently have staggered boards.[50] Arguments in favor of this practice are that it provides continuity by reducing the chance of an abrupt turnover in its membership and that it reduces the likelihood of electing people unfriendly to management (who might be interested in a hostile takeover) through cumulative voting. An argument against staggered boards is that they make it more difficult for concerned shareholders to curb a CEO's power—especially when that CEO is also Chairman of the Board. An increasing number of shareholder resolutions to replace staggered boards with annual elections of all board members are currently being passed at annual meetings.

A survey of directors of U.S. corporations revealed the following criteria in a good director:

- Is willing to challenge management when necessary (95%)
- Has special expertise important to the company (67%)
- Is available outside meetings to advise management (57%)
- Has expertise on global business issues (41%)
- Understands the firm's key technologies and processes (39%)
- Brings external contacts that are potentially valuable to the firm (33%)
- Has detailed knowledge of the firm's industry (31%)
- Has high visibility in his or her field (31%)
- Is accomplished at representing the firm to stakeholders (18%)[51]

Organization of the Board

The size of a board in the United States is determined by the corporation's charter and its bylaws, in compliance with state laws. Although some states require a minimum number of board members, most corporations have quite a bit of discretion in determining board size. The average large, publicly held U.S. firm has around 11 directors on its board. The average small/medium-size privately held company has approximately 7 to 8 members. Privately owned family businesses usually have only 4 board members. The average size of boards elsewhere is Japan, 14; Non-Japan Asia, 9; Germany, 16; UK, 10; and France, 11.[52]

Seventy-nine percent of the top executives of U.S. publicly held corporations hold the dual designation of chairman and CEO. (Only 5% of the firms in the UK have a combined chairman/CEO.[53]) The combined chair/CEO position is being increasingly criticized because of the potential for conflict of interest. The CEO is supposed to concentrate on strategy, planning, external relations, and responsibility to the board. The Chairman's responsibility is to ensure that the board and its committees perform their functions as stated in the board's charter. Further, the chairman schedules board meetings and presides over the annual shareholders' meeting. Critics of having one person in the two offices ask how the board can properly oversee top management if the Chairman is also a part of top management. For this reason, the Chairman and CEO roles are separated by law in Germany, the Netherlands, and Finland. A similar law has been considered in the United Kingdom and Australia. Although research is mixed regarding the impact of the combined Chair/CEO position on overall corporate financial performance, firm stock price and credit ratings both respond negatively to announcements of CEOs also assuming the Chair position.[54]

Many of those who prefer that the Chairman and CEO positions be combined agree that the outside directors should elect a **lead director**. This person is consulted by the Chairman/CEO regarding board affairs and coordinates the annual evaluation of the CEO.[55] The lead director position is very popular in the United Kingdom, where it originated. Of those U.S. companies combining the Chairman and CEO positions, 62% had a lead director in 2003, up from only 32% in 2002.[56] This is one way to give the board more power without undermining the power of the Chairman/CEO. The lead director becomes increasingly important because 87% of U.S. boards in 2003 (compared to only 41% in 2002) held executive sessions without the CEO being present.[57] Nevertheless, there are many ways in which an unscrupulous Chairman/CEO such as Dennis Kozlowski at Tyco can guarantee a director's loyalty. For example, Frank Walsh, the lead director of Tyco's board, was secretly paid $20 million (by Kozlowski and CFO Swartz) in exchange for his help in arranging an acquisition.[58] Research indicates that an increase in board independence often results in higher levels of CEO ingratiation behavior aimed at persuading directors to support CEO proposals. Long-tenured directors who support the CEO may use social pressure to persuade a new board member to conform to the group.[59] For example, more than half of the 16 board members at Walt Disney Productions had personal ties to CEO Michael Eisner or to the company—a big reason why Disney's board has been so strongly criticized. Even in those situations when the board has a nominating committee composed only of outsiders, the committee often obtains the CEO's approval for each new board candidate.[60]

The most effective boards accomplish much of their work through committees. Although they do not usually have legal duties, most committees are granted full power to act with the authority of the board between board meetings. Typical standing committees (in order of prevalence) are the audit (100%), compensation (99%), nominating (87%), stock options (85%), corporate governance (72%), and executive (52%) committees.[61] The executive committee is usually composed of two inside and two outside directors located nearby who can meet between board meetings to attend to matters that must be settled quickly. This committee acts as an extension of the board and, consequently, may have almost unrestricted authority in certain areas.[62] Although only the audit committee was 100% staffed by outsiders in 2003, this may soon become the rule for U.S. boards, given the recent requirements by the New York Stock Exchange and the SEC. Although each board committee typically meets four to five times annually, the average audit committee met seven times during 2003.[63]

Impact of the Sarbanes-Oxley Act on U.S. Corporate Governance

In response to the many corporate scandals uncovered since 2000, the U.S. Congress passed the **Sarbanes-Oxley Act** in June 2002. This act was designed to protect shareholders from the excesses and failed oversight that characterized failures at Enron, Tyco, WorldCom, Adelphia Communications, Qwest, and Global Crossing, among other prominent firms. Several key elements of Sarbanes-Oxley were designed to formalize greater board independence and oversight. For example, the act requires that all directors serving on the audit committee be independent of the firm and receive no fees other than for services of the director. In addition, boards may no longer grant loans to corporate officers (one of the problems at Tyco). The act has also established formal procedures for individuals (known as "whistle-blowers") to report incidents of questionable accounting or auditing. Firms are prohibited from retaliating against anyone reporting wrongdoing. Both the CEO and CFO must certify the corporation's financial information. The act bans auditors from providing both external and internal audit services to the same company. It also requires that a firm identify whether it has a "financial expert" serving on the audit committee who is independent from management.

Improving Governance

In implementing the Sarbanes-Oxley Act, the U.S. Securities and Exchange Commission (SEC) required in 2003 that a company disclose whether it has adopted a code of ethics that applies to the CEO and to the company's principal financial officer. Among other things, the SEC requires that the audit, nominating, and compensation committees be staffed *entirely* by outside directors. The New York Stock Exchange reinforced the mandates of Sarbanes-Oxley by requiring that companies have a Nominating/Governance Committee composed entirely of independent outside directors. Similarly, NASDAQ rules require that nominations for new directors be made by either a nominating committee of independent outsiders or by a majority of independent outside directors.[64]

Partially in response to Sarbanes-Oxley, a recent survey of directors of *Fortune 1000* U.S. companies by Mercer Delta Consulting and the University of Southern California revealed that 60% of directors spent more time on board matters in 2003 than the previous year, with 85% spending more time on their company's accounts, 83% more on governance practices, and 52% on monitoring financial performance.[65] Newly elected outside directors with financial management experience increased to 10% of all outside directors in 2003 from only 1% of outsiders in 1998.[66] Fifty-seven percent of *Fortune 1000* U.S. boards required in 2003 that directors own stock in the corporation—an increase from 51% the previous year.[67]

Evaluating Governance

To help investors evaluate a firm's corporate governance, a number of independent rating services, such as Standard & Poor's (S&P), Moody's, The Corporate Library, Institutional Shareholder Services (ISS), and Governance Metrics International (GMI), have established criteria for good governance. *Business Week* annually publishes a list of the best and worst boards of U.S. corporations. Whereas rating service firms like S&P, Moody's, and The Corporate Library use a wide mix of research data and criteria to evaluate companies, ISS and GMI have been criticized because they primarily use public records to score firms, using simple checklists.[68] In contrast, the S&P Corporate Governance Scoring System researches four major issues:

- Ownership Structure and Influence
- Financial Stakeholder Rights and Relations
- Financial Transparency and Information Disclosure
- Board Structure and Processes

Although the S&P scoring system is proprietary and confidential, independent research using generally accepted measures of S&P's four issues revealed that moving from the poorest- to the best-governed categories nearly doubled a firm's likelihood of receiving an investment-grade credit rating.[69]

An increasing number of boards are evaluating not only the performance of the CEO but also the performance of the board in total and that of individual directors. Korn/Ferry International reported that 82% of boards in 2003 had a formal process to evaluate CEO performance compared to 67% a year earlier. Regular formal evaluations of the full board were conducted in 2003 by 65% (37% in 2002) of U.S. boards compared to 37% of European boards and 41% of Asian boards. Individual directors were formally evaluated in 2003 by 29% of American boards compared to 41% of Asian boards, 52% of UK boards, 23% of French boards, and only 1% of German boards.[70]

Avoiding Governance Improvements

A number of corporations are concerned that various requirements to improve corporate governance will constrain top management's ability to effectively manage the company. For example, more U.S. public corporations have gone private in the years since the passage of Sarbanes-Oxley than before its passage. Other companies use multiple classes of stock to keep outsiders from having sufficient voting power to change the company. Insiders, usually the company's founders, get stock with extra votes, while others get second-class stock with fewer votes. For example, Brian Roberts, CEO of Comcast, owns "superstock" that represents only 0.4% of outstanding common stock but guarantees him one-third of the voting stock. The Investor Responsibility Research Center reports that 11.3% of the companies it monitored in 2004 had multiple classes, up from 7.5% in 1990.[71]

Another approach to sidestepping new governance requirements is being used by corporations such as Google, Infasource Services, Orbitz, and W&T Offshore. If a corporation in which an individual group or another company controls more than 50% of the voting shares decides to become a "controlled company," the firm is then exempt from requirements by the New York Stock Exchange and NASDAQ that a majority of the board and all members of key board committees be independent outsiders. According to governance authority Jay Lorsch, this will result in a situation in which "the majority shareholders can walk all over the minority."[72]

Trends in Corporate Governance

The role of the board of directors in the strategic management of a corporation is likely to be more active in the future. Although neither the composition of boards nor the board leadership structure has been consistently linked to firm financial performance, better governance does lead to higher credit ratings and stock prices. A McKinsey survey reveals that investors are willing to pay 16% more for a corporation's stock if it is known to have good corporate governance. The investors explained that they would pay more because, in their opinion (1) good governance leads to better performance over time, (2) good governance reduces the risk of the company getting into trouble, and (3) governance is a major strategic issue.[73]

Some of today's **trends in governance** (particularly prevalent in the United States and the United Kingdom) that are likely to continue include the following[74]:

- Boards are getting more involved not only in reviewing and evaluating company strategy but also in shaping it.

- Companies involved in class-action lawsuits by shareholders are making concessions in corporate governance as part of the settlements. For example, as part of its recent settlement, Sprint agreed to add a lead director, to elect directors annually, and to have only independent outsiders serve on key board committees.[75]

- Institutional investors, such as pension funds, mutual funds, and insurance companies, are becoming active on boards and are putting increasing pressure on top management to improve corporate performance. This trend is supported by a 2004 SEC requirement that a mutual fund must publicly disclose the proxy votes cast at company board meetings in its portfolio. This reduces the tendency for mutual funds to rubber-stamp management proposals.[76]

- Shareholders are demanding that directors and top managers own more than token amounts of stock in a corporation. Research indicates that when compensation committee members are significant shareholders, they tend to offer the CEO less salary but with a higher incentive component than do compensation committee members who own little to no stock.[77]

- Non-affiliated outside (non-management) directors are increasing their numbers and power in publicly held corporations as CEOs loosen their grip on boards. Outside members are taking charge of annual CEO evaluations. Except for the executive, finance, and investment committees, board committees are moving toward complete outsider composition. An increasing number of boards will be evaluating not only overall board performance but also that of individual directors.

- Boards are getting smaller—partially because of the reduction in the number of insiders but also because boards desire new directors to have specialized knowledge and expertise instead of general experience.

- Boards continue to take more control of board functions by either splitting the combined chair/CEO into two separate positions or establishing a lead outside director position.

- As corporations become more global, they are increasingly looking for board members with international experience.

- Instead of merely being able to vote for or against directors nominated by the board's nominating committee, shareholders may be allowed to nominate board members. Supported by the AFL-CIO, a more open nominating process would enable shareholders to vote out directors who ignore shareholder interests.[78]

- Society, in the form of special interest groups, increasingly expects boards of directors to balance the economic goal of profitability with the social needs of society. Issues dealing with workforce diversity and the environment are now reaching the board level.

2.2 | The Role of Top Management

The top management function is usually conducted by the CEO of the corporation in coordination with the Chief Operating Officer (COO) or president, executive vice president, and vice presidents of divisions and functional areas. Even though strategic management involves everyone in the organization, the board of directors holds top management primarily responsible for the strategic management of a firm.[79]

Responsibilities of Top Management

Top management responsibilities, especially those of the CEO, involve getting things accomplished through and with others in order to meet the corporate objectives. Top management's job is thus multidimensional and is oriented toward the welfare of the total organization. Specific top management tasks vary from firm to firm and are developed from an analysis of the mission, objectives, strategies, and key activities of the corporation. Tasks are typically divided among the members of the top management team. A diversity of skills can thus be very important. Research indicates that top management teams with a diversity of functional and educational backgrounds and length of time with the company tend to be significantly related to improvements in corporate market share and profitability.[80] In addition, highly diverse teams with some international experience tend to emphasize international growth strategies and strategic innovation, especially in uncertain environments, to boost financial performance.[81] The CEO, with the support of the rest of the top management team, must successfully handle two primary responsibilities that are crucial to the effective strategic management of the corporation: (1) provide executive leadership and a strategic vision and (2) manage the strategic planning process.

Executive Leadership and Strategic Vision

Executive leadership is the directing of activities toward the accomplishment of corporate objectives. Executive leadership is important because it sets the tone for the entire corporation. A **strategic vision** is a description of what the company is capable of becoming. It is often communicated in the company's mission and vision statements (as described in **Chapter 1**). People in an organization want to have a sense of mission, but only top management is in the position to specify and communicate this strategic vision to the general workforce. Top management's enthusiasm (or lack of it) about the corporation tends to be contagious. The importance of executive leadership is illustrated by Steve Reinemund, CEO of PepsiCo: "A leader's job is to define overall direction and motivate others to get there."[82]

Successful CEOs are noted for having a clear strategic vision, a strong passion for their company, and an ability to communicate with others. They are often perceived to be dynamic and charismatic leaders—which is especially important for high firm performance and investor confidence in uncertain environments.[83] They have many of the characteristics of **transformational leaders**—that is, leaders who provide change and movement in an organization by providing a vision for that change.[84] For instance, the positive attitude characterizing many well-known industrial leaders—such as Bill Gates at Microsoft, Anita Roddick at The Body Shop, Ted Turner at CNN, Steve Jobs at Apple Computer, Herb Kelleher at Southwest Airlines, and Louis Gerstner at IBM—has energized their respective corporations. These transformational leaders are able to command respect and to influence strategy formulation and implementation because they tend to have three key characteristics:

1. **The CEO articulates a strategic vision for the corporation:** The CEO envisions the company not as it currently is but as it can become. The new perspective that the CEO's vision brings to activities and conflicts gives renewed meaning to everyone's work and enables employees to see beyond the details of their own jobs to the functioning of the total corporation. Louis Gerstner proposed a new vision for IBM when he proposed that the company change its business model from computer hardware to services: "If customers were going to look to an integrator to help them envision, design, and build end-to-end solutions, then the companies playing that role would exert tremendous influence over the full range of technology decisions—from architecture and applications to hardware and software choices."[85] In a recent survey of 1,500 senior executives from 20 different countries, when asked the most important behavioral trait a CEO must have, 98% responded that the CEO must convey "a strong sense of vision."[86]

2. **The CEO presents a role for others to identify with and to follow:** The leader sets an example in terms of behavior, dress, and actions. The CEO's attitudes and values concerning the corporation's purpose and activities are clear-cut and constantly communicated in words and deeds. For example, when design engineers at General Motors had

problems with monitor resolution using the Windows operating system, Steve Ballmer, CEO of Microsoft, personally crawled under conference room tables to plug in PC monitors and diagnose the problem.[87] People know what to expect and have trust in their CEO. Research indicates that businesses in which the general manager has the trust of the employees have higher sales and profits with lower turnover than do businesses in which there is a lesser amount of trust.[88]

3. **The CEO communicates high performance standards and also shows confidence in the followers' abilities to meet these standards:** No leader ever improved performance by setting easily attainable goals that provided no challenge. Communicating high expectations to others can often lead to high performance.[89] The CEO must be willing to follow through by coaching people. As a result, employees view their work as very important and thus motivating.[90] Ivan Seidenberg, chief executive of Verizon Communications, was closely involved in deciding Verizon's strategic direction, and he showed his faith in his people by letting his key managers handle important projects and represent the company in public forums. "All of these people could be CEOs in their own right. They are warriors and they are on a mission," explained Steidenberg. Grateful for his faith in them, his managers were fiercely loyal both to him and the company.[91]

The negative side of confident executive leaders is that their very confidence may lead to *hubris*, in which their confidence blinds them to information that is contrary to a decided course of action. For example, overconfident CEOs tend to charge ahead with mergers and acquisitions even though they are aware that most acquisitions destroy shareholder value. Research by Tate and Malmendier found that "overconfident CEOs are more likely to conduct mergers than rational CEOs at any point in time . . . . Overconfident CEOs view their company as undervalued by outside investors who are less optimistic about the prospects of the firm." Overconfident CEOs were most likely to make acquisitions when they could avoid selling new stock to finance them, and they were more likely to do deals that diversified their firm's lines of businesses.[92] For an example of a once-excellent CEO who became overconfident, see STRATEGY HIGHLIGHT 2.2.

Managing the Strategic Planning Process

As business corporations adopt more of the characteristics of the learning organization, strategic planning initiatives can come from any part of an organization. A survey of 90 U.S. global corporations revealed that, in 90% of the firms, strategies were first proposed in the subsidiaries and sent to headquarters for approval.[93] However, unless top management encourages and supports the planning process, strategic management is not likely to result. In most corporations, top management must initiate and manage the strategic planning process. It may do so by first asking business units and functional areas to propose strategic plans for themselves, or it may begin by drafting an overall corporate plan within which the units can then build their own plans. Research suggests that bottom-up strategic planning may be most appropriate in multidivisional corporations operating in relatively stable environments but that top-down strategic planning may be most appropriate for firms operating in turbulent environments.[94] Other organizations engage in concurrent strategic planning in which all the organization's units draft plans for themselves after they have been provided with the organization's overall mission and objectives.

Regardless of the approach taken, the typical board of directors expects top management to manage the overall strategic planning process so that the plans of all the units and functional areas fit together into an overall corporate plan. Top management's job therefore includes the tasks of evaluating unit plans and providing feedback. To do this, it may require each unit to justify its proposed objectives, strategies, and programs in terms of how well they satisfy the organization's overall objectives in light of available resources.[95]

STRATEGY HIGHLIGHT 2.2

CEO Hubris at Disney?

When Michael Eisner was recruited from Paramount Pictures by Roy Disney (nephew of the late Walt Disney) and Stanley Gold in 1984, he worked quickly to put the faltering company back on its feet. Earnings per share had fallen from $4.16 in 1980 to $2.73 when Eisner took over. With Roy Disney's support and the help of his friend Frank Wells (previously Vice Chair of Warner Brothers) as President and COO, Eisner revitalized the failing animation division. The unit soon churned out successful films such as *The Little Mermaid*, *The Lion King*, *Aladdin*, and *Beauty and the Beast*. He expanded the theme park business and opened 681 new Disney stores full of merchandise. Eisner succeeded not only because he was an excellent manager but also because of his passion and enthusiasm for Disney values. He even took Walt's place as the emcee of Disney's television programs.

Following the death of his colleague Frank Wells, Eisner became even more like the late Walt Disney—increasingly autocratic. His tendency to micromanage the company drove away top executives such as Jeffrey Katzenberg and other studio heads. Taking advantage of Disney's growth in sales and profits, Eisner bought Miramax Films and the Anaheim Ducks hockey team, followed by the acquisition of Capital Cities/ABC in the early 1990s. Because the success of the company drove the stock price up significantly, Eisner's stock options were worth over $650 million when he cashed them in 1998–2000.

Over time, Eisner manipulated the board of directors to make sure that it supported his decisions. Although the board included few people with any knowledge of corporate finance, Eisner nominated to the board his personal lawyer, his architect, and the principal of the elementary school attended by his sons. He enabled his good friend Michael Ovitz to collect $140 million when he left the company after 15 months as its president. According to the Delaware Supreme Court, the board's willingness to follow Eisner's recommendation in giving Ovitz the largest payout allowed by his contract "[pushed] the envelope of judicial respect for the business judgment of directors in making compensation decisions." In 2003, the board chose not to re-nominate Andrea Van de Kamp as a board member because of her criticism of Eisner's decisions. The board reclassified Stanley Gold as an insider, thus forcing him to resign as chair of the powerful Governance and Nominating Committee. Critics wondered why Eisner's long-time critic was suddenly an insider when other board members who had closer financial or family ties to the company were deemed independent outsiders. For these and other reasons, the Walt Disney Company twice led *Business Week's* annual list of worst boards of directors.

From its peak in 1997, Disney's performance continued to slump. Although revenue grew 4% from 1997 to 2004,

operating profits fell 7% a year, and earnings per share stagnated. Analysts criticized Eisner for paying too much for acquisitions. Ratings at ABC continued to fall, as did theme parks' profit margins. Because the company refused to agree to a change in its distribution contract with Steve Jobs' Pixar, the maker of *Toy Story* and *Finding Nemo*, the contract was not renewed. Critics explained that Eisner was unable to work with Jobs because both men were supremely confident (some said arrogant) that their own judgment was correct—regardless of what others said. Harvey Weinstein of Miramax studios also indicated that he wanted out of his partnership with the Disney Company. Meanwhile, Disney's own animation unit was faltering and unable to match Pixar's new computer technology and creativity. Roy Disney and Stanley Gold left the board in 2003 in protest over Eisner's leadership. Early in 2004 Disney was the target of a takeover attempt by Comcast, a cable firm.

At its March 3, 2004, shareholders meeting, 45% of the votes withheld support for Eisner in his post as Disney chairman. Leading the fight were the pension funds of CALPERS and the Ohio Public Employees Retirement System. Soon thereafter, the Disney board announced that it was splitting the positions of CEO and Chairman of the Board. Eisner kept his title as CEO, but the Chairman's position went to George Mitchell, former Maine senator and a supporter of Eisner. According to California State Controller Steve Westly, "Major shareholders intend to keep pressure on Disney's audit committee, its compensation committee, and the management."

On September 10, 2004, 62-year-old Michael Eisner announced that he would step down as Disney CEO in late 2006. Critics responded that Eisner needed to be replaced sooner and that the board needed to be significantly strengthened. Roy Disney considered proposing a minority slate of board nominations for 2005 if the SEC changed the rules to allow investors to place their own candidates on the official ballot.

Sources: C. B. Shrader and J. D. Hunger, "Walt Disney Productions—1984," in T. L. Wheelen and J. D. Hunger, *Strategic Management and Business Policy*, 2nd edition (Reading, MA: Addison-Wesley Publishing, 1986), pp. 419–458; D. Lieberman, "Disney Tries to Work Magic with New Board Lineup," *USA Today* (March 3, 2003), pp. B1–B2; "The One Time Lion King," *Economist* (September 18, 2004), p. 70; R. Grover and T. Lowry, "Now It's Time to Say Goodbye," *Business Week* (March 15, 2004), pp. 31–32; "Finding Another Nemo," *Economist* (February 7, 2004), p. 64; R. Grover and A. Borrus, "Can Michael Eisner Hold the Fort?" *Business Week* (March 22, 2004), p. 96; M. McCarthy, "Disney Strips Chairmanship from Eisner," *USA Today* (March 4, 2004), pp. 1B–2B; K. Maney, "Who Can Save a Disney in Distress?" *USA Today* (March 3, 2004), p. 3B; R. Grover, "Eisner's Goofy Timetable," *Business Week* (September 27, 2004), p. 50.

Many large organizations have a **strategic planning staff** charged with supporting both top management and the business units in the strategic planning process. This planning staff typically consists of fewer than 10 people, headed by a senior vice president or director of corporate planning. The staff's major responsibilities are to:

1. Identify and analyze companywide strategic issues and suggest corporate strategic alternatives to top management.

2. Work as facilitators with business units to guide them through the strategic planning process.

2.3 | Conclusion

Who determines a corporation's performance? According to the popular press, the chief executive officer seems to be personally responsible for a company's success or failure. When a company is in trouble, one of the first alternatives usually presented is to fire the CEO. That was certainly the case at the Walt Disney Company under Michael Eisner. He was first viewed as a transformational leader who saved the company in the 1980s. By 2003, he was perceived to be the primary reason for the company's poor performance. The truth is not this simple.

According to research by Margarethe Wiersema, firing the CEO rarely solves a corporation's problems. In a study of CEO turnover caused by dismissals and retirements in the 500 largest public U.S. companies, 71% of the departures were involuntary. In those firms in which the CEO was fired or asked to resign and replaced by another, Wiersema found *no* significant improvement in the company's operating earnings or stock price. She couldn't find a single measure suggesting that CEO dismissal had a positive effect on corporate performance! Wiersema placed the blame for the poor results squarely on the shoulders of the boards of directors. Boards typically lack an in-depth understanding of the business and consequently rely too heavily on executive search firms that know even less about the business. According to Wiersema, boards that successfully managed the executive succession process had three things in common:

- The board set the criteria for candidate selection based on the strategic needs of the company.

- The board set realistic performance expectations rather than demanding a quick fix to please the investment community.

- The board developed a deep understanding of the business and provided strong strategic oversight of top management, including thoughtful annual reviews of CEO performance.[96]

As noted at the beginning of this chapter, corporate governance involves not just the CEO or the board of directors. It involves the combined active participation of the board, top management, and shareholders. One positive result of the many corporate scandals during 2001–2004 is the increased interest in governance. Institutional investors are no longer content to be passive shareholders. Thanks to new regulations, boards of directors are taking their responsibilities more seriously and including more independent outsiders on key oversight committees. Top managers are beginning to understand the value of working with boards as partners, not just as adversaries or as people to be manipulated. Although there will always be passive shareholders, rubber-stamp boards, and dominating CEOs, the simple truth is that good corporate governance means better strategic management.

Strategy Bits

- The frequency of CEO turnover has increased 53% since 1995.

- The average tenure of a U.S. *Fortune 500* CEO dropped from 9.5 years in 1995 to 7.3 years in 2002.[97]

- The average total compensation for a board member of a *Fortune 500* company approached $500,000 in 2005, up 14% from 2004.[98]

Discussion Questions

1. When does a corporation need a board of directors?

2. Who should and should not serve on a board of directors? What about environmentalists or union leaders?

3. Should a CEO be allowed to serve on another company's board of directors?

4. What would be the result if the only insider on a corporation's board were the CEO?

5. Should all CEOs be transformational leaders? Would you like to work for a transformational leader?

Strategic Practice Exercises

A. Think of the **best manager** for whom you have ever worked. What was it about that person that made him or her such a good boss? Consider the following statements as they pertain to that person. **Fill in the blank *in front of each* statement with one of the following values:**

**STRONGLY AGREE = 5; AGREE = 4; NEUTRAL = 3;
DISAGREE = 2; STRONGLY DISAGREE = 1.**

1. ___ I respect him/her personally and want to act in a way that merits his/her respect and admiration. ___

2. ___ I respect his/her competence about things with which he/she is more experienced than I. ___

3. ___ He/she can give special help to those who cooperate with him/her. ___

4. ___ He/she can apply pressure on those who cooperate with him/her. ___

5. ___ He/she has a legitimate right, considering his/her position, to expect that his/her suggestions will be carried out. ___

6. ___ I defer to his/her judgment in areas with which he/she is more familiar than I. ___

7. ___ He/she can make things difficult for me if I fail to follow his/her advice. ___

8. ___ Because of his/her job title and rank, I am obligated to follow his/her suggestions. ___

9. ___ I can personally benefit by cooperating with him/her. ___

10. ___ Following his/her advice results in better decisions. ___

11. ___ I cooperate with him/her because I have high regard for him/her as an individual. ___

12. ___ He/she can penalize those who do not follow his/her suggestions. ___

13. ___ I feel I have to cooperate with him/her. ___

14. ___ I cooperate with him/her because I wish to be identified with him/her. ___

15. ___ Cooperating with him/her can positively affect my performance. ___

Source: Questionnaire developed by J. D. Hunger from the article "Influence and Information: An Exploratory Investigation of the Boundary Role Person's Basis of Power" by Robert Spekman, *Academy of Management Journal*, March 1979. Copyright © 2004 by J. David Hunger.

B. Now think of the **worst manager** for whom you have ever worked. What was it about that person that made him or her such a poor boss? Consider the statements above as they pertain to that person. **Place a number *after each* statement with one of** the values from 5 = strongly agree to 1 = strongly disagree.

C. Add the values you marked for the best manager within each of the five categories of power below. Then do the same for the values you marked for the worst manager.

BEST MANAGER

Reward	Coercive	Legitimate	Referent	Expert
3.	4.	5.	1.	2.
9.	7.	8.	11.	6.
15.	12.	13.	14.	10.
Total	Total	Total	Total	Total

WORST MANAGER

Reward	Coercive	Legitimate	Referent	Expert
3.	4.	5.	1.	2.
9.	7.	8.	11.	6.
15.	12.	13.	14.	10.
Total	Total	Total	Total	Total

D. Consider the differences between how you rated your best and your worst manager. How different are the two profiles? In many cases, the best manager's profile tends to be similar to that of transformational leaders in that the best manager tends to score highest on referent, followed by expert and reward, power—especially when compared to the worst manager's profile. The worst manager often scores highest on coercive and legitimate power, followed by reward power. The results of this survey may help you to answer the fifth discussion question for this chapter.

Key Terms

affiliated director (p. 40)

agency theory (p. 39)

board of directors continuum (p. 37)

board of director responsibilities (p. 36)

codetermination (p. 42)

corporate governance (p. 36)

corporation (p. 36)

due care (p. 37)

executive leadership (p. 49)

family director (p. 40)

inside director (p. 39)

interlocking directorate (p. 43)

lead director (p. 45)

outside director (p. 39)

retired executive director (p. 40)

role of the board of directors in strategic management (p. 37)

Sarbanes-Oxley Act (p. 46)

staggered board (p. 44)

stewardship theory (p. 40)

strategic planning staff (p. 52)

strategic vision (p. 49)

top management responsibilities (p. 48)

transformational leader (p. 49)

trend in governance (p. 47)

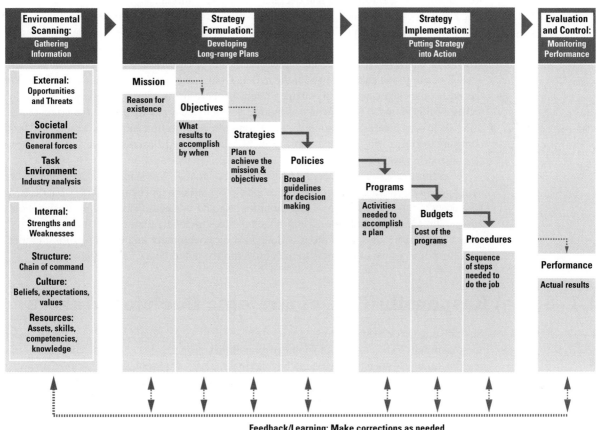

Feedback/Learning: Make corrections as needed

Learning Objectives

After reading this chapter, you should be able to:

- Compare and contrast Friedman's traditional view with Carroll's contemporary view of social responsibility
- Understand the relationship between social responsibility and corporate performance
- Be able to conduct a stakeholder analysis
- Explain why people may act unethically
- Describe different views of ethics according to the utilitarian, individual rights, and justice approaches

ONLY A FEW MILES FROM THE GLEAMING SKYSCRAPERS OF PROSPEROUS MINNEAPOLIS WAS a neighborhood littered with shattered glass from stolen cars and derelict houses used by drug lords. During the 1990s, the Hawthorne neighborhood became a no-man's-land where gun battles terrified local residents and raised the per capita murder rate 70% higher than that of New York.

Executives at General Mills became concerned when the murder rate reached a record high in 1996. The company's headquarters was located just five miles away from Hawthorne, then the city's most violent neighborhood. Working with law enforcement, politicians, community leaders, and residents, General Mills spent $2.5 million and donated thousands of employee hours to help clean up Hawthorne. Crack houses were demolished to make way for a new elementary school. Dilapidated houses in the neighborhood's core were rebuilt. General Mills provided grants to help people buy Hawthorne's houses. By 2003, homicides were down 32% and robberies had declined 56% in Hawthorne.

This story was nothing new for General Mills, a company listed in *Business Week's* 2003 list of most generous corporate philanthropists. In 2002 alone, the company donated $65 million out of revenues of $10.5 billion to causes ranging from education and the arts to social services. Every day, the company ships three truckloads of Cheerios, Wheaties, and other packaged goods to food banks throughout the nation. Community performance is even reflected in the performance reviews of top management. According to Christina Shea, president of General Mills Foundation, "We take as innovative approach to giving back to our communities as we do in our business." For joining with a nonprofit organization and a minority-owned food company to create 150 inner-city jobs, General Mills received *Business Ethics'* annual corporate citizenship award.[1]

Was this the best use of General Mills' time and money? At a time when companies were being pressured to cut costs and outsource jobs to countries with cheaper labor, what do business corporations owe their local communities? Should business firms give away shareholders' money, support social causes, and ask employees to donate their time to the community? Critics argue that this sort of thing is done best by government and not-for-profit charities. Isn't the primary goal of business to maximize profits, not to be a social worker?

3.1 | Social Responsibilities of Strategic Decision Makers

Should strategic decision makers be responsible only to shareholders, or do they have broader responsibilities? The concept of **social responsibility** proposes that a private corporation has responsibilities to society that extend beyond making a profit. Strategic decisions often affect more than just the corporation. A decision to retrench by closing some plants and discontinuing product lines, for example, affects not only the firm's workforce but also the communities where the plants are located and the customers with no other source for the discontinued product. Decisions to outsource manufacturing, software development, or customer service to contractors in other countries are likely to have a significant impact on more than just company profits. Such decisions can cause many to question the appropriateness of certain missions, objectives, and strategies of business corporations. Managers must be able to deal with these conflicting interests in an ethical manner to formulate a viable strategic plan.

Responsibilities of a Business Firm

What are the responsibilities of a business firm and how many of them must be fulfilled? Milton Friedman and Archie Carroll offer two contrasting views of the responsibilities of business firms to society.

Friedman's Traditional View of Business Responsibility

Urging a return to a laissez-faire worldwide economy with a minimum of government regulation, Milton Friedman argues against the concept of social responsibility. A business person who acts "responsibly" by cutting the price of the firm's product to prevent inflation, or by making expenditures to reduce pollution, or by hiring the hard-core unemployed, according to Friedman, is spending the shareholder's money for a general social interest. Even if the business person has shareholder permission or encouragement to do so, he or she is still acting from motives other than economic and may, in the long run, harm the very society the firm is trying to help. By taking on the burden of these social costs, the business becomes less efficient—either prices go up to pay for the increased costs or investment in new activities and research is postponed. These results negatively affect—perhaps fatally—the long-term efficiency of a business. Friedman thus referred to the social responsibility of business as a "fundamentally subversive doctrine" and stated:

> There is one and only one social responsibility of business—to use its resources and engage in activities designed to increase its profits so long as it stays within the rules of the game, which is to say, engages in open and free competition without deception or fraud.[2]

Following Friedman's reasoning, the management of General Mills was clearly guilty of misusing corporate assets and negatively affecting shareholder wealth. The millions spent in social services could have been invested in new product development or given back as dividends to the shareholders. Instead of General Mills' management acting on its own, shareholders could have decided which charities to support.

Carroll's Four Responsibilities of Business

Friedman's contention that the primary goal of business is profit maximization is only one side of an ongoing debate regarding corporate social responsibility (CSR). According to William J. Byron, Distinguished Professor of Ethics at Georgetown University and past-President of Catholic University of America, profits are merely a means to an end, not an end in itself. Just as a person needs food to survive and grow, so does a business corporation need profits to survive and grow. "Maximizing profits is like maximizing food." Thus, contends Byron, maximization of profits cannot be the primary obligation of business.[3]

As shown in **Figure 3–1**, Archie Carroll proposes that the managers of business organizations have four responsibilities: economic, legal, ethical, and discretionary.[4]

1. **Economic** responsibilities of a business organization's management are to produce goods and services of value to society so that the firm may repay its creditors and shareholders.

2. **Legal** responsibilities are defined by governments in laws that management is expected to obey. For example, U.S. business firms are required to hire and promote people based on their credentials rather than to discriminate on non-job-related characteristics such as race, gender, or religion.

Figure 3–1
**Responsibilities of
Business**

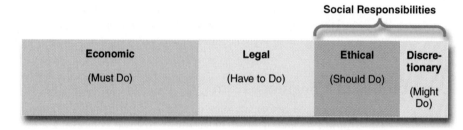

Source: *Adapted from A. B. Carroll, "A Three Dimensional Conceptual Model of Corporate Performance,"* Academy of Management Review *(October 1979), p. 499. Reprinted with permission.*

3. **Ethical** responsibilities of an organization's management are to follow the generally held beliefs about behavior in society. For example, society generally expects firms to work with the employees and the community in planning for layoffs, even though no law may require this. The affected people can get very upset if an organization's management fails to act according to generally prevailing ethical values.

4. **Discretionary** responsibilities are the purely voluntary obligations a corporation assumes. Examples are philanthropic contributions, training the hard-core unemployed, and providing day-care centers. The difference between ethical and discretionary responsibilities is that few people expect an organization to fulfill discretionary responsibilities, whereas many expect an organization to fulfill ethical ones.[5]

Carroll lists these four responsibilities *in order of priority*. A business firm must first make a profit to satisfy its economic responsibilities. To continue in existence, the firm must follow the laws, thus fulfilling its legal responsibilities. There is evidence that companies found guilty of violating laws have lower profits and sales growth after conviction.[6] To this point Carroll and Friedman are in agreement. Carroll, however, goes further by arguing that business managers have responsibilities beyond economic and legal ones.

Having satisfied the two basic responsibilities, according to Carroll, a firm should look to fulfilling its social responsibilities. Social responsibility, therefore, includes both ethical and discretionary, but not economic and legal, responsibilities. A firm can fulfill its ethical responsibilities by taking actions that society tends to value but has not yet put into law. When ethical responsibilities are satisfied, a firm can focus on discretionary responsibilities—purely voluntary actions that society has not yet decided are important. For example, when Cisco Systems decided to dismiss 6,000 full-time employees, it provided a novel severance package. Those employees who agreed to work for a local nonprofit organization for a year would receive one-third of their salaries plus benefits and stock options and be the first to be rehired. Nonprofits were delighted to hire such highly qualified people, and Cisco was able to maintain its talent pool for when it could hire once again.[7]

The discretionary responsibilities of today may become the ethical responsibilities of tomorrow. The provision of day-care facilities is, for example, moving rapidly from being a discretionary to an ethical responsibility. Carroll suggests that to the extent that business corporations fail to acknowledge discretionary or ethical responsibilities, society, through government, will act, making them legal responsibilities. Government may do this, moreover, without regard to an organization's economic responsibilities. As a result, the organization may have greater difficulty in earning a profit than it would have if it had voluntarily assumed some ethical and discretionary responsibilities.

Both Friedman and Carroll argue their positions based on the impact of socially responsible actions on a firm's profits. Friedman says that socially responsible actions hurt a firm's efficiency. Carroll proposes that a lack of social responsibility results in increased government regulations, which reduce a firm's efficiency.

Empirical research now indicates that socially responsible actions may have a positive effect on a firm's financial performance. Although a number of studies in the past have found no significant relationship,[8] an increasing number are finding a positive relationship.[9] A recent in-depth analysis by Margolis and Walsh of 127 studies found that "there is a positive association and very little evidence of a negative association between a company's social performance and its financial performance."[10] Another meta-analysis of 52 studies on social responsibility and performance reached this same conclusion.[11]

According to Porter and Kramer, "social and economic goals are not inherently conflicting, but integrally connected."[12] Being known as a socially responsible firm may provide a company with **social capital**, the goodwill of key stakeholders, that can be used for competitive advantage.[13] Target, for example, tries to attract socially concerned younger consumers by offering brands from companies that can boost ethical track records and community involvement.[14] A survey of more than 700 global companies by the Conference Board reported that 60% of the managers stated that citizenship activities had led to (1) goodwill that opened doors in local communities and (2) an enhanced reputation with consumers.[15] Another survey of 140 U.S. firms revealed that being more socially responsible resulted not only in competitive advantages but also in cost savings.[16] For example, companies that take the lead in being environmentally friendly, such as by using recycled materials, preempt attacks from environmental groups and enhance their corporate image. Programs to reduce pollution, for example, can actually reduce waste and maximize resource productivity. One study that examined 70 ecological initiatives taken by 43 companies found the average payback period to be 18 months.[17] Other examples of benefits received from being socially responsible are:

- Their environmental concerns may enable them to charge premium prices and gain brand loyalty (for example, Ben & Jerry's Ice Cream).
- Their trustworthiness may help them generate enduring relationships with suppliers and distributors without requiring them to spend a lot of time and money policing contracts (for example, Maytag).
- They can attract outstanding employees who prefer working for a responsible firm (for example, Procter & Gamble).
- They are more likely to be welcomed into a foreign country (for example, Levi Strauss).
- They can utilize the goodwill of public officials for support in difficult times. (For example, Minnesota supported Dayton Hudson's (now Target) fight to avoid being acquired by Dart Industries of Maryland.)
- They are more likely to attract capital infusions from investors who view reputable companies as desirable long-term investments (for example, 3M).[18]

Corporate Stakeholders

The concept that business must be socially responsible sounds appealing until we ask, "Responsible to whom?" A corporation's task environment includes a large number of groups with interest in a business organization's activities. These groups are referred to as **corporate stakeholders** because they affect or are affected by the achievement of the firm's objectives.[19] Should a corporation be responsible only to some of these groups, or does business have an equal responsibility to all of them? Does a company have any responsibility to the employees of suppliers (especially in other countries) to ensure that they are treated fairly and have safe working conditions?

A survey of the U.S. general public by Harris Poll revealed that 95% of the respondents felt that U.S. corporations owe something to their workers and the communities in which they operate and that they should sometimes sacrifice some profit for the sake of making things better for their workers and communities. People were concerned that business executives seemed to be more interested in making profits and boosting their own pay than they were in the safety and quality of the products made by their companies.[20] These negative feelings receive some support from a study which revealed that the CEOs at the 50 U.S. companies that outsourced the greatest number of jobs received a greater increase in pay (up 46%) from 2002 to 2003 than did the CEOs of 365 U.S. firms overall (only a 9% increase).[21]

In any one strategic decision, the interests of one stakeholder group can conflict with those of another. For example, a business firm's decision to use only recycled materials in its manufacturing process may have a positive effect on environmental groups but a negative effect on shareholder dividends. In another example, Maytag Corporation's top management decided to move refrigerator production from Galesburg, Illinois, to a lower-wage location in Mexico. On the one hand, shareholders were generally pleased with the decision because it would lower costs. On the other hand, officials and local union people were very unhappy at the loss of jobs when the Galesburg plant closed. Which group's interests should have priority?

Stakeholder Analysis

Stakeholder analysis is the identification and evaluation of corporate stakeholders. This can be done in a three-step process.

The *first step* in stakeholder analysis is to identify **primary stakeholders**, those who have a direct connection with the corporation and who have sufficient bargaining power to directly affect corporate activities. Primary stakeholders are directly affected by the corporation and usually include customers, employees, suppliers, shareholders, and creditors.

But who exactly are a firm's customers or employees and what do they want? This is not always a simple exercise. For example, Intel's customers were clearly computer manufacturers because that's to whom Intel sold its electronic chips. When a math professor found a small flaw in Intel's Pentium microprocessor in 1994, computer users demanded that Intel replace the defective chips. At first Intel refused to do so because it hadn't sold PCs to these individuals. According to then-CEO Andy Grove, "I got irritated and angry because of user demands that we take back a device we didn't sell." Intel wanted the PC users to follow the supply chain and complain to the firms from whom they had bought the computers. Gradually Grove was persuaded that Intel had a direct duty to these consumers. "Although we didn't sell to these individuals directly, we marketed to them. . . . It took me a while to understand this," explained Grove. In the end, Intel paid $450 million to replace the defective parts.[22]

Aside from the Intel example, business corporations usually know their primary stakeholders and what they want. The corporation systematically monitors these stakeholders because they are important to a firm's meeting its economic and legal responsibilities. Employees want a fair day's pay and fringe benefits. Customers want safe products and value for price paid. Shareholders want dividends and stock price appreciation. Suppliers want predictable orders and bills paid. Creditors want commitments to be met on time. In the normal course of affairs, the relationship between a firm and each of its primary stakeholders is regulated by written or verbal agreements and laws. Once a problem is identified, negotiation takes place based on costs and benefits to each party. (Government is not usually considered a primary stakeholder because laws apply to all in a category and usually cannot be negotiated.)

The *second step* in stakeholder analysis is to identify the **secondary stakeholders**—those who have only an indirect stake in the corporation but who are also affected by corporate activities. These usually include nongovernmental organizations (NGOs, such as Greenpeace), activists, local communities, trade associations, competitors, and governments. Because the corporation's relationship with each of these stakeholders is usually not covered by any written or verbal agreement, there is room for misunderstanding. As in the case of NGOs and activists, there actually may be no relationship until a problem develops—usually brought up by the stakeholder. In the normal course of events, these stakeholders do not affect the corporation's ability to meet its economic or legal responsibilities. Aside from competitors, these secondary stakeholders are not usually monitored by the corporation in any systematic fashion. As a result, relationships are usually based on a set of questionable assumptions about each other's needs and wants. Although these stakeholders may not directly affect a firm's short-term profitability, their actions could determine a corporation's reputation and thus its long-term performance. A number of companies, such as Nike, have been strongly criticized for purchasing their supplies from contractors (usually in developing nations) with unsafe manufacturing plants and "sweatshop" working conditions.

The *third step* in stakeholder analysis is to estimate the effect on each stakeholder group from any particular strategic decision. Because the primary decision criteria are typically economic, this is the point where secondary stakeholders may be ignored or discounted as unimportant. For a firm to fulfill its ethical or discretionary responsibilities, it must seriously consider the needs and wants of its secondary stakeholders in any strategic decision. For example, how much will specific stakeholder groups lose or gain? What other alternatives do they have to replace what may be lost?

Stakeholder Input

Once stakeholder impacts have been identified, managers should decide whether stakeholder input should be invited into the discussion of the strategic alternatives. A group is more likely to accept or even help implement a decision if it has some input into which alternative is chosen and how it is to be implemented. In the case of Maytag's decision to close its Galesburg, Illinois, refrigerator production, the community was not a part of the decision. Nevertheless, management decided to inform the local community of its decision three years in advance of the closing instead of the 60 days required by law. Although the announcement created negative attention, it gave the Galesburg employees and townspeople more time to adjust to the eventual closing.

Given the wide range of interests and concerns present in any organization's task environment, one or more groups, at any one time, probably will be dissatisfied with an organization's activities—even if management is trying to be socially responsible. A company may have some stakeholders of which it is only marginally aware. For example, McDonald's is known for its environmentally sound practices, its willingness to hire and train disabled workers, and its charitable donations. Nevertheless, the film documentary *Super Size Me* criticized the health benefits of eating McDonald's fast food and contributed to falling sales. Therefore, before making a strategic decision, strategic managers should consider how each alternative will affect various stakeholder groups. What seems at first to be the best decision because it appears to be the most profitable may actually result in the worst set of consequences to the corporation. One example of a company that does its best to consider its responsibilities to its primary and secondary stakeholders when making strategic decisions is Johnson & Johnson. See STRATEGY HIGHLIGHT 3.1 for the J&J credo.

3.2 | Ethical Decision Making

Some people joke that there is no such thing as "business ethics." They call it an oxymoron—a concept that combines opposite or contradictory ideas. Unfortunately, there is some truth to this sarcastic comment. For example, a survey by the Ethics Resource Center of 1,324 employees of 747 U.S. companies found that 48% of employees surveyed said that they had engaged in one or more unethical and/or illegal actions during the past year. The most common questionable behaviors involved cutting corners on quality (16%), covering up incidents (14%), abusing or lying about sick days (11%), and lying to or deceiving customers (9%).

STRATEGY HIGHLIGHT 3.1

The Johnson & Johnson Credo

We believe our first responsibility is to the doctors, nurses, and patients, to mothers and fathers and all others who use our products and services. In meeting their needs everything we do must be of high quality. We must constantly strive to reduce our costs in order to maintain reasonable prices. Customers' orders must be serviced promptly and accurately. Our suppliers and distributors must have an opportunity to make a fair profit.

We are responsible to our employees, the men and women who work with us throughout the world. Everyone must be considered as an individual. We must respect their dignity and recognize their merit. They must have a sense of security in their jobs. Compensation must be fair and adequate, and working conditions clean, orderly, and safe. We must be mindful of ways to help our employees fulfill their family responsibilities. Employees must feel free to make suggestions and complaints. There must be equal opportunity for employment, development, and advancement for those qualified. We must provide competent management, and their actions must be just and ethical.

We are responsible to the communities where we live and work and to the world community as well. We must be good citizens—support good works and charities and bear our fair share of taxes. We must encourage civic improvements and better health and education. We must maintain in good order the property we are privileged to use, protecting the environment and natural resources.

Our final responsibility is to our stockholders. Business must make a sound profit. We must experiment with new ideas. Research must be carried on, innovative programs developed, and mistakes paid for. New equipment must be purchased, new facilities provided, and new products launched. Reserves must be created for adverse times. When we operate according to these principles, the stockholders should realize a fair return.

Source: Johnson & Johnson Company web site (*www.jnj.com*), September 28, 2004. Reprinted by permission of Johnson & Johnson.

Some 56% of workers reported pressure to act unethically or illegally on the job.[23] In another survey, 53% of employees in corporations of all sizes admitted that they would be willing to misrepresent corporate financial statements if asked to do so by a superior.[24] A survey of 141 chief financial executives revealed that 17% had been pressured by their CEOs over a five-year period to misrepresent the company's financial results. Five percent admitted that they had succumbed to the request.[25]

In the past 10 years, there have been massive write-downs and restatements of profits caused by misclassification of expenses as capital expenditures. Top executives have appropriated corporate assets for personal gain. Illegal advantage has been given to large stakeholders in mutual funds to the financial disadvantage of smaller investors. Executive compensation has been perceived as being exorbitant and out of line with corporate performance. Stock dividends have been given to management without any improvement in corporate performance. It should be no surprise that in a recent survey of the U.S. general public, 70% of the respondents stated that they distrust business executives.[26] See **STRATEGY HIGHLIGHT 3.2** for examples of unethical practices at Enron and WorldCom.

Some Reasons for Unethical Behavior

Why are business people perceived to be acting unethically? It may be that the involved people are not even aware that they are doing something questionable. There is no worldwide standard of conduct for business people. This is especially important given that at least 22% of revenues of U.S. corporations come from other countries.[27] Cultural norms and values vary between countries and even between different geographic regions and ethnic groups within a country. For example, what is considered in one country to be a bribe to expedite service is sometimes considered in another country to be normal business practice. Some of these dif-

STRATEGY HIGHLIGHT 3.2

Unethical Practices at Enron and WorldCom Exposed by Whistle-Blowers

Corporate scandals at Enron, WorldCom, and Tyco, among other international companies, have caused people around the world to seriously question the ethics of business executives. Enron, in particular, has become infamous for the questionable actions of its top executives in the form of (1) off-balance sheet partnerships used to hide the company's deteriorating finances, (2) revenue from long-term contracts being recorded in the first year instead of being spread over multiple years, (3) financial reports being falsified to inflate executive bonuses, and (4) manipulation of the electricity market—leading to a California energy crisis. Only Sherron Watkins, an Enron accountant, was willing to speak out regarding the questionable nature of these practices. In a now-famous memo to then-CEO Kenneth Lay, Watkins warned:

I realize that we have had a lot of smart people looking at this and a lot of accountants including AA & Co. [Arthur Anderson] have blessed the accounting treatment. None

of that will protect Enron if these transactions are ever disclosed in the bright light of day.

At WorldCom, Cynthia Cooper, an internal auditor, noted that some of the company's capital expenditures should have been listed on the second-quarter financial statements as expenses. When she mentioned this to both WorldCom's controller and its chief financial officer, she was told to stop what she was doing and to delay the audit until the third quarter (when expensing the transactions would not be noticed). Instead, Cooper informed the board of directors' audit committee. Two weeks later, WorldCom announced that it was reducing earnings by $3.9 billion, the largest restatement in history.

Sources: G. Colvin, "Wonder Women of Whistleblowers," *Fortune* (August 12, 2002), p. 56; W. Zellner, "The Deadly Sins of Enron," *Business Week* (October 14, 2002), pp. 26–28; M. J. Mandel, "And the Enron Award Goes to . . . Enron," *Business Week* (May 20, 2002), p. 46.

ferences may derive from whether a country's governance system is rule based or relationship based. Relationship-based countries tend to be less transparent and have a higher degree of corruption than do rule-based countries.[28] See the **GLOBAL ISSUE** feature for an explanation of country governance systems and how they may affect business practices.

Another possible reason for what is often perceived to be unethical behavior lies in differences in values between business people and key stakeholders. Some business people may believe profit maximization is the key goal of their firm, whereas concerned interest groups may have other priorities, such as the hiring of minorities and women or the safety of their neighborhoods. Of the six values measured by the Allport-Vernon-Lindzey Study of Values test (aesthetic, economic, political, religious, social, and theoretical), both U.S. and UK executives consistently score highest on economic and political values and lowest on social and religious ones. This is similar to the value profile of managers from Japan, Korea, India, and Australia, as well as those of U.S. business school students. U.S. Protestant ministers, in contrast, score highest on religious and social values and very low on economic values.[29]

This difference in values can make it difficult for one group of people to understand another's actions. For example, even though some people feel that the advertising of cigarettes (especially to youth) is unethical, the people managing tobacco companies respond that they are simply offering a product; "Let the buyer beware" is a traditional saying in free-market capitalism. They argue that customers in a free-market democracy have the right to choose how they spend their money and live their lives. Social progressives may contend that business people working in tobacco, alcoholic beverages, and gambling industries are acting unethically by making and advertising products with potentially dangerous and expensive side effects, such as cancer, alcoholism, and addiction. People working in these industries could respond by asking whether it is ethical for people who don't smoke, drink, or gamble to reject another person's right to do so.

GL🌐BAL ISSUE

How Rule-Based and Relationship-Based Governance Systems Affect Ethical Behavior

The developed nations of the world operate under governance systems quite different from those used by developing nations. The developed nations and the business firms within them follow well-recognized rules in their dealings and financial reporting. To the extent that a country's rules force business corporations to publicly disclose in-depth information about the company to potential shareholders and others, that country's financial and legal system is said to be **transparent**. Transparency is said to simplify transactions and reduce the temptation to behave illegally or unethically. Finland, the United Kingdom, Hong Kong, the United States, and Australia have very transparent business climates. The Kurtzman Group, a consulting firm, developed an *opacity index* that measures the risks associated with unclear legal systems, regulations, economic policies, corporate governance standards, and corruption in 48 countries. The countries with the most opaque/least transparent ratings are Indonesia, Venezuela, China, Nigeria, India, Egypt, and Russia.

Developing nations tend to have **relationship-based governance**. Transactions are based on personal and implicit agreements, not on formal contracts enforceable by a court. Information about a business is largely local and private—thus cannot be easily verified by a third party. In contrast, **rule-based governance** relies on publicly verifiable information—the type of information that is typically not available in a developing country. The rule-based system has an infrastructure, based on accounting, auditing, ratings systems, legal cases, and codes, to provide and monitor this information. If present in a developing nation, the infrastructure is not very sophisticated. This is why investing in a developing country is very risky. The relationship-based system in a developing nation is inherently nontransparent due to the local and nonverifiable nature of its information. A business person needs to develop and nurture a wide network of personal relationships. *What* you know is less important than *who* you know.

The investment in time and money needed to build the necessary relationships to conduct business in a developing nation creates a high entry barrier for any newcomers to an industry. Thus, key industries in developing nations tend to be controlled by a small number of companies, usually privately owned, family-controlled conglomerates. Because public information is unreliable and insufficient for decisions, strategic decisions may depend more on a CEO playing golf with the prime minister than with questionable market share data. In a relationship-based system, the culture of the country (and the founder's family) strongly affects corporate culture and business ethics. What is "fair" depends on whether one is a family member, a close friend, a neighbor, or a stranger. Because behavior tends to be less controlled by laws and agreed-upon standards than by tradition, businesspeople from a rule-based developed nation perceive the relationship-based system in a developing nation to be less ethical and more corrupt. According to Larry Smeltzer, ethics professor at Arizona State University, "The lack of openness and predictable business standards drives companies away. . . . Why would you want to do business in, say, Libya, where you don't know the rules?"

Sources: S. Li, S. H. Park, and S. Li, "The Great Leap Forward: The Transition from Relation-Based Governance to Rule-Based Governance," *Organizational Dynamics*, Vol. 33, No. 1 (2003), pp. 63–78; M. Davids, "Global Standards, Local Problems," *Journal of Business Strategy* (January/February 1999), pp. 38–43; "The Opacity Index," *Economist* (September 18, 2004), p. 106.

Seventy percent of executives representing 111 diverse national and multinational corporations reported that they bend the rules to attain their objectives.[30] The three most common reasons given were:

- Organizational performance required it—74%
- Rules were ambiguous or out of date—70%
- Pressure from others and everyone does it—47%

The financial community's emphasis on short-term earnings performance is a significant pressure for executives to "manage" quarterly earnings. For example, a company achieving its forecasted quarterly earnings figure signals to the investment community that its strategy and operations are proceeding as planned. Failing to meet its target signals that the company is in trouble—thus causing the stock price to fall and shareholders to become worried. The company's exceeding its forecast in the fourth quarter of 2005 would raise analysts' expectations unrealistically high for the fourth quarter of 2006. Research by Degeorge and Patel involving more than 100,000 quarterly earnings reports revealed that a preponderance (82%) of reported earnings *exactly* matched analysts' expectations or exceeded them by only 1%. The disparity between the number of earnings reports that missed estimates by a penny and the number that exceeded them by a penny suggests that executives who risked falling short of forecasts "borrowed" earnings from future quarters.[31]

In explaining why executives at Enron engaged in unethical and illegal actions, former Enron Vice President Sherron Watkins used the "frogs in boiling water" analogy. If, for example, one were to toss a frog into a pan of boiling water, the frog would quickly jump out. It might be burned, but the frog would survive. However, if one put a frog in a pan of cold water and turned up the heat very slowly, the frog would not sense the increasing heat until it was too lethargic to jump out and would be boiled. According to Watkins:

> Enron's accounting moved from creative to aggressive, to fraudulent, like the pot of water moving from cool to lukewarm to boiling; those involved with the creative transactions soon found themselves working on the aggressive transactions and were finally in the uncomfortable situation of working on fraudulent deals.[32]

Moral Relativism

Some people justify their seemingly unethical positions by arguing that there is no one absolute code of ethics and that morality is relative. Simply put, **moral relativism** claims that morality is relative to some personal, social, or cultural standard and that there is no method for deciding whether one decision is better than another.

Adherents of moral relativism may believe that all moral decisions are deeply personal and that individuals have the right to run their own lives; each person should be allowed to interpret situations and act on his or her own moral values. They may also argue that social roles carry with them certain obligations to those roles only. A manager in charge of a department, for example, must put aside his or her personal beliefs and do instead what the role requires—that is, act in the best interests of the department. They could also argue that a decision is legitimate if it is common practice, regardless of other considerations ("everyone's doing it"). Some propose that morality itself is relative to a particular culture, society, or community. People should therefore understand the practices of other countries but not judge them. If the citizens of another country share certain norms and customs, what right does an outsider have to criticize them?

Although these arguments make some sense, moral relativism could enable a person to justify almost any sort of decision or action, so long as it is not declared illegal.

Kohlberg's Levels of Moral Development

Another reason some business people might be seen as unethical is that they may have no well-developed personal sense of ethics. A person's ethical behavior is affected by his or her level of moral development, certain personality variables, and such situational factors as the job itself, the supervisor, and the organizational culture.[33] Kohlberg proposes that a person progresses through three **levels of moral development**.[34] Similar in some ways to Maslow's hierarchy of needs, in Kohlberg's system, the individual moves from total self-centeredness to a concern for universal values. Kohlberg's three levels are as follows:

1. **The preconventional level:** This level is characterized by a concern for self. Small children and others who have not progressed beyond this stage evaluate behaviors on the basis of personal interest—avoiding punishment or quid pro quo.

2. **The conventional level:** This level is characterized by considerations of society's laws and norms. Actions are justified by an external code of conduct.

3. **The principled level:** This level is characterized by a person's adherence to an internal moral code. An individual at this level looks beyond norms or laws to find universal values or principles.

Kohlberg places most people in the conventional level, with fewer than 20% of U.S. adults in the principled level of development.[35]

Encouraging Ethical Behavior

Following Carroll's work, if businesspeople do not act ethically, government will be forced to pass laws regulating their actions—and usually increasing their costs. For self-interest, if for no other reason, managers should be more ethical in their decision making. One way to do that is by encouraging codes of ethics. Another is by providing guidelines for ethical behavior.

Codes of Ethics

A **code of ethics** specifies how an organization expects its employees to behave while on the job. Developing a code of ethics can be a useful way to promote ethical behavior, especially for people who are operating at Kohlberg's conventional level of moral development. Such codes are currently being used by more than half of U.S. corporations. A code of ethics (1) clarifies company expectations of employee conduct in various situations and (2) makes clear that the company expects its people to recognize the ethical dimensions in decisions and actions.[36]

Various studies indicate that an increasing number of companies are developing codes of ethics and implementing ethics training workshops and seminars. However, research also indicates that when faced with a question of ethics, managers tend to ignore codes of ethics and try to solve dilemmas on their own.[37] To combat this tendency, the management of a company that wants to improve its employees' ethical behavior should not only develop a comprehensive code of ethics but also communicate the code in its training programs, in its performance appraisal system, in policies and procedures, and through its own actions. It may even include key values in its values and mission statements (as discussed in **Chapter 1**). According to a 2004 survey of CEOs by the Business Roundtable Institute for Corporate Ethics, 74% of CEOs confirmed that their companies had made changes within the previous two years in how they handled or reported ethics issues. Specific changes reported were:

- Enhanced internal reporting and communications—33%
- Ethics hotlines—17%
- Improved compliance procedures—12%
- Greater oversight by the board of directors—10%[38]

A company's executives may also want to establish and enforce a code of ethical behavior for those companies with which it does business—especially if it outsources its manufacturing to a company in another country. For example, Reebok International has developed a set of production standards for the manufacturers that supply the company with its athletic shoes on a contract basis. In response to a report commissioned by Reebok (at a cost of $50,000) that found health and safety problems at two subcontractor plants in Indonesia, the two suppliers were forced to spend $500,000 in factory improvements in order to keep Reebok's business.[39]

Guidelines for Ethical Behavior

Ethics is defined as the consensually accepted standards of behavior for an occupation, a trade, or a profession. **Morality**, in contrast, is the precepts of personal behavior based on religious or philosophical grounds. **Law** refers to formal codes that permit or forbid certain behaviors and may or may not enforce ethics or morality.[40] Given these definitions, how do we arrive at a comprehensive statement of ethics to use in making decisions in a specific occupation, trade, or profession? A starting point for such a code of ethics is to consider the three basic approaches to ethical behavior[41]:

1. **Utilitarian Approach:** The **utilitarian approach** proposes that actions and plans should be judged by their consequences. People should therefore behave in a way that will produce the greatest benefit to society and produce the least harm or the lowest cost. A problem with this approach is the difficulty in recognizing all the benefits and costs of any particular decision. Research reveals that only the stakeholders who have the most *power* (ability to affect the company), *legitimacy* (legal or moral claim on company resources), and *urgency* (demand for immediate attention) are given priority by CEOs.[42] It is therefore likely that only the most obvious stakeholders will be considered, while others are ignored.

2. **Individual Rights Approach:** The **individual rights approach** proposes that human beings have certain fundamental rights that should be respected in all decisions. A particular decision or behavior should be avoided if it interferes with the rights of others. A problem with this approach is in defining "fundamental rights." The U.S. Constitution includes a Bill of Rights that may or may not be accepted throughout the world. The approach can also encourage selfish behavior when a person defines a personal need or want as a "right."

3. **Justice Approach:** The **justice approach** proposes that decision makers be equitable, fair, and impartial in the distribution of costs and benefits to individuals and groups. It follows the principles of *distributive justice* (people who are similar on relevant dimensions such as job seniority should be treated in the same way) and *fairness* (liberty should be equal for all persons). The justice approach can also include the concepts of *retributive justice* (punishment should be proportional to the offense) and *compensatory justice* (wrongs should be compensated in proportion to the offense). Affirmative action issues such as reverse discrimination are examples of conflicts between distributive and compensatory justice.

Cavanagh proposes that we solve ethical problems by asking the following three questions regarding an act or a decision:

1. **Utility:** Does it optimize the satisfactions of all stakeholders?
2. **Rights:** Does it respect the rights of the individuals involved?
3. **Justice:** Is it consistent with the canons of justice?

For example, is padding an expense account ethical? Using the utility criterion, this action increases the company's costs and thus does not optimize benefits for shareholders or customers. Using the rights approach, a person has no right to the money (otherwise, we wouldn't call it "padding"). Using the justice criterion, salary and commissions constitute ordinary compensation, but expense accounts only compensate a person for expenses incurred in doing his or her job—expenses that the person would not normally incur except in doing the job.[43]

Another approach to resolving ethical dilemmas is by applying the logic of the philosopher Immanuel Kant. Kant presents two principles (called **categorical imperatives**) to guide our actions:

1. A person's action is ethical only if that person is willing for that same action to be taken by everyone who is in a similar situation. This is same as the *Golden Rule*: Treat others as you would like them to treat you. For example, padding an expense account would be considered ethical if the person were also willing for everyone else to do the same if they

were the boss. Because it is very doubtful that any manager would be pleased with expense account padding, the action must be considered unethical.

2. A person should never treat another human being simply as a means but always as an end. This means that an action is morally wrong for a person if that person uses others merely as means for advancing his or her own interests. To be moral, the act should not restrict other people's actions so that they are disadvantaged in some way.[44]

3.3 | Conclusion

In his book *Defining Moments*, Joseph Badaracco states that most ethics problems deal with "right versus right" problems in which neither choice is wrong. These are what he calls "dirty hands problems" in which a person has to deal with very specific situations that are covered only vaguely in corporate credos or mission statements. For example, many mission statements endorse fairness but fail to define the term. At the personal level, *fairness* could mean playing by the rules of the game, following basic morality, treating everyone alike and not playing favorites, treating others as you would want to be treated, being sensitive to individual needs, providing equal opportunity for everyone, or creating a level playing field for the disadvantaged. According to Badaracco, codes of ethics are not always helpful because they tend to emphasize problems of misconduct and wrongdoing, not a choice between two acceptable alternatives, such as keeping an inefficient plant operating for the good of the community or closing the plant and relocating to a more efficient location to lower costs.[45]

This chapter provides a framework for understanding the social responsibilities of a business corporation. Following Carroll, it proposes that a manager should consider not only the economic and legal responsibilities of a firm but also its ethical and discretionary responsibilities. It also provides a method for making ethical choices, whether they are right versus right or some combination of right and wrong. It is important to consider Cavanaugh's questions, using the three approaches of utilitarian, rights, and justice, plus Kant's categorical imperatives when making a strategic decision. A corporation should try to move from Kohlberg's conventional to a principled level of ethical development. If nothing else, the frameworks should contribute to well-reasoned strategic decisions that a person can defend when interviewed by hostile media or questioned in a court room.

Strategy Bits

- In a survey of 192 U.S. companies, 92% monitored employees' use of e-mail and the Internet.
- Of the surveyed companies, 26% monitored their employees' electronic activities all the time.
- Almost none of the companies surveyed had checks in place to protect employees' privacy or to ensure that such monitoring was not abused.[46]

Discussion Questions

1. What is the relationship between corporate governance and social responsibility?

2. What is your opinion of Reebok's having production standards of human rights for its suppliers? What would Milton Friedman say? Contrast his view with Archie Carroll's view.

3. Does a company have to act selflessly to be considered socially responsible? For example, when building a

new plant, a corporation voluntarily invested in additional equipment that enabled it to reduce its pollution emissions beyond any current laws. Knowing that it would be very expensive for its competitors to do the same, the firm lobbied the government to make pollution regulations more restrictive on the entire industry. Is this company socially responsible? Were its managers acting ethically?

4. Are people living in a relationship-based governance system likely to be unethical in business dealings?

5. Given that people rarely use a company's code of ethics to guide their decision making, what good are the codes?

Strategic Practice Exercise

It is 1982. Zombie Savings and Loan is in trouble. This is a time when many savings and loans (S&Ls) are in financial difficulty. Zombie holds many 30-year mortgages at low fixed interest rates in its loan portfolio. Interest rates have risen significantly, and the Deregulation Act of 1980 has given Zombie and other S&Ls the right to make business loans and hold up to 20% of its assets as such. Because interest rates in general have risen, but the rate that Zombie receives on its old mortgages has not, Zombie must now pay out higher interest rates to its deposit customers or see them leave, and it has negative cash flow until rates fall below the rates in its mortgage portfolio or Zombie itself fails.

In present value terms, Zombie is insolvent, but the accounting rules of the time do not require marking assets to market, so Zombie is allowed to continue to operate and is faced with two choices: It can wait and hope interest rates fall before it is declared insolvent and is closed down, or it can raise fresh (insured) deposits and make risky loans that have high interest rates. Risky loans promise high payoffs (if they are repaid), but the probability of loss to Zombie and being closed later with greater loss to the Federal Savings & Loan Insurance Corporation (FSLIC) is high.

Zombie stays in business if its gamble pays off, and it loses no more than it has already lost if the gamble does not pay off. Indeed, if not closed, Zombie will raise increasingly greater new deposits and make more risky loans until it either wins or is shut down by the regulators.

Waiting for lower interest rates and accepting early closure if they do not arrive is certainly in the best interest of the FSLIC and of the tax payers, but the manager of Zombie has more immediate responsibilities, such as employees' jobs, mortgage customers, depositors, the local neighborhood, and his or her job. As a typical S&L, Zombie's depositors are its shareholders and vote according to how much money they have in savings accounts with Zombie. If Zombie closes, depositors may lose some, but not all, of their money, because their deposits are insured by the FSLIC. There is no other provider of home mortgages in the immediate area. What should the manager do?

Source: Adapted from D. W. Swanton, "Teaching Students the Nature of Moral Hazard: An Ethical Component for Finance Classes," paper presented to the annual meeting of the *Academy of Finance*, Chicago (March 13, 2003). Reprinted with permission.

Key Terms

categorical imperative (p. 67)
code of ethics (p. 66)
corporate stakeholders (p. 59)
ethics (p. 66)
individual rights approach (p. 67)
justice approach (p. 67)
law (p. 66)

levels of moral development (p. 65)
moral relativism (p. 65)
morality (p. 66)
primary stakeholder (p. 60)
relationship-based governance
  (p. 64)
rule-based governance (p. 64)

secondary stakeholder (p. 60)
social capital (p. 59)
social responsibility (p. 56)
stakeholder analysis (p. 60)
transparent (p. 64)
utilitarian approach (p. 67)

PART ENDING VIDEO CASE PART ONE

Newbury Comics, Inc.

STRATEGY BASICS

Newbury Comics was founded in 1978 by MIT roommates, Mike Dreese and John Brusger. With $2,000 and a comic book collection they converted a Newbury Street studio apartment in Boston's trendy Back Bay into the second organized comic book shop in the area. In 1979, Newbury Comics began selling punk and new wave music and quickly became the region's leading specialist in alternative music. By 1982, with a second store open in Harvard Square, the company's revenues were being generated mostly from cutting-edge music and rock-related merchandise.

Newbury Comics consists of 22 stores spanning the New England region and is known to be the place to shop for everything from the best of the underground/independent music scene to major label superstars. The chain also stocks a wide variety of non-music related items such as T-shirts, Dr. (doc) Martens shoes, posters, jewelry, cosmetics, books, magazines, and other trendy items.

The video features Cofounders Mike Dreese and John Brusger, as well as Jan Johannet, Manager of one of the New Hampshire stores, talking about the entrepreneurial beginning of Newbury Comics. They point out that the company wants its customers and its employees to "have a good time" in the store. Newbury Comics hires good people who like working in the store. The company attracts creative people because it is different from other retailers. Mike Dreese thinks of the company as expanding out of a comic book retailer into a lifestyle store emphasizing popular culture. He wants Newbury Comics to dominate its product categories and to be the retailer customers seek out in order to obtain what they want. He refers to an expression used throughout the company: "If you can't dominate it, don't do it." He wants the company to grow by looking for "incredible opportunities" (elephant hunting). This approach seems to work at Newbury Comics. The company sustained an annual growth rate of about 80% over the past 7 years resulting in 1,000% overall growth.

With some input from others at corporate headquarters, Mike Dreese develops the overall plan for the company by looking at where he would like the company to be in 3, 5, or 10 years. He analyzes the external environment in terms of competition, trends, and customer preferences. John Brusger then puts Mike's plan into action. The company identifies product growth areas by conducting dozens of experiments each month to learn what the customer wants.

Concepts Illustrated in the Video

- The Learning Organization
- Theories of Organizational Adaptation
- Model of Strategic Management
- Modes of Strategic Decision Making
- Strategic Decision Making Process
- Executive Leadership
- Strategic Vision

Study Questions

1. How is Newbury Comics an example of a learning organization?
2. What is the process of strategic management at Newbury Comics? Who is involved in each part?
3. What do you think might be the company's (a) current mission/vision, (b) objectives, (c) strategies, and (d) policies? Give an example of each from the video.
4. What theory of organizational adaptation is being followed by Mike Dreese?
5. Newbury Comics illustrates what mode of strategic decision making? Is it appropriate?

CHAPTER 4
Environmental Scanning and Industry Analysis

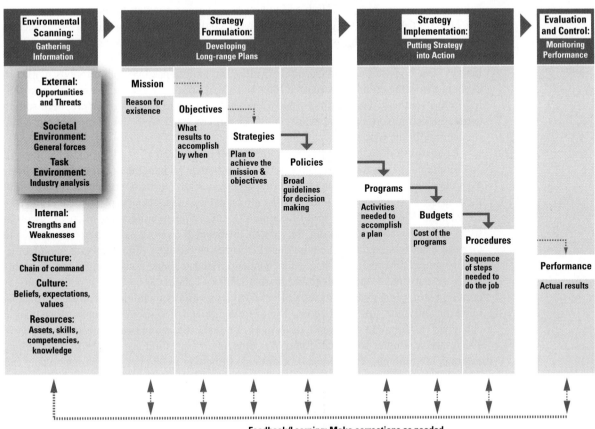

Environmental Scanning:	Strategy Formulation:	Strategy Implementation:	Evaluation and Control:
Gathering Information	Developing Long-range Plans	Putting Strategy into Action	Monitoring Performance

External:
Opportunities and Threats

Societal Environment:
General forces

Task Environment:
Industry analysis

Internal:
Strengths and Weaknesses

Structure:
Chain of command

Culture:
Beliefs, expectations, values

Resources:
Assets, skills, competencies, knowledge

Mission
Reason for existence

Objectives
What results to accomplish by when

Strategies
Plan to achieve the mission & objectives

Policies
Broad guidelines for decision making

Programs
Activities needed to accomplish a plan

Budgets
Cost of the programs

Procedures
Sequence of steps needed to do the job

Performance
Actual results

Feedback/Learning: Make corrections as needed

Learning Objectives

After reading this chapter, you should be able to:

- Recognize aspects of an organization's environment that can influence its long-term decisions
- Identify the aspects of an organization's environment that are most strategically important
- Conduct an industry analysis to understand the competitive forces that influence the intensity of rivalry within an industry
- Understand how industry maturity affects industry competitive forces
- Categorize international industries based on their pressures for coordination and local responsiveness
- Construct strategic group maps to assess the competitive positions of firms in an industry
- Identify key success factors and develop an industry matrix
- Use publicly available information to conduct competitive intelligence
- Know how to develop an industry scenario
- Construct an EFAS Table that summarizes external environmental factors

ROD SPRULES INVENTED JAVA-LOGS TO TAKE ADVANTAGE OF TWO INTERSECTING ENVIRON-mental trends—the increasing interest in recycling and the rapid growth of retail coffee houses throughout North America. The Java-Log is a fireplace log made primarily from recycled coffee grounds. It is different from traditional firewood in that it burns with a hotter, brighter flame, emits less carbon dioxide, and is made from a waste product. Sprules first learned of the high heat capacity of coffee grounds while working on a heated cold weather suit for his former employer. With coffee houses becoming popular, Sprules thought of finding a use for the used coffee grounds being produced daily in huge quantities at stores such as Starbucks. Together with his wife, Joanne Johnson, and business partner, Marcel Sbrollini, Sprules formed Robustion Products, Inc., in St. Laurent, Quebec, in 2000 to manufacture and market Java-Logs throughout Canada. Sbrollini, an experienced consumer goods marketer, explained how the company expanded into the United States: "We were just planning on selling in the Northeast United States, but we received so much publicity that we were selling across the entire Northeast and Midwest. By December 2003, we had sold most of our entire production for the season."[1]

Robustion Products is an example of an entrepreneurial firm that took advantage of environmental trends to create a successful new product. A changing environment can, however, also hurt a company. Many pioneering companies have gone out of business because of their failure to adapt to environmental change or, even worse, because of their failure to create change. For example, Baldwin Locomotive, the major manufacturer of steam locomotives, was very slow in making the switch to diesel locomotives. General Electric and General Motors soon dominated the diesel locomotive business. The dominant manufacturers of vacuum tubes failed to make the change to transistors and consequently lost that market. Eastman Kodak, the pioneer and market leader of chemical-based film photography, is currently struggling to make its transition to the newer digital technology. Failure to adapt is, however, only one side of the coin. The aforementioned Java-Logs example shows how a changing environment can create new opportunities at the same time it destroys old ones. The lesson is simple: To be successful over time, an organization needs to be in tune with its external environment. There must be a strategic fit between what the environment wants and what the corporation has to offer, as well as between what the corporation needs and what the environment can provide.

Current predictions are that the environment for all organizations will become even more uncertain with every passing year. What is **environmental uncertainty**? It is the *degree of complexity* plus the *degree of change* existing in an organization's external environment. As more and more markets become global, the number of factors a company must consider in any decision become huge and much more complex. With new technologies being discovered every year, markets change—and products must change with them.

On the one hand, environmental uncertainty is a threat to strategic managers because it hampers their ability to develop long-range plans and to make strategic decisions to keep the corporation in equilibrium with its external environment. On the other hand, environmental uncertainty is an opportunity because it creates a new playing field in which creativity and innovation can play a major part in strategic decisions.

4.1 | Environmental Scanning

Before an organization can begin strategy formulation, it must scan the external environment to identify possible opportunities and threats and its internal environment for strengths and weaknesses. **Environmental scanning** is the monitoring, evaluation, and dissemination of information from the external and internal environments to key people within the corporation. A corporation uses this tool to avoid strategic surprise and to ensure its long-term health. Research has found a positive relationship between environmental scanning and profits.[2]

Identifying External Environmental Variables

In undertaking environmental scanning, strategic managers must first be aware of the many variables within a corporation's societal and task environments. The **societal environment** includes general forces that do not directly touch on the short-run activities of the organization but that can, and often do, influence its long-run decisions. These, shown in **Figure 1–3**, are as follows:

- **Economic forces** that regulate the exchange of materials, money, energy, and information.
- **Technological forces** that generate problem-solving inventions.
- **Political–legal forces** that allocate power and provide constraining and protecting laws and regulations.
- **Sociocultural forces** that regulate the values, mores, and customs of society.

The **task environment** includes those elements or groups that directly affect a corporation and, in turn, are affected by it. These are governments, local communities, suppliers, competitors, customers, creditors, employees/labor unions, special-interest groups, and trade associations. A corporation's task environment is typically the industry within which the firm operates. **Industry analysis** (popularized by Michael Porter) refers to an in-depth examination of key factors within a corporation's task environment. Both the societal and task environments must be monitored to detect the strategic factors that are likely to have a strong impact on corporate success or failure.

Research indicates that high-performing chief executives vary their environmental scanning emphasis according to the level of dynamism they perceive in their external environment. In dynamic environments, successful CEOs pay more attention to the task environment, whereas in stable environments, CEOs focus on forces in the societal environment.[3]

Scanning the Societal Environment

The number of possible strategic factors in the societal environment is very high. The number becomes enormous when we realize that, generally speaking, each country in the world can be represented by its own unique set of societal forces—some of which are very similar to those of neighboring countries and some of which are very different.

For example, even though Korea and China share Asia's Pacific Rim area with Thailand, Taiwan, and Hong Kong (sharing many similar cultural values), they have very different views about the role of business in society. It is generally believed in Korea and China (and to a lesser extent in Japan) that the role of business is primarily to contribute to national development; however, in Hong Kong, Taiwan, and Thailand (and to a lesser extent in the Philippines, Indonesia, Singapore, and Malaysia), the role of business is primarily to make profits for the shareholders.[4] Such differences may translate into different trade regulations and varying difficulty in the **repatriation of profits** (the transfer of profits from a foreign subsidiary to a corporation's headquarters) from one group of Pacific Rim countries to another.

Monitoring Societal Trends. As shown in **Table 4–1**, large corporations categorize the societal environment in any one geographic region into four areas and focus their scanning in each area on trends that have corporatewide relevance. Obviously, trends in any one area may be very important to the firms in one industry but of lesser importance to firms in other industries.

Trends in the *economic* part of the societal environment can have an obvious impact on business activity. For example, an increase in interest rates means fewer sales of major home appliances. Why? A rising interest rate tends to be reflected in higher mortgage rates. Because higher mortgage rates increase the cost of buying a house, the demand for new and used houses tends to fall. Because most major home appliances are sold when people change houses, a reduction in house sales soon translates into a decline in sales of refrigerators, stoves, and dishwashers and reduced profits for everyone in the appliance industry.

The economic development of China and India is having a major impact on the rest of the world. By 2004, China had become the fourth-largest industrial producer in the world after the United States, Japan, and Germany. With India graduating more English-speaking scien-

TABLE 4–1 SOME IMPORTANT VARIABLES IN THE SOCIETAL ENVIRONMENT

Economic	Technological	Political–Legal	Sociocultural
GDP trends	Total government spending for R&D	Antitrust regulations	Lifestyle changes
Interest rates		Environmental protection laws	Career expectations
Money supply	Total industry spending for R&D		Consumer activism
Inflation rates		Tax laws	Rate of family formation
Unemployment levels	Focus of technological efforts	Special incentives	Growth rate of population
Wage/price controls	Patent protection	Foreign trade regulations	Age distribution of population
Devaluation/revaluation	New products	Attitudes toward foreign companies	Regional shifts in population
Energy availability and cost	New developments in technology transfer from lab to marketplace	Laws on hiring and promotion	Life expectancies
Disposable and discretionary income	Productivity improvements through automation	Stability of government	Birthrates
Currency markets	Internet availability	Outsourcing regulation	Pension plans
	Telecommunication infrastructure	Foreign "sweat shops"	Health care
	Computer hacking activity		Level of education

tists, engineers, and technicians than all other nations combined, it has become the primary location for the outsourcing of services, computer software, and telecommunications.[5]

Changes in the *technological* part of the societal environment can also have a great impact on multiple industries. Improvements in computer microprocessors have not only led to the widespread use of home computers but also to better automobile engine performance in terms of power and fuel economy through the use of microprocessors to monitor fuel injection. Digital technology allows movies and music to be available instantly over the Internet or through cable service, but it also means falling fortunes for video rental shops such as Blockbuster and CD stores such as Tower Records. Computer viruses developed by hackers create havoc in the information systems of corporations worldwide. Researchers at George Washington University have identified a number of breakthrough developments in technology that are already having a significant impact on many industries:

- **Portable Information Devices and Electronic Networking:** Combining the computing power of the personal computer, the networking of the Internet, the images of the television, and the convenience of the telephone, these appliances will soon be used by a majority of the population of industrialized nations to make phone calls, send e-mail, and transmit documents and other data. Even now, homes, autos, and offices are being connected (via wires and wirelessly) into intelligent networks that interact with one another. The traditional stand-alone desktop computer may soon join the manual typewriter as a historical curiosity.

- **Fuel Cells and Alternative Energy Sources:** The use of wind, geothermal, hydroelectric, solar, biomass, and other alternative energy sources should increase from the present level of 10% to about 30% by 2010. Once used exclusively to power spacecraft, fuel cells offer the prospect of pollution-free electrical power. Fuel cells chemically combine hydrogen and oxygen to produce electricity, with water as a byproduct. Although it will take a number of years before fuel cells replace gas-powered engines or vast power-generation plants, this technology is already providing an alternative source of power for large buildings.

- **Precision Farming:** The computerized management of crops to suit variations in land characteristics will make farming more efficient. Farm equipment dealers, such as Case and John Deere, add this equipment to tractors for an additional $6,000 or so. It enables farmers to reduce costs, increase yields, and decrease environmental impact. The old system of small, low-tech farming is becoming less viable as large corporate farms increase crop yields on limited farmland for a growing population.

- **Virtual Personal Assistants:** Very smart computer programs that monitor e-mail, faxes, and phone calls will be able to take over routine tasks, such as writing a letter, retrieving a file, making a phone call, or screening requests. Acting like a secretary, a person's virtual assistant could substitute for a person at meetings or in dealing with routine actions.

- **Genetically Altered Organisms:** A convergence of biotechnology and agriculture is creating a new field of life sciences. Plant seeds can be genetically modified to produce more needed vitamins or to be less attractive to pests and more able to survive. Animals (including people) could be similarly modified for desirable characteristics and to eliminate genetic disabilities and diseases.

- **Smart, Mobile Robots:** Robot development has been limited by a lack of sensory devices and sophisticated artificial intelligence systems. Improvements in these areas mean that robots will be created to perform more sophisticated factory work, run errands, do household chores, and assist the disabled.[6]

Trends in the *political–legal* part of the societal environment have a significant impact not only on the level of competition within an industry but also on which strategies might be

TABLE 4–2
CURRENT U.S.
GENERATIONS

Generation	Born	Age in 2005	Number
WW II/ Silent Generation	1932–1945	60–73	32 million
Baby Boomers	1946–1964	41–59	77 million
Generation X	1965–1977	28–40	45 million
Generation Y	1978–1994	11–27	70 million

Source: Developed from data listed in D. Parkinson, *Voices of Experience: Mature Workers in the Future Workforce* (New York: The Conference Board, 2002), p. 19.

successful.[7] For example, periods of strict enforcement of U.S. antitrust laws directly affect corporate growth strategy. As large companies find it more difficult to acquire another firm in the same or a related industry, they are typically driven to diversify into unrelated industries.[8] High levels of taxation and constraining labor laws in Western European countries stimulate companies to find better locations elsewhere. For example, France's statutory 35-hour work week led companies such as Robert Bosch, a German maker of car parts, to consider moving manufacturing to low-cost locations in Eastern Europe.[9]

Demographic trends are part of the *sociocultural* aspect of the societal environment. The demographic bulge in the U.S. population caused by the baby boom in the 1950s continues to affect market demand in many industries. This group of 77 million people in their 40s and 50s is the largest age group in all developed countries, especially in Europe. (See **Table 4–2**.) Although the median age in the United States will rise from 35 in 2000 to 40 by 2050, it will increase from 40 to 47 during the same time period in Germany, and it will increase up to 50 in Italy as soon as 2025.[10] With its low birthrate, Japan's population is expected to fall from 127.6 million in 2004 to around 100 million by 2050.[11] Companies with an eye on the future can find many opportunities to offer products and services to the growing number of "woofies" (well-off old folks)—defined as people over 50 with money to spend.[12] These people are very likely to purchase recreational vehicles (RVs), take ocean cruises, and enjoy leisure sports such as boating, fishing, and bowling, in addition to needing financial services and health care. Anticipating the needs of seniors for prescription drugs is one reason the Walgreen Company is opening a new corner pharmacy every 19 hours![13]

This trend can mean increasing sales for firms such as Winnebago (RVs), Carnival Cruise Lines, and Brunswick (sports equipment), among others. For example, the U.S. motor home industry sold more units in 2004 than it had in any year since 1978.[14] To attract older customers, retailers will need to place seats in their larger stores so aging shoppers can rest. Washrooms need to be more accessible. Signs need to be larger. Restaurants need to raise the level of lighting so people can read their menus. Home appliances need simpler and larger controls. Automobiles need larger door openings and more comfortable seats. Zimmer Holdings, an innovative manufacturer of artificial joints, is looking forward to its market growing rapidly over the next 20 years. According to J. Raymond Elliot, chair and CEO of Zimmer, "It's simple math. Our best years are still in front of us."[15]

Eight current sociocultural trends in the United States are transforming North America and the rest of the world:

1. **Increasing environmental awareness:** Recycling and conservation are becoming more than slogans. Busch Gardens, for example, has eliminated the use of disposable styrofoam trays in favor of washing and reusing plastic trays.

2. **Growing health consciousness:** Concerns about personal health fuel the trend toward physical fitness and healthier living. As a result, sales growth is slowing at fast-food

"burgers and fries" retailers such as McDonald's. Changing public tastes away from sugar-laden processed foods forced Interstate Bakeries, the maker of Twinkies and Wonder Bread, to declare bankruptcy in 2004. The European Union forbade the importation of genetically altered grain ("Frankenfood") because of possible side effects. The spread of AIDS to more than 40 million people worldwide adds even further impetus to the health movement.

3. **Expanding seniors market:** As their numbers increase, people over age 55 will become an even more important market. Already some companies are segmenting the senior population into Young Matures, Older Matures, and the Elderly—each having a different set of attitudes and interests. The desire for companionship by people whose children are grown is causing the pet care industry to grow 4.5% annually, and it is expected to reach about $36 billion in the United States by 2007.[16]

4. **Impact of the Generation Y boomlet:** Born between 1978 and 1994 to the baby boom and X generations, this cohort is almost as large as the baby boom generation. In 1957, the peak year of the postwar boom, 4.3 million babies were born. In 1990, there were 4.2 million births in Generation Y's peak year. By 2000, they were overcrowding elementary and high schools and entering college in numbers not seen since the baby boomers. Now in its teens and early 20s, this cohort is expected to have a strong impact on future products and services.

5. **Declining mass market:** Niche markets are defining the marketers' environment. People want products and services that are adapted more to their personal needs. For example, Estée Lauder's "All Skin" and Maybelline's "Shades of You" lines of cosmetic products are specifically made for African-American women. "Mass customization"—the making and marketing of products tailored to a person's requirements (for example, Dell and Gateway computers)—is replacing the mass production and marketing of the same product in some markets. Only 10% of the 6,200 magazines sold in the United States in 2004 were aimed at the mass market, down from 30% in the 1970s.[17]

6. **Changing pace and location of life:** Instant communication via e-mail, cell phones, and overnight mail enhances efficiency, but it also puts more pressure on people. Merging the personal computer with the communication and entertainment industries through telephone lines, satellite dishes, and cable television increases consumers' choices and allows workers to leave overcrowded urban areas for small towns and telecommute via personal computers and modems.

7. **Changing household composition:** Single-person households, especially those of single women with children, could soon become the most common household type in the United States. Married-couple households slipped from nearly 80% in the 1950s to 50.7% of all households in 2002.[18] A typical family household is no longer the same as it was once portrayed in *The Brady Bunch* in the 1970s or even *The Cosby Show* in the 1980s.

8. **Increasing diversity of workforce and markets:** Between now and 2050, minorities will account for nearly 90% of population growth in the United States. Over time, group percentages of the total U.S. population are expected to change as follows: Non-Hispanic Whites—from 90% in 1950 to 74% in 1995 to 53% by 2050; Hispanic Whites—from 9% in 1995 to 22% in 2050; Blacks—from 13% in 1995 to 15% in 2050; Asians—from 4% in 1995 to 9% in 2050; Native Americans—1%, with slight increase.[19] The number of Mexican immigrants residing illegally in the United States increased from 2.04 million in 1990 to 4.81 million in 2000.[20] Traditional minority groups are increasing their numbers in the workforce and are being identified as desirable target markets. For example, Sears, Roebuck transformed 97 of its stores in October 2004 into "multicultural stores" containing fashions for Hispanic, African-American, and Asian shoppers.[21]

International Societal Considerations. Each country or group of countries in which a company operates presents a unique societal environment with a different set of economic, technological, political–legal, and sociocultural variables for the company to face. International societal environments vary so widely that a corporation's internal environment and strategic management process must be very flexible. Cultural trends in Germany, for example, have resulted in the inclusion of worker representatives in corporate strategic planning. Because Islamic law (*sharia*) forbids interest (*riba*), loans of capital in Islamic countries must be arranged on the basis of profit-sharing instead of interest rates.[22] Differences in societal environments strongly affect the ways in which a **multinational corporation (MNC)**, a company with significant assets and activities in multiple countries, conducts its marketing, financial, manufacturing, and other functional activities. For example, the existence of regional associations such as the European Union, NAFTA in North America, Mercosur in South America, and ASEAN in Asia has a significant impact on the competitive rules of the game both for MNCs operating within and for MNCs wanting to enter these areas.

To account for the many differences among societal environments from one country to another, consider **Table 4–3**. It includes a list of economic, technological, political–legal, and sociocultural variables for any particular country or region. For example, an important economic variable for any firm investing in a foreign country is currency convertibility. Without convertibility, a company operating in Russia cannot convert its profits from rubles to dollars. In terms of sociocultural variables, many Asian cultures (especially China) are less concerned with the values of human rights than are European and North American cultures. Some Asians actually contend that U.S. companies are trying to impose Western human rights requirements on them in an attempt to make Asian products less competitive by raising their costs.[23]

Before planning its strategy for a particular international location, a company must scan the particular country environment(s) in question for opportunities and threats, and it must

TABLE 4–3 SOME IMPORTANT VARIABLES IN INTERNATIONAL SOCIETAL ENVIRONMENTS

Economic	Technological	Political–Legal	Sociocultural
Economic development	Regulations on technology transfer	Form of government	Customs, norms, values
Per capita income	Energy availability/cost	Political ideology	Language
Climate	Natural resource availability	Tax laws	Demographics
GDP trends	Transportation network	Stability of government	Life expectancies
Monetary and fiscal policies	Skill level of workforce	Government attitude toward foreign companies	Social institutions
Unemployment levels	Patent-trademark protection	Regulations on foreign ownership of assets	Status symbols
Currency convertibility	Internet availability		Lifestyle
Wage levels	Telecommunication infrastructure	Strength of opposition groups	Religious beliefs
Nature of competition	Computer hacking technology	Trade regulations	Attitudes toward foreigners
Membership in regional economic associations, e.g., EU, NAFTA, ASEAN		Protectionist sentiment	Literacy level
Membership in World Trade Organization (WTO)		Foreign policies	Human rights
Outsourcing capability		Terrorist activity	Environmentalism
		Legal system	"Sweat shops'
			Pension plans
			Health care

compare those with its own organizational strengths and weaknesses. For example, to operate successfully in a global industry such as automobiles, tires, electronics, or watches, a company must be prepared to establish a significant presence in the three developed areas of the world known collectively as the **Triad**. This term, coined by the Japanese management expert Kenichi Ohmae, refers to the three developed markets of Japan, North America, and Western Europe, which now form a single market with common needs.[24] Focusing on the Triad is essential for an MNC pursuing success in a global industry, according to Ohmae, because close to 90% of all high–value-added, high-technology manufactured goods are produced and consumed in North America, Western Europe, and Japan. Ideally, a company should have a significant presence in each of these regions so that it can develop, produce, and market its products simultaneously in all three areas. Otherwise, it will lose competitive advantage to Triad-oriented MNCs. No longer can an MNC develop and market a new product in one part of the world before it exports it to other developed countries.

Focusing only on the developed nations, however, causes a corporation to miss important market opportunities in the developing nations of the world. Although those nations may not have developed to the point that they have significant demand for a broad spectrum of products, they may very likely be on the threshold of rapid growth in the demand for specific products. This would be the ideal time for a company to enter this market—before competition is established. The key is to be able to identify the "trigger point" when demand for a particular product or service is ready to boom. See the GLOBAL ISSUE boxed highlight for an in-depth explanation of a technique to identify the optimum time to enter a particular market in a developing nation.

GL🌐BAL ISSUE

Identifying Potential Markets in Developing Nations

Research by the Deloitte & Touche Consulting Group reveals that the demand for a specific product increases exponentially at certain points in a country's development. Identifying this trigger point of demand is thus critical to entering emerging markets at the best time. A **trigger point** is the time when enough people have enough money to buy what a company has to sell but before competition is established. This can be determined by using the concept of **purchasing power parity (PPP)**, which measures the cost in dollars of the U.S.-produced equivalent volume of goods that an economy produces.

PPP offers an estimate of the material wealth a nation can purchase, rather than the financial wealth it creates, as is typically measured by Gross Domestic Product (GDP). As a result, restating a nation's GDP in PPP terms reveals much greater spending power than market exchange rates would suggest. For example, a shoe shine costing $5 to $10 in New York City can be purchased for 50¢ in Mexico City. Consequently, the people of Mexico City can enjoy the same standard of living (with respect to shoe shines) as people in New York City with only 5% to 10% of the money. Correcting for PPP restates all Mexican shoe shines at their U.S. purchase value of $5. If one million shoe shines were purchased in Mexico last year, using the PPP model would effectively increase the Mexican GDP by $5 million to $10 million. Using PPP, China becomes the world's second-largest economy after the United States, followed by Japan, India, and Germany.

A trigger point identifies when demand for a particular product is about to rapidly increase in a country. Identifying a trigger point can be a very useful technique for determining when to enter a new market in a developing nation. Trigger points vary for different products. For example, an apparent trigger point for long-distance telephone services is at $7,500 in GDP per capita—a point when demand for telecommunications services increases rapidly. Once national wealth surpasses $15,000 per capita, demand increases at a much slower rate with further increases in wealth. The trigger point for life insurance is around $8,000 in GDP per capita. At this point, the demand for life insurance increases between 200% and 300% above those countries with GDP per capita below the trigger point.

Source: D. Fraser and M. Raynor, "The Power of Parity," *Forecast* (May/June, 1996), pp. 8–12; "A Survey of the World Economy: The Dragon and the Eagle," Special Insert, *Economist* (October 2, 2004), p. 8; "The Big Mac Index: Food for Thought," *Economist* (May 29, 2004), pp. 71–72.

Creating a Scanning System How can anyone monitor and keep track of all the trends and factors in the worldwide societal environment? With the existence of the Internet, it is now possible to scan the entire world. Nevertheless, the vast amount of raw data makes scanning for information similar to drinking from a fire hose. It is a daunting task for even a large corporation with many resources. To deal with this problem, in 2002 IBM created a tool called *WebFountain* to help a company analyze the vast amounts of environmental data available on the Internet. WebFountain is an advanced information discovery system designed to help extract trends, detect patterns, and find relationships within vast amounts of raw data. For example, IBM sought to learn whether there was a trend toward more positive discussions about e-business. Within a week, the company had data that experts within the company used to replace their hunches with valid conclusions. The company uses WebFountain to:

- Locate negative publicity or investor discontent
- Track general trends
- Learn competitive information
- Identify emerging competitive threats
- Unravel consumer attitudes[25]

Scanning the Task Environment

As shown in **Figure 4–1**, a corporation's scanning of the environment includes analyses of all the relevant elements in the task environment. These analyses take the form of individual reports written by various people in different parts of the firm. At Procter & Gamble (P&G), for example, people from each of the brand management teams work with key people from the sales and market research departments to research and write a "competitive activity report" each quarter on each of the product categories in which P&G competes. People in purchasing also write similar reports concerning new developments in the industries that supply P&G. These and other reports are then summarized and transmitted up the corporate hierarchy for top management to use in strategic decision making. If a new development is reported regarding a particular product category, top management may then send memos asking people throughout the organization to watch for and

Figure 4–1
Scanning External Environment

report on developments in related product areas. The many reports resulting from these scanning efforts, when boiled down to their essentials, act as a detailed list of external strategic factors.

Identifying External Strategic Factors

The origin of competitive advantage lay in the ability to identify and respond to environmental change well in advance of competition.[26] Although this seems obvious, why are some companies better able to adapt than others? One reason is because of differences in the ability of managers to recognize and understand external strategic issues and factors. For example, in a 2002 global survey conducted by the Fuld-Gilad-Herring Academy of Competitive Intelligence, two-thirds of 140 corporate strategists admitted that their firms had been surprised by as many as three high-impact events in the past five years. Moreover, 97% stated that their companies had no early warning system in place.[27]

No firm can successfully monitor all external factors. Choices must be made regarding which factors are important and which are not. Even though managers agree that strategic importance determines what variables are consistently tracked, they sometimes miss or choose to ignore crucial new developments.[28] Personal values and functional experiences of a corporation's managers as well as the success of current strategies are likely to bias both their perception of what is important to monitor in the external environment and their interpretations of what they perceive.[29]

This willingness to reject unfamiliar as well as negative information is called **strategic myopia**.[30] If a firm needs to change its strategy, it might not be gathering the appropriate external information to change strategies successfully. One way to identify and analyze developments in the external environment is to use the **issues priority matrix** (see **Figure 4–2**) as follows:

1. Identify a number of likely trends emerging in the societal and task environments. These are strategic environmental issues—important trends that, if they occur, determine what the industry or the world will look like in the near future.

2. Assess the probability of these trends actually occurring, from low to medium to high.

3. Attempt to ascertain the likely impact (from low to high) of each of these trends on the corporation being examined.

Figure 4–2
Issues Priority Matrix

Probable Impact on Corporation

	High	Medium	Low
High	High Priority	High Priority	Medium Priority
Medium	High Priority	Medium Priority	Low Priority
Low	Medium Priority	Low Priority	Low Priority

Probability of Occurrence

A corporation's **external strategic factors** are the key environmental trends that are judged to have both a medium to high probability of occurrence and a medium to high probability of impact on the corporation. The issues priority matrix can then be used to help managers decide which environmental trends should be merely scanned (low priority) and which should be monitored as strategic factors (high priority). Those environmental trends judged to be a corporation's strategic factors are then categorized as opportunities and threats and are included in strategy formulation.

4.2 | Industry Analysis: Analyzing the Task Environment

An **industry** is a group of firms that produce a similar product or service, such as soft drinks or financial services. An examination of the important stakeholder groups, such as suppliers and customers, in a particular corporation's task environment is a part of industry analysis.

Porter's Approach to Industry Analysis

Michael Porter, an authority on competitive strategy, contends that a corporation is most concerned with the intensity of competition within its industry. The level of this intensity is determined by basic competitive forces, as depicted in **Figure 4–3**. "The collective strength of these forces," he contends, "determines the ultimate profit potential in the industry, where profit potential is measured in terms of long-run return on invested capital."[31] In carefully

Figure 4–3
Forces Driving Industry Competition

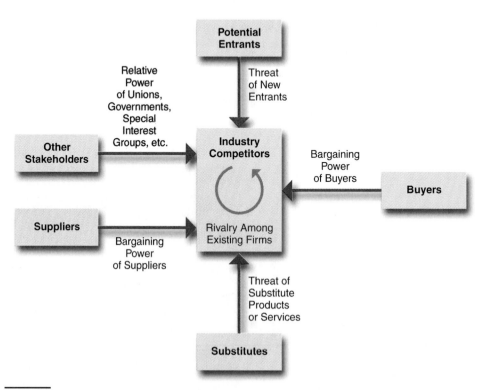

scanning its industry, a corporation must assess the importance to its success of each of the six forces: threat of new entrants, rivalry among existing firms, threat of substitute products or services, bargaining power of buyers, bargaining power of suppliers, and relative power of other stakeholders.[32] The stronger each of these forces, the more limited companies are in their ability to raise prices and earn greater profits. Although Porter mentions only five forces, a sixth—other stakeholders—is added here to reflect the power that governments, local communities, and other groups from the task environment wield over industry activities.

Using the model in **Figure 4–3**, a high force can be regarded as a threat because it is likely to reduce profits. A low force, in contrast, can be viewed as an opportunity because it may allow the company to earn greater profits. In the short run, these forces act as constraints on a company's activities. In the long run, however, it may be possible for a company, through its choice of strategy, to change the strength of one or more of the forces to the company's advantage. For example, Dell's early use of the Internet to market its computers was an effective way to negate the bargaining power of distributors in the PC industry.

A strategist can analyze any industry by rating each competitive force as high, medium, or low in strength. For example, the athletic shoe industry could be rated as follows: rivalry is high (Nike, Reebok, New Balance, and Adidas are strong competitors worldwide), threat of potential entrants is low (the industry has reached maturity/sales growth rate has slowed), threat of substitutes is low (other shoes don't provide support for sports activities), bargaining power of suppliers is medium but rising (suppliers in Asian countries are increasing in size and ability), bargaining power of buyers is medium but increasing (prices are falling; over half of consumers bought their sneakers on sale in 2002), and threat of other stakeholders is medium to high (government regulations and human rights concerns are growing). Based on current trends in each of these competitive forces, the industry's level of competitive intensity will continue to be high—meaning that sales increases and profit margins should continue to be modest for the industry as a whole.[33]

Threat of New Entrants

New entrants to an industry typically bring to it new capacity, a desire to gain market share, and substantial resources. They are, therefore, threats to an established corporation. The threat of entry depends on the presence of entry barriers and the reaction that can be expected from existing competitors. An **entry barrier** is an obstruction that makes it difficult for a company to enter an industry. For example, no new domestic automobile companies have been successfully established in the United States since the 1930s because of the high capital requirements to build production facilities and to develop a dealer distribution network. Some of the possible barriers to entry are:

- **Economies of Scale:** Scale economies in the production and sale of microprocessors, for example, gave Intel a significant cost advantage over any new rival.

- **Product Differentiation:** Corporations such as P&G and General Mills, which manufacture products such as Tide and Cheerios, create high entry barriers through their high levels of advertising and promotion.

- **Capital Requirements:** The need to invest huge financial resources in manufacturing facilities in order to produce large commercial airplanes creates a significant barrier to entry to any competitor for Boeing and Airbus.

- **Switching Costs:** Once a software program such as Excel or Word becomes established in an office, office managers are very reluctant to switch to a new program because of the high training costs.

- **Access to Distribution Channels:** Small entrepreneurs often have difficulty obtaining supermarket shelf space for their goods because large retailers charge for space on their shelves and give priority to the established firms that can pay for the advertising needed to generate high customer demand.

■ **Cost Disadvantages Independent of Size:** Once a new product earns sufficient market share to be accepted as the *standard* for that type of product, the maker has a key advantage. Microsoft's development of the first widely adopted operating system (MS-DOS) for the IBM-type personal computer gave it a significant competitive advantage over potential competitors. Its introduction of Windows helped to cement that advantage so that the Microsoft operating system is now on more than 90% of personal computers worldwide.

■ **Government Policy:** Governments can limit entry into an industry through licensing requirements by restricting access to raw materials, such as oil-drilling sites in protected areas.

Rivalry Among Existing Firms

In most industries, corporations are mutually dependent. A competitive move by one firm can be expected to have a noticeable effect on its competitors and thus may cause retaliation or counterefforts. For example, the entry by mail order companies such as Dell and Gateway into a PC industry previously dominated by IBM, Apple, and Compaq increased the level of competitive activity to such an extent that any price reduction or new product introduction was quickly followed by similar moves from other PC makers. The same is true of prices in the U.S. airline industry. According to Porter, intense rivalry is related to the presence of several factors, including:

■ **Number of Competitors:** When competitors are few and roughly equal in size, such as in the U.S. auto and major home appliance industries, they watch each other carefully to make sure that they match any move by another firm with an equal countermove.

■ **Rate of Industry Growth:** Any slowing in passenger traffic tends to set off price wars in the airline industry because the only path to growth is to take sales away from a competitor.

■ **Product or Service Characteristics:** A product can be very unique, with many qualities differentiating it from others of its kind, or it may be a **commodity**, a product whose characteristics are the same, regardless of who sells it. For example, most people choose a gas station based on location and pricing because they view gasoline as a commodity.

■ **Amount of Fixed Costs:** Because airlines must fly their planes on a schedule, regardless of the number of paying passengers for any one flight, they offer cheap standby fares whenever a plane has empty seats.

■ **Capacity:** If the only way a manufacturer can increase capacity is in a large increment by building a new plant (as in the paper industry), it will run that new plant at full capacity to keep its unit costs as low as possible—thus producing so much that the selling price falls throughout the industry.

■ **Height of Exit Barriers: Exit barriers** keep a company from leaving an industry. The brewing industry, for example, has a low percentage of companies that voluntarily leave the industry because breweries are specialized assets with few uses except for making beer.

■ **Diversity of Rivals:** Rivals that have very different ideas of how to compete are likely to cross paths often and unknowingly challenge each other's position. This happens often in the retail clothing industry when a number of retailers open outlets in the same location—thus taking sales away from each other. This is also likely to happen in some countries or regions when multinational corporations compete in an increasingly global economy.

Threat of Substitute Products or Services

A **substitute product** is a product that appears to be different but can satisfy the same need as another product. For example, e-mail is a substitute for the fax, Nutrasweet is a substitute for sugar, the Internet is a substitute for video stores, and bottled water is a substitute for a cola. According to Porter, "Substitutes limit the potential returns of an industry by placing a ceiling on the prices firms in the industry can profitably charge."[34] To the extent that switching costs are low, substitutes may have a strong effect on an industry. Tea can be considered a substitute for coffee. If the price of coffee goes up high enough, coffee drinkers will slowly begin switching to tea. The price of tea thus puts a price ceiling on the price of coffee. Sometimes a difficult task, the identification of possible substitute products or services means searching for products or services that can perform the same function, even though they have a different appearance and may not appear to be easily substitutable.

Bargaining Power of Buyers

Buyers affect an industry through their ability to force down prices, bargain for higher quality or more services, and play competitors against each other. A buyer or a group of buyers is powerful if some of the following factors hold true:

- A buyer purchases a large proportion of the seller's product or service (for example, oil filters purchased by a major auto maker).
- A buyer has the potential to integrate backward by producing the product itself (for example, a newspaper chain could make its own paper).
- Alternative suppliers are plentiful because the product is standard or undifferentiated (for example, motorists can choose among many gas stations).
- Changing suppliers costs very little (for example, office supplies are easy to find).
- The purchased product represents a high percentage of a buyer's costs, thus providing an incentive to shop around for a lower price (for example, gasoline purchased for resale by convenience stores makes up half their total costs).
- A buyer earns low profits and is thus very sensitive to costs and service differences (for example, grocery stores have very small margins).
- The purchased product is unimportant to the final quality or price of a buyer's products or services and thus can be easily substituted without affecting the final product adversely (for example, electric wire bought for use in lamps).

Bargaining Power of Suppliers

Suppliers can affect an industry through their ability to raise prices or reduce the quality of purchased goods and services. A supplier or supplier group is powerful if some of the following factors apply:

- The supplier industry is dominated by a few companies, but it sells to many (for example, the petroleum industry).
- Its product or service is unique and/or it has built up switching costs (for example, word processing software).
- Substitutes are not readily available (for example, electricity).
- Suppliers are able to integrate forward and compete directly with their present customers (for example, a microprocessor producer such as Intel can make PCs).
- A purchasing industry buys only a small portion of the supplier group's goods and services and is thus unimportant to the supplier (for example, sales of lawn mower tires are less important to the tire industry than are sales of auto tires).

Relative Power of Other Stakeholders

A sixth force should be added to Porter's list to include a variety of stakeholder groups from the task environment. Some of these groups are governments (if not explicitly included elsewhere), local communities, creditors (if not included with suppliers), trade associations, special-interest groups, unions (if not included with suppliers), shareholders, and complementors. According to Andy Grove, Chairman and past CEO of Intel, a **complementor** is a company (e.g., Microsoft) or an industry whose product works well with a firm's (e.g., Intel's) product and without which the product would lose much of its value.[35] An example of complementary industries is the tire and automobile industries. Key international stakeholders who determine many of the international trade regulations and standards are the World Trade Organization, the European Union, NAFTA, ASEAN, and Mercosur.

The importance of these stakeholders varies by industry. For example, environmental groups in Maine, Michigan, Oregon, and Iowa successfully fought to pass bills outlawing disposable bottles and cans, and thus deposits for most drink containers are now required. This effectively raised costs across the board, with the most impact on the marginal producers who could not internally absorb all these costs. The traditionally strong power of national unions in the U.S. auto and railroad industries has effectively raised costs throughout these industries but is of little importance in computer software.

Industry Evolution

Over time, most industries evolve through a series of stages from growth through maturity to eventual decline. The strength of each of the six forces mentioned earlier varies according to the stage of industry evolution. The industry life cycle is useful for explaining and predicting trends among the six forces that drive industry competition. For example, when an industry is new, people often buy the product, regardless of price, because it fulfills a unique need. This usually occurs in a **fragmented industry**—where no firm has large market share, and each firm serves only a small piece of the total market in competition with others (for example, cleaning services).[36] As new competitors enter the industry, prices drop as a result of competition. Companies use the experience curve (discussed in Chapter 5) and economies of scale to reduce costs faster than the competition. Companies integrate to reduce costs even further by acquiring their suppliers and distributors. Competitors try to differentiate their products from one another's in order to avoid the fierce price competition common to a maturing industry.

By the time an industry enters maturity, products tend to become more like commodities. This is now a **consolidated industry**—dominated by a few large firms, each of which struggles to differentiate its products from those of the competition. As buyers become more sophisticated over time, purchasing decisions are based on better information. Price becomes a dominant concern, given a minimum level of quality and features, and profit margins decline. The automobile, petroleum, and major home appliance industries are examples of mature, consolidated industries, each controlled by a few large competitors. In the case of the U.S. major home appliance industry, the industry changed from being a fragmented industry (pure competition) composed of hundreds of appliance manufacturers in the industry's early years to a consolidated industry (mature oligopoly) composed of four companies controlling over 98% of U.S. appliance sales. A similar consolidation is occurring now in European major home appliances.

As an industry moves through maturity toward possible decline, its products' growth rate of sales slows and may even begin to decrease. To the extent that exit barriers are low, firms begin converting their facilities to alternate uses or sell them to other firms. The industry tends to consolidate around fewer but larger competitors. The tobacco industry is an example of an industry currently in decline.

Categorizing International Industries

According to Porter, world industries vary on a continuum from multidomestic to global (see **Figure 4–4**).[37] **Multidomestic industries** are specific to each country or group of countries. This type of international industry is a collection of essentially domestic industries, such as retailing and insurance. The activities in a subsidiary of a multinational corporation (MNC) in this type of industry are essentially independent of the activities of the MNC's subsidiaries in other countries. Within each country, it has a manufacturing facility to produce goods for sale within that country. The MNC is thus able to tailor its products or services to the very specific needs of consumers in a particular country or group of countries having similar societal environments.

Global industries, in contrast, operate worldwide, with MNCs making only small adjustments for country-specific circumstances. In a global industry, an MNC's activities in one country are significantly affected by its activities in other countries. MNCs in global industries produce products or services in various locations throughout the world and sell them, making only minor adjustments for specific country requirements. Examples of global industries are commercial aircraft, television sets, semiconductors, copiers, automobiles, watches, and tires. The largest industrial corporations in the world in terms of sales revenue are, for the most part, MNCs operating in global industries.

The factors that tend to determine whether an industry will be primarily multidomestic or primarily global are:

1. *Pressure for coordination* within the MNCs operating in that industry
2. *Pressure for local responsiveness* on the part of individual country markets

To the extent that the pressure for coordination is strong and the pressure for local responsiveness is weak for MNCs within a particular industry, that industry will tend to become global. In contrast, when the pressure for local responsiveness is strong and the pressure for coordination is weak for multinational corporations in an industry, that industry will tend to be multidomestic. Between these two extremes lie a number of industries with varying characteristics of both multidomestic and global industries. The dynamic tension between these two factors is contained in the phrase "Think globally but act locally."

International Risk Assessment

Some firms, such as American Can Company and Mitsubishi Trading Company, develop elaborate information networks and computerized systems to evaluate and rank investment risks. Small companies can hire outside consultants such as Chicago's Associated Consultants International or Boston's Arthur D. Little, Inc., to provide political-risk assessments. Among the many systems that exist to assess political and economic risks are the Political System Stability Index, the Business Environment Risk Index, Business International's Country Assessment Service, the Economist Intelligence Unit, and Frost and Sullivan's World Political Risk Forecasts.[38] Business International provides subscribers with continuously

Figure 4–4
Continuum of International Industries

Multidomestic ←————————————————————→ **Global**
Industry in which companies tailor their products to the specific needs of consumers in a particular country. • Retailing • Insurance • Banking	Industry in which companies manufacture and sell the same products, with only minor adjustments made for individual countries around the world. • Automobiles • Tires • Television sets

updated information on conditions in 63 countries. Regardless of the source of data, a firm must develop its own method of assessing risk. It must decide on its most important risk factors and then assign weights to each.

Strategic Groups

A **strategic group** is a set of business units or firms that "pursue similar strategies with similar resources."[39] Categorizing firms in any one industry into a set of strategic groups is very useful as a way of better understanding the competitive environment.[40] Because a corporation's structure and culture tend to reflect the kinds of strategies it follows, companies or business units belonging to a particular strategic group within the same industry tend to be strong rivals and tend to be more similar to each other than to competitors in other strategic groups within the same industry.[41]

For example, although McDonald's and Olive Garden are a part of the same industry, the restaurant industry, they have different missions, objectives, and strategies, and thus they belong to different strategic groups. They generally have very little in common and pay little attention to each other when planning competitive actions. Burger King and Hardee's, however, have a great deal in common with McDonald's in terms of their similar strategy of producing a high volume of low-priced meals targeted for sale to the average family. Consequently, they are strong rivals and are organized to operate similarly.

Strategic groups in a particular industry can be mapped by plotting the market positions of industry competitors on a two-dimensional graph, using two strategic variables as the vertical and horizontal axes (see **Figure 4–5**):

1. Select two broad characteristics, such as price and menu, that differentiate the companies in an industry from one another.
2. Plot the firms, using these two characteristics as the dimensions.
3. Draw a circle around those companies that are closest to one another as one strategic group, varying the size of the circle in proportion to the group's share of total industry sales. (You could also name each strategic group in the restaurant industry with an identifying title, such as quick fast food or buffet-style service.)

Other dimensions, such as quality, service, location, or degree of vertical integration, could also be used in additional graphs of the restaurant industry to gain a better understanding of how the various firms in the industry compete. Keep in mind, however, that the two dimensions should not be highly correlated; otherwise, the circles on the map will simply lie along the diagonal, providing very little new information other than the obvious.

Strategic Types

In analyzing the level of competitive intensity within a particular industry or strategic group, it is useful to characterize the various competitors for predictive purposes. A **strategic type** is a category of firms based on a common strategic orientation and a combination of structure, culture, and processes consistent with that strategy. According to Miles and Snow, competing firms within a single industry can be categorized into one of four basic types on the basis of their general strategic orientation.[42] This distinction helps explain why companies facing similar situations behave differently and why they continue to do so over long periods of time. These general types have the following characteristics:

- **Defenders** are companies with limited product lines that *focus on improving the efficiency of their existing operations*. This cost orientation makes them unlikely to innovate in new areas. With its emphasis on efficiency, Lincoln Electric is an example of a defender.

Figure 4–5
Mapping Strategic Groups in the U.S. Restaurant Chain Industry

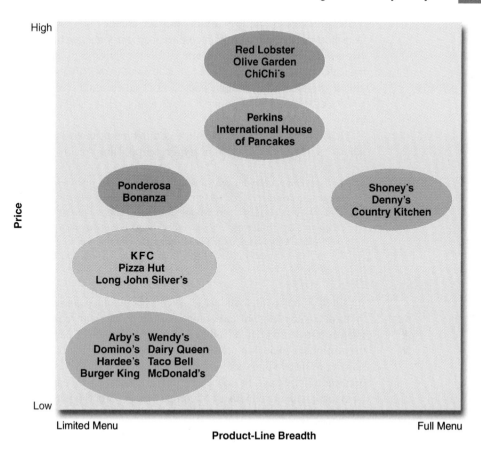

- **Prospectors** are companies with fairly broad product lines that *focus on product innovation and market opportunities*. This sales orientation makes them somewhat inefficient. They tend to emphasize creativity over efficiency. Rubbermaid's emphasis on new product development makes it an example of a prospector.

- **Analyzers** are corporations that *operate in at least two different product-market areas*, one stable and one variable. In the stable areas, efficiency is emphasized. In the variable areas, innovation is emphasized. Multidivisional firms, such as IBM and Procter & Gamble, which operate in multiple industries, tend to be analyzers.

- **Reactors** are corporations that *lack a consistent strategy–structure–culture relationship*. Their (often ineffective) responses to environmental pressures tend to be piecemeal strategic changes. Most major U.S. airlines have recently tended to be reactors—given the way they have been forced to respond to new entrants such as Southwest and JetBlue.

   Dividing the competition into these four categories enables a strategic manager not only to monitor the effectiveness of certain strategic orientations but also to develop scenarios of future industry developments (discussed later in this chapter).

Hypercompetition

Most industries today are facing an ever-increasing level of environmental uncertainty. They are becoming more complex and more dynamic. Industries that used to be multidomestic are becoming global. New flexible, aggressive, innovative competitors are moving into established markets to rapidly erode the advantages of large previously dominant firms. Distribution channels vary from country to country and are being altered daily through the use of sophisticated information systems. Closer relationships with suppliers are being forged to reduce costs, increase quality, and gain access to new technology. Companies learn to quickly imitate the successful strategies of market leaders, and it becomes harder to sustain any competitive advantage for very long. Consequently, the level of competitive intensity is increasing in most industries.

Richard D'Aveni contends that as this type of environmental turbulence reaches more industries, competition becomes **hypercompetition**. According to D'Aveni:

> *In hypercompetition the frequency, boldness, and aggressiveness of dynamic movement by the players accelerates to create a condition of constant disequilibrium and change. Market stability is threatened by short product life cycles, short product design cycles, new technologies, frequent entry by unexpected outsiders, repositioning by incumbents, and tactical redefinitions of market boundaries as diverse industries merge. In other words, environments escalate toward higher and higher levels of uncertainty, dynamism, heterogeneity of the players and hostility.*[43]

In hypercompetitive industries such as computers, competitive advantage comes from an up-to-date knowledge of environmental trends and competitive activity coupled with a willingness to risk a current advantage for a possible new advantage. Companies must be willing to **cannibalize** their own products (that is, replace popular products before competitors do so) in order to sustain their competitive advantage. As a result, competitive intelligence has never been more important. See **STRATEGY HIGHLIGHT 4.1** to learn how Microsoft is operating in the hypercompetitive industry of computer software. (Hypercompetition is discussed in more detail in **Chapter 6**.)

STRATEGY HIGHLIGHT 4.1

Microsoft in a Hypercompetitive Industry

Microsoft is an aggressive firm operating in a hypercompetitive industry. It has used its dominance in operating systems (DOS and Windows) to move into a very strong position in application programs such as word processing and spreadsheets (Word and Excel). Even though Microsoft held 90% of the market for personal computer operating systems in 1992, it still invested millions in developing the next generation—Windows 95 and Windows NT. These were soon followed by Windows Me and XP. Instead of trying to protect its advantage in the profitable DOS operating system, Microsoft actively sought to replace DOS with various versions of Windows. Before hypercompetition, most experts argued against cannibalization of a company's own product line because it destroys a very profitable product instead of harvesting it like a "cash cow." According to this line of thought, a company would be better off defending its older products. New products would be introduced only if it could be proven that they would not take sales away from

current products. Microsoft was one of the first companies to disprove this argument against cannibalization.

Bill Gates, Microsoft's co-founder, chair, and CEO, realized that if his company didn't replace its own DOS product line with a better product, someone else would (such as Linux or IBM's OS/2 Warp). He knew that success in the software industry depends not so much on company size as on moving aggressively to the next competitive advantage before a competitor does. "This is a hypercompetitive market," explained Gates. "Scale is not all positive in this business. Cleverness is the position in this business." By 2004, Microsoft still controlled over 90% of operating systems software and had achieved a dominant position in applications software as well.

Source: Adapted with permission of THE FREE PRESS, a Division of Simon & Schuster Adult Publishing Group, from HYPERCOMPETITION: Managing The Dynamics of Strategic Maneuvering by Richard D'Aveni. Copyright © 1994 by Richard A. D'Aveni. All rights reserved.

Using Key Success Factors to Create an Industry Matrix

Within any industry there are usually certain variables—key success factors—that a company's management must understand in order to be successful. **Key success factors** are variables that can significantly affect the overall competitive positions of companies within any particular industry. They typically vary from industry to industry and are crucial to determining a company's ability to succeed within that industry. They are usually determined by the economic and technological characteristics of the industry and by the competitive weapons on which the firms in the industry have built their strategies.[44] For example, in the major home appliance industry, a firm must achieve low costs, typically by building large manufacturing facilities dedicated to making multiple versions of one type of appliance, such as washing machines. Because 60% of major home appliances in the U.S. are sold through "power retailers" such as Sears and Best Buy, a firm must have a strong presence in the mass merchandiser distribution channel. It must offer a full line of appliances and provide a just-in-time delivery system to keep store inventory and ordering costs to a minimum. Because the consumer expects reliability and durability in an appliance, a firm must have excellent process R&D. Any appliance manufacturer that is unable to deal successfully with these key success factors will not survive long in the U.S. market.

An **industry matrix** summarizes the key success factors within a particular industry. As shown in **Table 4–4**, the matrix gives a weight for each factor, based on how important that factor is for success within the industry. The matrix also specifies how well various competitors in the industry are responding to each factor. To generate an industry matrix using two industry competitors (called A and B), complete the following steps for the industry being analyzed:

1. In **Column 1** (*Key Success Factors*), list the 8 to 10 factors that appear to determine success in the industry.

2. In **Column 2** (*Weight*), assign a weight to each factor, from **1.0** (Most Important) to **0.0** (Not Important), based on that factor's probable impact on the overall industry's current and future success. (**All weights must sum to 1.0, regardless of the number of strategic factors.**)

3. In **Column 3** (*Company A Rating*), examine a particular company within the industry—for example, Company A. Assign a rating to each factor, from **5** (Outstanding) to **1** (Poor)

TABLE 4–4 INDUSTRY MATRIX

Key Success Factors	Weight	Company A Rating	Company A Weighted Score	Company B Rating	Company B Weighted Score
	1	2	3	4	5	6
Total	1.00				

Source: T. L. Wheelen and J. D. Hunger, "Industry Matrix." Copyright © 1997, 2001, and 2005 by Wheelen and Hunger Associates. Reprinted with permission.

based on Company A's current response to that particular factor. Each rating is a judgment regarding how well that company is specifically dealing with each key success factor:

4. In **Column 4** (*Company A Weighted Score*), multiply the weight in **Column 2** for each factor by its rating in **Column 3** to obtain that factor's weighted score for Company A. This results in a weighted score for each key success factor, ranging from **5.0** (Outstanding) to **1.0** (Poor), with **3.0** as the average.

5. In **Column 5** (*Company B Rating*), examine a second company within the industry—in this case, Company B. Assign a rating to each key success factor, from **5.0** (Outstanding) to **1.0** (Poor), based on Company B's current response to each particular factor.

6. In **Column 6** (*Company B Weighted Score*), multiply the weight in **Column 2** for each factor by its rating in **Column 5** to obtain that factor's weighted score for Company B.

7. Finally, add the weighted scores for all the factors in **Columns 4 and 6** to determine the total weighted scores for companies A and B. **The total weighted score indicates how well each company is responding to current and expected key success factors in the industry's environment.** Check to ensure that the total weighted score truly reflects the company's current performance in terms of profitability and market share. The industry matrix can be expanded to include all the major competitors within an industry through the addition of two additional columns for each additional competitor.

4.3 | **Competitive Intelligence**

Much external environmental scanning is done on an informal and individual basis. Information is obtained from a variety of sources—suppliers, customers, industry publications, employees, industry experts, industry conferences, and the Internet.[45] For example, scientists and engineers working in a firm's R&D lab can learn about new products and competitors' ideas at professional meetings; someone from the purchasing department, speaking with supplier–representatives' personnel, may also uncover valuable bits of information about a competitor. A study of product innovation found that 77% of all product innovations in scientific instruments and 67% in semiconductors and printed circuit boards were initiated by the customer in the form of inquiries and complaints.[46] In these industries, the sales force and service departments must be especially vigilant.

Competitive intelligence is a formal program of gathering information on a company's competitors. Often called *business intelligence*, it is one of the fastest growing fields within strategic management. According to P&G Chairman John Pepper, "I can't imagine a time in history when the competencies, skills, and knowledge of the men and women in competitive intelligence are more needed and more relevant to a company being able to design a winning strategy and act on it."[47] At General Mills, for example, all employees have been trained to recognize and tap sources of competitive information. Janitors no longer simply place orders with suppliers of cleaning materials; they also ask about relevant practices at competing firms! A survey of large U.S. corporations revealed that 78% of them reported competitive intelligence activities within their firms.[48] As mentioned earlier, IBM uses its WebFountain software to scan the Internet for a variety of data, including competitor information and emerging competitive threats. According to a survey of corporate information officers by Merrill Lynch, business intelligence software topped the list of corporate software spending plans in 2003.[49]

Sources of Competitive Intelligence

Most corporations use outside organizations to provide them with environmental data. Firms such as A. C. Nielsen Co. provide subscribers with bimonthly data on brand share, retail prices, percentages of stores stocking an item, and percentages of stock-out stores. Strategists can use this data to spot regional and national trends as well as to assess market share. Information on market conditions, government regulations, industry competitors, and new products can be bought from "information brokers" such as Market Research.com (Findex), LexisNexis (company and country analyses), and Finsbury Data Services. Company and industry profiles are generally available from the Hoover's web site, at www.hoovers.com. Many business corporations have established their own in-house libraries and computerized information systems to deal with the growing mass of available information.

The Internet has changed the way strategists engage in environmental scanning. It provides the quickest means to obtain data on almost any subject. Although the scope and quality of Internet information is increasing geometrically, it is also littered with "noise," misinformation, and utter nonsense. For example, a number of corporate web sites are sending unwanted guests to specially constructed bogus web sites![50] Unlike the library, the Internet lacks the tight bibliographic control standards that exist in the print world. There is no ISBN or Dewey Decimal System to identify, search, and retrieve a document. Many web documents lack the name of the author and the date of publication. A web page providing useful information may be accessible on the web one day and gone the next. Unhappy ex-employees, far-out environmentalists, and prank-prone hackers create "blog" web sites to attack and discredit otherwise reputable corporations. Rumors with no basis in fact are spread via chat rooms and personal web sites. This creates a serious problem for researchers. How can one evaluate the information found on the Internet? For a way to evaluate intelligence information, see **STRATEGY HIGHLIGHT 4.2**.

Some companies choose to use industrial espionage or other intelligence-gathering techniques to get their information straight from their competitors. According to a survey by the American Society for Industrial Security, PricewaterhouseCoopers, and the U.S. Chamber of Commerce, Fortune 1000 companies lost an estimated $59 billion in one year alone due to the theft of trade secrets.[51] By using current or former competitors' employees and private contractors, some firms attempt to steal trade secrets, technology, business plans, and pricing strategies. For example, Avon Products hired private investigators to retrieve from a public dumpster documents (some of them shredded) that Mary Kay Corporation had thrown away. Studies reveal that 32% of the trash typically found next to copy machines contains confidential company data, in addition to personal data (29%) and gossip (39%).[52] Even P&G, which defends itself like a fortress from information leaks, is vulnerable. A competitor was able to learn the precise launch date of a concentrated laundry detergent in Europe when one of its people visited the factory where machinery was being made. Simply asking a few questions about what a certain machine did, whom it was for, and when it would be delivered was all that was necessary.

To combat the increasing theft of company secrets, the U.S. government passed the Economic Espionage Act in 1996. The law makes it illegal (with fines up to $5 million and 10 years in jail) to steal any material that a business has taken "reasonable efforts" to keep secret and that derives its value from not being known.[53] The Society of Competitive Intelligence

STRATEGY HIGHLIGHT 4.2

Evaluating Competitive Intelligence

A basic rule in intelligence gathering is that before a piece of information can be used in any report or briefing, it must first be evaluated in two ways. First, the source of the information should be judged in terms of its truthfulness and reliability. How trustworthy is the source? How well can a researcher rely on it for truthful and correct information? One approach is to rank the reliability of the source on a scale of A (extremely reliable), B (reliable), C (unknown reliability), D (probably unreliable), or E (very questionable reliability). The reliability of a source can be judged on the basis of the author's credentials, the organization sponsoring the information, and past performance, among other factors. Second, the information or data should be judged in terms of its likelihood of being correct. The correctness of the data may be ranked on a scale of 1 (correct), 2 (probably correct), 3 (unknown), 4 (doubtful), or 5 (extremely doubtful). The correctness of a piece of data or information can be judged on the basis of its agreement with other bits of separately obtained information or with a general trend supported by previous data. For every piece of information found on the Internet, for example, it is important to list not only the URL of the web page but also the evaluation of the information from A1 (good information) to E5 (bad information). Information found through library research in sources such as Moody's Industrials, Standard & Poor's, or

Value Line can generally be evaluated as having a reliability of A. The correctness of the data can still range anywhere from 1 to 5, but in most instances it is likely to be either 1 or 2, but probably no worse than 3 or 4. Web sites are quite different.

Web sites, such as those sponsored by the U.S. Securities and Exchange Commission (*www.sec.gov*) or Hoovers Online (*www.hoovers.com*) are extremely reliable. Company-sponsored web sites are generally reliable, but they are not the place to go for trade secrets, strategic plans, or proprietary information. For one thing, many firms think of their web sites primarily in terms of marketing and provide little data aside from product descriptions and distributors. Other companies provide their latest financial statements and links to other useful web sites. Nevertheless, some companies in very competitive industries may install software on their web site to ascertain a visitor's web address. Visitors from a competitor's domain name are thus screened before they are allowed to access certain web sites. They may not be allowed beyond the product information page, or they may be sent to a bogus web site containing misinformation. Cisco Systems, for example, uses its web site to send visitors from other high-tech firms to a special web page asking if they would like to apply for a job at Cisco.

Professionals (www.scip.org) urges strategists to stay within the law and to act ethically when searching for information. The society states that illegal activities are foolish because the vast majority of worthwhile competitive intelligence is available publicly via annual reports, web sites, and libraries. Unfortunately, a number of firms hire "kites," consultants with questionable reputations, who do what is necessary to get information when the selected methods do not meet SCIP ethical standards or are illegal. This allows the company that initiated the action to deny that it did anything wrong.[54]

Monitoring Competitors for Strategic Planning

The primary activity of a competitive intelligence unit is to monitor **competitors**—organizations that offer the same, similar, or substitutable products or services in the business area in which a particular company operates. To understand a competitor, it is important to answer the following 10 questions:

1. Why do your competitors exist? Do they exist to make profits or just to support another unit?

2. Where do they add customer value—higher quality, lower price, excellent credit terms, or better service?

3. Which of your customers are the competitors most interested in? Are they cherry-picking your best customers, picking the ones you don't want, or going after all of them?

4. What is their cost base and liquidity? How much cash do they have? How do they get their supplies?

5. Are they less exposed with their suppliers than your firm? Are their suppliers better than yours?

6. What do they intend to do in the future? Do they have a strategic plan to target your market segments? How committed are they to growth? Are there any succession issues?

7. How will their activity affect your strategies? Should you adjust your plans and operations?

8. How much better than your competitor do you need to be in order to win customers? Do either of you have a competitive advantage in the marketplace?

9. Will new competitors or new ways of doing things appear over the next few years? Who is a potential new entrant?

10. If you were a customer, would you choose your product over those offered by your competitors? What irritates your current customers? What competitors solve these particular customer complaints?[55]

To answer these and other questions, competitive intelligence professionals utilize a number of analytical techniques. In addition to the previously discussed SWOT analysis, Michael Porter's industry forces analysis, and strategic group analysis, some of these techniques are Porter's four corner exercise, Treacy and Wiersema's value disciplines, and Gilad's blind spot analysis. See **Appendix 4.A** for more information about these competitive analysis techniques.

Done right, competitive intelligence is a key input to strategic planning. Avnet, Inc., one of the world's largest distributors of electronic components, uses competitive intelligence in its growth by acquisition strategy. According to John Hovis, Avnet's senior vice president of corporate planning and investor relations:

> *Our competitive intelligence team has a significant responsibility in tracking all of the varied competitors, not just our direct competitors, but all the peripheral competitors that have a potential to impact our ability to create value. . . . One of the things we are about is finding new acquisition candidates, and our competitive intelligence unit is very much involved with our acquisition team, in helping to profile potential acquisition candidates.[56]*

4.4 | Forecasting

Environmental scanning provides reasonably hard data on the present situation and current trends, but intuition and luck are needed to accurately predict whether these trends will continue. The resulting forecasts are, however, usually based on a set of assumptions that may or may not be valid.

Danger of Assumptions

Faulty underlying assumptions are the most frequent cause of forecasting errors. Nevertheless, many managers who formulate and implement strategic plans rarely consider that their success is based on a series of assumptions. Many long-range plans are simply based on projections of the current situation.

One example of what can happen when a corporate strategy rests on the very questionable assumption that the future will simply be an extension of the present is that of Tupperware, the company that originated air-tight, easy-to-use plastic food storage containers. Much of the company's success had been based on Tupperware parties in the 1950s, when housewives gathered in each other's homes to socialize and play games while the local Tupperware lady demonstrated and sold new products. Management assumed during the following decades that Tupperware parties would continue being an excellent distribution channel. Its faith in this assumption blinded it to information about America's changing lifestyle (toward two-career families and single-parent households) and its likely impact on sales. Even in the 1990s, when Tupperware executives realized that their extrapolated sales forecasts were no longer justified, they were unable to improve their forecasting techniques until they changed their assumption that the best way to sell Tupperware was at a Tupperware party. Consequently, Rubbermaid and other competitors, which chose to market their containers in grocery and discount stores, continued to grow at the expense of Tupperware.[57]

Useful Forecasting Techniques

Various techniques are used to forecast future situations. Each has proponents and critics. A study of nearly 500 of the world's largest corporations revealed trend extrapolation to be the most widely practiced form of forecasting—more than 70% use this technique either occasionally or frequently.[58] Simply stated, **extrapolation** is the extension of present trends into the future. It rests on the assumption that the world is reasonably consistent and changes slowly in the short run. Time-series methods are approaches of this type; they attempt to carry a series of historical events forward into the future. The basic problem with extrapolation is that a historical trend is based on a series of patterns or relationships among so many different variables that a change in any one can drastically alter the future direction of the trend. As a rule of thumb, the further back into the past you can find relevant data supporting the trend, the more confidence you can have in the prediction.

Brainstorming, expert opinion, and statistical modeling are also very popular forecasting techniques. **Brainstorming** is a nonquantitative approach that requires simply the presence of people with some knowledge of the situation to be predicted. The basic ground rule is to propose ideas without first mentally screening them. No criticism is allowed. Ideas tend to build on previous ideas until a consensus is reached. This is a good technique to use with operating managers who have more faith in "gut feel" than in more quantitative number-crunching techniques. **Expert opinion** is a nonquantitative technique in which experts in a particular area attempt to forecast likely developments. This type of forecast is based on the ability of a knowledgeable person(s) to construct probable future developments based on the interaction of key variables. One application is the **Delphi technique**, in which separated experts independently assess the likelihoods of specified events. These assessments are combined and sent back to each expert for fine-tuning until agreement is reached. **Statistical modeling** is a quantitative technique that attempts to discover causal or at least explanatory factors that link two or more time series together. Examples of statistical modeling are regression analysis and other econometric methods. Although very useful in the grasping of historic trends, statistical modeling, like trend extrapolation, is based on historical data. As the patterns of relationships change, the accuracy of the forecast deteriorates. Other forecasting techniques, such as *cross-impact analysis (CIA)* and *trend-impact analysis (TIA)*, have not established themselves successfully as regularly employed tools.[59]

Scenario writing appears to be the most widely used forecasting technique after trend extrapolation. Originated by Royal Dutch Shell, *scenarios* are focused descriptions of different likely futures presented in a narrative fashion. A scenario thus may be merely a written description of some future state, in terms of key variables and issues, or it may be generated in combination with other forecasting techniques.

An **industry scenario** is a forecasted description of a particular industry's likely future. Such a scenario is developed by analyzing the probable impact of future societal forces on key groups in a particular industry. The process may operate as follows[60]:

1. Examine possible shifts in the societal variables globally.

2. Identify uncertainties in each of the six forces of the task environment (that is, potential entrants, competitors, likely substitutes, buyers, suppliers, and other key stakeholders).

3. Make a range of plausible assumptions about future trends.

4. Combine assumptions about individual trends into internally consistent scenarios.

5. Analyze the industry situation that would prevail under each scenario.

6. Determine the sources of competitive advantage under each scenario.

7. Predict competitors' behavior under each scenario.

8. Select the scenarios that are either most likely to occur or most likely to have a strong impact on the future of the company. Use these scenarios in strategy formulation.

4.5 | The Strategic Audit: A Checklist for Environmental Scanning

One way of scanning the environment to identify opportunities and threats is by using the Strategic Audit found in **Appendix 1.A** at the end of Chapter 1. The audit provides a checklist of questions by area of concern. For example, Part III of the audit examines the societal and task environments. It looks at the societal environment in terms of economic, technological, political-legal, and sociocultural forces. It also considers the task environment (industry) in terms of threat of new entrants, bargaining power of buyers and suppliers, threat of substitute products, rivalry among existing firms, and the relative power of other stakeholders.

4.6 | Synthesis of External Factors—EFAS

After strategic managers have scanned the societal and task environments and identified a number of likely external factors for their particular corporation, they may want to refine their analysis of these factors by using a form such as that given in **Table 4–5**. Using an **EFAS (External Factors Analysis Summary) Table** is one way to organize the external factors into the generally accepted categories of opportunities and threats as well as to analyze how well a particular company's management (rating) is responding to these specific factors in light of the perceived importance (weight) of these factors to the company. To generate an EFAS Table for the company being analyzed, complete the following steps:

1. In **Column 1 (*External Factors*)**, list the 8 to 10 most important opportunities and threats facing the company.

2. In **Column 2 (*Weight*)**, assign a weight to each factor, from **1.0** (Most Important) to **0.0** (Not Important), based on that factor's probable impact on a particular company's current strategic position. The higher the weight, the more important is this factor to the current and future success of the company. (**All weights must sum to 1.0, regardless of the number of factors.**)

3. In **Column 3 (*Rating*)**, assign a rating to each factor, from **5.0** (Outstanding) to **1.0** (Poor), based on that particular company's specific response to that particular factor. Each rating

TABLE 4–5 EXTERNAL FACTOR ANALYSIS SUMMARY (EFAS TABLE): MAYTAG AS EXAMPLE

External Factors	Weight	Rating	Weighted Score	Comments
	1	2	3	4	5
Opportunities				
• Economic integration of European Community	.20	4.1	.82	Acquisition of Hoover
• Demographics favor quality appliances	.10	5.0	.50	Maytag quality
• Economic development of Asia	.05	1.0	.05	Low Maytag presence
• Opening of Eastern Europe	.05	2.0	.10	Will take time
• Trend to "Super Stores"	.10	1.8	.18	Maytag weak in this channel
Threats				
• Increasing government regulations	.10	4.3	.43	Well positioned
• Strong U.S. competition	.10	4.0	.40	Well positioned
• Whirlpool and Electrolux strong globally	.15	3.0	.45	Hoover weak globally
• New product advances	.05	1.2	.06	Questionable
• Japanese appliance companies	.10	1.6	.16	Only Asian presence in Australia
Total Scores	**1.00**		**3.15**	

Notes:
1. List opportunities and threats (8–10) in Column 1.
2. Weight each factor from 1.0 (Most Important) to 0.0 (Not Important) in Column 2 based on that factor's probable impact on the company's strategic position. **The total weights must sum to 1.00**.
3. Rate each factor from 5.0 (Outstanding) to 1.0 (Poor) in Column 3 based on the company's response to that factor.
4. Multiply each factor's weight times its rating to obtain each factor's weighted score in Column 4.
5. Use Column 5 (comments) for rationale used for each factor.
6. Add the individual weighted scores to obtain the total weighted score for the company in Column 4. This tells how well the company is responding to the factors in its external environment.

Source: T. L. Wheelen and J. D. Hunger, "External Factors Analysis Summary (EFAS)." Copyright © 1987, 1988, 1989, 1990, and 2005 by T. L. Wheelen. Copyright © 1991, 2003, and 2005 by Wheelen and Hunger Associates. Reprinted by permission.

is a judgment regarding how well the company is currently dealing with each specific external factor.

| 5.0 | 4.5 | 4.0 | 3.5 | 3.0 | 2.5 | 2.0 | 1.5 | 1.0 |

Outstanding   **Above Average**   **Average**   **Below Average**   **Poor**

4. In **Column 4 (*Weighted Score*)**, multiply the weight in **Column 2** for each factor by its rating in Column 3 to obtain that factor's weighted score. This results in a weighted score for each factor ranging from **5.0** (Outstanding) to **1.0** (Poor), with **3.0** as average.

5. In **Column 5 (*Comments*)**, note why a particular factor was selected and how its weight and rating were estimated.

6. Finally, add the weighted scores for all the external factors in **Column 4** to determine the total weighted score for that particular company. ***The total weighted score* indicates how well a particular company is responding to current and expected factors in its external environment.** The score can be used to compare that firm to other firms in the industry. Check to ensure that the total weighted score truly reflects the company's current performance in terms of profitability and market share. ***The total weighted score for an average firm in an industry is always 3.0.***

As an example of this procedure, **Table 4–5** includes a number of external factors for Maytag Corporation, with corresponding weights, ratings, and weighted scores provided. This table is appropriate for 1995, before Maytag sold its European and Australian operations. Note that Maytag's total weight was 3.15, meaning that the corporation was slightly above average in the major home appliance industry at that time.

4.7 | Conclusion

Wayne Gretzky was one of the most famous people ever to play professional ice hockey. He wasn't very fast. His shot was fairly weak. He was usually last in his team in strength training. He tended to operate in the back of his opponent's goal, anticipating where his team members would be long before they got there and fed them passes so unsuspected that he would often surprise his own team members. In an interview with *Time* magazine, Gretzky stated that the key to winning is *skating not to where the puck is but to where it is going to be*. "People talk about skating, puck handling and shooting, but the whole sport is angles and caroms, forgetting the straight direction the puck is going, calculating where it will be diverted, factoring in all the interruptions," explained Gretzky.[61]

Environmental scanning involves monitoring, collecting, and evaluating information in order to understand the current trends in the societal and task environments. The information is then used to forecast whether these trends will continue or whether others will take their place. What will an industry look like in 10 to 20 years? What kind of developments can we expect in the societal environment to affect the industry? Who will be the key competitors? Who is likely to fall by the wayside? We use this information to make certain assumptions about the future—assumptions that are then used in strategic planning. In many ways, success in the business world is like ice hockey: The key to winning is not to assume that your industry will continue as it is now but to assume that the industry will change and to make sure that your company will be in position to take advantage of that change.

Strategy Bits

How much richer is the average person in America versus China? Because prices tend to be lower in poor economies, a dollar of spending in China is worth more than a dollar in the United States. A better method is to use Purchasing Power Parity (PPP), which takes account of price differences. The Big Mac PPP is the exchange rate that would leave the burger in any country costing the same as in the United States. In 2005, what was the average price of a Big Mac in U.S. dollars?[62]

Brazil: $2.39	Egypt: $1.55	Malaysia: $1.38	Turkey: $2.98
Britain: $3.44	Euro area: $2.92	Mexico: $2.58	USA: $3.06
Canada: $2.63	Hong Kong: $1.54	Russia: $1.48	
Czech Republic: $2.30	Japan: $2.34	Switzerland: $5.05	

Discussion Questions

1. Discuss how a development in a corporation's societal environment can affect the corporation through its task environment.

2. According to Porter, what determines the level of competitive intensity in an industry?

3. According to Porter's discussion of industry analysis, is Pepsi Cola a substitute for Coca-Cola?

4. How can a decision maker identify strategic factors in a corporation's external international environment?

5. Compare and contrast trend extrapolation with the writing of scenarios as forecasting techniques.

Strategic Practice Exercise

How far should people in a business firm go in gathering competitive intelligence? Where do you draw the line?

Evaluate each of the following approaches that a person could use to gather information about competitors. For each approach, mark your feeling about its appropriateness:

1 (DEFINITELY NOT APPROPRIATE), 2 (PROBABLY NOT APPROPRIATE), 3 (UNDECIDED), 4 (PROBABLY APPROPRIATE), OR 5 (DEFINITELY APPROPRIATE)

The business firm should try to get useful information about competitors by:

1. ___ Carefully studying trade journals

2. ___ Wiretapping the telephones of competitors

3. ___ Posing as a potential customer to competitors

4. ___ Getting loyal customers to put out a phony "request for proposal," soliciting competitors' bids

5. ___ Buying competitors' products and taking them apart

6. ___ Hiring management consultants who have worked for competitors

7. ___ Rewarding competitors' employees for useful "tips"

8. ___ Questioning competitors' customers and/or suppliers

9. ___ Buying and analyzing competitors' garbage

10. ___ Advertising and interviewing for nonexistent jobs

11. ___ Taking public tours of competitors' facilities

12. ___ Releasing false information about the company in order to confuse competitors

13. ___ Questioning competitors' technical people at trade shows and conferences

14. ___ Hiring key people away from competitors

15. ___ Analyzing competitors' labor union contracts

16. ___ Having employees date persons who work for competitors

17. ___ Studying aerial photographs of competitors' facilities

After marking each of the preceding approaches, compare your responses to those of other people in your class. For each approach, the people marking 4 or 5 should say why they thought this particular act would be appropriate. Those who marked 1 or 2 should then state why they thought this act would be inappropriate.

Go to the web site of the Society for Competitive Intelligence Professionals (www.scip.org). What does SCIP say about these approaches?

Source: Developed from W. A. Jones, Jr., and N. B. Bryan, Jr., "Business Ethics and Business Intelligence: An Empirical Study of Information-Gathering Alternatives," *International Journal of Management* (June 1995), pp. 204–208. For actual examples of some of these activities, see J. Kerstetter, P. Burrows, J. Greene, G. Smith, and M. Conlin, "The Dark Side of the Valley," *Business Week* (July 17, 2000), pp. 42–43.

Key Terms

brainstorming (p. 96)
cannibalize (p. 90)
commodity (p. 84)
competitive intelligence (p. 92)
competitor (p. 94)
complementor (p. 86)
consolidated industry (p. 86)
Delphi technique (p. 96)
EFAS Table (p. 97)
entry barrier (p. 83)
environmental scanning (p. 73)
environmental uncertainty (p. 72)
exit barrier (p. 84)
expert opinion (p. 96)
external strategic factor (p. 82)

extrapolation (p. 96)
fragmented industry (p. 86)
global industry (p. 87)
hypercompetition (p. 90)
industry (p. 82)
industry analysis (p. 73)
industry matrix (p. 91)
industry scenario (p. 96)
issues priority matrix (p. 81)
key success factor (p. 91)
multidomestic industry (p. 87)
multinational corporation (MNC) (p. 78)
new entrant (p. 83)
purchasing power parity (PPP)(p. 79)

repatriation of profits (p. 74)
scenario writing (p. 96)
societal environment (p. 73)
statistical modeling (p. 96)
strategic group (p. 88)
strategic myopia (p. 81)
strategic type (p. 88)
substitute product (p. 85)
task environment (p. 73)
Triad (p. 78)
trigger point (p. 79)

APPENDIX 4.A
Competitive
Analysis Techniques

Analytical techniques commonly used in competitive intelligence are *SWOT analysis*, *Porter's industry forces*, and *strategic group analysis* (also called *competitive cluster analysis*). In addition to these are Porter's *four-corner exercise*, Treacy and Wiersema's *value disciplines*, and Gilad's *blind spot analysis*. These can be used in a strategic war game in which people role-play different competitors and their possible future strategies.

Porter's four-corner exercise involves analyzing a specific competitor's future goals, assumptions, current strategies, and capabilities in order to compile a competitor's response profile. See **Figure 4–6**.

Figure 4–6
Four-Corner Exercise: Porter's Components of Competitor Analysis

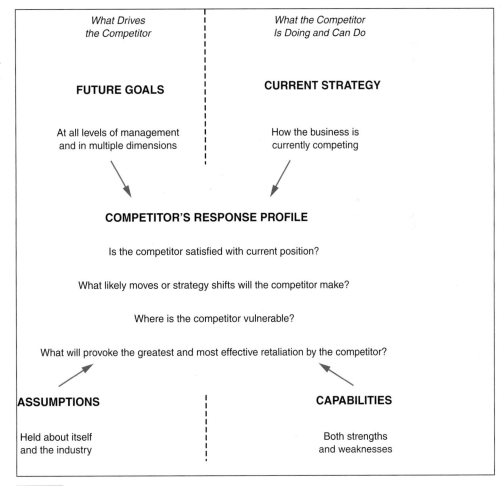

What Drives the Competitor	*What the Competitor Is Doing and Can Do*
FUTURE GOALS	**CURRENT STRATEGY**
At all levels of management and in multiple dimensions	How the business is currently competing

COMPETITOR'S RESPONSE PROFILE

Is the competitor satisfied with current position?

What likely moves or strategy shifts will the competitor make?

Where is the competitor vulnerable?

What will provoke the greatest and most effective retaliation by the competitor?

ASSUMPTIONS	**CAPABILITIES**
Held about itself and the industry	Both strengths and weaknesses

101

Having knowledge of a competitor's goals allows predictions about how likely the competitor is to change strategy and respond to changing conditions. Identifying a competitor's assumptions about itself and the industry can reveal blind spots about how management perceives its environment. Considering a competitor's current strategy and how long it has been in place may indicate whether the company is likely to continue in its current direction. If a strategy is not stated explicitly, one should consider its actions and policies in order to note its implicit strategy. The last step is to objectively evaluate a competitor's capabilities in terms of strengths and weaknesses. The competitor's goals, assumptions, and current strategy influence the likelihood, timing, nature, and intensity of a competitor's reactions. Its strengths and weaknesses determine its ability to initiate or react to strategic moves and to deal with environmental changes.[63]

Treacy and Wiersema's value disciplines involves the evaluation of a competitor in terms of three dimensions: product leadership, operational excellence, and customer intimacy. (See **Figure 4–7**.) After analyzing 80 market-leading companies, Treacy and Wiersema noted that each of these firms developed a compelling and unmatched value proposition on one dimension but was able to maintain acceptable standards on the other two dimensions. *Operationally excellent* companies deliver a combination of quality, price, and ease of purchase that no other can match in their market. An example is Dell Computer, a master of operational excellence. A *product leader* consistently strives to provide its market with leading-edge products or new applications of existing products or services. Johnson & Johnson is an example of a product leader that finds new ideas, develops them quickly, and then looks for ways to

Figure 4–7
Value Discipline Triad

"Best product"

Product Leadership

Product differentiation

Operational Competence

Customer Responsive

Operational Excellence

"Best total cost"

Customer Intimacy

"Best total solution"

Source: Figure reprinted by permission of Michael Treacy from The Discipline of Market Leaders, *Figure 5, p. 45, by Michael Treacy and Fred Wiersema. Published by Addison-Wesley Publishing Company, Inc. Copyright © 1997 by Michael Treacy.*

improve them. A company that delivers value through *customer intimacy* bonds with its customers and develops high customer loyalty. IBM is an example of a company that pursues excellence in customer intimacy. IBM's current strategy is to provide a total information technology service to its customers so that customers can totally rely on IBM to take care of any information technology (IT) problems.[64] According to Wayne Rosenkrans, past president of SCIP, it is possible to mark a spot on each of the three value dimensions shown in Figure 4-7 for each competitor being analyzed. Then one can draw lines connecting each of the marks, resulting in a triangle that reveals that competitor's overall value proposition.[65]

Gilad's blind spot analysis is based on the premise that the assumptions held by decision makers regarding their own company and their industry may act as perceptual biases or blind spots. As a result, (1) the firm may not be aware of strategically important developments, (2) the firm may inaccurately perceive strategically important developments, or (3) even if the firm is aware of important developments, it may learn too slowly to allow for a timely response. It is important to gather sufficient information about a competitor and its executives to be able to list top management's assumptions about buyers' preferences, the nature of the supply chain, the industry's key success factors, barriers to entry, and the threat appeal of substitutes to customers. One should analyze the industry objectively without regard to these assumptions. Any gap between an objective industry analysis and a competitor's top management assumptions is a potential blind spot. One should include these blind spots when considering how this competitor might respond to environmental change.[66]

Rosenkrans suggests that an analyst should first use Porter's industry forces technique to develop the four-corner analysis. Then the analyst should use the four corner analysis to generate a strategic group (cluster) analysis. Finally, the analyst should include the three value dimensions to develop a blind spot analysis.

These techniques can be used to conduct a war game simulating the various competitors in the industry. Gather people from various functional areas in your own corporation and put them into teams identified as industry competitors. Each company team should perform a complete analysis of the competitor it is role-playing. Each company team first creates starting strategies for its company and presents it to the entire group. Each company team then creates counter-strategies and presents them to the entire group. After all the presentations are complete, the full group creates new strategic considerations to be included as items to monitor in future environmental scanning.[67]

Some competitive intelligence analysts take the war game approach one step further by creating an "invented" company that could appear in the future but does not exist today. A team brainstorms what type of strategy the invented competitor might employ. The strategy is often based on a new breakthrough product that is radically different from current offerings. Its goals, strategies, and competitive posture should be different from any currently being used in the industry. According to Liam Fahey, an authority on competitive intelligence, "the invented competitor is proving to be a spur to bold and innovative thinking."[68]

CHAPTER 5
Internal Scanning: Organizational Analysis

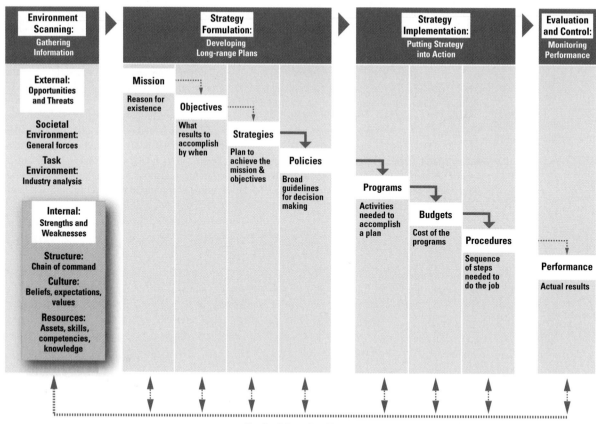

| Environment Scanning: Gathering Information | Strategy Formulation: Developing Long-range Plans | Strategy Implementation: Putting Strategy into Action | Evaluation and Control: Monitoring Performance |

External: Opportunities and Threats

Societal Environment: General forces

Task Environment: Industry analysis

Internal: Strengths and Weaknesses

Structure: Chain of command

Culture: Beliefs, expectations, values

Resources: Assets, skills, competencies, knowledge

Mission
Reason for existence

Objectives
What results to accomplish by when

Strategies
Plan to achieve the mission & objectives

Policies
Broad guidelines for decision making

Programs
Activities needed to accomplish a plan

Budgets
Cost of the programs

Procedures
Sequence of steps needed to do the job

Performance
Actual results

Feedback/Learning: Make corrections as needed

Learning Objectives

After reading this chapter, you should be able to:

- Apply the resource view of the firm to determine core and distinctive competencies
- Use the VRIO framework and the value chain to assess an organization's competitive advantage and how it can be sustained
- Understand a company's business model and how it could be imitated
- Assess a company's corporate culture and how it might affect a proposed strategy
- Scan functional resources to determine their fit with a firm's strategy
- Construct an IFAS Table that summarizes internal factors

ON AUGUST 12, 2004, HEWLETT-PACKARD COMPANY (HP) ANNOUNCED NOT ONLY THAT it had failed to meet its quarterly earnings estimates but also that it was lowering its earnings outlook for the remainder of the year. Its acquisition of Compaq was not growing the company's personal computer (PC) business as planned. At the same time, Dell Inc. announced not only that it achieved its profit targets but also that it would continue to do so in the coming quarters.[1] While other PC firms, such as HP and Gateway, were struggling to make money in the PC business, Dell continued to be "the little engine that could." Since 1995, Dell had gained 12.6 points of market share in desktops, laptops, and PC servers, to 16%—the same market share as HP and Compaq combined. IBM, the creator of the PC standard, divested its PC business and was now focusing on the selling of services and solutions instead of machines. Unhappy about the way Dell was taking large chunks out of the market for Windows servers, Oracle CEO Larry Ellison explained, "If you want to be in the PC business, you have to compete against Dell and that is very difficult."[2] What was the secret of Dell's success?

Dell's business model is simple: Dell machines are made to order and delivered directly to the customer. It has no distributors or retail stores. Dell's PCs have consistently been listed among the best PCs on the market by *PC World* and *PC Magazine*. Cash flow is never a problem. Customers pay Dell long before Dell pays its suppliers. The company holds virtually no parts inventory. As a result, Dell makes computers more quickly and cheaply than any other company.

Dell is the master of process engineering and value chain management. It spends only $440 million annually on R&D contrasted to $4 billion spent annually by HP, and it focuses all its spending on improving its manufacturing processes. It has many patents on its operations' methods. Instead of spending its money on new computer technology, Dell waits until a new technology becomes a standard. Founder and CEO Michael Dell explained that soon after a technology product arrives on the market, it is a high-priced, high-margin item that is made differently by each company. Over time, the technology standardizes—the way PCs standardized around Intel microprocessors and Microsoft operating systems. At a certain point between the development of the standard and its becoming a commodity, that technology is ripe for Dell. When the leaders are earning 40% or 50% profit margins, they are vulnerable to Dell making a profit on far smaller margins. Dell drives down costs further by perfecting its manufacturing processes and using its buying power to obtain cheaper parts. Its reduction of overhead expenses to only 9.6% of revenue means that Dell earns nearly $1 million in revenue per employee—three times the revenue per employee at IBM and almost twice HP's rate.[3] Explains Dell's President, Kevin Rollins: "Our business model excels in that transition."[4]

Given that the secret to Dell's success is well known and fairly simple, why doesn't someone else imitate its success? Explained Michael Dell, "If you look at a lot of truly great businesses, others can understand what they do, but they can't do it."[5] Gateway tried to follow the same business model as Dell but almost went bankrupt. Like Wal-Mart in retailing and Southwest in airlines, Dell has created a distinctive competency and used it to dominate the industry. So far, no other PC maker has been able to copy Dell's success.

5.1 | A Resource-Based Approach to Organizational Analysis

Scanning and analyzing the external environment for opportunities and threats is not enough to provide an organization a competitive advantage. Analysts must also look within the corporation itself to identify **internal strategic factors**—critical *strengths* and *weaknesses* that are likely to determine whether a firm will be able to take advantage of opportunities while avoiding threats. This internal scanning, often referred to as **organizational analysis**, is concerned with identifying and developing an organization's resources and competencies.

Core and Distinctive Competencies

Resources are an organization's assets and are thus the basic building blocks of the organization. They include *physical assets*, such as plant, equipment, and location; *human assets*, in terms of the number of employees and their skills; and *organizational assets*, such as culture and reputation. **Capabilities** refer to a corporation's ability to exploit its resources. They consist of business processes and routines that manage the interaction among resources to turn inputs into outputs. For example, a company's marketing capability can be based on the interaction among its marketing specialists, information technology, and financial resources. A capability is functionally based and is resident in a particular function. Thus, there are marketing capabilities, manufacturing capabilities, and human resource management capabilities. A **competency** is a cross-functional integration and coordination of capabilities. For example, a competency in new product development in one division of a corporation may be the consequence of integrating management of information systems (MIS) capabilities, marketing capabilities, R&D capabilities, and production capabilities within the division. A **core competency** is a collection of competencies that crosses divisional boundaries, is widespread within the corporation, and is something that the corporation can do exceedingly well. Thus new product development is a core competency if it goes beyond one division.[6] For example, a core competency of Avon Products is its expertise in door-to-door selling. FedEx has a core competency in its application of information technology to all its operations. A company must continually reinvest in a core competency or risk its becoming a *core rigidity* or *deficiency*—that is, a strength that over time matures and may become a weakness.[7] Although it is typically not an asset in the accounting sense, a core competency is a very valuable resource—it does not "wear out" with use. In general, the more core competencies are used, the more refined they get, and the more valuable they become. When core competencies are superior to those of the competition, they are called **distinctive competencies**. For example, General Electric is well known for its distinctive competency in management development. Its executives are sought out by other companies hiring top managers.[8]

Barney, in his **VRIO framework** of analysis, proposes four questions to evaluate a firm's competencies:

1. **Value:** Does it provide customer value and competitive advantage?
2. **Rareness:** Do other competitors possess it?
3. **Imitability:** Is it costly for others to imitate?
4. **Organization:** Is the firm organized to exploit the resource?

If the answer to each of these questions is *yes* for a particular competency, it is considered to be a strength and thus a distinctive competence.[9]

It is important to evaluate the importance of a company's resources, capabilities, and competencies to ascertain whether they are internal strategic factors—that is, particular strengths and weaknesses that will help determine the future of the company. This can be done by comparing measures of these factors with measures of (1) the company's past performance, (2) the company's key competitors, and (3) the industry as a whole. To the extent that a resource (such as a firm's cash situation), capability, or competency is significantly different from the firm's own past, its key competitors, or the industry average, that resource is likely to be a strategic factor and should be considered in strategic decisions.

Even though a distinctive competency is certainly considered to be a corporation's key strength, a key strength may not always be a distinctive competency. As competitors attempt to imitate another company's competency (especially during hypercompetition), what was once a distinctive competency becomes a minimum requirement to compete in the industry.[10] Even though the competency may still be a core competency and thus a strength, it is no longer unique. For example, when Maytag Company alone made high-quality home appliances, this ability was a distinctive competency. As other appliance makers imitated Maytag's quality control and design processes, this continued to be a key strength (that is, a core competency) of Maytag, but it was less and less a distinctive competency.

Using Resources to Gain Competitive Advantage

Proposing that a company's sustained competitive advantage is primarily determined by its resource endowments, Grant proposes a five-step, resource-based approach to strategy analysis:

1. Identify and classify the firm's resources in terms of strengths and weaknesses.
2. Combine the firm's strengths into specific capabilities and core competencies.
3. Appraise the profit potential of these capabilities and competencies in terms of their potential for sustainable competitive advantage and the ability to harvest the profits resulting from their use. Are there any distinctive competencies?
4. Select the strategy that best exploits the firm's capabilities and competencies relative to external opportunities.
5. Identify resource gaps and invest in upgrading weaknesses.[11]

Where do these competencies come from? A corporation can gain access to a distinctive competency in four ways:

- It may be an asset endowment, such as a key patent, coming from the founding of the company. For example, Xerox grew on the basis of its original copying patent.

- It may be acquired from someone else. For example, Whirlpool bought a worldwide distribution system when it purchased Philips's appliance division.

- It may be shared with another business unit or alliance partner. For example, Apple Computer worked with a design firm to create the special appeal of its Apple II and Mac computers.

- It may be carefully built and accumulated over time within the company. For example, Honda carefully extended its expertise in small motor manufacturing from motorcycles to autos and lawnmowers.[12]

The desire to build or upgrade a core competency is one reason entrepreneurial and other fast-growing firms often tend to locate close to their competitors. They form **clusters**—geographic concentrations of interconnected companies and industries. Examples in the United States are computer technology in Silicon Valley in northern California; light aircraft in Wichita, Kansas; financial services in New York City; agricultural equipment in Iowa and Illinois; and home furniture in North Carolina. According to Michael Porter, clusters provide access to employees, suppliers, specialized information, and complementary products.[13] Being close to one's competitors makes it easier to measure and compare performance against rivals. Capabilities may thus be formed externally through a firm's network resources. An example is the presence of many venture capitalists located in Silicon Valley who provide financial support and assistance to high-tech startup firms in the region. Employees from competitive firms in these clusters often socialize. As a result, companies learn from each other while competing with each other. Interestingly, research reveals that companies with core competencies have little to gain from locating in a cluster with other firms and therefore do not do so. In contrast, firms with the weakest technologies, human resources, training programs, suppliers, and distributors are strongly motivated to cluster. They have little to lose and a lot to gain from locating close to their competitors.[14]

Determining the Sustainability of an Advantage

Just because a firm is able to use its resources, capabilities, and competencies to develop a competitive advantage does not mean it will be able to sustain it. Two characteristics determine the sustainability of a firm's distinctive competency(ies): durability and imitability.

Durability is the rate at which a firm's underlying resources, capabilities, or core competencies depreciate or become obsolete. New technology can make a company's core competency obsolete or irrelevant. For example, Intel's skills in using basic technology developed by others to manufacture and market quality microprocessors was a crucial capability until management realized that the firm had taken current technology as far as possible with the Pentium chip. Without basic R&D of its own, it would slowly lose its competitive advantage to others. It thus formed a strategic alliance with HP to gain access to a needed technology.

Imitability is the rate at which a firm's underlying resources, capabilities, or core competencies can be duplicated by others. To the extent that a firm's distinctive competency gives it competitive advantage in the marketplace, competitors will do what they can to learn and imitate that set of skills and capabilities. Competitors' efforts may range from **reverse engineering** (which involves taking apart a competitor's product in order to find out how it works), to hiring employees from the competitor, to outright patent infringement. A core competency can be easily imitated to the extent that it is transparent, transferable, and replicable:

- **Transparency** is the speed with which other firms can understand the relationship of resources and capabilities supporting a successful firm's strategy. For example, Gillette has always supported its dominance in the marketing of razors with excellent R&D. A competitor could never understand how the Sensor or Mach 3 razor was produced simply by taking one apart. Gillette's razor design is very difficult to copy, partially because the manufacturing equipment needed to produce it is so expensive and complicated.

- **Transferability** is the ability of competitors to gather the resources and capabilities necessary to support a competitive challenge. For example, it may be very difficult for a wine maker to duplicate a French winery's key resources of land and climate, especially if the imitator is located in Iowa.

- **Replicability** is the ability of competitors to use duplicated resources and capabilities to imitate the other firm's success. For example, even though many companies have tried to imitate Procter & Gamble's (P&G's) success with brand management by hiring brand managers away from P&G, they have often failed to duplicate P&G's success. The competitors have failed to identify less visible P&G coordination mechanisms or to realize that P&G's brand management style conflicted with the competitor's own corporate culture. Another example is Wal-Mart's sophisticated *cross-docking system*, which provides the company a substantial cost advantage by improving its ability to reduce shipping and handling cost. A truck arriving from a supplier transfers its goods not into Wal-Mart's warehouse but into other trucks that move the goods directly to Wal-Mart's stores. While Wal-Mart has the same resources in terms of retail space, employee skills, and equipment as many other discount chains, it has the unique capability to manage its resources for maximum productivity.[15]

It is relatively easy to learn and imitate another company's core competency or capability if it comes from **explicit knowledge**—that is, knowledge that can be easily articulated and communicated. This is the type of knowledge that competitive intelligence activities can quickly identify and communicate. **Tacit knowledge**, in contrast, is knowledge that is *not* easily communicated because it is deeply rooted in employee experience or in a corporation's culture.[16] Tacit knowledge is more valuable and more likely to lead to a sustainable competitive advantage than is explicit knowledge because it is much harder for competitors to imitate.[17] As explained in a Michael Dell quote earlier in this chapter, "others can understand what they do, but they can't do it." The knowledge may be complex and combined with other types of knowledge in an unclear fashion such that even management cannot clearly explain the competency.[18] This can be a problem. Because P&G's successful approach to brand management is primarily composed of tacit knowledge, the firm's top management is very reluctant to make any significant modifications to it—fearing that they might destroy the very thing they would be trying to improve!

An organization's resources and capabilities can be placed on a continuum to the extent that they are durable and can't be imitated (that is, aren't transparent, transferable, or replicable) by another firm. This **continuum of sustainability** is depicted in **Figure 5–1**. At one extreme are slow-cycle resources, which are sustainable because they are shielded by patents, geography, strong brand names, or tacit knowledge. These resources and capabilities form distinctive competencies because they provide a sustainable competitive advantage. Gillette's razor technology is a good example of a product built around slow-cycle resources. The other extreme includes fast-cycle resources, which face the highest imitation pressures because they are based on a concept or technology that can be easily duplicated, such as Sony's Walkman. To the extent that a company has fast-cycle resources, the primary way it can compete successfully is through increased speed from lab to marketplace. Otherwise, it has no real sustainable competitive advantage.

With its low-cost position, good service, and reputation for quality PCs, Dell has successfully built a sustainable competitive advantage based on relatively slow-cycle patented manufacturing process resources—resources that are durable and can't be easily imitated because they lack transparency, transferability, and replicability.

Figure 5–1
Continuum of Resource Sustainability

Source: Suggested by J. R. Williams, "How Sustainable Is Your Competitive Advantage?" California Management Review *(Spring 1992), p. 33. Copyright © 1992 by the Regents of the University of California. Reprinted from the* California Management Review, *Vol. 34, No. 3. By permission of The Regents. All rights reserved.*

5.2 | Business Models

When analyzing a company, it is helpful to learn what sort of business model it is following. This is especially important when analyzing Internet-based companies. A **business model** is a company's method for making money in the current business environment. It includes the key structural and operational characteristics of a firm—how it earns revenue and makes a profit. A business model is usually composed of five elements:

- Who it serves
- What it provides
- How it makes money
- How it differentiates and sustains competitive advantage
- How it provides its product/service[19]

The simplest business model is to provide a good or service that can be sold so that revenues exceed costs and expenses. Other models can be much more complicated. Some of the many possible business models are:

- *Customer Solutions Model:* IBM uses this model to make money not by selling IBM products but by selling its expertise to improve its customers' operations. This is a consulting model.

- *Profit Pyramid Model:* General Motors offers a full line of automobiles in order to close out any niches where a competitor might find a position. The key is to get customers to buy in at the low-priced, low-margin entry point (Saturn's basic sedans) and move them up to high-priced, high-margin products (SUVs and pickup trucks), where the company makes its money.

- *Multi-Component System/Installed Base Model:* Gillette invented this classic model to sell razors at break-even pricing in order to make money on higher-margin razor blades. HP does the same with printers and printer cartridges. The product is thus a system, not just one product, with one component providing most of the profits.

- *Advertising Model:* Similar to the multi-component system/installed base model, this model offers its basic product free in order to make money on advertising. Originating in the newspaper industry, this model is used heavily in commercial radio and television. This was a key model of the dot.com boom when web sites offered free services to users in order to expose them to the advertising that paid the bills. This model is analogous to Mary Poppins' "spoonful of sugar helps the medicine go down."

- *Switchboard Model:* In this model a firm acts as an intermediary to connect multiple sellers to multiple buyers. Financial planners juggle a wide range of products for sale to multiple customers with different needs.

- *Time Model:* Product R&D and speed are the keys to success in the time model. Being the first to market with a new innovation allows a pioneer such as Sony to earn high margins. Once others enter the market with process R&D and lower margins, it's time to move on.

- *Efficiency Model:* In this model, a company waits until a product becomes standardized and then enters the market with a low-priced, low-margin product that appeals to the mass market. This model is used by Wal-Mart, Dell, and Southwest.

- *Blockbuster Model:* In some industries, such as pharmaceuticals and motion picture studios, profitability is driven by a few key products. The focus is on high investment in a few products with high potential payoffs—especially if they can be protected by patents.

- ***Profit Multiplier Model:*** The idea of this model is to develop a concept that may or may not make money on its own but can spin off many profitable products. Walt Disney invented this concept by using cartoon characters to develop high-margin theme parks, merchandise, and licensing opportunities.

- ***Entrepreneurial Model:*** In this model, a company offers specialized products/services to market niches that are too small to be worthwhile to large competitors but have the potential to grow quickly. Small, local brew pubs have been very successful in a mature industry dominated by Anheuser-Busch. This model has been used by small high-tech firms that develop innovative prototypes in order to sell off the companies (without ever selling a product) to Microsoft or DuPont.

- ***De Facto Standard Model:*** In this model, a company offers products free or at a very low price in order to saturate the market and become the industry standard. Once users are locked in, the company offers higher-margin products using this standard. For example, Microsoft packaged Internet Explorer free with its Windows software in order to take market share from Netscape's web browser.[20]

In order to understand how some of these business models work, it is important to learn where on the value chain the company makes its money. Although a company might offer a large number of products and services, one product (such as HP's printers) might contribute most of the profits.

5.3 | **Value-Chain Analysis**

A **value chain** is a linked set of value-creating activities that begin with basic raw materials coming from suppliers, move on to a series of value-added activities involved in producing and marketing a product or service, and end with distributors getting the final goods into the hands of the ultimate consumer. See **Figure 5–2** for an example of a typical value chain for a manufactured product. The focus of value-chain analysis is to examine the corporation in the context of the overall chain of value-creating activities, of which the firm may be only a small part.

Very few corporations include a product's entire value chain. Ford Motor Company did when it was managed by its founder, Henry Ford I. During the 1920s and 1930s, the company owned its own iron mines, ore-carrying ships, and a small rail line to bring ore to its mile-long River Rouge plant in Detroit. Visitors to the plant would walk along an elevated walkway, where they could watch iron ore being dumped from the rail cars into huge furnaces. The resulting steel was poured and rolled out onto a moving belt to be fabricated into auto frames and parts while the visitors watched in awe. As visitors walked along the walkway, they observed an automobile being built piece by piece. Reaching the end of the moving line, the finished automobile was driven out of the plant into a vast adjoining parking lot. Ford trucks would then load the cars for delivery to dealers. Although the Ford dealers were not employees of the company, they had almost no power in the arrangement. Dealerships were awarded by the company and taken away if a dealer was at all disloyal. Ford Motor Company at that

Figure 5–2
Typical Value Chain for a Manufactured Product

Raw Materials → Primary Manufacturing → Fabrication → Distributor → Retailer

time was completely vertically integrated—that is, it controlled (usually by ownership) every stage of the value chain, from the iron mines to the retailers.

Industry Value-Chain Analysis

The value chains of most industries can be split into two segments: *upstream* and *downstream* segments. In the petroleum industry, for example, *upstream* refers to oil exploration, drilling, and moving of the crude oil to the refinery, and *downstream* refers to refining the oil plus transporting and marketing gasoline and refined oil to distributors and gas station retailers. Even though most large oil companies are completely integrated, they often vary in the amount of expertise they have at each part of the value chain. Amoco, for example, had strong expertise downstream in marketing and retailing. British Petroleum, in contrast, was more dominant in upstream activities like exploration. That's one reason the two companies merged to form BP Amoco.

An industry can be analyzed in terms of the profit margin available at any point along the value chain. For example, the U.S. auto industry's revenues and profits are divided among many value-chain activities, including manufacturing, new and used car sales, gasoline retailing, insurance, after-sales service and parts, and lease financing. From a revenue standpoint, auto manufacturers dominate the industry, accounting for almost 60% of total industry revenues. Profits, however, are a different matter. Auto leasing is the most profitable activity in the value chain, followed by insurance and auto loans. The core activities of manufacturing and distribution, however, earn significantly smaller shares of the total industry profits than they do of total revenues. For example, because auto sales have become marginally profitable, dealerships are now emphasizing service and repair. As a result of various differences along the industry value chain, manufacturers have moved aggressively into auto financing.[21] Ford, for example, generated $3.3 billion in profits from financial services in 2003 compared to a loss of $2 billion from automobiles, even though financing accounted for less than 16% of the company's revenues!

In analyzing the complete value chain of a product, note that even if a firm operates up and down the entire industry chain, it usually has an area of primary expertise where its primary activities lie. A company's **center of gravity** is the part of the chain that is most important to the company and the point where its greatest expertise and capabilities lie—its core competencies. According to Galbraith, a company's center of gravity is usually the point at which the company started. After a firm successfully establishes itself at this point by obtaining a competitive advantage, one of its first strategic moves is to move forward or backward along the value chain in order to reduce costs, guarantee access to key raw materials, or guarantee distribution.[22] This process, called *vertical integration*, is discussed in more detail in **Chapter 7**.

In the paper industry, for example, Weyerhaeuser's center of gravity is in the raw materials and primary manufacturing parts of the value chain, as shown in **Figure 5–2**. Weyerhaeuser's expertise is in lumbering and pulp mills, which is where the company started. It integrated forward by using its wood pulp to make paper and boxes, but its greatest capability still lay in getting the greatest return from its lumbering activities. In contrast, P&G is primarily a consumer products company that also owned timberland and operated pulp mills. Its expertise is in the product producer and marketer distributor parts of the **Figure 5–2** value chain. P&G purchased these assets to guarantee access to the large quantities of wood pulp it needed to expand its disposable diaper, toilet tissue, and napkin products. P&G's strongest capabilities have always been in the downstream activities of product development, marketing, and brand management. It has never been as efficient in upstream paper activities as Weyerhauser. It had no real distinctive competence on that part of the value chain. When paper supplies became more plentiful (and competition got rougher), P&G gladly sold its land

and mills to focus more on the part of the value chain where it could provide the greatest value at the lowest cost—creating and marketing innovative consumer products. As was the case with P&G's experience in the paper industry, it makes sense for a company to outsource any weak areas it may control internally on the industry value chain.

Corporate Value-Chain Analysis

Each corporation has its own internal value chain of activities. See **Figure 5–3** for an example of a corporate value chain. Porter proposes that a manufacturing firm's **primary activities** usually begin with inbound logistics (raw materials handling and warehousing), go through an operations process in which a product is manufactured, and continue on to outbound logistics (warehousing and distribution), to marketing and sales, and finally to service (installation, repair, and sale of parts). Several **support activities**, such as procurement (purchasing), technology development (R&D), human resource management, and firm infrastructure (accounting, finance, strategic planning), ensure that the primary value-chain activities operate effectively and efficiently. Each of a company's product lines has its own distinctive value chain. Because most corporations make several different products or services, an internal analysis of the firm involves analyzing a series of different value chains.

The systematic examination of individual value activities can lead to a better understanding of a corporation's strengths and weaknesses. According to Porter, "Differences among competitor value chains are a key source of competitive advantage."[23] Corporate value-chain analysis involves the following three steps:

1. *Examine each product line's value chain in terms of the various activities involved in producing that product or service.* Which activities can be considered strengths (core competencies) or weaknesses (core deficiencies)? Do any of the strengths provide competitive advantage, and can they thus be labeled distinctive competencies?

2. *Examine the linkages within each product line's value chain.* **Linkages** are the connections between the way one value activity (for example, marketing) is performed and the

Figure 5–3
A Corporation's Value Chain

Firm Infrastructure
(general management, accounting, finance, strategic planning)

Human Resource Management
(recruiting, training, development)

Technology Development
(R&D, product and process improvement)

Procurement
(purchasing of raw materials, machines, supplies)

Support Activities

| Inbound Logistics (raw materials handling and warehousing) | Operations (machining, assembling, testing) | Outbound Logistics (warehousing and distribution of finished product) | Marketing and Sales (advertising, promotion, pricing, channel relations) | Service (installation, repair, parts) |

Profit Margin

Primary Activities

Source: Adapted with the permission of The Free Press, a Division of Simon & Schuster Adult Publishing Group, from COMPETITIVE ADVANTAGE: Creating and Sustaining Superior Performance *by Michael Porter. Copyright © 1985, 1988 by Michael E. Porter. All rights reserved.*

cost of performance of another activity (for example, quality control). In seeking ways for a corporation to gain competitive advantage in the marketplace, the same function can be performed in different ways with different results. For example, quality inspection of 100% of output by the workers themselves instead of the usual 10% by quality control inspectors might increase production costs, but that increase could be more than offset by the savings obtained from reducing the number of repair people needed to fix defective products and increasing the amount of salespeople's time devoted to selling instead of exchanging already-sold but defective products.

3. *Examine the potential synergies among the value chains of different product lines or business units.* Each value element, such as advertising or manufacturing, has an inherent economy of scale in which activities are conducted at their lowest possible cost per unit of output. If a particular product is not being produced at a high enough level to reach economies of scale in distribution, another product could be used to share the same distribution channel. This is an example of economies of scope, which result when the value chains of two separate products or services share activities, such as the same marketing channels or manufacturing facilities. For example, the cost of joint production of multiple products can be lower than the cost of separate production.

5.4 | Scanning Functional Resources and Capabilities

The simplest way to begin an analysis of a corporation's value chain is by carefully examining its traditional functional areas for potential strengths and weaknesses. Functional resources and capabilities include not only the financial, physical, and human assets in each area but also the ability of the people in each area to formulate and implement the necessary functional objectives, strategies, and policies. These resources and capabilities include the knowledge of analytical concepts and procedural techniques common to each area as well as the ability of the people in each area to use them effectively. If used properly, these resources and capabilities serve as strengths to carry out value-added activities and support strategic decisions. In addition to the usual business functions of marketing, finance, R&D, operations, human resources, and information systems, we also discuss structure and culture as key parts of a business corporation's value chain.

Basic Organizational Structures

Although there is an almost infinite variety of structural forms, certain basic types predominate in modern complex organizations. **Figure 5–4** illustrates three basic **organizational structures**. The conglomerate structure is a variant of divisional structure and is thus not depicted as a fourth structure. Generally speaking, each structure tends to support some corporate strategies over others:

- **Simple structure** has no functional or product categories and is appropriate for a small, entrepreneur-dominated company with one or two product lines that operates in a reasonably small, easily identifiable market niche. Employees tend to be generalists and jacks-of-all-trades. In terms of stages of development (discussed in **Chapter 9**), this is a Stage I company.

- **Functional structure** is appropriate for a medium-sized firm with several product lines in one industry. Employees tend to be specialists in the business functions that are important to that industry, such as manufacturing, marketing, finance, and human resources. In terms of stages of development (discussed in **Chapter 9**), this is a Stage II company.

Figure 5–4
Basic Organizational Structures

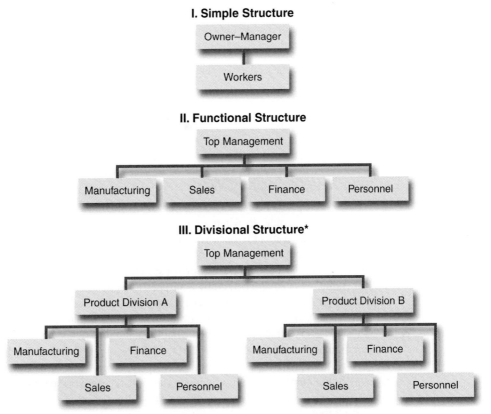

*Strategic Business Units and the conglomerate structure are variants of the divisional structure.

- **Divisional structure** is appropriate for a large corporation with many product lines in several related industries. Employees tend to be functional specialists organized according to product/market distinctions. General Motors, for example, groups its various auto lines into the separate divisions of Saturn, Chevrolet, Pontiac, Buick, and Cadillac. Management attempts to find some synergy among divisional activities through the use of committees and horizontal linkages. In terms of stages of development (discussed in **Chapter 9**), this is a Stage III company.

- **Strategic business units (SBUs)** are a modification of the divisional structure. SBUs are divisions or groups of divisions composed of independent product-market segments that are given primary responsibility and authority for the management of their own functional areas. An SBU may be of any size or level, but it must have (1) a unique mission, (2) identifiable competitors, (3) an external market focus, and (4) control of its business functions.[24] The idea is to decentralize on the basis of strategic elements rather than on the basis of size, product characteristics, or span of control and to create horizontal linkages among units previously kept separate. For example, rather than organize products on the basis of packaging technology, such as frozen foods, canned foods, and bagged foods, General Foods organized its products into SBUs on the basis of consumer-oriented menu segments: breakfast foods, beverages, main meals, desserts, and pet foods. In terms of stages of development (discussed in **Chapter 9**), this is also a Stage III company.

- **Conglomerate structure** is appropriate for a large corporation with many product lines in several unrelated industries. A variant of the divisional structure, the conglomerate structure (sometimes called a holding company) is typically an assemblage of legally independent firms (subsidiaries) operating under one corporate umbrella but controlled through the subsidiaries' boards of directors. The unrelated nature of the subsidiaries prevents any attempt at gaining synergy among them. In terms of stages of development (discussed in **Chapter 9**), this is also a Stage III company.

If the current basic structure of a corporation does not easily support a strategy under consideration, top management must decide whether the proposed strategy is feasible or whether the structure should be changed to a more advanced structure, such as a matrix or network. (Advanced structural designs such as the matrix and network are discussed in **Chapter 9**.)

Corporate Culture: The Company Way

There is an oft-told story of a person new to a company asking an experienced co-worker what an employee should do when a customer calls. The old-timer responded: "There are three ways to do any job—the right way, the wrong way, and the company way. Around here, we always do things the company way." In most organizations, the "company way" is derived from the corporation's culture. **Corporate culture** is the collection of beliefs, expectations, and values learned and shared by a corporation's members and transmitted from one generation of employees to another. The corporate culture generally reflects the values of the founder(s) and the mission of the firm.[25] It gives a company a sense of identity: "This is who we are. This is what we do. This is what we stand for." The culture includes the dominant orientation of the company, such as R&D at HP, customer service at Nordstrom, or product quality at Maytag. It often includes a number of informal work rules (forming the "company way") that employees follow without question. These work practices over time become part of a company's unquestioned tradition. The culture, therefore, reflects the company's values

Corporate culture has two distinct attributes: intensity and integration.[26] **Cultural intensity** is the degree to which members of a unit accept the norms, values, or other culture content associated with the unit. This shows the culture's depth. Organizations with strong norms promoting a particular value, such as quality at Maytag, have intensive cultures, whereas new firms (or those in transition) have weaker, less intensive cultures. Employees in an intensive culture tend to exhibit consistent behavior—that is, they tend to act similarly over time. **Cultural integration** is the extent to which units throughout an organization share a common culture. This is the culture's breadth. Organizations with a pervasive dominant culture may be hierarchically controlled and power oriented, such as a military unit, and have highly integrated cultures. All employees tend to hold the same cultural values and norms. In contrast, a company that is structured into diverse units by functions or divisions usually exhibits some strong subcultures (for example, R&D versus manufacturing) and a less integrated corporate culture.

Corporate culture fulfills several important functions in an organization:

1. Conveys a sense of identity for employees.
2. Helps generate employee commitment to something greater than themselves.
3. Adds to the stability of the organization as a social system.
4. Serves as a frame of reference for employees to use to make sense of organizational activities and to use as a guide for appropriate behavior.[27]

Corporate culture shapes the behavior of people in a corporation. Because these cultures have a powerful influence on the behavior of people at all levels, they can strongly affect a corporation's ability to shift its strategic direction. A strong culture should not only promote survival, but it should also create the basis for a superior competitive position by increasing motivation and facilitating coordination and control.[28] For example, a culture emphasizing

GL🌐BAL ISSUE

Managing Corporate Culture for Global Competitive Advantage: ABB Versus Matsushita

Zurich-based ABB Asea Brown Boveri AG is a worldwide builder of power plants, electrical equipment, and industrial factories in 140 countries. By establishing one set of multicultural values throughout its global operations, ABB's management believes that the company will gain an advantage over its rivals Siemens AG of Germany, France's Alcatel-Alsthom NV, and the U.S.'s General Electric Company. ABB is a company with no geographic base. Instead, it has many "home" markets that can draw on expertise from around the globe. ABB created a set of 500 global managers who could adapt to local cultures while executing ABB's global strategies. These people are multilingual and move around each of ABB's 5,000 profit centers in 140 countries. Their assignment is to cut costs, improve efficiency, and integrate local businesses with the ABB worldview.

Few multinational corporations are as successful as ABB in getting global strategies to work with local operations. In agreement with the resource-based view of the firm, ABB Chair Percy Barnevik states, "Our strength comes from pulling together. . . . If you can make this work real well, then you get a competitive edge out of the organization which is very, very difficult to copy."

Contrast ABB's globally oriented corporate culture with the more Japanese-oriented parochial culture of Matsushita Electric Industrial Corporation of Japan (MEI). Operating under the brand names of Panasonic and Technic, MEI is the third-largest electrical company in the world. Konosuke Matsushita founded the company in 1918. His management philosophy led to the company's success but became institutionalized in the corporate culture—a culture that was more focused on Japanese values than on cross-cultural globalization. As a result, MEI's corporate culture does not adapt well to local conditions. Not only is MEI's top management *exclusively* Japanese, its subsidiary managers are *overwhelmingly* Japanese. The company's distrust of non-Japanese managers in the United States and some European countries results in a "rice-paper ceiling" that prevents non-Japanese people from being promoted into MEI subsidiaries' top management. Foreign employees are often confused by the corporate philosophy that has not been adapted to suit local realities. MEI's corporate culture perpetuates a cross-cultural divide that separates the Japanese from the non-Japanese managers, leaving the non-Japanese managers feeling frustrated and undervalued. This divide prevents the flow of knowledge and experience from regional operations to the headquarters and may hinder MEI's ability to compete globally.

Sources: Summarized from J. Guyon, "ABB Fuses Units with One Set of Values," *Wall Street Journal* (October 2, 1996), p. A15, and N. Holden, "Why Globalizing with a Conservative Corporate Culture Inhibits Localization of Management: The Telling Case of Matsushita Electric," *International Journal of Cross Cultural Management*, Vol. 1, No. 1 (2001), pp. 53–72.

constant renewal may help a company adapt to a changing, hypercompetitive environment.[29] To the extent that a corporation's distinctive competence is embedded in an organization's culture, it will be a form of tacit knowledge and very difficult for a competitor to imitate.[30] The GLOBAL ISSUE feature shows the differences between ABB Asea Brown Boveri AG and Matsushita Electric in terms of how they manage their corporate cultures in a global industry.

A change in mission, objectives, strategies, or policies is not likely to be successful if it is in opposition to the accepted culture of a firm. Foot-dragging and even sabotage may result, as employees fight to resist a radical change in corporate philosophy. As with structure, if an organization's culture is compatible with a new strategy, it is an internal strength. But if the corporate culture is not compatible with the proposed strategy, it is a serious weakness. Corporate culture is also important when considering an acquisition. The merging of two dissimilar cultures, if not handled wisely, can be a recipe for disaster.

Strategic Marketing Issues

The marketing manager is a company's primary link to the customer and the competition. The manager, therefore, must be especially concerned with the market position and marketing mix of the firm as well as with the overall reputation of the company and its brands.

Market Position and Segmentation

Market position deals with the question, "Who are our customers?" It refers to the selection of specific areas for marketing concentration and can be expressed in terms of market, product, and geographic locations. Through market research, corporations are able to practice **market segmentation** with various products or services so that managers can discover what niches to seek, which new types of products to develop, and how to ensure that a company's many products do not directly compete with one another.

Marketing Mix

Marketing mix refers to the particular combination of key variables under a corporation's control that can be used to affect demand and to gain competitive advantage. These variables are product, place, promotion, and price. Within each of these four variables are several sub-variables, listed in **Table 5–1**, that should be analyzed in terms of their effects on divisional and corporate performance.

Product Life Cycle

One of the most useful concepts in marketing, insofar as strategic management is concerned, is the **product life cycle.** As depicted in **Figure 5–5**, the product life cycle is a graph showing time plotted against the monetary sales of a product as it moves from introduction through growth and maturity to decline. This concept enables a marketing manager to examine the marketing mix of a particular product or group of products in terms of its position in its life cycle.

Brand and Corporate Reputation

A **brand** is a name given to a company's product which identifies that item in the mind of the consumer. Over time and with proper advertising, a brand connotes various characteristics in the consumers' minds. For example, Maytag means quality home appliances. Disney stands for family entertainment. Ivory suggests "pure" soap. BMW means high-performance autos. A brand can thus be an important corporate resource. If done well, a brand name is connected to the product to such an extent that a brand may stand for an entire product category, such as Kleenex for facial tissue. The objective is for the customer to ask for the brand name (Coke or Pepsi) instead of the product category (cola). The world's 10 most valuable brands

TABLE 5–1
MARKETING MIX
VARIABLES

Product	Place	Promotion	Price
Quality	Channels	Advertising	List price
Features	Coverage	Personal selling	Discounts
Options	Locations	Sales promotion	Allowances
Style	Inventory	Publicity	Payment periods
Brand name	Transport		Credit items
Packaging			
Sizes			
Services			
Warranties			
Returns			

Source: Philip Kotler, *MARKETING MANAGEMENT*, 11th edition © 2003, p. 16. Reprinted by Pearson Education, Inc., Upper Saddle River, NJ.

Figure 5–5
Product Life Cycle

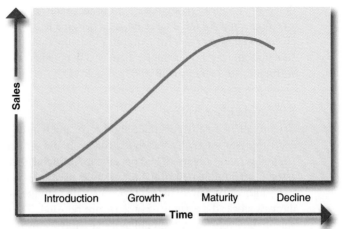

* The right end of the Growth stage is often called Competitive Turbulence because of price and distribution competition that shakes out the weaker competitors. For further information, see C. R. Wasson, *Dynamic Competitive Strategy and Product Life Cycles,* 3rd ed. (Austin, TX: Austin Press, 1978).

in 2004 were Coca-Cola, Microsoft, IBM, GE, Intel, Disney, McDonald's, Nokia, Toyota, and Marlboro, in that order. According to *Business Week*, the Coca-Cola brand is worth $67.4 billion.[31]

A **corporate brand** is a type of brand in which the company's name serves as the brand. Of the world's top 10 brands listed previously, all except Marlboro are corporate brands. The rest, such as Microsoft and IBM, are company names. The value of a corporate brand is that it typically stands for consumers' impressions of a company and can thus be extended onto products not currently offered—regardless of the company's actual expertise. For example, Caterpillar, a manufacturer of heavy earth-moving equipment, used consumer associations with the Caterpillar brand (*rugged, masculine, construction-related*) to market work boots. Thus, consumer impressions of a brand can suggest new product categories to enter even though a company may have no competencies in making or marketing that type of product or service.[32]

A **corporate reputation** is a widely held perception of a company by the general public. A good corporate reputation can be a strategic resource. It can serve in marketing as both a signal and an entry barrier. Reputation is especially important when the quality of a company's product or service is not directly observable and can be learned only through experience. For example, retail stores are willing to stock a new product from P&G or Anheuser-Busch because they know that both companies market only good-quality products that are highly advertised. Like tacit knowledge, reputation tends to be long lasting and hard for others to duplicate—thus providing sustainable competitive advantage.[33] Research reveals a positive relationship between corporate reputation and financial performance.[34]

Strategic Financial Issues

A financial manager must ascertain the best sources of funds, uses of funds, and control of funds. All strategic issues have financial implications. Cash must be raised from internal or external (local and global) sources and allocated for different uses. The flow of funds in the operations of an organization must be monitored. To the extent that a corporation is involved in international activities, currency fluctuations must be dealt with to ensure that profits aren't wiped out by the rise or fall of the dollar versus the yen, euro, or other currencies. Benefits in the form of returns, repayments, or products and services must be given to the sources of outside financing. All these tasks must be handled in a way that complements and supports overall corporate strategy. A firm's capital structure (amounts of debt and equity) can influence its strategic choices. For example, increased debt tends to increase risk aversion and decrease the willingness of management to invest in R&D.[35]

Financial Leverage

The mix of externally generated short-term and long-term funds in relationship to the amount and timing of internally generated funds should be appropriate to the corporate objectives, strategies, and policies. The concept of **financial leverage** (the ratio of total debt to total assets) is helpful in describing how debt is used to increase the earnings available to common shareholders. When a company finances its activities by sales of bonds or notes instead of through stock, the earnings per share are boosted: The interest paid on the debt reduces taxable income, but fewer shareholders share the profits than if the company had sold more stock to finance its activities. The debt, however, does raise the firm's break-even point above what it would have been if the firm had financed from internally generated funds only. High leverage may therefore be perceived as a corporate strength in times of prosperity and ever-increasing sales or as a weakness in times of recession and falling sales. This is because leverage acts to magnify the effect on earnings per share of an increase or decrease in monetary sales. Research indicates that greater leverage has a positive impact on performance for firms in stable environments but a negative impact for firms in dynamic environments.[36]

Capital Budgeting

Capital budgeting is the analyzing and ranking of possible investments in fixed assets such as land, buildings, and equipment in terms of the additional outlays and additional receipts that will result from each investment. A good finance department will be able to prepare such capital budgets and to rank them on the basis of some accepted criteria or hurdle rate (for example, years to pay back investment, rate of return, or time to break-even point) for the purpose of strategic decision making. Most firms have more than one hurdle rate and vary it as a function of the type of project being considered. Projects with high strategic significance, such as entering new markets or defending market share, often have low hurdle rates.[37]

Strategic Research and Development (R&D) Issues

An R&D manager is responsible for suggesting and implementing a company's technological strategy in light of its corporate objectives and policies. The manager's job, therefore, involves (1) choosing among alternative new technologies to use within the corporation, (2) developing methods of embodying the new technology in new products and processes, and (3) deploying resources so that the new technology can be successfully implemented.

R&D Intensity, Technological Competence, and Technology Transfer

A company must make available the resources necessary for effective research and development. A company's **R&D intensity** (that is, its spending on R&D as a percentage of sales revenue) is a principal means of gaining market share in global competition. The amount spent on R&D often varies by industry. For example, the U.S. computer software industry spends an average of 13.5% of its sales dollars for R&D, whereas the paper and forest products industry spends only 1.0%.[38] A good rule of thumb for R&D spending is that a corporation should spend at a "normal" rate for that particular industry, unless its strategic plan calls for unusual expenditures.

Simply spending money on R&D or new projects does not mean, however, that the money will produce useful results. For example, Pharmacia Upjohn spent more of its revenues on research than any other company in any industry (18%), but it was ranked low in innovation.[39] A company's R&D unit should be evaluated for **technological competence** in both the development and the use of innovative technology. Not only should the corporation make a consistent research effort (as measured by reasonably constant corporate expenditures that result in usable innovations), it should also be proficient in managing research personnel and integrating their innovations into its day-to-day operations. If a company is not proficient in **technology transfer**—the process of taking a new technology from the laboratory to the marketplace—it will not gain much advantage from new technological advances. For example, Xerox Corporation has been criticized for failing to take advantage of various innovations (such as the mouse and the graphical user interface for PCs) developed originally in its sophisticated Palo Alto Research Center. See Strategy Highlight 5.1 for a classic example of how Apple Computer's ability to imitate a core competency of Xerox gave it a competitive advantage (which was sustainable until Microsoft launched Windows 95).

R&D Mix

Basic R&D is conducted by scientists in well-equipped laboratories where the focus is on theoretical problem areas. The best indicators of a company's capability in this area are its patents and research publications. **Product R&D** concentrates on marketing and is concerned with product or product-packaging improvements. The best measurements of ability in this area are the number of successful new products introduced and the percentage of total sales and profits coming from products introduced within the past five years. **Engineering (or process) R&D** is concerned with engineering, concentrating on quality control and the development of design specifications and improved production equipment. A company's capability in this area can be measured by consistent reductions in unit manufacturing costs and by the number of product defects.

Most corporations have a mix of basic, product, and process R&D, and this mix varies by industry, company, and product line. The balance of these types of research is known as the **R&D mix** and should be appropriate to the strategy being considered and to each product's life cycle. For example, it is generally accepted that product R&D normally dominates the early stages of a product's life cycle (when the product's optimal form and features are still being

STRATEGY HIGHLIGHT 5.1

A Problem of Technology Transfer at Xerox Corporation

In the mid-1970s, Xerox Corporation's Palo Alto Research Center (PARC) had developed Alto, a new type of computer with some innovative features. Although Alto was supposed to serve as a research prototype, it became so popular among PARC personnel that some researchers began to develop Alto as a commercial product. Unfortunately, this put PARC into direct conflict with Xerox's product development group, which was at the same time developing a rival machine called the Star. Because the Star was in line with the company's expressed product development strategy, top management, which placed all its emphasis on the Star, ignored Alto.

In 1979, Steve Jobs, co-founder of Apple Computer, Inc., made a now-legendary tour of the normally very secretive PARC. Researchers gave Jobs a demonstration of the Alto. Unlike the computers that Apple was then building, Alto had the power of a minicomputer. Its user-friendly software generated crisp text and bright graphics. Jobs fell in love with the machine. He promptly asked Apple's engineers to duplicate the look and feel of Alto. The result was the Macintosh—a personal computer that soon revolutionized the industry.

―――――――――――

Note: See the 1999 motion picture *The Pirates of Silicon Valley* for the fuller story of how Apple Computer imitated the features of the Alto and how Microsoft, in turn, imitated the "look and feel" of Apple's Macintosh.

debated), whereas process R&D becomes especially important in the later stages (when the product's design is solidified and the emphasis is on reducing costs and improving quality).

Impact of Technological Discontinuity on Strategy

An R&D manager must determine when to abandon present technology and when to develop or adopt new technology. Richard Foster of McKinsey and Company states that the displacement of one technology by another (**technological discontinuity**) is a frequent and strategically important phenomenon. Such a discontinuity occurs when a new technology cannot simply be used to enhance the current technology but actually substitutes for that technology to yield better performance. For each technology within a given field or industry, according to Foster, the plotting of product performance against research effort/expenditures on a graph results in an S-shaped curve. He describes the process depicted in **Figure 5–6**:

> Early in the development of the technology a knowledge base is being built and progress requires a relatively large amount of effort. Later, progress comes more easily. And then, as the limits of that technology are approached, progress becomes slow and expensive. That is when R&D dollars should be allocated to technology with more potential. That is also—not so incidentally—when a competitor who has bet on a new technology can sweep away your business or topple an entire industry.[40]

Computerized information technology is currently on the steep upward slope of its S-curve, in which relatively small increments in R&D effort result in significant improvement in performance. This is an example of Moore's Law, which states that silicon chips (microprocessors) double in complexity every 18 months.[41] The presence of a technological discontinuity in the world's steel industry during the 1960s explains why the large capital expenditures by U.S. steel companies failed to keep them competitive with the Japanese firms that adopted the new technologies. As Foster points out, "History has shown that as one technology nears the end of its S-curve, competitive leadership in a market generally changes hands."[42]

Figure 5–6
Technological Discontinuity

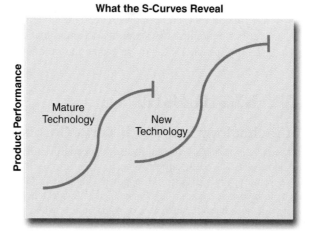

What the S-Curves Reveal

Product Performance

Mature Technology

New Technology

Research Effort/Expenditure

In the corporate planning process, it is generally assumed that incremental progress in technology will occur. But past developments in a given technology cannot be extrapolated into the future because every technology has its limits. The key to competitiveness is to determine when to shift resources to a technology that has more potential.

Source: From "Are You Investing in the Wrong Technology?" P. Pascarella, Industry Week, *July 25, 1983. Reprinted by permission of Penton Media, Inc.*

Christensen explains in *The Innovator's Dilemma* why this transition occurs when a "disruptive technology" enters an industry. In a study of computer disk drive manufacturers, he explains that established market leaders are typically reluctant to move in a timely manner to a new technology. This reluctance to switch technologies (even when the firm is aware of the new technology and may have even invented it!) is because the resource allocation process in most companies gives priority to those projects (typically based on the old technology) with the greatest likelihood of generating a good return on investment—those projects that appeal to the firm's current customers (whose products are also based on the characteristics of the old technology). For example, in the 1980s a disk drive manufacturer's customers (PC manufacturers) wanted a better, faster $5\frac{1}{4}''$ drive with greater capacity. These PC makers were not interested in the new $3\frac{1}{2}''$ drives based on the new technology because (at that time) the smaller drives were slower and had less capacity. Smaller size was irrelevant because these companies primarily made desktop PCs that were designed to hold large drives.

New technology is generally riskier and of little appeal to the current customers of established firms. Products derived from the new technology are more expensive and do not meet the customers' requirements—requirements based on the old technology. New entrepreneurial firms are typically more interested in the new technology because it is one way to appeal to a developing market niche in a market currently dominated by established companies. Even though the new technology may be more expensive to develop, it offers performance improvements in areas that are attractive to this small niche but of no consequence to the customers of the established competitors.

This was the case with the entrepreneurial manufacturers of $3\frac{1}{2}''$ disk drives. These smaller drives appealed to the PC makers who were trying to increase their small PC market share by offering laptop computers. Size and weight were more important to these customers than were capacity and speed. By the time the new technology was developed to the point that the $3\frac{1}{2}''$ drive matched and even surpassed the $5\frac{1}{4}''$ drive in terms of speed and capacity (in addition to size and weight), it was too late for the established $5\frac{1}{4}''$ disk drive firms to switch to the new technology. Once their customers begin demanding smaller products using the new technology, the established firms were unable to respond quickly and lost their leadership position in the industry. They were able to remain in the industry (with a much reduced market share) only if they were able to utilize the new technology to be competitive in the new product line.[43]

Strategic Operations Issues

The primary task of an operations (manufacturing or service) manager is to develop and operate a system that will produce the required number of products or services, with a certain quality, at a given cost, within an allotted time. Many of the key concepts and techniques popularly used in manufacturing can be applied to service businesses.

In very general terms, manufacturing can be intermittent or continuous. In **intermittent systems** (job shops), an item is normally processed sequentially, but the work and sequence of the process vary. An example is an auto body repair shop. At each location, the tasks determine the details of processing and the time required for them. These job shops can be very labor intensive. For example, a job shop usually has little automated machinery and thus a small amount of fixed costs. It has a fairly low break-even point, but its variable cost line (composed of wages and costs of special parts) has a relatively steep slope. Because most of the costs associated with the product are variable (many employees earn piece-rate wages), a job shop's variable costs are higher than those of automated firms. Its advantage over other firms is that it can operate at low levels and still be profitable. After a job shop's sales reach the break-even point, however, the huge variable costs as a percentage of total costs keep the profit per unit at a relatively low level. In terms of strategy, such a firm should look for a niche in the marketplace for which it can produce and sell a reasonably small quantity of goods.

In contrast, **continuous systems** are those laid out as lines on which products can be continuously assembled or processed. An example is an automobile assembly line. A firm using continuous systems invests heavily in fixed investments such as automated processes and highly sophisticated machinery. Its labor force, relatively small but highly skilled, earns salaries rather than piece-rate wages. Consequently, this firm has a high amount of fixed costs. It also has a relatively high break-even point, but its variable cost line rises slowly. This is an example of **operating leverage**, the impact of a specific change in sales volume on net operating income. The advantage of high operating leverage is that once the firm reaches the break-even point, its profits rise faster than do those of less automated firms having lower operating leverage. Continuous systems reap benefits from economies of scale. In terms of strategy, such a firm needs to find a high-demand niche in the marketplace for which it can produce and sell a large quantity of goods. However, a firm with high operating leverage is likely to suffer huge losses during a recession. During an economic downturn, a firm with less automation and thus less leverage is more likely to survive comfortably because a drop in sales primarily affects variable costs. It is often easier to lay off labor than to sell off specialized plants and machines.

Experience Curve

A conceptual framework that many large corporations have used successfully is the experience curve (originally called the learning curve). The **experience curve** suggests that unit production costs decline by some fixed percentage (commonly 20%–30%) each time the total accumulated volume of production in units doubles. The actual percentage varies by industry and is based on many variables: the amount of time it takes a person to learn a new task, scale economies, product and process improvements, and lower raw materials costs, among others. For example, in an industry with an 85% experience curve, a corporation might expect a 15% reduction in unit costs for every doubling of volume. The total costs per unit can be expected to drop from $100 when the total production is 10 units, to $85 ($100 × 85%) when production increases to 20 units, and to $72.25 ($85 × 85%) when it reaches 40 units. Achieving these results often means investing in R&D and fixed assets; higher fixed costs and less flexibility thus result. Nevertheless, the manufacturing strategy is one of building capacity ahead of demand in order to achieve the lower unit costs that develop from the experience curve. On the basis of some future point on the experience curve, a corporation should price its product or service very low to preempt competition and increase market demand. The resulting high number of units sold and high market share should result in high profits, based on the low unit costs.

Management commonly uses the experience curve in estimating the production costs of (1) a product never before made with the present techniques and processes or (2) current products produced by newly introduced techniques or processes. The concept was first applied in the airframe industry and can be applied in the service industry as well. For example, a cleaning company can reduce its costs per employee by having its workers use the same equipment and techniques to clean many adjacent offices in one office building rather than just cleaning a few offices in multiple buildings. Although many firms have used experience curves extensively, an unquestioning acceptance of the industry norm (such as 80% for the airframe industry or 70% for integrated circuits) is very risky. The experience curve of an industry as a whole might not hold true for a particular company for a variety of reasons.

Flexible Manufacturing for Mass Customization

The use of large, continuous, mass-production facilities to take advantage of experience-curve economies has recently been criticized. The use of Computer-Assisted Design and Computer-Assisted Manufacturing (CAD/CAM) and robot technology means that learning times are shorter and products can be economically manufactured in small, customized batches in a process called **mass customization**—the low-cost production of individually customized goods and services.[44] **Economies of scope** (in which common parts of the manufacturing activities of various products are combined to gain economies even though small numbers of each product are made) replace **economies of scale** (in which unit costs are reduced by making large numbers of the same product) in flexible manufacturing. **Flexible manufacturing** permits the low-volume output of custom-tailored products at relatively low unit costs through economies of scope. It is thus possible to have the cost advantages of continuous systems with the customer-oriented advantages of intermittent systems.

Strategic Human Resource Management (HRM) Issues

The primary task of a manager of human resources is to improve the match between individuals and jobs. Research indicates that companies with good HRM practices have higher profits and a better survival rate than do firms without these practices.[45] A good HRM department should know how to use attitude surveys and other feedback devices to assess employees' satisfaction with their jobs and with the corporation as a whole. HRM managers should also use job analysis to obtain job description information about what each job needs to accomplish in terms of quality and quantity. Up-to-date job descriptions are essential not only for proper employee selection, appraisal, training, and development for wage and salary administration, as well as for labor negotiations, but also for summarizing the corporatewide human resources in terms of employee-skill categories. Just as a company must know the number, type, and quality of its manufacturing facilities, it must also know the kinds of people it employs and the skills they possess. The best strategies are meaningless if employees do not have the skills to carry them out or if jobs cannot be designed to accommodate the available workers. For example, HP uses employee profiles to ensure that it has the right mix of talents to implement its planned strategies.

Increasing Use of Teams

Management is beginning to realize that it must be more flexible in its utilization of employees in order for human resources to be a strength. Human resource managers, therefore, need to be knowledgeable about work options such as part-time work, job sharing, flex-time, extended leaves, and contract work, and especially about the proper use of teams. More than two-thirds of large U.S. companies are successfully using **autonomous (self-managing) work teams**, in which a group of people work together without a supervisor to plan, coordinate, and evaluate their own work.[46] Northern Telecom found productivity and quality to increase with work teams to such an extent that it was able to reduce the number of quality inspectors by 40%.[47]

As a way to move a product more quickly through its development stage, companies such as Motorola, Chrysler, NCR, Boeing, and General Electric are using **cross-functional work teams**. Instead of developing products in a series of steps—beginning with a request from sales, which leads to design, then to engineering and on to purchasing, and finally to manufacturing (and often resulting in a costly product rejected by the customer)—companies are tearing down the traditional walls separating the departments so that people from each discipline can get involved in projects early on. In a process called **concurrent engineering**, the once-isolated specialists now work side by side and compare notes constantly in an effort to design cost-effective products with features customers want. Taking this approach enabled Chrysler Corporation to reduce its product development cycle from 60 to 36 months.[48] For such cross-functional work teams to be successful, the groups must receive training and coaching. Otherwise, poorly implemented teams may worsen morale, create divisiveness, and raise the level of cynicism among workers.[49]

Virtual teams are groups of geographically and/or organizationally dispersed co-workers that are assembled using a combination of telecommunications and information technologies to accomplish an organizational task.[50] In the United States alone, more than half of companies that have more than 5,000 employees use virtual teams—involving around 8.4 million people.[51] Internet, intranet, and extranet systems are combining with other new technologies such as desktop videoconferencing and collaborative software to create a new workplace in which teams of workers are no longer restrained by geography, time, or organizational boundaries. As more companies outsource some of the activities previously conducted internally, the traditional organizational structure is being replaced by a series of virtual teams that rarely, if ever, meet face to face. Such teams may be established as temporary groups to accomplish a specific task or may be more permanent to address continuing issues such as strategic planning. Membership on these teams is often fluid, depending on the task to be accomplished. They may include not only employees from different functions within a company but also members of various stakeholder groups, such as suppliers, customers, and law or consulting firms. The use of virtual teams to replace traditional face-to-face work groups is being driven by five trends:

1. Flatter organizational structures with increasing cross-functional coordination needs
2. Turbulent environments requiring more interorganizational cooperation
3. Increasing employee autonomy and participation in decision making
4. Higher knowledge requirements derived from a greater emphasis on service
5. Increasing globalization of trade and corporate activity[52]

Union Relations and Temporary/Part-Time Workers

If a corporation is unionized, a good human resource manager should be able to work closely with the union. Even though union membership had dropped to only 13% of the U.S. workforce by 2003 compared to 24% in 1973, it still included 16 million people.[53] To save jobs, U.S. unions are increasingly willing to support new strategic initiatives and employee involvement programs. For example, United Steel Workers hired Ron Bloom, an investment banker, to propose a strategic plan to make Goodyear Tire & Rubber globally competitive in a way that would preserve as many jobs as possible. In a contract ratified in September 2003, the union gave up $1.15 billion in wage and benefit concessions over three years in return for a promise by Goodyear's top management to invest in 12 of its 14 U.S. factories, to limit imports from its factories in Brazil and Asia, and to maintain 85% of its 19,000-person workforce. The company also agreed to aggressively restructure the firm's $5 billion debt by 2007. According to Bloom, "We told Goodyear, 'We'll make you profitable, but you're going to adopt this strategy.'. . . We think the company should be a patient, long-term builder of value for the employees and shareholders."[54]

Outside the United States, the average proportion of unionized workers among major industrialized nations is around 50%. European unions tend to be militant, politically oriented, and much less interested in working with management to increase efficiency. Nationwide strikes can occur quickly. In contrast, Japanese unions are typically tied to individual companies and are usually supportive of management. These differences among countries have significant implications for the management of multinational corporations.

To increase flexibility, avoid layoffs, and reduce labor costs, corporations are using more temporary (also known as contingent) workers. Ninety percent of U.S. firms use temporary workers in some capacity; 43% use them in professional and technical functions.[55] Approximately 13% of those in the U.S. workforce are part-time workers. The percentage is even higher in some European countries, such as the Netherlands, where more than one-third of all employees work part time.[56] Labor unions are concerned that companies use temps to avoid hiring costlier unionized workers. At United Parcel Service, for example, 80% of the jobs created from 1993 to 1997 were staffed by part-timers, whose pay rates hadn't changed since 1982. Fully 10% of the company's 128,000 part-timers worked 30 hours or more per week but were still paid at a lower rate than were full-time employees.[57]

Quality of Work Life and Human Diversity

Human resource departments have found that to reduce employee dissatisfaction and unionization efforts (or, conversely, to improve employee satisfaction and existing union relations), they must consider the **quality of work life** in the design of jobs. Partially a reaction to the traditionally heavy emphasis on technical and economic factors in job design, quality of work life emphasizes improving the human dimension of work. A knowledgeable human resource manager, therefore, should be able to improve a corporation's quality of work life by (1) introducing participative problem solving, (2) restructuring work, (3) introducing innovative reward systems, and (4) improving the work environment. It is hoped that these improvements will lead to a more participative corporate culture and thus higher productivity and quality products. Ford Motor Company, for example, rebuilt and modernized its famous River Rouge plant by using flexible equipment and new processes. Employees work in teams and use Internet-connected PCs on the shop floor to share their concerns instantly with suppliers or product engineers. Workstations were redesigned to make them more ergonomic and reduce repetitive-strain injuries. "If you feel good while you're working, I think quality and productivity will increase, and Ford thinks that too, otherwise, they wouldn't do this," observed Jerry Sullivan, president of United Auto Workers Local 600.[58]

Human diversity refers to the mix in the workplace of people from different races, cultures, and backgrounds. Realizing that the demographics are changing toward an increasing percentage of minorities and women in the workforce, companies are now concerned with hiring and promoting people without regard to ethnic background. According to a study reported by *Fortune* magazine, companies that pursue diversity outperform the S&P 500.[59] In a survey of 131 leading European companies, 67.2% stated that a diverse workforce can provide competitive advantage.[60] A manager from Nestle stated, "To deliver products that meet the needs of individual consumers, we need people who respect other cultures, embrace diversity, and never discriminate on any basis."[61] Good human resource managers should be working to ensure that people are treated fairly on the job and are not harassed by prejudiced co-workers or managers. Otherwise, they may find themselves subject to lawsuits. Coca-Cola Company, for example, agreed to pay $192.5 million because of discrimination against African-American salaried employees in pay, promotions, and evaluations from 1995 to 2000. According to Chairman and CEO Douglas Daft, "Sometimes things happen in an unintentional manner. And I've made it clear that can't happen anymore."[62]

An organization's human resources may be the key to achieving a sustainable competitive advantage. Advances in technology are copied almost immediately by competitors around the world. However, people are not always willing to move to other companies in other countries. This means that the only long-term resource advantage remaining to corporations operating in industrialized nations may lie in the area of skilled human resources. Research reveals that competitive strategies are more successfully executed in companies with a high level of commitment to their employees than in firms with less commitment.[63]

Strategic Information Systems/Technology Issues

The primary task of a manager of information systems/technology is to design and manage the flow of information in an organization in ways that improve productivity and decision making. Information must be collected, stored, and synthesized in such a manner that it will answer important operating and strategic questions. A corporation's information system can be a strength or a weakness in multiple areas of strategic management. It can not only aid in environmental scanning and in controlling a company's many activities, it can also be used as a strategic weapon in gaining competitive advantage.

Impact on Performance

Information systems/technology offers four main contributions to corporate performance. *First* (beginning in the 1970s with mainframe computers), it is used to automate existing back-office processes, such as payroll, human resource records, and accounts payable and receivable, and to establish huge databases. *Second* (beginning in the 1980s), it is used to automate individual tasks, such as keeping track of clients and expenses, through the use of PCs with word processing and spreadsheet software. Corporate databases are accessed to provide sufficient data to analyze the data and create what-if scenarios. These first two contributions tend to focus on reducing costs. *Third* (beginning in the 1990s), it is used to enhance key business functions, such as marketing and operations. This third contribution focuses on productivity improvements. The system provides customer support and help in distribution and logistics. For example, FedEx found that by allowing customers to directly access its package-tracking database via its Internet web site instead of their having to talk to a human operator, the company saved up to $2 million annually.[64] Business processes are analyzed to increase efficiency and productivity via reengineering. Enterprise resource planning (ERP) application software, such as SAP, PeopleSoft, Oracle, Baan, and J.D. Edwards, are used to integrate worldwide business activities so that employees need to enter information only once, and then that information is available to all corporate systems (including accounting) around the world. *Fourth* (beginning in 2000), it is used to develop competitive advantage. For example, American Hospital Supply (AHS), a leading manufacturer and distributor of a broad line of products for doctors, laboratories, and hospitals, developed an order-entry distribution system that directly linked the majority of its customers to AHS computers. The system was successful because it simplified ordering processes for customers, reduced costs for both AHS and customers, and allowed AHS to provide pricing incentives to the customer. As a result, customer loyalty was high, and AHS' share of the market became large.

A current trend in corporate information systems is the increasing use of the Internet for marketing, intranets for internal communication, and extranets for logistics and distribution. An **intranet** is an information network within an organization that also has access to the external worldwide Internet. An intranet typically begins as a way to provide employees with company information such as lists of product prices, employee benefits, and company policies. It is likely to be converted into an extranet for supply-chain management. An **extranet** is an information network within an organization that is available to key suppliers and customers. The key issue in building an extranet is the creation of fire walls to block extranet users from accessing the firm's or other users' confidential data. Once this is accomplished, the company can allow employees, customers, and suppliers to access information and conduct business on the Internet in a completely automated manner. By connecting these groups, a company hopes to obtain a competitive advantage by reducing the time needed to design and bring new products to market, slashing inventories, customizing manufacturing, and entering new markets.[65]

Supply-Chain Management

The expansion of the marketing-oriented Internet into intranets and extranets is making significant contributions to organizational performance through supply chain management. **Supply-chain management** is the forming of networks for sourcing raw materials, manufacturing products or creating services, storing and distributing goods, and delivering goods to customers and consumers.[66] In a 2003 survey, more than 85% of senior executives stated that improving their firm's supply-chain performance was a top priority. Companies, such as Wal-Mart, Dell, and Toyota, that are known to be exemplars in supply-chain management spend only 4% of their revenues on supply-chain costs compared to 10% by the average firm.[67]

Industry leaders are integrating modern information systems into their corporate value chains to harmonize companywide efforts and to achieve competitive advantage. For example, Heineken distributors input actual depletion figures and replenishment orders to the Netherlands brewer through their linked web pages. This interactive planning system generates time-phased orders based on actual usage rather than on projected demand. Distributors are then able to modify plans based on local conditions or changes in marketing. Heineken uses these modifications to adjust brewing and supply schedules. As a result of this system, lead times have been reduced from the traditional 10–12 weeks to 4–6 weeks. This time savings is especially useful in an industry competing on product freshness. In another example, P&G participates in an information network to move the company's line of consumer products through Wal-Mart's many stores. As part of the network with Wal-Mart, P&G knows by cash register and by store what products have passed through the system every hour of each day. The network is linked by satellite communications on a real-time basis. With actual point-of-sale information, products are replenished to meet current demand and minimize stockouts while maintaining exceptionally low inventories.[68]

5.5 | The Strategic Audit: A Checklist for Organizational Analysis

One way of conducting an organizational analysis to ascertain a company's strengths and weaknesses is by using a Strategic Audit, as shown in **Appendix 1.A** at the end of **Chapter 1**. The audit provides a checklist of questions, by area of concern. For example, Part IV of the audit examines corporate structure, culture, and resources. It looks at organizational resources and capabilities in terms of the functional areas of marketing, finance, R&D, operations, human resources, and information systems, among others.

5.6 | Synthesis of Internal Factors

After strategists have scanned the internal organizational environment and identified factors for their particular corporation, they may want to summarize their analysis of these factors by using a form such as that given in **Table 5–2**. This **IFAS (Internal Factor Analysis Summary) Table** is one way to organize the internal factors into the generally accepted categories of strengths and weaknesses as well as to analyze how well a particular company's management is responding to these specific factors in light of the perceived importance of these factors to the company. Strategists can use the VRIO framework (Value, Rareness, Imitability, & Organization) to assess the importance of each of the factors that might be considered strengths. Except for its internal orientation, an IFAS Table is built the same way as the EFAS Table described in **Chapter 4** (in **Table 4–5**). To use an IFAS Table, complete the following steps:

1. In **Column 1 (*Internal Factors*)**, list the 8 to 10 most important strengths and weaknesses facing the company.

TABLE 5–2 INTERNAL FACTOR ANALYSIS SUMMARY (IFAS TABLE): MAYTAG AS EXAMPLE

Internal Factors	Weight	Rating	Weighted Score	Comments
	1	2	3	4	5
Strengths				
• Quality Maytag culture	.15	5.0	.75	Quality key to success
• Experienced top management	.05	4.2	.21	Know appliances
• Vertical integration	.10	3.9	.39	Dedicated factories
• Employer relations	.05	3.0	.15	Good, but deteriorating
• Hoover's international orientation	.15	2.8	.42	Hoover name in cleaners
Weaknesses				
• Process-oriented R&D	.05	2.2	.11	Slow on new products
• Distribution channels	.05	2.0	.10	Superstores replacing small dealers
• Financial position	.15	2.0	.30	High debt load
• Global positioning	.20	2.1	.42	Hoover weak outside the United Kingdom and Australia
• Manufacturing facilities	.05	4.0	.20	Investing now
Total Scores	**1.00**		**3.05**	

Notes:

1. List strengths and weaknesses (8–10) in Column 1.
2. Weight each factor from **1.0** (Most Important) to **0.0** (Not Important) in Column 2 based on that factor's probable impact on the company's strategic position. **The total weights must sum to 1.00**.
3. Rate each factor from **5.0** (Outstanding) to **1.0** (Poor) in Column 3 based on the company's response to that factor.
4. Multiply each factor's weight times its rating to obtain each factor's weighted score in Column 4.
5. Use Column 5 (comments) for rationale used for each factor.
6. Add the individual weighted scores to obtain the total weighted score for the company in Column 4. This tells how well the company is responding to the factors in its internal environment.

Source: T. L. Wheelen and J. D. Hunger, "Internal Factor Analysis Summary (IFAS)." Copyright © 1987, 1988, 1989, 1990, and 2005 by T. L. Wheelen. Copyright © 1991, 2003, and 2005 by Wheelen and Hunger Associates. Reprinted by permission.

2. In **Column 2** (*Weight*), assign a weight to each factor, from 1.0 (Most Important) to 0.0 (Not Important), based on that factor's probable impact on the particular company's current strategic position. The higher the weight, the more important this factor is to the current and future success of the company. (**All weights must sum to 1.0, regardless of the number of factors.**)

3. In **Column 3** (*Rating*), assign a rating to each factor from 5.0 (Outstanding) to 1.0 (Poor), based on management's specific response to that particular factor. Each rating is a judgment regarding how well the company's management is currently dealing with each specific internal factor.

4. In **Column 4** (*Weighted Score*), multiply the weight in **Column 2** for each factor by its rating in **Column 3** to obtain that factor's weighted score. This results in a weighted score for each factor ranging from **5.0** (Outstanding) to **1.0** (Poor), with 3.0 as Average.

5. In **Column 5** (*Comments*), note why a particular factor was selected and how its weight and rating were estimated.

6. Finally, add the weighted scores for all the internal factors in **Column 4** to determine the total weighted score for that particular company. The **total weighted score** indicates how well a particular company is responding to current and expected factors in its internal environment. The score can be used to compare that firm to other firms in its industry. Check to ensure that the total weighted score truly reflects the company's current performance in terms of profitability and market share. **The total weighted score for an average firm in an industry is always 3.0.**

As an example of this procedure, **Table 5–2** includes a number of internal factors for Maytag Corporation in 1995 (before Maytag sold its European and Australian operations), with corresponding weights, ratings, and weighted scores provided. Note that Maytag's total weighted score is 3.05, meaning that the corporation is about average compared to the strengths and weaknesses of others in the major home appliance industry.

5.7 | Conclusion

In 1991, Kentucky Fried Chicken changed its name to KFC in an attempt to broaden its image away from fried chicken. KFC management had noted the societal trend toward healthier eating and was worried that its signature item was in decline. The company responded to this trend by introducing "Colonel's Rotisserie Gold" chicken but was forced to drop it after the roasters kept breaking down. Not wanting to give up, management later introduced an "Oven-Roasted" line of chicken. After promoting the product for only three months, CEO David Novak admitted that the roasted line was a disappointment. "We don't think we came out of the box in the roasted category with the best effort that we could have," explained Novak. Deciding to refocus on its signature fried chicken items, management aired a new pool of television commercials extolling the health benefits of its fried chicken—only to be charged by the Federal Trade Commission of making false claims. Nevertheless, the company continued its preparations for a new line of salads being introduced later in 2004.[69]

Monitoring the external environment is only one part of environmental scanning. Strategists also need to scan a corporation's internal environment to identify its resources, capabilities, and competencies. What are its strengths and weaknesses? At KFC, management clearly noted that the environment was changing in a way that made its primary product less desirable. In attempting to offer a product that was more in line with the changing market, it failed to effectively deal with its weaknesses in new product development and marketing. Its two attempts to introduce roasted chicken were failures. Management's next mistake was using advertising to try to convince the public that its fried chicken was a health food. This is a classic example of a "reactor" company attempting to stay in business by jumping from one ill-advised strategy to another, without realizing that it didn't have the capabilities in key functional areas to support a new strategy.

Strategy Bits

- Countries with the highest percentages of their populations in the workforce are China (56.5%), Switzerland (56.1%), Thailand (54.4%), Iceland (54.2%), and Denmark (53.8%). Canada ranks 8th, at 52.4%, and the United States ranks 25th, at 49.0%.

- Countries with the highest percentages of women in the workforce are Belarus (52.9%), Cambodia (51.6%), Malawi (50.2%), Moldova (50.1%), and The Bahamas (49.4%). The United States ranks 19th, at 46.6%, and Canada ranks 23rd, at 46.0%.[70]

Discussion Questions

1. What is the relevance of the resource-based view of a firm to strategic management in a global environment?

2. How can value-chain analysis help identify a company's strengths and weaknesses?

3. In what ways can a corporation's structure and culture be internal strengths or weaknesses?

4. What are the pros and cons of management's using the experience curve to determine strategy?

5. How might a firm's management decide whether it should continue to invest in current known technology or in new, but untested, technology? What factors might encourage or discourage such a shift?

Strategic Practice Exercises

1. Based on the information presented in the Conclusion to this chapter, what would you recommend to the management of KFC? Should it continue to experiment with healthier menu items, or should it just "stick to its knitting" by staying with fried food? What resources and competencies are needed to adopt a health food strategy?

2. Can you analyze a corporation by using the Internet? Try the following exercise:

   a. Form into teams of around three to five people. Select a well-known publicly owned company to research. Inform the instructor of your choice.

   b. Assign each person a separate task. One might be to find the latest financial statements. Another would be to learn as much as possible about the company's top management and board of directors. Another might be to identify its business model. Another might be to identify its key competitors.

   c. Conduct research on the company by *using the Internet only*.

   d. Meet with your team members to discuss what you have found. What are the company's opportunities,

threats, strengths, and weaknesses? Go back to the Internet for more information, if needed.

   e. Prepare a three- to five-page typed report of the company. The report should include information that answers the following questions:

      i. Does the firm have any core competencies? Are any of these distinctive (better than the competition) competencies? Does the firm have any competitive advantage? Provide a SWOT analysis, using EFAS and IFAS Tables.

      ii. What is the likely future of this firm if it continues on its current path?

      iii. Would you buy stock in this company? Assume that your team has $25,000 to invest. Allocate the money among the four to five primary competitors in this industry. List the companies, the number of shares you would purchase of each, the cost of each share as of a given date, and the total cost for each purchase, assuming a typical commission used by an Internet broker, such as E-Trade.

Key Terms

autonomous (self-managing) work team (p. 125)

basic R&D (p. 121)

brand (p. 118)

business model (p. 110)

capability (p. 106)

capital budgeting (p. 120)

center of gravity (p. 112)

cluster (p. 107)

competency (p. 106)

concurrent engineering (p. 125)

conglomerate structure (p. 115)

continuous system (p. 124)

continuum of sustainability (p. 109)

core competency (p. 106)

corporate brand (p. 119)

corporate culture (p. 116)

corporate reputation (p. 119)

cross-functional work team (p. 125)

cultural integration (p. 116)

cultural intensity (p. 116)

distinctive competency (p. 106)

divisional structure (p. 115)

durability (p. 108)

economy of scale (p. 125)

economy of scope (p. 125)

engineering (or process) R&D (p. 121)

experience curve (p. 124)

explicit knowledge (p. 109)

extranet (p. 128)

financial leverage (p. 120)

flexible manufacturing (p. 125)

functional structure (p. 114)

human diversity (p. 127)

IFAS Table (p. 129)

imitability (p. 108)

intermittent system (p. 123)

internal strategic factor (p. 106)

intranet (p. 128)

linkage (p. 113)

market position (p. 118)

market segmentation (p. 118)

marketing mix (p. 118)

mass customization (p. 125)

operating leverage (p. 124)
organizational analysis (p. 106)
organizational structure (p. 114)
primary activity (p. 113)
product life cycle (p. 118)
product R&D (p. 121)
quality of work life (p. 127)
R&D intensity (p. 120)
R&D mix (p. 121)

replicability (p. 108)
resource (p. 106)
reverse engineering (p. 108)
simple structure (p. 114)
strategic business unit (SBU) (p. 115)
support activity (p. 113)
supply-chain management (p. 128)
tacit knowledge (p. 109)

technological competence (p. 121)
technological discontinuity (p. 122)
technology transfer (p. 121)
transferability (p. 108)
transparency (p. 108)
value chain (p. 111)
VRIO framework (p. 106)
virtual team (p. 126)

PART ENDING VIDEO CASE PART TWO

Newbury Comics, Inc.

ENVIRONMENTAL SCANNING AND ORGANIZATIONAL ANALYSIS

Newbury Comics Cofounders, Mike Dreese and John Brusger, parlayed $2,000 and a comic book collection into a thriving chain of 22 stores spanning the New England region. Known to be *the* place to shop for everything from the best of the underground/independent music scene to major label superstars, the chain also stocks a wide variety of non-music related items such as T-shirts, Dr. (doc) Martens shoes, posters, jewelry, cosmetics, books, magazines, and other trendy items.

In Part Two, **"Scanning the Environment,"** the video case addresses the identification of external environmental variables, industry analysis, and organizational analysis. Newbury Comics, Inc., Cofounders Mike and John, and Jan Johannet, Manager for one of the New Hampshire stores, reveal more about the development of the company. They discuss factors contributing to the successful growth of Newbury Comics. They describe how their diverse customers plus the emergence of bootlegging (selling illegal copies) and burning discs (copying 1 CD onto another CD) led the company to begin offering used CDs in its stores.

Used CDs have become a very important business for Newbury Comics. Mike Dreese reports that used CDs account for $6 to 7 million in annual sales and $4 million in annual gross profits for the company. This fact is remarkable given that the firm's overall annual sales and pre-tax profits are $75 million and $8 million, respectively. According to John Brusger and Jan Johannet, the new CD market turned "soft" when mass merchandisers like Target and Best Buy began selling CDs and Internet companies, such as Napster, offered the downloading of music. John and Mike wanted another product to supplement their sales of new CDs. They scanned their environment to learn if it made sense to enter this business.

They asked the owners of local specialty music stores for information. These "mom and pop" retailers had been buying and selling used CDs for years and were very familiar with this product. Mike refers to the local mom and pop retailers as his "strategic alliance of information sources." According to John, surveys of current customers revealed that a large number of Newbury Comics customers wanted the company to be in the used CD business. Management analyzed the competition for used CDs in Newbury Comics' market area. Used CDs appeared to have high sales potential. The immediate competition was composed of mom and pop specialty music retailers; no chain stores offered used CDs at that time. According to Mike Dreese, the local stores weren't doing a good job of marketing used CDs.

According to Mike and Jan, Newbury Comics has several internal strengths, which uniquely fit the used CD market. The stores have a wide variety of customers and a staff with "knowledge of the street." The employees live the lifestyle of Newbury Comics' discriminating customers and are thus able to identify trends before the public at large learns of them. Consequently, the stores are able to purchase an excellent selection of underground music in addition to the usual top 50 and older CDs. Mike Dreese states that new entrant specialist shops into the used CD business are "not a threat to us." He is concerned that established chains such as Tower Records, Best Buy, and Music Land might someday enter the used CD business.

Concepts Illustrated in the Video

- Environmental Scanning
- Industry Analysis
- Organizational Analysis
- Identifying Societal Trends
- Rivalry Among Existing Firms

- Threat of New Entrants/Entry Barriers
- Threat of Substitute Products
- Industry Evolution
- Core and Distinctive Competencies
- Corporate Culture

Study Questions

1. How does Newbury Comics conduct environmental scanning? How well is it doing it?

2. Describe the competitors in Newbury Comics' market area. Do they form strategic groups? How do the actions of competitors affect Newbury Comics (and vice versa)?

3. What are the substitutes for CDs? Are they a threat or an opportunity for Newbury Comics?

4. What external factors played a role in the decision to enter the used CD business? What other businesses should the company consider entering?

5. What are the core competencies of Newbury Comics? Are they distinctive? Why?

CHAPTER 6
Strategy Formulation: Situation Analysis and Business Strategy

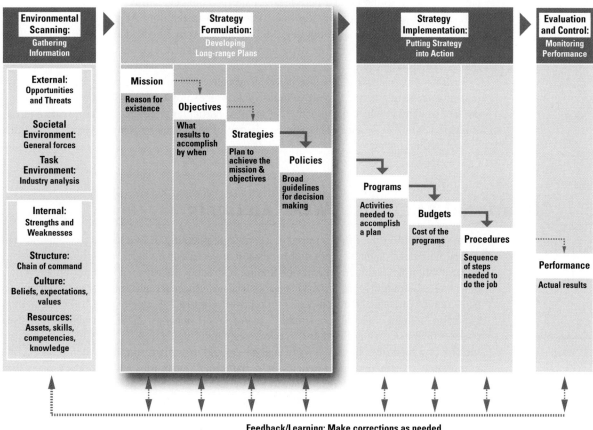

Feedback/Learning: Make corrections as needed

Learning Objectives

After reading this chapter, you should be able to:

- Organize environmental and organizational information by using SWOT analysis and an SFAS Matrix
- Generate strategic options by using the TOWS matrix
- Understand the competitive and cooperative strategies available to corporations
- List the competitive tactics that would accompany competitive strategies
- Identify the basic types of strategic alliances

MIDAMAR CORPORATION IS A FAMILY-OWNED COMPANY IN CEDAR RAPIDS, IOWA, THAT has carved out a growing niche for itself in the world food industry: supplying food prepared according to strict religious standards. The company specializes in halal foods, which are produced and processed according to Islamic law for sale to Muslims. Why did it focus on this one type of food? According to owner-founder Bill Aossey, "It's a big world, and you can only specialize in so many places." Although halal foods are not as widely known as kosher foods (processed according to Judaic law), their market is growing along with Islam, the world's fastest-growing religion. Midamar purchases halal-certified meat from Midwestern companies certified to conduct halal processing. Certification requires practicing Muslims schooled in halal processing to slaughter the livestock and to oversee meat and poultry processing.

Aossey is a practicing Muslim who did not imagine such a vast market when he founded his business in 1974. "People thought it would be a passing fad," remarked Aossey. The company has grown to the point where it now exports halal-certified beef, lamb, and poultry to hotels, restaurants, and distributors in 30 countries throughout Asia, Africa, Europe, and North America. Its customers include McDonald's, Pizza Hut, and KFC. McDonald's, for example, uses Midamar's turkey strips as a bacon-alternative in a breakfast product recently introduced in Singapore.[1]

Midamar is successful because its chief executive formulated a strategy designed to give it an advantage in a very competitive industry. It is an example of a differentiation focus competitive strategy in which a company focuses on a particular target market to provide a differentiated product or service. This strategy is one of the business competitive strategies discussed in this chapter.

6.1 | Situational Analysis: SWOT Analysis

Strategy formulation, often referred to as strategic planning or long-range planning, is concerned with developing a corporation's mission, objectives, strategies, and policies. It begins with situation analysis: the process of finding a strategic fit between external opportunities and internal strengths while working around external threats and internal weaknesses. As shown in the Strategic Decision-Making Process in **Figure 1–5**, step 5(a) is "analyzing strategic factors in light of the current situation, using SWOT analysis." **SWOT** is an acronym used to describe the particular Strengths, Weaknesses, Opportunities, and Threats that are strategic factors for a specific company. SWOT analysis should not only result in the identification of a corporation's distinctive competencies—the particular capabilities and resources that a firm possesses and the superior way in which they are used—but also in the identification of opportunities that the firm is not currently able to take advantage of due to a lack of appropriate resources. Over the years, SWOT analysis has proven to be the most enduring analytical technique using in strategic management. For example, a survey of 113 manufacturing and service companies in the United Kingdom reported the five most-used tools and techniques in strategic analysis to be (1) spreadsheet what-if analysis, (2) analysis of key or critical success factors, (3) financial analysis of competitors, (4) SWOT analysis, and (5) core capabilities analysis.[2] It is very likely that these have a similar rate of usage in the rest of the world.

It can be said that the essence of strategy is opportunity divided by capacity.[3] An opportunity by itself has no real value unless a company has the capacity (i.e., resources) to take advantage of that opportunity. This approach, however, considers only opportunities and strengths when considering alternative strategies. By itself, a distinctive competency in a key resource or capability is no guarantee of competitive advantage. Weaknesses in other resource areas can prevent a strategy from being successful. SWOT can thus be used to take a broader view of strategy through the formula SA = O/(S–W) that is, (Strategic Alternative equals Opportunity divided by Strengths minus Weaknesses). This reflects an important issue strategic managers face: Should we invest more in our strengths to make them even stronger (a distinctive competence) or should we invest in our weaknesses to at least make them competitive?

SWOT analysis, by itself, is not a panacea. Some of the primary criticisms of SWOT analysis are:

- It generates lengthy lists.
- It uses no weights to reflect priorities.
- It uses ambiguous words and phrases.
- The same factor can be placed in two categories (e.g., a strength may also be a weakness).
- There is no obligation to verify opinions with data or analysis.
- It requires only a single level of analysis.
- There is no logical link to strategy implementation.[4]

Generating a Strategic Factors Analysis Summary (SFAS) Matrix

The EFAS and IFAS Tables plus the SFAS Matrix have been developed to deal with the criticisms of SWOT analysis. When used together, they are a powerful analytical set of tools for strategic analysis. The **SFAS (Strategic Factors Analysis Summary) Matrix** summarizes an organization's strategic factors by combining the external factors from the EFAS Table with the internal factors from the IFAS Table. The EFAS and IFAS examples given of Maytag Corporation (as it was in 1995) in **Tables 4–5** and **5–2** list a total of 20 internal and external factors. These are too many factors for most people to use in strategy formulation. The SFAS Matrix requires a strategic decision maker to condense these strengths, weaknesses, opportunities, and threats into fewer than 10 strategic factors. This is done by reviewing and revising the weight given each factor. The revised weights reflect the priority of each factor as a determinant of the company's future success. The highest-weighted EFAS and IFAS factors should appear in the SFAS Matrix.

As shown in **Figure 6–1**, you can create an SFAS Matrix by following these steps:

1. In **Column 1 (*Strategic Factors*)**, list the most important EFAS and IFAS items. After each factor, indicate whether it is a Strength (**S**), a Weakness (**W**), an Opportunity (**O**), or a Threat (**T**).

2. In **Column 2 (*Weight*)**, assign weights for all the internal and external strategic factors. As with the EFAS and IFAS Tables presented earlier, **the weight column must total 1.00**. This means that the weights calculated earlier for EFAS and IFAS will probably have to be adjusted.

3. In **Column 3 (*Rating*)** assign a rating of how the company's management is responding to each of the strategic factors. These ratings will probably (but not always) be the same as those listed in the EFAS and IFAS Tables.

TABLE 5–2 **INTERNAL FACTOR ANALYSIS SUMMARY (IFAS): MAYTAG AS EXAMPLE (SELECTION OF STRATEGIC FACTORS)***

Internal Strategic Factors	Weight	Rating	Weighted Score	Comments
	1	2	3	4	5
Strengths				
S1 Quality Maytag culture	.15	5.0	.75	Quality key to success
S2 Experienced top management	.05	4.2	.21	Know appliances
S3 Vertical integration	.10	3.9	.39	Dedicated factories
S4 Employee relations	.05	3.0	.15	Good, but deteriorating
S5 Hoover's international orientation	.15	2.8	.42	Hoover name in cleaners
Weaknesses				
W1 Process-oriented R&D	.05	2.2	.11	Slow on new products
W2 Distribution channels	.05	2.0	.10	Superstores replacing small dealers
W3 Financial position	.15	2.0	.30	High debt load
W4 Global positioning	.20	2.1	.42	Hoover weak outside the United Kingdom and Australia
W5 Manufacturing facilities	.05	4.0	.20	Investing now
Total Scores	1.00		3.05	

TABLE 4–5 **EXTERNAL FACTOR ANALYSIS SUMMARY (EFAS): MAYTAG AS EXAMPLE (SELECTION OF STRATEGIC FACTORS)***

External Strategic Factors	Weight	Rating	Weighted Score	Comments
	1	2	3	4	5
Opportunities				
O1 Economic integration of European Community	.20	4.1	.82	Acquisition of Hoover
O2 Demographics favor quality appliances	.10	5.0	.50	Maytag quality
O3 Economic development of Asia	.05	1.0	.05	Low Maytag presence
O4 Opening of Eastern Europe	.05	2.0	.10	Will take time
O5 Trend to "Super Stores"	.10	1.8	.18	Maytag weak in this channel
Threats				
T1 Increasing government regulations	.10	4.3	.43	Well positioned
T2 Strong U.S. competition	.10	4.0	.40	Well positioned
T3 Whirlpool and Electrolux strong globally	.15	3.0	.45	Hoover weak globally
T4 New product advances	.05	1.2	.06	Questionable
T5 Japanese appliance companies	.10	1.6	.16	Only Asian presence is Australia
Total Scores	1.00		3.15	

*The most important external and internal factors are identified in the EFAS and IFAS tables as shown here by shading these factors.

Figure 6–1 **Strategic Factor Analysis Summary (SFAS) Matrix**

Strategic Factors (Select the most important opportunities/threats from EFAS, Table 4–5 and the most important strengths and weaknesses from IFAS, Table 5–2)	Weight	Rating	Weighted Score	Duration SHORT	INTERMEDIATE	LONG	Comments
S1 Quality Maytag culture (S)	.10	5.0	.50			X	Quality key to success
S5 Hoover's international orientation (S)	.10	2.8	.28	X	X		Name recognition
W3 Financial position (W)	.10	2.0	.20	X	X		High debt
W4 Global positioning (W)	.15	2.2	.33		X	X	Only in N.A., U.K., and Australia
O1 Economic integration of European Community (O)	.10	4.1	.41			X	Acquisition of Hoover
O2 Demographics favor quality (O)	.10	5.0	.50		X		Maytag quality
O5 Trend to super stores (O + T)	.10	1.8	.18	X			Weak in this channel
T3 Whirlpool and Electrolux (T)	.15	3.0	.45	X			Dominate industry
T5 Japanese appliance companies (T)	.10	1.6	.16			X	Asian presence
Total Scores	1.00		3.01				

Notes:
1. List each of the most important factors developed in your IFAS and EFAS Tables in Column 1.
2. Weight each factor from 1.0 (Most Important) to 0.0 (Not Important) in Column 2 based on that factor's probable impact on the company's strategic position. **The total weights must sum to 1.00.**
3. Rate each factor from 5.0 (Outstanding) to 1.0 (Poor) in Column 3 based on the company's response to that factor.
4. Multiply each factor's weight times its rating to obtain each factor's weighted score in Column 4.
5. For duration in Column 5, check appropriate column (short term—less than 1 year; intermediate—1 to 3 years; long term—over 3 years).
6. Use Column 6 (comments) for rationale used for each factor.

Source: T. L. Wheelen and J. D. Hunger, "Strategic Factors Analysis Summary (SFAS)." Copyright © 1987, 1988, 1989, 1990, 1991, 1992, 1993, 1994, 1995, 1996 and 2005 by T. L. Wheelen. Copyright © 1997 and 2005 by Wheelen and Hunger Associates. Reprinted by permission.

4. In **Column 4 (*Weighted Score*)** multiply the weight in **Column 2** for each factor by its rating in **Column 3** to obtain the factor's rated score. This results in a weighted score for each factor ranging from **5.0** (outstanding) to **1.0** (Poor), with **3.0** as average.

5. In **Column 5 (*Duration*)**, depicted in **Figure 6–1**, indicate **short-term** (less than one year), **intermediate-term** (one to three years), or **long-term** (three years and beyond).

6. In **Column 6 (*Comments*)**, repeat or revise your comments for each strategic factor from the previous EFAS and IFAS Tables. **The total weighted score for the average firm in an industry is always 3.0**

The resulting SFAS Matrix is a listing of the firm's external and internal strategic factors in one table. The example given in **Figure 6–1** is for Maytag Corporation in 1995, before the firm sold its European and Australian operations. The SFAS Matrix includes only the most important factors gathered from environmental scanning and thus provides information that is essential for strategy formulation. The use of EFAS and IFAS Tables together with the SFAS Matrix deals with some of the criticisms of SWOT analysis. For example, the use of the SFAS Matrix reduces the list of factors to a manageable number, puts weights on each factor, and allows one factor to be listed as both a strength and a weakness (or as an opportunity and a threat).

Finding a Propitious Niche

One desired outcome of analyzing strategic factors is identifying a niche where an organization can use its core competencies to take advantage of a particular market opportunity. A niche is a need in the marketplace that is currently unsatisfied. The goal is to find a **propitious niche**—an extremely favorable niche that is so well suited to the firm's internal and external environment that other corporations are not likely to challenge or dislodge it.[5] A niche is propitious to the extent that it currently is just large enough for one firm to satisfy its demand. After a firm has found and filled that niche, it is not worth a potential competitor's time or money to also go after the same niche.

Finding such a niche is not always easy. A firm's management must be always looking for a **strategic window**—that is, a unique market opportunity that is available only for a particular time. The first firm through a strategic window can occupy a propitious niche and discourage competition (if the firm has the required internal strengths). One company that has successfully found a propitious niche is Frank J. Zamboni & Company, the manufacturer of the machines that smooth the ice at ice skating rinks. Frank Zamboni invented the unique tractor-like machine in 1949, and no one has found a substitute for what it does. Before the machine was invented, people had to clean and scrape the ice by hand to prepare the surface for skating. Now hockey fans look forward to intermissions just to watch "the Zamboni" slowly drive up and down the ice rink, turning rough, scraped ice into a smooth mirror surface—almost like magic. So long as Zamboni's company is able to produce the machines in the quantity and quality desired, at a reasonable price, it's not worth another company's while to go after Frank Zamboni & Company's propitious niche.

As a niche grows, so can a company within that niche—by increasing its operations' capacity or through alliances with larger firms. The key is to identify a market opportunity in which the first firm to reach that market segment can obtain and keep dominant market share. For example, Church & Dwight was the first company in the United States to successfully market sodium bicarbonate for use in cooking. Its Arm & Hammer brand baking soda is still found in 95% of all U.S. households. The propitious niche concept is crucial to the software industry. Small initial demand in emerging markets allows new entrepreneurial ventures to go after niches too small to be noticed by established companies. When Microsoft developed its first disk operating system (DOS) in 1980 for IBM's personal computers, for example, the demand for such open systems software was very small—a small niche for a then very small Microsoft. The company was able to fill that niche and to successfully grow with it.

Niches can also change—sometimes faster than a firm can adapt to that change. A company's management may discover in their situation analysis that they need to invest heavily in the firm's capabilities to keep them competitively strong in a changing niche. South African Breweries (SAB), for example, took this approach when management realized that the only way to keep competitors out of its market was to continuously invest in increased productivity and infrastructure in order to keep its prices very low. See the GLOBAL ISSUE feature to see how SAB was able to successfully defend its market niche during significant changes in its environment.

GL🌐BAL ISSUE

SAB Defends Its Propitious Niche

Out of 50 beers drunk by South Africans, 49 are brewed by South African Breweries (SAB). Founded more than a century ago, SAB controlled most of the local beer market by 1950 with brands such as Castle and Lion. When the government repealed the ban on the sale of alcohol to blacks in the 1960s, SAB and other brewers competed for the rapidly growing market. SAB fought successfully to retain its dominance of the market. With the end of apartheid, foreign brewers have been tempted to break SAB's near-monopoly but have been deterred by the entry barriers SAB has erected:

Entry Barrier #1: Every year for the past two decades SAB has reduced its prices. The "real" (adjusted for inflation) price of its beer is now half what it was during the 1970s. SAB has been able to achieve this through a continuous emphasis on productivity improvements—boosting production while cutting the workforce almost in half. Keeping prices low has been key to SAB's avoiding charges of abusing its monopoly.

Entry Barrier #2: In South Africa's poor and rural areas, roads are rough, and electricity is undependable. SAB has long experience in transporting crates to remote villages along bad roads and making sure that distributors have refrigerators (and electricity generators if needed). Many of its distributors are former employees who have been helped by the company to start their own trucking businesses.

Entry Barrier #3: Most of the beer sold in South Africa is sold through unlicensed pubs called *shebeens*—most of which date back to apartheid, when blacks were not allowed licenses. Although the current government of South Africa would be pleased to grant pub licenses to blacks, the shebeen owners don't want them. They enjoy not paying any taxes. SAB cannot sell directly to the shebeens, but it does so indirectly through wholesalers. The government, in turn, ignores the situation, preferring that people drink SAB beer than potentially deadly moonshine.

To break into South Africa, a new entrant would have to build large breweries and a substantial distribution network. SAB would, in turn, probably reduce its prices still further to defend its market. The difficulties of operating in South Africa are too great, the market is growing too slowly, and (given SAB's low cost position) the likely profit margin is too low to justify entering the market. Some foreign brewers, such as Heineken, would rather use SAB to distribute their products throughout South Africa. With its home market secure, SAB purchased Miller Brewing to secure a strong presence in North America.

Source: Summarized from "Big Lion, Small Cage," *The Economist* (August 12, 2000), p. 56, and other sources.

6.2 | Review of Mission and Objectives

A reexamination of an organization's current mission and objectives must be made before alternative strategies can be generated and evaluated. Even when formulating strategy, decision makers tend to concentrate on the alternatives—the action possibilities—rather than on a mission to be fulfilled and objectives to be achieved. This tendency is so attractive because it is much easier to deal with alternative courses of action that exist right here and now than to really think about what you want to accomplish in the future. The end result is that we often choose strategies that set our objectives for us rather than having our choices incorporate clear objectives and a mission statement.

Problems in performance can derive from an inappropriate statement of mission, which may be too narrow or too broad. If the mission does not provide a *common thread* (a unifying theme) for a corporation's businesses, managers may be unclear about where the company is heading. Objectives and strategies might be in conflict with each other. Divisions might be competing against one another rather than against outside competition—to the detriment of the corporation as a whole.

A company's objectives can also be inappropriately stated. They can either focus too much on short-term operational goals or be so general that they provide little real guidance. There may be a gap between planned and achieved objectives. When such a gap occurs, either the strategies have to be changed to improve performance or the objectives need to be adjusted downward to be more realistic. Consequently, objectives should be constantly reviewed to ensure their usefulness. This is what happened at Coca-Cola Company in 2004, when management failed to note the growing consumer desire for alternatives to soda pop. In a statement to investors, Chairman and CEO Neville Isdell reported that "the emerging consumer trends in health and wellness were missed. . . . We stopped driving carbonated soft drinks, and we're the world leader." Isdell then indicated that weak results should persist into 2005 in the key markets of North America, Germany, and the Philippines. He reported that the company had consequently reduced its sales growth objective for 2005 to 3.5%, down from 5.5%. Operating income growth was also reduced from 10% to 7%. In addition, earnings per share growth was reduced from 12% to less than 10%. Isdell concluded by stating that 2005 "is not going to deliver the kinds of returns that are going to be acceptable to me, as a shareholder."[6]

6.3 | Generating Alternative Strategies by Using a TOWS Matrix

Thus far we have discussed how a firm uses SWOT analysis to assess its situation. SWOT can also be used to generate a number of possible alternative strategies. The **TOWS Matrix** (TOWS is just another way of saying SWOT) illustrates how the external opportunities and threats facing a particular corporation can be matched with that company's internal strengths and weaknesses to result in four sets of possible strategic alternatives. (See **Figure 6–2**.) This is a good way to use brainstorming to create alternative strategies that might not otherwise be considered. It forces strategic managers to create various kinds of growth as well as retrenchment strategies. It can be used to generate corporate as well as business strategies.

To generate a TOWS Matrix for Maytag Corporation in 1995, for example, use the External Factor Analysis Summary (EFAS) Table listed in **Table 4–5** from **Chapter 4** and the Internal Factor Analysis Summary (IFAS) Table listed in **Table 5–2** from **Chapter 5**. To build **Figure 6–2**, take the following steps:

Figure 6–2
TOWS Matrix

INTERNAL FACTORS (IFAS) / EXTERNAL FACTORS (EFAS)	Strengths (S) List 5 – 10 *internal* strengths here	Weaknesses (W) List 5 – 10 *internal* weaknesses here
Opportunities (O) List 5 – 10 *external* opportunities here	**SO Strategies** Generate strategies here that use **strengths** to take **advantage** of **opportunities**	**WO Strategies** Generate strategies here that take **advantage** of **opportunities** by **overcoming weaknesses**
Threats (T) List 5 – 10 *external* threats here	**ST Strategies** Generate strategies here that use **strengths** to **avoid threats**	**WT Strategies** Generate strategies here that **minimize weaknesses** and **avoid threats**

Source: Reprinted from Long-Range Planning, *Vol. 15, No. 2, 1982, Weihrich "The TOWS Matrix—A Tool For Situational Analysis," p. 60. Copyright © 1982 with permission of Elsevier.*

1. In the Opportunities (O) block, list the external opportunities available in the company's or business unit's current and future environment from the EFAS Table (**Table 4–5**).

2. In the Threats (T) block, list the external threats facing the company or unit now and in the future from the EFAS Table (**Table 4–5**).

3. In the Strengths (S) block, list the specific areas of current and future strength for the company or unit from the IFAS Table (**Table 5–2**).

4. In the Weaknesses (W) block, list the specific areas of current and future weakness for the company or unit from the IFAS Table (**Table 5–2**).

5. Generate a series of possible strategies for the company or business unit under consideration based on particular combinations of the four sets of factors:

   - **SO Strategies** are generated by thinking of ways in which a company or business unit could use its strengths to take advantage of opportunities.

   - **ST Strategies** consider a company's or unit's strengths as a way to avoid threats.

   - **WO Strategies** attempt to take advantage of opportunities by overcoming weaknesses.

   - **WT Strategies** are basically defensive and primarily act to minimize weaknesses and avoid threats.

The TOWS Matrix is very useful for generating a series of alternatives that the decision makers of a company or business unit might not otherwise have considered. It can be used for the corporation as a whole (as is done in **Figure 6–3** with Maytag Corporation before it sold Hoover Europe), or it can be used for a specific business unit within a corporation (such as Hoover's floor care products). Nevertheless, using a TOWS Matrix is only one of many ways to generate alternative strategies. Another approach is to evaluate each business unit within a corporation in terms of possible competitive and cooperative strategies.

6.4 | Business Strategies

Business strategy focuses on improving the competitive position of a company's or business unit's products or services within the specific industry or market segment that the company or business unit serves. Business strategy can be competitive (battling against all competitors for advantage) and/or cooperative (working with one or more companies to gain advantage against other competitors). Just as corporate strategy asks what industry(ies) the company should be in, business strategy asks how the company or its units should compete or cooperate in each industry.

Porter's Competitive Strategies

Competitive strategy raises the following questions:

- Should we compete on the basis of lower cost (and thus price), or should we differentiate our products or services on some basis other than cost, such as quality or service?

- Should we compete head to head with our major competitors for the biggest but most sought-after share of the market, or should we focus on a niche in which we can satisfy a less sought-after but also profitable segment of the market?

Michael Porter proposes two "generic" competitive strategies for outperforming other corporations in a particular industry: lower cost and differentiation.[7] These strategies are

TABLE 5–2 INTERNAL FACTOR ANALYSIS SUMMARY (IFAS): MAYTAG AS EXAMPLE (SELECTION OF STRATEGIC FACTORS)*

Internal Strategic Factors	Weight	Rating	Weighted Score	Comments
	1	2	3	4	5
Strengths				
S1 Quality Maytag culture	.15	5.0	.75	Quality key to success
S2 Experienced top management	.05	4.2	.21	Know appliances
S3 Vertical integration	.10	3.9	.39	Dedicated factories
S4 Employee relations	.05	3.0	.15	Good, but deteriorating
S5 Hoover's international orientation	.15	2.8	.42	Hoover name in cleaners
Weaknesses				
W1 Process-oriented R&D	.05	2.2	.11	Slow on new products
W2 Distribution channels	.05	2.0	.10	Superstores replacing small dealers
W3 Financial position	.15	2.0	.30	High debt load
W4 Global positioning	.20	2.1	.42	Hoover weak outside the United Kingdom and Australia
W5 Manufacturing facilities	.05	4.0	.20	Investing now
Total Scores	1.00		3.05	

TABLE 4–5 EXTERNAL FACTOR ANALYSIS SUMMARY (EFAS): MAYTAG AS EXAMPLE (SELECTION OF STRATEGIC FACTORS)*

External Strategic Factors	Weight	Rating	Weighted Score	Comments
	1	2	3	4	5
Opportunities				
O1 Economic integration of European Community	.20	4.1	.82	Acquisition of Hoover
O2 Demographics favor quality appliances	.10	5.0	.50	Maytag quality
O3 Economic development of Asia	.05	1.0	.05	Low Maytag presence
O4 Opening of Eastern Europe	.05	2.0	.10	Will take time
O5 Trend to "Super Stores"	.10	1.8	.18	Maytag weak in this channel
Threats				
T1 Increasing government regulations	.10	4.3	.43	Well positioned
T2 Strong U.S. competition	.10	4.0	.40	Well positioned
T3 Whirlpool and Electrolux strong globally	.15	3.0	.45	Hoover weak globally
T4 New product advances	.05	1.2	.06	Questionable
T5 Japanese appliance companies	.10	1.6	.16	Only Asian presence is Australia
Total Scores	1.00		3.15	

*The most important external and internal factors are identified in the EFAS and IFAS Tables as shown here by shading these factors.

Figure 6–3 Generating TOWS Matrix for Maytag Corporation

Strengths⟶
Weaknesses⟶

Internal Factors (IFAS Table 5–2) External Factors (EFAS Table 4–5)	Strengths (S) S1 Quality Maytag culture S2 Experienced top management S3 Vertical integration S4 Employee relations S5 Hoover's international orientation	Weaknesses (W) W1 Process-oriented R&D W2 Distribution channels W3 Financial position W4 Global positioning W5 Manufacturing facilities
Opportunities (O) O1 Economic integration of European Community O2 Demographics favor quality O3 Economic development of Asia O4 Opening of Eastern Europe O5 Trend toward super stores	**SO Strategies** • *Use worldwide Hoover distribution channels to sell both Hoover and Maytag major appliances.* • *Find joint venture partners in Eastern Europe and Asia.*	**WO Strategies** • *Expand Hoover's presence in continental Europe by improving Hoover quality and reducing manufacturing and distribution costs.* • *Emphasize superstore channel for all non-Maytag brands.*
Threats (T) T1 Increasing government regulation T2 Strong U.S. competition T3 Whirlpool and Electrolux positioned for global economy T4 New product advances T5 Japanese appliance companies	**ST Strategies** • *Acquire Raytheon's appliance business to increase U.S. market share.* • *Merge with a Japanese major home appliance company.* • *Sell off all non-Maytag brands and strongly defend Maytag's U.S. niche.*	**WT Strategies** • *Sell off Dixie-Narco Division to reduce debt.* • *Emphasize cost reduction to reduce break-even point.* • *Sell out to Raytheon or a Japanese firm.*

called generic because they can be pursued by any type or size of business firm, even by not-for-profit organizations:

- **Lower cost strategy** is the ability of a company or a business unit to design, produce, and market a comparable product more efficiently than its competitors.
- **Differentiation strategy** is the ability of a company to provide unique and superior value to the buyer in terms of product quality, special features, or after-sale service.

Porter further proposes that a firm's competitive advantage in an industry is determined by its **competitive scope**—that is, the breadth of the company's or business unit's target market. Before using one of the two generic competitive strategies (lower cost or differentiation), the firm or unit must choose the range of product varieties it will produce, the distribution channels it will employ, the types of buyers it will serve, the geographic areas in which it will sell, and the array of related industries in which it will also compete. This should reflect an understanding of the firm's unique resources. Simply put, a company or business unit can choose a broad target (that is, aim at the middle of the mass market) or a narrow target (that is, aim at a market niche). Combining these two types of target markets with the two competitive strategies results in the four variations of generic strategies depicted in **Figure 6–4**. When the lower-cost and differentiation strategies have a broad mass-market target, they are simply called *cost leadership* and *differentiation*. When they are focused on a market niche (narrow

Figure 6–4
**Porter's Generic
Competitive
Strategies**

Competitive Advantage

target), however, they are called *cost focus* and *differentiation focus*. Although research indicates that established firms pursuing broad-scope strategies outperform firms following narrow-scope strategies in terms of ROA (Return on Assets), new entrepreneurial firms have a better chance of surviving if they follow a narrow-scope rather than a broad-scope strategy.[8]

Cost leadership is a lower-cost competitive strategy that aims at the broad mass market and requires "aggressive construction of efficient-scale facilities, vigorous pursuit of cost reductions from experience, tight cost and overhead control, avoidance of marginal customer accounts, and cost minimization in areas like R&D, service, sales force, advertising, and so on."[9] Because of its lower costs, the cost leader is able to charge a lower price for its products than its competitors and still make a satisfactory profit. Although it may not necessarily have the lowest costs in the industry, it has lower costs than its competitors. Some companies successfully following this strategy are Wal-Mart, Dell (computers), Alamo (rental cars), Aldi (grocery stores), Southwest Airlines, and Timex (watches). Having a lower-cost position also gives a company or business unit a defense against rivals. Its lower costs allow it to continue to earn profits during times of heavy competition. Its high market share means that it will have high bargaining power relative to its suppliers (because it buys in large quantities). Its low price will also serve as a barrier to entry because few new entrants will be able to match the leader's cost advantage. As a result, cost leaders are likely to earn above-average returns on investment.

Differentiation is aimed at the broad mass market and involves the creation of a product or service that is perceived throughout its industry as unique. The company or business unit may then charge a premium for its product. This specialty can be associated with design or brand image, technology, features, a dealer network, or customer service. Differentiation is a viable strategy for earning above-average returns in a specific business because the resulting brand loyalty lowers customers' sensitivity to price. Increased costs can usually be passed on to the buyers. Buyer loyalty also serves as an entry barrier; new firms must develop their own distinctive competence to differentiate their products in some way in order to compete successfully. Examples of companies that successfully use a differentiation strategy are Walt Disney Productions, Maytag, Nike, Apple Computer, and Mercedes-Benz. Research suggests that a differentiation strategy is more likely to generate higher profits than is a low-cost strategy because differentiation creates a better entry barrier. A low-cost strategy is more likely, however, to generate increases in market share.[10]

Cost focus is a low-cost competitive strategy that focuses on a particular buyer group or geographic market and attempts to serve only that niche, to the exclusion of others. In using cost focus, a company or business unit seeks a cost advantage in its target segment. A good example of this strategy is Potlach Corporation, a manufacturer of toilet tissue. Rather than compete directly against Procter & Gamble's Charmin, Potlach makes the house brands for Albertson's, Safeway, Jewel, and many other grocery store chains. It matches the quality of the well-known brands but keeps costs low by eliminating advertising and promotion expenses. As a result, Spokane-based Potlach makes 92% of the private-label bathroom tissue and one-third of all bathroom tissue sold in Western U.S. grocery stores.[11]

Differentiation focus, like cost focus, concentrates on a particular buyer group, product line segment, or geographic market. This is the strategy successfully followed by Midamar Corporation, Morgan Motor Car Company (a manufacturer of classic British sports cars), Nickelodeon (a cable channel for children), and local ethnic grocery stores. In using differentiation focus, a company or business unit seeks differentiation in a targeted market segment. This strategy is valued by those who believe that a company or a unit that focuses its efforts is better able to serve the special needs of a narrow strategic target more effectively than can its competition. As explained in STRATEGY HIGHLIGHT 6.1, this strategy is followed by Poison, Incorporated, in the marketing of its Grim Reaper cigarettes to a very small segment of the tobacco market: serious risk takers!

Risks in Competitive Strategies

No one competitive strategy is guaranteed to achieve success, and some companies that have successfully implemented one of Porter's competitive strategies have found that they could not sustain the strategy. As shown in **Table 6–1**, each of the generic strategies has risks. For example, a company following a differentiation strategy must ensure that the higher price it charges for its higher quality is not too far above the price of the competition; otherwise, customers will not see the extra quality as worth the extra cost. This is what is meant in **Table 6–1** by the term **cost proximity**. P&G's use of R&D and advertising to differentiate its products had been very successful for many years, until customers in the value-conscious 1990s turned to cheaper private brands. As a result, P&G was forced to reduce costs until it could get prices back in line with customer expectations.

STRATEGY HIGHLIGHT 6.1

Grim Reaper Uses Focused Differentiation Strategy

Cigarettes are bad for your health. The U.S. Surgeon General, many research studies, and practically all health agencies agree that smoking is a primary cause of cancer. So, why would anyone buy a new brand of cigarettes called *Grim Reaper*, with a black-hooded death's head on its package?

After running a construction business for many years in Castle Hayne, North Carolina, Dan Norris founded Poison, Incorporated, to sell cigarettes to risk takers. He came up with this radical idea when he read a news report about a multi-billion-dollar judgment against Philip Morris by a man who claimed that he had no idea cigarettes were hazardous. Poison sold 12,000 cartons in 2003. Norris explains:

My product is just telling you the truth. . . . Our target market is a person who understands the dangers of smoking cigarettes, but is willing to take the chance for the experience of smoking. . . . The smokers of our cigarettes are the ones who climb Mount Everest, scuba through the canyons of Abez, hang glide off the cliffs of Montejerno, and know they have lived their lives to the fullest when they take the final ride with the Reaper.

Source: Summarized from A. G. Breed, "Little Tobacco," *The (Ames, IA) Tribune* (January 17, 2004), p. C7.

TABLE 6–1 RISKS OF GENERIC COMPETITIVE STRATEGIES

Risks of Cost Leadership	Risks of Differentiation	Risks of Focus
Cost leadership is not sustained: • Competitors imitate. • Technology changes. • Other bases for cost leadership erode.	Differentiation is not sustained: • Competitors imitate. • Bases for differentiation become less important to buyers.	The focus strategy is imitated. The target segment becomes structurally unattractive: • Structure erodes. • Demand disappears.
Proximity in differentiation is lost.	Cost proximity is lost.	Broadly targeted competitors overwhelm the segment: • The segment's differences from other segments narrow. • The advantages of a broad line increase.
Cost focusers achieve even lower cost in segments.	Differentiation focusers achieve even greater differentiation in segments.	New focusers subsegment the industry.

Source: Adapted with the permission of The Free Press, A Division of Simon & Schuster Adult Publishing Group, from *COMPETITIVE ADVANTAGE: Creating and Sustaining Superior Performance* by Michael Porter. Copyright © 1985, 1998 by Michael E. Porter. All rights reserved.

Issues in Competitive Strategies

Porter argues that to be successful, a company or business unit must achieve one of the previously mentioned generic competitive strategies. It is especially difficult to move between a narrow-target strategy and a broad-target strategy. Otherwise, the company or business unit is **stuck in the middle** of the competitive marketplace, with no competitive advantage, and is doomed to below-average performance. An example of a company that is stuck in the middle is Hewlett-Packard (HP). After its acquisition of Compaq in 2002, HP lost its direction and was squeezed between Dell and IBM. Dell stood for low priced simple PCs in an industry where PCs were becoming a commodity. IBM stood for weaving together multiple subsystems in a complex industry to provide integrative customer solutions. HP could neither match Dell's low cost nor IBM's differentiation on the basis of quality service. In referring to CEO Carly Fiorina's attempt to offer "the best customer experience," one analyst stated: "Her problem, in a nutshell, is that HP is trying to be all things to all kinds of customers, and is leaving them more and more plain confused."[12]

Although it may be difficult to move from a narrow- to a broad-target scope strategy (and vice versa) successfully, research does not support the argument that a firm or unit must chose between differentiation and lower cost in order to be successful.[13] What of companies that attempt to achieve *both* a low-cost and a high-differentiation position? The Toyota and Honda auto companies are often presented as examples of successful firms able to achieve both of these generic strategies. Thanks to advances in technology, a company may be able to design quality into a product or service in such a way that it can achieve both high quality and high market share—thus lowering costs.[14] Although Porter agrees that it is possible for a company or a business unit to achieve low cost and differentiation simultaneously, he continues to argue that this state is often temporary.[15] Porter does admit, however, that many different kinds of potentially profitable competitive strategies exist. Although there is generally room for only one company to successfully pursue the mass-market cost leadership strategy (because it is so dependent on achieving dominant market share), there is room for an almost unlimited number of differentiation and focus strategies (depending on the range of possible desirable features and the number of identifiable market niches). Quality, alone, has eight different dimen-

TABLE 6–2
THE EIGHT
DIMENSIONS OF
QUALITY

1. Performance	Primary operating characteristics, such as a washing machine's cleaning ability.
2. Features	"Bells and whistles," such as cruise control in a car, that supplement the basic functions.
3. Reliability	Probability that the product will continue functioning without any significant maintenance.
4. Conformance	Degree to which a product meets standards. When a customer buys a product out of the warehouse, it should perform identically to that viewed on the showroom floor.
5. Durability	Number of years of service a consumer can expect from a product before it significantly deteriorates. Differs from reliability in that a product can be durable but still need a lot of maintenance.
6. Serviceability	Product's ease of repair.
7. Aesthetics	How a product looks, feels, sounds, tastes, or smells.
8. Perceived Quality	Product's overall reputation. Especially important if there are no objective, easily used measures of quality.

Source: Adapted with the permission of The Free Press, A Division of Simon & Schuster Adult Publishing Group, from *MANAGING QUALITY: The Strategic and Competitive Edge* by David A. Garvin. Copyright © 1988 by David A. Garvin. All rights reserved.

sions—each with the potential of providing a product with a competitive advantage (see **Table 6–2**).

Most entrepreneurial ventures follow focus strategies. The successful ones differentiate their product from those of other competitors in the areas of quality and service, and they focus the product on customer needs in a segment of the market, thereby achieving a dominant share of that part of the market. Adopting guerrilla warfare tactics, these companies go after opportunities in market niches too small to justify retaliation from the market leaders. Veteran entrepreneur Norm Brodsky argues that it's often much easier for a small company to compete against a big company than against a well-run small company. "We beat the giants on service. We beat them on flexibility. We beat them on location and price."[16]

Industry Structure and Competitive Strategy

Although each of Porter's generic competitive strategies may be used in any industry, certain strategies are more likely to succeed than others in some instances. In a **fragmented industry**, for example, where many small- and medium-sized local companies compete for relatively small shares of the total market, focus strategies will likely predominate. Fragmented industries are typical for products in the early stages of their life cycles. If few economies are to be gained through size, no large firms will emerge, and entry barriers will be low—allowing a stream of new entrants into the industry. Chinese restaurants, veterinary care, used-car sales, ethnic grocery stores, and funeral homes are examples. Even though P.F. Chang's (97 outlets) and the Panda Restaurant Group (600 outlets) have firmly established themselves as chains in the United States, local, family-owned restaurants still comprise 87% of Asian casual dining restaurants.[17]

If a company is able to overcome the limitations of a fragmented market, however, it can reap the benefits of a broadly targeted cost leadership or differentiation strategy. Until Pizza Hut was able to use advertising to differentiate itself from local competitors, the pizza fast-food business was a fragmented industry composed primarily of locally owned pizza parlors, each with its own distinctive product and service offering. Subsequently, Domino's used the cost leader strategy to achieve U.S. national market share.

As an industry matures, fragmentation is overcome, and the industry tends to become a **consolidated industry** dominated by a few large companies. Although many industries start out being fragmented, battles for market share and creative attempts to overcome local or niche market boundaries often increase the market share of a few companies. After product standards become established for minimum quality and features, competition shifts to a greater emphasis on cost and service. Slower growth, overcapacity, and knowledgeable buyers combine to put a premium on a firm's ability to achieve cost leadership or differentiation along the dimensions most desired by the market. R&D shifts from product to process improvements. Overall product quality improves, and costs are reduced significantly.

The **strategic rollup** was developed in the mid-1990s as an efficient way to quickly consolidate a fragmented industry. With the aid of money from venture capitalists, an entrepreneur acquires hundreds of owner-operated small businesses. The resulting large firm creates economies of scale by building regional or national brands, applies best practices across all aspects of marketing and operations, and hires more sophisticated managers than the small businesses could previously afford. Rollups differ from conventional mergers and acquisitions in three ways: (1) they involve large numbers of firms, (2) the acquired firms are typically owner operated, and (3) the objective is not to gain incremental advantage but to reinvent an entire industry.[18] Rollups are currently under way in the funeral industry, led by Service Corporation International, Stewart Enterprises, and the Loewen Group; and in the veterinary care industries, by Veterinary Centers of America. Of the 16,000 pet hospitals in the United States, Veterinary Centers of American had acquired 317 by June 2004 and was in the process of buying at least 25 more each year for the foreseeable future.[19]

Once consolidated, an industry has become one in which cost leadership and differentiation tend to be combined to various degrees. A firm can no longer gain high market share simply through low price. The buyers are more sophisticated and demand a certain minimum level of quality for price paid. The same is true for firms emphasizing high quality. Either the quality must be high enough and valued by the customer enough to justify the higher price or the price must be dropped (through lowering costs) to compete effectively with the lower-priced products. This consolidation is taking place worldwide in the automobile, airline, and home appliance industries.

Hypercompetition and Competitive Strategy

In his book *Hypercompetition*, D'Aveni proposes that it is becoming increasingly difficult to sustain a competitive advantage for very long. "Market stability is threatened by short product life cycles, short product design cycles, new technologies, frequent entry by unexpected outsiders, repositioning by incumbents, and tactical redefinitions of market boundaries as diverse industries merge."[20] Consequently, a company or business unit must constantly work to improve its competitive advantage. It is not enough to be just the lowest-cost competitor. Through continuous improvement programs, competitors are usually working to lower their costs as well. Firms must find new ways not only to reduce costs further but also to add value to the product or service being provided.

The same is true of a firm or unit that is following a differentiation strategy. Maytag Corporation, for example, was successful for many years by offering the most reliable brand in major home appliances. It was able to charge the highest prices for Maytag brand washing machines. When other competitors improved the quality of their products, however, it became increasingly difficult for customers to justify Maytag's significantly higher price. Consequently, Maytag Corporation was forced not only to add new features to its products but also to reduce costs through improved manufacturing processes so that its prices were no longer out of line with those of the competition.

D'Aveni contends that when industries become hypercompetitive, they tend to go through escalating stages of competition. Firms initially compete on cost and quality, until an abundance of high-quality, low-priced goods result. This occurred in the U.S. major home appliance industry by 1980. In a second stage of competition, the competitors move into untapped markets. Others usually imitate these moves until the moves become too risky or expensive. This epitomized the major home appliance industry during the 1980s and 1990s, as firms moved first to Europe and then into Asia and South America.

According to D'Aveni, firms then raise entry barriers to limit competitors. Economies of scale, distribution agreements, and strategic alliances made it all but impossible for a new firm to enter the major home appliance industry by the end of the 20th century. After the established players have entered and consolidated all new markets, the next stage is for the remaining firms to attack and destroy the strongholds of other firms. Maytag's 1995 decision to divest its European division and acquire Amana was a prelude to building a North American stronghold, while Whirlpool, GE, and Electrolux were distracted by European and worldwide investments. Eventually, according to D'Aveni, the remaining large global competitors work their way to a situation of perfect competition in which no one has any advantage and profits are minimal.

Before hypercompetition, strategic initiatives provided competitive advantage for many years, perhaps for decades. This is no longer the case. According to D'Aveni, as industries become hypercompetitive, there is no such thing as a sustainable competitive advantage. Successful strategic initiatives in this type of industry typically last only months to a few years. According to D'Aveni, the only way a firm in this kind of dynamic industry can sustain any competitive advantage is through a continuous series of multiple short-term initiatives aimed at replacing a firm's current successful products with the next generation of products before the competitors can do so. Intel and Microsoft are taking this approach in the hypercompetitive computer industry.

Hypercompetition views competition, in effect, as a distinct series of ocean waves on what used to be a fairly calm stretch of water. As industry competition becomes more intense, the waves grow higher and require more dexterity to handle. Although a strategy is still needed to sail from point A to point B, more turbulent water means that a craft must continually adjust course to suit each new large wave. One danger of D'Aveni's concept of hypercompetition, however, is that it may lead to an overemphasis on short-term tactics (discussed in the next section) over long-term strategy. Too much of an orientation on the individual waves of hypercompetition could cause a company to focus too much on short-term temporary advantage and not enough on achieving its long-term objectives through building sustainable competitive advantage.

Which Competitive Strategy Is Best?

Before selecting one of Porter's generic competitive strategies for a company or business unit, management should assess its feasibility in terms of company or business unit resources and capabilities. Porter lists some of the commonly required skills and resources, as well as organizational requirements, in **Table 6–3**.

Competitive Tactics

Studies of decision making report that half the decisions made in organizations fail because of poor tactics.[21] A **tactic** is a specific operating plan that details how a strategy is to be implemented in terms of when and where it is to be put into action. By their nature, tactics are narrower in scope and shorter in time horizon than are strategies. Tactics, therefore, may be viewed (like policies) as a link between the formulation and implementation of strategy. Some of the tactics available to implement competitive strategies are timing tactics and market location tactics.

TABLE 6–3 REQUIREMENTS FOR GENERIC COMPETITIVE STRATEGIES

Generic Strategy	Commonly Required Skills and Resources	Common Organizational Requirements
Overall Cost Leadership	• Sustained capital investment and access to capital • Process engineering skills • Intense supervision of labor • Products designed for ease of manufacture • Low-cost distribution system	• Tight cost control • Frequent, detailed control reports • Structured organization and responsibilities • Incentives based on meeting strict quantitative targets
Differentiation	• Strong marketing abilities • Product engineering • Creative flair • Strong capability in basic research • Corporate reputation for quality or technological leadership • Long tradition in the industry or unique combination of skills drawn from other businesses • Strong cooperation from channels	• Strong coordination among functions in R&D, product development, and marketing • Subjective measurement and incentives instead of quantitative measures • Amenities to attract highly skilled labor, scientists, or creative people
Focus	• Combination of the above policies directed at the particular strategic target	• Combination of the above policies directed at the particular strategic target

Source: Adapted with the permission of The Free Press, A Division of Simon & Schuster Adult Publishing Group, from *COMPETITIVE STRATEGY: Techniques for Analyzing Industries and Competitors* by Michael Porter. Copyright © 1980, 1998 by The Free Press. All rights reserved.

Timing Tactics: When to Compete

A **timing tactic** deals with *when* a company implements a strategy. The first company to manufacture and sell a new product or service is called the **first mover** (or pioneer). Some of the advantages of being a first mover are that the company is able to establish a reputation as an industry leader, move down the learning curve to assume the cost leader position, and earn temporarily high profits from buyers who value the product or service very highly. A successful first mover can also set the standard for all subsequent products in the industry. A company that sets the standard "locks in" customers and is then able to offer further products based on that standard.[22] Microsoft was able to do this in software with its Windows operating system, and Netscape garnered over an 80% share of the Internet browser market by being first to commercialize the product successfully. Research indicates that moving first or second into a new industry or foreign country results in greater market share and shareholder wealth than does moving later.[23] Being first provides a company profit advantages for about 10 years in consumer goods and about 12 years in industrial goods.[24] This is only true, however, if the first mover has sufficient resources to both exploit the new market and defend its position against later arrivals with greater resources.[25] Gillette, for example, has been able to keep its leadership of the razor category (70% market share) by continuously introducing new products.[26]

Being a first mover does, however, have disadvantages. These disadvantages can be, conversely, advantages enjoyed by late-mover firms. **Late movers** may be able to imitate the technological advances of others (and thus keep R&D costs low), keep risks down by waiting until a new market is established, and take advantage of the first mover's natural inclination to ignore market segments.[27] Research indicates that successful late movers tend to be large firms with considerable resources and related experience.[28] Microsoft is one example. Once Netscape had established itself as the standard for Internet browsers in the 1990s, Microsoft used its huge resources to directly attack Netscape's position with its Internet Explorer. It did not want Netscape to also set the standard in the developing and highly lucrative intranet market inside corporations. By 2004, Microsoft's Internet Explorer dominated web browsers, and Netscape was only a minor presence. Nevertheless, research suggests that the advantages and disadvantages of first and late movers may not always generalize across industries because of differences in entry barriers and the resources of the specific competitors.[29]

Market Location Tactics: Where to Compete

A **market location tactic** deals with *where* a company implements a strategy. A company or business unit can implement a competitive strategy either offensively or defensively. An **offensive tactic** usually takes place in an established competitor's market location. A **defensive tactic** usually takes place in the firm's own current market position as a defense against possible attack by a rival.[30]

Offensive Tactics. Some of the methods used to attack a competitor's position are:

- **Frontal Assault:** The attacking firm goes head to head with its competitor. It matches the competitor in every category, from price to promotion to distribution channel. To be successful, the attacker must have not only superior resources but also the willingness to persevere. This is generally a very expensive tactic and may serve to awaken a sleeping giant, depressing profits for the whole industry. This is what Kimberly-Clark did when it introduced Huggies disposable diapers against P&G's market-leading Pampers. The resulting competitive battle between the two firms depressed Kimberly-Clark's profits.[31]

- **Flanking Maneuver:** Rather than going straight for a competitor's position of strength with a frontal assault, a firm may attack a part of the market where the competitor is weak. AMD followed this tactic with its entry into the microprocessor market—a market then almost totally dominated by Intel. Rather than going directly after Intel's microprocessor business, AMD developed low-priced chips to go after the customers Intel didn't mind losing. To be successful, the flanker must be patient and willing to carefully expand out of the relatively undefended market niche or else face retaliation by an established competitor.

- **Bypass Attack:** Rather than directly attacking the established competitor frontally or on its flanks, a company or business unit may choose to change the rules of the game. This tactic attempts to cut the market out from under the established defender by offering a new type of product that makes the competitor's product unnecessary. For example, instead of competing directly against Microsoft's Pocket PC and Palm Pilot for the handheld computer market, Apple introduced the iPod as a personal digital music player. It was the most radical change to the way people listen to music since the Sony Walkman. By redefining the market, Apple successfully sidestepped both Intel and Microsoft, leaving them to play catch-up.[32]

- **Encirclement:** Usually evolving out of a frontal assault or flanking maneuver, encirclement occurs as an attacking company or unit encircles the competitor's position in terms of products or markets or both. The encircler has greater product variety (e.g., a complete product line, ranging from low to high price) and/or serves more markets (e.g., dominates every secondary market). For example, Steinway was a major manufacturer of pianos in the United States until Yamaha entered the market with a broader range of pianos, keyboards, and other musical instruments. Although Steinway still dominates concert halls, it has only a 2% share of the U.S. market.[33]

- **Guerrilla Warfare:** Instead of a continual and extensive resource-expensive attack on a competitor, a firm or business unit may choose to "hit and run." Guerrilla warfare is characterized by the use of small, intermittent assaults on different market segments held by the competitor. In this way, a new entrant or small firm can make some gains without seriously threatening a large, established competitor and evoking some form of retaliation. To be successful, the firm or unit conducting guerrilla warfare must be patient enough to accept small gains and to avoid pushing the established competitor to the point that it must respond or else lose face. Microbreweries, which make beer for sale to local customers, use this tactic against national brewers such as Anheuser-Busch.

Defensive Tactics. According to Porter, defensive tactics aim to lower the probability of attack, divert attacks to less threatening avenues, or lessen the intensity of an attack. Instead of increasing competitive advantage per se, they make a company's or business unit's competitive advantage more sustainable by causing a challenger to conclude that an attack is unattractive. These tactics deliberately reduce short-term profitability to ensure long-term profitability[34]:

- **Raise Structural Barriers:** Entry barriers act to block a challenger's logical avenues of attack. Some of the most important, according to Porter, are to:
  1. Offer a full line of products in every profitable market segment to close off any entry points (for example, Coca Cola offers unprofitable noncarbonated beverages to keep competitors off store shelves);
  2. Block channel access by signing exclusive agreements with distributors;
  3. Raise buyer switching costs by offering low-cost training to users;
  4. Raise the cost of gaining trial users by keeping prices low on items new users are most likely to purchase;
  5. Increase scale economies to reduce unit costs;
  6. Foreclose alternative technologies through patenting or licensing;
  7. Limit outside access to facilities and personnel;
  8. Tie up suppliers by obtaining exclusive contracts or purchasing key locations;
  9. Avoid suppliers that also serve competitors; and
  10. Encourage the government to raise barriers, such as safety and pollution standards or favorable trade policies.

- **Increase Expected Retaliation:** This tactic is any action that increases the perceived threat of retaliation for an attack. For example, management may strongly defend any erosion of market share by drastically cutting prices or matching a challenger's promotion through a policy of accepting any price-reduction coupons for a competitor's product. This counterattack is especially important in markets that are very important to the defending company or business unit. For example, when Clorox Company challenged P&G in the detergent market with Clorox Super Detergent, P&G retaliated by test marketing its liquid bleach, Lemon Fresh Comet, in an attempt to scare Clorox into retreating from the detergent market. Research suggests that retaliating quickly is not as successful in slowing market share loss as a slower but more concentrated and aggressive response.[35]

- **Lower the Inducement for Attack:** A third type of defensive tactic is to reduce a challenger's expectations of future profits in the industry. Like Southwest Airlines, a company can deliberately keep prices low and constantly invest in cost-reducing measures. With prices kept very low, there is little profit incentive for a new entrant.

Cooperative Strategies

A company uses competitive strategies and tactics to gain competitive advantage within an industry by battling against other firms. These are not, however, the only business strategy options available to a company or business unit for competing successfully within an industry.

A company can also use **cooperative strategies** to gain competitive advantage within an industry by working with other firms. The two general types of cooperative strategies are collusion and strategic alliances.

Collusion

Collusion is the active cooperation of firms within an industry to reduce output and raise prices in order to get around the normal economic law of supply and demand. Collusion may be explicit, in which case firms cooperate through direct communication and negotiation, or tacit, in which case firms cooperate indirectly through an informal system of signals. Explicit collusion is illegal in most countries and in a number of regional trade associations, such as the European Union. For example, Archer Daniels Midland (ADM), the large U.S. agricultural products firm, conspired with its competitors to limit the sales volume and raise the price of the food additive lysine. Executives from three Japanese and South Korean lysine manufacturers admitted meeting in hotels in major cities throughout the world to form a "lysine trade association." The three companies were fined more than $20 million by the U.S. federal government.[36] In another example, Denver-based Qwest signed agreements favoring competitors that agreed not to oppose Qwest's merger with U.S. West or its entry into the long-distance business in its 14-state region. In one agreement, Qwest agreed to pay McLeodUSA almost $30 million to settle a billing dispute in return for McLeod's withdrawing its objections to Qwest's purchase of U.S. West.[37]

Collusion can also be tacit, in which case there is no direct communication among competing firms. According to Barney, tacit collusion in an industry is most likely to be successful if (1) there are a small number of identifiable competitors, (2) costs are similar among firms, (3) one firm tends to act as the price leader, (4) there is a common industry culture that accepts cooperation, (5) sales are characterized by a high frequency of small orders, (6) large inventories and order backlogs are normal ways of dealing with fluctuations in demand, and (7) there are high entry barriers to keep out new competitors.[38]

Even tacit collusion can, however, be illegal. For example, when General Electric wanted to ease price competition in the steam turbine industry, it widely advertised its prices and publicly committed not to sell below those prices. Customers were even told that if GE reduced turbine prices in the future, it would give customers a refund equal to the price reduction. GE's message was not lost on Westinghouse, the major competitor in steam turbines. Both prices and profit margins remained stable for the next 10 years in this industry. The U.S. Department of Justice then sued both firms for engaging in "conscious parallelism" (following each other's lead to reduce the level of competition) in order to reduce competition.

Strategic Alliances

A **strategic alliance** is a partnership of two or more corporations or business units to achieve strategically significant objectives that are mutually beneficial.[39] Alliances between companies or business units have become a fact of life in modern business. The number of strategic alliances grew to more than 10,200 in 2000 alone. Each of the top 500 global business firms now average 60 major alliances.[40] Fully two-thirds of companies surveyed in 2003 expected their dependence on alliances of some sort to increase over the next three years.[41] Some alliances are very short term, only lasting long enough for one partner to establish a beachhead in a new market. Over time, conflicts over objectives and control often develop among the partners. For these and other reasons, around half of all alliances (including international alliances) perform unsatisfactorily.[42] Others are more long lasting and may even be preludes to full mergers between companies.

Many alliances increase profitability of the members and have a positive effect on firm value.[43] A study by Cooper and Lybrand found that firms involved in strategic alliances had

11% higher revenue and 20% higher growth rate than did companies not involved in alliances.[44] It is likely that forming and managing strategic alliances is a capability that is learned over time. Research reveals that the more experience a firm has with strategic alliances, the more likely its alliances will be successful.[45]

Companies or business units may form a strategic alliance for a number of reasons, including:

1. **To obtain technology and/or manufacturing capabilities:** For example, Intel formed a partnership with HP to use HP's capabilities in RISC technology in order to develop the successor to Intel's Pentium microprocessor. A study found that firms with strategic alliances had more modern manufacturing technologies than did firms without alliances.[46]

2. **To obtain access to specific markets:** Rather than buy a foreign company or build breweries of its own in other countries, Anheuser-Busch chose to license the right to brew and market Budweiser to other brewers, such as Labatt in Canada, Modelo in Mexico, and Kirin in Japan. In a survey by the *Economist Intelligence Unit*, 59% of executives stated that their primary reason for engaging in alliances was the need for fast and low-cost expansion into new markets.[47]

3. **To reduce financial risk:** For example, because the costs of developing new large jet airplanes were becoming too high for any one manufacturer, Aerospatiale of France, British Aerospace, Construcciones Aeronáuticas of Spain, and Daimler-Benz Aerospace of Germany formed a joint consortium called Airbus Industrie to design and build such planes. Using alliances with suppliers is a popular means of outsourcing an expensive activity.

4. **To reduce political risk:** Forming alliances with local partners is a good way to overcome deficiencies in resources and capabilities when expanding into international markets.[48] To gain access to China while ensuring a positive relationship with the often-restrictive Chinese government, Maytag Corporation formed a joint venture with the Chinese appliance maker RSD.

5. **To learn new capabilities:** For example, Pittsburgh Brewing Company, maker of Iron City Beer, partnered with Alcoa to produce aluminum bottles that keep beer colder for 50 minutes longer than conventional bottles.[49]

Cooperative arrangements between companies and business units fall along a continuum from weak and distant to strong and close. (See **Figure 6–5**.) The types of alliances range from mutual service consortia to joint ventures and licensing arrangements to value-chain partnerships.[50]

Mutual Service Consortia. A **mutual service consortium** is a partnership of similar companies in similar industries that pool their resources to gain a benefit that is too expensive to develop alone, such as access to advanced technology. For example, IBM of the United States,

Figure 6–5
Continuum of Strategic Alliances

Mutual Service Consortia	Joint Venture, Licensing Arrangement	Value-Chain Partnership

Weak and Distant   **Strong and Close**

Source: Reprinted by permission of the Harvard Business Review. From "Collaborative Advantage: The Art of Alliances," by R.M. Kanter, July–August 1994. Copyright © 1994 by the Harvard Business School Publishing Corporation; all rights reserved.

Toshiba of Japan, and Siemens of Germany formed a consortium to develop new generations of computer chips. As part of this alliance, IBM offered Toshiba its expertise in chemical mechanical polishing to help develop a new manufacturing process using ultraviolet lithography to etch tiny circuits in silicon chips. IBM then transferred the new technology to a facility in the United States.[51] The mutual service consortia is a fairly weak and distant alliance—appropriate for partners that wish to work together but not share their core competencies. There is very little interaction or communication among the partners.

Joint Ventures. A **joint venture** is a "cooperative business activity, formed by two or more separate organizations for strategic purposes, that creates an independent business entity and allocates ownership, operational responsibilities, and financial risks and rewards to each member, while preserving their separate identity/autonomy."[52] Along with licensing arrangements, joint ventures lay at the midpoint of the continuum and are formed to pursue an opportunity that needs a capability from two companies or business units, such as the technology of one and the distribution channels of another.

Joint ventures are the most popular form of strategic alliance. They often occur because the companies involved do not want to or cannot legally merge permanently. Joint ventures provide a way to temporarily combine the different strengths of partners to achieve an outcome of value to both. For example, Toys 'Я' Us and Amazon.com formed a joint venture called Toysrus.com to act as an online toy store. Amazon agreed to include the joint venture on its web site, ship the products, and handle customer service. In turn, Toys 'R' Us agreed to choose and buy the toys, using its parents' purchasing power to get the most desired toys at the best price.[53]

Extremely popular in international undertakings because of financial and political–legal constraints, forming joint ventures is a convenient way for corporations to work together without losing their independence. Disadvantages of joint ventures include loss of control, lower profits, probability of conflicts with partners, and the likely transfer of technological advantage to the partner. Joint ventures are often meant to be temporary, especially by some companies that may view them as a way to rectify a competitive weakness until they can achieve long-term dominance in the partnership. Partially for this reason, joint ventures have a high failure rate. Research indicates, however, that joint ventures tend to be more successful when both partners have equal ownership in the venture and are mutually dependent on each other for results.[54]

Licensing Arrangements. A **licensing arrangement** is an agreement in which the licensing firm grants rights to another firm in another country or market to produce and/or sell a product. The licensee pays compensation to the licensing firm in return for technical expertise. Licensing is an especially useful strategy if the trademark or brand name is well known but the MNC does not have sufficient funds to finance its entering the country directly. Anheuser-Busch uses this strategy to produce and market Budweiser beer in the United Kingdom, Japan, Israel, Australia, Korea, and the Philippines. This strategy also becomes important if the country makes entry via investment either difficult or impossible. The danger always exists, however, that the licensee might develop its competence to the point that it becomes a competitor to the licensing firm. Therefore, a company should never license its distinctive competence, even for some short-run advantage.

Value-Chain Partnerships. A **value-chain partnership** is a strong and close alliance in which one company or unit forms a long-term arrangement with a key supplier or distributor for mutual advantage. For example, P&G, the maker of Folgers and Millstone coffee, worked with coffee appliance makers Mr. Coffee, Krups, and Hamilton Beach to use technology licensed from Black & Decker to market a pressurized, single-serve coffee-making system called Home Cafe. This was an attempt to reverse declining at-home coffee consumption at a time when coffeehouse sales were rising.[55]

To improve the quality of parts it purchases, companies in the U.S. auto industry, for example, have decided to work more closely with fewer suppliers and to involve them more in product design decisions. Activities that had previously been done internally by an auto maker are now being outsourced to suppliers specializing in those activities. The benefits of such relationships do not just accrue to the purchasing firm. Research suggests that suppliers that engage in long-term relationships are more profitable than suppliers with multiple short-term contracts.[56]

All forms of strategic alliances involve uncertainty. Many issues need to be dealt with when an alliance is initially formed, and others emerge later. Many problems revolve around the fact that a firm's alliance partners may also be its competitors, either immediately or in the future. According to Peter Lorange, an authority in strategy, one thorny issue in any strategic alliance is how to cooperate without giving away the company or business unit's core competence: "Particularly when advanced technology is involved, it can be difficult for partners in an alliance to cooperate and openly share strategic know-how, but it is mandatory if the joint venture is to succeed."[57] It is therefore important that a company or business unit that is interested in joining or forming a strategic alliance consider the strategic alliance success factors listed in **Table 6–4**.

TABLE 6–4 STRATEGIC ALLIANCE SUCCESS FACTORS

- Have a clear strategic purpose. Integrate the alliance with each partner's strategy. Ensure that mutual value is created for all partners.

- Find a fitting partner with compatible goals and complementary capabilities.

- Identify likely partnering risks and deal with them when the alliance is formed.

- Allocate tasks and responsibilities so that each partner can specialize in what it does best.

- Create incentives for cooperation to minimize differences in corporate culture or organization fit.

- Minimize conflicts among the partners by clarifying objectives and avoiding direct competition in the marketplace.

- In an international alliance, ensure that those managing it have comprehensive cross-cultural knowledge.

- Exchange human resources to maintain communication and trust. Don't allow individual egos to dominate.

- Operate with long-term time horizons. The expectation of future gains can minimize short-term conflicts.

- Develop multiple joint projects so that any failures are counterbalanced by successes.

- Agree on a monitoring process. Share information to build trust and keep projects on target. Monitor customer responses and service complaints.

- Be flexible in terms of willingness to renegotiate the relationship in terms of environmental changes and new opportunities.

- Agree on an exit strategy for when the partners' objectives are achieved or the alliance is judged a failure.

Source: Compiled from B. Gomes-Casseres, "Do You Really Have an Alliance Strategy?" *Strategy & Leadership* (September/October 1998), pp. 6–11; L. Segil, "Strategic Alliances for the 21st Century," *Strategy & Leadership* (September/October 1998), pp. 12–16; and A. C. Inkpen and K-Q Li, "Joint Venture Formation: Planning and Knowledge Gathering for Success," *Organizational Dynamics* (Spring 1999), pp. 33–47. Inkpen and Li provide a checklist of 17 questions on p. 46.

6.5 | Conclusion

Once environmental scanning is completed, situational analysis calls for the integration of this information. SWOT analysis is the most popular method for examining external and internal information. We recommend using the SFAS Matrix as one way to identify a corporation's strategic factors. Using the TOWS matrix to identify a propitious niche is one way to develop a sustainable competitive advantage by using those strategic factors.

Business strategy is composed of both competitive and cooperative strategy. As the external environment becomes more uncertain, an increasing number of corporations are choosing to simultaneously compete *and* cooperate with their competitors. These firms may cooperate to obtain efficiency in some areas, while each firm simultaneously tries to differentiate itself for competitive purposes. Raymond Noorda, Novell's founder and former CEO, coined the term **co-opetition** to describe such simultaneous competition and cooperation among firms.[58] A careful balancing act, co-opetition involves the careful management of alliance partners so that each partner obtains sufficient benefits to keep the alliance together. A long-term view is crucial. An unintended transfer of knowledge could be enough to provide one partner a significant competitive advantage over the others.[59] Unless that company forebears from using that knowledge against its partners, the alliance will be doomed.

Strategy Bits

- Countries with the highest levels of global competitiveness are Finland, the United States, Sweden, Taiwan, Denmark, Norway, and Singapore, in that order.[60]

- Countries with the highest percentages of pirated software are Vietnam (94%), China (92%), Indonesia (88%), Russia and Ukraine (87%), and Pakistan (83%).[61]

Discussion Questions

1. What industry forces might cause a propitious niche to disappear?

2. Is it possible for a company or business unit to follow a cost leadership strategy and a differentiation strategy simultaneously? Why or why not?

3. Is it possible for a company to have a sustainable competitive advantage when its industry becomes hyper-competitive?

4. What are the advantages and disadvantages of being a first mover in an industry? Give some examples of first-mover and late-mover firms. Were they successful?

5. Why are many strategic alliances temporary?

Strategic Practice Exercise

THE PROBLEM

On January 22, 2002, Kmart Corporation became the largest retailer in U.S. history to seek bankruptcy protection. In Kmart's petition for reorganization under Chapter 11 of the U.S. Bankruptcy Code, Kmart management announced that they would outline a plan for repaying Kmart's creditors, reducing Kmart's size, and restructuring its business so that it could leave court protection as a viable competitor in discount mass-market retailing. Emerging from bankruptcy in May 2003, Kmart still lacked a business strategy to succeed in an extremely competitive marketplace.

By 2004, the discount department store industry had reached maturity, and Kmart no longer possessed a clearly defined position within that industry. Its primary competitors were Wal-Mart, Sears, Target, Kohl's, and JCPenney, with secondary competitors in certain categories. Wal-Mart, an extremely efficient retailer, was known for consistently having the lowest costs (reflected in low prices) and the highest sales in the industry. Having started in rural

America, Wal-Mart was now actively growing internationally. Sears, with the second-highest annual sales, had a strong position in hard goods, such as home appliances and tools. Around 40% of all major home appliance sales continued to be controlled by Sears. Nevertheless, Sears was struggling with slumping sales as customers turned from Sears' mall stores to stand-alone, big-box retailers, such as Lowe's and Home Depot, to buy their hard goods. Target, third in sales but second in profits, behind Wal-Mart, had distinguished itself as a merchandiser of stylish upscale products. Along with Wal-Mart, Target had flourished to such an extent that Dayton-Hudson, its parent company, had changed its corporate name to Target. Kohl's, a relatively new entrant to the industry, operated 420 family-oriented stores in 32 states. JCPenney operated more than 1,000 stores in all 50 states. Both Kohl's and JCPenney emphasized soft goods, such as clothing and related items.

Kmart was also challenged by "category killers" that competed in only one or a few industry categories but in greater depth within any category than could any department store. Some of these were Toys 'Я' Us, Home Depot, Lowe's, and drug stores such as Rite Aid, CVS, Eckerd, and Walgreens.

Kmart had been established in 1962 by its parent company S.S. Kresge as a discount department store offering the most variety of goods at the lowest prices. Unlike Sears, the company chose not to locate in shopping centers but to establish its discount stores in highly visible corner locations. During the 1960s, '70s, and '80s, Kmart prospered. By 1990, however, when Wal-Mart first surpassed Kmart in annual sales, Kmart's stores had become dated and lost their appeal.

Other well-known discount stores, such as Korvette's, Grant's, Woolco, Ames, Bradlees, and Montgomery Ward, had gone out of business as the industry had consolidated and reached maturity. Attempting to avoid this fate, Kmart management updated and enlarged the stores, added name brands, and hired Martha Stewart as its lifestyle consultant. None of these changes improved Kmart's financial situation. By the time it declared bankruptcy, it had lost money in 5 of the past 10 years.

Out of bankruptcy, Kmart became profitable—primarily by closing or selling (to Sears and Home Depot) around 600 of its retail stores. Management had been unable to invigorate sales in its stores. Declared guilty of insider trading, Martha Stewart went to prison just before the 2004 Christmas season. In a surprise move, Edward Lampert, Kmart's Chairman of the Board and a major shareholder of Sears, initiated the acquisition of Sears by Kmart for $11 billion in November 2004. The new company was to be called Sears Holdings Corporation. Even though management predicted that the combined company's costs could be reduced by $500 million annually within three years through supplier and administrative economies, analysts wondered how these two struggling firms could ever be successful.[62]

THE ASSIGNMENT

What business competitive strategies were used by each of Kmart's competitors? What business strategy(ies) do you recommend for the new company? Should Kmart and Sears keep their own identities and have unique competitive strategies, or should they be combined in some manner with a new competitive strategy? Defend your answer.

Key Terms

business strategy (p. 145)

collusion (p. 157)

competitive scope (p. 147)

competitive strategy (p. 145)

consolidated industry (p. 152)

cooperative strategy (p. 157)

co-opetition (p. 161)

cost focus (p. 149)

cost leadership (p. 148)

cost proximity (p. 149)

defensive tactic (p. 155)

differentiation (p. 148)

differentiation focus (p. 149)

differentiation strategy (p. 147)

first mover (p. 154)

fragmented industry (p. 151)

joint venture (p. 159)

late mover (p. 154)

licensing arrangement (p. 159)

lower cost strategy (p. 147)

market location tactic (p. 155)

mutual service consortium (p. 158)

offensive tactic (p. 155)

propitious niche (p. 142)

SFAS (Strategic Factors Analysis Summary) Matrix (p. 139)

SO, ST, WO, WT Strategies (p. 145)

strategic alliance (p. 157)

strategic rollup (p. 152)

strategic window (p. 142)

strategy formulation (p. 138)

stuck in the middle (p. 150)

SWOT (p. 138)

tactic (p. 153)

timing tactics (p. 154)

TOWS Matrix (p. 144)

value-chain partnership (p. 159)

CHAPTER 7
Strategy Formulation: Corporate Strategy

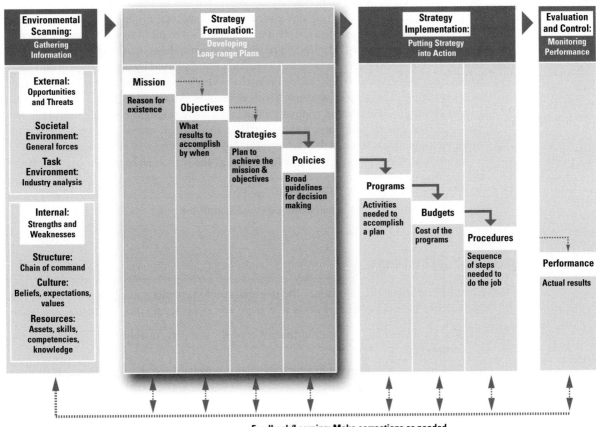

Environmental Scanning: Gathering Information	Strategy Formulation: Developing Long-range Plans	Strategy Implementation: Putting Strategy into Action	Evaluation and Control: Monitoring Performance

External: Opportunities and Threats

Societal Environment: General forces

Task Environment: Industry analysis

Internal: Strengths and Weaknesses

Structure: Chain of command

Culture: Beliefs, expectations, values

Resources: Assets, skills, competencies, knowledge

Mission Reason for existence

Objectives What results to accomplish by when

Strategies Plan to achieve the mission & objectives

Policies Broad guidelines for decision making

Programs Activities needed to accomplish a plan

Budgets Cost of the programs

Procedures Sequence of steps needed to do the job

Performance Actual results

Feedback/Learning: Make corrections as needed

Learning Objectives

After reading this chapter, you should be able to:

- Understand the three aspects of corporate strategy.
- Apply the directional strategies of growth, stability, and retrenchment
- Understand the differences between vertical and horizontal growth as well as concentric and conglomerate diversification
- Identify strategic options to enter a foreign country
- Apply portfolio analysis to guide decisions in companies with multiple products and businesses
- Develop a parenting strategy for a multiple-business corporation

WHAT IS THE BEST WAY FOR A COMPANY TO GROW IF ITS PRIMARY BUSINESS IS MATURING? A study of 1,850 companies by Zook and Allen revealed two conclusions: First, the most sustained profitable growth occurs when a corporation pushes out of the boundary around its core business into adjacent businesses. Second, those corporations that consistently outgrow their rivals do so by developing a formula for expanding those boundaries in a predicable, repeatable manner.[1]

Nike is a classic example of this process. Despite its success in athletic shoes, no one expected Nike to be successful when it diversified in 1995 from shoes into golf apparel, balls, and equipment. Only a few years later, it was acknowledged to be a major player in the new business. According to researchers Zook and Allen, the key to Nike's success was a formula for growth that the company had applied and adapted successfully in a series of entries into sports markets, from jogging to volleyball to tennis to basketball to soccer and, most recently, to golf. First, Nike established a leading position in athletic shoes in the target market—in this case, golf shoes. Second, Nike launched a clothing line endorsed by the sports' top athletes—in this case, Tiger Woods. Third, the company formed new distribution channels and contracts with key suppliers in the new business. Nike's reputation as a strong marketer of new products gave it credibility. Fourth, the company introduced higher-margin equipment into the new market. In the case of golf clubs, it started with irons and then moved to drivers. Once it had captured a significant share in the U.S. market, Nike's next step was global distribution.

Zook and Allen propose that this formula was the reason Nike moved past Reebok in the sporting goods industry. In 1987, Nike's operating profits were only $164 million, compared to Reebok's much larger $309 million. Fifteen years later, Nike's profits had grown to $1.1 billion while Reebok's had declined to $247 million.[2]

7.1 | Corporate Strategy

The vignette about Nike illustrates the importance of corporate strategy to a firm's survival and success. Corporate strategy deals with three key issues facing the corporation as a whole:

1. The firm's overall orientation toward growth, stability, or retrenchment (*directional strategy*).

2. The industries or markets in which the firm competes through its products and business units (*portfolio strategy*).

3. The manner in which management coordinates activities and transfers resources and cultivates capabilities among product lines and business units (*parenting strategy*).

Corporate strategy is primarily about the choice of direction for a firm as a whole and the management of its business or product portfolio.[3] This is true whether the firm is a small company or a large multinational corporation (MNC). In a large multiple-business company, in particular, corporate strategy is concerned with managing various product lines and business units for maximum value. In this instance, corporate headquarters must play the role of the organizational "parent," in that it must deal with various product and business unit "children." Even though each product line or business unit has its own competitive or cooperative strategy that it uses to obtain its own competitive advantage in the marketplace, the corporation must coordinate these different business strategies so that the corporation as a whole succeeds as a "family."[4]

Corporate strategy, therefore, includes decisions regarding the flow of financial and other resources to and from a company's product lines and business units. Through a series of coordinating devices, a company transfers skills and capabilities developed in one unit to other units that need such resources. In this way, it attempts to obtain synergy among numerous product lines and business units so that the corporate whole is greater than the sum of its individual business unit parts.[5] All corporations, from the smallest company offering one product in only one industry to the largest conglomerate operating in many industries with many products, must at one time or another consider one or more of these issues.

To deal with each of the key issues, this chapter is organized into three parts that examine corporate strategy in terms of *directional strategy* (orientation toward growth), *portfolio analysis* (coordination of cash flow among units), and *corporate parenting* (the building of corporate synergies through resource sharing and development).[6]

7.2 | Directional Strategy

Just as every product or business unit must follow a business strategy to improve its competitive position, every corporation must decide its orientation toward growth by asking the following three questions:

1. Should we expand, cut back, or continue our operations unchanged?
2. Should we concentrate our activities within our current industry, or should we diversify into other industries?
3. If we want to grow and expand nationally and/or globally, should we do so through internal development or through external acquisitions, mergers, or strategic alliances?

A corporation's **directional strategy** is composed of three general orientations (sometimes called *grand strategies*):

- **Growth strategies** expand the company's activities.
- **Stability strategies** make no change to the company's current activities.
- **Retrenchment strategies** reduce the company's level of activities.

Having chosen the general orientation (such as growth), a company's managers can select from several more specific corporate strategies, such as concentration within one product line/industry or diversification into other products/industries. (See **Figure 7–1**.) These strategies are useful both to corporations operating in only one industry with one product line and to those operating in many industries with many product lines.

Growth Strategies

By far the most widely pursued corporate directional strategies are those designed to achieve growth in sales, assets, profits, or some combination. Companies that do business in expanding industries must grow to survive. Continuing growth involves increasing sales and a chance

Figure 7–1
Corporate Directional Strategies

• GROWTH	• STABILITY	• RETRENCHMENT

Concentration
  Vertical Growth
  Horizontal Growth
Diversification
  Concentric
  Conglomerate
	Pause/Proceed with Caution
	No Change
	Profit
		Turnaround
		Captive Company
		Sell-Out/Divestment
		Bankruptcy/Liquidation

to take advantage of the experience curve to reduce the per-unit cost of products sold, thereby increasing profits. This cost reduction becomes extremely important if a corporation's industry is growing quickly or consolidating and if competitors are engaging in price wars in attempts to increase their shares of the market. Firms that have not reached "critical mass" (that is, gained the necessary economy of large-scale production) face large losses unless they can find and fill a small, but profitable, niche where higher prices can be offset by special product or service features. That is why Oracle wanted to acquire PeopleSoft, a rival software firm, in 2004. Although still growing, the software industry was maturing around a handful of large firms. According to CEO Larry Ellison, Oracle needed to double or even triple in size by buying smaller and weaker rivals if it was to compete with SAP and Microsoft.[7]

A corporation can grow internally by expanding its operations both globally and domestically, or it can grow externally through mergers, acquisitions, and strategic alliances. A **merger** is a transaction involving two or more corporations in which stock is exchanged but in which only one corporation survives. Mergers usually occur between firms of somewhat similar size and are usually "friendly." The resulting firm is likely to have a name derived from its composite firms. One example is the merging of Allied Corporation and Signal Companies to form Allied Signal. An **acquisition** is the purchase of a company that is completely absorbed as an operating subsidiary or division of the acquiring corporation. Examples are Procter & Gamble's (P&G's) acquisition of Richardson-Vicks, known for its Oil of Olay and Vidal Sassoon brands, and Noxell Corporation, known for Noxzema and Cover Girl.

Acquisitions usually occur between firms of different sizes and can be either friendly or hostile. Hostile acquisitions are often called *takeovers*. A strategic alliance is a partnership between two or more corporations or business units to achieve strategically significant objectives that are mutually beneficial. See **Chapter 6** for a detailed discussion of strategic alliances.

Growth is a very attractive strategy for two key reasons:

- Growth based on increasing market demand may mask flaws in a company—flaws that would be immediately evident in a stable or declining market. A growing flow of revenue into a highly leveraged corporation can create a large amount of **organization slack** (unused resources) that can be used to quickly resolve problems and conflicts between departments and divisions. Growth also provides a big cushion for turnaround in case a strategic error is made. Larger firms also have more bargaining power than do small firms and are more likely to obtain support from key stakeholders in case of difficulty.

- A growing firm offers more opportunities for advancement, promotion, and interesting jobs. Growth itself is exciting and ego-enhancing for CEOs. The marketplace and potential investors tend to view a growing corporation as a "winner" or "on the move." Executive compensation tends to get bigger as an organization increases in size. Large firms are also more difficult to acquire than are smaller ones; thus an executive's job in a large firm is more secure.

The two basic growth strategies are **concentration** on the current product line(s) in one industry and **diversification** into other product lines in other industries.

Concentration

If a company's current product lines have real growth potential, concentration of resources on those product lines makes sense as a strategy for growth. The two basic concentration strategies are vertical growth and horizontal growth. Growing firms in a growing industry tend to choose these strategies before they try diversification.

Vertical Growth.   Vertical growth can be achieved by taking over a function previously provided by a supplier or by a distributor. The company, in effect, grows by making its own supplies and/or by distributing its own products. This may be done in order to reduce costs, gain control over a scarce resource, guarantee quality of a key input, or obtain access to potential customers. This growth can be achieved either internally by expanding current operations or externally through acquisitions. Henry Ford, for example, used internal company resources to build his River Rouge plant outside Detroit. The manufacturing process was integrated to the point that iron ore entered one end of the long plant, and finished automobiles rolled out the other end, into a huge parking lot. In contrast, Cisco Systems, a maker of Internet hardware, chose the external route to vertical growth by purchasing Radiata, Inc., a maker of chip sets for wireless networks. This acquisition gave Cisco access to technology permitting wireless communications at speeds previously possible only with wired connections.[8]

Vertical growth results in **vertical integration**—the degree to which a firm operates vertically in multiple locations on an industry's value chain, from extracting raw materials to manufacturing to retailing. More specifically, assuming a function previously provided by a supplier is called **backward integration** (going backward on an industry's value chain). The purchase of Carroll's Foods for its hog-growing facilities by Smithfield Foods, the world's largest pork processor, is an example of backward integration.[9] Assuming a function previously provided by a distributor is labeled **forward integration** (going forward on an industry's value chain). FedEx, for example, used forward integration when it purchased Kinko's in order to provide store-front package drop-off and delivery services for the small-business market.[10]

Vertical growth is a logical strategy for a corporation or business unit with a strong competitive position in a highly attractive industry—especially when technology is predictable and markets are growing.[11] To keep and even improve its competitive position, a company may use backward integration to minimize resource acquisition costs and inefficient operations as well as forward integration to gain more control over product distribution. The firm, in effect, builds on its distinctive competence by expanding along the industry's value chain to gain greater competitive advantage.

Although backward integration is often more profitable than forward integration (because of typical low margins in retailing), it can reduce a corporation's strategic flexibility. The resulting encumbrance of expensive assets that might be hard to sell could create an exit barrier, preventing the corporation from leaving that particular industry. Examples of single-use assets are blast furnaces and breweries. When demand drops in either of these industries (steel or beer), these assets have no alternative use but continue to cost money in terms of debt payments, property taxes, and security expenses.

Transaction cost economics proposes that vertical integration is more efficient than contracting for goods and services in the marketplace when the transaction costs of buying goods on the open market become too great. When highly vertically integrated firms become excessively large and bureaucratic, however, the costs of managing the internal transactions may become greater than simply purchasing the needed goods externally—thus justifying outsourcing over vertical integration. This is why vertical integration and outsourcing are situation specific. Neither approach is best for all companies in all situations.[12] STRATEGY HIGHLIGHT **7.1** shows how transaction cost economics helps explain why firms vertically integrate or outsource important activities.

STRATEGY HIGHLIGHT 7.1

Transaction Cost Economics Analyzes Vertical Growth Strategy

Why do corporations use vertical growth to permanently own suppliers or distributors when they could simply purchase individual items when needed on the open market? Transaction cost economics is a branch of institutional economics that attempts to answer this question. Transaction cost economics proposes that owning resources through vertical growth is more efficient than contracting for goods and services in the marketplace when the transaction costs of buying goods on the open market become too great. Transaction costs include the basic costs of drafting, negotiating, and safeguarding a market agreement (a contract) as well as the later managerial costs when the agreement is creating problems (e.g., goods aren't being delivered on time or quality is lower than needed), renegotiation costs (e.g., costs of meetings and phone calls), and the costs of settling disputes (e.g., lawyers' fees and court costs).

According to Williamson, three conditions must be met before a corporation will prefer internalizing a vertical transaction through ownership over contracting for the transaction in the marketplace: (1) A high level of uncertainty must surround the transaction, (2) assets involved in the transaction must be highly specialized to the transaction, and (3) the transaction must occur frequently. If there is a high level of uncertainty, it will be impossible to write a contract covering all contingencies, and it is likely that the contractor will act opportunistically to exploit any gaps in the written agreement—thus creating problems and increasing costs. If the assets being contracted for are highly specialized (e.g., goods or services with few alter-

nate uses), there are likely to be few alternative suppliers—thus allowing the contractor to take advantage of the situation and increase costs. The more frequent the transactions, the more opportunity for the contractor to demand special treatment and thus increase costs further.

Vertical integration is not always more efficient than the marketplace, however. When highly vertically integrated firms become excessively large and bureaucratic, the costs of managing the internal transactions may become greater than simply purchasing the needed goods externally—thus justifying outsourcing over ownership. The usually hidden management costs (e.g., excessive layers of management, endless committee meetings needed for interdepartmental coordination, and delayed decision making due to excessively detailed rules and policies) add to the internal transaction costs—thus reducing the effectiveness and efficiency of vertical integration. The decision to own or to outsource is, therefore, based on the particular situation surrounding the transaction and the ability of the corporation to manage the transaction internally both effectively and efficiently.

Sources: O. E. Williamson and S. G. Winter, eds., *The Nature of the Firm: Origins, Evolution, and Development* (New York: Oxford University Press, 1991); E. Mosakowski, "Organizational Boundaries and Economic Performance: An Empirical Study of Entrepreneurial Computer Firms," *Strategic Management Journal* (February 1991), pp. 115–133; P. S. Ring and A. H. Van de Ven, "Structuring Cooperative Relationships Between Organizations," *Strategic Management Journal* (October 1992), pp. 483–498.

Harrigan proposes that a company's degree of vertical integration can range from total ownership of the value chain needed to make and sell a product to no ownership at all.[13] (See **Figure 7–2.**) Under **full integration**, a firm internally makes 100% of its key supplies and completely controls its distributors. Large oil companies, such as BP Amoco and Royal Dutch Shell, are fully integrated. They own the oil rigs that pump the oil out of the ground, the ships and pipelines that transport the oil, the refineries that convert the oil to gasoline, and the trucks that deliver the gasoline to company-owned and franchised gas stations. If a corporation does not want the disadvantages of full vertical integration, it may choose either taper or quasi-integration strategies.

With **taper integration**, a firm internally produces less than half of its own requirements and buys the rest from outside suppliers (backward taper integration). In the case of Smithfield

Figure 7–2
Vertical Integration Continuum

Full Integration	Taper Integration	Quasi-Integration	Long-Term Contract

Source: Suggested by K.R. Harrigan, Strategies for Vertical Integration *(Lexington, MA: Lexington Books, D.C. Heath, 1983), pp. 16–21. Reprinted by permission of Rowman & Littlefield Publishing Group.*

Foods, its purchase of Carroll's allows it to produce 27% of the hogs it needs to process into pork. In terms of forward taper integration, a firm may sell part of its goods through company-owned stores and the rest through general wholesalers. Although Apple Computer opened 25 company-owned stores in 2001, most of the company's sales continued to be through national chains such as CompUSA and Circuit City and through independent local and regional dealers specializing in Macs.[14]

With **quasi-integration**, a company does not make any of its key supplies but purchases most of its requirements from outside suppliers that are under its partial control (backward quasi-integration). For example, by purchasing 20% of the common stock of a key supplier, In Focus Systems, Motorola guaranteed its access to In Focus' technology, which enabled Motorola to establish a joint venture with In Focus to manufacture flat-panel video displays.[15] An example of forward quasi-integration would be a large pharmaceutical firm acquiring part interest in a drugstore chain in order to guarantee that its drugs have access to the distribution channel. Purchasing part interest in a key supplier or distributor usually provides a company with a seat on the other firm's board of directors, thus guaranteeing the acquiring firm both information and control. A company may not want to invest in suppliers or distributors, but it still wants to guarantee access to needed supplies or distribution channels. In this case, it may use contractual agreements.

Long-term contracts are agreements between two firms to provide agreed-upon goods and services to each other for a specified period of time. This cannot really be considered to be vertical integration unless it is an *exclusive* contract that specifies that the supplier or distributor cannot have a similar relationship with a competitive firm. In that case, the supplier or distributor is really a *captive company* that, although officially independent, does most of its business with the contracted firm and is formally tied to the other company through a long-term contract.

Recently there has been a movement away from vertical growth strategies (and thus vertical integration) toward cooperative contractual relationships with suppliers and even with competitors. These relationships range from **outsourcing**, in which resources are purchased from outsiders through long-term contracts instead of being made in-house (for example, Hewlett-Packard buys its laser engines from Canon for HP's laser jet printers), to strategic alliances, in which partnerships, technology licensing agreements, and joint ventures supplement a firm's capabilities (for example, Toshiba has used strategic alliances with GE, Siemens, Motorola, and Ericsson to become one of the world's leading electronic companies).[16]

Horizontal Growth. A firm can achieve **horizontal growth** by expanding its products into other geographic locations and/or by increasing the range of products and services it offers to current markets. In the latter case, the company expands sideways at the same location on the industry's value chain. One example is Blockbuster's 2004 bid for its rival in movie rentals, Hollywood Entertainment. In another example, General Motors followed a horizontal growth strategy when it extended its operations to China. After it launched Buick in China in 1999, it invested more than $2 billion into an expanded lineup of 14 cars, ranging from the Chevrolet Spark mini car to luxurious Cadillacs. Along with its Chinese partners, GM is investing an additional $3 billion to raise production, develop new engines, and expand R&D in Shanghai.[17] A company can grow horizontally through internal development or externally through acquisitions or strategic alliances with other firms in the same industry.

Horizontal growth results in **horizontal integration**—the degree to which a firm operates in multiple geographic locations at the same point on an industry's value chain. Horizontal integration for a firm may range from full to partial ownership to long-term contracts. For example, KLM, the Dutch airline, purchased a controlling stake (partial ownership) in Northwest Airlines to obtain access to American and Asian markets. KLM was unable to acquire all of Northwest's stock because of U.S. government regulations forbidding foreign ownership of a domestic airline (for defense reasons). Many small commuter airlines engage in long-term contracts with major airlines in order to offer a complete arrangement for travelers. For example, Mesa Airlines arranged a five-year agreement with United Airlines to be listed on United's computer reservations as United Express through the Denver airport.

Diversification Strategies

When an industry consolidates and becomes mature, most of the surviving firms have reached the limits of growth using vertical and horizontal growth strategies. Unless the competitors are able to expand internationally into less mature markets, they may have no choice but to diversify into different industries if they want to continue growing. The two basic diversification strategies are concentric and conglomerate.

Concentric (Related) Diversification. Growth through **concentric diversification** into a related industry may be a very appropriate corporate strategy when a firm has a strong competitive position but industry attractiveness is low. Research indicates that the probability of succeeding by moving into a related business is a function of a company's position in its core business. For companies in leadership positions, the chances for success are nearly three times higher than those for followers.[18] By focusing on the characteristics that have given the company its distinctive competence, the company uses those very strengths as its means of diversification. The firm attempts to secure strategic fit in a new industry where the firm's product knowledge, its manufacturing capabilities, and the marketing skills it used so effectively in the original industry can be put to good use.[19] The corporation's products or processes are related in some way: They possess some common thread.

The search is for **synergy**, the concept that two businesses will generate more profits together than they could separately. The point of commonality may be similar technology, customer usage, distribution, managerial skills, or product similarity. This is the rationale taken by Quebec-based Bombardier, the world's third-largest aircraft manufacturer. In the 1980s, the company expanded beyond snowmobiles into making light rail equipment. Defining itself as a transportation company, it entered the aircraft business in 1986, with its purchase of Canadair, then best known for its fire-fighting airplanes. It later bought Learjet, a well-known maker of business jets. Over a 14-year period, Bombardier launched 14 new aircraft. By 2004, the company was planning to build slightly larger versions of its successful 100-seat commuter jets to directly compete with Airbus and Boeing.[20]

A firm may choose to diversify concentrically through either internal or external means. Bombardier, for example, diversified externally through acquisitions. Toro, in contrast, grew internally in North America by using its current manufacturing processes and distributors to make and market snow blowers in addition to lawn mowers. For some criteria to use when considering concentric diversification alternatives, see STRATEGY HIGHLIGHT 7.2.

Conglomerate (Unrelated) Diversification. When management realizes that the current industry is unattractive and that the firm lacks outstanding abilities or skills that it could easily transfer to related products or services in other industries, the most likely strategy is **conglomerate diversification**—diversifying into an industry unrelated to its current one. Rather than maintaining a common thread throughout their organization, strategic managers who adopt this strategy are primarily concerned with financial considerations of cash flow or risk reduction. This is also a good strategy for a firm that is able to transfer its own excellent management system into less well-managed acquired firms. General Electric and Berkshire Hathaway are examples of companies that have used conglomerate diversification to grow successfully. Managed by Warren Buffet, Berkshire Hathaway has interests in furniture retailing, razor blades, airlines, paper, broadcasting, soft drinks, and publishing.[21]

STRATEGY HIGHLIGHT 7.2

Screening Criteria for Concentric Diversification

Market Attractiveness

1. Is the market large enough to be attractive?
2. Is the market growing faster than the economy?
3. Does it offer the potential to increase revenue from current customers?
4. Does it provide the ability to sell existing services to new customers?
5. Does it create a recurring revenue stream?
6. Are average earnings in the industry/market higher than in current businesses?
7. Is the market already taken by strong competitors?
8. Does it strengthen relationships with existing value-chain players?

Market Feasibility

1. Can the company enter the market within a year?
2. Are there any synergies in the geographic region where the market is located?
3. Can existing capabilities be leveraged for market entry?
4. Can existing assets be leveraged for market entry?
5. Can existing employees be used to support this opportunity?
6. Will current and future laws and regulations affect entry?
7. Is there a need for a strong brand in the new market?
8. If there is a need for partners, can the company secure and manage partner relationships?

Source: Summarized from N. J. Kaplan, "Surviving and Thriving When Your Customers Contract," *Journal of Business Strategy* (January/February 2003), p. 20. Republished with permission, Emerald Group Publishing Limited.

The emphasis in conglomerate diversification is on sound investment and value-oriented management rather than on the product–market synergy common to concentric diversification. A cash-rich company with few opportunities for growth in its industry might, for example, move into another industry where opportunities are great but cash is hard to find. Another instance of conglomerate diversification might be when a company with a seasonal and, therefore, uneven cash flow purchases a firm in an unrelated industry with complementing seasonal sales that will level out the cash flow. CSX management considered the purchase of a natural gas transmission business (Texas Gas Resources) by CSX Corporation (a railroad-dominated transportation company) to be a good fit because most of the gas transmission revenue was realized in the winter months—the lean period in the railroad business.

International Entry Options

In today's world, growth usually has international implications. Research indicates that going international is positively associated with firm profitability.[22] A corporation can select from several strategic options the most appropriate method to use in entering a foreign market or establishing manufacturing facilities in another country. The options vary from simple exporting to acquisitions to management contracts. As in the case of KLM's purchase of stock in Northwest Airlines, this can be a part of the corporate strategies previously discussed. See the GLOBAL ISSUE feature to see how Wal-Mart is using international entry options in a horizontal growth strategy to expand throughout the world. Some of the most popular options for international entry are as follows:

- **Exporting:** A good way to minimize risk and experiment with a specific product is **exporting**, shipping goods produced in the company's home country to other countries for marketing. The company could choose to handle all critical functions itself, or it could contract these functions to an export management company. Exporting is becoming

GL🌐BAL ISSUE

Wal-Mart Looks to International Markets for Growth

How can Wal-Mart continue to grow? From its humble beginnings in Bentonville, Arkansas, the company has successfully grown such that its discount stores can now be found in most every corner of the nation. Wal-Mart long ago surpassed Sears as the largest retailer in the United States. Eight out of ten U.S. households shop at Wal-Mart at least once a year. With $256 billion in annual sales, it is the world's biggest company. Its core domestic discount store business made up 65% of the firm's sales and 85% of its profits in 2004.

According to A. T. Kearney, Wal-Mart's three biggest sources of cost advantage were low corporate overhead, supply-chain efficiencies, and low labor costs. Increasing attempts to unionize Wal-Mart's workers, 8,000 employee lawsuits, and the need to reduce its employee turnover are likely to erode its labor cost advantage. (The company has to hire 600,000 employees every year just to stay at its current size.) The company's expanding human resources, public relations, and legal departments were adding to the firm's overhead costs and eroding its entrepreneurial culture. In addition, Wal-Mart had fewer locations left in the United States on which to build stores. These factors suggested that the company's domestic growth could not be sustained past 2007. Then what?

Wal-Mart's management realized that an increasing percentage of Wal-Mart's growth must come from international markets. Unfortunately, the company's first attempts to expand outside the country in the early 1990s flopped miserably. Wal-Mart offered the wrong products, such as tennis balls that wouldn't bounce in high-altitude Mexico City and 110-volt appliances in Argentina, where 220 volts is the norm. Learning from those early attempts, Wal-Mart opened stores in Canada, Mexico, China, Brazil, Japan, Germany, and Britain.

After closing a losing operation in Indonesia, management altered its strategy to focus on becoming a major retailer in Europe. In December 1997, Wal-Mart purchased the 21-store German Tertkauf chain. A year later, it strengthened its hold in Germany by acquiring 74 Interspar stores. It took months of remodeling the stores with wider aisles, better lighting, and more check-out counters before the stores were re-christened Wal-Mart. Unfortunately, Wal-Mart was unable to make these stores profitable; even by 2004. German price controls, rigid labor laws, and restrictive zoning regulations made it very difficult for Wal-Mart to compete with well-established rivals such as Metro and Aldi. Wal-Mart's expatriate managers suffered from culture-clash, which was not helped by their refusal to learn German. Hiring employees was difficult due to relatively low pay and a frugal policy on managers' business expenses.

Interestingly, Wal-Mart did better in the United Kingdom than in Germany. In 1999, it bought Britain's 229-store Asda Group, the country's third-largest grocery chain. Already a strong retailer, Wal-Mart's Asda soon overtook struggling J. Sainsbury to become the second-largest supermarket chain after Tesco in the UK.

Worldwide, more than 100 million customers visit Wal-Mart stores every week. Of its 4,906 total stores, in 2004, 1,375 (28%) were located outside the United States in nine countries (including 623 in Mexico and 34 in China). In 2004, Wal-Mart's management planned to open 50 new discount stores and more than 220 new supercenters in North America, plus around 140 stores overseas.

Sources: "How Big Can It Grow?" *Economist* (April 17, 2004), pp. 67–69; L. Kim, "Crossing the Rhine," *U.S. News & World Report* (August 14, 2000), p. 39; "Wal-Mart to Buy British Food Chain," *Des Moines Register* (June 15, 1999), p. 9S; P. Geitner, "Wal-Mart Rises in Germany," *Des Moines Register* (December 11, 1999), p. 12S; *Money* (December 1999), p. 162.

increasingly popular for small businesses because of the Internet, fax machines, toll-free numbers, and overnight express services, which reduce the once-formidable costs of going international.

- **Licensing:** Under a **licensing** agreement, the licensing firm grants rights to another firm in the host country to produce and/or sell a product. The licensee pays compensation to the licensing firm in return for technical expertise. This is an especially useful strategy if the trademark or brand name is well known but the company does not have sufficient funds to finance its entering the country directly. Anheuser-Busch uses this strategy to produce and market Budweiser beer in the United Kingdom, Japan, Israel, Australia, Korea, and the Philippines. This strategy is also important if the country makes entry via investment either difficult or impossible.

- **Franchising:** Under a **franchising** agreement, the franchiser grants rights to another company to open a retail store using the franchiser's name and operating system. In exchange, the franchisee pays the franchiser a percentage of its sales as a royalty. Franchising provides an opportunity for a firm to establish a presence in countries where the population or per capita spending is not sufficient for a major expansion effort.[23] Franchising accounts for 40% of total U.S. retail sales. Close to half of U.S. franchisers, such as Toys 'Я' Us, franchise internationally.[24]

- **Joint Ventures:** Forming a joint venture between a foreign corporation and a domestic company is the most popular strategy used to enter a new country.[25] Companies often form joint ventures to combine the resources and expertise needed to develop new products or technologies. A joint venture may also enable a firm to enter a country that restricts foreign ownership. The corporation can enter another country with fewer assets at stake and thus lower risk. For example, when Mexico privatized its railroads in 1996 (two years after the North American Free Trade Agreement was ratified), the Kansas City Southern (KCS) saw an opportunity to form one complete railroad from Mexico's industrialized northeast to Canada. KCS jointly bid with the Mexican shipping line Transportacion Maritima Mexicana (with which it would jointly operate the Mexican rail system) to purchase 80% of Grupo Transportacion Ferroviaria Mexicana (TFM). KCS then formed an alliance with Canadian National Railway to complete the route.[26] A joint venture may be an association between a company and a firm in the host country or a government agency in that country. A quick method of obtaining local management, it also reduces the risks of expropriation and harassment by host country officials.

- **Acquisitions:** A relatively quick way to move into an international area is through acquisitions—purchasing another company already operating in that area. Synergistic benefits can result if the company acquires a firm with strong complementary product lines and a good distribution network. For example, South Africa Breweries (SAB) paid $5.6 billion to purchase Miller Brewing from Philip Morris in 2002. With this acquisition, SAB became SABMiller and obtained a strong position in North America without having to build breweries and a distribution network. It also moved ahead of Anheuser-Busch as the world's second-largest brewer, after Belgium's Interbrew. SABMiller's next international strategic move was to bid for China's Harbin Brewery Group in 2004.[27] Research suggests that wholly owned subsidiaries are more successful in international undertakings than are strategic alliances, such as joint ventures.[28] This is one reason firms more experienced in international markets take a higher ownership position when making a foreign investment.[29] Cross-border acquisitions now account for 19% of all acquisitions in the United States—up from only 6% in 1985.[30] In some countries, however, acquisitions can be difficult to arrange because of a lack of available information about potential candidates. Government restrictions on ownership, such as the U.S. requirement that limits foreign ownership of U.S. airlines to 49% of nonvoting and 25% of voting stock, can also discourage acquisitions.

- **Green-Field Development:** If a company doesn't want to purchase another company's problems along with its assets, it may choose **green-field development**—building its own manufacturing plant and distribution system. Research indicates that firms possessing high levels of technology, multinational experience, and diverse product lines prefer greenfield development to acquisitions.[31] This is usually a far more complicated and expensive operation than acquisition, but it allows a company more freedom in designing the plant, choosing suppliers, and hiring a workforce. For example, Nissan, Honda, and Toyota built auto factories in rural areas of Great Britain and then hired a young workforce with no experience in the industry.

- **Production Sharing:** Coined by Peter Drucker, the term **production sharing** means the process of combining the higher labor skills and technology available in developed countries with the lower-cost labor available in developing countries. It is often called *outsourcing*. One example is Maytag's moving some of its refrigeration production to a new plant in Reynosa, Mexico, in order to reduce labor costs. A current trend is to move data processing and programming activities "offshore" to places such as Ireland, India, Barbados, Jamaica, the Philippines, and Singapore, where wages are lower, English is spoken, and telecommunications are in place.

- **Turnkey Operations: Turnkey operations** are typically contracts for the construction of operating facilities in exchange for a fee. The facilities are transferred to the host country or firm when they are complete. The customer is usually a government agency of, for example, a Middle Eastern country that has decreed that a particular product must be produced locally and under its control. For example, Fiat built an auto plant in Russia to produce an older model of Fiat under a Russian brand name. MNCs that perform turnkey operations are frequently industrial equipment manufacturers that supply some of their own equipment for the project and that commonly sell replacement parts and maintenance services to the host country. They thereby create customers as well as future competitors.

- **BOT Concept:** The **BOT (Build, Operate, Transfer) concept** is a variation of the turnkey operation. Instead of turning the facility (usually a power plant or toll road) over to the host country when completed, the company operates the facility for a fixed period of time, during which it earns back its investment plus a profit. It then turns the facility over to the government at little or no cost to the host country.[32]

- **Management Contracts:** A large corporation operating throughout the world is likely to have a large amount of management talent at its disposal. **Management contracts** offer a means through which a corporation can use some of its personnel to assist a firm in a host country for a specified fee and period of time. Management contracts are common when a host government expropriates part or all of a foreign-owned company's holdings in its country. The contracts allow the firm to continue to earn some income from its investment and keep the operations going until local management is trained.

Controversies in Directional Growth Strategies

Is vertical growth better than horizontal growth? Is concentric diversification better than conglomerate diversification? Although the research is not in complete agreement, growth into areas related to a company's current product lines is generally more successful than is growth into completely unrelated areas.[33] For example, one study of various growth projects examined how many were considered successful—that is, still in existence after 22 years. The results were vertical growth, 80%; horizontal growth, 50%; concentric diversification, 35%; and conglomerate diversification, 28%.[34]

In terms of diversification strategies, research suggests that the relationship between relatedness and performance is curvilinear, in the shape of an inverted U-shaped curve. If a new business is very similar to that of the acquiring firm, it adds little new to the corporation and only marginally improves performance. If the new business is completely different from the acquiring company's businesses, there may be very little potential for any synergy. If, however, the new business provides new resources and capabilities in a different, but similar, business, the likelihood of a significant performance improvement is high.[35]

Is internal growth better than external growth? Corporations can follow the growth strategies of either concentration or diversification through the internal development of new products and services, or through external acquisitions, mergers, and strategic alliances. The value of global acquisitions and mergers has steadily increased from less than $1 trillion in 1990 to

$3.5 trillion in 2000.[36] Research generally concludes, however, that firms growing through acquisitions do not perform financially as well as firms that grow through internal means.[37] For example, on September 3, 2001, the day *before* HP announced that it was purchasing Compaq, HP's stock was selling at $23.11. After the announcement, the stock price fell to $18.87. Three years later, on September 21, 2004, the shares sold at $18.70, down 19% from the first of the year.[38] One reason for this poor performance may be that acquiring firms tend to spend less on R&D than do other firms.[39] Another reason may be the typically high price of the acquisition itself. Studies reveal that over one-half to two-thirds of acquisitions are failures primarily because the premiums paid were too high for them to earn their cost of capital.[40] Another reason for the poor stock performance is that 50% of the customers of a merged firm are less satisfied with the combined company's service two years after the merger.[41] Other research indicates, however, that acquisitions have a higher survival rate than do new internally generated business ventures.[42] It is likely that neither strategy is best by itself and that some combination of internal and external growth strategies is better than using one or the other.[43]

What can improve acquisition performance? A study by Bain & Company of more than 11,000 acquisitions by companies throughout the world concluded that successful acquirers make small, low-risk acquisitions before moving on to larger ones.[44] Research by Porrini reveals that previous experience between an acquirer and a target firm in terms of R&D, manufacturing, or marketing alliances improves the likelihood of a successful acquisition.[45] Realizing that an acquired company must be carefully assimilated into the acquiring firm's operations, Cisco uses three criteria to judge whether a company is a suitable candidate for takeover:

- It must be relatively small.
- It must be comparable in organizational culture.
- It must be physically close to one of the existing affiliates.[46]

Stability Strategies

A corporation may choose stability over growth by continuing its current activities without any significant change in direction. Although sometimes viewed as a lack of strategy, the stability family of corporate strategies can be appropriate for a successful corporation operating in a reasonably predictable environment.[47] They are very popular with small business owners who have found a niche and are happy with their success and the manageable size of their firms. Stability strategies can be very useful in the short run, but they can be dangerous if followed for too long (as many small-town businesses discovered when Wal-Mart came to town). Some of the more popular of these strategies are the pause/proceed-with-caution, no-change, and profit strategies.

Pause/Proceed-with-Caution Strategy

A **pause/proceed-with-caution strategy** is, in effect, a timeout—an opportunity to rest before continuing a growth or retrenchment strategy. It is a very deliberate attempt to make only incremental improvements until a particular environmental situation changes. It is typically conceived as a temporary strategy to be used until the environment becomes more hospitable or to enable a company to consolidate its resources after prolonged rapid growth. This was the strategy Dell followed after its growth strategy had resulted in more growth than it could handle. Explained CEO Michael Dell, "We grew 285% in two years, and we're having some growing pains." Selling personal computers by mail enabled Dell to underprice Compaq and IBM, but it could not keep up with the needs of a $2 billion, 5,600-employee company selling PCs in 95 countries. Dell did not give up on its growth strategy; it merely put it temporarily in limbo until the company was able to hire new managers, improve the structure, and build new facilities.[48]

No-Change Strategy

A **no-change strategy** is a decision to do nothing new—a choice to continue current operations and policies for the foreseeable future. Rarely articulated as a definite strategy, a no-change strategy's success depends on a lack of significant change in a corporation's situation. The relative stability created by the firm's modest competitive position in an industry facing little or no growth encourages the company to continue on its current course, making only small adjustments for inflation in its sales and profit objectives. There are no obvious opportunities or threats, nor is there much in the way of significant strengths or weaknesses. Few aggressive new competitors are likely to enter such an industry. The corporation has probably found a reasonably profitable and stable niche for its products. Unless the industry is undergoing consolidation, the relative comfort a company in this situation experiences is likely to encourage the company to follow a no-change strategy in which the future is expected to continue as an extension of the present. Most small-town businesses probably follow this strategy before Wal-Mart moves into their areas.

Profit Strategy

A **profit strategy** is a decision to do nothing new in a worsening situation but instead to act as though the company's problems are only temporary. The profit strategy is an attempt to artificially support profits when a company's sales are declining by reducing investment and short-term discretionary expenditures. Rather than announce the company's poor position to shareholders and the investment community at large, top management may be tempted to follow this very seductive strategy. Blaming the company's problems on a hostile environment (such as anti-business government policies, unethical competitors, finicky customers, and/or greedy lenders), management defers investments and/or cuts expenses (such as R&D, maintenance, and advertising) to stabilize profits during this period. It may even sell one of its product lines for the cash-flow benefits. For example, Kmart sold some of its retail stores to Home Depot and Sears at a time when its store sales were declining. Obviously, the profit strategy is useful only to help a company get through a temporary difficulty. It may also be a way to boost the value of a company in preparation for going public via an initial public offering (IPO). Unfortunately, the strategy is seductive, and if continued long enough, it will lead to a serious deterioration in a corporation's competitive position. The profit strategy thus tends to be top management's passive, short-term, and often self-serving response to a difficult situation.

Retrenchment Strategies

A company may pursue retrenchment strategies when it has a weak competitive position in some or all of its product lines, resulting in poor performance—sales are down and profits are becoming losses. These strategies impose a great deal of pressure to improve performance. In an attempt to eliminate the weaknesses that are dragging the company down, management may follow one of several retrenchment strategies, ranging from turnaround or becoming a captive company to selling out, bankruptcy, or liquidation.

Turnaround Strategy

Turnaround strategy emphasizes the improvement of operational efficiency and is probably most appropriate when a corporation's problems are pervasive but not yet critical. Research shows that poorly performing firms in mature industries have been able to improve their performance by cutting costs and expenses and by selling assets.[49] Analogous to a weight-reduction diet, the two basic phases of a turnaround strategy are contraction and consolidation.[50]

Contraction is the initial effort to quickly "stop the bleeding" with a general, across-the-board cutback in size and costs. The second phase, **consolidation**, implements a program to stabilize the now-leaner corporation. To streamline the company, plans are developed to reduce unnecessary overhead and to make functional activities cost-justified. This is a crucial time for the organization. If the consolidation phase is not conducted in a positive manner, many of the best people leave the organization. An overemphasis on downsizing and cutting costs coupled with a heavy hand by top management is usually counterproductive and can actually hurt performance.[51] If, however, all employees are encouraged to get involved in productivity improvements, the firm is likely to emerge from this retrenchment period a much stronger and better-organized company. It has improved its competitive position and is able once again to expand the business.[52] See **STRATEGY HIGHLIGHT 7.3** for a description of IBM's effective use of the turnaround strategy.

Captive Company Strategy

A **captive company strategy** involves giving up independence in exchange for security. A company with a weak competitive position may not be able to engage in a full-blown turnaround strategy. The industry may not be sufficiently attractive to justify such an effort from either the current management or investors. Nevertheless, a company in this situation faces poor sales and increasing losses unless it takes some action. Management desperately searches for an "angel" by offering to be a captive company to one of its larger customers in

STRATEGY HIGHLIGHT 7.3

Turnaround Strategy at IBM

During the 1970s and 1980s, IBM dominated the computer industry worldwide. It was the market leader in both large mainframe and small personal computers (PCs). Along with Apple Computer, IBM set the standard for all PCs. Even until recently—when IBM no longer dominates the field—PCs are still identified as being either Apple or IBM-style PCs.

IBM's problems came to a head in the early 1990s. The company's computer sales were falling. More companies were choosing to replace their large, expensive mainframe computers with PCs, but they weren't buying the PCs from IBM. An increasing number of firms, such as HP, Dell, Gateway, and Compaq, had entered the industry. They offered IBM-style PC "clones" that were considerably cheaper and often more advanced than IBM's PCs. IBM's falling revenues meant corporate losses—$15 billion in cumulative losses from 1991 through 1993. Industry experts perceived the company as a bureaucratic dinosaur that could no longer adapt to changing conditions. Its stock price fell to $40, with no end in sight.

IBM's board of directors in 1993 hired a new CEO, Louis Gerstner, to lead a corporate turnaround strategy at "Big Blue" (the nickname IBM had earned because of its rigid dress code policies). To stop the flow of red ink, the company violated its long-held "no layoffs" policy by reducing its workforce by 40%. Under Gerstner, IBM reorganized its sales force around specific industries, such as retailing and banking. Decision making was made easier. Previously, according to Joseph Formichelli, a top executive with the PC division, he had "had to go through seven layers to get things done." Firing incompetent employees could take a year, "so you pawned them off on another group." Strategy presentations were hashed over so many times, "they got watered down to nothing." Under Gerstner, however, formal presentations were no longer desired. The emphasis switched to quicker decision making and a stronger customer orientation.

From 1994 to 2000, the company transformed itself from being a besieged computer maker to a dominant service provider. Its Global Services unit grew from almost nothing to a $30 billion business with more than 135,000 employees. In 2004, it divested its PC business.

Source: G. Hamel, "Waking Up IBM," *Harvard Business Review* (July–August 2000), pp. 137–146; I. Sager, "Inside IBM: Internet Business Machines," *Business Week E.Biz* (December 13, 1999), pp. EB20–EB40; B. Ziegler, "Gerstner's IBM Revival: Impressive, Incomplete," *Wall Street Journal* (March 25, 1997), pp. B1, B4.

order to guarantee the company's continued existence with a long-term contract. In this way, the corporation may be able to reduce the scope of some of its functional activities, such as marketing, thus significantly reducing costs. The weaker company gains certainty of sales and production in return for becoming heavily dependent on another firm for at least 75% of its sales. For example, to become the sole supplier of an auto part to General Motors, Simpson Industries of Birmingham, Michigan, agreed to let a special team from GM inspect its engine parts facilities and books and interview its employees. In return, nearly 80% of the company's production was sold to GM through long-term contracts.[53]

Sell-Out/Divestment Strategy

If a corporation with a weak competitive position in an industry is unable either to pull itself up by its bootstraps or to find a customer to which it can become a captive company, it may have no choice but to sell out. The **sell-out strategy** makes sense if management can still obtain a good price for its shareholders and the employees can keep their jobs by selling the entire company to another firm. The hope is that another company will have the necessary resources and determination to return the company to profitability.

If the corporation has multiple business lines and it chooses to sell off a division with low growth potential, this is called **divestment**. This was the strategy Quaker Oats used when it sold its struggling Snapple beverage unit for $300 million—$1.4 billion less than it had paid for the business. When Quaker's management had purchased Snapple, they believed that they could use Quaker's resources to continue Snapple's phenomenal growth. They had hoped to transform the stately old oatmeal company into a soft-drink power. Unfortunately for Quaker, the soft drink market was changing rapidly. New entrants, such as Arizona Iced Tea, Mystic, and Nantucket Nectars, imitated Snapple, while Coke and Pepsi formed alliances with Nestea and Lipton to enter the market.[54]

Bankruptcy/Liquidation Strategy

When a company finds itself in the worst possible situation, with a poor competitive position in an industry with few prospects, management has only a few alternatives—all of them distasteful. Because no one is interested in buying a weak company in an unattractive industry, the firm must pursue a bankruptcy or liquidation strategy. **Bankruptcy** involves giving up management of the firm to the courts in return for some settlement of the corporation's obligations. Top management hopes that once the court decides the claims on the company, the company will be stronger and better able to compete in a more attractive industry. Faced with high debt and declining sales of its Wonder Bread, Twinkies, and Hostess Cup Cakes, Interstate Bakeries declared Chapter 11 bankruptcy in 2004. Because the company had been unable to reduce its high overhead costs, its products were no longer cost-competitive. A new CEO was appointed to do what Interstate's management had been unable to do: slash labor and manufacturing costs while boosting distribution to Wal-Mart and other discount retailers.[55]

In contrast to bankruptcy, which seeks to perpetuate a corporation, **liquidation** is the termination of a firm. When the industry is unattractive and the company is too weak to be sold as a going concern, management may choose to convert as many saleable assets as possible to cash, which is then distributed to the shareholders after all obligations are paid. Liquidation is a prudent strategy for distressed firms with a small number of choices, all of which are problematic.[56] The benefit of liquidation over bankruptcy is that the board of directors, as representatives of the shareholders, together with top management make the decisions instead of turning them over to the bankruptcy court, which may choose to ignore shareholders completely.

At times, top management must be willing to select one of these less desirable retrenchment strategies. Unfortunately, many top managers are unwilling to admit that their company has serious weaknesses for fear that they may be personally blamed. Even worse, top management may not even perceive that crises are developing. When these top managers eventually notice trouble, they are prone to attribute the problems to temporary environmental disturbances and tend to follow profit strategies. Even when things are going terribly wrong, top management is greatly tempted to avoid liquidation in the hope of a miracle. Top management enters a *cycle of decline*, in which it goes through a process of secrecy and denial, followed by blame and scorn, avoidance and turf protection, ending with passivity and helplessness.[57] Thus, a corporation needs a strong board of directors who, to safeguard shareholders' interests, can tell top management when to quit.

7.3 | Portfolio Analysis

Chapter 6 deals with how individual product lines and business units can gain competitive advantage in the marketplace by using competitive and cooperative strategies. Companies with multiple product lines or business units must also ask themselves how these various products and business units should be managed to boost overall corporate performance:

- How much of our time and money should we spend on our best products and business units to ensure that they continue to be successful?

- How much of our time and money should we spend developing new costly products, most of which will never be successful?

One of the most popular aids to developing corporate strategy in a multiple-business corporation is portfolio analysis. Although its popularity has dropped since the 1970s and 1980s, when more than half of the largest business corporations used portfolio analysis, it is still used by around 27% of Fortune 500 firms in corporate strategy formulation.[58] Portfolio analysis puts the corporate headquarters into the role of an internal banker. In **portfolio analysis**, top management views its product lines and business units as a series of investments from which it expects a profitable return. The product lines/business units form a portfolio of investments that top management must constantly juggle to ensure the best return on the corporation's invested money. A McKinsey & Company study of the performance of the 200 largest U.S. corporations found that companies that actively managed their business portfolios through acquisitions and divestitures created substantially more shareholder value than companies that passively held their businesses.[59]

Two of the most popular portfolio approaches are the BCG Growth-Share Matrix and GE Business Screen.

BCG Growth-Share Matrix

Using the **BCG (Boston Consulting Group) Growth-Share Matrix**, depicted in **Figure 7–3**, is the simplest way to portray a corporation's portfolio of investments. Each of a corporation's product lines or business units is plotted on a matrix according to both the growth rate of the industry in which it competes and its relative market share. A unit's relative competitive position is defined as its market share in the industry divided by that of the largest other competitor. By this calculation, a relative market share above 1.0 belongs to the market leader. The business growth rate is the percentage of market growth—that is, the percentage by which sales of a particular business unit classification of products have increased. The matrix assumes that, other things being equal, a growing market is attractive.

The line separating areas of high and low relative competitive position is set at 1.5 times. A product line or business unit must have relative strengths of this magnitude to ensure that it

Figure 7–3
BCG Growth-Share Matrix

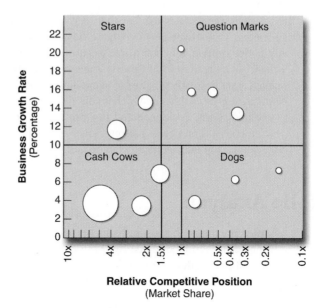

Source: Reprinted from Long Range Planning, *Vol. 10, No. 2, 1977, Hedley, "Strategy and the Business Portfolio," p. 12. Copyright © 1977 with permission from Elsevier.*

will have the dominant position needed to be a "star" or "cash cow." On the other hand, a product line or unit having a relative competitive position less than 1.0 has "dog" status.[60] Each product or unit is represented in **Figure 7–3** by a circle. The area of the circle represents the relative significance of each business unit or product line to the corporation in terms of assets used or sales generated.

The BCG Growth-Share Matrix has a lot in common with the product life cycle. As a product moves through its life cycle, it is categorized into one of four types for the purpose of funding decisions:

- **Question marks** (sometimes called "problem children" or "wildcats") are new products with the potential for success, but they need a lot of cash for development. If such a product is to gain enough market share to become a market leader and thus a star, money must be taken from more mature products and spent on the question mark.

- **Stars** are market leaders that are typically at the peak of their product life cycle and are usually able to generate enough cash to maintain their high share of the market. When their market growth rate slows, stars become cash cows. HP's printer business has been called HP's "crown jewel" by CEO Carleton Fiorina because in 2002 it provided 105% of HP's profits (other units lost money) while accounting for only 28% of HP's sales.[61]

- **Cash cows** typically bring in far more money than is needed to maintain their market share. In this declining stage of their life cycle, these products are "milked" for cash that will be invested in new question marks. Question marks unable to obtain dominant market share (and thus become stars) by the time the industry growth rate inevitably slows become dogs.

- **Dogs** have low market share and do not have the potential (because they are in an unattractive industry) to bring in much cash. According to the BCG Growth-Share Matrix, dogs should be either sold off or managed carefully for the small amount of cash they can generate. For example, DuPont, the inventor of nylon, sold its textiles unit in 2003 because the company wanted to eliminate its low-margin products and focus more on its growing biotech business.[62]

Underlying the BCG Growth-Share Matrix is the concept of the experience curve (discussed in **Chapter 5**). The key to success is assumed to be market share. Firms with the highest market share tend to have a cost leadership position based on economies of scale, among other things. If a company is able to use the experience curve to its advantage, it should be able to manufacture and sell new products at a price low enough to garner early market share leadership (assuming no successful imitation by competitors). Once the product becomes a star, it is destined to be very profitable, considering its inevitable future as a cash cow.

Having plotted the current positions of its product lines or business units on a matrix, a company can project its future positions, assuming no change in strategy. Present and projected matrixes can thus be used to help identify major strategic issues facing the organization. The goal of any company is to maintain a balanced portfolio so it can be self-sufficient in cash and always working to harvest mature products in declining industries to support new ones in growing industries.

The BCG Growth-Share Matrix is a very well-known portfolio concept with some clear advantages. It is quantifiable and easy to use. *Cash cow*, *dog*, and *star* are easy-to-remember terms for referring to a corporation's business units or products. Unfortunately, the BCG Growth-Share Matrix also has some serious limitations:

■ The use of highs and lows to form four categories is too simplistic.

■ The link between market share and profitability is questionable.[63] Low-share businesses can also be profitable.[64] For example, Olivetti is still profitably selling manual typewriters through mail-order catalogs.

■ Growth rate is only one aspect of industry attractiveness.

■ Product lines or business units are considered only in relation to one competitor: the market leader. Small competitors with fast-growing market shares are ignored.

■ Market share is only one aspect of overall competitive position.

GE Business Screen

General Electric, with the assistance of the McKinsey & Company consulting firm, developed a more complicated matrix. As depicted in **Figure 7–4**, the **GE Business Screen** includes nine cells based on long-term industry attractiveness and business strength/competitive position. The GE Business Screen, in contrast to the BCG Growth-Share Matrix, includes much more data in its two key factors than just business growth rate and comparable market share. For example, at GE, industry attractiveness includes market growth rate, industry profitability, size, and pricing practices, among other possible opportunities and threats. Business strength or competitive position includes market share as well as technological position, profitability, and size, among other possible strengths and weaknesses.[65]

The individual product lines or business units are identified by a letter and plotted as circles on the GE Business Screen. The area of each circle is in proportion to the size of the industry in terms of sales. The pie slices within the circles depict the market shares of the product lines or business units.

To plot product lines or business units on the GE Business Screen, follow these four steps:

1. Select criteria to rate the industry for each product line or business unit. Assess overall industry attractiveness for each product line or business unit on a scale from 1 (very unattractive) to 5 (very attractive).

2. Select the key factors needed for success in each product line or business unit. Assess business strength/competitive position for each product line or business unit on a scale of 1 (very weak) to 5 (very strong).

Figure 7–4
General Electric's Business Screen

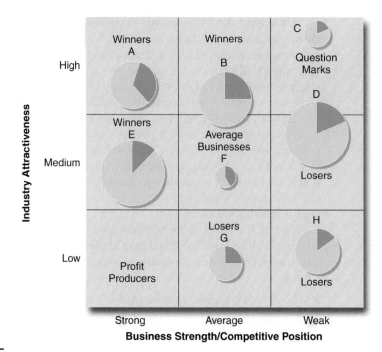

Figure 7–4
General Electric's Business Screen

Source: Adapted from Strategic Management in GE, *Corporate Planning and Development, General Electric Corporation. Reprinted by permission of General Electric Company.*

3. Plot each product line's or business unit's current position on a matrix like that depicted in **Figure 7–4**.

4. Plot the firm's future portfolio, assuming that present corporate and business strategies remain unchanged. Is there a performance gap between projected and desired portfolios? If so, this gap should serve as a stimulus to seriously review the corporation's current mission, objectives, strategies, and policies.

Overall the nine-cell GE Business Screen is an improvement over the BCG Growth-Share Matrix. The GE Business Screen considers many more variables and does not lead to such simplistic conclusions. It recognizes, for example, that the attractiveness of an industry can be assessed in many different ways (other than simply using growth rate), and it thus allows users to select whatever criteria they feel are most appropriate to their situation. This portfolio matrix, however, does have some shortcomings:

- It can get quite complicated and cumbersome.
- The numerical estimates of industry attractiveness and business strength/competitive position give the appearance of objectivity, but they are in reality subjective judgments that may vary from one person to another.
- It cannot effectively depict the positions of new products or business units in developing industries.

Advantages and Limitations of Portfolio Analysis

Portfolio analysis is commonly used in strategy formulation because it offers certain *advantages*:

- It encourages top management to evaluate each of the corporation's businesses individually and to set objectives and allocate resources for each.
- It stimulates the use of externally oriented data to supplement management's judgment.

- It raises the issue of cash-flow availability for use in expansion and growth.

- Its graphic depiction facilitates communication.

Portfolio analysis does, however, have some very real *limitations* that have caused some companies to reduce their use of this approach:

- Defining product/market segments is difficult.

- It suggests the use of standard strategies that can miss opportunities or be impractical.

- It provides an illusion of scientific rigor when in reality positions are based on subjective judgments.

- Its value-laden terms, such as cash cow and dog, can lead to self-fulfilling prophecies.

- It is not always clear what makes an industry attractive or where a product is in its life cycle.

- Naively following the prescriptions of a portfolio model may actually reduce corporate profits if they are used inappropriately. For example, General Mills' Chief Executive H. Brewster Atwater cited his company's Bisquick brand baking mix as a product that would have been written off years ago based on portfolio analysis. "This product is 57 years old. By all rights it should have been overtaken by newer products. But with the proper research to improve the product and promotion to keep customers excited, it's doing very well."[66]

7.4 | Corporate Parenting

Campbell, Goold, and Alexander, authors of *Corporate-Level Strategy: Creating Value in the Multibusiness Company*, contend that corporate strategists must address two crucial questions:

- What businesses should this company own and why?

- What organizational structure, management processes, and philosophy will foster superior performance from the company's business units?[67]

Portfolio analysis attempts to answer these questions by examining the attractiveness of various industries and by managing business units for cash flow—that is, by using cash generated from mature units to build new product lines. Unfortunately, portfolio analysis fails to deal with the question of what industries a corporation should enter or with how a corporation can attain synergy among its product lines and business units. As suggested by its name, portfolio analysis tends to primarily view matters financially, regarding business units and product lines as separate and independent investments.

Corporate parenting, in contrast, views a corporation in terms of resources and capabilities that can be used to build business unit value as well as generate synergies across business units. According to Campbell, Goold, and Alexander:

> *Multibusiness companies create value by influencing—or parenting—the businesses they own. The best parent companies create more value than any of their rivals would if they owned the same businesses. Those companies have what we call parenting advantage.*[68]

Corporate parenting generates corporate strategy by focusing on the core competencies of the parent corporation and on the value created from the relationship between the parent and its businesses. In the form of corporate headquarters, the parent has a great deal of power in this relationship. According to Campbell, Goold, and Alexander, if there is a good fit between the parent's skills and resources and the needs and opportunities of the business units, the corporation is likely to create value. If, however, there is not a good fit, the corporation is likely to destroy value.[69] Research indicates that companies that have a good fit between their strategy and their parenting roles are better performers than companies that do not have a good fit.[70] This approach to corporate strategy is useful not only in deciding what new businesses to acquire but also in choosing how each existing business unit should be best managed. This appears to be the secret to the success of General Electric under CEO Jack Welch. According to one analyst, "He and his managers really add value by imposing tough standards of profitability and by disseminating knowledge and best practice quickly around the GE empire. If some manufacturing trick cuts costs in GE's aero-engine repair shops in Wales, he insists it be applied across the group."[71]

The primary job of corporate headquarters is, therefore, to obtain synergy among the business units by providing needed resources to units, transferring skills and capabilities among the units, and coordinating the activities of shared unit functions to attain economies of scope (as in centralized purchasing).[72] This is in agreement with the concept of the learning organization discussed in **Chapter 1** in which the role of a large firm is to facilitate and transfer the knowledge assets and services throughout the corporation.[73] This is especially important given that 75% or more of a modern company's market value stems from its intangible assets—the organization's knowledge and capabilities.[74]

Developing a Corporate Parenting Strategy

Campbell, Goold, and Alexander recommend that the search for appropriate corporate strategy involves three analytical steps:

1. **Examine each business unit (or target firm, in the case of acquisition) in terms of its strategic factors:** People in the business units probably identified strategic factors when they were generating business strategies for their units. One popular approach is to establish centers of excellence throughout a corporation. According to Frost, Birkinshaw, and Ensign, a **center of excellence** is "an organizational unit that embodies a set of capabilities that has been explicitly recognized by the firm as an important source of value creation, with the intention that these capabilities be leveraged by and/or disseminated to other parts of the firm."[75]

2. **Examine each business unit (or target firm) in terms of areas in which performance can be improved:** These are considered to be parenting opportunities. For example, two business units might be able to gain economies of scope by combining their sales forces. In another instance, a unit may have good, but not great, manufacturing and logistics skills. A parent company having world-class expertise in these areas could improve that unit's performance. The corporate parent could also transfer some people from one business unit who have the desired skills to another unit that is in need of those skills. People at corporate headquarters may, because of their experience in many industries, spot areas where improvements are possible that even people in the business unit may not have noticed. Unless specific areas are significantly weaker than the competition, people in the business units may not even be aware that these areas could be improved, especially if each business unit monitors only its own particular industry.

3. **Analyze how well the parent corporation fits with the business unit (or target firm):** Corporate headquarters must be aware of its own strengths and weaknesses in terms of resources, skills, and capabilities. To do this, the corporate parent must ask whether it has the characteristics that fit the parenting opportunities in each business unit. It must also ask whether there is a misfit between the parent's characteristics and the strategic factors of each business unit.

Horizontal Strategy and Multipoint Competition

A **horizontal strategy** is a corporate strategy that cuts across business unit boundaries to build synergy across business units and to improve the competitive position of one or more business units.[76] When used to build synergy, it acts like a parenting strategy. When used to improve the competitive position of one or more business units, it can be thought of as a corporate competitive strategy. In **multipoint competition**, large multi-business corporations compete against other large multi-business firms in a number of markets. These multipoint competitors are firms that compete with each other not only in one business unit but in a number of business units. At one time or another, a cash-rich competitor may choose to build its own market share in a particular market, to the disadvantage of another corporation's business unit. Although each business unit has primary responsibility for its own business strategy, it may sometimes need some help from its corporate parent, especially if the competitor business unit is getting heavy financial support from its corporate parent. In such an instance, corporate headquarters develops a horizontal strategy to coordinate the various goals and strategies of related business units.

For example, P&G, Kimberly-Clark, Scott Paper, and Johnson & Johnson (J&J) compete with one another in varying combinations of consumer paper products, from disposable diapers to facial tissue. If (purely hypothetically) J&J just developed a toilet tissue with which it chose to challenge P&G's high-share Charmin brand in a particular district, it might charge a low price for its new brand to build sales quickly. P&G might not choose to respond to this attack on its share by cutting prices on Charmin. Because of Charmin's high market share, P&G would lose significantly more sales dollars in a price war than J&J would with its initially low-share brand. To retaliate, P&G might thus challenge J&J's high-share baby shampoo with P&G's own low-share brand of baby shampoo in a different district. Once J&J had perceived P&G's response, it might choose to stop challenging Charmin so that P&G would stop challenging J&J's baby shampoo.

Multipoint competition and the resulting use of horizontal strategy may actually slow the development of hypercompetition in an industry. The realization that an attack on a market leader's position could result in a response in another market leads to mutual forbearance in which managers behave more conservatively toward multimarket rivals and competitive rivalry is reduced.[77] In one industry, for example, multipoint competition resulted in firms being less likely to exit a market. "Live and let live" replaced strong competitive rivalry.[78] Multipoint competition is likely to become even more prevalent in the future, as corporations become global competitors and expand into more markets through strategic alliances.[79]

7.5 | Conclusion

Corporate strategy is primarily about the choice of direction for the firm as a whole. It deals with three key issues that a corporation faces: (1) the firm's overall orientation toward growth, stability, or retrenchment; (2) the industries or markets in which the firm competes through its products and business units; and (3) the manner in which management coordinates activities and transfers resources and cultivates capabilities among product lines and business units. These issues are dealt with through directional strategy, portfolio analysis, and corporate parenting.

One impact of the growth of computers and the Internet is that corporations are rethinking what industries they should be in. For example, Emerson Electric, the 110-year-old St. Louis manufacturer of electric motors, refrigeration components, and industrial tools, recently positioned itself in power backup systems for computers. Realizing that the growth potential of its traditional product lines was limited, Emerson's management decided to move into a more attractive industry. With the power grid reaching its capacity, electrical outages are expected to become more commonplace in the United States as the economy expands. First, the company purchased Jordan Industries Inc.'s telecommunications-products business. Emerson then bought the power supply division of Swedish phone maker Ericsson.

Emerson's acquisitions meant that the company could provide reliable power backup capability for its customers. When the power goes out, Emerson's components act to switch the power from one source to another and regulate the voltage. Emerson provides the generators and fuel cells to generate the temporary electricity. These products have become crucial for any company that relies on the Internet for conducting business. Intira Corp., a St. Louis web-hosting company, suffered a seven-hour outage due to a malfunctioning transformer, but it was able to stay online thanks to Emerson equipment. According to John Steensen, Intira's chief technology officer, "All of our affected customers would have gotten a month of free service if we had gone down, costing us hundreds of thousands of dollars." The acquisitions significantly increased Emerson's sales and made the power unit the largest and fastest-growing of Emerson's five SBUs. Cisco Systems, MCI, and Intel are Emerson customers. Emerson's management is estimating that its high-tech power-systems business will grow at 15% to 20% annually for the foreseeable future.[80]

Strategy Bits

- The least corrupt countries in the world are Finland, New Zealand, Denmark, Iceland, Singapore, and Sweden.[81]

- The most corrupt countries in the world are Angola, Democratic Republic of Congo, Ivory Coast, Georgia, Indonesia, and Tajikistan.[82]

Discussion Questions

1. How does horizontal growth differ from vertical growth as a corporate strategy? from concentric diversification?

2. What are the tradeoffs between an internal and an external growth strategy? Which approach is best as an international entry strategy?

3. Is stability really a strategy or just a term for no strategy?

4. Compare and contrast SWOT analysis with portfolio analysis.

5. How is corporate parenting different from portfolio analysis? How is it alike? Is it a useful concept in a global industry?

Strategic Practice Exercise

On March 14, 2000, Stephen King, the horror writer, published his new book, *Riding the Bullet*, on the Internet before it appeared in print. Within 24 hours, around 400,000 people had downloaded the book—even though most of them needed to download software in order to read the book. The unexpected demand crashed servers. According to Jack Romanos, president of Simon & Schuster, "I don't think anybody could have anticipated how many people were out there who are willing to accept the written word in a paperless format." To many, this announced the coming of the electronic novel. Environmentalists applauded that e-books would soon replace paper books and newspapers, thus reducing pollution coming from paper mills and landfills. The King book was easy to download, and the download took less time than a trip to the bookstore. Critics argued that the King book used the Internet because at 66 pages, it was too short to be a standard printed novel. It was also free, so there was nothing to discourage natural curiosity. Some people in the industry estimated that 75% of those who downloaded the book did not read it.[83]

1. Form into small groups in the class to discuss the future of Internet publishing.

2. Consider the following questions as discussion guides:

   ■ What are the pros and cons of electronic publishing?

   ■ Should newspaper and book publishers convert to electronic publishing over paper? (The *Wall Street Journal* and others publish in both paper and electronic formats. Is this a success?)

   ■ Would you prefer this textbook and others in an electronic format?

   ■ What business model should publishers use to make money publishing on the Internet?

3. Present your group's conclusions to the class.

Key Terms

acquisition (p. 166)

backward integration (p. 167)

bankruptcy (p. 178)

BCG (Boston Consulting Group) Growth-Share Matrix (p. 179)

BOT (Build, Operate, Transfer) concept (p. 174)

captive company strategy (p. 177)

cash cow (p. 180)

center of excellence (p. 184)

concentration (p. 166)

concentric diversification (p. 170)

conglomerate diversification (p. 170)

consolidation (p. 177)

contraction (p. 177)

corporate parenting (p. 183)

corporate strategy (p. 164)

directional strategy (p. 165)

diversification (p. 166)

divestment (p. 178)

dog (p. 180)

exporting (p. 171)

forward integration (p. 167)

franchising (p. 173)

full integration (p. 168)

GE business screen (p. 181)

green-field development (p. 173)

growth strategy (p. 165)

horizontal growth (p. 169)

horizontal integration (p. 169)

horizontal strategy (p. 185)

licensing (p. 172)

liquidation (p. 178)

long-term contract (p. 169)

management contract (p. 174)

merger (p. 166)

multipoint competition (p. 185)

no-change strategy (p. 176)

organization slack (p. 166)

outsourcing (p. 169)

pause/proceed-with-caution strategy (p. 175)

portfolio analysis (p. 179)

production sharing (p. 174)

profit strategy (p. 176)

quasi-integration (p. 169)

question mark (p. 180)

retrenchment strategy (p. 165)

sell-out strategy (p. 178)

stability strategy (p. 165)

star (p. 180)

synergy (p. 170)

taper integration (p. 168)

transaction cost economics (p. 167)

turnaround strategy (p. 176)

turnkey operation (p. 174)

vertical growth (p. 167)

vertical integration (p. 167)

CHAPTER 8
Strategy Formulation: Functional Strategy and Strategic Choice

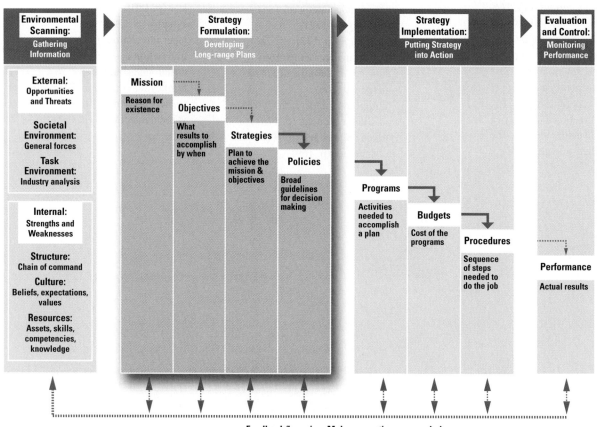

Environmental Scanning: Gathering Information	Strategy Formulation: Developing Long-range Plans	Strategy Implementation: Putting Strategy into Action	Evaluation and Control: Monitoring Performance
External: Opportunities and Threats	**Mission** Reason for existence		
Societal Environment: General forces	**Objectives** What results to accomplish by when		
Task Environment: Industry analysis	**Strategies** Plan to achieve the mission & objectives		
Internal: Strengths and Weaknesses	**Policies** Broad guidelines for decision making	**Programs** Activities needed to accomplish a plan	
Structure: Chain of command		**Budgets** Cost of the programs	
Culture: Beliefs, expectations, values		**Procedures** Sequence of steps needed to do the job	**Performance** Actual results
Resources: Assets, skills, competencies, knowledge			

Feedback/Learning: Make corrections as needed

Learning Objectives

After reading this chapter, you should be able to:

- Identify a variety of functional strategies that can be used to achieve organizational goals and objectives
- Understand what activities and functions are appropriate to outsource in order to gain or strengthen competitive advantage
- Recognize strategies to avoid and understand why they are dangerous
- Construct corporate scenarios to evaluate strategic options
- Use a stakeholder priority matrix to aid in strategic decision making
- Develop policies to implement corporate, business, and functional strategies

FOR ALMOST 150 YEARS, THE CHURCH & DWIGHT COMPANY HAS BEEN BUILDING MARKET share on a brand name whose products are in 95% of all U.S. households. Yet if you asked the average person what products this company makes, few would know. Although Church & Dwight may not be a household name, the company's ubiquitous orange box of Arm & Hammer[1] brand baking soda is common throughout North America. Church & Dwight provides a classic example of a marketing functional strategy called *product development*. Shortly after its introduction in 1878, Arm & Hammer Baking Soda became a fundamental item on the pantry shelf as people found many uses for sodium bicarbonate other than baking, such as cleaning, deodorizing, and tooth brushing. Hearing of the many uses people were finding for its product, the company advertised that its baking soda was good not only for baking but also for deodorizing refrigerators—simply by leaving an open box in the refrigerator. In a brilliant marketing move, the firm then suggested that consumers buy the product and throw it away—deodorize a kitchen sink by dumping Arm & Hammer baking soda down the drain!

The company did not stop there. It looked for other uses of its sodium bicarbonate in new products. Church & Dwight has achieved consistent growth in sales and earnings through the use of *line extensions*, putting the Arm & Hammer brand first on baking soda and then on laundry detergents, toothpaste, and deodorants. By the beginning of the 21st century, Church & Dwight had become a significant competitor in markets previously dominated only by giants such as Procter & Gamble, Unilever, and Colgate-Palmolive—using only one brand name. Was there a limit to this growth? Was there a point at which these continuous line extensions would begin to eat away at the integrity of the Arm & Hammer name?

8.1 | Functional Strategy

Functional strategy is the approach a functional area takes to achieve corporate and business unit objectives and strategies by maximizing resource productivity. It is concerned with developing and nurturing a functional capability to provide a company or business unit with a competitive advantage. Just as a multidivisional corporation has several business units, each with its own business strategy, each business unit has its own set of departments, each with its own functional strategy.

The orientation of a functional strategy is dictated by its parent business unit's strategy.[2] For example, a business unit following a competitive strategy of differentiation through high quality needs a manufacturing functional strategy that emphasizes expensive quality assurance processes over cheaper, high-volume production; a human resource functional strategy that emphasizes the hiring and training of a highly skilled, but costly, workforce; and a marketing functional strategy that emphasizes distribution channel "pull," using advertising to increase consumer demand, over "push," using promotional allowances to retailers. If a business unit were to follow a low-cost competitive strategy, however, a different set of functional strategies would be needed to support the business strategy.

Just as competitive strategies may need to vary from one region of the world to another, functional strategies may need to vary from region to region. When Mr. Donut expanded into Japan, for example, it had to market donuts not as breakfast but as snack food. Because the Japanese had no breakfast coffee and donut custom, they preferred to eat the donuts in the afternoon or evening. Mr. Donut restaurants were thus located near railroad stations and supermarkets. All signs were in English, to appeal to the Western interests of the Japanese.

Marketing Strategy

Marketing strategy deals with pricing, selling, and distributing a product. Using a **market development** strategy, a company or business unit can (1) capture a larger share of an existing market for current products through market saturation and market penetration or (2) develop new markets for current products. Consumer product giants such as P&G, Colgate-Palmolive, and Unilever are experts at using advertising and promotion to implement a market saturation/penetration strategy to gain the dominant market share in a product category. As seeming masters of the product life cycle, these companies are able to extend product life almost indefinitely through "new and improved" variations of product and packaging that appeal to most market niches. These companies also follow the second market development strategy by taking a successful product they market in one part of the world and marketing it elsewhere. Noting the success of their presoak detergents in Europe, for example, both P&G and Colgate successfully introduced this type of laundry product to North America under the trade names of Biz and Axion.

Using the **product development** strategy, a company or unit can (1) develop new products for *existing markets* or (2) develop new products for *new markets*. Church & Dwight has had great success by following the first product development strategy, developing new products to sell to its current customers in its existing markets. Acknowledging the widespread appeal of its Arm & Hammer brand baking soda, the company has generated new uses for its sodium bicarbonate by reformulating it as toothpaste, deodorant, and detergent. Using a successful brand name to market other products is called **line extension**, and it is a good way to appeal to a company's current customers. Sara Lee Corporation (famous for its frozen cheesecake) has taken the same approach by putting the Sara Lee name on various food products, such as premium meats and fresh baked goods. Arm & Hammer has successfully followed the second product development strategy by developing new pollution-reduction products (using sodium bicarbonate compounds) for sale to coal-fired electric utility plants—a very different market from grocery stores.

There are numerous other marketing strategies. For advertising and promotion, for example, a company or business unit can choose between "push" and "pull" marketing strategies. Many large food and consumer products companies in the United States and Canada have followed a **push strategy** by spending a large amount of money on trade promotion in order to gain or hold shelf space in retail outlets. Trade promotion includes discounts, in-store special offers, and advertising allowances designed to "push" products through the distribution system. The Kellogg Company decided a few years ago to change its emphasis from a push to a **pull strategy**, in which advertising "pulls" the products through the distribution channels. The company now spends more money on consumer advertising designed to build brand awareness so that shoppers will ask for the products. Research has indicated that a high level of advertising (a key part of a pull strategy) is beneficial to leading brands in a market.[3]

Other marketing strategies deal with distribution and pricing. Should a company use distributors and dealers to sell its products, or should it sell directly to mass merchandisers or even straight to the consumers via the Internet? Using multiple channels simultaneously can lead to problems. In order to increase the sales of its lawn tractors and mowers, for example, John Deere decided to sell the products not only through its current dealer network but also through mass merchandisers such as Home Depot. Deere's dealers were furious. They considered Home Depot to be a key competitor. The dealers were concerned that Home Depot's ability to underprice them would eventually lead to their becoming little more than repair facilities for their competition and left with insufficient sales to stay in business.[4]

When pricing a new product, a company or business unit can follow one of two strategies. For new-product pioneers, **skim pricing** offers the opportunity to "skim the cream" from the top of the demand curve with a high price while the product is novel and competitors are few. **Penetration pricing**, in contrast, attempts to hasten market development and offers the pioneer the opportunity to use the experience curve to gain market share with a low price and then dominate the industry. Depending on corporate and business unit objectives and strategies, either of these choices may be desirable to a particular company or unit. Penetration pricing is, however, more likely than skim pricing to raise a unit's operating profit in the long term.[5] The use of the Internet to market goods directly to consumers allows a company to use **dynamic pricing**, a practice in which prices vary frequently based upon demand, market segment, and product availability.[6]

Financial Strategy

Financial strategy examines the financial implications of corporate and business-level strategic options and identifies the best financial course of action. It can also provide competitive advantage through a lower cost of funds and a flexible ability to raise capital to support a business strategy. Financial strategy usually attempts to maximize the financial value of a firm.

The trade-off between achieving the desired debt-to-equity ratio and relying on internal long-term financing via cash flow is a key issue in financial strategy. Many small- and medium-sized family-owned companies such as Urschel Laboratories try to avoid all external sources of funds in order to avoid outside entanglements and to keep control of the company within the family. Many financial analysts believe, however, that only by financing through long-term debt can a corporation use financial leverage to boost earnings per share—thus raising stock price and the overall value of the company. Research indicates that higher debt levels not only deter takeover by other firms (by making the company less attractive) but also lead to improved productivity and improved cash flows by forcing management to focus on core businesses.[7]

Research reveals that a firm's financial strategy is influenced by its corporate diversification strategy. Equity financing, for example, is preferred for related diversification, whereas debt financing is preferred for unrelated diversification.[8] The recent trend away from unrelated to related acquisitions explains why the number of acquisitions being paid for entirely with stock increased from only 2% in 1988 to 50% in 1998.[9]

A very popular financial strategy is the leveraged buyout (LBO). In a **leveraged buyout**, a company is acquired in a transaction financed largely by debt, usually obtained from a third party, such as an insurance company or an investment banker. Ultimately the debt is paid with money generated from the acquired company's operations or by sales of its assets. The acquired company, in effect, pays for its own acquisition. Management of the LBO is then under tremendous pressure to keep the highly leveraged company profitable. Unfortunately, the huge amount of debt on the acquired company's books may actually cause its eventual decline by focusing management's attention on short-term matters. One study of LBOs (also called MBOs [Management Buy Outs]) revealed that the financial performance of the typical LBO usually falls below the industry average in the fourth year after the buyout. The firm declines because of inflated expectations, utilization of all slack, management burnout, and a lack of strategic management.[10] Often the only solution is to go public once again by selling stock to finance growth.[11]

The management of dividends and stock price is an important part of a corporation's financial strategy. Corporations in fast-growing industries such as computers and computer software often do not declare dividends. They use the money they might have spent on dividends to finance rapid growth. If the company is successful, its growth in sales and profits is reflected in a higher stock price, eventually resulting in a hefty capital gain when shareholders sell their common stock. Other corporations, such as Maytag Corporation, that do not face rapid growth must support the value of their stock by offering consistent dividends. Like Maytag, they may even go into debt to finance these dividends.

A number of firms are supporting the price of their stock by using **reverse stock splits**. Contrasted with a typical forward 2-for-1 stock split in which an investor receives an additional share for every share owned (with each share being worth only half as much), in a reverse 1-for-2 stock split, an investor's shares are split in half for the same total amount of money (with each share now being worth twice as much). Thus, 100 shares of stock worth $10 each are exchanged for 50 shares worth $20 each. A reverse stock split may successfully raise a company's stock price, but does not solve underlying problems. A study by Credit Suisse First Boston revealed that almost all 800 companies that had reverse stock splits in a five-year period underperformed their peers over the long term.[12]

A recent financial strategy being used by large established corporations to highlight a high-growth business unit in a popular sector of the stock market is to establish a tracking stock. A **tracking stock** is a type of common stock tied to one portion of a corporation's business. This strategy allows established companies to highlight a high-growth business unit without selling the business. By keeping the unit as a subsidiary with its common stock separately identified, the corporation is able to keep control of the subsidiary and yet allow the subsidiary the ability to fund its own growth with outside money. It goes public as an IPO and pays dividends based on the unit's performance. Because the tracking stock is actually an equity interest in the parent company (not the subsidiary), another company cannot acquire the subsidiary by buying its shares. Examples of corporations that use tracking stocks as part of their financial strategy are AT&T (AT&T Wireless), Sprint (Sprint PCS), JCPenney (CVS Drugs), and Staples (Staples.com).[13]

Research and Development (R&D) Strategy

R&D strategy deals with product and process innovation and improvement. It also deals with the appropriate mix of different types of R&D (basic, product, or process) and with the question of how new technology should be accessed—through internal development, external acquisition, or strategic alliances.

One of the R&D choices is to be either a **technological leader**, pioneering an innovation, or a **technological follower**, imitating the products of competitors. Porter suggests that deciding to become a technological leader or follower can be a way of achieving either overall low cost or differentiation. (See **Table 8–1**.)

One example of an effective use of the *leader* R&D functional strategy to achieve a differentiation competitive advantage is Nike, Inc. Nike spends more than most in the industry on R&D to differentiate the performance of its athletic shoes from that of its competitors. As a result, its products have become the favorite of serious athletes. An example of the use of the *follower* R&D functional strategy to achieve a low-cost competitive advantage is Dean Foods Company. "We're able to have the customer come to us and say, 'If you can produce X, Y, and Z product for the same quality and service, but at a lower price and without that expensive label on it, you can have the business,'" says Howard Dean, president of the company.[14]

TABLE 8–1
RESEARCH AND
DEVELOPMENT
STRATEGY AND
COMPETITIVE
ADVANTAGE

	Technological Leadership	**Technological Followership**
Cost Advantage	Pioneer the lowest-cost production design. Be the first down the learning curve. Create low-cost ways of performing value activities.	Lower the cost of the product or value activities by learning from the leader's experience. Avoid R&D costs through imitation.
Differentiation	Pioneer a unique product that increases buyer value. Innovate in other activities to increase buyer value.	Adapt the product or delivery system more closely to buyer needs by learning from the leader's experience.

Source: Adapted with the permission of The Free Press, A Division of Simon & Schuster Adult Publishing Group, from *COMPETITIVE ADVANTAGE: Creating and Sustaining Superior Performance* by Michael Porter. Copyright © 1985, 1998 by Michael E. Porter. All rights reserved.

An increasing number of companies are working with their suppliers to help them keep up with changing technology. They are beginning to realize that a firm cannot be competitive technologically only through internal development. For example, Chrysler Corporation's skillful use of parts suppliers to design everything from car seats to drive shafts has enabled it to spend consistently less money than its competitors to develop new car models. Using strategic technology alliances is one way to combine the R&D capabilities of two companies. Maytag Company worked with one of its suppliers to apply fuzzy logic technology to its IntelliSense™ dishwasher. The partnership enabled Maytag to complete the project in a shorter amount of time than if it had tried to do it alone.[15]

A new approach to R&D is **open innovation**, in which a firm uses alliances and connections with corporate, government, and academic labs to learn about new developments. For example, Intel opened four small-scale research facilities adjacent to universities to promote the cross-pollination of ideas. Mattel, Wal-Mart, and other toy manufacturers and retailers use idea brokers such as Big Idea Group to scout for new toy ideas. Big Idea Group invites inventors to submit ideas to its web site (www.bigideagroup.net). It then refines and promotes to its clients the most promising ideas.[16] To open its own labs to ideas being generated elsewhere, P&G's CEO Art Lafley decreed that half of the company's ideas must come from outside, up from 10% in 2000. P&G instituted the use of *technology scouts* to search beyond the company for promising innovations.[17] A slightly different approach is for a large firm such as IBM or Microsoft to purchase minority stakes in relatively new high-tech entrepreneurial ventures that need capital to continue operation. Investing corporate venture capital is one way to gain access to promising innovations at a lower cost than by developing them internally.[18]

Operations Strategy

Operations strategy determines how and where a product or service is to be manufactured, the level of vertical integration in the production process, the deployment of physical resources, and relationships with suppliers. It should also deal with the optimum level of technology the firm should use in its operations processes. See the GLOBAL ISSUE feature to see how differences in national conditions can lead to differences in product design and manufacturing facilities from one country to another.

Advanced Manufacturing Technology (AMT) is revolutionizing operations worldwide and should continue to have a major impact as corporations strive to integrate diverse business

GL🌐BAL ISSUE

International Differences Alter Whirlpool's Operations Strategy

To better penetrate the growing markets in developing nations, Whirlpool decided to build a "world washer." This new type of washing machine was to be produced in Brazil, Mexico, and India. Lightweight, with substantially fewer parts than its U.S. counterpart, its performance was to be equal to or better than anything on the world market while being competitive in price with the most popular models in these markets. The goal was to develop a complete product, process, and facility design package that could be used in different countries with low initial investment. Originally the plan had been to make the same low-cost washer in identical plants in each of the three countries.

Significant differences in each of the three countries forced Whirlpool to change its product design to adapt to each nation's situation. According to Lawrence Kremer, Senior Vice President of Global Technology and Operations, "Our Mexican affiliate, Vitromatic, has porcelain and glass-making capabilities. Porcelain baskets made sense for them. Stainless steel became the preferred material for the others." Costs also affected decisions. "In India, for example, material costs may run as much as 200% to 800% higher than else-

where, while labor and overhead costs are comparatively minimal," added Kremer. Another consideration were the garments to be washed in each country. For example, saris—the 18-foot lengths of cotton or silk with which Indian women drape themselves—needed special treatment in an Indian washing machine, forcing additional modifications.

Manufacturing facilities also varied from country to country. Brastemp, Whirlpool's Brazilian partner, built its plant of precast concrete to address the problems of high humidity. In India, however, the construction crew cast the concrete, allowed it to cure, and then, using chain, block, and tackle, five or six men raised each three-ton slab into place. Instead of using one building, Mexican operations used two—one housing the flexible assembly lines and stamping operations, and an adjacent facility housing the injection molding and extrusion processes.

Source: WHEELEN, TOM; HUNGER, J. DAVID, *STRATEGIC MANAGEMENT AND BUSINESS POLICY*, 9th Edition, © 2004, p. 172. Reprinted by permission of Pearson Education, Inc., Upper Saddle River, NJ.

---

activities by using computer-assisted design and manufacturing (CAD/CAM) principles. The use of CAD/CAM, flexible manufacturing systems, computer numerically controlled systems, automatically guided vehicles, robotics, manufacturing resource planning (MRP II), optimized production technology, and just-in-time techniques contribute to increased flexibility, quick response time, and higher productivity. Such investments also act to increase the company's fixed costs and could cause significant problems if the company is unable to achieve economies of scale or scope. Baldor Electric Company, the largest maker of industrial electric motors in the United States, built a new factory by using new technology to eliminate undesirable jobs with high employee turnover. With one-tenth the employees of its foreign plants, the plant was cost-competitive with plants producing motors in Mexico and China.[19]

A firm's manufacturing strategy is often affected by a product's life cycle. As the sales of a product increase, there will be an increase in production volume ranging from lot sizes as low as one in a **job shop** (one-of-a-kind production using skilled labor) through **connected line batch flow** (components are standardized; each machine functions like a job shop but is positioned in the same order as the parts are processed) to lot sizes as high as 100,000 or more per year for **flexible manufacturing systems** (parts are grouped into manufacturing families to produce a wide variety of mass-produced items) and **dedicated transfer lines** (highly automated assembly lines that make one mass-produced product using little human labor). According to this concept, the product becomes standardized into a commodity over time in conjunction with increasing demand. Flexibility thus gives way to efficiency.[20]

Increasing competitive intensity in many industries has forced companies to switch from traditional mass production using dedicated transfer lines to a continuous improvement production strategy. A **mass-production** system was an excellent method to produce a large number of low-cost, standard goods and services. Employees worked on narrowly defined, repetitive tasks under close supervision in a bureaucratic and hierarchical structure. Quality, however, often tended to be fairly low. Learning how to do something better was the prerogative of management; workers were expected only to learn what was assigned to them. This system tended to dominate manufacturing until the 1970s. Under the **continuous improvement** system developed by Japanese firms, empowered cross-functional teams strive constantly to improve production processes. Managers are more like coaches than like bosses. The result is a large quantity of low-cost, standard goods and services, but with high quality. The key to continuous improvement is the acknowledgment that workers' experience and knowledge can help managers solve production problems and contribute to tightening variances and reducing errors. Because continuous improvement enables firms to use the same low-cost competitive strategy as do mass-production firms but at a significantly higher level of quality, it is rapidly replacing mass production as an operations strategy.

The automobile industry is currently experimenting with the strategy of **modular manufacturing** in which pre-assembled sub-assemblies are delivered as they are needed (i.e., Just-In-Time) to a company's assembly-line workers, who quickly piece the modules together into a finished product. For example, General Motors built a new automotive complex in Brazil to make its new subcompact, the Celta. Sixteen of the 17 buildings were occupied by suppliers, including Delphi, Lear, and Goodyear. These suppliers delivered pre-assembled modules (which comprised 85% of the final value of each car) to GM's building for assembly. In a process new to the industry, the suppliers acted as a team to build a single module comprising the motor, transmission, fuel lines, rear axle, brake-fluid lines, and exhaust system, which was then installed as one piece. GM hoped that this manufacturing strategy would enable it to produce 100 vehicles annually per worker compared to the standard rate of 30 to 50 autos per worker.[21] Ford and Chrysler have opened similar modular facilities in Brazil.

The concept of a product's life cycle eventually leading to one-size-fits-all mass production is being increasingly challenged by the new concept of mass customization. Appropriate for an ever-changing environment, mass customization requires that people, processes, units, and technology reconfigure themselves to give customers exactly what they want, when they want it. In the case of Dell Computer, customers use the Internet to design their own computers. In contrast to continuous improvement, mass customization requires flexibility and quick responsiveness. Managers coordinate independent, capable individuals. An efficient linkage system is crucial. The result is low-cost, high-quality, customized goods and services.

Purchasing Strategy

Purchasing strategy deals with obtaining the raw materials, parts, and supplies needed to perform the operations function. Purchasing strategy is important because materials and components purchased from suppliers comprise 50% of total manufacturing costs of manufacturing companies in the United Kingdom, United States, Australia, Belgium, and Finland.[22] The basic purchasing choices are multiple, sole, and parallel sourcing. Under **multiple sourcing**, the purchasing company orders a particular part from several vendors. Multiple sourcing has traditionally been considered superior to other purchasing approaches because (1) it forces suppliers to compete for the business of an important buyer, thus reducing purchasing costs, and (2) if one supplier cannot deliver, another usually can, thus guaranteeing that parts and supplies are always on hand when needed. Multiple sourcing has been one way for a purchasing firm to control the relationship with its suppliers. So long as suppliers can provide evidence that they can meet the product specifications, they are kept on the purchaser's list of acceptable vendors for specific parts and supplies. Unfortunately, the common practice of accepting the lowest bid often compromises quality.

W. Edwards Deming, a well-known management consultant, strongly recommended **sole sourcing** as the only manageable way to obtain high supplier quality. Sole sourcing relies on only one supplier for a particular part. Given his concern with designing quality into a product in its early stages of development, Deming argued that the buyer should work closely with the supplier at all stages. This reduces both cost and time spent on product design, and it also improves quality. It can also simplify the purchasing company's production process by using the **Just-In-Time (JIT)** concept of having the purchased parts arrive at the plant just when they are needed rather than keeping inventories. The concept of sole sourcing is taken one step further in JIT II, in which vendor sales representatives actually have desks next to the purchasing company's factory floor, attend production status meetings, visit the R&D lab, and analyze the purchasing company's sales forecasts. These in-house suppliers then write sales orders for which the purchasing company is billed. Developed by Lance Dixon at Bose Corporation, JIT II is also being used at IBM, Honeywell, and Ingersoll-Rand. Karen Dale, purchasing manager for Honeywell's office supplies, said she was very concerned about confidentiality when JIT II was first suggested to her. Now she has 5 suppliers working with her 20 buyers and reports few problems.[23]

Sole sourcing reduces transaction costs and builds quality by having the purchaser and supplier work together as partners rather than as adversaries. With sole sourcing, more companies will have longer relationships with fewer suppliers. Sole sourcing does, however, have limitations. If a supplier is unable to deliver a part, the purchaser has no alternative but to delay production. Multiple suppliers can provide the purchaser with better information about new technology and performance capabilities. The limitations of sole sourcing have led to the development of parallel sourcing. In **parallel sourcing**, two suppliers are the sole suppliers of two different parts, but they are also backup suppliers for each other's parts. If one vendor cannot supply all of its parts on time, the other vendor is asked to make up the difference.[24]

The Internet is being increasingly used both to find new sources of supply and to keep inventories replenished. For example, Hewlett-Packard introduced a Web-based procurement system to enable its 84,000 employees to buy office supplies from a standard set of suppliers. The new system enabled the company to save $60 to $100 million annually in purchasing costs.[25] See STRATEGY HIGHLIGHT 8.1 to learn how David Crosier, Vice President for Supply-chain Management at Staples, used the Internet to keep the retailer in Post-It Notes and Scotch tape from 3M.

Logistics Strategy

Logistics strategy deals with the flow of products into and out of the manufacturing process. Three trends related to this strategy are evident: centralization, outsourcing, and the use of the Internet. To gain logistical synergies across business units, corporations began centralizing logistics in the headquarters group. This centralized logistics group usually contains specialists with expertise in different transportation modes, such as rail or trucking. They work to aggregate shipping volumes across the entire corporation to gain better contracts with shippers. Companies such as Georgia-Pacific, Marriott, and Union Carbide view the logistics function as an important way to differentiate themselves from the competition, to add value, and to reduce costs.

Many companies have found that outsourcing logistics reduces costs and improves delivery time. For example, HP contracted with Roadway Logistics to manage its in-bound raw materials warehousing in Vancouver, Canada. Nearly 140 Roadway employees replaced 250 HP workers, who were transferred to other HP activities.[26]

Many companies are using the Internet to simplify their logistical system. For example, Ace Hardware created an online system for its retailers and suppliers. An individual hardware store can now see on the web site that ordering 210 cases of wrenches is cheaper than ordering 200 cases. Because a full pallet is composed of 210 cases of wrenches, an order for a full pallet means that the supplier doesn't have to pull 10 cases off a pallet and repackage them

STRATEGY HIGHLIGHT 8.1

Staples Uses Internet to Replenish Inventory from 3M

David Crosier was mad. As the Vice President for Supply-chain Management for Staples, the office supplies retailer, Crosier couldn't even find a Post-It Note to write down the complaint that his stores were consistently low on 3M products. Crosier would send an order to the Minnesota Mining & Manufacturing Company (3M) for 10,000 rolls of Scotch tape and receive only 8,000. Even worse, the supplies from 3M often arrived late, causing "stock outs" of popular products. Crosier then discovered 3M's new online ordering system for office supplies. The web site enabled 3M to reduce customer frustration caused by paper forms and last-minute phone calls by eliminating error-prone steps in purchasing. Since using 3M's web site, Staples' Crosier reports that 3M's fill rate has improved by 20% and that its on-time performance has almost doubled. "The technology takes a lot of inefficiencies out of the supply-chain process."

This improvement at 3M was initiated by Allen Messerli, information manager at 3M, over a five-year period. Since 1997, 3M has invested $30 million in the project. Ongoing maintenance costs of keeping the system current are $2.6 million. Before implementing this online system, 3M had serious problems with its finished goods inventory, distribution, and customer service. For example, nearly 40% of its customer records (in the U.S. alone) had invalid addresses. Bloated finished goods inventory in 1998 caused a 45% drop in earnings. With more than 70,000 employees around the world, 3M had difficulty linking employees, managers, and customers because of incompatible networks. With its new Global Enterprise Data Warehouse, 3M is now delivering customer, product, sales, inventory, and financial data directly to its employees and partners, who can access the information via the Internet (at www.3m.com). The company reports saving $10 million annually in maintenance and customer-service costs. More accurate and current sales reporting is saving an additional $2.5 million per year. The new technology has improved productivity, boosting global sales. Supply-chain managers such as David Crosier at Staples are pleased with making the Internet an important part of their purchasing strategy.

Source: D. Little, "3M: Glued to the Web" *Business Week E.Biz* (November 2000), pp. EB65–EB70.

for storage. There is less chance that loose cases will be lost in delivery, and the paperwork doesn't have to be redone. As a result, Ace's transportation costs are down 18%, and warehouse costs have been cut 28%.[27] As shown in **STRATEGY HIGHLIGHT 8.1**, 3M's new system enabled it to save $10 million annually in maintenance and customer-service costs.

Human Resource Management (HRM) Strategy

HRM strategy, among other things, addresses the issue of whether a company or business unit should hire a large number of low-skilled employees who receive low pay, perform repetitive jobs, and most likely quit after a short time (the McDonald's restaurant strategy) or hire skilled employees who receive relatively high pay and are cross-trained to participate in *self-managing work teams*. As work increases in complexity, the more suited it is for teams, especially in the case of innovative product development efforts. Multinational corporations are increasingly using self-managing work teams in their foreign affiliates as well as in home country operations.[28] Research indicates that the use of work teams leads to increased quality and productivity as well as to higher employee satisfaction and commitment.[29]

Companies following a competitive strategy of differentiation through high quality use input from subordinates and peers in performance appraisals to a greater extent than do firms following other business strategies.[30] A complete **360-degree appraisal**, in which input is gathered from multiple sources, is now being used by more than 10% of U.S. corporations, and has become one of the most popular tools in developing new managers.[31]

Companies are finding that having a *diverse workforce* can be a competitive advantage. Research reveals that firms with a high degree of racial diversity following a growth strategy have higher productivity than do firms with less racial diversity.[32] Avon Company, for example, was able to turn around its unprofitable inner-city markets by putting African-American and Hispanic managers in charge of marketing to these markets.[33] Diversity in terms of age and national origin also offers benefits. DuPont's use of multinational teams has helped the company develop and market products internationally. McDonald's has discovered that older workers perform as well as if not better than younger employees. According to Edward Rensi, CEO of McDonald's USA, "We find these people to be particularly well motivated, with a sort of discipline and work habits hard to find in younger employees."[34]

Information Technology Strategy

Corporations are increasingly using **information technology strategy** to provide business units with competitive advantage. When FedEx first provided its customers with PowerShip computer software to store addresses, print shipping labels, and track package location, its sales jumped significantly. UPS soon followed with its own MaxiShips software. Viewing its information system as a distinctive competency, FedEx continued to push for further advantage over UPS by using its web site to enable customers to track their packages. FedEx uses this competency in its advertisements by showing how customers can track the progress of their shipments. (Soon thereafter, UPS provided the same service.) Although it can be argued that information technology has now become so pervasive that it no longer offers companies a competitive advantage, corporations worldwide continue to spend over $2 trillion annually on information technology.[35]

Multinational corporations are finding that having a sophisticated intranet allows employees to practice *follow-the-sun management*, in which project team members living in one country can pass their work to team members in another country in which the work day is just beginning. Thus, night shifts are no longer needed.[36] The development of instant translation software is also enabling workers to have online communication with co-workers in other countries who use a different language.[37] For example, Mattel has cut the time it takes to develop new products by 10% by enabling designers and licensees in other countries to collaborate on toy design. IBM uses its intranet to allow its employees to collaborate and improve their skills, thus reducing its training and travel expenses.[38]

Many companies, such as Lockheed Martin and Whirlpool, use information technology to form closer relationships with both their customers and suppliers through sophisticated extranets. For example, General Electric's Trading Process Network allows suppliers to electronically download GE's requests for proposals, view diagrams of parts specifications, and communicate with GE purchasing managers. According to Robert Livingston, GE's head of worldwide sourcing for the Lighting Division, going on the web reduces processing time by one-third.[39]

8.2 | The Sourcing Decision: Location of Functions

For a functional strategy to have the best chance of success, it should be built on a capability residing within that functional area. If a corporation does not have a strong capability in a particular functional area, that functional area could be a candidate for outsourcing.

Outsourcing is purchasing from someone else a product or service that had been previously provided internally. Outsourcing is becoming an increasingly important part of strategic decision making and an important way to increase efficiency and often quality. Firms competing in global industries must in particular search worldwide for the most appropriate suppliers. In a study of 30 firms, outsourcing resulted on average in a 9% reduction in costs and a 15% increase in capacity and quality.[40] For example, Boeing is using outsourcing as a way to reduce the cost of designing and manufacturing its new 787 Dreamliner. Up to 70% of the plane is being outsourced. In a break from past practice, suppliers make large parts of the fuselage, including plumbing, electrical, and computer systems, and ship them to Seattle for assembly by Boeing. Outsourcing enables Boeing to build a 787 in 4 months instead of the usual 12.[41]

According to an American Management Association survey of member companies, 94% of the responding firms outsource at least one activity. The outsourced activities are general and administrative (78%), human resources (77%), transportation and distribution (66%), information systems (63%), manufacturing (56%), marketing (51%), and finance and accounting (18%). The survey also reveals that 25% of the respondents have been disappointed in their outsourcing results. Fifty-one percent of the firms reported bringing an outsourced activity back in-house. Nevertheless, authorities not only expect the number of companies engaging in outsourcing to increase, they also expect companies to outsource an increasing number of functions, especially those in customer service, bookkeeping, financial/clerical, sales/telemarketing, and the mailroom.[42] Software programming and customer service, in particular, are being outsourced to India. For example, General Electric's back-office services unit, GE Capital International Services, is one of the oldest and biggest of India's outsourcing companies. From only $26 million in 1999, its annual revenues grew to over $420 million in 2004.[43] As part of this trend, in 2004 IBM acquired Daksh eServices Ltd., one of India's biggest suppliers of remote business services.[44]

Outsourcing does have disadvantages. For example, mounting complaints forced Dell Computer to stop routing corporate customers to a technical support call center in Bangalore, India.[45] GE's introduction of a new washing machine was delayed three weeks because of production problems at a supplier's company to which it had contracted out key work. Some companies have found themselves locked into long-term contracts with outside suppliers that were no longer competitive.[46] Some authorities propose that the cumulative effects of continued outsourcing steadily reduce a firm's ability to learn new skills and to develop new core competencies.[47] A survey of 129 outsourcing firms revealed that half the outsourcing projects undertaken in 2003 failed to deliver anticipated savings. Another survey of software projects, by MIT, found that the median Indian project had 10% more software bugs than did comparable U.S. projects.[48] A study of 91 outsourcing efforts conducted by European and North American firms found seven major outsourcing errors that should be avoided[49]:

1. **Outsourcing activities that should not be outsourced:** Companies failed to keep core activities in-house.
2. **Selecting the wrong vender:** Vendors were not trustworthy or lacked state-of-the-art processes.
3. **Writing a poor contract:** Companies failed to establish a balance of power in the relationship.
4. **Overlooking personnel issues:** Employees lost commitment to the firm.
5. **Losing control over the outsourced activity:** Qualified managers failed to manage the outsourced activity.[50]
6. **Overlooking the hidden costs of outsourcing:** Transaction costs overwhelmed other savings.
7. **Failing to plan an exit strategy:** Companies failed to build reversibility clauses into their contracts.

Sophisticated strategists, according to Quinn, are no longer thinking just of market share or vertical integration as the keys to strategic planning:

Instead they concentrate on identifying those few core service activities where the company has or can develop: (1) a continuing strategic edge and (2) long-term streams of new products to satisfy future customer demands. They develop these competencies in greater depth than anyone else in the world. Then they seek to eliminate, minimize, or outsource activities where the company cannot be preeminent, unless those activities are essential to support or protect the chosen areas of strategic focus.[51]

The key to outsourcing is to purchase from outside only those activities that are not key to the company's distinctive competencies. Otherwise, the company may give up the very capabilities that made it successful in the first place, thus putting itself on the road to eventual decline. This is supported by research reporting that companies that have more experience with a particular manufacturing technology tend to keep manufacturing in-house.[52] J. P. Morgan Chase & Company terminated a seven-year technology outsourcing agreement with IBM because the bank's management realized that information technology (IT) was too important strategically to be outsourced.[53] Therefore, in determining functional strategy, the strategist must:

- Identify the company's or business unit's core competencies
- Ensure that the competencies are continually being strengthened
- Manage the competencies in a way that best preserves the competitive advantage they create

An outsourcing decision depends on the fraction of total value added that the activity under consideration represents and on the amount of potential competitive advantage in that activity for the company or business unit. See the proposed outsourcing matrix in **Figure 8–1**. A firm should consider outsourcing any activity or function that has low potential for competitive advantage. If that activity constitutes only a small part of the total value of the firm's products or services, it should be purchased on the open market (assuming that quality providers of the activity are plentiful). If, however, the activity contributes highly to the company's products or services, the firm should purchase it through long-term contracts with trusted suppliers or distributors. A firm should always produce at least some of the activity or function (i.e., taper vertical integration) if that activity has the potential for providing the company some competitive advantage. However, full vertical integration should be considered

Figure 8–1
Proposed Outsourcing Matrix

Activity's Total Value-Added to Firm's Products and Services

	Low	High
High (Activity's Potential for Competitive Advantage)	**Taper Vertical Integration:** Produce Some Internally	**Full Vertical Integration:** Produce All Internally
Low	**Outsource Completely:** Buy on Open Market	**Outsource Completely:** Purchase with Long-Term Contracts

Source: J. D. Hunger and T. L. Wheelen, "Proposed Outsourcing Matrix." Copyright © 1996 and 2005 by Wheelen and Hunger Associates. Reprinted by permission.

only when that activity or function adds significant value to the company's products or services in addition to providing competitive advantage.

8.3 | Strategies to Avoid

Several strategies that could be considered corporate, business, or functional are very dangerous. Managers who have made poor analyses or lack creativity may be trapped into considering some of the following **strategies to avoid:**

- **Follow the Leader:** Imitating a leading competitor's strategy might seem to be a good idea, but it ignores a firm's particular strengths and weaknesses and the possibility that the leader may be wrong. Fujitsu Ltd., the world's second-largest computer maker, had been driven since the 1960s by the sole ambition of catching up to IBM. Like IBM, Fujitsu competed primarily as a mainframe computer maker. So devoted was it to catching IBM, however, that it failed to notice that the mainframe business had reached maturity by 1990 and was no longer growing.

- **Hit Another Home Run:** If a company is successful because it pioneered an extremely successful product, it tends to search for another super product that will ensure growth and prosperity. As in betting on long shots in horse races, the probability of finding a second winner is slight. Polaroid spent a lot of money developing an "instant" movie camera, but the public ignored it in favor of the camcorder.

- **Arms Race:** Entering into a spirited battle with another firm for increased market share might increase sales revenue, but that increase will probably be more than offset by increases in advertising, promotion, R&D, and manufacturing costs. Since the deregulation of airlines, price wars and rate specials have contributed to the low profit margins and bankruptcies of many major airlines, such as Eastern, Pan American, TWA, and United.

- **Do Everything:** When faced with several interesting opportunities, management might tend to leap at all of them. At first, a corporation might have enough resources to develop each idea into a project, but money, time, and energy are soon exhausted as the many projects demand large infusions of resources. The Walt Disney Company's expertise in the entertainment industry led it to acquire the ABC network. As the company churned out new motion pictures and television programs such as *Who Wants to Be a Millionaire*, it spent $750 million to build new theme parks and buy a cruise line and a hockey team. By 2000, even though corporate sales had continued to increase, net income was falling.[54]

- **Losing Hand:** A corporation might have invested so much in a particular strategy that top management is unwilling to accept its failure. Believing that it has too much invested to quit, management may continue to throw "good money after bad." Pan American Airlines, for example, chose to sell its Pan Am Building and Intercontinental Hotels, the most profitable parts of the corporation, to keep its money-losing airline flying. Continuing to suffer losses, the company followed this profit strategy of shedding assets for cash until it had sold off everything and went bankrupt.

8.4 | Strategic Choice: Selecting the Best Strategy

After the pros and cons of the potential strategic alternatives have been identified and evaluated, one must be selected for implementation. By now, it is likely that many feasible alternatives will have emerged. How is the best strategy determined?

Perhaps the most important criterion is the capability of the proposed strategy to deal with the specific strategic factors developed earlier, in the SWOT analysis. If the alternative doesn't take advantage of environmental opportunities and corporate strengths/competencies, and lead away from environmental threats and corporate weaknesses, it will probably fail.

Another important consideration in the selection of a strategy is the ability of each alternative to satisfy agreed-on objectives with the least resources and the fewest negative side effects. It is, therefore, important to develop a tentative implementation plan in order to address the difficulties that management is likely to face. This should be done in light of societal trends, the industry, and the company's situation, based on the construction of scenarios.

Constructing Corporate Scenarios

Corporate scenarios are *pro forma* (estimated) balance sheets and income statements that forecast the effect each alternative strategy and its various programs will likely have on division and corporate return on investment. (Pro forma financial statements are discussed in **Chapter 15**.) In a survey of *Fortune 500* firms, 84% reported using computer simulation models in strategic planning. Most of these were simply spreadsheet-based simulation models dealing with what-if questions.[55]

The recommended scenarios are simply extensions of the industry scenarios discussed in **Chapter 4**. If, for example, industry scenarios suggest the probable emergence of a strong market demand in a specific country for certain products, a series of alternative strategy scenarios can be developed. The alternative of acquiring another firm having these products in that country can be compared with the alternative of a green-field development (e.g., building new operations in that country). By using three sets of estimated sales figures (Optimistic, Pessimistic, and Most Likely) for the new products over the next five years, the two alternatives can be evaluated in terms of their effect on future company performance as reflected in the company's probable future financial statements. Pro forma balance sheets and income statements can be generated with spreadsheet software, such as Excel, on a personal computer.

To construct a corporate scenario, follow these steps:

1. Use industry scenarios (as discussed in **Chapter 4**) to develop a set of assumptions about the task environment (in the specific country under consideration). For example, 3M requires the general manager of each business unit to describe annually what his or her industry will look like in 15 years. List *optimistic*, *pessimistic*, and *most likely* assumptions for key economic factors such as the GDP (Gross Domestic Product), CPI (Consumer Price Index), and prime interest rate and for other key external strategic factors such as governmental regulation and industry trends. This should be done for every country/region in which the corporation has significant operations that will be affected by each strategic alternative. These same underlying assumptions should be listed for each of the alternative scenarios to be developed.

2. Develop common-size financial statements (as discussed in **Chapter 15**) for the company's or business unit's previous years, to serve as the basis for the trend analysis projections of pro forma financial statements. Use the *Scenario Box* form shown in **Table 8–2**:

   a. Use the historical common-size percentages to estimate the level of revenues, expenses, and other categories in estimated pro forma statements for future years.

   b. Develop for each strategic alternative a set of *optimistic*, *pessimistic*, and *most likely* assumptions about the impact of key variables on the company's future financial statements.

   c. Forecast three sets of sales and cost of goods sold figures for at least five years into the future.

TABLE 8–2 SCENARIO BOX FOR USE IN GENERATING FINANCIAL PRO FORMA STATEMENTS

Factor	Last Year	Historical Average	Trend Analysis	Projections[1]									Comments
				200–			200–			200–			
				O	P	ML	O	P	ML	O	P	ML	
GDP													
CPI													
Other													
Sales units													
Dollars													
COGS													
Advertising and marketing													
Interest expense													
Plant expansion													
Dividends													
Net profits													
EPS													
ROI													
ROE													
Other													

Note:
1. **O** = Optimistic; **P** = Pessimistic; **ML** = Most Likely.

Source: T. L. Wheelen and J. D. Hunger. Copyright © 1987, 1988, 1989, 1990, 1992, and 2005 by T. L Wheelen. Copyright © 1993 and 2005 by Wheelen and Hunger Associates. Reprinted with permission.

    d. Analyze historical data and make adjustments based on the environmental assumptions listed earlier. Do the same for other figures that can vary significantly.

    e. Assume for other figures that they will continue in their historical relationship to sales or some other key determining factor. Plug in expected inventory levels, accounts receivable, accounts payable, R&D expenses, advertising and promotion expenses, capital expenditures, and debt payments (assuming that debt is used to finance the strategy), among others.

    f. Consider not only historical trends but also programs that might be needed to implement each alternative strategy (such as building a new manufacturing facility or expanding the sales force).

3. Construct detailed pro forma financial statements for each strategic alternative:

    a. List the actual figures from this year's financial statements in the left column of the spreadsheet.

    b. List to the right of this column the optimistic figures for years 1 through 5.

    c. Go through this same process with the same strategic alternative, but now list the pessimistic figures for the next five years.

d. Do the same with the most likely figures.

e. Develop a similar set of *optimistic* (O), *pessimistic* (P), and *most likely* (ML) pro forma statements for the second strategic alternative. This process generates six different pro forma scenarios reflecting three different situations (O, P, and ML) for two strategic alternatives.

f. Calculate financial ratios and common-size income statements, and create balance sheets to accompany the pro forma statements.

g. Compare the assumptions underlying the scenarios with the financial statements and ratios to determine the feasibility of the scenarios. For example, if cost of goods sold drops from 70% to 50% of total sales revenue in the pro forma income statements, this drop should result from a change in the production process or a shift to cheaper raw materials or labor costs rather than from a failure to keep the cost of goods sold in its usual percentage relationship to sales revenue when the predicted statement was developed.

The result of this detailed scenario construction should be anticipated net profits, cash flow, and net working capital for each of three versions of the two alternatives for five years into the future. A strategist might want to go further into the future if the strategy is expected to have a major impact on the company's financial statements beyond five years. The result of this work should provide sufficient information on which forecasts of the likely feasibility and probable profitability of each of the strategic alternatives could be based.

Obviously, these scenarios can quickly become very complicated, especially if three sets of acquisition prices and development costs are calculated. Nevertheless, this sort of detailed what if analysis is needed to realistically compare the projected outcome of each reasonable alternative strategy and its attendant programs, budgets, and procedures. Regardless of the quantifiable pros and cons of each alternative, the actual decision will probably be influenced by several subjective factors such as those described in the following sections.

Management's Attitude Toward Risk

The attractiveness of a particular strategic alternative is partially a function of the amount of risk it entails. **Risk** is composed not only of the *probability* that the strategy will be effective but also of the *amount of assets* the corporation must allocate to that strategy and the *length of time* the assets will be unavailable for other uses. Because of variation among countries in terms of customs, regulations, and resources, companies operating in global industries must deal with a greater amount of risk than firms operating only in one country.[56] The greater the assets involved and the longer they are committed, the more likely top management is to demand a high probability of success. Managers with no ownership position in a company are unlikely to have much interest in putting their jobs in danger with risky decisions. Research indicates that managers who own a significant amount of stock in their firms are more likely to engage in risk-taking actions than are managers with no stock.[57]

A high level of risk was why Intel's board of directors found it difficult to vote for a proposal in the early 1990s to commit $5 billion to making the Pentium microprocessor chip—five times the amount of money needed for its previous chip. In looking back on that board meeting, then-CEO Andy Grove remarked, "I remember people's eyes looking at that chart and getting big. I wasn't even sure I believed those numbers at the time." The proposal committed the company to building new factories—something Intel had been reluctant to do. A wrong decision would mean that the company would end up with a killing amount of overcapacity. Based on Grove's presentation, the board decided to take the gamble. Intel's resulting manufacturing expansion eventually cost $10 billion but resulted in Intel's obtaining 75% of the microprocessor business and huge cash profits.[58]

Risk might be one reason that significant innovations occur more often in small firms than in large, established corporations. A small firm managed by an entrepreneur is often willing to accept greater risk than is a large firm of diversified ownership run by professional managers.[59] It is one thing to take a chance if you are the primary shareholder and are not concerned with periodic changes in the value of the company's common stock. It is something else if the corporation's stock is widely held and acquisition-hungry competitors or takeover artists surround the company like sharks every time the company's stock price falls below some external assessment of the firm's value.

A new approach to evaluating alternatives under conditions of high environmental uncertainty is to use real-options theory. According to the **real-options approach**, when the future is highly uncertain, it pays to have a broad range of options open. This is in contrast to using **net present value (NPV)** to calculate the value of a project by predicting its payouts, adjusting them for risk, and subtracting the amount invested. By boiling everything down to one scenario, NPV doesn't provide any flexibility in case circumstances change. NPV is also difficult to apply to projects in which the potential payoffs are currently unknown. The real-options approach, however, deals with these issues by breaking an investment into stages. Management allocates a small amount of funding to initiate multiple projects, monitors their development, and then cancels the projects that aren't successful and funds those that are doing well. This approach is very similar to the way venture capitalists fund an entrepreneurial venture in stages of funding based on the venture's performance.

A survey of 4,000 CFOs found that 27% of them always or almost always used some sort of options approach to evaluating and deciding on growth opportunities.[60] Research indicates that the use of the real-options approach does improve organizational performance.[61] Some of the corporations using the real-options approach are Chevron for bidding on petroleum reserves, Airbus for calculating the costs of airlines changing their orders at the last minute, and the Tennessee Valley Authority for outsourcing electricity generation instead of building its own plant. Because of its complexity, the real-options approach is not worthwhile for minor decisions or for projects requiring a full commitment at the beginning.[62]

Pressures from Stakeholders

The attractiveness of a strategic alternative is affected by its perceived compatibility with the key stakeholders in a corporation's task environment. Creditors want to be paid on time. Unions exert pressure for comparable wage and employment security. Governments and interest groups demand social responsibility. Shareholders want dividends. All these pressures must be given some consideration in the selection of the best alternative.

Stakeholders can be categorized in terms of their (1) interest in a corporation's activities and (2) relative power to influence the corporation's activities.[63] With the **Stakeholder Priority Matrix** depicted in **Figure 8–2**, each stakeholder group can be placed in one of the nine cells.

Strategic managers should ask four questions to assess the importance of stakeholder concerns in a particular decision:

1. How will this decision affect each stakeholder, especially those given high and medium priority?
2. How much of what each stakeholder wants is he or she likely to get under this alternative?
3. What are the stakeholders likely to do if they don't get what they want?
4. What is the probability that they will do it?

Strategy makers should choose strategic alternatives that minimize external pressures and maximize the probability of gaining stakeholder support. In addition, top management can propose a political strategy to influence its key stakeholders. A **political strategy** is a plan to bring stakeholders into agreement with a corporation's actions. Some of the most commonly

Figure 8–2
**Stakeholder
Priority Matrix**

	Low Power	**Medium Power**	**High Power**
High Interest	Medium Priority	High Priority	High Priority
Medium Interest	Low Priority	Medium Priority	High Priority
Low Interest	Low Priority	Low Priority	Medium Priority

Source: ACADEMY OF MANAGEMENT EXECUTIVE: THE THINKING MANAGER'S SOURCE by C. ANDERSON. Copyright 1997 by ACAD OF MGMT. Reproduced with permission of ACAD OF MGMT in the format Textbook via Copyright Clearance Center.

used political strategies are constituency building, political action committee contributions, advocacy advertising, lobbying, and coalition building.

Pressures from the Corporate Culture

If a strategy is incompatible with a company's corporate culture, the likelihood of its success is very low. Foot-dragging and even sabotage will result as employees fight to resist a radical change in corporate philosophy. Precedents from the past tend to restrict the kinds of objectives and strategies that can be seriously considered.[64] The "aura" of the founders of a corporation can linger long past their lifetimes because their values are imprinted on a corporation's members.

In evaluating a strategic alternative, strategy makers must consider corporate culture pressures and assess a strategy's compatibility with the corporate culture. If there is little fit, management must decide if it should:

- Take a chance on ignoring the culture
- Manage around the culture and change the implementation plan
- Try to change the culture to fit the strategy
- Change the strategy to fit the culture

Further, a decision to proceed with a particular strategy without a commitment to change the culture or manage around the culture (both very tricky and time-consuming) is dangerous. Nevertheless, restricting a corporation to only those strategies that are completely compatible with its culture might eliminate from consideration the most profitable alternatives. (See **Chapter 10** for more information on managing corporate culture.)

Needs and Desires of Key Managers

Even the most attractive alternative might not be selected if it is contrary to the needs and desires of important top managers. Personal characteristics and experience affect a person's assessment of an alternative's attractiveness.[65] A person's ego may be tied to a particular proposal to the extent that all other alternatives are strongly lobbied against. As a result, the person may have unfavorable forecasts altered so that they are more in agreement with the desired alternative.[66] A key executive might influence other people in top management to favor a particular alternative so that objections to it are overruled. For example, one CEO was able to locate the corporation's 500-person national headquarters in Washington, DC, so that it would be close to his own home.

Industry and cultural backgrounds affect strategic choice. For example, executives with strong ties within an industry tend to choose strategies commonly used in that industry. Other executives who have come to the firm from another industry and have strong ties outside the industry tend to choose different strategies from what is being currently used in their industry.[67] County of origin often affects preferences. For example, Japanese managers prefer a cost-leadership strategy more than do U.S. managers.[68] Research reveals that executives from Korea, the United States, Japan, and Germany tend to make different strategic choices in similar situations because they use different decision criteria and weights. For example, Korean executives emphasize industry attractiveness, sales, and market share in their decisions, whereas U.S. executives emphasize projected demand, discounted cash flow, and ROI.[69]

There is a tendency to maintain the status quo, which means that decision makers continue with existing goals and plans beyond the point when an objective observer would recommend a change in course. Some executives show a self-serving tendency to attribute the firm's problems not to their own poor decisions but to environmental events out of their control, such as government policies or a poor economic climate.[70] Negative information about a particular course of action to which a person is committed may be ignored because of a desire to appear competent or because of strongly held values regarding consistency. It may take a crisis or an unlikely event to cause strategic decision makers to seriously consider an alternative they had previously ignored or discounted.[71] For example, it wasn't until the CEO of ConAgra, a multinational food products company, had a heart attack that ConAgra started producing the Healthy Choice line of low-fat, low-cholesterol, low-sodium frozen-food entrees.

Process of Strategic Choice

There is an old story told at General Motors:

> At a meeting with his key executives, CEO Alfred Sloan proposed a controversial strategic decision. When asked for comments, each executive responded with supportive comments and praise. After announcing that they were all in apparent agreement, Sloan stated that they were not going to proceed with the decision. Either his executives didn't know enough to point out potential downsides of the decision, or they were agreeing to avoid upsetting the boss and disrupting the cohesion of the group. The decision was delayed until a debate could occur over the pros and cons.[72]

Strategic choice is the evaluation of alternative strategies and selection of the best alternative. There is mounting evidence that when an organization is facing a dynamic environment, the best strategic decisions are not arrived at through **consensus** when everyone agrees on one alternative. They actually involve a certain amount of heated disagreements—and even conflict.[73] This is certainly the case for firms operating in global industries. Because unmanaged conflict often carries a high emotional cost, authorities in decision making propose that strategic managers use "programmed conflict" to raise different opinions, regardless of the personal feelings of the people involved.[74] Two techniques help strategic managers avoid the consensus trap that Alfred Sloan found:

1. **Devil's Advocate:** The idea of the **devil's advocate** originated in the medieval Roman Catholic Church as a way of ensuring that impostors were not canonized as saints. One trusted person was selected to find and present all the reasons a person should *not* be

canonized. When this process is applied to strategic decision making, a devil's advocate (who may be an individual or a group) is assigned to identify potential pitfalls and problems with a proposed alternative strategy in a formal presentation.

2. **Dialectical Inquiry:** The dialectical philosophy, which can be traced back to Plato and Aristotle and more recently to Hegel, involves combining two conflicting views—the thesis and the antithesis—into a synthesis. When applied to strategic decision making, **dialectical inquiry** requires that two proposals using different assumptions be generated for each alternative strategy under consideration. After advocates of each position present and debate the merits of their arguments before key decision makers, either one of the alternatives or a new compromise alternative is selected as the strategy to be implemented.

Research generally supports the conclusion that the devil's advocate and dialectical inquiry methods are equally superior to consensus in decision making, especially when the firm's environment is dynamic. The debate itself, rather than its particular format, appears to improve the quality of decisions by formalizing and legitimizing constructive conflict and by encouraging critical evaluation. Both lead to better assumptions and recommendations and to a higher level of critical thinking among the people involved.[75]

Regardless of the process used to generate strategic alternatives, each resulting alternative must be rigorously evaluated in terms of its ability to meet four criteria:

1. **Mutual exclusivity:** Doing any one alternative would preclude doing any other.

2. **Success:** It must be doable and have a good probability of success.

3. **Completeness:** It must take into account all the key strategic issues.

4. **Internal consistency:** It must make sense on its own as a strategic decision for the entire firm and not contradict key goals, policies, and strategies currently being pursued by the firm or its units.[76]

8.5 | Developing Policies

The selection of the best strategic alternative is not the end of strategy formulation. The organization must then engage in developing policies. Policies define the broad guidelines for implementation. Flowing from the selected strategy, policies provide guidance for decision making and actions throughout the organization. They are the principles under which the corporation operates on a day-to-day basis. At General Electric, for example, Chairman Jack Welch initiated the policy that any GE business unit be Number One or Number Two in whatever market it competes. This policy gives clear guidance to managers throughout the organization. Another example of such a policy is Casey's General Stores' policy that a new service or product line may be added to its stores only when the product or service can be justified in terms of increasing store traffic.

When crafted correctly, an effective policy accomplishes three things:

- It forces trade-offs between competing resource demands.
- It tests the strategic soundness of a particular action.
- It sets clear boundaries within which employees must operate while granting them freedom to experiment within those constraints.[77]

Policies tend to be rather long lived and can even outlast the particular strategy that created them. These general policies—such as "The customer is always right" (Nordstrom) or "Low prices, every day" (Wal-Mart)—can become, in time, part of a corporation's culture.

Such policies can make the implementation of specific strategies easier. They can also restrict top management's strategic options in the future. Thus a change in strategy should be followed quickly by a change in policies. Managing policy is one way to manage the corporate culture.

8.5 | Conclusion

This chapter completes the part of this book on strategy formulation and sets the stage for strategy implementation. Functional strategies must be formulated to support business and corporate strategies; otherwise, the company will move in multiple directions and eventually pull itself apart. For a functional strategy to have the best chance of success, it should be built on a capability residing within that functional area. If a corporation does not have a strong capability in a particular functional area, that functional area could be a candidate for outsourcing.

When evaluating a strategic alternative, the most important criterion is the ability of the proposed strategy to deal with the specific strategic factors developed earlier, in the SWOT analysis. If the alternative doesn't take advantage of environmental opportunities and corporate strengths/competencies and lead away from environmental threats and corporate weaknesses, it will probably fail. Developing corporate scenarios and pro forma projections for each alternative are rational aids for strategic decision making. This logical approach fits Mintzberg's planning mode of strategic decision making, as discussed in Chapter 1. Nevertheless, some strategic decisions are inherently risky and may be resolved on the basis of one person's "gut feel." This is an aspect of the entrepreneurial mode and may be used in large, established corporations as well as in new venture startups. Various management studies have found that executives routinely rely on their intuition to solve complex problems. According to Ralph Larsen, Chairman and CEO of Johnson & Johnson, "Often there is absolutely no way that you could have the time to thoroughly analyze every one of the options or alternatives available to you. So you have to rely on your business judgment."[78]

For example, when Bob Lutz, President of Chrysler Corporation, was enjoying a fast drive in his Cobra roadster one weekend in 1988, he wondered why Chrysler's cars were so dull. "I felt guilty: there I was, the president of Chrysler, driving this great car that had such a strong Ford association," said Lutz, referring to the original Cobra's Ford V-8 engine. That Monday, Lutz enlisted allies at Chrysler to develop a muscular, outrageous sports car that would turn heads and stop traffic. Others in management argued that the $80 million investment would be better spent elsewhere. The sales force warned that no U.S. auto maker had ever succeeded in selling a $50,000 car. With only his gut instincts to support him, he pushed the project forward with unwavering commitment. The result was the Dodge Viper—a car that single-handedly changed the public's perception of Chrysler. Years later, Lutz had trouble describing exactly how he had made this critical decision. "It was this subconscious, visceral feeling. And it just felt right," explained Lutz.[79]

Strategy Bits

- Forrester Research projects that 3.3 million U.S. jobs will be outsourced offshore by 2015.[80]

- Deloitte Research projects more than 800,000 financial services jobs and high-tech jobs will migrate from Western Europe to cheaper labor markets in India, Eastern Europe, China, Africa, and Latin America.[81]

Discussion Questions

1. Are functional strategies interdependent, or can they be formulated independently of other functions?

2. Why is penetration pricing more likely than skim pricing to raise a company's or a business unit's operating profit in the long run?

3. How does mass customization support a business unit's competitive strategy?

4. When should a corporation or business unit outsource a function or an activity?

5. What is the relationship of policies to strategies?

Strategic Practice Exercise

Levi Strauss & Company, the California gold rush outfitter whose trademark blue jeans have been an American clothing staple for generations, had fallen on hard times by 2004 and needed a change in strategic direction. At the end of 2003, the company had undergone seven straight years of declining sales after its sales peaked in 1996 at $7.1 billion. Although the company earned $311 million in operating profits in 2003 on $4 billion in revenues, it posted a record $349 million in net losses, largely due to non-cash charges for accounting purposes. The firm's global workforce had shrunk from more than 37,000 in 1996 to around 12,000. According to Walter Loeb, a retail analyst, "There was a time when Levi's was the fashion garment of the day. The exclusivity of the Levi's brand is no longer as important to customers."

Management responded to the decline by moving its manufacturing plants offshore and by introducing a new line of discount jeans. In the early 1980s, the company had 63 manufacturing plants in the United States. Beset by strong competition in the 1990s, the company had hoped to cut costs and invigorate sales by steadily shifting production to overseas contractors. On January 8, 2004, the company closed its San Antonio, Texas, plant, its last U.S. plant. Levi's continued to base its headquarters staff, designers, and sales employees in the United States. According to company spokesperson Jeff Beckman, the company's identity would also stay in the United States. "We're still an American brand, but we're also a brand and a company whose products have been adopted by consumers around the world. We have to operate as a global company," said Beckman.

In July 2003, the company introduced its new line of Signature jeans at Wal-Mart, priced at $21 to $23 a pair. The company had traditionally sold its products in department stores, where prices ranged from $35 for the 501 jeans to $44 for 599 Giant Fit baggy jeans. In 2004, management was considering selling its $1 billion Dockers casual-pants unit in order to reduce its $2.2 billion debt and to refocus on the jeans business.[82]

1. What is Levi's problem?

2. What do you think of its actions to completely outsource its manufacturing overseas and to introduce a new low-priced line of jeans in discount stores?

3. Should it sell its Dockers unit?

4. What would you recommend to Levi's top management to boost company sales and profits?

Key Terms

360-degree appraisal (p. 197)
connected line batch flow (p. 194)
consensus (p. 207)
continuous improvement (p. 195)
corporate scenario (p. 202)
dedicated transfer line (p. 194)
devil's advocate (p. 207)
dialectical inquiry (p. 208)
dynamic pricing (p. 191)
financial strategy (p. 191)

flexible manufacturing system (p. 194)
functional strategy (p. 189)
HRM strategy (p. 197)
information technology strategy (p. 198)
job shop (p. 194)
Just-In-Time (JIT) (p. 196)
leveraged buyout (LBO) (p. 191)
line extension (p. 190)

logistics strategy (p. 196)
market development (p. 190)
marketing strategy (p. 190)
mass production (p. 194)
modular manufacturing (p. 195)
multiple sourcing (p. 195)
net present value (NPV) (p. 205)
open innovation (p. 193)
operations strategy (p. 193)
outsourcing (p. 198)

parallel sourcing (p. 196)
penetration pricing (p. 191)
political strategy (p. 205)
product development (p. 190)
pull strategy (p. 190)
purchasing strategy (p. 195)
push strategy (p. 190)

R&D strategy (p. 192)
real-options approach (p. 205)
reverse stock split (p. 192)
risk (p. 204)
skim pricing (p. 191)
sole sourcing (p. 195)
Stakeholder priority matrix (p. 205)

strategic choice (p. 207)
strategies to avoid (p. 201)
technological follower (p. 192)
technological leader (p. 192)
tracking stock (p. 192)

PART ENDING VIDEO CASE PART THREE

Newbury Comics, Inc.

STRATEGY FORMULATION

Newbury Comics Cofounders Mike Dreese and John Brusger parlayed $2,000 and a comic book collection into a thriving chain of 22 stores spanning the New England region, known to be *the* place to shop for everything from the best of the underground/independent music scene to major label superstars. The chain also stocks a wide variety of non-music related items such as T-shirts, Dr. (doc) Martens shoes, posters, jewelry, cosmetics, books, magazines, and other trendy items.

In Part Three, **"Strategy Formulation,"** the video addresses strategy formulation in terms of situation analysis, business, corporate, and functional strategy. Mike, John, and Jan conduct a SWOT analysis of Newbury Comics in terms of Strengths, Weaknesses, Opportunities, and Threats and how strategy is formulated. They are very much aware of how the company's core competencies provide competitive advantage. Mike explains that he dislikes setting three-year revenue targets (objectives), but prefers to formulate strategy on an experimental basis. Note that even when discussing strategy formulation, Mike talks about implementation. He tells how he assigned the development of the used CD implementation plan to Duncan Brown, Senior Vice President. Brown was to look for long-run roadblocks in case the strategy was successful in the short run. Newbury Comics is a good example of the value of SWOT analysis when formulating strategy. Most of the information, such as the employees' knowledge and competition, was presented in the earlier video dealing with environmental scanning. Some of the threats, however, are mentioned for the first time. Mike notes that the vendor community (suppliers of new CDs) may decide to make it difficult for any retailer to buy new CDs if that retailer sells used ones. He also notes that in four to five years, Napster-type operators who deal in digit-to-digit downloads instead of CDs may dominate the business of music distribution.

The management of Newbury Comics definitely believes that the company has a competitive advantage (edge) in its market. Jan states that the company's prices are cheaper than the mall music stores plus it offers used CDs. Even when competitors like Best Buy have similar prices, Newbury Comics has a better selection plus used CDs. Mike again points out that the company's corporate culture attracts employees with a "knowledge of the street." One-third of the employees play in bands. John adds that Newbury Comics offers hard-to-find material that is sold in "onesies" and "twosies" to the discriminating buyer.

Concepts Illustrated in the Video

- Strategy Formulation
- SWOT Analysis
- Propitious Niche
- Competitive Strategy
- Competitive Tactics (timing)

- Corporate Growth Strategy
- Marketing Strategy
- Human Resource Management Strategy
- Information Systems Strategy
- Management's Attitude Toward Risk

Study Questions

1. Has Newbury Comics found a "propitious niche"?

2. Conduct a SWOT analysis of Newbury Comics. Did you list anything that management failed to list?

3. The video casually mentions mission and objectives for the company. Formulate a mission statement for Newbury Comics.

4. What competitive strategy is being followed by Newbury Comics?

5. What corporate strategy is being followed by Newbury Comics?

CHAPTER 9
Strategy Implementation: Organizing for Action

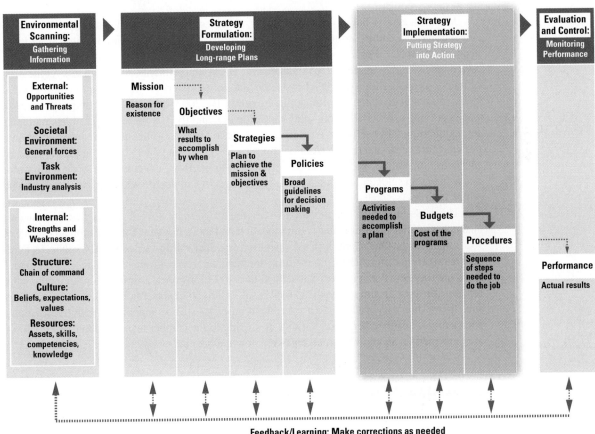

Environmental Scanning: Gathering Information	Strategy Formulation: Developing Long-range Plans	Strategy Implementation: Putting Strategy into Action	Evaluation and Control: Monitoring Performance

External: Opportunities and Threats

Societal Environment: General forces

Task Environment: Industry analysis

Internal: Strengths and Weaknesses

Structure: Chain of command

Culture: Beliefs, expectations, values

Resources: Assets, skills, competencies, knowledge

Mission
Reason for existence

Objectives
What results to accomplish by when

Strategies
Plan to achieve the mission & objectives

Policies
Broad guidelines for decision making

Programs
Activities needed to accomplish a plan

Budgets
Cost of the programs

Procedures
Sequence of steps needed to do the job

Performance
Actual results

Feedback/Learning: Make corrections as needed

Learning Objectives

After reading this chapter, you should be able to:

- Develop programs, budgets, and procedures to implement strategic change
- Understand the importance of achieving synergy during strategy implementation
- List the stages of corporate development and the structure that characterizes each stage
- Identify the blocks to changing from one stage to another
- Construct matrix and network structures to support flexible and nimble organizational strategies
- Decide when and if programs such as reengineering, Six Sigma, and job redesign are appropriate methods of strategy implementation
- Understand the centralization versus decentralization issue in multinational corporations

JOHNSON & JOHNSON (J&J) IS ONE OF THE MOST SUCCESSFUL HEALTH-CARE COMPANIES IN the world. Founded in 1886, it is composed of 204 different business units, organized into 3 groups: pharmaceutical drugs, medical devices and diagnostics, and consumer products. Although most people know J&J for its Band-Aids and baby powder, its competitors know the company as a fierce rival that combines scientific expertise with intelligent marketing. It regularly develops or acquires innovative products and then sells them more aggressively than most companies. Even though hospitals might prefer to purchase surgical tools from one company and sutures from another, it will likely buy them both from J&J because J&J offers favorable prices to hospitals that buy the whole package. Johnson & Johnson's reputation as an ethical company makes it easy for the company to persuade physicians and consumers to try its new products.

J&J's success is based on its unique structure and culture. J&J is structured as a divisional company, and its authority is very decentralized. Each of its units operates as an independent enterprise. For example, each unit establishes its own business strategy and has its own finance and human resource management (HRM) departments. Although this duplication of functions creates high overhead costs, the autonomy fosters an entrepreneurial attitude that keeps the company intensely competitive overall. By 2003, however, the company's growth was beginning to level off. Drug sales were slowing, and there were fewer feasible candidates for acquisition. CEO William Weldon and his top management team decided that additional growth must come internally, from obtaining synergy among J&J's many units. As head of J&J's drug operation, Weldon had earlier worked to get R&D executives to work with senior managers from sales and marketing on a new committee to decide which projects to push and which to drop.

The cross-functional collaboration within the drug group worked so well that Weldon created new systems to foster better communication and more frequent collaboration among all of J&J's many units. One result of this cooperation was J&J's drug-coated stent, Cypher. J&J created teams from different units in the drug and medical device groups to collaborate on manufacturing this new type of stent. The device not only props open arteries after angioplasty but releases the drug sirolimus into the blood vessel wall to block the creation of excessive scar tissue. "If we didn't have all this expertise, we'd probably still be negotiating with outside companies to put this together," said Weldon. Referring to the Cypher team, Weldon stated: "They are the experts who know the marketplace, know the hospitals, and know the cardiologists."[1]

9.1 | Strategy Implementation

Strategy implementation is the sum total of the activities and choices required for the execution of a strategic plan. It is the process by which objectives, strategies, and policies are put into action through the development of programs, budgets, and procedures. Although implementation is usually considered after strategy has been formulated, implementation is a key part of strategic management. Strategy formulation and strategy implementation should thus be considered as two sides of the same coin.

Poor implementation has been blamed for a number of strategic failures. For example, studies show that half of all acquisitions fail to achieve what was expected of them, and one out of four international ventures does not succeed.[2] The most-mentioned problems reported in postmerger integration were poor communication, unrealistic synergy expectations, structural problems, missing master plan, lost momentum, lack of top management commitment, and unclear strategic fit. A study by A. T. Kearney found that a company has just two years in which to make an acquisition perform. After the second year, the window of opportunity for forging synergies has mostly closed. Kearney's study was supported by further independent research by Bert, MacDonald, and Herd. Among the most successful acquirers studied, 70% to 85% of all merger synergies were realized within the first 12 months, with the remainder being realized in year 2.[3]

To begin the implementation process, strategy makers must consider these questions:

- *Who* are the people who will carry out the strategic plan?
- *What* must be done to align the company's operations in the new intended direction?
- *How* is everyone going to work together to do what is needed?

These questions and similar ones should have been addressed initially when the pros and cons of strategic alternatives were analyzed. They must also be addressed again before appropriate implementation plans can be made. Unless top management can answer these basic questions satisfactorily, even the best-planned strategy is unlikely to provide the desired outcome.

A survey of 93 *Fortune 500* firms revealed that more than half of the corporations experienced the following 10 problems when they attempted to implement a strategic change. These problems are listed in order of frequency:

1. Implementation took more time than originally planned.
2. Unanticipated major problems arose.
3. Activities were ineffectively coordinated.
4. Competing activities and crises took attention away from implementation.
5. The involved employees had insufficient capabilities to perform their jobs.
6. Lower-level employees were inadequately trained.
7. Uncontrollable external environmental factors created problems.
8. Departmental managers provided inadequate leadership and direction.
9. Key implementation tasks and activities were poorly defined.
10. The information system inadequately monitored activities.[4]

9.2 | Who Implements Strategy?

Depending on how a corporation is organized, those who implement strategy will probably be a much more diverse set of people than those who formulate it. In most large, multi-industry corporations, the implementers are everyone in the organization. Vice presidents of functional areas and directors of divisions or strategic business units (SBUs) work with their subordinates to put together large-scale implementation plans. Plant managers, project managers, and unit heads put together plans for their specific plants, departments, and units. Therefore, every operational manager down to the first-line supervisor and every employee is involved in some way in the implementation of corporate, business, and functional strategies.

Many of the people in the organization who are crucial to successful strategy implementation probably have little to do with the development of the corporate and even business strategy. Therefore, they might be entirely ignorant of the vast amount of data and work that went into the formulation process. Unless changes in mission, objectives, strategies, and policies and their importance to the company are communicated clearly to all operational managers, there can be a lot of resistance and foot-dragging. Managers might hope to influence top management into abandoning its new plans and returning to its old ways. This is one reason why involving people from all organizational levels in the formulation and implementation of strategy tends to result in better organizational performance.

9.3 | **What Must Be Done?**

The managers of divisions and functional areas work with their fellow managers to develop programs, budgets, and procedures for the implementation of strategy. They also work to achieve synergy among the divisions and functional areas in order to establish and maintain a company's distinctive competence.

Developing Programs, Budgets, and Procedures

Strategy implementation involves establishing programs to create a series of new organizational activities, budgets to allocate funds to the new activities, and procedures to handle the day-to-day details.

Programs

The purpose of a **program** is to make a strategy action oriented. For example, when Xerox Corporation undertook a turnaround strategy, it needed to significantly reduce its costs and expenses. In 2002 management introduced a program called *Lean Six Sigma*. This program was developed to identify and improve a poorly performing process. Xerox first trained its top executives in the program and then launched around 250 individual Six Sigma projects throughout the corporation. The result was $6 million in saving in 2003, with even more expected in 2004.[5] (Six Sigma is explained later in this chapter.)

One way to examine the likely impact new programs will have on an existing organization is to compare proposed programs and activities with current programs and activities. Brynjolfsson, Renshaw, and Van Alstyne proposed a **matrix of change** to help managers decide how quickly change should proceed, in what order changes should take place, whether to start at a new site, and whether the proposed systems are stable and coherent. As shown in **Figure 9–1**, target practices (new programs) for a manufacturing plant are drawn on the vertical axis, and existing practices (current activities) are drawn on the horizontal axis. As shown, any new strategy will likely involve a sequence of new programs and activities. Any one of these may conflict with existing practices/activities—and that creates implementation problems. Use the following steps to create the matrix:

1. Compare the new programs/target practices with each other to see if they are complementary (+), interfering (−), or have no effect on each other (leave blank).

2. Examine existing practices/activities for their interactions with each other, using the same symbols as in step 1.

3. Compare each new program/target practice with each existing practice/activity for any interaction effects. Place the appropriate symbols in the cells in the lower-right part of the matrix.

Figure 9–1
**The Matrix of
Change**

4. Evaluate each program/activity in terms of its relative importance to achieving the strategy or getting the job accomplished.

5. Examine the overall matrix to identify problem areas where proposed programs are likely to interfere with each other or with existing practices/activities. Note in **Figure 9–1** that the proposed program of installing flexible equipment interferes with the proposed program of assembly-line rationalization. The two new programs need to be changed so that they no longer conflict with each other. Note also that the amount of change necessary to carry out the proposed implementation programs (target practices) is a function of the number of times each program interferes with existing practices/activities. That is, the more minus signs and the fewer plus signs in the matrix, the more implementation problems can be expected.

The matrix of change can be used to address the following types of questions:

- **Feasibility:** Do the proposed programs and activities constitute a coherent, stable system? Are the current activities coherent and stable? Is the transition likely to be difficult?

- **Sequence of Execution:** Where should the change begin? How does the sequence affect success? Are there reasonable stopping points?

- **Location:** Are we better off instituting the new programs at a new site, or can we reorganize the existing facilities at a reasonable cost?

- **Pace and Nature of Change:** Should the change be slow or fast, incremental or radical? Which blocks of current activities must be changed at the same time?
- **Stakeholder Evaluations:** Have we overlooked any important activities or interactions? Should we get further input from interested stakeholders? Which new programs and current activities offer the greatest sources of value?

The matrix offers useful guidelines on where, when, and how fast to implement change.[6]

Budgets

After programs have been developed, the **budget** process begins. Planning a budget is the last real check a corporation has on the feasibility of its selected strategy. An ideal strategy might be found to be completely impractical only after specific implementation programs are costed in detail.

Procedures

After the program, divisional, and corporate budgets are approved, **procedures** must be developed. Often called **Standard Operating Procedures (SOPs)**, they typically detail the various activities that must be carried out to complete a corporation's programs. Also known as *organizational routines*, procedures are the primary means by which organizations accomplish much of what they do.[7] Once in place, procedures must be updated to reflect any changes in technology as well as in strategy. For example, a company following a differentiation competitive strategy manages its sales force more closely than does a firm following a low-cost strategy. Differentiation requires long-term customer relationships created out of close interaction with the sales force. An in-depth understanding of the customer needs provides the foundation for product development and improvement.[8] In a retail store, procedures ensure that the day-to-day store operations will be consistent over time (that is, next week's work activities will be the same as this week's) and consistent among stores (that is, each store will operate in the same manner as the others). For example, to ensure that its policies are carried out to the letter in every one of its fast-food retail outlets, McDonald's has done an excellent job of developing very detailed procedures (and policing them!).

Before a new strategy can be successfully implemented, current procedures may need to be changed. For example, in order to implement Home Depot's strategic move into services, such as kitchen and bathroom installation, the company had to first improve its productivity. Store managers were drowning in paperwork designed for a smaller and simpler company. "We'd get a fax, an e-mail, a call, and a memo, all on the same project," reported store manager Michael Jones. One executive used just three weeks of memos to wallpaper an entire conference room, floor to ceiling—windows included. CEO Robert Nardelli told his top managers to eliminate duplicate communications and streamline work projects. Directives not related to work orders had to be sent separately and only once a month. The company also spent $2 million on workload-management software.[9]

Achieving Synergy

One of the goals to be achieved in strategy implementation is synergy between and among functions and business units. This is the reason corporations commonly reorganize after an acquisition. **Synergy** is said to exist for a divisional corporation if the return on investment (ROI) of each division is greater than what the return would be if each division were an independent business. According to Goold and Campbell, synergy can take place in one of six forms:

- **Shared Know-How:** Combined units often benefit from sharing knowledge or skills. This is a leveraging of core competencies.

- **Coordinated Strategies:** Aligning the business strategies of two or more business units may provide a corporation significant advantage by reducing inter-unit competition and developing a coordinated response to common competitors (horizontal strategy).

- **Shared Tangible Resources:** Combined units can sometimes save money by sharing resources, such as a common manufacturing facility or R&D lab.

- **Economies of Scale or Scope:** Coordinating the flow of products or services of one unit with that of another unit can reduce inventory, increase capacity utilization, and improve market access.

- **Pooled Negotiating Power:** Combined units can combine their purchasing to gain bargaining power over common suppliers to reduce costs and improve quality. The same can be done with common distributors.

- **New Business Creation:** Exchanging knowledge and skills can facilitate new products or services by extracting discrete activities from various units and combining them in a new unit or by establishing joint ventures among internal business units.[10]

Johnson & Johnson's program to improve collaboration among its 204 business units is one example of how J&J hoped to obtain all six forms of synergy, but especially the last one, new business creation.

9.4 | How Is Strategy to Be Implemented? Organizing for Action

Before plans can lead to actual performance, a corporation should be appropriately organized, programs should be adequately staffed, and activities should be directed toward achieving desired objectives. (Organizing activities are reviewed briefly in this chapter; staffing, directing, and control activities are discussed in **Chapters 10** and **11**.)

Any change in corporate strategy is very likely to require some sort of change in the way an organization is structured and in the kind of skills needed in particular positions. Managers must, therefore, closely examine the way their company is structured in order to decide what, if any, changes should be made in the way work is accomplished. Should activities be grouped differently? Should the authority to make key decisions be centralized at headquarters or decentralized to managers in distant locations? Should the company be managed like a "tight ship" with many rules and controls, or "loosely" with few rules and controls? Should the corporation be organized into a "tall" structure with many layers of managers, each having a narrow span of control (that is, few employees per supervisor) to better control his or her subordinates; or should it be organized into a "flat" structure with fewer layers of managers, each having a wide span of control (that is, more employees per supervisor) to give more freedom to his or her subordinates?

Structure Follows Strategy

In a classic study of large U.S. corporations such as DuPont, General Motors, Sears, and Standard Oil, Alfred Chandler concluded that **structure follows strategy**—that is, changes in corporate strategy lead to changes in organizational structure.[11] He also concluded that organizations follow a pattern of development from one kind of structural arrangement to another as they expand. According to Chandler, these structural changes occur because the old structure, having been pushed too far, has caused inefficiencies that have become too obviously detrimental to bear. Chandler, therefore, proposed the following as the sequence of what occurs:

1. New strategy is created.
2. New administrative problems emerge.
3. Economic performance declines.
4. New appropriate structure is invented.
5. Profit returns to its previous level.

Chandler found that in their early years, corporations such as DuPont tend to have a centralized functional organizational structure that is well suited to producing and selling a limited range of products. As they add new product lines, purchase their own sources of supply, and create their own distribution networks, they become too complex for highly centralized structures. To remain successful, this type of organization needs to shift to a decentralized structure with several semiautonomous divisions (referred to in **Chapter 5** as *divisional structure*).

Alfred P. Sloan, past CEO of General Motors, detailed how GM conducted such structural changes in the 1920s.[12] He saw decentralization of structure as "centralized policy determination coupled with decentralized operating management." After top management had developed a strategy for the total corporation, the individual divisions (Chevrolet, Buick, and so on) were free to choose how to implement that strategy. Patterned after DuPont, GM found the decentralized multidivisional structure to be extremely effective in allowing the maximum amount of freedom for product development. Return on investment (ROI) was used as a financial control. (ROI is discussed in more detail in **Chapter 11**.)

Research generally supports Chandler's proposition that structure follows strategy (as well as the reverse proposition that structure influences strategy).[13] As mentioned earlier, changes in the environment tend to be reflected in changes in a corporation's strategy, thus leading to changes in a corporation's structure. Strategy, structure, and the environment need to be closely aligned; otherwise, organizational performance will likely suffer.[14] For example, a business unit following a differentiation strategy needs more freedom from headquarters to be successful than does another unit following a low-cost strategy.[15]

Although it is agreed that organizational structure must vary with different environmental conditions, which, in turn, affect an organization's strategy, there is no agreement about an optimal organizational design. What was appropriate for DuPont and General Motors in the 1920s might not be appropriate today. Firms in the same industry do, however, tend to organize themselves similarly to one another. For example, automobile manufacturers tend to emulate General Motors' divisional concept, whereas consumer-goods producers tend to emulate the brand-management concept (a type of matrix structure) pioneered by Procter & Gamble Company. The general conclusion seems to be that firms following similar strategies in similar industries tend to adopt similar structures.

Stages of Corporate Development

Successful corporations tend to follow a pattern of structural development as they grow and expand. Beginning with the simple structure of the entrepreneurial firm (in which everybody does everything), successful corporations usually get larger and organize along functional lines, with marketing, production, and finance departments. With continuing success, the company adds new product lines in different industries and organizes itself into interconnected divisions. The differences among these three structural **stages of corporate development** in terms of typical problems, objectives, strategies, reward systems, and other characteristics are specified in detail in **Table 9–1**.

TABLE 9–1 **FACTORS DIFFERENTIATING STAGE I, II, AND III COMPANIES**

Function	Stage I	Stage II	Stage III
1. Sizing up: Major problems	Survival and growth dealing with short-term operating problems.	Growth, rationalization, and expansion of resources, providing for adequate attention to product problems.	Trusteeship in management and investment and control of large, increasing, and diversified resources. Also, important to diagnose and take action on problems at division level.
2. Objectives	Personal and subjective.	Profits and meeting functionally oriented budgets and performance targets.	ROI, profits, earnings per share.
3. Strategy	Implicit and personal; exploitation of immediate opportunities seen by owner-manager.	Functionally oriented moves restricted to "one product" scope; exploitation of one basic product or service field.	Growth and product diversification; exploitation of general business opportunities.
4. Organization: Major characteristic of structure	One unit, "one-man show."	One unit, functionally specialized group.	Multiunit general staff office and decentralized operating divisions.
5. (a) Measurement and control	Personal, subjective control based on simple accounting system and daily communication and observation.	Control grows beyond one person; assessment of functional operations necessary; structured control systems evolve.	Complex formal system geared to comparative assessment of performance measures, indicating problems and opportunities and assessing management ability of division managers.
5. (b) Key performance indicators	Personal criteria, relationships with owner, operating efficiency, ability to solve operating problems.	Functional and internal criteria such as sales, performance compared to budget, size of empire, status in group, personal, relationships, etc.	More impersonal application of comparisons such as profits, ROI, P/E ratio, sales, market share, productivity, product leadership, personnel development, employee attitudes, public responsibility.
6. Reward-punishment system	Informal, personal, subjective; used to maintain control and divide small pool of resources for key performers to provide personal incentives	More structured; usually based to a greater extent on agreed policies as opposed to personal opinion and relationships.	Allotment by "due process" of a wide variety of different rewards and punishments on a formal and systematic basis. Companywide policies usually apply to many different classes of managers and workers with few major exceptions for individual cases.

Source: Donald H. Thain, "Stages of Corporate Development," *Ivey Business Journal* (formerly *Ivey Business Quarterly*), Winter 1969, p. 37. Copyright © 1969, Ivey Management Services. One time permission to reproduce granted by Ivey Management Services.

Stage I: Simple Structure

Stage I is typified by the entrepreneur, who founds a company to promote an idea (a product or a service). The entrepreneur tends to make all the important decisions personally and is involved in every detail and phase of the organization. The Stage I company has little formal structure, which allows the entrepreneur to directly supervise the activities of every employee (see **Figure 5–4** for an illustration of the simple, functional, and divisional structures). Planning is usually short range or reactive. The typical managerial functions of planning, organizing, directing, staffing, and controlling are usually performed to a very limited degree, if at all. The greatest strengths of a Stage I corporation are its flexibility and dynamism. The drive of the entrepreneur energizes the organization in its struggle for growth. Its greatest weakness is its extreme reliance on the entrepreneur to decide general strategies as well as detailed procedures. If the entrepreneur falters, the company usually flounders. This is labeled by Greiner as a **crisis of leadership**.[16]

Stage I describes Oracle Corporation, the computer software firm, under the management of its co-founder and CEO Lawrence Ellison. The company adopted a pioneering approach to retrieving data, called Structured Query Language (SQL). When IBM made SQL its standard, Oracle's success was assured. Unfortunately, Ellison's technical wizardry was not sufficient to manage the company. Often working at home, he lost sight of details outside his technical interests. Although the company's sales were rapidly increasing, its financial controls were so weak that management had to restate an entire year's results to rectify irregularities. After the company recorded its first loss, Ellison hired a set of functional managers to run the company while he retreated to focus on new product development.

Stage II: Functional Structure

Stage II is the point when the entrepreneur is replaced by a team of managers who have functional specializations. The transition to this stage requires a substantial managerial style change for the chief officer of the company, especially if he or she was the Stage I entrepreneur. He or she must learn to delegate; otherwise, having additional staff members yields no benefits to the organization. The previous example of Ellison's retreat from top management at Oracle Corporation to new product development manager is one way that technically brilliant founders are able to get out of the way of the newly empowered functional managers. In Stage II, the corporate strategy favors protectionism through dominance of the industry, often through vertical and horizontal growth. The great strength of a Stage II corporation lies in its concentration and specialization in one industry. Its great weakness is that all its eggs are in one basket.

By concentrating on one industry while that industry remains attractive, a Stage II company, such as Oracle Corporation in computer software, can be very successful. Once a functionally structured firm diversifies into other products in different industries, however, the advantages of the functional structure break down. A **crisis of autonomy** can now develop, in which people managing diversified product lines need more decision-making freedom than top management is willing to delegate to them. The company needs to move to a different structure.

Stage III: Divisional Structure

Stage III is typified by the corporation's managing diverse product lines in numerous industries; it decentralizes the decision-making authority. Stage III organizations grow by diversifying their product lines and expanding to cover wider geographical areas. They move to a divisional structure with a central headquarters and decentralized operating divisions—with each division or business unit a functionally organized Stage II company. They may also use a conglomerate structure if top management chooses to keep its collection of Stage II subsidiaries operating autonomously. A **crisis of control** can now develop, in which the various units act to optimize their own sales and profits without regard to the overall corporation, whose headquarters seems far away and almost irrelevant.

Recently, divisions have been evolving into SBUs to better reflect product-market considerations. Headquarters attempts to coordinate the activities of its operating divisions or SBUs through performance- and results-oriented control and reporting systems and by stressing corporate planning techniques. The units are not tightly controlled but are held responsible for their own performance results. Therefore, to be effective, the company has to have a decentralized decision process. The greatest strength of a Stage III corporation is its almost unlimited resources. Its most significant weakness is that it is usually so large and complex that it tends to become relatively inflexible. General Electric, DuPont, and General Motors are examples of Stage III corporations.

Stage IV: Beyond SBUs

Even with its evolution into SBUs during the 1970s and 1980s, the divisional structure is not the last word in organization structure. The use of SBUs may result in a **red tape crisis** in which the corporation has grown too large and complex to be managed through formal programs and rigid systems, and procedures take precedence over problem solving. Under conditions of (1) increasing environmental uncertainty, (2) greater use of sophisticated technological production methods and information systems, (3) the increasing size and scope of worldwide business corporations, (4) a greater emphasis on multi-industry competitive strategy, and (5) a more educated cadre of managers and employees, new advanced forms of organizational structure are emerging. These structures emphasize collaboration over competition in the managing of an organization's multiple overlapping projects and developing businesses.

The matrix and the network are two possible candidates for a fourth stage in corporate development—a stage that not only emphasizes horizontal over vertical connections between people and groups but also organizes work around temporary projects in which sophisticated information systems support collaborative activities. According to Greiner, it is likely that this stage of development will have its own crisis as well—a sort of **pressure-cooker crisis**. He predicts that employees in these collaborative organizations will eventually grow emotionally and physically exhausted from the intensity of teamwork and the heavy pressure for innovative solutions.[17]

Blocks to Changing Stages

Corporations often find themselves in difficulty because they are blocked from moving into the next logical stage of development. Blocks to development may be internal (such as lack of resources, lack of ability, or refusal of top management to delegate decision making to others) or external (such as economic conditions, labor shortages, and lack of market growth). For example, Chandler noted in his study that the successful founder/CEO in one stage was rarely the person who created the new structure to fit the new strategy, and as a result, the transition from one stage to another was often painful. This was true of General Motors Corporation under the management of William Durant, Ford Motor Company under Henry Ford I, Polaroid Corporation under Edwin Land, Apple Computer under Steven Jobs, and Hayes Microcomputer Products under Dennis Hayes. (See **Strategy Highlight 9.1** for what happened to the company founded by the inventor of the modem.)

Entrepreneurs who start businesses generally have four tendencies that work very well for small new ventures but become Achilles' heels for these same individuals when they try to manage a larger firm with diverse needs, departments, priorities, and constituencies:

- **Loyalty to comrades:** This is good at the beginning but soon becomes a liability as "favoritism."
- **Task oriented:** Focusing on the job is critical at first but then becomes excessive attention to detail.
- **Single-mindedness:** A grand vision is needed to introduce a new product but can become tunnel vision as the company grows into more markets and products.
- **Working in isolation:** This is good for a brilliant scientist but disastrous for a CEO with multiple constituencies.[18]

STRATEGY HIGHLIGHT 9.1

The Founder of the Modem Blocks Transition to Stage II

Would there be an Internet without the modem? Although most large organizations now rent digital T1 lines for fast Internet access, many individuals and small business owners still access the World Wide Web through the same type of modem and command set invented by Dennis Hayes.

Dennis Hayes is legendary not only for inventing the personal computer modem but also for driving his company into bankruptcy—not once but twice. Hayes and retired partner Dale Heatherington founded Hayes Microcomputer Products 20 years ago, when they invented a device called the Hayes Smartmodem that allowed personal computers to communicate with each other through telephone lines via the Hayes Standard AT Command Set. The modem was needed to convert voice analog data into the digital data needed by computers. Modem sales boomed from $4.8 million in 1981 to $150 million in 1985. When competitors developed low-cost modems, Hayes delayed until the early 1990s to respond with its own low-priced version. Sales and profits plummeted. Hayes lost its dominant position to U.S. Robotics. Management problems mounted. Creditors and potential investors looking into the company's books and operations found them a shambles. According to one investment banker, "The factory was in complete disarray." The company reported its first loss in 1994, by which time the company had nearly $70 million in debt. In November 1994, Hayes applied for protection from creditors under Chapter 11 of the U.S. Bankruptcy Code.

Still under the leadership of its founder, the company underwent a turnaround during 1995. Still in second place with a 9.3% market share of modem sales in North America, Dennis Hayes put his company up for sale. He turned down a bid of $140 million from rival Diamond Multimedia Systems and instead accepted only $30 million for 49% of the company from Asian investors. Although the offer required Mr. Hayes to relinquish the title of CEO, Hayes would still be Chairman of the Board. He explained his decision as deriving from his unwillingness to completely let go of his baby. "I'll be able to have input, through the board and as chairman, that will best use my abilities. What I was concerned about was that someone would come in and . . . slash a part of the company without understanding how it fit in."

The company, renamed Hayes Corporation, continued to suffer losses. On October 9, 1998, the company declared **Chapter 11** bankruptcy for the last time. Unable to find further financing to turn things around, the company was forced to sell its brands, manufacturing facilities, and distribution offices to the Canadian firm Zoom Technologies (www.zoom.com), for $5.3 million. It sold its web site domain name, Hayes.com, its service center, and its spare parts inventories to Modem Express (www.modemexpress.com), a seller of refurbished "orphan" products. The company founded by Dennis Hayes now exists only as a division of another company.

Source: D. McDermott, "Asians Rejuvenate Hayes Microcomputer," *Wall Street Journal* (May 6, 1996), p. A10, plus information gathered from company web sites and Hayes Company documents within the SEC's Edgar database.

This difficulty in moving to a new stage is compounded by the founder's tendency to maneuver around the need to delegate by carefully hiring, training, and grooming his or her own team of managers. The team tends to maintain the founder's influence throughout the organization long after the founder is gone. This is what happened at Walt Disney Productions when the family continued to emphasize Walt's policies and plans long after he was dead. Although this may often be an organization's strength, it may also be a weakness—to the extent that the culture supports the status quo and blocks needed change.

Organizational Life Cycle

Instead of considering stages of development in terms of structure, the organizational life cycle approach places the primary emphasis on the dominant issue facing the corporation. Organizational structure is only a secondary concern. The **organizational life cycle** describes how organizations grow, develop, and eventually decline. It is the organizational equivalent of the product life cycle in marketing. These stages are Birth (Stage I), Growth (Stage II), Maturity (Stage III), Decline (Stage IV), and Death (Stage V). The impact of these stages on

TABLE 9–2 ORGANIZATIONAL LIFE CYCLE

	Stage I	Stage II	Stage III*	Stage IV	Stage V
Dominant Issue	Birth	Growth	Maturity	Decline	Death
Popular Strategies	Concentration in a niche	Horizontal and vertical growth	Concentric and conglomerate diversification	Profit strategy followed by retrenchment	Liquidation or bankruptcy
Likely Structure	Entrepreneur dominated	Functional management emphasized	Decentralization into profit or investment centers.	Structural surgery	Dismemberment of structure

Note: *An organization may enter a Revival phase either during the Maturity or Decline stages and thus extend the organization's life.

corporate strategy and structure is summarized in **Table 9–2**. Note that the first three stages of the organizational life cycle are similar to the three commonly accepted stages of corporate development mentioned previously. The only significant difference is the addition of the Decline and Death stages to complete the cycle. Even though a company's strategy may still be sound, its aging structure, culture, and processes may be such that they prevent the strategy from being executed properly. Its core competencies become *core ridgities* that are no longer able to adapt to changing conditions—thus the company moves into Decline.[19]

Movement from Growth to Maturity to Decline and finally to Death is not, however, inevitable. A Revival phase may occur sometime during the Maturity or Decline stages. The corporation's life cycle can be extended by managerial and product innovations.[20] This often occurs during the implementation of a turnaround strategy. This is what happened at Lionel, the maker of toy electric trains. Founded by Joshua Lionel Cowen in 1900 to make electrical devices, Lionel came to define the toy electric train. In 1953, Lionel sold three million engines and freight cars, making it the biggest toy manufacturer in the world. By the mid-1960s, the company was in decline. Electric trains were becoming a historical curiosity. Slot cars and space toys were in demand. Train hobbyists preferred the smaller HO gauge electric train over Lionel's larger train because HO gauge trains were more realistic and used less space. The company barely managed to remain in business over the next three decades. In 1999, Lionel's new owners hired Richard Maddox, a lifelong train enthusiast and an executive close to retirement at toy company Bachmann Industries. Maddox and his executive team worked to update Lionel's trains with new models and the latest technology. He improved the catalog and established dozens of licensing agreements. "We're trying to excel in things whimsical, clever," says Maddox. The unofficial Lionel historian, Todd Wagner, discovered long-forgotten blueprints of trains from the 1920s and 1930s that were gathering dust in old Lionel storerooms. The company decided to use those plans to build more authentic historical models. The reinvigorated company soon saw increased sales and profits.[21]

Unless a company is able to resolve the critical issues facing it in the Decline stage, it is likely to move into Stage V, Death—also known as bankruptcy. This is what happened to Montgomery Ward, Pan American Airlines, Macy's Department Stores, Baldwin-United, Eastern Airlines, Colt's Manufacturing, Orion Pictures, and Wheeling-Pittsburgh Steel, as well as many other firms. So many Internet ventures went bankrupt during 2000 that *Fortune* magazine listed 135 Internet companies on its "Dot-Com Deathwatch."[22] As in the cases of Johns-Manville, International Harvester, Macy's, and Kmart—all of which went bankrupt—a corporation can rise like a phoenix from its own ashes and live again under the same or a different name. The company may be reorganized or liquidated, depending on individual circumstances. For example, Kmart emerged from Chapter 11 bankruptcy in 2003 with a new

CEO and a plan to sell a number of its stores to Home Depot and Sears. These sales earned the company close to $1 billion. Although store sales continued to erode, Kmart had sufficient cash reserves to continue with its turnaround.[23] It used that money to acquire Sears in 2005. Unfortunately, however, fewer than 20% of firms entering Chapter 11 bankruptcy in the United States emerge as going concerns; the rest are forced into liquidation.[24]

Few corporations move through these five stages in order. Some corporations, for example, might never move past Stage II. Others, like General Motors, might go directly from Stage I to Stage III. A large number of entrepreneurial ventures jump from Stage I or II directly into Stage IV or V. Hayes Microcomputer Products, for example, went from the Growth (Stage II) to Decline stage (Stage IV) under its founder Dennis Hayes. The key is to be able to identify indications that a firm is in the process of changing stages and to make the appropriate strategic and structural adjustments to ensure that corporate performance is maintained or even improved. This is what the successful Internet auction firm eBay did when it hired Meg Whitman from Hasbro as CEO to professionalize its management and to improve its marketing.

Advanced Types of Organizational Structures

The basic structures (simple, functional, divisional, and conglomerate) are discussed in **Chapter 5** and summarized under the first three stages of corporate development in this chapter. A new strategy may require more flexible characteristics than the traditional functional or divisional structure can offer. Today's business organizations are becoming less centralized, with a greater use of cross-functional work teams. **Table 9–3** depicts some of the changing structural characteristics of modern corporations. Although many variations and hybrid structures contain these characteristics, two forms stand out: the matrix structure and the network structure.

Matrix Structure

Most organizations find that organizing around either functions (in the functional structure) or products and geography (in the divisional structure) provides an appropriate organizational structure. The matrix structure, in contrast, may be very appropriate when organizations conclude that neither functional nor divisional forms, even when combined with horizontal linking mechanisms such as SBUs, are right for their situations. In **matrix structures**,

TABLE 9–3
CHANGING STRUCTURAL CHARACTERISTICS OF MODERN CORPORATIONS

Old Organization Design	New Organization Design
One large corporation	Minibusiness units and cooperative relationships
Vertical communication	Horizontal communication
Centralized, top-down decision making	Decentralized participative decision making
Vertical integration	Outsourcing and virtual organizations
Work/quality teams	Autonomous work teams
Functional work teams	Cross-functional work teams
Minimal training	Extensive training
Specialized job design focused on individuals	Value-chain team-focused job design

Source: Reprinted from *RESEARCH IN ORGANIZATIONAL CHANGE AND DEVELOPMENT*, Vol. 7, No. 1, 1993, Macy and Izumi, "Organizational Change, Design, and Work Innovation: A Meta-Analysis of 131 North American Field Studies—1961–1991," p. 298. Copyright © 1993 with permission from Elsevier.

Figure 9–2
**Matrix and
Network Structures**

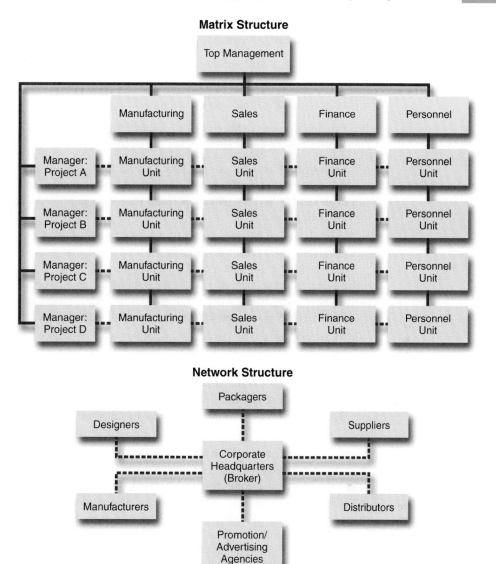

functional and product forms are combined simultaneously at the same level of the organization. (See **Figure 9–2**.) Employees have two superiors, a product or project manager, and a functional manager. The "home" department—that is, engineering, manufacturing, or sales—is usually functional and is reasonably permanent. People from these functional units are often assigned temporarily to one or more product units or projects. The product units or projects are usually temporary and act like divisions in that they are differentiated on a product-market basis.

Pioneered in the aerospace industry, the matrix structure was developed to combine the stability of the functional structure with the flexibility of the product form. The matrix structure is very useful when the external environment (especially its technological and market aspects) is very complex and changeable. It does, however, produce conflicts revolving around duties, authority, and resource allocation. To the extent that the goals to be achieved are vague and the technology used is poorly understood, a continuous battle for power between product and functional managers is likely. The matrix structure is often found in an organization or SBU when the following three conditions exist:

- Ideas need to be cross-fertilized across projects or products.
- Resources are scarce.
- Abilities to process information and to make decisions need to be improved.[25]

Davis and Lawrence, authorities on the matrix form of organization, propose that *three distinct phases* exist in the development of the matrix structure[26]:

1. **Temporary Cross-functional Task Forces:** These are initially used when a new product line is being introduced. A project manager is in charge as the key horizontal link. J&J's experience with cross-functional teams in its drug group led it to emphasize teams crossing multiple units.

2. **Product/brand Management:** If the cross-functional task forces become more permanent, the project manager becomes a product or brand manager, and a second phase begins. In this arrangement, function is still the primary organizational structure, but product or brand managers act as the integrators of semi-permanent products or brands. Considered by many a key to the success of P&G, brand management has been widely imitated by other consumer products firms around the world.

3. **Mature Matrix:** The third and final phase of matrix development involves a true dual-authority structure. Both the functional and product structures are permanent. All employees are connected to both a vertical functional superior and a horizontal product manager. Functional and product managers have equal authority and must work well together to resolve disagreements over resources and priorities. Boeing and TRW Systems are example of companies that use a mature matrix.

Network Structure—The Virtual Organization

A newer and somewhat radical organizational design, the **network structure** (see **Figure 9–2**) is an example of what could be termed a "non-structure" because of its virtual elimination of in-house business functions. Many activities are outsourced. A corporation organized in this manner is often called a **virtual organization** because it is composed of a series of project groups or collaborations linked by constantly changing nonhierarchical, cobweb-like electronic networks.[27]

The network structure becomes most useful when the environment of a firm is unstable and is expected to remain so.[28] Under such conditions, there is usually a strong need for innovation and quick response. Instead of having salaried employees, the company may contract with people for a specific project or length of time. Long-term contracts with suppliers and distributors replace services that the company could provide for itself through vertical integration. Electronic markets and sophisticated information systems reduce the transaction costs of the marketplace, thus justifying a "buy" over a "make" decision. Rather than being located in a single building or area, the organization's business functions are scattered worldwide. The organization is, in effect, only a shell, with a small headquarters acting as a "broker," electronically connected to some completely owned divisions, partially owned subsidiaries, and other independent companies. In its ultimate form, a network organization is a series of independent firms or business units linked together by computers in an information system that designs, produces, and markets a product or service.[29]

An example of a complete network organization is Just Toys. This New York City company licenses characters such as Disney's Little Mermaid, Hanna-Barbera's Flintstones, and Marvel Entertainment's Spiderman to make bendable polyvinyl chloride figures called Bend-Ems. The manufacturing and administrative work for Bend-Ems is contracted out. The company has only 30 employees. If a toy isn't selling well, production can be reduced and shipments stopped almost immediately. It would take Mattel and Hasbro months to react in a similar situation.

Other companies, such as Nike, Reebok, and Benetton, use the network structure in their operations function by subcontracting (outsourcing) manufacturing to other companies in low-cost locations around the world. For control purposes, the Italian-based Benetton maintains what it calls an "umbilical cord" by assuring production planning for all its subcontractors, planning materials requirements for them, and providing them with bills of labor and standard prices and costs, as well as technical assistance to make sure their quality is up to Benetton's standards.

The network organizational structure provides an organization with increased flexibility and adaptability to cope with rapid technological change and shifting patterns of international trade and competition. It allows a company to concentrate on its distinctive competencies while gathering efficiencies from other firms that are concentrating their efforts in their areas of expertise. The network does, however, have disadvantages. Some believe that the network is really only a transitional structure because it is inherently unstable and subject to tensions.[30] The availability of numerous potential partners can be a source of trouble. Contracting out individual activities to separate suppliers or distributors may keep the firm from discovering internal synergies by combining these activities. If a particular firm overspecializes on only a few functions, it runs the risk of choosing the wrong functions and thus becoming noncompetitive.

Cellular Organization: A New Type of Structure?

Miles and Snow et al. propose that the evolution of organizational forms is leading from the matrix and the network to the cellular organizational form. According to them, "a **cellular organization** is composed of cells (self-managing teams, autonomous business units, etc.) which can operate alone but which can interact with other cells to produce a more potent and competent business mechanism." This combination of independence and interdependence allows the cellular organizational form to generate and share the knowledge and expertise needed to produce continuous innovation. The cellular form includes the dispersed entrepreneurship of the divisional structure, customer responsiveness of the matrix, and self-organizing knowledge and asset sharing of the network.[31] As proposed, the cellular structure is similar to a current trend in industry of using internal joint ventures to temporarily combine specialized expertise and skills within a corporation to accomplish a task that individual units alone could not accomplish.[32]

According to Miles and Snow et al., the impetus for such a new structure is the pressure for a continuous process of innovation in all industries. Each cell has an entrepreneurial responsibility to the larger organization. Beyond knowledge creation and sharing, the cellular form adds value by keeping the firm's total knowledge assets more fully in use than any other type of structure. It is beginning to appear in firms that are focused on rapid product and service innovation—providing unique or state-of-the-art offerings.

Reengineering and Strategy Implementation

Reengineering is the radical redesign of business processes to achieve major gains in cost, service, or time. It is not in itself a type of structure, but it is an effective way to implement a turnaround strategy.

Business process reengineering strives to break away from the old rules and procedures that develop and become ingrained in every organization over the years. These may be a combination of policies, rules, and procedures that have never been seriously questioned because they were established years earlier. They may range from "Credit decisions are made by the credit department" to "Local inventory is needed for good customer service." These rules of organization and work design may have been based on assumptions about technology, people, and organizational goals that may no longer be relevant. Rather than attempting to fix existing problems through minor adjustments and fine-tuning of existing processes, the key to reengineering is asking, "If this were a new company, how would we run this place?"

Michael Hammer, who popularized the concept of reengineering, suggests the following principles for reengineering:

- **Organize around outcomes, not tasks:** Design a person's or a department's job around an objective or outcome instead of a single task or series of tasks.

- **Have those who use the output of the process perform the process:** With computer-based information systems, processes can now be reengineered so that the people who need the result of the process can do it themselves.

- **Subsume information-processing work into the real work that produces the information:** People or departments that produce information can also process it for use instead of just sending raw data to others in the organization to interpret.

- **Treat geographically dispersed resources as though they were centralized:** With modern information systems, companies can provide flexible service locally while keeping the actual resources in a centralized location for coordination purposes.

- **Link parallel activities instead of integrating their results:** Instead of having separate units perform different activities that must eventually come together, have them communicate while they work so that they can do the integrating.

- **Put the decision point where the work is performed and build control into the process:** The people who do the work should make the decisions and be self-controlling.

- **Capture information once and at the source:** Instead of having each unit develop its own database and information processing activities, the information can be put on a network so that all can access it.[33]

Studies of the performance of reengineering programs show mixed results. Several companies have had success with business process reengineering. For example, the Mossville Engine Center, a business unit of Caterpillar, Inc., used reengineering to decrease process cycle times by 50%, reduce the number of process steps by 45%, reduce human effort by 8%, and improve cross-divisional interactions and overall employee decision making.[34]

One study of North American financial firms found that "the average reengineering project took 15 months, consumed 66 person-months of effort, and delivered cost savings of 24%."[35] In a survey of 782 corporations using reengineering, 75% of the executives said their companies had succeeded in reducing operating expenses and increasing productivity. Although only 47% stated that their companies had succeeded in generating revenue growth and 37% at raising market share, 70% of the respondents stated that their companies planned to use reengineering in the future.[36] A study of 134 large and small Canadian companies found that reengineering programs resulted in (1) an increase in productivity and product quality, (2) cost reductions, and (3) an increase in overall organization quality, for both large and small firms.[37] Other studies report, however, that anywhere from 50% to 70% of reengineering programs fail to achieve their objectives.[38]

Six Sigma

Originally conceived by Motorola as a quality improvement program in the mid-1980s, Six Sigma has become a cost-saving program for all types of manufacturers. Briefly, **Six Sigma** is an analytical method for achieving near-perfect results on a production line. Although the emphasis is on reducing product variance in order to boost quality and efficiency, it is increasingly being applied to accounts receivable, sales, and R&D. In statistics, the Greek letter *sigma* denotes variation in the standard bell-shaped curve. One sigma equals 690,000 defects per 1 million. Most companies are only able to achieve three sigma, or 66,000 errors per million. Six Sigma reduces the defects to only 3.4 per million—thus saving money by preventing waste. The process of Six Sigma encompasses five steps:

1. *Define* a process where results are poorer than average.
2. *Measure* the process to determine exact current performance.
3. *Analyze* the information to pinpoint where things are going wrong.
4. *Improve* the process and eliminate the error.
5. *Establish* controls to prevent future defects from occurring.[39]

At Dow Chemical, each Six Sigma project has resulted in cost savings of $500,000 in the first year. Six Sigma experts at 3M have been able to speed up R&D and analyze why its top sales people sold more than others. A disadvantage of the program is that training costs in the beginning may outweigh any savings. The expense of compiling and analyzing data, especially in areas where a process cannot be easily standardized, may exceed what is saved.[40]

A new program called **Lean Six Sigma** is becoming increasingly popular in companies. This program incorporates the statistical approach of Six Sigma with the lean manufacturing program originally developed by Toyota. Like reengineering, it includes the removal of unnecessary steps in any process and fixing those that remain. This is the "lean" addition to Six Sigma. Xerox used Lean Six Sigma to resolve a problem with a $500,000 printing press it had just introduced. Teams from supply, manufacturing, and R&D development used Lean Six Sigma to find the cause of the problem and to resolve it by working with a supplier to change the chemistry of the oil on a roller.[41]

Designing Jobs to Implement Strategy

Organizing a company's activities and people to implement strategy involves more than simply redesigning a corporation's overall structure; it also involves redesigning the way jobs are done. With the increasing emphasis on reengineering, many companies are beginning to rethink their work processes, with an eye toward phasing unnecessary people and activities out of the process. Process steps that have traditionally been performed sequentially can be improved by performing them concurrently using cross-functional work teams. Harley-Davidson, for example, has managed to reduce total plant employment by 25% while reducing by 50% the time needed to build a motorcycle. Restructuring through needing fewer people requires broadening the scope of jobs and encouraging teamwork. The design of jobs and subsequent job performance are, therefore, increasingly being considered as sources of competitive advantage.

Job design refers to the study of individual tasks in an attempt to make them more relevant to the company and to the employee(s). To minimize some of the adverse consequences of task specialization, corporations have turned to new job design techniques: **job enlargement** (combining tasks to give a worker more of the same type of duties to perform), **job rotation** (moving workers through several jobs to increase variety), and **job enrichment** (altering the jobs by giving the worker more autonomy and control over activities). The **job characteristics model** is a good example of job enrichment. (See STRATEGY HIGHLIGHT 9.2.) Although each of these methods has its adherents, no one method seems to work in all situations.

A good example of modern job design is the introduction of team-based production by the glass manufacturer Corning, Inc., in its Blacksburg, Virginia, plant. With union approval, Corning reduced job classifications from 47 to 4 to enable production workers to rotate jobs

STRATEGY HIGHLIGHT 9.2

Designing Jobs with the Job Characteristics Model

The job characteristics model is an advanced approach to job design based on the belief that tasks can be described in terms of certain objective characteristics and that these characteristics affect employee motivation. In order for a job to be motivating, (1) the worker needs to feel a sense of responsibility, feel the task to be meaningful, and receive useful feedback on his or her performance, and (2) the job has to satisfy needs that are important to the worker. The model proposes that managers follow five principles for redesigning work:

1. Combine tasks to increase task variety and to enable workers to identify with what they are doing.

2. Form natural work units to make a worker more responsible and accountable for the performance of the job.

3. Establish client relationships so the worker will know what performance is required and why.

4. Vertically load the job by giving workers increased authority and responsibility over their activities.

5. Open feedback channels by providing workers with information on how they are performing.

Research supports the job characteristics model as a way to improve job performance through job enrichment. Although there are several other approaches to job design, practicing managers seem increasingly to follow the prescriptions of this model as a way of improving productivity and product quality.

———————

Source: J. R. Hackman and G. R. Oldham, *Work Redesign* (Reading, MA: Addison-Wesley, 1980), pp. 135–141; G. Johns, J. L. Xie, and Y. Fang, "Mediating and Moderating Effects in Job Design," *Journal of Management* (December 1992), pp. 657–676; R. W. Griffin, "Effects of Work Redesign on Employee Perceptions, Attitudes, and Behaviors: A Long-Term Investigation," *Academy of Management Journal* (June 1991), pp. 425–435.

after learning new skills. The workers were divided into 14-member teams that, in effect, managed themselves. The plant had only two levels of management: Plant Manager Robert Hoover and two line leaders who only advised the teams. Employees worked demanding $12\frac{1}{2}$-hour shifts, alternating three-day and four-day weeks. The teams made managerial decisions, imposed discipline on fellow workers, and were required to learn three "skill modules" within two years or else lose their jobs. As a result of this new job design, a Blacksburg team, made up of workers with interchangeable skills, can retool a line to produce a different type of filter in only 10 minutes—six times faster than workers in a traditionally designed filter plant. The Blacksburg plant earned a $2 million profit in its first eight months of production instead of losing the $2.3 million projected for the startup period. The plant performed so well that Corning's top management acted to convert the company's 27 other factories to team-based production.[42]

9.5 | International Issues in Strategy Implementation

An international company is one that engages in any combination of activities, from exporting/importing to full-scale manufacturing, in foreign countries. A **multinational corporation (MNC)**, in contrast, is a highly developed international company with a deep involvement throughout the world, plus a worldwide perspective in its management and decision making. For an MNC to be considered global, it must manage its worldwide operations as if they were totally interconnected. This approach works best when the industry has moved from being *multidomestic* (each country's industry is essentially separate from the same industry in other countries; an example is retailing) to *global* (each country is a part of one worldwide industry; an example is consumer electronics).

The design of an organization's structure is strongly affected by the company's stage of development in international activities and the types of industries in which the company is involved. Strategic alliances may complement or even substitute for an internal functional activity. The issue of centralization versus decentralization becomes especially important for an MNC operating in both multidomestic and global industries.

International Strategic Alliances

Strategic alliances, such as joint ventures and licensing agreements, between an MNC and a local partner in a host country are becoming increasingly popular as a means by which a corporation can gain entry into other countries, especially less developed countries. The key to the successful implementation of these strategies is the selection of the local partner. Each party needs to assess not only the strategic fit of each company's project strategy but also the fit of each company's respective resources. A successful joint venture may require as much as two years of prior contacts between the parties. Research reveals that firms favor past partners when forming new alliances.[43] Key drivers for strategic fit between alliance partners are the following:

- Partners must agree on fundamental values and have a shared vision about the potential for joint value creation.
- Alliance strategy must be derived from business, corporate, and functional strategy.
- The alliance must be important to both partners, especially to top management.
- Partners must be mutually dependent for achieving clear and realistic objectives.
- Joint activities must have added value for customers and the partners.
- The alliance must be accepted by key stakeholders.
- Partners contribute key strengths but protect core competencies.[44]

Stages of International Development

Corporations operating internationally tend to evolve through five common stages, both in their relationships with widely dispersed geographic markets and in the manner in which they structure their operations and programs. These **stages of international development** are:

- **Stage 1 (Domestic Company):** The primarily domestic company exports some of its products through local dealers and distributors in the foreign countries. The impact on the organization's structure is minimal because an export department at corporate headquarters handles everything.
- **Stage 2 (Domestic Company with Export Division):** Success in Stage 1 leads the company to establish its own sales company with offices in other countries to eliminate the middlemen and to better control marketing. Because exports have now become more important, the company establishes an export division to oversee foreign sales offices.
- **Stage 3 (Primarily Domestic Company with International Division):** Success in earlier stages leads the company to establish manufacturing facilities in addition to sales and service offices in key countries. The company now adds an international division with responsibilities for most of the business functions conducted in other countries.
- **Stage 4 (Multinational Corporation with Multidomestic Emphasis):** Now a full-fledged MNC, the company increases its investments in other countries. The company establishes a local operating division or company in the host country, such as Ford of Britain, to better serve the market. The product line is expanded, and local manufacturing capacity is established. Managerial functions (product development, finance, marketing, and so on) are organized locally. Over time, the parent company acquires other related businesses, broadening the base of the local operating division. As the subsidiary in the

host country successfully develops a strong regional presence, it achieves greater autonomy and self-sufficiency. The operations in each country are, nevertheless, managed separately as if each were a domestic company.

- **Stage 5 (Multinational Corporation with Global Emphasis):** The most successful MNCs move into a fifth stage in which they have worldwide personnel, R&D, and financing strategies. Typically operating in a global industry, the MNC denationalizes its operations and plans product design, manufacturing, and marketing around worldwide considerations. Global considerations now dominate organizational design. The global MNC structures itself in a matrix form around some combination of geographic areas, product lines, and functions. All managers are responsible for dealing with international as well as domestic issues.

Research provides some support for the concept of the stages of international development, but it does not necessarily support the preceding sequence of stages. For example, a company may initiate production and sales in multiple countries without having gone through the steps of exporting or having local sales subsidiaries. In addition, any one corporation can be at different stages simultaneously, with different products in different markets at different levels. Firms may also leapfrog across stages to a global emphasis. Developments in information technology are changing the way business is being done internationally. See the GLOBAL ISSUE feature for a possible sixth stage of international development, in which an MNC locates its headquarters and key functions at multiple locations around the world. Nevertheless, the stages concept provides a useful way to illustrate some of the structural changes corporations undergo when they increase their involvement in international activities.

Centralization Versus Decentralization

A basic dilemma an MNC faces is how to organize authority centrally so that it operates as a vast interlocking system that achieves synergy and at the same time decentralize authority so that local managers can make the decisions necessary to meet the demands of the local mar-

GL🌐BAL ISSUE

Multiple Headquarters: A Sixth Stage of International Development?

In what could be a sixth stage of international development, an increasing number of MNCs are relocating their headquarters and headquarters functions at multiple locations around the world. Of the 800 corporate headquarters established in 2002, 200 of them were in developing nations. The antivirus software company Trend Micro, for example, spreads its top executives, engineers, and support staff throughout the world to improve its ability to respond to new virus threats. "With the Internet, viruses became global. To fight them, we had to become a global company," explained Chairman Steve Chang. Trend Micro's financial headquarters is in Tokyo, where it went public. Its product development is in Taiwan, and its sales headquarters is in America's Silicon Valley.

C. K. Prahalad, strategy professor at the University of Michigan, proposes that this is a new stage of international development. "There is a fundamental rethinking about what

is a multinational company. Does it have a home country? What does headquarters mean? Can you fragment your corporate functions globally?" Corporate headquarters are now becoming virtual, with executives and core corporate functions dispersed throughout various world regions. These primarily technology companies are using geography to obtain competitive advantage through the availability of talent or capital, low costs, or proximity to most important customers. Logitech, for example, has its manufacturing headquarters in Taiwan to capitalize on low-cost Asian manufacturing; its business-development headquarters in Switzerland, where it has a series of strategic technology partnerships; and a third headquarters in Fremont, California.

Sources: S. Hamm, "Borders Are So 20th Century," *Business Week* (January 22, 2003), pp. 68–70; "Globalization from the Top Down," *Futurist* (November–December 2003), p. 13.

ket or host government.[45] To deal with this problem, MNCs tend to structure themselves either along product groups or geographic areas. They may even combine both in a matrix structure—the design chosen by 3M Corporation and Asea Brown Boveri (ABB), among others.[46] One side of 3M's matrix represents the company's product divisions; the other side includes the company's international country and regional subsidiaries.

Two examples of the usual international structure are Nestlé and American Cyanamid. Nestlé's structure is one in which significant power and authority have been decentralized to geographic entities. This structure is similar to that depicted in **Figure 9–3**, in which each geographic set of operating companies has a different group of products. In contrast, American Cyanamid has a series of centralized product groups with worldwide responsibilities. To depict Cyanamid's structure, the geographical entities in **Figure 9–3** would have to be replaced by product groups or SBUs.

The **product-group structure** of American Cyanamid enables the company to introduce and manage a similar line of products around the world. This enables the corporation to centralize decision making along product lines and to reduce costs. The **geographic-area structure** of Nestlé, in contrast, allows the company to tailor products to regional differences and to achieve regional coordination. For instance, Nestlé markets 200 different varieties of its instant coffee, Nescafé. The geographic-area structure decentralizes decision making to the local subsidiaries.

As industries move from being multidomestic to more globally integrated, MNCs are increasingly switching from the geographic-area to the product-group structure. Nestlé, for example, found that its decentralized structure had become increasingly inefficient. As a result, operating margins at Nestlé trailed those at rivals Unilever, Group Danone, and Kraft Foods by as much as 50%. CEO Peter Brabeck-Letmathe acted to eliminate country-by-country responsibilities for many functions. In one instance, he established five centers worldwide to handle most coffee and cocoa purchasing. Nevertheless, Nestlé is still using three different versions of accounting, planning, and inventory software for each of its main regions—Europe, the Americas, and Asia, Oceania, and Africa.[47]

Figure 9–3
Geographic Area Structure for an MNC

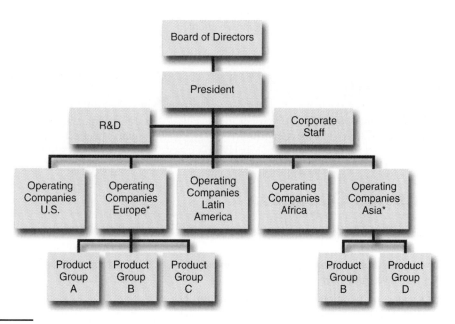

Note: Because of space limitations, product groups for only Europe and Asia are shown here.

Simultaneous pressures for decentralization to be locally responsive and centralization to be maximally efficient are causing interesting structural adjustments in most large corporations. This is what is meant by the phrase "think globally, act locally." Companies are attempting to decentralize those operations that are culturally oriented and closest to the customers—manufacturing, marketing, and human resources. At the same time, the companies are consolidating less visible internal functions, such as research and development, finance, and information systems, where there can be significant economies of scale.

9.6 | Conclusion

Strategy implementation is where "the rubber hits the road." Environmental scanning and strategy formulation are crucial to strategic management but by themselves are only the beginning of the process. The failure to carry a strategic plan into the day-to-day operations of the workplace is a major reason why strategic planning often fails to achieve its objectives. It is discouraging to note that in one study nearly 70% of the strategic plans were never successfully implemented.[48]

For a strategy to be successfully implemented, it must be made action oriented. This is done through a series of programs that are funded through specific budgets and contain new detailed procedures. This chapter explains how jobs and organizational units can be designed to support a change in strategy. This is what Edward Zander did when he took over as CEO of Motorola in 2003. He knew that in order to turn around Motorola's recent poor performance, he had to dismantle Motorola's bureaucracy and its culture of interdepartmental rivalry. The units were referred to as *smokestacks* or *warring tribes*, with very little inter-unit cooperation but a lot of conflict. Zander's plan was to replace Motorola's product-based divisions with customer-based divisions. He hoped that this structural change would promote a more cooperative atmosphere so that the company could implement its new concept of "seamless mobility," in which people could transfer home phone calls, digital music, or television programs to a mobile phone as they leave the house. Zander followed through by making cooperation a key factor in raises and bonuses.[49] Like Zander, we will continue with issues in strategy implementation in the next two chapters.

Strategy Bits

- The implementation of a strategic decision usually takes from 2 to 16 months for completion.[50]

- Most corporate headquarters have around 10 to 30 programs in effect at any one time.[51]

Discussion Questions

1. How should a corporation attempt to achieve synergy among functions and business units?

2. How should an owner–manager prepare a company for its movement from Stage I to Stage II?

3. How can a corporation keep from sliding into the Decline stage of the organizational life cycle?

4. Is reengineering just another management fad, or does it offer something of lasting value?

5. How is the cellular organization different from the network structure?

Strategic Practice Exercise

The Synergy Game
Yolanda Sarason and Catherine Banbury

SETUP
Put three to five chairs on either side of a room, facing each other, in the front of the class. Put a table in the middle, with a bell in the middle of the table.

PROCEDURE
The instructor/moderator divides the class into teams of three to five people. Each team selects a name for itself. The instructor/moderator lists the team names on the board. The first two teams come to the front and sit in the chairs facing each other. The instructor/moderator reads a list of products or services being provided by an actual company. The winning team must identify (1) possible sources of synergy and (2) the actual company being described. For example, if the products/services listed are family restaurants, airline catering, hotels, and retirement centers, the synergy is ***standardized food service and hospitality settings*** and the company is **The Marriott Corporation**. The first team to successfully name the company *and* the synergy wins the round.

After one practice session, the game begins. Each of the teams is free to discuss the question with other team members. When one of the two teams thinks that it has the answer to both parts of the question, it must be the first to ring the bell in order to announce its answer. If it gives the correct answer, it is deemed the winner of round one. Both parts of the answer must be given for a team to have the correct answer. If a team correctly provides only one part, that answer is still wrong—no partial credit. The instructor/moderator does not say which part of the answer, if either, was

correct. The second team then has the opportunity to state the answer. If the second team is wrong, both teams may try once more. If neither chooses to try again, the instructor/moderator may (1) declare no round winner and both teams sit down, (2) allow the next two teams to provide the answer to round one, or (3) go on to the next round with the same two teams. Two new teams then come to the front for the next round. Once all groups have played once, the winning teams play each other. Rounds continue until there is a grand champion. The instructor should provide a suitable prize, such as candy bars, for the winning team.

Source: This exercise was developed by Professors Yolanda Sarason of Colorado State University and Catherine Banbury of St. Mary's College and Purdue University and presented at the Organizational Behavior Teaching Conference, June 1999. Copyright © 1999 by Yolanda Sarason and Catherine Banbury. Adapted with permission.

Note from Wheelen and Hunger
The *Instructors' Manual* for this book contains a list of products and services with their synergy and the name of the company. In case your instructor does not use this exercise, try the following examples:

> Example 1: Motorcycles, autos, lawn mowers, generators

> Example 2: Athletic footwear, Rockport shoes, Greg Norman clothing, sportswear

For each example, did you guess the company providing these products/services and the synergy obtained? The answers are printed here, upside down:

Example 1: Engine technology by Honda

Example 2: Marketing and distribution for the athletically oriented by Reebok

Key Terms

CHAPTER 10
Strategy Implementation: Staffing and Directing

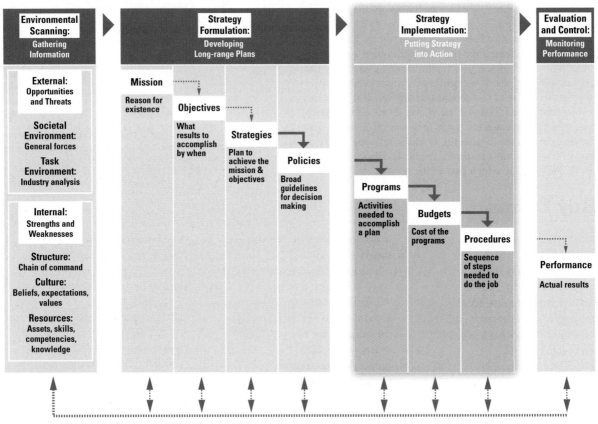

Environmental Scanning: Gathering Information	Strategy Formulation: Developing Long-range Plans	Strategy Implementation: Putting Strategy into Action	Evaluation and Control: Monitoring Performance

External: Opportunities and Threats

Societal Environment: General forces

Task Environment: Industry analysis

Internal: Strengths and Weaknesses

Structure: Chain of command

Culture: Beliefs, expectations, values

Resources: Assets, skills, competencies, knowledge

Mission
Reason for existence

Objectives
What results to accomplish by when

Strategies
Plan to achieve the mission & objectives

Policies
Broad guidelines for decision making

Programs
Activities needed to accomplish a plan

Budgets
Cost of the programs

Procedures
Sequence of steps needed to do the job

Performance
Actual results

Feedback/Learning: Make corrections as needed

Learning Objectives

After reading this chapter, you should be able to:

- Understand the link between strategy and staffing decisions
- Match the appropriate manager to the strategy
- Understand how to implement an effective downsizing program
- Discuss important issues in effectively staffing and directing international expansion
- Assess and manage the corporate culture's fit with a new strategy
- Decide when and if programs such as MBO and TQM are appropriate methods of strategy implementation
- Formulate action plans

HAVE YOU HEARD OF ENTERPRISE RENT-A-CAR? YOU WON'T FIND IT AT THE AIRPORT WITH Hertz, Avis, or National Car Rental operations. Yet Enterprise owns more cars and operates in more locations than Hertz or Avis. It is the largest rental car company in North America. In ignoring the highly competitive airport market, Enterprise has chosen a differentiation competitive strategy by marketing to people in need of a spare car. Instead of locating many cars at a few high-priced locations at airports, Enterprise sets up inexpensive offices throughout metropolitan areas. As a result, cars are rented for 30% less than they cost at airports. As soon as one branch office grows to about 150 cars, the company opens another rental office a few miles away. People are increasingly renting from Enterprise even when their current car works fine. According to CEO Andy Taylor, "We call it a 'virtual car.' Small-business people who have to pick up clients call us when they want something better than their own car." Why is Enterprise able to follow this competitive strategy so successfully without attracting Hertz and Avis into its market?

The secret to Enterprise's success is its well-executed strategy implementation. Clearly laid-out programs, budgets, and procedures support the company's competitive strategy by making Enterprise stand out in the mind of the consumer. When a new rental office opens, employees spend time developing relationships with the service managers of every auto dealership and body shop in the area. Enterprise employees bring pizza and doughnuts to workers at auto garages across the country. Enterprise forms agreements with dealers to provide replacements for cars brought in for service. At major accounts, the company actually staffs an office at the dealership and has cars parked outside so customers don't have to go to an Enterprise office to complete paperwork.

One key to implementation at Enterprise is *staffing*—hiring and promoting a certain kind of person. Virtually every Enterprise employee is a college graduate, usually from the bottom half of the class. According to COO Donald Ross, "We hire from the half of the college class that makes the upper half possible. We want athletes, fraternity types—especially fraternity presidents and social directors. People people." These new employees begin as management trainees. Instead of regular raises, their pay is tied to branch office profits.

Another key to implementation at Enterprise is *leading*—specifying clear performance objectives and promoting a team-oriented corporate culture. The company stresses promotion from within and advancement based on performance. Every Enterprise employee, including top executives, starts at the bottom. As a result, a bond of shared experience connects all employees and managers. To reinforce a cohesive culture of camaraderie, senior executives routinely do "grunt work" at branch offices. Even Andy Taylor, the CEO, joins the work. "We were visiting an office in Berkeley and it was mobbed, so I started cleaning cars," says Taylor. "As it was happening, I wondered if it was a good use of my time, but the effect on morale was tremendous." Because the financial results of every branch office and every region are available to all, the collegial culture stimulates good-natured competition. "We're this close to beating out Middlesex," grins Woody Erhardt, an area manager in New Jersey. "I want to pound them into the ground. If they lose, they have to throw a party for us, and we get to decide what they wear."[1]

This example from Enterprise Rent-A-Car illustrates how a strategy must be implemented with carefully considered programs in order to succeed. This chapter discusses strategy implementation in terms of staffing and leading. **Staffing** focuses on the selection and use of employees. **Leading** emphasizes the use of programs to better align employee interests and attitudes with a strategy.

10.1 | Staffing

The implementation of new strategies and policies often calls for new human resource management priorities and a different use of personnel. Such staffing issues can involve hiring new people with new skills, firing people with inappropriate or substandard skills, and/or training existing employees to learn new skills.

If growth strategies are to be implemented, new people may need to be hired and trained. Experienced people with the necessary skills need to be found for promotion to newly created managerial positions. When a corporation follows a growth through acquisition strategy, it may find that it needs to replace several managers in the acquired company. The percentage of an acquired company's top management team that either quit or was asked to leave is around 25% after the first year, 35% after the second year, 48% after the third year, 55% after the fourth year, and 61% after five years.[2] In addition, executives who join an acquired company after the acquisition quit at significantly higher-than-normal rates beginning in their second year. Executives continue to depart at higher-than-normal rates for nine years after the acquisition.[3] Turnover rates of executives in firms acquired by foreign firms are significantly higher than for firms acquired by domestic firms, primarily in the fourth and fifth years after the acquisition.[4]

It is one thing to lose excess employees after a merger, but it is something else to lose highly skilled people who are difficult to replace. To deal with problems such as this, some companies are appointing special integration managers to shepherd companies through the implementation process. The job of the integrator is to prepare a competitive profile of the combined company in terms of its strengths and weaknesses, draft an ideal profile of what the combined company should look like, develop action plans to close the gap between the actuality and the ideal, and establish training programs to unite the combined company and to make it more competitive.[5] To be a successful **integration manager**, a person should have (1) a deep knowledge of the acquiring company, (2) a flexible management style, (3) an ability to work in cross-functional project teams, (4) a willingness to work independently, and (5) sufficient emotional and cultural intelligence to work well with people from all backgrounds.[6]

If a corporation adopts a retrenchment strategy, however, a large number of people may need to be laid off or fired (in many instances, being laid off is the same as being fired); and top management, as well as the divisional managers, needs to specify the criteria to be used in making these personnel decisions. Should employees be fired on the basis of low seniority or on the basis of poor performance? Sometimes corporations find it easier to close or sell off an entire division than to choose which individuals to fire.

Staffing Follows Strategy

As in the case of structure, staffing requirements are likely to follow a change in strategy. For example, promotions should be based not only on current job performance but also on whether a person has the skills and abilities to do what is needed to implement the new strategy.

Changing Hiring and Training Requirements

Having formulated a new strategy, a corporation may find that it needs to either hire different people or retrain current employees to implement the new strategy. Consider the introduction of team-based production at Corning's filter plant mentioned in **Chapter 9**.

Employee selection and training were crucial to the success of the new manufacturing strategy. Plant Manager Robert Hoover sorted through 8,000 job applications before hiring 150 people with the best problem-solving ability and a willingness to work in a team setting. Those selected received extensive training in technical and interpersonal skills. During the first year of production, 25% of all hours worked were devoted to training, at a cost of $750,000.[7]

One way to implement a company's business strategy, such as overall low cost, is through training and development. A study of 51 corporations in the UK found that 71% of "leading" companies rated staff learning and training as important or very important compared to 62% of the other companies.[8] Another study of 155 U. S. manufacturing firms revealed that those with training programs had 19% higher productivity than did those without such programs. Another study found that a doubling of formal training per employee resulted in a 7% reduction in scrap.[9] Training is especially important for a differentiation strategy emphasizing quality or customer service. For example, Motorola, with annual sales of $17 billion, spends 4% of its payroll on training by providing at least 40 hours of training a year to each employee. There is a very strong connection between strategy and training at Motorola. For example, after setting a goal to reduce product development cycle time, Motorola created a two-week course to teach its employees how to accomplish that goal. It brought together marketing, product development, and manufacturing managers to create an action learning format in which the managers worked together instead of separately. The company is especially concerned with attaining the highest quality possible in all its operations. Realizing that it couldn't hit quality targets with poor parts, Motorola developed a class for its suppliers on statistical process control. The company estimates that every $1 it spends on training delivers $30 in productivity gains within three years.[10]

Training is also important when implementing a retrenchment strategy. As suggested earlier, successful downsizing means that a company has to invest in its remaining employees. General Electric's Aircraft Engine Group used training to maintain its share of the market even though it had cut its workforce from 42,000 to 33,000 in the 1990s.[11]

Matching the Manager to the Strategy

It is possible that a current CEO may not be appropriate to implement a new strategy. Research indicates that there may be a career life cycle for top executives. During the early years of executives' tenure, for example, they tend to experiment intensively with product lines to learn about their business. This is their *learning stage*. Later, their accumulated knowledge allows them to reduce experimentation and increase performance. This is their *harvest stage*. They enter a *decline stage* in their later years, when they reduce experimentation still further, and performance declines. Thus, there is an inverted U-shaped relationship between top executive tenure and the firm's financial performance. Some executives retire before any decline occurs. Others stave off decline longer than their counterparts. Because the length of time spent in each stage varies among CEOs, it is up to the board to decide when a top executive should be replaced.[12]

The most appropriate type of general manager needed to effectively implement a new corporate or business strategy depends on the desired strategic direction of that firm or business unit. Executives with a particular mix of skills and experiences may be classified as an **executive type** and paired with a specific corporate strategy. For example, a corporation following a concentration strategy emphasizing vertical or horizontal growth would probably want an aggressive new chief executive with a great deal of experience in that particular industry—a **dynamic industry expert**. A diversification strategy, in contrast, might call for someone with an analytical mind who is highly knowledgeable in other industries and can manage diverse product lines—an **analytical portfolio manager**. A corporation choosing to follow a stability strategy would probably want as its CEO a **cautious profit planner**, a person with a conservative style, a production or engineering background, and experience with controlling budgets, capital expenditures, inventories, and standardization procedures.

Weak companies in a relatively attractive industry tend to turn to a type of challenge-oriented executive known as a **turnaround specialist** to save the company. For example, Burger King's new CEO, Gregory Brenneman, was hired in 2004 to fix the ailing company because he had built a reputation as a turnaround wizard. After helping Continental Airlines return to profitability in the 1990s, he engineered the sale of PricewaterhouseCoopers to IBM in 2002. Burger King's hamburger market share had fallen from 18.5% in 2001 to 15.6% in 2003—and had taken profits with it. In his first 90 days at Burger King, Brenneman developed a turnaround plan that he hoped to complete with a public offering of Burger King shares in 2006. His plan included improving food offerings and buying back some stores from franchisees to give the company greater control over menus and store design.[13]

If a company cannot be saved, a **professional liquidator** might be called on by a bankruptcy court to close the firm and liquidate its assets. This is what happened to Montgomery Ward, Inc., the nation's first catalog retailer, which closed its stores for good in 2001, after declaring bankruptcy for the second time. Research tends to support the conclusion that as a firm's environment changes, it tends to change the type of top executive to implement a new strategy.[14] For example, during the 1990s, when the emphasis was on growth in a company's core products/services, the most desired background for a U.S. CEO was either in marketing or international experience, contrasted with finance during the 1980s, when conglomerate diversification was popular.[15]

This approach is in agreement with Chandler, who proposes (see **Chapter 9**) that the most appropriate CEO of a company changes as a firm moves from one stage of development to another. Because priorities certainly change over an organization's life, successful corporations need to select managers who have skills and characteristics appropriate to the organization's particular stage of development and position in its life cycle. For example, founders of firms tend to have functional backgrounds in technological specialties, whereas successors tend to have backgrounds in marketing and administration.[16] A change in the environment leading to a change in a company's strategy also leads to a change in the top management team. For example, a change in the U.S. utility industry's environment in 1992, supporting internally focused, efficiency-oriented strategies, led to top management teams being dominated by older managers with longer company and industry tenure, with efficiency-oriented backgrounds in operations, engineering, and accounting.[17] Research reveals that executives having a specific personality characteristic (external locus of control) are more effective in regulated industries than are executives with a different characteristic (internal locus of control).[18]

Other studies have found a link between the type of CEO and a firm's overall strategic type. (Strategic types are presented in **Chapter 4**). For example, successful prospector firms tended to be headed by CEOs from research/engineering and general management backgrounds. High-performance defenders tended to have CEOs with accounting/finance, manufacturing/production, and general management experience. Analyzers tended to have CEOs with a marketing/sales background.[19]

A study of 173 firms over a 25-year period revealed that CEOs in these companies tended to have the same functional specialization as the former CEO, especially when the past CEO's strategy continued to be successful. This may be a pattern for successful corporations.[20] In particular, it explains why so many prosperous companies tend to recruit their top executives from one particular area. At Procter & Gamble (P&G)—a good example of an analyzer firm—for example, the route to the CEO's position has traditionally been through brand management, with a strong emphasis on marketing—and more recently international experience. In other firms, the route may be through manufacturing, marketing, accounting, or finance—depending on what the corporation has always considered its core capability (and its overall strategic orientation).

Selection and Management Development

Selection and development are important not only to ensure that people with the right mix of skills and experiences are initially hired but also to help them grow on the job so that they might be prepared for future promotions.

Executive Succession: Insiders Versus Outsiders

Executive succession is the process of replacing a key top manager. The average tenure of a chief executive of a large U.S. company declined from nearly nine years in 1980 to just over seven years in 2001.[21] Given that two-thirds of all major corporations worldwide replace their CEO at least once in a five-year period, it is important that the firm plan for this eventuality.[22] It is especially important for a company that usually promotes from within to prepare its current managers for promotion. For example, companies using relay executive succession, in which a candidate is groomed to take over the CEO position, have significantly higher performance than those that hire someone from the outside or hold a competition between internal candidates.[23] These "heirs apparent" are provided special assignments, including membership on other firms' boards of directors.[24]

Companies known for being excellent training grounds for executive talent are AlliedSignal, Bain & Company, Bankers Trust, Bristol Myers Squibb, Citicorp, General Electric, Hewlett-Packard, McDonald's, McKinsey & Company, Microsoft, Nike, PepsiCo, Pfizer, and P&G. For example, one study showed that hiring 19 GE executives into CEO positions added $24.5 billion to the share prices of the companies that hired them. One year after people from GE started their new jobs, 11 of the 19 companies they joined were outperforming their competitors and the overall market.[25]

Some of the best practices for top management succession are encouraging boards to help the CEO create a succession plan, identifying succession candidates below the top layer, measuring internal candidates against outside candidates to ensure the development of a comprehensive set of skills, and providing appropriate financial incentives.[26] A survey of U.S. boards by Korn/Ferry International found that 77% had some sort of succession-planning process in place in 2003, compared to only 33% two years earlier.[27] Succession planning has become the most important topic discussed by boards of directors.[28] See **STRATEGY HIGHLIGHT 10.1** to see how Hewlett-Packard identifies those with potential for executive leadership positions.

Prosperous firms tend to look outside for CEO candidates only if they have no obvious internal candidates. For example, only 10% of *Fortune* 100 companies have CEOs appointed from the outside.[29] Hiring an outsider to be a CEO is a risky gamble. CEOs from the outside tend to introduce significant change and high turnover among the current top management.[30] A study of 392 large U.S. firms revealed that only 16.6% of them had hired outsiders to be their CEOs. The outsiders tended to perform slightly worse than insiders but had a very high variance in performance. Compared to that of insiders, the performance of outsiders tended to be either very good or very poor. Although outsiders performed much better (in terms of shareholder returns) than insiders in the first half of their tenures, they did much worse in their second half. As a result, the average tenure of an outsider was 6.6 years compared to 10.9 years for insiders.[31]

Firms in trouble, however, overwhelmingly choose outsiders to lead them.[32] For example, one study of 22 firms undertaking turnaround strategies over a 13-year period found that the CEO was replaced in all but 2 companies. Of 27 changes of CEO (several firms had more than 1 CEO during this period), only 7 were insiders—20 were outsiders.[33] The probability of an outsider being chosen to lead a firm in difficulty increases if there is no internal heir apparent, if the last CEO was fired, and if the board of directors is composed of a large percentage of outsiders.[34] Boards realize that the best way to force a change in strategy is to hire a new CEO

STRATEGY HIGHLIGHT 10.1

How Hewlett-Packard Identifies Potential Executives

Hewlett-Packard identifies those with high potential for executive leadership by looking for six broad competencies that the company believes are necessary:

1. *Practice the HP Way* by building trust and respect, focusing on achievement, demonstrating integrity, being innovative with customers, contributing to the community, and developing organizational decision making.

2. *Lead change and learning* by recognizing and acting on signals for change, leading organizational change, learning from organizational experience, removing barriers to change, developing self, and challenging and developing others.

3. *Know the internal and external environments* by anticipating global trends, acting on trends, and learning from others.

4. *Lead strategy setting* by inspiring breakthrough business strategy, leading the strategy-making process,

committing to business vision, creating long-range strategies, building financial strategies, and defining a business-planning system.

5. *Align the organization* by working across boundaries, implementing competitive cost structures, developing alliances and partnerships, planning and managing core business, and designing the organization.

6. *Achieve results* by building a track record, establishing accountability, supporting calculated risks, making tough individual decisions, and resolving performance problems.

Source: Summarized from R. M. Fulmer, P. A. Gibbs, and M. Goldsmith, "The New HP Way: Leveraging Strategy with Diversity, Leadership Development and Decentralization," *Strategy & Leadership* (October/November/December, 1999), pp. 21–29.

who has no connections to the current strategy.[35] For example, outsiders have been found to be very effective in leading strategic change for firms in Chapter 11 bankruptcy.[36]

Identifying Abilities and Potential

A company can identify and prepare its people for important positions in several ways. One approach is to establish a sound **performance appraisal system** to identify good performers with promotion potential. A survey of 34 corporate planners and human resource executives from 24 large U.S. corporations revealed that approximately 80% made some attempt to identify managers' talents and behavioral tendencies so that they could place a manager with a likely fit to a given competitive strategy.[37] Companies select those people with promotion potential to be in their executive development training program. Approximately 10,000 of GE's 276,000 employees take at least one class at the company's famous Leadership Development Center in Crotonville, New York.[38] Doug Pelino, chief talent officer at Xerox, keeps a list of about 100 managers in middle management and at the vice presidential levels who have been selected to receive special training, leadership experience, and mentorship to become the next generation of top management.[39]

A company should examine its human resource system to ensure not only that people are being hired without regard to their racial, ethnic, or religious background but also that they are being identified for training and promotion in the same manner. Management diversity could be a competitive advantage in a multiethnic world. With more women in the workplace, an increasing number are moving into top management. Recent studies are suggesting that female executives score higher than men on motivating others, fostering communication, producing high-quality work, and listening to others, while there is no difference between male and female executives in strategic planning or analyzing issues.[40]

Many large organizations are using **assessment centers** to evaluate a person's suitability for an advanced position. Corporations such as AT&T, Standard Oil, IBM, Sears, and GE have successfully used assessment centers. Because each is specifically tailored to its corporation, these assessment centers are unique. They use special interviews, management games, in-basket exercises, leaderless group discussions, case analyses, decision-making exercises, and oral presentations to assess the potential of employees for specific positions. Promotions into these positions are based on performance levels in the assessment center. Assessment centers have generally been able to accurately predict subsequent job performance and career success.[41]

Job rotation—moving people from one job to another—is also used in many large corporations to ensure that employees are gaining the appropriate mix of experiences to prepare them for future responsibilities. Rotating people among divisions is one way that a corporation can improve the level of organizational learning. General Electric, for example, routinely rotates its executives from one sector to a completely different one to learn the skills of managing in different industries. Jeffrey Immelt, who took over as CEO from Jack Welch, had managed businesses in plastics, appliances, and medical systems.[42] Companies that pursue related diversification strategies through internal development make greater use of interdivisional transfers of people than do companies that grow through unrelated acquisitions. Apparently, the companies that grow internally attempt to transfer important knowledge and skills throughout the corporation in order to achieve some sort of synergy.[43]

Problems in Retrenchment

Downsizing (sometimes called "rightsizing") refers to the planned elimination of positions or jobs. This program is often used to implement retrenchment strategies. Because the financial community is likely to react favorably to announcements of downsizing from a company in difficulty, such a program may provide some short-term benefits, such as raising the company's stock price. If not done properly, however, downsizing may result in less, rather than more, productivity. One study found that a 10% reduction in people resulted in only a 1.5% reduction in costs, profits increased in only half the firms downsizing, and the stock prices of downsized firms increased over three years, but not as much as did those of firms that did not downsize.[44] Why were the results so marginal?

A study of downsizing at automobile-related U.S. industrial companies revealed that at 20 out of 30 companies, either the wrong jobs were eliminated or blanket offers of early retirement prompted managers, even those considered invaluable, to leave. After the layoffs, the remaining employees had to do not only their work but also the work of the people who had gone. Because the survivors often didn't know how to do the departeds' work, morale and productivity plummeted.[45] Downsizing can seriously damage the learning capacity of organizations.[46] Creativity drops significantly (affecting new product development), and it becomes very difficult to keep high performers from leaving the company.[47] In addition, cost-conscious executives tend to defer maintenance, skimp on training, delay new product introductions, and avoid risky new businesses—all of which leads to lower sales and eventually to lower profits.

A good retrenchment strategy can thus be implemented well in terms of organizing but poorly in terms of staffing. A situation can develop in which retrenchment feeds on itself and acts to further weaken instead of strengthen the company. Research indicates that companies undertaking cost-cutting programs are four times more likely than others to cut costs again, typically by reducing staff.[48] This happened at Eastman Kodak and Xerox during the 1990s, but 10 years later the companies were still working to regain their profitable past performance. In contrast, successful downsizing firms undertake a strategic reorientation, not just a bloodletting of employees. Research shows that when companies use downsizing as part of a larger restructuring program to narrow company focus, they enjoy better performance.[49]

Consider the following guidelines that have been proposed for successful downsizing:

- **Eliminate unnecessary work instead of making across-the-board cuts:** Spend the time to research where money is going and eliminate the task, not the workers, if it doesn't add value to what the firm is producing. Reduce the number of administrative levels rather than the number of individual positions. Look for interdependent relationships before eliminating activities. Identify and protect core competencies.

- **Contract out work that others can do cheaper:** For example, Bankers Trust of New York has contracted out its mailroom and printing services and some of its payroll and accounts payable activities to a division of Xerox. Outsourcing may be cheaper than vertical integration.

- **Plan for long-run efficiencies:** Don't simply eliminate all postponable expenses, such as maintenance, R&D, and advertising, in the unjustifiable hope that the environment will become more supportive. Continue to hire, grow, and develop—particularly in critical areas.

- **Communicate the reasons for actions:** Tell employees not only why the company is downsizing but also what the company is trying to achieve. Promote educational programs.

- **Invest in the remaining employees:** Because most "survivors" in a corporate downsizing will probably be doing different tasks from what they were doing before the change, firms need to draft new job specifications, performance standards, appraisal techniques, and compensation packages. Additional training is needed to ensure that everyone has the proper skills to deal with expanded jobs and responsibilities. Empower key individuals/groups and emphasize team building. Identify, protect, and mentor people who have leadership talent.

- **Develop value-added jobs to balance out job elimination:** When no other jobs are currently available within the organization to transfer employees to, management must consider other staffing alternatives. For example, Harley-Davidson worked with the company's unions to find other work for surplus employees by moving into Harley plants work that had previously been done by suppliers.[50]

International Issues in Staffing

Implementing a strategy of international expansion takes a lot of planning and can be very expensive. Nearly 80% of midsize and larger companies send their employees abroad, and 45% plan to increase the number they have on foreign assignment. A complete package for one executive working in another country costs from $300,000 to $1 million annually. Nevertheless, between 10% and 20% of all U.S. managers sent abroad returned early because of job dissatisfaction or difficulties in adjusting to a foreign country. Of those who stayed for the duration of their assignment, nearly one-third did not perform as well as expected. One-fourth of those completing an assignment left their company within one year of returning home—often leaving to join a competitor.[51] One common mistake is failing to educate the person about the customs and values in other countries.

Because of cultural differences, managerial style and human resource practices must be tailored to fit the particular situations in other countries. Because only 11% of human resource managers have ever worked abroad, most have little understanding of a global assignment's unique personal and professional challenges and thus fail to develop the training necessary for such an assignment.[52] Ninety percent of companies select employees for an international assignment based on their technical expertise while ignoring other areas.[53] A lack of knowledge of national and ethnic differences can make managing an international operation extremely difficult. For example, the three ethnic groups living in Malaysia (Malay, Chinese, and Indian) share different religions, attend different schools, and do not like to work in the same factories with each other. Because of the importance of cultural distinctions such as these, multinational corporations (MNCs) are now putting more emphasis on intercultural training for managers being sent on an assignment to a foreign country. This type of training is one of the commonly cited reasons for the lower expatriate failure rates—6% or less—for European and Japanese MNCs, which have emphasized cross-cultural experiences, compared with a 35% failure rate for U.S.-based MNCs.[54]

To improve organizational learning, many MNCs are providing their managers with international assignments lasting as long as five years. Upon their return to headquarters, these expatriates have an in-depth understanding of the company's operations in another part of the world. This has value to the extent that these employees communicate this understanding to others in decision-making positions. Research indicates that an MNC performs at a higher level when its CEO has international experience.[55] Unfortunately, not all corporations appropriately manage international assignments. While out of the country, a person may be overlooked for an important promotion (out of sight, out of mind). Upon his or her return to the home country, co-workers may deprecate the out-of-country experience as a waste of time. The perceived lack of organizational support for international assignments increases the likelihood that an expatriate will return home early.[56]

Out of their study of 750 U.S., Japanese, and European companies, Black and Gregersen found that the companies that do a good job of managing foreign assignments follow three general practices:

- When making international assignments, they focus on transferring knowledge and developing global leadership.
- They make foreign assignments to people whose technical skills are matched or exceeded by their cross-cultural abilities.
- They end foreign assignments with a deliberate repatriation process, with career guidance and jobs where the employees can apply what they learned in their assignments.[57]

Once a corporation has established itself in another country, it hires and promotes people from the host country into higher-level positions. For example, most large MNCs attempt to fill managerial positions in their subsidiaries with well-qualified citizens of the host countries. Unilever and IBM take this approach to international staffing. This policy serves to placate nationalistic governments and to better attune management practices to the host country's culture. The danger in using primarily foreign nationals to staff managerial positions in subsidiaries is the increased likelihood of suboptimization (the local subsidiary ignores the needs of the larger parent corporation). This makes it difficult for an MNC to meet its long-term, worldwide objectives. To a local national in an MNC subsidiary, the corporation as a whole is an abstraction. Communication and coordination across subsidiaries become more difficult. As it becomes harder to coordinate the activities of several international subsidiaries, an MNC will have serious problems operating in a global industry.

Another approach to staffing the managerial positions of MNCs is to use people with an "international" orientation, regardless of their country of origin or host country assignment. This is a widespread practice among European firms. For example, Electrolux, a Swedish firm, had a French director in its Singapore factory. Using third-country "nationals" can allow for more opportunities for promotion than does Unilever's policy of hiring local people, but it can also result in more misunderstandings and conflicts with the local employees and with the host country's government.

Some U.S. corporations take advantage of immigrants and their children to staff key positions when negotiating entry into another country and when selecting an executive to manage the company's new foreign operations. For example, when General Motors wanted to learn more about business opportunities in China, it turned to Shirley Young, a Vice President of Marketing at GM. Born in Shanghai and fluent in Chinese language and customs, Young was instrumental in helping GM negotiate a $1 billion joint venture with Shanghai Automotive to build a Buick plant in China. With other Chinese-Americans, Young formed a committee to advise GM on relations with China. Although just a part of a larger team of GM employees working on the joint venture, Young coached GM employees on Chinese customs and traditions.[58]

MNCs with a high level of international interdependence among activities need to provide their managers with significant international assignments and experiences as part of their training and development. Such assignments provide future corporate leaders with a series of valuable international contacts in addition to a better personal understanding of international issues and global linkages among corporate activities.[59] Research reveals that corporations using cross-national teams, whose members have international experience and communicate frequently with overseas managers, have greater product development capabilities than others.[60] Executive recruiters report that more major corporations are now requiring candidates to have international experience.[61]

10.2 | Leading

Implementation also involves leading through coaching people to use their abilities and skills most effectively and efficiently to achieve organizational objectives. Without direction, people tend to do their work according to their personal view of what tasks should be done, how, and in what order. They may approach their work as they have in the past or emphasize those tasks that they most enjoy—regardless of the corporation's priorities. This can create real problems, particularly if the company is operating internationally and must adjust to customs and traditions in other countries. This direction may take the form of management leadership, communicated norms of behavior from the corporate culture, or agreements among workers in autonomous work groups. It may also be accomplished more formally through action planning or through programs such as Management By Objectives (MBO), and Total Quality Management (TQM).

Managing Corporate Culture

Because an organization's culture can exert a powerful influence on the behavior of all employees, it can strongly affect a company's ability to shift its strategic direction. A problem for a strong culture is that a change in mission, objectives, strategies, or policies is not likely to be successful if it is in opposition to the accepted culture of the company. Corporate culture has a strong tendency to resist change because its very reason for existence often rests on preserving stable relationships and patterns of behavior. For example, the male-dominated, Japanese-centered corporate culture of the giant Mitsubishi Corporation created problems for the company when it implemented its growth strategy in North America. The alleged sexual harassment of its female employees by male supervisors resulted in a lawsuit by the U.S. Equal Employment Opportunity Commission and a boycott of the company's automobiles by the National Organization for Women.[62]

There is no one best corporate culture. An optimal culture is one that best supports the mission and strategy of the company of which it is a part. This means that, like structure and staffing, corporate culture should support the strategy. Unless strategy is in complete agreement with the culture, any significant change in strategy should be followed by a modification of the organization's culture. Although corporate culture can be changed, it may often take a

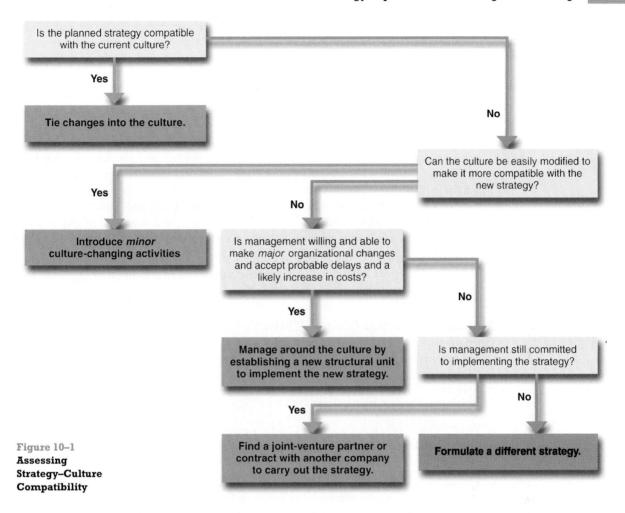

Figure 10–1
**Assessing
Strategy–Culture
Compatibility**

long time, and it requires much effort. A key job of management involves managing corporate culture. In doing so, management must evaluate what a particular change in strategy means to the corporate culture, assess whether a change in culture is needed, and decide whether an attempt to change the culture is worth the likely costs.

Assessing Strategy–Culture Compatibility

When implementing a new strategy, a company should take the time to assess **strategy–culture compatibility**. (See **Figure 10–1**.) Consider the following questions regarding a corporation's culture:

1. **Is the planned strategy compatible with the company's current culture?** *If yes*, full steam ahead. Tie organizational changes into the company's culture by identifying how the new strategy will achieve the mission better than the current strategy does. *If not . . .*

2. **Can the culture be easily modified to make it more compatible with the new strategy?** *If yes*, move forward carefully by introducing a set of culture-changing activities such as minor structural modifications, training and development activities, and/or hiring new managers who are more compatible with the new strategy. When P&G's top

management decided to implement a strategy aimed at reducing costs, for example, it made some changes in how things were done, but it did not eliminate its brand-management system. The culture adapted to these modifications over a couple years, and productivity increased. *If not . . .*

3. **Is management willing and able to make major organizational changes and accept probable delays and a likely increase in costs?** *If yes*, manage around the culture by establishing a new structural unit to implement the new strategy. At General Motors, for example, top management realized the company had to make some radical changes to be more competitive. Because the current structure, culture, and procedures were very inflexible, management decided to establish a completely new division (GM's first new division since 1918) called Saturn to build its new auto. In cooperation with the United Auto Workers, an entirely new labor agreement was developed, based on decisions reached by consensus. Carefully selected employees received from 100 to 750 hours of training, and a whole new culture was built, piece by piece. *If not . . .*

4. **Is management still committed to implementing the strategy?** *If yes*, find a joint-venture partner or contract with another company to carry out the strategy. *If not*, formulate a different strategy.

Managing Cultural Change Through Communication

Communication is key to the effective management of change. Rationale for strategic changes should be communicated to workers not only in newsletters and speeches but also in training and development programs. This is especially important in decentralized firms where a large number of employees work in far-flung business units.[63] Companies in which major cultural changes have successfully taken place had the following characteristics in common:

- The CEO and other top managers had a strategic vision of what the company could become and communicated that vision to employees at all levels. The current performance of the company was compared to that of its competition and constantly updated.

- The vision was translated into the key elements necessary to accomplish that vision. For example, if the vision called for the company to become a leader in quality or service, aspects of quality and service were pinpointed for improvement, and appropriate measurement systems were developed to monitor them. These measures were communicated widely through contests, formal and informal recognition, and monetary rewards, among other devices.[64]

For example, when Pizza Hut, Taco Bell, and KFC were purchased by Tricon Global Restaurants (now Yum! Brands) from PepsiCo, the new management knew that it had to create a radically different culture than the one at PepsiCo if the company was to succeed. To begin, management formulated a statement of shared values—"How We Work Together" principles. They declared their differences with the "mother country" (PepsiCo) and wrote a "Declaration of Independence" stating what the new company would stand for. Restaurant managers participated in team-building activities at the corporate headquarters and finished by signing the company's "Declaration of Independence" as "founders" of the company. Since then, "Founder's Day" has become an annual event celebrating the culture of the company. Headquarters was renamed the "Restaurant Support Center," signifying the cultural value that the restaurants were the central focus of the company. People measures were added to financial measures and customer measures, reinforcing the "putting people first" value. In an unprecedented move in the industry, restaurant managers were given stock options and added to the list of performance incentives. The company created values-focused 360-degree performance reviews, which were eventually pushed to the restaurant manager level.[65]

Managing Diverse Cultures Following an Acquisition

When merging with or acquiring another company, top management must give some consideration to a potential clash of corporate cultures. According to a Hewitt Associates survey of 218 major U.S. corporations, integrating culture was a top challenge for 69% of the reporting companies.[66] Cultural differences are even more problematic when a company acquires a firm in another country. DaimlerChrysler's purchase of a controlling interest in Mitsubishi Motors in 2001 was insufficient to overcome Mitsubishi's resistance to change. After investing $2 billion to cut Mitsubishi's costs and improve its product development, DaimlerChrysler gave up. According to one executive, "It's an absolute disaster. We can't sell it. It's worth nothing."[67] It's dangerous to assume that the firms can simply be integrated into the same reporting structure. The greater the gap between the cultures of the acquired firm and the acquiring firm, the faster executives in the acquired firm quit their jobs and valuable talent is lost. Conversely, when corporate cultures are similar, performance problems are minimized.[68]

There are four general methods of managing two different cultures. (See **Figure 10–2**.) The choice of which method to use should be based on (1) how much members of the acquired firm value preserving their own culture and (2) how attractive they perceive the culture of the acquirer to be[69]:

1. **Integration** involves a relatively balanced give-and-take of cultural and managerial practices between the merger partners—and no strong imposition of cultural change on either company. It merges the two cultures in such a way that the separate cultures of both firms are preserved in the resulting culture. This is what occurred when France's Renault purchased a controlling interest in Japan's Nissan Motor Company and installed Carlos Ghosn as Nissan's new CEO to turn around the company. Ghosn was very sensitive to Nissan's culture and allowed the company room to develop a new corporate culture based on the best elements of Japan's national culture. His goal was to form one successful auto group from two very distinct companies.[70]

Figure 10–2
Methods of Managing the Culture of an Acquired Firm

How Much Members of the Acquired Firm Value Preservation of Their Own Culture

	Very Much	Not at All
Very Attractive	Integration	Assimilation
Not at All Attractive	Separation	Deculturation

Perception of the Attractiveness of the Acquirer

Source: ACADEMY OF MANAGEMENT REVIEW by *A. NAHAVARDI, A. R. MALEKZADEH. Copyright 1988 by the ACAD OF MGMT. Reproduced with permission of ACAD OF MGMT in the format Textbook via Copyright Clearance Center.*

2. **Assimilation** involves the domination of one organization over the other. The domination is not forced, but it is welcomed by members of the acquired firm, who may feel for many reasons that their culture and managerial practices have not produced success. The acquired firm surrenders its culture and adopts the culture of the acquiring company. See STRATEGY HIGHLIGHT 10.2 describes this method of acculturation when Admiral was acquired by Maytag Corporation.

3. **Separation** is characterized by a separation of the two companies' cultures. They are structurally separated, without cultural exchange. In the Shearson–American Express merger, both parties agreed to keep the fast-paced Shearson completely separate from the planning-oriented American Express. This approach allowed American Express to easily divest Shearson once it discovered that the merger was not working.

4. **Deculturation** involves the disintegration of one company's culture, resulting from unwanted and extreme pressure from the other to impose its culture and practices. This is the most common and most destructive method of dealing with two different cultures. It is often accompanied by much confusion, conflict, resentment, and stress. This is a primary reason so many executives tend to leave after their firm is acquired.[71] Such a merger typically results in poor performance by the acquired company and its eventual divestment. This is what happened when AT&T acquired NCR Corporation in 1990 for its computer business. It replaced NCR managers with an AT&T management team, reorganized sales, forced employees to adhere to the AT&T code of values (called the "Common Bond"), and even dropped the proud NCR name (successor to National Cash Register) in favor of a sterile GIS (Global Information Solutions) nonidentity. By 1995, AT&T was forced to take a $1.2 billion loss and lay off 10,000 people.[72] The NCR unit was sold in 1996.

STRATEGY HIGHLIGHT 10.2

Admiral Assimilates Maytag's Culture

Maytag's corporate culture had been dominated almost from the birth of the company by the concept of quality. Maytag employees took great pride in being known as the "dependability people." Over the years, Maytag Company consistently advertised that its repairmen were "lonely" because Maytag products rarely, if ever, needed repair.

Admiral's history had, however, been quite different from Maytag's. Prior to Maytag's purchase of Magic Chef (and thus Admiral) in 1986, Admiral had been owned by three different corporations. Its manufacturing plant in Galesburg, Illinois, had deteriorated to a dismal level by the time Maytag acquired it. Refrigerators sometimes rolled off the assembly line with screws driven in crooked and temperature balances askew.

Maytag's management had always wanted to have its own Maytag brand refrigerator. That was one reason it purchased Admiral. But it was worried that Admiral might not be able to produce a quality product to Maytag's specifications. To improve Admiral's quality, Maytag's top management decided to integrate Admiral directly into Maytag Company operations. As a result, all Admiral functional departments except marketing reported directly to the Maytag Company president.

Under the direction of Leonard Hadley, while he was serving as Maytag President, a project was initiated to design and manufacture a refrigerator for the Maytag brand at the Admiral plant. When Hadley first visited Admiral's facilities to discuss the design of a Maytag line of refrigerators, Admiral personnel asked Hadley when the name on their plant's water tower would be changed from Admiral to Maytag. Hadley, acknowledging Maytag's cultural concerns regarding quality, responded: "When you earn it."

The refrigerator resulting from the Maytag–Admiral collaboration was a huge success. The project crystallized corporate management's philosophy for forging synergies among the Maytag units, while simultaneously allowing the individual expertise of those units to flourish. Admiral's employees were willing to accept the dominance of Maytag's strong quality-oriented culture because they respected it. In turn, they expected to be treated with some respect for their tradition of skill in refrigeration technology.

Action Planning

Activities can be directed toward accomplishing strategic goals through action planning. At a minimum, an **action plan** states what actions are going to be taken, by whom, during what time frame, and with what expected results. After a program has been selected to implement a particular strategy, an action plan should be developed to put the program in place. **Table 10–1** shows an example of an action plan for a new advertising and promotion program. Take the example of a company choosing forward vertical integration through the acquisition of a retailing chain as its growth strategy. Once it owns its own retail outlets, it must integrate the stores into the company. One of the many programs it would have to develop is a new advertising

TABLE 10–1 EXAMPLE OF AN ACTION PLAN

Action Plan for Jan Lewis, Advertising Manager, and Rick Carter, Advertising Assistant, Ajax Continental

Program Objective: To Run a New Advertising and Promotion Campaign for the Combined Jones Surplus/Ajax Continental Retail Stores for the Coming Christmas Season Within a Budget of $XX.

Program Activities:
1. Identify Three Best Ad Agencies for New Campaign.
2. Ask Three Ad Agencies to Submit a Proposal for a New Advertising and Promotion Campaign for Combined Stores.
3. Agencies Present Proposals to Marketing Manager.
4. Select Best Proposal and Inform Agencies of Decision.
5. Agency Presents Winning Proposal to Top Management.
6. Ads Air on TV and Promotions Appear in Stores.
7. Measure Results of Campaign in Terms of Viewer Recall and Increase in Store Sales.

Action Steps	Responsibility	Start–End
1. A. Review previous programs	Lewis & Carter	1/1–2/1
B. Discuss with boss	Lewis & Smith	2/1–2/3
C. Decide on three agencies	Lewis	2/4
2. A. Write specifications for ad	Lewis	1/15–1/20
B. Assistant writes ad request	Carter	1/20–1/30
C. Contact ad agencies	Lewis	2/5–2/8
D. Send request to three agencies	Carter	2/10
E. Meet with agency acct. execs	Lewis & Carter	2/16–2/20
3. A. Agencies work on proposals	Acct. Execs	2/23–5/1
B. Agencies present proposals	Carter	5/1–5/15
4. A. Select best proposal	Lewis	5/15–5/20
B. Meet with winning agency	Lewis	5/22–5/30
C. Inform losers	Carter	6/1
5. A. Fine-tune proposal	Acct. Exec	6/1–7/1
B. Presentation to management	Lewis	7/1–7/3
6. A. Ads air on TV	Lewis	9/1–12/24
B. Floor displays in stores	Carter	8/20–8/30
7. A. Gather recall measures of ads	Carter	9/1–12/24
B. Evaluate sales data	Carter	1/1–1/10
C. Prepare analysis of campaign	Carter	1/10–2/15

program for the stores. The resulting action plan to develop a new advertising program should include much of the following information:

1. **Specific actions to be taken to make the program operational:** One action might be to contact three reputable advertising agencies and ask them to prepare a proposal for a new radio and newspaper ad campaign based on the theme "Jones Surplus is now a part of Ajax Continental. Prices are lower. Selection is better."

2. **Dates to begin and end each action:** Time would have to be allotted not only to select and contact three agencies but to allow them sufficient time to prepare a detailed proposal. For example, allow one week to select and contact the agencies plus three months for them to prepare detailed proposals to present to the company's marketing director. Also allow some time to decide which proposal to accept.

3. **Person (identified by name and title) responsible for carrying out each action:** List someone—such as Jan Lewis, advertising manager—who can be put in charge of the program.

4. **Person responsible for monitoring the timeliness and effectiveness of each action:** Indicate that Jan Lewis is responsible for ensuring that the proposals are of good quality and are priced within the planned program budget. She will be the primary company contact for the ad agencies and will report on the progress of the program once a week to the company's marketing director.

5. **Expected financial and physical consequences of each action:** Estimate when a completed ad campaign will be ready to show top management and how long it will take after approval to begin to air the ads. Estimate also the expected increase in store sales over the six-month period after the ads are first aired. Indicate whether "recall" measures will be used to help assess the ad campaign's effectiveness plus how, when, and by whom the recall data will be collected and analyzed.

6. **Contingency plans:** Indicate how long it will take to get an acceptable ad campaign to show top management if none of the initial proposals is acceptable.

Action plans are important for several reasons. First, action plans serve as a link between strategy formulation and evaluation and control. Second, an action plan specifies what needs to be done differently from the way operations are currently carried out. Third, during the evaluation and control process that comes later, an action plan helps in both the appraisal of performance and the identification of any remedial actions, as needed. In addition, the explicit assignment of responsibilities for implementing and monitoring the programs may contribute to better motivation.

Management By Objectives

Management By Objectives (MBO) is a technique that encourages participative decision making through shared goal setting at all organizational levels and performance assessment based on the achievement of stated objectives.[73] MBO links organizational objectives and the behavior of individuals. Because it is a system that links plans with performance, it is a powerful implementation technique.

The MBO process involves:

1. Establishing and communicating organizational objectives.
2. Setting individual objectives (through superior–subordinate interaction) that help implement organizational ones.

3. Developing an action plan of activities needed to achieve the objectives.

4. Periodically (at least quarterly) reviewing performance as it relates to the objectives and including the results in the annual performance appraisal.[74]

MBO provides an opportunity for the corporation to connect the objectives of people at each level to those at the next higher level. MBO, therefore, acts to tie together corporate, business, and functional objectives, as well as the strategies developed to achieve them. Although MBO originated the 1950s, 90% of surveyed practicing managers feel that MBO is applicable today.[75] The principles of MBO are a part of self-managing work teams and quality circles.[76]

One of the real benefits of MBO is that it can reduce the amount of internal politics operating within a large corporation. Political actions within a firm can cause conflict and create divisions between the very people and groups who should be working together to implement strategy. People are less likely to jockey for position if the company's mission and objectives are clear and they know that the reward system is based not on game playing but on achieving clearly communicated, measurable objectives.

Total Quality Management

Total Quality Management (TQM) is an operational philosophy committed to *customer satisfaction* and *continuous improvement*. TQM is committed to quality/excellence and to being the best in all functions. Because TQM aims to reduce costs and improve quality, it can be used as a program to implement an overall low-cost or a differentiation business strategy. About 92% of manufacturing companies and 69% of service firms have implemented some form of quality management practices.[77] Not all have been successes. McKinsey & Company reported that two-thirds of the TQM programs it examined had failed to produce expected improvements. In contrast, a recent study of TQM in 193 hospitals found a positive relationship between the degree of TQM implementation and organizational performance.[78] An analysis of the successes and failures of TQM concluded that the key is top management. Successful TQM programs occur in companies in which "top managers move beyond defensive and tactical orientations to embrace a developmental orientation."[79]

TQM has four objectives:

1. Better, less variable quality of the product and service
2. Quicker, less variable response in processes to customer needs
3. Greater flexibility in adjusting to customers' shifting requirements
4. Lower cost through quality improvement and elimination of non–value-adding work[80]

According to TQM, faulty processes, not poorly motivated employees, are the cause of defects in quality. The program involves a significant change in corporate culture, requiring strong leadership from top management, employee training, empowerment of lower-level employees (giving people more control over their work), and teamwork in order to succeed in a company. TQM emphasizes prevention, not correction. Inspection for quality still takes place, but the emphasis is on improving the process to prevent errors and deficiencies. Thus quality circles or quality improvement teams are formed to identify problems and to suggest how to improve the processes that may be causing the problems.

TQM's essential ingredients are:

- **An intense focus on customer satisfaction:** Everyone (not just people in the sales and marketing departments) understands that their jobs exist only because of customer needs. Thus all jobs must be approached in terms of how they will affect customer satisfaction.

- **Internal as well as external customers:** An employee in the shipping department may be the internal customer of another employee who completes the assembly of a product, just as a person who buys the product is a customer of the entire company. An employee must be just as concerned with pleasing the internal customer as in satisfying the external customer.

- **Accurate measurement of every critical variable in a company's operations:** This means that employees have to be trained in what to measure, how to measure, and how to interpret the data. A rule of TQM is that *you only improve what you measure.*

- **Continuous improvement of products and services:** Everyone realizes that operations need to be continuously monitored to find ways to improve products and services.

- **New work relationships based on trust and teamwork:** Important is the idea of empowerment—giving employees wide latitude in how they go about achieving the company's goals. Research indicates that the keys to TQM success lie in executive commitment, an open organizational culture, and employee empowerment.[81]

International Considerations in Leading

In a study of 53 different national cultures, Hofstede found that each nation's unique culture could be identified using five dimensions. He found that national culture is so influential that it tends to overwhelm even a strong corporate culture. (See the numerous sociocultural societal variables that compose another country's culture that are listed in **Chapter 4's Table 4–3**.) In measuring the differences among these **dimensions of national culture** from country to country, Hofstede was able to explain why a certain management practice might be successful in one nation but fail in another[82]:

1. **Power distance (PD)** is the extent to which a society accepts an unequal distribution of power in organizations. Malaysia and Mexico scored highest, whereas Germany and Austria scored lowest. People in countries scoring high on this dimension tend to prefer autocratic to more participative managers.

2. **Uncertainty avoidance (UA)** is the extent to which a society feels threatened by uncertain and ambiguous situations. Greece and Japan scored highest on disliking ambiguity, whereas the United States and Singapore scored lowest. People in nations scoring high on this dimension tend to want career stability, formal rules, and clear-cut measures of performance.

3. **Individualism-collectivism (I-C)** is the extent to which a society values individual freedom and independence of action compared with a tight social framework and loyalty to the group. The United States and Canada scored highest on individualism, whereas Mexico and Guatemala scored lowest. People in nations scoring high on individualism tend to value individual success through competition, whereas people scoring low on individualism (thus high on collectivism) tend to value group success through collective cooperation.

4. **Masculinity-femininity (M-F)** is the extent to which society is oriented toward money and things (which Hofstede labels masculine) or toward people (which Hofstede labels feminine). Japan and Mexico scored highest on masculinity, whereas France and Sweden scored lowest (thus highest on femininity). People in nations scoring high on masculinity tend to value clearly defined sex roles where men dominate and to emphasize performance and independence, whereas people scoring low on masculinity (and thus high on femininity) tend to value equality of the sexes where power is shared and to emphasize the quality of life and interdependence.

5. **Long-term orientation (LT)** is the extent to which society is oriented toward the long versus the short term. Hong Kong and Japan scored highest on long-term orientation, whereas Pakistan scored the lowest. A long-term time orientation emphasizes the importance of hard work, education, and persistence as well as the importance of thrift. Nations with a long-term time orientation tend to value strategic planning and other management techniques with a long-term payback.

Hofstede's work is being extended by Project GLOBE, a team of 150 researchers who are collecting data on cultural values and practices and leadership attributes from 18,000 managers in 62 countries. The project is studying the nine cultural dimensions of assertiveness, future orientation, gender differentiation, uncertainty avoidance, power distance, institutional emphasis on collectivism versus individualism, in-group collectivism, performance orientation, and humane orientation.[83]

The dimensions of national culture help explain why some management practices work well in some countries but not in others. For example, MBO, which originated in the United States, has succeeded in Germany, according to Hofstede, because the idea of replacing the arbitrary authority of the boss with the impersonal authority of mutually agreed-upon objectives fits the low power distance that is a dimension of the German culture. It has failed in France, however, because the French are used to high power distances; they are used to accepting orders from a highly personalized authority. In countries with high levels of uncertainty avoidance, such as Switzerland and Austria, communication should be clear and explicit, based on facts. Meetings should be planned in advance and have clear agendas. In contrast, in low-uncertainty-avoidance countries, such as Greece or Russia, people are not used to structured communication and prefer more open-ended meetings. Because Thailand has a high level of power distance, Thai managers feel that communication should go from the top to the bottom of a corporation. As a result, 360-degree performance appraisals are seen as dysfunctional.[84] Some of the difficulties experienced by U.S. companies in using Japanese-style quality circles in TQM may stem from the extremely high value U.S. culture places on individualism. The differences between the United States and Mexico in terms of the power distance (Mexico 104 vs. U.S. 46) and individualism–collectivism (U.S. 91 vs. Mexico 30) dimensions may help explain why some companies operating in both countries have difficulty adapting to the differences in customs.[85] In addition, research has found that technology alliance formation is strongest in countries that value cooperation and avoid uncertainty.[86]

When one successful company in one country merges with another successful company in another country, the clash of corporate cultures is compounded by the clash of national cultures. For example, when two companies, one from a high-uncertainty-avoidance society and one from a low-uncertainty-avoidance country, are considering a merger, they should investigate each other's management practices to determine potential areas of conflict. With the value of cross-border mergers and acquisitions totaling $720 billion annually, the management of cultures is becoming a key issue in strategy implementation.[87] See the GLOBAL ISSUE feature to learn how differences in national and corporate cultures created conflict when Upjohn Company of the United States and Pharmacia AB of Sweden merged.

MNCs must pay attention to the many differences in cultural dimensions around the world and adjust their management practices accordingly. Cultural differences can easily go unrecognized by a headquarters staff that may interpret these differences as personality defects, whether the people in the subsidiaries are locals or expatriates. When conducting strategic planning in an MNC, top management must be aware that the process will vary based on the culture of the nation where a subsidiary is located. For example, in one MNC, the French expect concepts and key questions and answers. North American managers provide heavy financial analysis. Germans give precise dates and financial analysis. Information is usually late from Spanish and Moroccan operations, and quotas are typically inflated. It is up to management to adapt to the

GL🌐BAL ISSUE

Cultural Differences Create Implementation Problems in Merger

When Upjohn Pharmaceuticals of Kalamazoo, Michigan, and Pharmacia AB of Stockholm, Sweden, merged in 1995, employees of both sides were optimistic for the newly formed Pharmacia & Upjohn, Inc. Both companies were second-tier competitors fighting for survival in a global industry. Together, the firms would create a global company that could compete scientifically with its bigger rivals.

Because Pharmacia had acquired an Italian firm in 1993, it also had a large operation in Milan. U.S. executives scheduled meetings throughout the summer of 1996—only to cancel them when their European counterparts could not attend. Although it was common knowledge in Europe that most Swedes take the entire month of July for vacation and that Italians take off all of August, this was not common knowledge in Michigan. Differences in management styles became a special irritant. Swedes were used to an open system, with autonomous work teams. Executives sought the whole group's approval before making an important decision. Upjohn executives followed the more traditional American top-down approach. Upon taking command of the newly merged firm, Dr. Zabriskie (who had been Upjohn's CEO), divided the company into departments reporting to the new London headquarters. He required frequent reports, budgets, and staffing updates. The Swedes reacted negatively to this top-down management hierarchical style. "It was degrading," said Stener Kvinnsland, head of Pharmacia's cancer research in Italy before he quit the new company.

The Italian operations baffled the Americans, even though the Italians felt comfortable with a hierarchical management style. Italy's laws and unions made layoffs difficult. Italian data and accounting were often inaccurate. Because the Americans didn't trust the data, they were constantly asking for verification. In turn, the Italians were concerned that the Americans were trying to take over Italian operations. At Upjohn, all workers were subject to testing for drug and alcohol abuse. Upjohn also banned smoking. At Pharmacia's Italian business center, however, waiters poured wine freely every afternoon in the company dining room. Pharmacia's boardrooms were stocked with humidors for executives who smoked cigars during long meetings. After a brief attempt to enforce Upjohn's policies, the company dropped both the no-drinking and no-smoking policies for European workers.

Although the combined company had cut annual costs by $200 million, overall costs of the merger reached $800 million, some $200 million more than projected. Nevertheless, Jan Eckberg, CEO of Pharmacia before the merger, remained confident of the new company's ability to succeed. He admitted, however, that "we have to make some smaller changes to release the full power of the two companies."

Source: Summarized from R. Frank and T. M. Burton, "Cross-Border Merger Results in Headaches for a Drug Company," *Wall Street Journal* (February 4, 1997), pp. A1, A12.

---

differences.[88] The values embedded in his or her national culture have a profound and enduring effect on an executive's orientation, regardless of the impact of industry experience or corporate culture.[89] Hofstede and Bond conclude: "Whether they like it or not, the headquarters of multinationals are in the business of multicultural management."[90]

10.3 | Conclusion

Strategy is implemented through structural change (organizing), selecting the appropriate people to carry out the strategy (staffing), and clear communication regarding how the strategy can be put into action (leading). A number of programs, such as organizational and job design, reengineering, Six Sigma, MBO, TQM, and action planning, can be used to implement a new strategy. Executives must manage the corporate culture and find the right mix of qualified people to put a strategy in place.

Research on executive succession reveals that it is very risky to hire new top managers from outside the corporation. Although this is often done when a company is in trouble, it can be dangerous for a successful firm. This is also true when hiring people for non-executive positions. An in-depth study of 1,052 star stock analysts at 78 investment banks revealed that hiring a star (an outstanding performer) from another company did not improve the hiring company's performance. When a company hires a star, the star's performance plunges, there is a sharp decline in the functioning of the team the person works with, and the company's market value declines. Their performance dropped about 20% and did not return to the level before the job change—even after 5 years. Interestingly, around 36% of the stars left the investment banks that hired them within 36 months. Another 29% quit in the next 24 months.

This phenomenon occurs not because a star doesn't suddenly become less intelligent when switching firms, but because the star cannot take to the new firm the firm-specific resources that contributed to her or his achievements at the previous company. As a result, the star is unable to repeat the high performance in another company until he or she learns the new system. This may take years, but only if the new company has a good support system in place. Otherwise, the performance may never improve. For these reasons, companies cannot obtain competitive advantage by hiring stars from the outside. Instead, they should emphasize growing their own talent and developing the infrastructure necessary for high performance.[91]

It is important not to ignore the 75% of the workforce who, while not being stars, are the solid performers that keep a company going over the years. An undue emphasis on attracting stars wastes money and destroys morale. The CEO of McKesson, a pharmaceutical wholesaler, calls these B players "performers in place. . . . They are happy living in Dubuque. I have more time and admiration for them than the A player who is at my desk every six months asking for the next promotion." Coaches who try to forge a sports team composed of stars court disaster. According to Karen Freeman, former head coach of women's basketball at Wake Forest University, "During my coaching days, the most dysfunctional teams were the ones who had no respect for the B players." In basketball or business, when the team goes into a slump, the stars are the first to whine, Freeman reports.[92]

Strategy Bits

- The number of students leaving their home countries for higher education will triple from 2 million to nearly 6 million per year by 2020.

- The countries attracting the largest number of international students are the United States followed by the United Kingdom.[93]

Discussion Questions

1. What skills should a person have for managing a business unit following a differentiation strategy? Why? What should a company do if no one is available internally and the company has a policy of promotion from within?

2. When should someone from outside a company be hired to manage the company or one of its business units?

3. What are some ways to implement a retrenchment strategy without creating a lot of resentment and conflict with labor unions?

4. How can corporate culture be changed?

5. Why is an understanding of national cultures important in strategic management?

Strategic Practice Exercise

Staffing involves finding the person with the right blend of characteristics, such as personality, training, and experience, to implement a particular strategy. The Keirsey Temperament Sorter is designed to identify different kinds of personality temperament. It is similar to other instruments derived from Carl Jung's theory of psychological types, such as the Myers-Briggs, the Singer-Loomis, and the Grey-Wheelright. The questionnaire identifies four temperament types: **Guardian (SJ)**, **Artisan (SP)**, **Idealist (NF)**, and **Rational (NT)**. *Guardians* have natural talent in managing goods and services. They are dependable and trustworthy. *Artisans* have keen senses and are at home with tools, instruments, and vehicles. They are risk-takers and like action. *Idealists* are concerned with growth and development and like to work with people. They prefer friendly cooperation over confrontation and conflict.

Rationalists are problem solvers who like to know how things work. They work tirelessly to accomplish their goals. Each of these four types has four variants.[94]

Keirsey challenges the assumption that people are basically the same in the ways that they think, feel, and approach problems. Keirsey argues that it is far less desirable to attempt to change others (because it has little likelihood of success) than to attempt to understand, work with, and take advantage of normal differences. Companies can use this type of questionnaire to help team members understand how each person can contribute to team performance. For example, Lucent Technology used the Myers-Briggs Type Indicator to help build trust and understanding among 500 engineers in 13 time zones and 3 continents in a distributed development project.

1. Access the Keirsey Temperament Sorter using your Internet browser. Type in the following URL: *www.advisorteam.com*

2. Complete and score the questionnaire. Print the description of your personality type.

3. Read the information on the web site about each personality type. Become familiar with each.

4. Bring to class a sheet of paper containing your name and your personality type: Guardian, Artisan, Idealist, or Rational. Your instructor will either put you into a group containing people with the same predominant style or into a group with representatives from each type. He or she may then give each group a number. The instructor will then give the teams a project to accomplish. Each group will have approximately 30 minutes to do the project. It may be to solve a problem, analyze a short case, or propose a new entrepreneurial venture. The instructor will provide you with very little guidance other than to form and number the groups, give them the project, and keep track of time. He or she may move from group to group to sit in on each team's progress. When the time is up, the instructor will ask a spokesperson from each group to (1) describe the process the group went through and (2) present orally each group's ideas. After each group makes its presentation, the instructor may choose one or more of the following:

- On a sheet of paper, each person in the class should identify his or her personality type and vote which team did the best on the project.

- The class as a whole should try to identify each group's dominant decision-making style in terms of how it did its assignment. See how many people vote for one of the four types for each team.

- Each member of a group should guess whether he or she was put into a team composed of the same personality types or in one composed of all four personality types.

Key Terms

action plan (p. 253)

analytical portfolio manager (p. 241)

assessment center (p. 244)

assimilation (p. 252)

cautious profit planner (p. 241)

deculturation (p. 252)

dimensions of national culture (p. 256)

downsizing (p. 245)

dynamic industry expert (p. 241)

executive succession (p. 243)

executive type (p. 241)

individualism–collectivism (p. 256)

integration (p. 251)

integration manager (p. 240)

job rotation (p. 245)

leading (p. 240)

long-term orientation (p. 257)

Management By Objectives (p. 254)

masculinity–femininity (p. 256)

performance appraisal system (p. 244)

power distance (p. 256)

professional liquidator (p. 242)

separation (p. 252)

staffing (p. 240)

strategy–culture compatibility (p. 249)

Total Quality Management (p. 255)

turnaround specialist (p. 242)

uncertainty avoidance (p. 256)

CHAPTER 11
Evaluation and Control

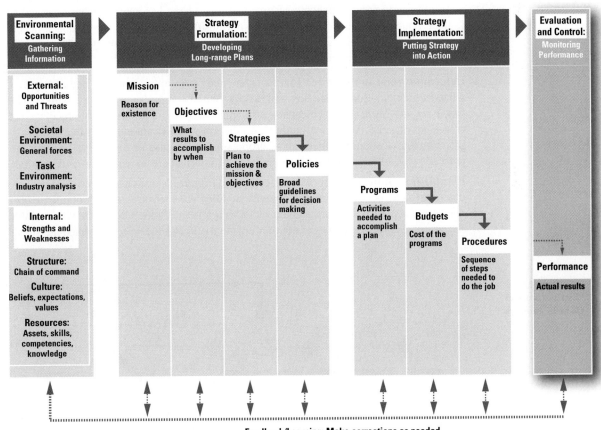

Environmental Scanning: Gathering Information	Strategy Formulation: Developing Long-range Plans				Strategy Implementation: Putting Strategy into Action			Evaluation and Control: Monitoring Performance

Environmental Scanning:
Gathering Information

External:
Opportunities and Threats

Societal Environment:
General forces

Task Environment:
Industry analysis

Internal:
Strengths and Weaknesses

Structure:
Chain of command

Culture:
Beliefs, expectations, values

Resources:
Assets, skills, competencies, knowledge

Strategy Formulation:
Developing Long-range Plans

Mission
Reason for existence

Objectives
What results to accomplish by when

Strategies
Plan to achieve the mission & objectives

Policies
Broad guidelines for decision making

Strategy Implementation:
Putting Strategy into Action

Programs
Activities needed to accomplish a plan

Budgets
Cost of the programs

Procedures
Sequence of steps needed to do the job

Evaluation and Control:
Monitoring Performance

Performance
Actual results

Feedback/Learning: Make corrections as needed

Learning Objectives

After reading this chapter, you should be able to:

- Understand the basic control process
- Choose among traditional measures, such as ROI, and shareholder value measures, such as economic value added, to properly assess performance
- Use the balanced scorecard approach to develop key performance measures
- Apply the benchmarking process to a function or an activity
- Understand the impact of problems with measuring performance
- Develop appropriate control systems to support specific strategies

NUCOR CORPORATION, ONE OF THE MOST SUCCESSFUL STEEL FIRMS OPERATING IN THE United States, keeps its evaluation and control process simple and easy to manage. According to Kenneth Iverson, Chairman of the Board:

> We try to keep our focus on what really matters—bottom-line performance and long-term survival. That's what we want our people to be thinking about. Management takes care not to distract the company with a lot of talk about other issues. We don't clutter the picture with lofty vision statements or ask employees to pursue vague, intermediate objectives like "excellence" or burden them with complex business strategies. Our competitive strategy is to build manufacturing facilities economically and to operate them efficiently. Period. Basically, we ask our employees to produce more product for less money. Then we reward them for doing that well.[1]

The **evaluation and control process** ensures that a company is achieving what it set out to accomplish. It compares performance with desired results and provides the feedback necessary for management to evaluate results and take corrective action, as needed. This process can be viewed as a five-step feedback model, as depicted in **Figure 11–1**:

1. **Determine what to measure:** Top managers and operational managers need to specify what implementation processes and results will be monitored and evaluated. The processes and results must be capable of being measured in a reasonably objective and consistent manner. The focus should be on the most significant elements in a process— the ones that account for the highest proportion of expense or the greatest number of problems. Measurements must be found for all important areas, regardless of difficulty.

2. **Establish standards of performance:** Standards used to measure performance are detailed expressions of strategic objectives. They are measures of acceptable performance results. Each standard usually includes a tolerance range that defines acceptable deviations. Standards can be set not only for final output but also for intermediate stages of production output.

Figure 11–1
Evaluation and Control Process

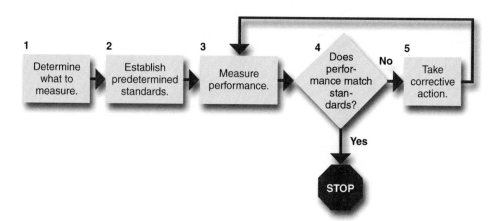

3. **Measure actual performance:** Measurements must be made at predetermined times.

4. **Compare actual performance with the standard:** If actual performance results are within the desired tolerance range, the measurement process stops here.

5. **Take corrective action:** If actual results fall outside the desired tolerance range, action must be taken to correct the deviation. The following questions must be answered:

   a. Is the deviation only a chance fluctuation?

   b. Are the processes being carried out incorrectly?

   c. Are the processes appropriate to the achievement of the desired standard? Action must be taken that will not only correct the deviation but also prevent its happening again.

   d. Who is the best person to take corrective action?

Top management is often better at the first two steps of the control model than it is at the last two follow-through steps. It tends to establish a control system and then delegate the implementation to others. This can have unfortunate results. Nucor is unusual in its ability to deal with the entire evaluation and control process.

11.1 | Evaluation and Control in Strategic Management

Evaluation and control information consists of performance data and activity reports (gathered in Step 3 in **Figure 11–1**). If undesired performance results because the strategic management processes were inappropriately used, operational managers must know about it so that they can correct the employee activity. Top management need not be involved. If, however, undesired performance results from the processes themselves, top managers, as well as operational managers, must know about it so that they can develop new implementation programs or procedures. Evaluation and control information must be relevant to what is being monitored. One of the obstacles to effective control is the difficulty in developing appropriate measures of important activities and outputs.

An application of the control process to strategic management is depicted in **Figure 11–2**. It provides strategic managers with a series of questions to use in evaluating an implemented strategy. Such a strategy review is usually initiated when a gap appears between a company's financial objectives and the expected results of current activities. After answering the proposed set of questions, a manager should have a good idea of where the problem originated and what must be done to correct the situation.

11.2 | Measuring Performance

Performance is the end result of activity. Which measures to select to assess performance depends on the organizational unit to be appraised and the objectives to be achieved. The objectives that were established earlier in the strategy formulation part of the strategic management process (dealing with profitability, market share, and cost reduction, among others) should certainly be used to measure corporate performance once the strategies have been implemented.

Appropriate Measures

Some measures, such as return on investment (ROI), are appropriate for evaluating a corporation's or division's ability to achieve a profitability objective. This type of measure, however, is inadequate for evaluating additional corporate objectives such as social responsibility or

Figure 11–2
Evaluating an Implemented Strategy

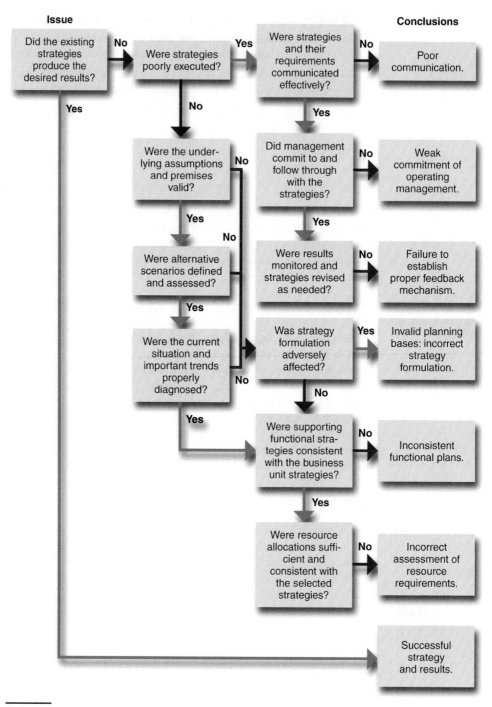

Source: From "The Strategic Review," Planning Review, Jeffrey A. Schmidt, 1998 © MCB University Press Limited. Republished with permission of Emerald Group Publishing Ltd.

employee development. Even though profitability is a corporation's major objective, ROI can be computed only after profits are totaled for a period. It tells what happened after the fact—not what is happening or what will happen. A firm, therefore, needs to develop measures that predict likely profitability. These are referred to as **steering controls** because they measure variables that influence future profitability.

One example of a steering control used by retail stores is the *inventory turnover ratio*, in which a retailer's cost of goods sold is divided by the average value of its inventories. This measure shows how hard an investment in inventory is working; the higher the ratio, the better. Not only does quicker-moving inventory tie up less cash in inventories, it also reduces the risk that the goods will grow obsolete before they're sold—a crucial measure for computers and other technology items. For example, Office Depot increased its inventory turnover ratio from 6.9 in 2003 to 7.5 in 2004, leading to increased profits for the year.[2]

Types of Controls

Controls can be established to focus on actual performance results (output), on the activities that generate the performance (behavior), or on resources that are used in performance (input). **Behavior controls** specify how something is to be done through policies, rules, standard operating procedures, and orders from a superior. **Output controls** specify what is to be accomplished by focusing on the end result of the behaviors through the use of objectives and performance targets or milestones. **Input controls** focus on resources, such as knowledge, skills, abilities, values, and motives of employees.[3]

Behavior, output, and input controls are not interchangeable. Behavior controls (such as following company procedures, making sales calls to potential customers, and getting to work on time) are most appropriate when performance results are hard to measure but the cause–effect connection between activities and results is clear. Output controls (such as sales quotas, specific cost-reduction or profit objectives, and surveys of customer satisfaction) are most appropriate when specific output measures have been agreed on but the cause–effect connection between activities and results is not clear. Input controls (such as number of years of education and experience) are most appropriate when output is difficult to measure and there is no clear cause–effect relationship between behavior and performance (such as in college teaching). Corporations following the strategy of conglomerate diversification tend to emphasize output controls with their divisions and subsidiaries (presumably because they are managed independently of each other), whereas corporations following concentric diversification use all three types of controls (presumably because synergy is desired).[4] Even if all three types of controls are used, one or two of them may be emphasized more than another, depending on the circumstances. For example, Muralidharan and Hamilton propose that as a multinational corporation (MNC) moves through its stages of development, its emphasis on control should shift from being primarily output at first, to behavioral, and finally to input control.[5]

Examples of increasingly popular behavior controls are the ISO 9000 and 14000 Standards Series on quality and environmental assurance developed by the International Standards Association of Geneva, Switzerland. Using the **ISO 9000 Standards Series** (composed of five sections, from 9000 to 9004) is a way of objectively documenting a company's high level of quality operations. Using the **ISO 14000 Standards Series** is a way to document the company's impact on the environment. A company wanting ISO 9000 certification would document its process for product introductions, among other things. ISO 9001 would require this firm to separately document design input, design process, design output, and design verification—a large amount of work. ISO 14001 would specify how companies should establish, maintain, and continually improve an environmental management system. Although the average total cost for a company to be ISO 9000 certified is close to $250,000, the annual savings are around $175,000 per company.[6] Overall, ISO 14001–related savings are about equal to the costs, reports Tim Delawder, Vice President of SWD, Inc., a metal finishing company in Addison, Illinois.[7]

Many corporations view ISO 9000 certification as assurance that a supplier sells quality products. Firms such as DuPont, Hewlett-Packard, and 3M have facilities registered to ISO standards. Companies in more than 60 countries, including Canada, Mexico, Japan, the United States (including the entire U.S. auto industry), and the European Union, require ISO 9000 certification of their suppliers.[8] The same is happening for ISO 14000. Both Ford and General Motors require their suppliers to follow ISO 14001. In a survey of manufacturing executives, 51% of the executives found that ISO 9000 certification increased their international competitiveness. Other executives noted that it signaled their commitment to quality and gave them a strategic advantage over noncertified competitors.[9] Since its ISO 14000 certification, SWD, Inc., has become a showplace for environmental awareness. According to SWD's Delawder, ISO 14000 certification improves environmental awareness among employees, reduces risks of violating regulations, and improves the firm's image among customers and the local community.[10]

Another example of a behavior control is a company's monitoring of employee phone calls and PCs to ensure that employees are behaving according to company guidelines. In a study by the American Management Association, nearly 75% of U.S. companies actively monitored their workers' communications and on-the-job activities. Around 54% tracked individual employees' Internet connections, and 38% admitted storing and reviewing their employees' e-mail. About 45% of the companies surveyed had disciplined workers (16% had fired them). For example, Xerox fired 40 employees for visiting pornographic web sites.[11]

Activity-Based Costing

Activity-based costing (ABC) is a recently developed accounting method for allocating indirect and fixed costs to individual products or product lines based on the value-added activities going into that product.[12] This accounting method is thus very useful in doing a value-chain analysis of a firm's activities for making outsourcing decisions. Traditional cost accounting, in contrast, focuses on valuing a company's inventory for financial reporting purposes. To obtain a unit's cost, cost accountants typically add direct labor to the cost of materials. Then they compute overhead from rent to R&D expenses, based on the number of direct labor hours it takes to make a product. To obtain unit cost, they divide the total by the number of items made during the period under consideration.

Traditional cost accounting is useful when direct labor accounts for most of total costs and a company produces just a few products requiring the same processes. This may have been true of companies during the early part of the twentieth century, but it is no longer relevant today, when overhead may account for as much as 70% of manufacturing costs. According to Bob Van Der Linde, CEO of a contract manufacturing services firm in San Diego, California: "Overhead is 80% to 90% in our industry, so allocation errors lead to pricing errors, which could easily bankrupt the company."[13] The appropriate allocation of indirect costs and overhead has thus become crucial for decision making. The traditional volume-based cost-driven system systematically understates the cost per unit of products with low sales volumes and products with a high degree of complexity. Similarly, it overstates the cost per unit of products with high sales volumes and a low degree of complexity.[14] When Chrysler used ABC, it discovered that the true cost of some of the parts used in making cars was 30 times what the company had previously estimated.[15]

ABC accounting allows accountants to charge costs more accurately than the traditional method because it allocates overhead far more precisely. For example, imagine a production line in a pen factory where black pens are made in high volume and blue pens in low volume. Assume that it takes eight hours to retool (reprogram the machinery) to shift production from one kind of pen to the other. The total costs include supplies (the same for both pens), the direct labor of the line workers, and factory overhead. In this instance, a very significant part of the overhead cost is the cost of reprogramming the machinery to switch from one pen to another. If the company produces 10 times as many black pens as blue pens, 10 times the cost of the reprogramming expenses will be allocated to the black pens as to the blue pens under traditional cost accounting methods. This approach underestimates, however, the true cost of making the blue pens.

ABC accounting, in contrast, first breaks down pen manufacturing into its activities. It is then very easy to see that it is the activity of changing pens that triggers the cost of retooling. The ABC accountant calculates an average cost of setting up the machinery and charges it against each batch of pens that requires retooling, regardless of the size of the run. Thus a product carries only those costs for the overhead it actually consumes. Management is now able to discover that its blue pens cost almost twice as much as do the black pens. Unless the company is able to charge a higher price for its blue pens, it cannot make a profit on these pens. Unless there is a strategic reason why it must offer blue pens (such as a key customer who must have a small number of blue pens with every large order of black pens or a marketing trend away from black to blue pens), the company will earn significantly greater profits if it completely stops making blue pens.[16]

Enterprise Risk Management

Enterprise Risk Management (ERM) is a corporatewide, integrated process for managing the uncertainties that could negatively or positively influence the achievement of a corporation's objectives. In the past, managing risk was done in a fragmented manner within functions or business units. Individuals would manage process risk, safety risk, and insurance, financial, and other assorted risks. As a result of this fragmented approach, companies would take huge risks in some areas of the business while overmanaging substantially smaller risks in other areas. ERM is being adopted because of the increasing amount of environmental uncertainty that can affect an entire corporation. As a result, the position Chief Risk Officer is one of the fastest-growing executive positions in U.S. corporations.[17] Microsoft uses scenario analysis to identify key business risks. According to Microsoft's treasurer, Brent Callinicos, "The scenarios are really what we're trying to protect against."[18] The scenarios were the possibility of an earthquake in the Seattle region and a major downturn in the stock market.

The process of rating risks involves three steps:

1. Identify the risks, using scenario analysis or brainstorming or by performing risk self-assessments.
2. Rank the risks, using some scale of impact and likelihood.
3. Measure the risks, using some agreed-upon standard.

Some companies are using value at risk, or VAR (effect of unlikely events in normal markets), and stress testing (effect of plausible events in abnormal markets) methodologies to measure the potential impact of the financial risks they face. DuPont uses earnings at risk (EAR) measuring tools to measure the effect of risk on reported earnings. It can then manage risk to a specified earnings level, based on the company's "risk appetite." With this integrated view, DuPont can view how risks affect the likelihood of achieving certain earnings targets.[19]

Primary Measures of Corporate Performance

The days when simple financial measures such as ROI or EPS were used alone to assess overall corporate performance are coming to an end. Analysts now recommend a broad range of methods to evaluate the success or failure of a strategy. Some of these methods are stakeholder measures, shareholder value, and the balanced scorecard approach. Even though each of these methods has supporters as well as detractors, the current trend is clearly toward more complicated financial measures and an increasing use of non-financial measures of corporate performance. For example, research indicates that companies pursuing strategies founded on innovation and new product development now tend to favor non-financial over financial measures.[20]

Traditional Financial Measures

The most commonly used measure of corporate performance (in terms of profits) is **return on investment (ROI)**. It is simply the result of dividing net income before taxes by the total amount invested in the company (typically measured by total assets). Although using ROI has several advantages, it also has several distinct limitations. (See **Table 11–1**.) Although ROI gives the impression of objectivity and precision, it can be easily manipulated.

Earnings per share (EPS), which involves dividing net earnings by the amount of common stock, also has several deficiencies as an evaluation of past and future performance. First, because alternative accounting principles are available, EPS can have several different but equally acceptable values, depending on the principle selected for its computation. Second, because EPS is based on accrual income, the conversion of income to cash can be near term or delayed. Therefore, EPS does not consider the time value of money. **Return on equity (ROE)**, which involves dividing net income by total equity, also has limitations because it is also derived from accounting-based data. In addition, EPS and ROE are often unrelated to a company's stock price.

Operating cash flow, which involves the amount of money generated by a company before the cost of financing and taxes, is a broad measure of a company's funds. This is the

TABLE 11–1 **ADVANTAGES AND LIMITATIONS OF USING ROI AS A MEASURE OF CORPORATE PERFORMANCE**	Before using Return on Investment (ROI) as a measure of corporate performance, consider its advantages and limitations. **Advantages** • ROI is a single, comprehensive number that includes all revenues, costs, and expenses. • It can be used to evaluate the performance of a general manager of a division or SBU. • It can be compared across companies to see which firms are performing better. • It provides an incentive to use current assets efficiently and to acquire new assets only when they would increase profits significantly. **Limitations** • ROI is very sensitive to depreciation policy. ROI can be increased by writing down the value of assets through accelerated depreciation. • It can discourage investment in new facilities or the upgrading of old ones. Older plants with depreciated assets have an advantage over newer plants in earning a higher ROI. • It provides an incentive for division managers to set transfer prices for goods sold to other divisions as high as possible and to lobby for corporate policy favoring in-house transfers over purchases from other firms. • Managers tend to focus more on ROI in the short-run over its use in the long-run. This provides an incentive for goal displacement and other dysfunctional consequences. • ROI is not comparable across industries which operate under different conditions of favorability. • It is influenced by the overall economy and will tend to be higher in prosperity and lower in a recession. • It is affected by inventory practices (LIFO or FIFO) and inflation.

company's net income plus depreciation plus depletion, amortization, interest expense, and income tax expense.[21] Some takeover specialists look at a much narrower **free cash flow**: the amount of money a new owner can take out of the firm without harming the business. This is net income plus depreciation, depletion, and amortization less capital expenditures and dividends. The free cash flow ratio is very useful in evaluating the stability of an entrepreneurial venture.[22] Although cash flow may be harder to manipulate than earnings, the number can be increased by selling accounts receivable, classifying outstanding checks as accounts payable, trading securities, and capitalizing certain expenses, such as direct-response advertising.[23]

Because of these and other limitations, ROI, EPS, ROE, and operating cash flow are not by themselves adequate measures of corporate performance. At the same time, these traditional financial measures are very appropriate when used with complementary financial and non-financial measures. (See STRATEGY HIGHLIGHT 11.1 for an example of weird performance measures that have been used instead of the traditional financial measures.)

Stakeholder Measures

Each stakeholder has its own set of criteria to determine how well the corporation is performing. These criteria typically deal with the direct and indirect impacts of corporate activities on stakeholder interests. Top management should establish one or more simple **stakeholder measures** for each stakeholder category so that it can keep track of stakeholder concerns. (See **Table 11–2**.)

Shareholder Value

Because of the belief that accounting-based numbers such as ROI, ROE, and EPS are not reliable indicators of a corporation's economic value, many corporations are using shareholder value as a better measure of corporate performance and strategic management effectiveness. **Shareholder value** can be defined as the present value of the anticipated future stream of cash flows from the business plus the value of the company if liquidated. Arguing that the purpose

STRATEGY HIGHLIGHT 11.1

Eyeballs and MUUs: Questionable Performance Measures

When Amazon.com's investor-relations team went to Denver in September 2000 to seek funding from Marsico Capital Management, a mutual fund company, it presented its usual performance story. Even though the company had never shown a profit, the team told how Amazon.com had a "first to market" advantage and that its web site received an extremely high number of "monthly unique visitors" and "eyeballs." Although such presentations had in the past raised millions of dollars for the company in stock purchases, this one failed. Marsico was more concerned with when the company would become profitable. The Amazon.com team left empty-handed.

Until 2000, investors had been so enamored with new Internet firms that they had made decisions based on novel measures of performance and firm valuation. They looked at measures such as *stickiness* (length of web site visit),

eyeballs (number of people who visit a web site), and *mindshare* (brand awareness). Mergers and acquisitions were priced on multiples of *MUUs* (monthly unique users) or even on registered users. Since practically all the dot.com (Internet) firms failed to earn a profit, investors and analysts used these measures to estimate what the firms might be worth sometime in the future. Once analysts realized that these valuations were worthless, stock prices dropped to almost nothing, and by 2001 most of the dot.com firms were out of business.

Sources: E. Schonfeld, "How Much Are Your Eyeballs Worth?" *Fortune* (February 21, 2000), pp. 197–204; N. Byrnes, "Eyeballs, Bah! Figuring Dot-Coms' Real Worth," *Business Week* (October 30, 2000), p. 62; R. Barker, "Amazon: Cheaper—But Cheap Enough?" *Business Week* (December 4, 2000), p. 172.

TABLE 11–2 A SAMPLE SCORECARD FOR "KEEPING SCORE" WITH STAKEHOLDERS

Stakeholder Category	Possible Near-Term Measures	Possible Long-Term Measures
Customers	Sales ($ and volume) New customers Number of new customer needs met ("tries")	Growth in sales Turnover of customer base Ability to control price

Suppliers	Cost of raw material
	Delivery time
	Inventory
	Availability of raw material
		Growth rates of:
		    Raw material costs
		    Delivery time
		    Inventory
		New ideas from suppliers

Financial community	EPS Stock price Number of "buy" lists ROE	Ability to convince Wall Street of strategy Growth in ROE
Employees	Number of suggestions Productivity Number of grievances	Number of internal promotions Turnover
Congress	Number of new pieces of legislation that affect the firm Access to key members and staff	Number of new regulations that affect industry Ratio of "cooperative" vs. "competitive" encounters
Consumer advocate (CA)	Number of meetings Number of "hostile" encounters Number of times coalitions formed Number of legal actions	Number of changes in policy due to CA Number of CA-initiated "calls for help"
Environmentalists	Number of meetings Number of hostile encounters Number of times coalitions formed Number of EPA complaints Number of legal actions	Number of changes in policy due to environmentalists Number of environmentalist "calls for help"

Source: R. E. Freeman, *Strategic Management: A Stakeholder Approach* (Boston: Ballinger Publishing Company, 1984), p. 179. Copyright © 1984 by R. E. Freeman. Reprinted by permission of R. Edward Freeman.

of a company is to increase shareholder wealth, shareholder value analysis concentrates on cash flow as the key measure of performance. The value of a corporation is thus the value of its cash flows discounted back to their present value, using the business's cost of capital as the discount rate. As long as the returns from a business exceed its cost of capital, the business will create value and be worth more than the capital invested in it.

The New York consulting firm Stern Stewart & Company devised and popularized two shareholder value measures: economic value added (EVA) and market value added (MVA). A basic tenet of EVA and MVA is that businesses should not invest in projects unless they can generate a profit above the cost of capital. Stern Stewart argues that a deficiency of traditional accounting-based measures is that they assume the cost of capital to be zero.[24] Well-known companies, such as Coca-Cola, General Electric, AT&T, Whirlpool, Quaker Oats, Eli Lilly, Georgia-Pacific, Polaroid, Sprint, Teledyne, and Tenneco have adopted MVA and/or EVA as the best yardstick for corporate performance. According to Sprint's CFO, Art Krause, "Unlike EPS, which measures accounting results, MVA gauges true economic performance."[25]

Economic value added (EVA) has become an extremely popular shareholder value method of measuring corporate and divisional performance and may be on its way to replacing ROI as the standard performance measure. EVA measures the difference between the pre-strategy and poststrategy values for the business. Simply put, EVA is after-tax operating income minus the total annual cost of capital. The formula to measure EVA is:

$$\text{EVA} = \text{after-tax operating income} - (\text{investment in assets} \times \text{weighted average cost of capital})^{26}$$

The cost of capital combines the cost of debt and equity. The annual cost of borrowed capital is the interest charged by the firm's banks and bondholders. To calculate the cost of equity, assume that shareholders generally earn about 6% more on stocks than on government bonds. If long-term treasury bills are selling at 7.5%, the firm's cost of equity should be 13.5%—more if the firm is in a risky industry. A corporation's overall cost of capital is the weighted-average cost of the firm's debt and equity capital. The investment in assets is the total amount of capital invested in the business, including buildings, machines, computers, and investments in R&D and training (allocating costs annually over their useful life). Because the typical balance sheet understates the investment made in a company, Stern Stewart has identified 150 possible adjustments, before EVA is calculated.[27] Multiply the firm's total investment in assets by the weighted-average cost of capital. Subtract that figure from after tax operating income. If the difference is positive, the strategy (and the management employing it) is generating value for the shareholders. If it is negative, the strategy is destroying shareholder value.[28]

Roberto Goizueta, past-CEO of Coca-Cola, explained, "We raise capital to make concentrate, and sell it at an operating profit. Then we pay the cost of that capital. Shareholders pocket the difference."[29] Managers can improve their company's or business unit's EVA by (1) earning more profit without using more capital, (2) using less capital, and (3) investing capital in high-return projects. Studies have found that companies using EVA outperform their median competitor by an average of 8.43% of total return annually.[30] EVA does, however, have some limitations. For one thing, it does not control for size differences across plants or divisions. As with ROI, managers can manipulate the numbers. As with ROI, EVA is an after-the-fact measure and cannot be used as a steering control.[31] Although proponents of EVA argue that EVA (unlike Return on Investment, Equity, or Sales) has a strong relationship to stock price, other studies do not support this contention.[32]

Market value added (MVA) is the difference between the market value of a corporation and the capital contributed by shareholders and lenders. Like net present value, it measures the stock market's estimate of the net present value of a firm's past and expected capital investment projects. As such, MVA is the present value of future EVA.[33] To calculate MVA,

1. Add all the capital that has been put into a company—from shareholders, bondholders, and retained earnings.

2. Reclassify certain accounting expenses, such as R&D, to reflect that they are actually investments in future earnings. This provides the firm's total capital. So far, this is the same approach taken in calculating EVA.

3. Using the current stock price, total the value of all outstanding stock, adding it to the company's debt. This is the company's market value. If the company's market value is greater than all the capital invested in it, the firm has a positive MVA—meaning that management (and the strategy it is following) has created wealth. In some cases, however, the market value of the company is actually less than the capital put into it, which means shareholder wealth is being destroyed.

Microsoft, General Electric, Intel, and Coca-Cola tend to have high MVAs in the United States, whereas General Motors and RJR Nabisco have low ones.[34] Studies have shown that EVA is a predictor of MVA. Consecutive years of positive EVA generally lead to a soaring

MVA.[35] Research also reveals that CEO turnover is significantly correlated with MVA and EVA, whereas ROA and ROE are not. This suggests that EVA and MVA may be more appropriate measures of the market's evaluation of a firm's strategy and its management than are the traditional measures of corporate performance.[36] Nevertheless, these measures consider only the financial interests of the shareholder and ignore other stakeholders, such as environmentalists and employees.

Balanced Scorecard Approach: Using Key Performance Measures

Rather than evaluate a corporation using a few financial measures, Kaplan and Norton argue for a "balanced scorecard" that includes non-financial as well as financial measures.[37] This approach is especially useful given that research indicates that non-financial assets explain 50% to 80% of a firm's value.[38] The **balanced scorecard** combines financial measures that tell the results of actions already taken with operational measures on customer satisfaction, internal processes, and the corporation's innovation and improvement activities—the drivers of future financial performance. Management should develop goals or objectives in each of four areas:

1. **Financial:** How do we appear to shareholders?
2. **Customer:** How do customers view us?
3. **Internal Business Perspective:** What must we excel at?
4. **Innovation and Learning:** Can we continue to improve and create value?

Each goal in each area (for example, avoiding bankruptcy in the financial area) is then assigned one or more measures, as well as a target and an initiative. These measures can be thought of as **key performance measures**—measures that are essential for achieving a desired strategic option.[39] For example, a company could include cash flow, quarterly sales growth, and ROE as measures for success in the financial area. It could include market share (competitive position goal) and percentage of new sales coming from new products (customer acceptance goal) as measures under the customer perspective. It could include cycle time and unit cost (manufacturing excellence goal) as measures under the internal business perspective. It could include time to develop next-generation products (technology leadership objective) under the innovation and learning perspective.

A survey by Bain & Company reported that 50% of *Fortune 1000* companies in North America and about 40% in Europe use a version of the balanced scorecard.[40] Another survey reported that the balanced scorecard is used by over half of *Fortune's Global 1000* companies.[41] A study of the *Fortune 500* firms in the United States and the *Post 300* firms in Canada revealed the most popular non-financial measures to be customer satisfaction, customer service, product quality, market share, productivity, service quality, and core competencies. New product development, corporate culture, and market growth were not far behind.[42] CIGNA, for example, uses the balanced scorecard to determine employee bonuses.[43] Corporate experience with the balanced scorecard reveals that a firm should tailor the system to suit its situation, not just adopt it as a cookbook approach. When the balanced scorecard complements corporate strategy, it improves performance. Using the method in a mechanistic fashion without any link to strategy hinders performance and may even decrease it.[44]

Evaluating Top Management and the Board of Directors

Through its strategy, audit, and compensation committees, a board of directors closely evaluates the job performance of the CEO and the top management team. Of course, it is concerned primarily with overall corporate profitability as measured quantitatively by ROI, ROE, EPS, and shareholder value. The absence of short-run profitability certainly contributes to the firing of any CEO. The board, however, is also concerned with other factors.

Members of the compensation committees of today's boards of directors generally agree that a CEO's ability to establish strategic direction, build a management team, and provide leadership are more critical in the long run than are a few quantitative measures. The board should evaluate top management not only on the typical output-oriented quantitative measures but also on behavioral measures—factors relating to its strategic management practices. The specific items that a board uses to evaluate its top management should be derived from the objectives that both the board and top management agreed on earlier. If better relations with the local community and improved safety practices in work areas were selected as objectives for the year (or for five years), these items should be included in the evaluation. In addition, other factors that tend to lead to profitability might be included, such as market share, product quality, or investment intensity. Although the number of boards conducting systematic evaluations of their CEO is increasing, it is estimated that no more than half of the boards do so.

Only 40% of large corporations conduct formal performance evaluations of their boards of directors. Individual director evaluations are even less common. Corporations that have successfully used board performance appraisal systems are Target, Bell South, Raytheon, and Gillette.[45] *Business Week* annually publishes a list of the best and worst boards of directors in the United States.

Chairman–CEO Feedback Instrument. An increasing number of companies are evaluating their CEO by using a 17-item questionnaire developed by Ram Charan, an authority on corporate governance. The questionnaire focuses on four key areas: (1) company performance, (2) leadership of the organization, (3) team building and management succession, and (4) leadership of external constituencies.[46] After taking an hour to complete the questionnaire, the board of KeraVision, Inc., used it as a basis for a lengthy discussion with the CEO, Thomas Loarie. The board criticized Loarie for "not tempering enthusiasm with reality" and urged Loarie to develop a clear management succession plan. The evaluation caused Loarie to more closely involve the board in setting the company's primary objectives and discussing "where we are, where we want to go, and the operating environment."[47]

Management Audit. **Management audits** are very useful to boards of directors in evaluating management's handling of various corporate activities. Management audits have been developed to evaluate activities such as corporate social responsibility, functional areas such as the marketing department, and divisions such as the international division. These can be helpful if the board has selected particular functional areas or activities for improvement.

Strategic Audit. The strategic audit presented in the Chapter 1 **Appendix 1.A** is a type of management audit. A strategic audit provides a checklist of questions, by area or issue, that enables a systematic analysis of various corporate functions and activities to be made. It is a type of management audit and is extremely useful as a diagnostic tool to pinpoint corporatewide problem areas and to highlight organizational strengths and weaknesses and environmental opportunities and threats (SWOT).[48] A strategic audit can help determine why a certain area is creating problems for a corporation and help generate solutions to the problem. As such, it can be very useful in evaluating the performance of top management.

Primary Measures of Divisional and Functional Performance

Companies use a variety of techniques to evaluate and control performance in divisions, strategic business units (SBUs), and functional areas. If a corporation is composed of SBUs or divisions, it will use many of the same performance measures (ROI or EVA, for instance) that it uses to assess overall corporate performance. To the extent that it can isolate specific functional units such as R&D, the corporation may develop responsibility centers. It will also use typical functional measures such as market share and sales per employee (marketing), unit costs and percentage of defects (operations), percentage of sales from new products and number of patents (R&D), and turnover and job satisfaction (HRM). For example, FedEx uses Enhanced Tracker software with its COSMOS database to track the progress of its 2.5 to 3.5 million shipments daily. As a courier is completing her or his day's activities, the Enhanced Tracker asks whether the person's package count equals the Enhanced Tracker's count. If the count is off, the software helps reconcile the differences.[49]

During strategy formulation and implementation, top management approves a series of programs and supporting **operating budgets** from its business units. During evaluation and control, actual expenses are contrasted with planned expenditures, and the degree of variance is assessed. This is typically done on a monthly basis. In addition, top management will probably require **periodic statistical reports** summarizing data on such key factors as the number of new customer contracts, the volume of received orders, and productivity figures.

Responsibility Centers

Control systems can be established to monitor specific functions, projects, or divisions. Budgets are one type of control system that is typically used to control the financial indicators of performance. **Responsibility centers** are used to isolate a unit so that it can be evaluated separately from the rest of the corporation. Each responsibility center, therefore, has its own budget and is evaluated on its use of budgeted resources. It is headed by the manager responsible for the center's performance. The center uses resources (measured in terms of costs or expenses) to produce a service or a product (measured in terms of volume or revenues). There are five major types of responsibility centers. The type is determined by the way the corporation's control system measures these resources and services or products:

1. **Standard cost centers: Standard cost centers** are primarily used in manufacturing facilities. Standard (or expected) costs are computed for each operation on the basis of historical data. In evaluating the center's performance, its total standard costs are multiplied by the units produced. The result is the expected cost of production, which is then compared to the actual cost of production.

2. **Revenue centers:** With **revenue centers**, production, usually in terms of unit or dollar sales, is measured without consideration of resource costs (for example, salaries). The center is thus judged in terms of effectiveness rather than efficiency. The effectiveness of a sales region, for example, is determined by comparing its actual sales to its projected or previous year's sales. Profits are not considered because sales departments have very limited influence over the cost of the products they sell.

3. **Expense centers:** Resources are measured in dollars, without consideration for service or product costs. Thus budgets will have been prepared for engineered expenses (costs that can be calculated) and for discretionary expenses (costs that can be only estimated). Typical **expense centers** are administrative, service, and research departments. They cost a company money, but they only indirectly contribute to revenues.

4. **Profit centers:** Performance is measured in terms of the difference between revenues (which measure production) and expenditures (which measure resources). A **profit center** is typically established whenever an organizational unit has control over both its resources and its products or services. By having such centers, a company can be organized into divisions of separate product lines. The manager of each division is given autonomy to the extent that he or she is able to keep profits at a satisfactory (or better) level.

   Some organizational units that are not usually considered potentially autonomous can, for the purpose of profit center evaluations, be made so. A manufacturing department, for example, can be converted from a standard cost center (or expense center) into a profit center; it is allowed to charge a transfer price for each product it "sells" to the sales department. The difference between the manufacturing cost per unit and the agreed-upon transfer price is the unit's "profit."

Transfer pricing is commonly used in vertically integrated corporations and can work well when a price can be easily determined for a designated amount of product. Even though most experts agree that market-based transfer prices are the best choice, only 30%–40% of companies use market price to set the transfer price. (Of the rest, 50% use cost; 10%–20% use negotiation.)[50] When a price cannot be set easily, however, the relative bargaining power of the centers, rather than strategic considerations, tends to influence the agreed-upon price. Top management has an obligation to make sure that these political considerations do not overwhelm the strategic ones. Otherwise, profit figures for each center will be biased and provide poor information for strategic decisions at both the corporate and divisional levels.

5. **Investment centers:** Because many divisions in large manufacturing corporations use significant assets to make their products, their asset base should be factored into their performance evaluation. Thus it is insufficient to focus only on profits, as in the case of profit centers. An **investment center's** performance is measured in terms of the difference between its resources and its services or products. For example, two divisions in a corporation made identical profits, but one division owns a $3 million plant, whereas the other owns a $1 million plant. Both make the same profits, but one is obviously more efficient; the smaller plant provides the shareholders with a better return on their investment. The most widely used measure of investment center performance is ROI.

Most single-business corporations, such as Apple Computer, tend to use a combination of cost, expense, and revenue centers. In these corporations, most managers are functional specialists and manage against a budget. Total profitability is integrated at the corporate level. Multidivisional corporations with one dominating product line (such as Anheuser-Busch) that have diversified into a few businesses but that still depend on a single product line (such as beer) for most of their revenue and income generally use a combination of cost, expense, revenue, and profit centers. Multidivisional corporations, such as General Electric, tend to emphasize investment centers—although in various units throughout the corporation other types of responsibility centers are also used. One problem with using responsibility centers, however, is that the separation needed to measure and evaluate a division's performance can diminish the level of cooperation among divisions that is needed to attain synergy for the corporation as a whole. (This problem is discussed later in this chapter, under "Suboptimization.")

Using Benchmarking to Evaluate Performance

According to Xerox Corporation, the company that pioneered this concept in the United States, **benchmarking** is "the continual process of measuring products, services, and practices against the toughest competitors or those companies recognized as industry leaders."[51] Benchmarking, an increasingly popular program, is based on the concept that it makes no sense to reinvent something that someone else is already using. It involves openly learning how others do something better than one's own company so that the company not only can imitate but perhaps even improve on its current techniques. The benchmarking process usually involves the following steps:

1. Identify the area or process to be examined. It should be an activity that has the potential to determine a business unit's competitive advantage.

2. Find behavioral and output measures of the area or process and obtain measurements.

3. Select an accessible set of competitors and best-in-class companies against which to benchmark. These may very often be companies that are in completely different industries

but perform similar activities. For example, when Xerox wanted to improve its order fulfillment, it went to L.L.Bean, the successful mail-order firm, to learn how it achieved excellence in this area.

4. Calculate the differences among the company's performance measurements and those of the best-in-class companies and determine why the differences exist.

5. Develop tactical programs for closing performance gaps.

6. Implement the programs and then compare the resulting new measurements with those of the best-in-class companies.

Benchmarking has been found to produce best results in companies that are already well managed. Apparently, poorer-performing firms tend to be overwhelmed by the discrepancy between their performance and the benchmark—and tend to view the benchmark as too difficult to reach.[52] Nevertheless, a survey by Bain & Company of 460 companies of various sizes across all U.S. industries indicated that more than 70% were using benchmarking in either a major or limited manner.[53] Cost reductions range from 15% to 45%.[54] Benchmarking can also increase sales, improve goal setting, and boost employee motivation.[55] The average cost of a benchmarking study is around $100,000 and involves 30 weeks of effort.[56] Manco, Inc., a small Cleveland-area producer of duct tape, regularly benchmarks itself against Wal-Mart, Rubbermaid, and PepsiCo to enable it to better compete with giant 3M. The American Productivity & Quality Center, a Houston research group, established the Open Standards Benchmarking Collaborative database, composed of more than 1,200 commonly used measures and individual benchmarks, to track the performance of core operational functions. Firms can submit their performance data to this online database to learn how they compare to top performers and industry peers (see *www.apqc.org*).

International Measurement Issues

The three most widely used techniques for international performance evaluation are ROI, budget analysis, and historical comparisons. In one study, 95% of the corporate officers interviewed stated that they use the same evaluation techniques for foreign and domestic operations. Rate of return was mentioned as the single most important measure.[57] However, ROI can cause problems when it is applied to international operations: Because of foreign currencies, different rates of inflation, different tax laws, and the use of transfer pricing, both the net income figure and the investment base may be seriously distorted.[58]

A study of 79 MNCs revealed that **international transfer pricing** from one country unit to another is primarily used not to evaluate performance but to minimize taxes.[59] Taxes are an important issue for MNCs, given that corporate tax rates vary from over 40% in Canada, Japan, Italy, and the United States to 25% in Bolivia, 15% in Chile, and 10%–15% in Zambia.[60] For example, the U.S. Internal Revenue Service contends that many Japanese firms doing business in the United States have artificially inflated the value of U.S. deliveries in order to reduce the profits and thus the taxes of their American subsidiaries.[61] Parts made in a subsidiary of a Japanese MNC in a low-tax country such as Singapore can be shipped to its subsidiary in a high-tax country such as the United States at such a high price that the U.S. subsidiary reports very little profit (and thus pays few taxes), while the Singapore subsidiary reports a very high profit (but also pays few taxes because of the lower tax rate). A Japanese MNC can, therefore, earn more profit worldwide by reporting less profit in high-tax countries and more profit in low-tax countries. Transfer pricing is an important factor, given that 56% of all trade in the Triad and one-third of all international trade is composed of intercompany transactions.[62] Transfer pricing can thus be one way the parent company can reduce taxes and "capture profits" from a subsidiary. Other common ways of transferring profits to the parent company (often referred to as the **repatriation of profits**) are through dividends, royalties, and management fees.[63]

Among the most important barriers to international trade are the different standards for products and services. There are at least three categories of standards: safety/environmental, energy efficiency, and testing procedures. Existing standards have been drafted by such bodies as the British Standards Institute (BSI-UK) in the United Kingdom, Japanese Industrial Standards Committee (JISC), AFNOR in France, DIN in Germany, CSA in Canada, and American Standards Institute in the United States. These standards traditionally created entry barriers that served to fragment various industries, such as major home appliances, by country. The International Electrotechnical Commission (IEC) standards were created to harmonize standards in the European Union and eventually to serve as worldwide standards, with some national deviations to satisfy specific needs. Because the European Union (EU) was the first to harmonize the many different standards of its member countries, the EU is shaping standards for the rest of the world. In addition, the International Organization for Standardization (ISO) is preparing and publishing international standards. These standards provide a foundation for regional associations to build upon. CANENA, the Council for Harmonization of Electrotechnical Standards of the Nations of the Americas, was created in 1992 to further coordinate the harmonization of standards in North and South America. Efforts are also under way in Asia to harmonize standards.[64]

An important issue in international trade is **piracy**. Firms in developing nations around the world make money by making counterfeit copies of well-known name brand products and selling them globally. See the GLOBAL ISSUE feature to learn how this is being done.

GL🌐BAL ISSUE

Piracy: 15%–20% of China's Goods Are Counterfeit

"There's more counterfeiting going on in China now than we've ever seen anywhere," states Dan Chow, a law professor at Ohio State University. "We know that 15 to 20 percent of all goods in China are counterfeit." This includes products from Tide detergent and Budweiser beer to Marlboro cigarettes. Yamaha estimates that five out of every six bikes bearing its brand name are fake. Procter & Gamble estimates that 15% of the soaps and detergents under its Head & Shoulders, Vidal Sassoon, Safeguard, and Tide brands in China are counterfeit, costing the company $150 million in lost sales. In Yiwu, a few hours from Shanghai, one person admitted to a *60 Minutes* reporter that she could make 1,000 pairs of counterfeit Nike shoes in 10 days for $4.00 a pair. According to Joseph M. Johnson, president of the China division of Bestfoods Asia Ltd, "We are spending millions of dollars to combat counterfeiting."

Tens of thousands of counterfeiters are currently active in China. They range from factories mixing shampoo and soap in back rooms to large state-owned enterprises making copies of soft drinks and beer. Other factories make everything from car batteries to automobiles. Mobile CD factories with optical disc-mastering machines counterfeit music and software. *60 Minutes* found a small factory in Donguan making fake Callaway golf clubs and bags at a rate of 500 bags per week. Factories in southern Guangdong or Fujian provinces truck their products to a central distribution center, such as the one in Yiwu. They may also be shipped across the border into Russia, Pakistan, Vietnam, or Burma. Chinese counterfeiters have developed a global reach through their connections with organized crime.

According to the market research firm Automotive Resources, the profit margins on counterfeit shock absorbers can reach 80% versus only 15% for the real ones. Counterfeiters charge up to 80% less for an oil filter for a Mercedes than the $24 for an authentic filter.

Counterfeit products can be found around the world—not just in China. The worldwide cost of software piracy is around $12 million annually. For example, 27% of the software sold in the United States is pirated. That figure increases to around 50% in Brazil, Singapore, and Poland, and to over 80% in Vietnam (94%), China (92%), Indonesia (88%), Russia (87%), Ukraine (87%), and Pakistan (83%).

Sources: "The World's Greatest Fakes," *60 Minutes*, CBS News (August 8, 2004); "Business Software Piracy," *Pocket World in Figures 2004* (London: Economist & Profile Book, 2003), p. 60; D. Roberts, F. Balfour, P. Magnusson, P. Engardio, and J. Lee, "China's Piracy Plague," *Business Week* (June 5, 2000), pp. 44–48; "Emerging Market Indicators: Software Piracy," *The Economist* (June 27, 1998), p. 108; "Piracy's Big-Business Victims," *Futurist Update* (December 2000).

Authorities in international business recommend that the control and reward systems used by a global MNC be different from those used by a multidomestic MNC.[65] A *multidomestic MNC* should use loose controls on its foreign units. The management of each geographic unit should be given considerable operational latitude, but it should be expected to meet some performance targets. Because profit and ROI measures are often unreliable in international operations, it is recommended that the MNC's top management, in this instance, emphasize budgets and non-financial measures of performance such as market share, productivity, public image, employee morale, and relations with the host country government.[66] Multiple measures should be used to differentiate between the worth of the subsidiary and the performance of its management.

A *global MNC*, however, needs tight controls over its many units. To reduce costs and gain competitive advantage, it is trying to spread the manufacturing and marketing operations of a few fairly uniform products around the world. Therefore, its key operational decisions must be centralized. Its environmental scanning must include research not only into each of the national markets in which the MNC competes but also into the "global arena" of the interaction between markets. Foreign units are thus evaluated more as cost centers, revenue centers, or expense centers than as investment or profit centers because MNCs operating in a global industry do not often make the entire product in the country in which it is sold.

11.3 | Strategic Information Systems

Before performance measures can have any impact on strategic management, they must first be communicated to the people responsible for formulating and implementing strategic plans. Strategic information systems can perform this function. They can be computer based or manual, formal or informal. One of the key reasons given for the bankruptcy of International Harvester was the inability of the corporation's top management to precisely determine its income by major class of similar products. Because of this inability, management kept trying to fix ailing businesses and was unable to respond flexibly to major changes and unexpected events. In contrast, one of the key reasons for the success of Wal-Mart has been management's use of the company's sophisticated information system to control purchasing decisions. Cash registers in Wal-Mart retail stores transmit information hourly to computers at company headquarters. Consequently, managers know every morning exactly how many of each item were sold the day before, how many have been sold so far in the year, and how this year's sales compare to last year's. The information system allows all reordering to be done automatically by computers, without any managerial input. It also allows the company to experiment with new toys without committing to big orders in advance. In effect, the system allows the customers to decide through their purchases what gets reordered.

Enterprise Resource Planning (ERP)

Many corporations around the world have adopted **enterprise resource planning (ERP)** software. ERP unites all of a company's major business activities, from order processing to production, within a single family of software modules. The system provides instant access to critical information to everyone in the organization, from the CEO to the factory floor worker. Because of the ability of ERP software to use a common information system throughout a company's many operations around the world, it is becoming the business information systems' global standard. The major providers of this software are SAP AG, Oracle, J. D. Edwards, Peoplesoft, Baan, and SSA.

The German company SAP AG originated the concept with its R/3 software system. Microsoft, for example, used R/3 to replace a tangle of 33 financial tracking systems in 26 subsidiaries. Even though it cost the company $25 million and took 10 months to install, R/3 annually saves Microsoft $18 million. Coca-Cola uses the R/3 system to enable a manager in Atlanta to use her personal computer to check the latest sales of 20-ounce bottles of Coke Classic in India. Owens-Corning envisions that its R/3 system will allow salespeople to learn what is available at any plant or warehouse and to quickly assemble orders for customers.

ERP is, nevertheless, not for every company. The system is extremely complicated and demands a high level of standardization throughout a corporation. Its demanding nature often forces companies to change the way they do business. There are three reasons ERP could fail: (1) insufficient tailoring of the software to fit the company, (2) inadequate training, and (3) insufficient implementation support.[67] Over the two-year period of installing R/3, Owens-Corning had to completely overhaul its operations. Because R/3 was incompatible with Apple Computer's very organic corporate culture, the company was only able to apply it to its order management and financial operations, but not to manufacturing. Other companies that had difficulty installing and using ERP are Whirlpool, Hershey Foods, and Stanley Works. At Whirlpool, SAP's software led to missed and delayed shipments, causing Home Depot to cancel its agreement for selling Whirlpool products.[68]

Divisional and Functional IS Support

At the divisional or SBU level of a corporation, the information system should be used to support, reinforce, or enlarge its business-level strategy through its decision support system. An SBU pursuing a strategy of overall cost leadership could use its information system to reduce costs either by improving labor productivity or improving the use of other resources such as inventory or machinery. Merrill Lynch took this approach when it developed PRISM software to provide its 500 U.S. retail offices with quick access to financial information in order to boost brokers' efficiency. Another SBU, in contrast, might want to pursue a differentiation strategy. It could use its information system to add uniqueness to the product or service and contribute to quality, service, or image through the functional areas. FedEx wanted to use superior service to gain a competitive advantage. It invested significantly in several types of information systems to measure and track the performance of its delivery service. Together, these information systems gave FedEx the fastest error-response time in the overnight delivery business.

11.4 | **Problems in Measuring Performance**

The measurement of performance is a crucial part of evaluation and control. The lack of quantifiable objectives or performance standards and the inability of the information system to provide timely and valid information are two obvious control problems. According to Meg Whitman, CEO of eBay, "If you can't measure it, you can't control it." That's why eBay has a multitude of measures, from total revenues and profits to *take rate*, the ratio of revenues to the value of goods traded on the site.[69] Without objective and timely measurements, it would be extremely difficult to make operational, let alone strategic, decisions. Nevertheless, the use of timely, quantifiable standards does not guarantee good performance. The very act of monitoring and measuring performance can cause side effects that interfere with overall corporate performance. Among the most frequent negative side effects are a short-term orientation and goal displacement.

Short-Term Orientation

Top executives report that in many situations, they analyze neither the long-term implications of present operations on the strategy they have adopted nor the operational impact of a strategy on the corporate mission. Long-run evaluations are often not conducted because executives (1) don't realize their importance, (2) believe that short-run considerations are more important than long-run considerations, (3) aren't personally evaluated on a long-term basis, or (4) don't have the time to make a long-run analysis.[70] There is no real justification for the first and last reasons. If executives realize the importance of long-run evaluations, they make the time needed to conduct them. Even though many chief executives point to immediate pressures from the investment community and to short-term incentive and promotion plans to support the second and third reasons, evidence does not always support their claims.[71]

At one international heavy-equipment manufacturer, managers were so strongly motivated to achieve their quarterly revenue target that they shipped unfinished products from their plant in England to a warehouse in the Netherlands for final assembly. By shipping the incomplete products, they were able to realize the sales before the end of the quarter—thus fulfilling their budgeted objective and making their bonuses. Unfortunately, the high cost of assembling the goods at a distant location (requiring not only renting the warehouse but also paying additional labor) ended up reducing the company's overall profit.[72]

Many accounting-based measures encourage a **short-term orientation** in which managers consider only current tactical or operational issues and ignore long-term strategic ones. **Table 11–1** indicates that one of the limitations of ROI as a performance measure is its short-term nature. In theory, ROI is not limited to the short run, but in practice it is often difficult to use this measure to realize long-term benefits for a company. Because managers can often manipulate both the numerator (earnings) and the denominator (investment), the resulting ROI figure can be meaningless. Advertising, maintenance, and research efforts can be reduced. Estimates of pension-fund profits, unpaid receivables, and old inventory are easy to adjust. Optimistic estimates of returned products, bad debts, and obsolete inventory inflate the present year's sales and earnings.[73] Expensive retooling and plant modernization can be delayed as long as a manager can manipulate figures on production defects and absenteeism.

Mergers can be undertaken that will do more for the present year's earnings (and the next year's paycheck) than for the division's or corporation's future profits. For example, research on 55 firms that engaged in major acquisitions revealed that even though the firms performed poorly after the acquisition, the acquiring firms' top management still received significant increases in compensation.[74] Determining CEO compensation on the basis of firm size rather than performance is typical and is particularly likely for firms that are not monitored closely by independent analysts.[75]

Research supports the conclusion that many CEOs and their friends on the board of directors' compensation committee manipulate information to provide themselves a pay raise. For example, CEOs tend to announce bad news—thus reducing the company's stock price—just before the issuance of stock options. Once the options are issued, the CEOs tend to announce good news—thus raising the stock price and making their options more valuable.[76] Board compensation committees tend to expand the peer group comparison outside their industry to include lower-performing firms to justify a high raise to the CEO. They tend to do this when the company performs poorly, the industry performs well, the CEO is already highly paid, and shareholders are powerful and active.[77]

Goal Displacement

If not carefully done, monitoring and measuring of performance can actually result in a decline in overall corporate performance. **Goal displacement** is the confusion of means with ends and occurs when activities originally intended to help managers attain corporate objectives become ends in themselves—or are adapted to meet ends other than those for which they were intended. Two types of goal displacement are behavior substitution and suboptimization.

Behavior Substitution

Behavior substitution refers to a phenomenon when people substitute activities that do not lead to goal accomplishment for activities that do lead to goal accomplishment because the wrong activities are being rewarded. Managers, like most other people, tend to focus more of their attention on behaviors that are clearly measurable than on those that are not. Employees often receive little or no reward for engaging in hard-to-measure activities such as cooperation and initiative. However, easy-to-measure activities might have little or no relationship to the desired good performance. Rational people, nevertheless, tend to work for the rewards that the system has to offer. Therefore, people tend to substitute behaviors that are recognized and rewarded for behaviors that are ignored, without regard to their contribution to goal accomplishment. A research study of 157 corporations revealed that most of the companies made little attempt to identify areas of non-financial performance that might advance their chosen strategy. Only 23% consistently built and verified cause-and-effect relationships between intermediate controls (such as number of patents filed or product flaws) and company performance.[78]

A U.S. Navy quip sums up this situation: "What you inspect (or reward) is what you get." If the reward system emphasizes quantity while merely asking for quality and cooperation, the system is likely to produce a large number of low-quality products and unsatisfied customers.[79] A proposed law governing the effect of measurement on behavior is that quantifiable measures drive out non-quantifiable measures.

A classic example of behavior substitution happened a few years ago at Sears. Sears' management thought that it could improve employee productivity by tying performance to rewards. It, therefore, paid commissions to its auto shop employees as a percentage of each repair bill. Behavior substitution resulted as employees altered their behavior to fit the reward system. The results were over-billed customers, charges for work never done, and a scandal that tarnished Sears' reputation for many years.[80]

Suboptimization

Suboptimization refers to the phenomenon of a unit optimizing its goal accomplishment to the detriment of the organization as a whole. The emphasis in large corporations on developing separate responsibility centers can create some problems for the corporation as a whole. To the extent that a division or functional unit views itself as a separate entity, it might refuse to cooperate with other units or divisions in the same corporation if cooperation could in some way negatively affect its performance evaluation. The competition between divisions to achieve a high ROI can result in one division's refusal to share its new technology or work process improvements. One division's attempt to optimize the accomplishment of its goals can cause other divisions to fall behind and thus negatively affect overall corporate performance. One common example of suboptimization occurs when a marketing department approves an early shipment date to a customer as a means of getting an order and forces the manufacturing department into overtime production for that one order. Production costs are raised, which reduces the manufacturing department's overall efficiency. The end result might be that, although marketing achieves its sales goal, the corporation as a whole fails to achieve its expected profitability.

11.5 | **Guidelines for Proper Control**

In designing a control system, top management should remember that controls should follow strategy. Unless controls ensure the use of the proper strategy to achieve objectives, there is a strong likelihood that dysfunctional side effects will completely undermine the implementation of the objectives. The following guidelines are recommended:

1. **Control should involve only the minimum amount of information needed to give a reliable picture of events:** Too many controls create confusion. Focus on the strategic factors by following the **80/20 rule**: Monitor those 20% of the factors that determine 80% of the results. See STRATEGY HIGHLIGHT 11.2 for some additional rules of thumb used by strategists.

2. **Controls should monitor only meaningful activities and results, regardless of measurement difficulty:** If cooperation between divisions is important to corporate performance, some form of qualitative or quantitative measure should be established to monitor cooperation.

3. **Controls should be timely so that corrective action can be taken before it is too late:** Steering controls, controls that monitor or measure the factors influencing performance, should be stressed so that advance notice of problems is given.

4. **Long-term *and* short-term controls should be used:** If only short-term measures are emphasized, a short-term managerial orientation is likely.

5. **Controls should aim at pinpointing exceptions:** Only activities or results that fall outside a predetermined tolerance range should call for action.

6. **Emphasize the reward of meeting or exceeding standards rather than punishment for failing to meet standards:** Heavy punishment of failure typically results in goal displacement. Managers will "fudge" reports and lobby for lower standards.

STRATEGY HIGHLIGHT 11.2

Some Rules of Thumb in Strategy

Managers use many rules of thumb, such as the 80/20 rule, in making strategic decisions. These "rules" are primarily approximations based on years of practical experience by many managers. Although most of these rules have no objective data to support them, they are often accepted by practicing managers as a way of estimating the cost or time necessary to conduct certain activities. They may be useful because they can help narrow the number of alternatives into a shorter list for more detailed analysis. Some of the rules of thumb used by experienced strategists are described here.

Indirect Costs of Strategic Initiatives

■ The R&D Rule of Sevens is that for every $1 spent in developing a new prototype, $7 will be needed to get a product ready for market, and $7 additional will be required to get to the first sale. These estimates don't cover working capital requirements for stocking distributor inventories.

■ First-year costs for promoting a new consumer goods product are 33% of anticipated first-year sales. Second-year costs should be 20%, and third year costs 15%.

■ A reasonably successful patent-based innovation will require $2 million in legal defense costs.

Safety Margins for New Business Initiatives

■ A new manufacturing business should have sufficient startup capital to cover one year of costs.

■ A new consumer goods business should have sufficient capital to cover two years of business.

■ A new professional services business should have sufficient capital to cover three years of costs.

Source: R. West and F. Wolek, "Rules of Thumb in Strategic Thinking," *Strategy & Leadership* (March/April 1999), p. 34. Republished with permission, Emerald Group Publishing Limited.

If the culture complements and reinforces the strategic orientation of a firm, there is less need for an extensive formal control system. In their book *In Search of Excellence*, Peters and Waterman state that "the stronger the culture and the more it was directed toward the marketplace, the less need was there for policy manuals, organization charts, or detailed procedures and rules. In these companies, people way down the line know what they are supposed to do in most situations because the handful of guiding values is crystal clear."[81] For example, at Eaton Corporation, the employees are expected to enforce the rules themselves. If someone misses too much work or picks fights with co-workers, other members of the production team point out the problem. According to Randy Savage, a long-time Eaton employee, "They say there are no bosses here, but if you screw up, you find one pretty fast."[82]

11.6 | Strategic Incentive Management

To ensure congruence between the needs of a corporation as a whole and the needs of the employees as individuals, management and the board of directors should develop an incentive program that rewards desired performance. This reduces the likelihood of the agency problems (when employees act to feather their own nests instead of building shareholder value) mentioned in **Chapter 2**. Incentive plans should be linked in some way to corporate and divisional strategy. Research reveals that firm performance is affected by its compensation policies.[83] Companies using different business strategies tend to adopt different pay policies. For example, a survey of 600 business units indicates that the pay mix associated with a growth strategy emphasizes bonuses and other incentives over salary and benefits, whereas the pay mix associated with a stability strategy has the reverse emphasis.[84] Research indicates that SBU managers having long-term performance elements in their compensation program favor a long-term perspective and thus greater investments in R&D, capital equipment, and employee training.[85] The typical CEO pay package is composed of 21% salary, 27% short-term annual incentives, 16% long-term incentives, and 36% stock options.[86]

The following three approaches are tailored to help match measurements and rewards with explicit strategic objectives and time frames[87]:

1. **Weighted-factor method:** The **weighted-factor method** is particularly appropriate for measuring and rewarding the performance of top SBU managers and group-level executives when performance factors and their importance vary from one SBU to another. One corporation's measurements might contain the following variations: the performance of high-growth SBUs is measured in terms of market share, sales growth, designated future payoff, and progress on several future-oriented strategic projects; the performance of low-growth SBUs, in contrast, is measured in terms of ROI and cash generation; and the performance of medium-growth SBUs is measured for a combination of these factors. (See **Table 11–3**.)

2. **Long-term evaluation method:** The **long-term evaluation method** compensates managers for achieving objectives set over a multiyear period. An executive is promised some company stock or "performance units" (convertible into money or stock) in amounts to be based on long-term performance. A board of directors, for example, might set a particular objective in terms of growth in earnings per share during a five-year period. The giving of awards would be contingent on the corporation's meeting that objective within the designated time. Any executive who leaves the corporation before the objective is met receives nothing. The typical emphasis on stock price makes this approach more applicable to top management than to business unit managers. Because rising stock markets tend to raise the stock prices of mediocre companies, there is a developing trend to index stock

TABLE 11–3
WEIGHTED-
FACTOR
APPROACH TO
STRATEGIC
INCENTIVE
MANAGEMENT

Strategic Business Unit Category	Factor	Weight
High Growth	Return on assets	10%
	Cash flow	0%
	Strategic-funds programs (developmental expenses)	45%
	Market-share increase	45%
	Total	**100%**
Medium Growth	Return on assets	25%
	Cash flow	25%
	Strategic-funds programs (developmental expenses)	25%
	Market-share increase	25%
	Total	**100%**
Low Growth	Return on assets	50%
	Cash flow	50%
	Strategic-funds programs (developmental expenses)	0%
	Market-share increase	0%
	Total	**100%**

Source: Reprinted from *ORGANIZATIONAL DYNAMICS*, Vol. 13, No. 4, 1984, Paul J. Stonich, "The Performance Measurement and Reward System: Critical to Strategic Management," p. 51. Copyright © 1984 with permission of Elsevier.

options to competitors or to the Standard & Poor's 500.[88] General Electric, for example, offered its CEO 250,000 performance share units (PSUs) tied to performance targets achieved over five years. Half of the PSUs convert into GE stock only if GE achieves 10% average annual growth in operations. The other half converts to stock only if total shareholder return meets or beats the S&P 500.[89]

3. **Strategic-funds method:** The **strategic-funds method** encourages executives to look at developmental expenses as being different from expenses required for current operations. The accounting statement for a corporate unit enters strategic funds as a separate entry below the current ROI. It is, therefore, possible to distinguish between expense dollars consumed in the generation of current revenues and those invested in the future of a business. Therefore, a manager can be evaluated on both a short- and a long-term basis and has an incentive to invest strategic funds in the future. (See **Table 11–4**.)

TABLE 11–4
STRATEGIC-FUNDS
APPROACH TO AN
SBU'S PROFIT-
AND-LOSS
STATEMENT

Sales	$12,300,000
Cost of sales	−6,900,000
Gross margin	$ 5,400,000
General and administrative expenses	−3,700,000
Operating profit (return on sales)	$ 1,700,000
Strategic funds (development expenses)	−1,000,000
Pretax profit	$ 700,000

Source: Reprinted from *ORGANIZATIONAL DYNAMICS*, Vol. 13, No. 4, 1984, Paul J. Stonich, "The Performance Measurement and Reward System: Critical to Strategic Management," p. 52. Copyright © 1984 with permission of Elsevier.

An effective way to achieve the desired strategic results through a reward system is to combine the three approaches:

1. Segregate strategic funds from short-term funds, as is done in the strategic-funds method.
2. Develop a weighted-factor chart for each SBU.
3. Measure performance on three bases: The pretax profit indicated by the strategic-funds approach, the weighted factors, and the long-term evaluation of the SBUs' and the corporation's performance.

Genentech, General Electric, Adobe, IBM, and Textron are some firms in which top management compensation is contingent upon the company's achieving strategic objectives.[90]

11.7 | Conclusion

Having strategic management without evaluation and control is like playing football without any goalposts. Unless strategic management improves performance, it is only an exercise. In business, the bottom-line measure of performance is making a profit. If people aren't willing to pay more than what it costs to make a product or provide a service, that business will not continue to exist. **Chapter 1** explains that organizations engaging in strategic management outperform those that do not. The sticky issue is: How should we measure performance? Is measuring profits sufficient? Does an income statement tell us what we need to know? The accrual method of accounting enables us to count a sale even when the cash has not yet been received. Therefore, a firm might be profitable but still go bankrupt because it can't pay its bills. Is profits the amount of cash on hand at the end of the year after paying costs and expenses? But what if you made a big sale in December and must wait until January to get paid? Like retail stores, perhaps we need to use a fiscal year ending January 31 (to include returned Christmas items that were bought in December) instead of a calendar year ending December 31. Should two managers receive the same bonus when their divisions earn the same profit, even though one division is much smaller than the other? What of the manager who is managing a new product introduction that won't make a profit for another two years?

Evaluation and control is one of the most difficult parts of strategic management. No one measure can tell us what we need to know. That's why we need to use not only the traditional measures of financial performance, such as net earnings, ROI, and EPS, but we need to consider using EVA or MVA and a balanced scorecard, among other possibilities. On top of that, science informs us that just attempting to measure something changes what is being measured. The measurement of performance can and does result in short-term–oriented actions and goal displacement. That's why experts suggest that we use multiple measures of only those things that provide a meaningful and reliable picture of events: Measure those 20% of the factors that determine 80% of the results. Once the appropriate performance measurements are taken, it is possible to learn whether the strategy was successful. As shown in the model of strategic management depicted at the beginning of this chapter, the measured results of corporate performance allow us to decide whether we need to reformulate the strategy, improve its implementation, or gather more information about our competition.

Strategy Bits

- The five busiest airports in the world are Atlanta Hartsfield, Chicago O'Hare, London Heathrow, Tokyo Haneda, and Los Angeles International, in that order.[91]
- The countries with the most crowded road networks (number of vehicles per kilometer of road) are Hong Kong (286.7), United Arab Emirates (231.6), Germany (194.5), Lebanon (190.6), and Singapore (168.9). The United States ranks 42nd, at only 34.1 vehicles per kilometer (1 kilometer = 0.62 mile).[92]

Discussion Questions

1. Is **Figure 11–1** a realistic model of the evaluation and control process?

2. What are some examples of behavior controls? Output controls? Input controls?

3. Is EVA an improvement over ROI, ROE, or EPS?

4. How much faith can a manager place in a transfer price as a substitute for a market price in measuring a profit center's performance?

5. Is the evaluation and control process appropriate for a corporation that emphasizes creativity? Are control and creativity compatible?

Strategic Practice Exercise

Each year, *Fortune* magazine publishes an article titled, "America's Most Admired Companies." It lists the 10 most admired companies in the United States. Another article lists the top 10 in the world. *Fortune*'s rankings are based on scoring publicly held companies on what it calls "eight key attributes of reputation": innovativeness, quality of management, employee talent, quality of products/services, long-term investment value, financial soundness, social responsibility, and use of corporate assets. *Fortune* asks Clark, Martire & Bartolomeo to survey more than 10,000 executives, directors, and securities analysts. Respondents are asked to choose the companies they admire most, regardless of industry. *Fortune* has been publishing this list since 1982. The *2004 Fortune* list of the top 10 most admired were (starting with number 1) Wal-Mart, Berkshire Hathaway, Southwest Airlines, General Electric, Dell Computer, Microsoft, Johnson & Johnson, Starbucks, FedEx, and IBM. The top 10 outside the United States were Toyota Motor, BMW, Sony, Nokia, Nestlé, Honda Motor, British Petroleum, Singapore Airlines, Cannon, and L'Oreal.[93]

Try one of these exercises:
1. Go to the library and find a "Most Admired Companies" *Fortune* article from the 1980s or early 1990s and compare that list to the latest one. (See *www.fortune.com* for the latest list.) Which companies have fallen out of the top 10? Pick one of the companies and investigate why it is no longer on the list.

2. How much of the evaluation is dominated by the profitability of the company? See how many of the top 10 are very profitable. How many of these companies also appear in *Fortune*'s "The 100 Best Companies to Work For"?

3. Why was Wal-Mart the most admired company in the United States in both 2003 and 2004 (up from 6th place in 1999)? Wal-Mart was sued more than 6,000 times in 2002. It is said to squeeze its suppliers to death and destroy its competitors (often small, local mom-and-pop stores) through brute force. It imports many of its goods from China, thus contributing to the outsourcing of jobs.[94] Shouldn't the most admired company also score highly in "The 100 Best Companies to Work For"?

4. Compare *Fortune*'s list to other lists of corporate reputations. Other lists are compiled by the Reputation Institute (*www.reputationinstitute.com*) and by PricewaterhouseCoopers and Financial Times (available through the web site of the Reputation Institute). Note that the Reputation Institute lists J&J as number 1, whereas PricewaterhouseCoopers/FT lists GE as its most respected company. Why is there a difference among the three ratings?

Key Terms

80/20 rule (p. 282)
activity-based costing (p. 266)
balanced scorecard (p. 272)
behavior control (p. 265)
behavior substitution (p. 281)
benchmarking (p. 275)
earnings per share (p. 268)
economic value added (p. 271)
enterprise resource planning (p. 278)
enterprise risk management (p. 267)

evaluation and control information (p. 263)
evaluation and control process (p. 262)
expense center (p. 274)
free cash flow (p. 269)
goal displacement (p. 280)
input control (p. 265)
international transfer pricing (p. 276)
investment center (p. 275)

ISO 9000 Standards Series (p. 265)
ISO 14000 Standards Series (p. 265)
key performance measure (p. 272)
long-term evaluation method (p. 283)
management audit (p. 273)
market value added (p. 271)
operating budget (p. 274)
operating cash flow (p. 269)
output control (p. 265)

performance (p. 263)

periodic statistical report (p. 274)

piracy (p. 277)

profit center (p. 274)

repatriation of profit (p. 277)

responsibility center (p. 274)

return on equity (p. 268)

return on investment (p. 268)

revenue center (p. 274)

shareholder value (p. 269)

short-term orientation (p. 280)

stakeholder measure (p. 269)

standard cost center (p. 274)

steering control (p. 264)

strategic-funds method (p. 283)

suboptimization (p. 280)

transfer pricing (p. 275)

weighted-factor method (p. 283)

PART ENDING VIDEO CASE PART FOUR

Newbury Comics, Inc

IMPLEMENTATION AND CONTROL

Newbury Comics cofounders Mike Dreese and John Brusger parlayed $2,000 and a comic book collection into a thriving chain of 22 stores spanning the New England region, known to be *the* place to shop for everything from the best of the underground/independent music scene to major label superstars. The chain also stocks a wide variety of non-music related items such as T-shirts, Dr. (doc) Martens shoes, posters, jewelry, cosmetics, books, magazines, and other trendy items.

In Part Four, **"Strategy Implementation and Control,"** the video focuses on Newbury Comics' used CD business. Mike, John, and Jan discuss the development of procedures and control processes for introducing the used CD program. Budgeting is indirectly mentioned in terms of huge expenditures made at the six-month point to greatly expand the program. The video also highlights the importance of having the right staff to implement a strategy.

As pointed out in Part 3 of the Video Case, the project of developing an implementation plan was assigned to Duncan Brown, Senior Vice President. Part of this plan was to begin the used CD program in a few stores and then evaluate how well the program was working. This was a very ad hoc approach to implementation, but it fit the very loose entrepreneurial approach Newbury Comics takes toward strategy formulation. Mike tells us that he is more interested in "continuous improvement" than in setting specific sales or profit objectives. He admits that one reason he wanted to enter the used CD business was because he likes being a "pioneer" (i.e., first mover). But being a pioneer has its problems.

Jan points out that when the used CD program was started, a store would just put up signs saying that it now bought and sold used CDs. It was then up to the manager to set both the buying and selling price for each CD (with no help from any computer). The main office would then print tags for that store. As a result, stores (even the same store) would offer the same CD for a different price. Following Mike's belief in encouraging creativity and individual initiative, there were no attempts to place blame during this implementation period.

Mike points out that the used CD business is much more complicated than dealing with new CDs. Although management saw it as a risky business, they also believed that its potential for the company outweighed the risk. Because of the many complications of the used CD business, it resulted in a series of new activities in implementation, evaluation, and control, such as choosing what CDs to buy at what price, cleaning, and packaging them. These new activities resulted in adding new job duties at the store level, warehouse, and main office—thus changing the structure of the organization from one of being fairly decentralized at the store level to one with much more centralization of decision making at headquarters. The main office took control of pricing. The IBM AS-400 computer was part of the information system developed for the used CD bar code program to integrate information from all the stores. Duties were expanded and positions were added at the headquarters office and warehouse to deal with finding sources of bulk shipments, setting prices, and sorting, cleaning, and packaging used CDs. Special relationships were developed with some bulk suppliers of used CDs to make sure that Newbury Comics would get the first look at a new batch in return for paying more than other purchasers. A system of procedures was developed to sell non-selling used CDs to other retailers.

Concepts Illustrated in the Video

- Strategy Implementation: Programs, Budgets, and Procedures
- Achieving Synergy
- Job Design
- Staffing Follows Strategy
- Evaluation and Control: Measuring Performance
- Strategic Information Systems

Study Questions

1. Why was the used CD program at Newbury Comics a success?
2. What programs and procedures did management use to implement the growth strategy?
3. How important is staffing to this company's success?
4. How does the structure of Newbury Comics help or hinder the company's growth?
5. How is synergy achieved throughout the company?

CHAPTER 12
Strategic Issues in Managing Technology and Innovation

Learning Objectives

After reading this chapter, you should be able to:

- List the differences between successful and unsuccessful innovations
- Understand the importance of lead users and market research as sources of new ideas
- Assess the importance of product and process R&D for success within an industry
- Decide when to innovate internally and when to use alliances
- Propose an appropriate structure and culture to support innovative ideas and products
- Apply appropriate techniques and measures to manage new product development

MOST PEOPLE HAVE TASTED PEPSI COLA, LAY'S POTATO CHIPS, AND FRITO'S CORN CHIPS, but have they tried Quaker Soy Crisps or Gatorade Xtremo Thirst Quencher? These are just 2 of the more than 200 new product variations that PepsiCo annually adds to its already large global portfolio of products. Why does PepsiCo introduce so many new products when its current products are still in demand? According to PepsiCo's Chairman and CEO, Steven Reinemund, "Innovation is what consumers are looking for, particularly in the small, routine things of their life." This emphasis on product development seems to be paying off. PepsiCo's double-digit earnings have been consistent over the years and show no sign of slowing. (Its earnings increased 19% from 2002 to 2003 on a 7% increase in sales.) In 2004, PepsiCo was included in *Business Week*'s list of the 50 best-performing public companies.

PepsiCo constantly monitors its environment for changing tastes and fashions. It then tailors its products to suit those changes. When the public became concerned with obesity, its Frito-Lay division developed several low-fat chips and led its competitors by removing all trans fats from its Lay's, Ruffles, and Doritos brands. In June 2004, it introduced "low-carb" Doritos, Cheetos, and Tostitos. The company looks for new products both internally and externally. To capitalize on the growing market for New Age herbal-enhanced beverages, it acquired SoBe Beverages in 2001. Since then, PepsiCo has used brand extension to offer the energy drink SoBe No Fear to the school-aged market and SoBe Fuerte to the Hispanic market. Noting that the foreign-born segment of the 46 million U.S. Hispanic market didn't like PepsiCo's Latin-flavored versions of Lay's and Doritos chips, the company looked to its Mexican subsidiary, Sabritas. Not wanting to cannibalize Frito-Lay's core U.S. brands, the company limited the distribution of products such as Sabritones chile and lime puffed wheat snacks to smaller retail stores in Mexican-dominated areas. Despite no advertising and minimal distribution, U.S. sales of Sabritas brands doubled from $50 million in 2002 to $100 million in 2004. Distribution increased from 10% to one-third of the U.S. population. Because they were marketed as an ethnic specialty rather than as a Frito-Lay line extension, the Sabritas brands were able to win extra shelf space in grocery stores. Analysts agree that PepsiCo has developed a strong capability in product development. According to Robert van Brugge of Sanford C. Bernstein & Company, "They have been early to see trends and aggressive in targeting them."[1]

PepsiCo is a good example of a company successfully using its resources to create new products for new and existing markets. Properly managing technology and innovation is crucial in a fast-moving global environment. In the high-pressure toys and games industry, for example, about 40% of all products on the market are less than one year old.[2] Over the past 15 years, the top 20% of firms in an annual innovation poll conducted by *Fortune* magazine achieved double the shareholder returns of their peers.[3] Nevertheless, many large firms find it difficult to be continually innovative. A recent survey of business executives reveals that a significant majority are concerned that their companies are losing growth opportunities because they are not able to properly manage new technology (see **Table 12–1**).[4] A survey of 700 companies by Arthur D. Little found that 85% of the executives were "dissatisfied with their ability to manage innovation."[5] Even innovative established companies, such as 3M, Procter & Gamble (P&G), and Rubbermaid, have experienced a slowing in their rate of successful new product introductions.[6]

TABLE 12–1 EXECUTIVES FEAR THEIR COMPANIES ARE BECOMING LESS INNOVATIVE	A survey of business executives conducted by *Fortune* with the consulting firm Integral, Inc., revealed the percentages of those responding either **agree** or **strongly agree** to the following five statements:	
	Your company has recently lost relatively low-value customers in small market niches or low-end market segments.	55%
	Your organization passes up growth opportunities it would have pursued when the company was smaller because the opportunities are now "too small to be interesting."	60%
	There is a disconnect between the kind of innovations your frontline troops suggest and the types of innovations upper management invests in.	64%
	When your organization sees a potentially disruptive technology, it defines it as a technical problem ("Will our customers accept the product?") instead of a market problem.	58%
	New entrants have exploited opportunities where uncertainty over market size and customer needs resulted in inaction by your company.	68%
	Source: "Don't Leave Us Behind," *Fortune* (April 3, 2000), p. 250.	

In this chapter, we examine strategic issues in technology and innovation as they affect environmental scanning, strategy formulation, strategy implementation, and evaluation and control.

12.1 | The Role of Management

Due to increased competition and accelerated product development cycles, innovation and the management of technology are becoming crucial to corporate success. Research conducted by Forbes, Ernst & Young, and the Wharton School of Business found the most important driver of corporate value for both durable and non-durable companies to be innovation.[7] New product development is positively associated with corporate performance.[8] Approximately half the profits of all U.S. companies come from products launched in the previous 10 years.[9] What is less obvious is how a company can generate a significant return from investment in R&D as well as an overall sense of enthusiasm for innovative behavior and risk-taking. One way is to include innovation in the corporation's mission statement. See STRATEGY HIGHLIGHT 12.1 for mission statements from well-known companies. Another way is by establishing policies that support the innovative process. For example, 3M has a policy of generating at least 25% of its revenue from products introduced in the preceding three years. To support this policy, this $13 billion corporation annually spends nearly $1 billion.[10]

The importance of technology and innovation must be emphasized by people at the very top and reinforced by people throughout a corporation. If top management and the board are not interested in these topics, managers below them tend to echo their lack of interest. When growth in sales and profits stalled at P&G several years ago, the new CEO, Art Lafley, realized that product development was no longer a core competency of the company. In 2002, just 12 of the firm's 250-some brands generated half of P&G's sales and an even larger percentage of its profits.[11] Lafley urged product groups to "connect and develop" by pulling in experts from unrelated brands to help with new product creation. One example of the impact of Lafley's directive was the decision to enter the home car-care business. Instead of a project team trying to develop a new product on its own, P&G looked for and found expertise in different parts of the company. The company's PuR unit's water filter experts knew how to

STRATEGY HIGHLIGHT 12.1

Examples of Innovation Emphasis in Mission Statements

To emphasize the importance of technology, creativity, and innovation to overall future corporate success, some well-known firms have added sections to this effect in their published mission statements. Some of these are listed here:

Proctor & Gamble: "Our success is based on a deep understanding of consumers, their habits, and product needs; our ability to attract and support the best innovations in the world; out ability to acquire, develop, and apply technology across P & G's broad array of product categories; and our capability to collaborate with external innovation partners."

IBM: "We strive to lead in the creation, development, and manufacture of the industry's most advanced information technologies, including computer systems, software, networking systems, storage devices and microelectronics."

Intel: "Delight our customers, employees, and shareholders by relentlessly delivering the platform and technology advancements that become essential to the way we work and live."

Hewlett-Packard: "We want to create the best technology on the planet — and be the best at selling, servicing, and supporting that technology."

Merck & Co: "The mission of Merck is to provide society with superior products and services by developing innovations and solutions that improve the quality of life and satisfy customer needs, and to provide employees with meaningful work and advancement opportunities, and investors with a superior return."

Sources: Intel: All rights reserved. Intel Corporation, 2200 Mission College Blvd., Santa Clara, CA 95052-8119, USA. Used with permission
Reprinted by permission of Merck and Company

---

deionize water to get rid of minerals. Its Cascade brand unit already had a compound in its dishwasher detergent that reduced water spots. The project team combined both technologies to make the Mr. Clean AutoDry handheld sprayer, a device that sprays soap on cars and then rinses them without spotting. The result was a doubling of Mr. Clean brand sales in a year.[12]

Management has an obligation to not only encourage new product development but also develop a system to ensure that technology is being used most effectively, with the consumer in mind. Between 33% and 60% of all new products that reach the market fail to make a profit.[13] A study by Chicago consultants Kuczmarski & Associates of 11,000 new products marketed by 77 manufacturing, service, and consumer-product firms revealed that only 56% of all newly introduced products were still being sold five years later. Only 1 in 13 new product ideas ever made it into test markets. Although some authorities argue that this percentage of successful new products needs to be improved, others contend that too high a percentage means that a company isn't taking the risks necessary to develop a really new product.[14]

A study of 111 successful and 86 unsuccessful product innovations found that the *successful innovations* had some or all of the following features:

- They were moderately new to the market.
- They were based on tried-and-tested technology.
- They saved money, met customers' needs, and supported existing practices.

In contrast, the *unsuccessful innovations* had a different set of characteristics:

- They were based on cutting-edge or untested technology.
- They followed a "me-too" approach.
- They were created with no clearly defined solution in mind.[15]

The importance of top management's providing appropriate direction is exemplified by Steve Jobs' management of Apple Computer. Ever since he co-founded the company, Jobs has pushed Apple to provide not just a product but a complete system. For example, Apple decided in 2001 to make a digital music player, the iPod, that would be as easy to use for digital media as the Sony Walkman was for cassette tapes. Jobs realized, however, that the company could not succeed by just making and selling hardware. The digital player would be worthless without an online download store. By painstakingly negotiating digital-rights issues with reluctant record companies, he achieved something never before accomplished: providing easy, legal access to over 1 million songs. By 2004, Apple sold 3.7 million iPods valued at $1 billion in sales. Commenting on the iPod's success, Jobs explained, "We can invent a complete solution that works."[16]

12.2 | Environmental Scanning

Issues in innovation and technology influence both external and internal environmental scanning.

External Scanning

Corporations need to continually scan their external societal and task environments for new developments in technology that may have some application to their current or potential products. Research reveals that firms that scan their external environment are more innovative than those that focus inward on their core competencies as a way to generate new products or processes.[17] Stakeholders, especially customers, can be important participants in the new product development process.

Technological Developments

Motorola, a company well known for its ability to invest in profitable new technologies and manufacturing improvements, has a sophisticated scanning system. Its intelligence department monitors the latest technological developments introduced at scientific conferences, in journals, and in trade gossip. This information helps it build "technology roadmaps" that assess where breakthroughs are likely to occur, when they can be incorporated into new products, how much money their development will cost, and which of the developments is being worked on by the competition.[18]

A company's focusing its scanning efforts too closely on its current product line is dangerous. Most new developments that threaten existing business practices and technologies do not come from existing competitors or even from within traditional industries. A new technology that can substitute for an existing technology at a lower cost and provide higher quality can change the very basis for competition in an industry. Managers therefore need to actively scan the periphery for new product ideas because this is where breakthrough innovations will be found.[19] Consider, for example, the impact of Internet technology on the personal computer software industry. Microsoft Corporation had ignored the developing Internet technology during the 1980s and early 1990s while battling successfully with IBM, Lotus, and WordPerfect to dominate operating system software via Windows 95 as well as word processing and spreadsheet programs via Microsoft Office. Ironically, just as Microsoft introduced its new Windows 95 operating system, newcomer Netscape used Java applets in its user-friendly, graphically oriented browser program with the potential to make operating systems unnecessary. By the time Microsoft realized the significance of this threat, Netscape had already established itself as the industry standard for browsers. Microsoft was forced to spend huge amounts of time and resources trying to catch up to Netscape's dominant market share with its own Internet Explorer browser.

One way to learn about new technological developments in an industry is to locate part of a company's R&D or manufacturing in those locations making a strong impact on product development. Large multinational corporations (MNCs) undertake between 5% and 25% of their R&D outside their home country.[20] For example, automobile companies like to have design centers in southern California and in Italy, key areas for automotive styling. Software companies throughout the world know that they must have a programming presence in California's Silicon Valley if they are to compete on the leading edge of technology. The same is true of the semiconductor industry in terms of manufacturing.[21]

Impact of Stakeholders on Innovation

A company should look to its stakeholders, especially its customers, suppliers, and distributors, for sources of product and service improvements. These groups of people have the most to gain from innovative new products or services. Under certain circumstances, they may propose new directions for product development. Some of the methods of gathering information from key stakeholders are using lead users, market research, and new product experimentation.

Lead Users. Research by Von Hippel indicates that customers are a key source of innovation in many industries. For example, 77% of the innovations developed in the scientific instruments industry came from the users of the products. Suppliers are often important sources as well. Suppliers accounted for 36% of innovations in the thermoplastics industry, according to Von Hippel.[22] One way to commercialize a new technology is through early and in-depth involvement with a firm's customers in a process called co-development.[23] This type of customer is called a "lead user."

Von Hipple proposes that companies should look to lead users for help in product development, especially in high-technology industries where things move so quickly that a product is becoming obsolete by the time it arrives on the market. These **lead users** are "companies, organizations, or individuals that are well ahead of market trends and have needs that go far beyond those of the average user."[24] They are the first to adopt a product because they benefit significantly from its use—even if it is not fully developed. At Dow Chemical, for example, scientists solicit feedback from customers before developing a new product in the lab. Once the product is ready for commercialization, Dow gives its lead users the first opportunity to use the product and suggest further development.[25]

At 3M, a product development team in 3M's Medical Surgical Markets Division was charged with creating a breakthrough in the area of surgical drapes—the material that prevents infections from spreading during surgery. At the time, 3M dominated the market but had not developed a new product improvement in almost a decade. After spending six weeks learning about the cause and prevention of infections, the project team spent six more weeks investigating trends in infection control. The team then worked to identify lead users—doctors in developing nations and veterinarians who couldn't afford the current expensive drapes. The team invited several lead users to a $2\frac{1}{2}$-day workshop focused on "Can we find a revolutionary, low-cost approach to infection control?" The workshop generated concepts for six new product lines and a radical new approach to infection control. The team chose the three strongest concepts for presentation to senior management. 3M has successfully applied the lead user method in 8 of its 55 divisions.

Lead user teams are typically composed of four to six people from marketing and technical departments, with one person serving as project leader. Team members usually spend 12 to 15 hours per week on the project for its duration. For planning purposes, a team should allow four to six weeks for each phase and four to six months for the entire project. The four phases of the lead user process are:

1. **Lay the Foundation:** Identify target markets and the type and level of innovations desired.

2. **Determine the Trends:** Research the field and talk with experts who have a broad view of emerging technologies and leading-edge applications.

3. **Identify Lead Users:** Talk with users at the leading edge of the target and related markets to understand their needs.

4. **Develop the Breakthrough:** Host a two- to three-day workshop with several lead users and a half-dozen marketing and technical people. Participants first work in small groups and then as a whole to design the final concepts that fit the company's and the users' needs.[26]

Market Research.   A more traditional method of obtaining new product ideas is to use **market research** to survey current users regarding what they would like in a new product. This method has been successfully used by companies, such as P&G, to identify consumer preferences. It is especially useful in directing incremental improvements to existing products. For example, the auto maker BMW solicits suggestions from BMW owners to improve its current offerings and to obtain ideas for new products.

Market research may not, however, necessarily provide the information needed for truly innovative products or services (radical innovation). According to Sony executive Kozo Ohsone, "When you introduce products that have never been invented before, what good is market research?" For example, Hal Sperlich took the concept of the minivan from Ford to Chrysler when Ford refused to develop the concept. According to Sperlich,

> [Ford] lacked confidence that a market existed because the product didn't exist. The auto industry places great value on historical studies of market segments. Well, we couldn't prove there was a market for the minivan because there was no historical segment to cite. In Detroit most product-development dollars are spent on modest improvements to existing products, and most market research money is spent on studying what customers like among available products. In ten years of developing the minivan we never once got a letter from a housewife asking us to invent one. To the skeptics, that proved there wasn't a market out there.[27]

A heavy emphasis on being customer driven could actually prevent companies from developing innovative new products. A study of the impact of technological discontinuity (explained in **Chapter 5**) in various industries revealed that the leading firms failed to switch to the new technology not because management was ignorant of the new development but because they listened too closely to their current customers. In all of these firms, a key task of management was to decide which of the many product and development programs continually being proposed to them should receive financial resources. The criterion used for the decision was the total return perceived in each project, adjusted by the perceived riskiness of the project. Projects targeted at the known needs of key customers in established markets consistently won the most resources. Sophisticated systems for planning and compensation favored this type of project every time. As a result, the leading companies continued to use the established technology to make the products its current customers demanded, allowing smaller entrepreneurial competitors to develop the new, more risky technology.[28]

Because the market for the innovative products based on the new technology was fairly small at first, new ventures had time to fine-tune product design, build sufficient manufacturing capacity, and establish the product as the industry standard (as Netscape did with its Internet browser). As the marketplace began to embrace the new standard, the customers of the leading companies began to ask for products based on the new technology. Although some established manufacturers were able to defend their market share positions through aggressive product development and marketing activity (as Microsoft did against Netscape), many firms, finding that the new entrants had developed insurmountable advantages in manufacturing cost and design experience, were forced out of the market. Even the established manufacturers that converted to the new technology were unable to win a significant share of the new market.[29]

New Product Experimentation and Acquisition.   Instead of using lead users or market research to test the potential of innovative products, some successful companies are using speed and flexibility to gain market information. These companies have developed their products by probing potential markets with early versions of the products, learning from the probes, and probing again.[30] For example, Seiko's only market research is surprisingly simple. The company introduces hundreds of new models of watches into the marketplace. It makes more of the models that sell; it drops those that don't.

The consulting firm Arthur D. Little found that the use of standard market research techniques has resulted in a success rate of only 8% for new cereals—92% of all new cereals fail. As a result, innovative firms, such as Keebler and the leading cereal makers, are reducing their expenditures for market research and working to reduce the cost of launching new products by making their manufacturing processes more flexible.[31]

Microsoft has successfully followed a strategy of monitoring the competition for new developments. It follows an *embrace and extend* strategy of imitating new products developed by pioneers, refining them, and outmarketing the competition. (This approach is nothing new. P&G used Mr. Clean to defeat the newly introduced Lestoil.) Microsoft's distinctive competency is its ability to change directions and adjust priorities when the market changes.[32] Another approach to new product development is to simply acquire new technology from others. Cisco Systems, for example, kept itself on the cutting edge of making and selling Internet routers by buying a number of high-tech startups. In effect, Cisco outsourced its R&D to California's venture capitalists.[33]

Internal Scanning

In addition to scanning the external environment, strategists should also assess their company's ability to innovate effectively by asking the following questions:

1. Has the company developed the resources needed to try new ideas?
2. Do the managers allow experimentation with new products or services?
3. Does the corporation encourage risk-taking and tolerate mistakes?
4. Are people more concerned with new ideas or with defending their turf?
5. Is it easy to form autonomous project teams?[34]

In addition to answering these questions, strategists should assess how well company resources are internally allocated and evaluate the organization's ability to develop and transfer new technology in a timely manner into the generation of innovative products and services. These issues are important, given that it takes on average seven ideas to generate a new commercial product, according to the Product and Development Management Association.[35]

Resource Allocation Issues

A company must make available the resources necessary for effective research and development. Research indicates that a company's **R&D intensity** (its spending on R&D as a percentage of sales revenue) is a principal means of gaining market share in global competition.[36] The amount of money spent on R&D often varies by industry. For example, the computer software and drug industries spend an average of 11% to 13% of their sales revenue for R&D. Others, such as the food and the containers and packaging industries, spend less than 1%. A good rule of thumb for R&D spending is that a corporation should spend at a "normal" rate for that particular industry, unless its competitive strategy dictates otherwise.[37] Research indicates that consistency in R&D strategy and resource allocation across lines of business improves corporate performance by enabling the firm to better develop synergies among product lines and business units.[38]

Simply spending money on R&D or new projects does not, however, guarantee useful results. One study found that although large firms spent almost twice as much per R&D patent than did smaller firms, the smaller firms used more of their patents. The innovation rate of small businesses was 322 innovations per million employees versus 225 per million for large companies.[39] A recent study by the U.S. Small Business Administration reported that patents obtained by small firms were twice as likely to be among the top 1% of the most widely cited patents as patents obtained by large firms.[40] One explanation for this phenomenon is that large (especially older) firms tend to spend development money on extensions of their current products (incremental innovation) or to increase the efficiency of existing performance.[41] In contrast, small firms tend to apply technology to improving effectiveness through developing completely new products (radical innovation).[42] Other studies reveal that the maximum innovator in various industries often was the middle-sized firm. These firms were generally more effective and efficient than others in technology transfer. Very small firms often do not have sufficient resources to exploit new concepts (unless supported by venture capitalists with deep pockets), whereas the bureaucracy present in large firms rewards consistency over creativity.[43] From these studies, Hitt, Hoskisson, and Harrison propose the existence of an inverted U-shaped relationship between size and innovation. According to Hitt et al., "This suggests that organizations are flexible and responsive up to some threshold size but encounter inertia after that point."[44]

In some cases, firms waste their R&D spending. For example, between 1950 and 1979, the U.S. steel industry spent 20% more on plant maintenance and upgrading for each ton of production capacity added or replaced than did the Japanese steel industry. Nevertheless, the top management of U.S. steel firms failed to recognize and adopt two breakthroughs in steelmaking—the basic oxygen furnace and continuous casting. Their hesitancy to adopt new technology caused them to lose the world steel market.[45]

Time-to-Market Issues

In addition to money, another important consideration in the effective management of R&D is **time to market**. During the 1980s, the time from inception to profitability of a specific R&D program was generally accepted to be 7 to 11 years. According to Karlheinz Kaske, CEO of Siemens AG, however, the time available to complete the cycle is getting shorter. Companies no longer can assume that competitors will allow them the number of years needed to recoup their investment. In the past, Kaske says, "ten to fifteen years went by before old products were replaced by new ones . . . now, it takes only four or five years."[46] Time to market is an important issue because 60% of patented innovations are generally imitated within four years at 65% of the cost of innovation.[47] In the 1980s, Japanese auto manufacturers gained incredible competitive advantage over U.S. manufacturers by reducing new products' time to market to only three years. (U.S. auto companies needed five years.)[48]

12.3 | Strategy Formulation

R&D strategy deals not only with the decision to be a leader or a follower in terms of technology and market entry (discussed in **Chapter 8**, in the R&D strategy section) but also with the source of the technology. Should a company develop its own technology or purchase it from others? The strategy also takes into account a company's particular mix of basic versus applied and product versus process R&D (discussed in **Chapter 5**). The particular mix should suit the level of industry development and the firm's particular corporate and business strategies.

Product Versus Process R&D

As illustrated in **Figure 12–1**, the proportion of product and process R&D tends to vary as a product moves along its life cycle. In the early stages, **product innovations** are most important because the product's physical attributes and capabilities most affect financial performance. Later, **process innovations** such as improved manufacturing facilities, increasing

Figure 12–1
**Product and
Process R&D in the
Innovation Life
Cycle**

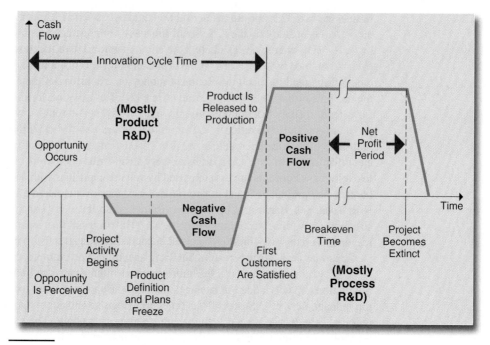

Source: Adapted from M. L. Patterson, "Lessons from the Assembly Line," Journal of Business Strategy *(May/June 1993), p. 43. Republished with permission, Emerald Group Publishing Limited.*

product quality, and faster distribution become important to maintaining the product's economic returns. Generally, product R&D has been key to achieving differentiation strategies, whereas process R&D has been at the core of successful cost-leadership strategies.

Historically, U.S. corporations have not been as skillful at process innovations as have German and Japanese companies. The primary reason has been a function of the amount of money invested in each form of R&D. U.S. firms spend, on the average, 70% of their R&D budgets on product R&D and only 30% on process R&D; German firms, 50% on each form; and Japanese firms, 30% on product and 70% on process R&D.[49] The traditionally heavy emphasis by U.S. major home appliance manufacturers on process R&D is one reason they have such a strong position in the North American market. The emphasis on quality and durability, coupled with a reluctance to make major design changes simply for the sake of change, has resulted in products with an average life expectancy of 20 years for refrigerators and 15 years for washers and dryers. Even though quality has improved significantly over the past 20 years, the average washer, dryer, and refrigerator cost no more than they did 20 years ago and yet last almost twice as long.

To be competitive, companies must find the proper mix of product and process R&D. Research indicates that too much emphasis by a firm on efficiency-oriented process R&D can drive out product R&D.[50] Even though the key to the success of the U.S. major home appliance industry has been its emphasis on process innovation, significant product innovation is more likely to result in a first-mover advantage.[51] For example, Maytag's introduction of the Neptune, a new type of front-loading washing machine, gave it a significant marketing advantage even after Whirlpool and General Electric introduced their versions of the new product.

Technology Sourcing

Technology sourcing, typically a make-or-buy decision, can be important in a firm's R&D strategy. Although in-house R&D has traditionally been an important source of technical knowledge (resulting in valuable patents) for companies, firms can also tap the R&D capabilities of competitors, suppliers, and other organizations through contractual agreements (such as licensing, R&D agreements, and joint ventures) or acquisitions. Each approach has advantages and disadvantages.[52] One example of technology acquisition was Motorola's purchase in 2004 of MeshNetworks, Inc., to obtain a Wi-Fi technology needed in Motorola's government contracting business.[53] When technological cycles were longer, a company was more likely to choose an independent R&D strategy not only because it gave the firm a longer lead time before competitors copied it but also because it was more profitable in the long run. In today's world of shorter innovation life cycles and global competition, a company may no longer have the luxury of waiting to reap a long-term profit.

Firms that are unable to finance alone the huge costs of developing a new technology may coordinate their R&D with other firms through a **strategic R&D alliance**. By the 1990s, more than 150 cooperative alliances involving 1,000 companies were operating in the United States, and many more were operating throughout Europe and Asia.[54] These alliances can be (1) joint programs or contracts to develop a new technology, (2) joint ventures establishing a separate company to take a new product to market, or (3) minority investments in innovative firms wherein the innovator obtains needed capital and the investor obtains access to valuable research. For example, the biotech company Amgen uses strategic alliances as part of its growth strategy. It uses its collegial corporate culture to court entrepreneurial ventures that are normally shy of big companies. "We're trying to have a small company feel," explains Amgen CEO Kevin Sharer. By 2003, Amgen had formed partnerships with 100 companies. It developed its latest drug, Cinacalcet, a treatment for a kidney-related condition called secondary hyperparathyroidism, from a license with one of its partners, NPS Pharmaceuticals.[55]

When should a company buy or license technology from others instead of developing it internally? Following the resource-based view of the firm discussed in **Chapter 5**, a company should buy technologies that are commonly available but make (and protect) those that are rare, valuable, and hard to imitate and that have no close substitutes. In addition, outsourcing technology may be appropriate when:

- The technology is of low significance to competitive advantage.
- The supplier has proprietary technology.
- The supplier's technology is better and/or cheaper and reasonably easy to integrate into the current system.
- The company's strategy is based on system design, marketing, distribution, and service—not on development and manufacturing.
- The technology development process requires special expertise.
- The technology development process requires new people and new resources.[56]

Licensing technology to other companies may be an excellent R&D strategy—especially in a turbulent high-tech environment where being the first firm to establish the standard dominant design may bring competitive advantage.[57] Matsushita successfully used this strategy to overcome the technologically superior Sony beta format with the VHS format for VCRs. When Matsushita freely licensed the VHS format to all other VCR makers, Sony was relegated to a minority position in the market, and Matsushita (through its Panasonic brand) became a dominant VCR manufacturer.[58] Licensing enables a company to enter foreign markets that might not otherwise be possible due to high tariffs, import prohibitions and restrictions, or the high cost and risk of investing in foreign factories. Licensing is an alternative international strategy in situations when exports or local production through a subsidiary or joint venture are impractical.[59]

A serious issue in the sourcing of new technology is the use of another company's intellectual property without paying for it. **Intellectual property** is special knowledge used in a new product or process developed by a company for its own use and is usually protected by a patent, copyright, trademark, or trade secret. It can be licensed to another firm for a fee. As mentioned earlier, making and selling an imitation of someone else's product (such as Nike shoes) is considered to be piracy. Both the recording industry and the motion picture industry are extremely threatened by the illegal duplication of their products.

The number of patents being issued in the United States is growing at 6% annually and running at nearly twice the level of a decade ago. Similar growth is happening elsewhere in the world. Patents are global. Although a U.S. patent does not function outside the United States, the same idea cannot in theory be patented anywhere else.[60] Countries joining the World Trade Organization (WTO) must agree to Trips (trade-related aspects of intellectual property rights), an international agreement that establishes minimum standards for the legal protection of intellectual property.[61] Because China has recently joined the WTO, a number of companies are attempting to enforce their patents in that country. See the GLOBAL ISSUE feature for an example of a Chinese company that was sued by Cisco Systems for intellectual property violations.

Importance of Technological Competence

Firms that emphasize growth through acquisitions over internal development tend to be less innovative than others in the long run.[62] Research suggests that companies must have at least a minimal R&D capability if they are to correctly assess the value of technology developed by others. This is called a company's "absorptive capacity" and is a valuable by-product of rou-

GL🌐BAL ISSUE

Use of Intellectual Property at Huawei Technologies

Xu Danhua, chief of the pre-research department at Huawei Technologies, works to develop products for digital homes. He is using technologies to link PCs, TVs, stereos, and other devices to the Internet and to each other throughout a building or an apartment. "I like to face the challenges of new technology," says Xu. "Huawei is a company that very quickly takes on the trends of the industry." This is a relatively new direction for a company that until recently was a low-cost manufacturer of equipment developed elsewhere. Huawei intends to sell sophisticated electronic products to international customers. According to the company's head of R&D, "Huawei is a global company with global markets in mind." To take advantage of skilled people in other parts of the world, it is building development centers in Europe, India, and the United States.

Cisco Systems, a maker of networking equipment, launched a lawsuit against Huawei in December 2002, alleging patent and copyright infringement and asking for an injunction to remove certain Huawei products from the market. Cisco had already lined up support from the Chinese government. Having just joined the World Trade Organization (WTO) in 2001, China was eager to shed its image as the world's leading haven for pirated goods. According to an official with China's Ministry of Information Industry, "The government will not give any political help to Huawei."

Huawei protested its innocence but soon announced a global joint venture with Cisco's rival, 3Com Corporation. The venture provides Huawei with 3Com's distribution system, along with a strong base in the United States. When Cisco's Executive Vice President, Charles Giancarlo, was informed of the Huawei–3Com alliance, he said, "I was so mad I couldn't speak for three days." Keeping up the pressure, Cisco filed another suit in east Texas, near Huawei's Dallas office. Huawei typically undersells Western rivals by 30% or more and has a reputation for selling products that look and feel like Cisco's products. It was a major competitor in DSL equipment. "Huawei is a threat to everyone," says Christine Heckart, Vice President for Marketing at Juniper Networks. "They bid on everything that moves."

For Huawei, the lawsuits were part of a painful and risky transition from a position of cheap labor, government support, and lax intellectual property protection in China to the tougher rules of global markets. Eager to shed its "me-too" reputation, Huawei agreed to settle the lawsuit with Cisco Systems in 2004.

Sources: Summarized from P. Burrows and B. Einhorn, "Cisco: In Hot Pursuit of a Chinese Rival," *Business Week* (May 19, 2003), pp. 62–63, and B. Einhorn, M. Kripalani, and J. Ewing, "Huawei: More Than a Local Hero," *Business Week* (October 11, 2004), pp. 180–184.

tine in-house R&D activity.[63] **Absorptive capacity** is a firm's ability to recognize, assimilate, and utilize new external knowledge.[64] Firms that have absorptive capacity are able to use knowledge obtained externally to increase the productivity of their research expenditures.[65] Further, without this capacity, firms could become locked out in their ability to assimilate the technology at a later time. Therefore, a company's absorptive capacity is a dynamic capability that influences the nature and sustainability of that company's competitive advantage.[66]

A corporation that purchases an innovative technology must have the **technological competence** to make good use of it. Some companies that introduce the latest technology into their processes do not adequately assess the competence of their people to handle it. For example, a survey conducted in the United Kingdom in the 1980s found that 44% of all companies that started to use robots met with initial failure, and that 22% of those firms abandoned the use of robots altogether, mainly because of inadequate technological knowledge and skills.[67] One U.S. company built a new plant equipped with computer-integrated manufacturing and statistical process controls, but the employees could not operate the equipment because 25% of them were illiterate.[68]

Categories of Innovation

Innovation can range from incremental to radical. As shown in **Figure 12–2**, a corporation's *capabilities* (existing or new) interact with its *strategic scope* (limited or unlimited) to form four basic categories of innovation. A corporation may emphasize one of these categories or operate in all of them.[69]

Quadrant 1: Improving Core Businesses. This type of innovation focuses on incremental innovations that can be developed rapidly and inexpensively. It includes line extensions and more convenient packaging and is often a part of a horizontal growth strategy. Its potential weakness is market myopia—its emphasis on current products and customers. As illustrated earlier in this chapter, PepsiCo is the master of this type of innovation.

Quadrant 2: Exploiting Strategic Advantages. This type of innovation focuses on taking existing brands and product lines to new customers and markets without requiring major change in current capabilities. It means moving beyond the company's current strategic scope

Figure 12–2
Categories of Innovation

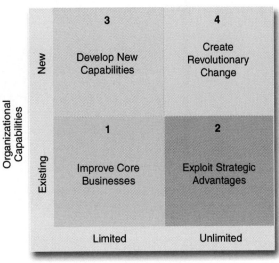

Source: Adapted from C. Hickman and C. Raia, "Incubating Innovation," Journal of Business Strategy *(May/June 2002), p. 15. Reprinted with permission, Emerald Group Publishing Limited.*

by leveraging capabilities by spreading them across a broader range of markets and customers via concentric diversification. Its potential weakness is the relative ease with which competitors with similar capabilities can imitate the innovation. Coleman and Toro are examples of companies that have leveraged their capabilities in camping (Coleman) and lawn (Toro) equipment to move into new products and new markets, such as Coleman gas grills and Toro snow blowers.

Quadrant 3: Developing New Capabilities. This type of innovation focuses on deepening customer satisfaction and loyalty to the brand or product line by adding new organizational capabilities without introducing major changes in strategic scope. The company may develop or purchase new technologies, talents, or businesses to better serve the firm's current scope of customers and markets. It may involve a vertical growth strategy. Its potential weakness is the investment cost and implementation time. Microsoft follows an embrace-and-extend policy to either acquire or imitate a new product in order to offer it to its current customers in the next version of Windows or Office software.

Quadrant 4: Creating Revolutionary Change. This type of innovation focuses on radical innovations that transcend current product lines or brands to make fundamental changes in both its strategic scope and its capabilities. This can mean a new business model and a revolutionary new future for the company. Its potential weakness is a high risk of failure. Sony

Figure 12–3
**Product/Market
Evolution Portfolio
Matrix**

Source: C. W. Hofer and D. Schendel, Strategy Formulation: Analytical Concepts (St. Paul, MN: West Publishing Co., 1978), p. 34. From C. W. Hofer, "Conceptual Constructs for Formulating Corporate and Business Strategies" (Dover, MA: Case Publishing), no. BP-0041, p. 3. Copyright © 1977 by Charles W. Hofer. Reprinted by permission.

Corporation is the master of radical innovation. Its pioneering products, such as the Walkman, the Airboard, and the robo-pet Aibo, introduce whole new product categories.

Product Portfolio

Developed by Hofer and based on the product life cycle, the 15-cell **product/market evolution matrix** (shown in **Figure 12–3**) depicts the types of developing products that cannot be easily shown on other portfolio matrixes. Products are plotted in terms of their competitive positions and their stages of product/market evolution. As on the GE Business Screen, the circles represent the sizes of the industries involved, and the pie wedges represent the market shares of the firm's business product lines. Present and future matrixes can be developed to identify strategic issues. In response to **Figure 12–3**, for example, we could ask why Product B does not have a greater share of the market, given its strong competitive position. We could also ask why the company has only one product in the developmental stage. A limitation of this matrix is that the product life cycle does not always hold for every product. Many products, for example, do not inevitably fall into decline but (like Tide detergent and Colgate toothpaste) are revitalized and put back on a growth track.

12.4 | **Strategy Implementation**

If a corporation decides to develop innovations internally, it must make sure that its structure and culture are suitable for such a strategy. It must make sufficient resources available for new products, provide collaborative structures and processes, and incorporate innovation into its overall corporate strategy.[70] It must ensure that its R&D operations are managed appropriately. It must establish procedures to support all six **stages of new product development**. (See **Table 12–2.**) If, like most large corporations, the culture is too bureaucratic and rigid to support entrepreneurial projects, top management must reorganize so that innovative projects can be free to develop.

Developing an Innovative Entrepreneurial Culture

To create a more innovative corporation, top management must develop an entrepreneurial culture—one that is open to the transfer of new technology into company activities and products and services. The company must be flexible and accepting of change. It should include a willingness to withstand a certain percentage of product failures on the way to success. It should be able to manage small, incremental innovations in existing products as well

TABLE 12–2
SIX STAGES OF NEW PRODUCT DEVELOPMENT

1. **Idea Generation.** New product concepts are identified and refined.
2. **Concept Evaluation.** Screening techniques are used to determine the concept's validity and market opportunity. Preliminary market research is conducted, and a strategy is developed. A business plan is developed to present to management.
3. **Preliminary Design.** A new venture team is formed to prepare desired product specifications.
4. **Prototype Build and Test.** A functioning model of the product is built and subjected to numerous tests.
5. **Final Design and Pilot Production.** Final product and process designs are developed to produce small numbers of the product for use in test marketing. Suggestions from the users are fed back to the design team for possible inclusion in the final product.
6. **New Business Development.** The entire company is energized to launch the product.

Source: Managing Corporate Culture, Innovation, and Intrapreneurship, Howard W. Oden. Copyright © 1997 by Quorum Books. Reproduced with permission of Greenwood Publishing, Inc., Westport, CT.

as radical advances that may alter the basis for competition in an industry.[71] Largeness is not a disadvantage. In his classic book *Diffusion of Innovations*, Rogers reveals that innovative organizations tend to have the following characteristics:

- Positive attitude toward change
- Decentralized decision making
- Complexity
- Informal structure
- Interconnectedness
- Organizational slack (unused resources)
- Large size
- System openness[72]

Such a culture has been noted in 3M Corporation and Texas Instruments, among others. R&D in these companies is managed quite differently from traditional methods. First, employees are dedicated to a particular project outcome rather than to innovation in general. Second, employees are often responsible for all functional activities and for all phases of the innovation process. Time is allowed to be sacrificed from regular duties to spend on innovative ideas. If the ideas are feasible, employees are temporarily reassigned to help develop them. These people may become project champions who fight for resources to make the project a success. Third, these internal ventures are often separated from the rest of the company to provide them with greater independence, freedom for short-term pressures, different rewards, improved visibility, and access to key decision makers.[73]

The innovative process often involves individuals at different organizational levels who fulfill three different types of entrepreneurial roles: product champion, sponsor, and orchestrator. A **product champion** is a person who generates a new idea and supports it through many organizational obstacles. A **sponsor** is usually a department manager who recognizes the value of the idea, helps obtain funding to develop the innovation, and facilitates its implementation. An **orchestrator** is someone in top management who articulates the need for innovation, provides funding for innovating activities, creates incentives for middle managers to sponsor new ideas, and protects idea/product champions from suspicious or jealous executives. Unless all these roles are present in a company, major innovations are unlikely to occur.[74]

Companies are finding that one way to overcome the barriers to successful product innovation is by using multifunctional teams with significant autonomy dedicated to a project. In a survey of 701 companies from Europe, the United States, and Japan, 85% of the respondents have used this approach, with 62% rating it as successful.[75] Research reveals that cross-functional teams are best for designing and developing innovative new products, whereas the more traditional bureaucratic structures seem to be best for developing modifications to existing products, line extensions, and me-too products.[76] Chrysler Corporation was able to reduce the development time for new vehicles by 40% by using cross-functional teams and by developing a partnership approach to new projects.[77] International Specialty Products, a maker of polymers, used "product express" teams composed of chemists and representatives from manufacturing and engineering to cut development time in half. "Instead of passing a baton, we bring everyone into the commercialization process at the same time," explained John Tancredi, vice president for R&D. "We are moving laterally, like rugby players, instead of like runners in a relay race."[78]

Organizing for Innovation: Corporate Entrepreneurship

Corporate entrepreneurship (also called intrapreneurship) is defined by Guth and Ginsberg as "the birth of new businesses within existing organizations, that is, internal innovation or venturing; and the transformation of organizations through renewal of the key ideas on which they are

Figure 12–4
**Organizational
Designs for
Corporate
Entrepreneurship**

Strategic Importance

		Very Important	Uncertain	Not Important
Operational Relatedness	Unrelated	**3** Special Business Units	**6** Independent Business Units	**9** Complete Spin-off
	Partly Related	**2** New Product Business Department	**5** New Venture Division	**8** Contracting
	Strongly Related	**1** Direct Integration	**4** Micro New Ventures Department	**7** Nurturing and Contracting

*Source: Reprinted from R. A. Burgelman, "Designs for Corporate Entrepreneurship in Established Firms."
Copyright © 1984, by the Regents of the University of California. Reprinted from the* California Management
Review, *Vol. 26, No. 3. By permission of The Regents. All rights reserved.*

built, that is, strategic renewal."[79] A large corporation that wants to encourage innovation and creativity within its firm must choose a structure that will give the new business unit an appropriate amount of freedom while maintaining some degree of control at headquarters. Research reveals that corporate entrepreneurship has a positive impact on a company's financial performance.[80]

Burgelman proposes (see **Figure 12–4**) that the use of a particular organizational design should be determined by (1) the strategic importance of the new business to the corporation and (2) the relatedness of the unit's operations to those of the corporation.[81] The combination of these two factors results in nine organizational designs for corporate entrepreneurship:

1. **Direct Integration:** A new business with a great deal of strategic importance and operational relatedness must be a part of the corporation's mainstream. Product champions—people who are respected by others in the corporation and who know how to work the system—are needed to manage these projects. Janiece Webb championed the incorporation of Internet web browsers in Motorola's mobile phones and is now in charge of Motorola's Personal Networks Group. Because Webb's unit only makes software, she works with other divisions to shape their "product maps," which show what they hope to bring to market and when.[82]

2. **New Product Business Department:** A new business with a great deal of strategic importance and partial operational relatedness should be a separate department, organized around an entrepreneurial project in the division where skills and capabilities can be shared. Maytag Corporation did this when it built a new plant near its current Newton, Iowa, washer plant to manufacture the wholly new Neptune line of energy- and water-efficient front-loading washing machines.

3. **Special Business Units:** A new business with a great deal of strategic importance and low operational relatedness should be a special new business unit with specific objectives and time horizons. Teradyne tried this with a new product called Integra. The new product was based on a new, low-cost technology—something that might be good enough in a few years to replace Teradyne's current technology. Because the technology wasn't good enough for Teradyne's high-end applications, Teradyne's management treated

Integra like an entrepreneurial venture. Integra's general manager, Marc Levine, reported to a board of directors composed of Teradyne's top executives. Instead of a budget, Levine had a business plan and venture capital (from Teradyne). This governance structure allowed Integra to operate autonomously by recruiting and purchasing from outside the company. According to Levine, "The idea was to think of this as a business from the start, not an R&D project. The board setup allows more of a coaching attitude." Says Teradyne's Vice President, Edward Rogas, "A division is always pressed to do the next logical thing—and make it compatible with the existing line. We told Marc: Be aggressive on the technology; do something no one else has done."[83]

4. **Micro New Ventures Department:** A new business with uncertain strategic importance and high operational relatedness should be a peripheral project that is likely to emerge in the operating divisions on a continuous basis. Each division thus has its own new ventures department. Xerox Corporation, for example, uses its SBUs to generate and nurture new ideas. Small product-synthesis teams within each SBU test the feasibility of new ideas. Those concepts receiving a "go" are managed by an SBU product-delivery team, headed by a chief engineer, that takes the prototype from development through manufacturing.

5. **New Venture Division:** A new business with uncertain strategic importance that is only partly related to present corporate operations belongs in a new venture division. It brings together projects that either exist in various parts of the corporation or can be acquired externally; sizable new businesses are built. Lucent established an internal venture capital operation to fund the ideas of researchers from its Bell Labs R&D unit that didn't fit into existing business units. One new venture, Visual Insights, sells software that can detect billing fraud by analyzing patterns in large amounts of data. Another, Veridicom, does fingerprint authentication.[84]

6. **Independent Business Units:** Uncertain strategic importance coupled with no relationship to present corporate activities can make external arrangements attractive. Hewlett-Packard established printers as an independent business unit in Boise, Idaho (far from its Palo Alto, California, headquarters), because management was unsure of the desktop printer's future. According to Richard Belluzzo, head of HP's printer business, "We had the resources of a big company, but we were off on our own. There wasn't central planning . . . , so we could make decisions really fast."[85]

7. **Nurturing and Contracting:** When an entrepreneurial proposal might not be important strategically to the corporation but is strongly related to present operations, top management might help the entrepreneurial unit to spin off from the corporation. This allows a friendly competitor, instead of one of the corporation's major rivals, to capture a small niche. Techtronix has extensively used this approach. Because of research revealing that related spin-offs tend to be poorer performers than nonrelated spin-offs (presumably owing to the loss of benefits enjoyed with a larger company), it is especially important that the parent company continue to support the development of the spun-off unit in this cell.[86]

8. **Contracting:** As the required capabilities and skills of the new business are less related to those of the corporation, the parent corporation may spin off the strategically unimportant unit yet keep some relationship through a contractual arrangement with the new firm. The connection is useful in case the new firm eventually develops something of value to the corporation. For example, B.F. Goodrich offered manufacturing rights plus a long-term purchasing agreement to a couple of its managers for a specific raw material Goodrich still used (in declining quantities) in its production process but no longer wanted to manufacture internally.

9. **Complete Spin-off:** If both the strategic importance and the operational relatedness of the new business are negligible, the corporation is likely to completely sell off the business to

STRATEGY HIGHLIGHT 12.2

How *Not* to Develop an Innovative Organization

In their book *Corporate Venturing*, researchers Block and MacMillan state that fostering an organizationwide commitment to new business development means more than paying lip service to innovation. They argue that a superficial commitment is almost worse than no commitment at all. They noted that unsuccessful companies tend to follow the following "rules of the road to certain failure":

1. Announce to the company that from now on, it is going to "become entrepreneurial."

2. Create a separate venture department charged with the job of developing new businesses. Hold no one else responsible.

3. Bring in a horde of consultants and self-professed experts to harangue management and employees at all levels to aggressively seek new business ideas.

4. Hold several one-day senior management retreats to discuss the need to become more entrepreneurial.

5. Make no further changes in management practices or the behavior of senior managers.

Source: Reprinted by permission of the Harvard Business School Press. From "Corporate Venturing: Creating New Business Within the Firm," by Z. Block and I. C. MacMillan, Boston MA, 1993, p. 36. Copyright © 1993 by the Harvard Business School Publishing Corporation.

another firm or to the present employees in some form of Employee Stock Ownership Plan (ESOP). The corporation could also sell off the unit through a leveraged buyout (executives of the unit buy the unit from the parent company with money from a third source, to be repaid out of the unit's anticipated earnings). Because 3M wanted to focus its development money on areas with more profit potential, it decided to spin off its money-losing data storage and medical imaging divisions as a new company called Imation.

Organizing for innovation has become especially important for corporations that want to become more innovative but whose age and size have made them highly bureaucratic, with a culture that discourages creative thinking. These new structural designs for corporate entrepreneurship cannot work by themselves, however. The entrepreneurial units must also have the support of management and sufficient resources. They must also have employees who are risk-takers, willing to purchase an ownership interest in the new venture, and a corporate culture that supports new ventures. This is in contrast to corporations in which top management makes only a superficial commitment to innovation by demanding new ideas without providing the culture necessary to support their development. See STRATEGY HIGHLIGHT 12.2 for how *not* to develop an innovative organization.

12.5 | Evaluation and Control

For innovations to succeed, appropriate evaluation and control techniques must be used to ensure that the end product is what was originally planned. Some of these techniques are the stage-gate process and the house of quality. Appropriate measures are also needed to evaluate the effectiveness of the R&D process. Today's global information technology enables executives to continually assess performance as a product moves from the idea to the finished product stage.

Evaluation and Control Techniques

The **stage-gate process** is a method of managing new product development to increase the likelihood of launching new products quickly and successfully. The process is a series of steps to move products through the six stages of new product development listed in **Table 12–2**. A new concept cannot move beyond any stage until it has been evaluated thoroughly. The stage-gate process is used by companies such as IBM, 3M, General Motors, Corning, and P&G. Corning's managers believe that the process enables them to better estimate the potential payback of any project under consideration. They report that the stage-gate process reduces development time, allows identification of questionable projects, and increases the ratio of internally generated products that result in commercially successful products. It is especially useful for a major platform project (such as a line of new cars) that could be used to create multiple derivative products.[87]

The **house of quality** is another method of managing new product development.[88] Originally developed at Mitsubishi's Kobe shipyards, it is a tool to help project teams make important design decisions by getting them to think about what users want and how to get it to them most effectively.[89] It enhances communication and coordination among engineering, marketing, and manufacturing and ensures better product/customer fit. As shown in **Figure 12–5**, the house of quality is a matrix that maps customer requirements against product attributes. The first step is to identify product requirements and to weight their relative importance from the customer's perspective. For example, market research identified five attributes that customers want from a car door. Each of these are listed in the left column of **Figure 12–5**. The second step is to identify the engineering attributes in measurable terms. As shown in **Figure 12–5**, engineering lists four attributes of the door. In the third step, the team fills in the body of the central matrix (the body of the house). Each cell in the matrix indicates both the direction and the strength of a relationship between an engineering attribute and a customer requirement. **Figure 12–5** shows two negative signs between "easy to open" and "weight of the door," indicating that heavy doors are generally harder to open. The fourth step is to fill in the roof of the house by showing the interaction between design parameters. Thus, the negative sign between door weight and hinge stiffness indicates that a heavy door reduces the stiffness of the hinge. The final bit of information is depicted on the far right side of the house of quality and is a summary of the company's existing product compared with that of its competitors.

Figure 12–5 **House of Quality**

The house of quality provides a common framework within which the project team can interact. It makes the relationship between customer requirements and product attributes clear, emphasizes design trade-offs, highlights the competitive shortcomings of current products, and helps identify what steps should be taken to improve the design. It is very useful for cross-functional project teams and a good technique to ensure that both the customer's desires and production feasibility are included in the end result.[90]

Evaluation and Control Measures

Companies want to gain more productivity at a faster pace from their R&D activities. But how do we measure the effectiveness or efficiency of a company's R&D? This is a problem, given that a company shouldn't expect more than one in seven product ideas from basic research to make it to the marketplace. Some companies measure the proportion of their sales attributable to new products. For example, Hewlett-Packard measures how much of its revenues come from products introduced in the past three years.[91] At BellCore, the effectiveness of basic research is measured by how often the lab's research is cited in other scientists' work. This measure is compiled and published by the Institute for Scientific Information. Other companies judge the quality of research by counting how many patents they file annually.

Pittiglio Rabin Todd & McGrath (PRTM), a high-tech consulting firm, proposes an **index of R&D effectiveness**. The index is calculated by dividing the percentage of total revenue spent on R&D into new product profitability, which is expressed as a percentage. When this measure was applied to 45 large electronics manufacturers, only 9 companies scored 1.0 or higher, indicating that only 20% received a positive payback from their R&D spending. The top companies kept spending on marginal products to a minimum by running frequent checks on product versus market opportunities and canceling questionable products quickly. They

TABLE 12–3

THIRTEEN "BEST PRACTICES" FOR IMPROVING R&D

1. Corporate and business unit strategies are well defined and clearly communicated.
2. Core technologies are defined and communicated to R&D.
3. Investments are made in developing multinational R&D capabilities to tap ideas throughout the world.
4. Funding for basic research comes from corporate sources to ensure a long-term focus; funding for development comes from business units to ensure accountability.
5. Basic and applied research are performed either at a central facility or at a small number of labs, each focused on a particular discipline of science or technology. Development work is usually performed at business unit sites.
6. Formal, cross-functional teams are created for basic, applied, and developmental projects.
7. Formal mechanisms exist for regular interaction among scientists, and between R&D and other functions.
8. Analytical tools are used for selecting projects as well as for ongoing project evaluation.
9. The transfer of technology to business units is the most important measure of R&D performance.
10. Effective measures of career development are in place at all levels of R&D.
11. Recruiting of new people is from diverse universities and from other companies when specific experience or skills are required that would take a long time to develop internally.
12. Some basic research is performed internally, but there are also many university and third-party relationships.
13. Formal mechanisms are used for monitoring external technological developments.

Source: From "Benchmarking R&D Productivity," I. Krause and J. Liu, 1993 © MCB University Press Limited. Republished with permission of Emerald Group Publishing Ltd.

also moved new products to market in half the time of the others. As a result, revenue growth among the top 20% of the companies was double the average of all 45 companies.[92]

A study of 15 multinational companies with successful R&D operations focused on three measures of R&D success: (1) improving technology transfer from R&D to business units, (2) accelerating time to market for new products and processes, and (3) institutionalizing cross-functional participation in R&D. The companies participated in basic, applied, and developmental research activities. The study revealed 13 **best practices** that all the companies followed.[93] Listed in **Table 12–3**, they provide a benchmark for a company's R&D activities.

12.6 | Conclusion

The management of technology and innovation is crucial in today's fast-moving global environment. In every industry, the leading competitors are the innovators. The list of today's innovators, well-known companies such as Dell, Southwest Airlines, and Starbucks, lead their industry now but will eventually cede this advantage to other companies with even better ideas. The real challenge for strategic management is *sustained innovation*.[94]

Royal Dutch/Shell had traditionally been better at investing in large, low-risk projects yielding a modest return than in small, high-risk projects with the potential to transform the entire industry. In an effort to emphasize radical innovation, the company introduced a new approach called *GameChanger*.[95] Six teams of six people each meet every week at the Exploration and Production Divisions in Houston, Texas, and in Rijswijk, the Netherlands, to consider ideas that have been sent to them by e-mail. Out of these GameChanger teams have come four business initiatives for the corporation. One of them is Shell's new "Light Touch" oil-discovery method—a way of using lasers to sense hydrocarbon emissions released naturally in the air from underground reserves.

Increasing numbers of companies are using the Internet to stimulate and manage innovation. The concept is for small entrepreneurial teams to drive innovation at a rate never before experienced in large corporations. According to Christensen, author of *The Innovator's Dilemma*, "The trend now is to decentralize operations, to build idea factories, or idea markets. This is a way to bring the startup mentality inside."[96]

Companies such as Nortel Networks and P&G are adopting this "knowledge market" approach to innovation. Nortel allocates *phantom stock* to those who volunteer for special high-risk innovative projects. Nortel buys the stock as if the project were an IPO. Employees are paid in chits redeemable for cash once when the project is finished and again after it has been on the market about a year. P&G has created a Corporate New Ventures (CNV) unit as an autonomous idea lab with a mission of encouraging new ideas for products and putting them into speedy production. Ideas bubbling up from P&G's worldwide workforce of 110,000 people are routed to the CNV innovation panel via *My Idea*, a corporate collaboration network. Employees submitting winning ideas are rewarded with stock options. CNV teams then analyze the ideas by using the Internet to analyze markets, demographics, and cost information to learn whether the idea is a feasible opportunity. Once the team agrees on an idea, a project is launched within days. The CNV has the authority to tap any resources in the company to bring a product to market. So far, CNV has generated 58 products into the market. One of these, a cleaning product called Swiffer, was commercialized in just 10 months, less than half the usual time. Swiffer is a disposable cloth that generates static electricity to attract dust and dirt. The idea for it was generated by P&G's paper and cleaning-agent experts during a discussion on the Internet. According to Craig Wynett, CNV President, "It was an exercise in speed, in breaking down the company's traditional division-by-division territories to come up with new ideas."[97]

Strategy Bits

- Japan is the world's robotics leader, with 350,000 industrial robots in 2003. Germany is second, with 105,000, and the United States is third, with 104,000 robots.[98]

- In 2004, 607,000 household robots were in use. Most of these were vacuum cleaner and lawn mower robots.

The UN Commission for Europe and the International Federation of Robotics predict that 4.1 million domestic robots will be in use by the end of 2007.[99]

- In 2004, 692,000 companion or entertainment robots, such as Sony's dog-like Aibo, were in use throughout the world.[100]

Discussion Questions

1. How should a corporation scan the external environment for new technological developments? Who should be responsible?

2. What is technology research and how does it differ from market research?

3. What is the importance of product and process R&D to competitive strategy?

4. What factors help determine whether a company should outsource a technology?

5. How can a company develop an entrepreneurial culture?

Strategic Practice Exercise

How Creative Is Your Organization?

One of the keys to managing technology and innovation is to have a creative organization in which people are free to propose and try new ideas. The following questionnaire is taken from "Building a Creative Hothouse" by Barton Kunstler in the January–February 2001 issue of *The Futurist*. It is a simplified version of the Hothouse Assessment Instrument presented in greater detail in the Spring 2000 issue of *Futures Research Quarterly*. This version describes many of the elements of a highly creative organization.

If you work or have worked full time in an organization, answer this questionnaire in light of your experience with that organization. If you have not worked full time anywhere, find someone who is working full time and ask that person to complete this questionnaire. Then discuss the person's answers with him or her.

To assess the level of creativity in your organization's culture, score your level of agreement or disagreement with the statements below as follows: **Strongly Agree** (5 points), **Mildly Agree** (4 points), **Neutral** (3 points), **Mildly Disagree** (2 points), **Strongly Disagree** (1 point).

(1) VALUES

1. ___ We believe that our work can change the world.

2. ___ The organization actively promotes a positive quality of life in our surrounding communities.

3. ___ People here really believe our products and services are vital to others' well-being.

4. ___ Virtually all who work here continually study and question the basic nature of their job and the technologies—human, organizational, technical—they work with.

5. ___ Working here fills me with a sense of personal well-being and commitment to my higher values.

(2) MISSION AND VISION

6. ___ Principles of justice and compassion directly and significantly influence strategy, design, and development.

7. ___ We explore the fundamental practices and principles of our industry and its disciplines as a source of creativity, values, and purpose.

8. ___ We can fail without fear for our jobs.

9. ___ My organization takes the long view.

10. ___ Employees are free to develop their own vision of what their jobs entail.

(3) IDEAS

11. ___ This organization cultivates the growth of knowledge into wisdom and views wisdom as a guide to action.

12. ___ Organizational structure is shaped by innovative, idea-driven approaches to our challenges and tasks.

13. ___ Organizational responses to crises are thoughtful and imaginative, not reactive and typical.

14. ___ The organization respects thinkers.

15. ___ I am respected for all my talents, whether or not they contribute to the bottom line.

(4) EXCHANGE

16. ____ My organization rewards those who display mastery at their jobs and seeks their advice, whatever their title or position.

17. ____ Institutionalized procedures enable anyone to make suggestions or raise objections.

18. ____ Intellectually exciting and stimulating conversation directly influences product development and delivery.

19. ____ "Idea people" share their vision with other employees and invite feedback.

20. ____ The group uses conflict as an opportunity for personal and organizational growth.

(5) PERCEPTION

21. ____ How we perceive our tasks, our expertise, and the group itself is a legitimate object of inquiry.

22. ____ Whole-minded thinking, including activities based on movement and heightening awareness of the five senses, is encouraged.

23. ____ Employees are taught and encouraged to think creatively.

24. ____ We continually re-vision our group's place within its industry and society as a whole.

25. ____ Clear problem-solving algorithms are taught, practiced, developed, and applied wherever a need is perceived, without regard to concerns of status, tradition, or company politics.

(6) LEARNING

26. ____ To be viewed as a "continuous learner" at work benefits one's career.

27. ____ We regularly challenge group norms, and anyone can initiate this process.

28. ____ My organization is constantly engaged in learning about itself and the environments in which it operates.

29. ____ The organization allocates resources toward employee involvement in cultural events as attendees, participants, or learners.

30. ____ Projects are undertaken by integrated teams whose members bring multiple disciplines and diverse perspectives to the task.

(7) SOCIAL

31. ____ Our relationships at work are relaxed, irreverent, warm, and crackling with ideas.

32. ____ People from different departments and organizational levels socialize together, either during or after work.

33. ____ Committee meetings are reasonably productive and amicable.

34. ____ When we form teams to work on special projects, the work is integrated into our day-to-day schedules.

35. ____ We always produce effective leadership when and where we need it.

(8) FESTIVA

36. ____ Social occasions are planned and designed in highly creative ways.

37. ____ The line between work and play is virtually nonexistent.

38. ____ Developments in art, politics, science, and other fields not directly related to our work are discussed in relation to their impact upon our organization and industry.

39. ____ We have a strong group vocabulary of terms and symbols that promotes communication, community, and creativity.

40. ____ We are encouraged to play whimsically with ideas, materials, and objects as well as with new ways of doing things.

_____ **TOTAL POINTS**

Scoring Your Organization's Creativity

If You Scored:	Organization Is in the Creative . . .
40–79	*Dead Zone*—a place where it is virtually impossible for creativity to flourish
80–159	*I-Zone*—where management thinks in terms of the next quarter and creativity is seldom transmitted from one person or department to another* OR . . . *O-Zone*—where creativity is valued but not consistently incorporated into the organization's strategy*
160–200	*Hot Zone*—where creativity is intense and productive

Note: I-Zone organizations score higher on Values, Ideas, Perception, and Social questions. O-Zone organizations score higher on Mission and Vision, Learning, Exchange, and Festiva questions.

Source: B. Kunstler, "Building a Creative Hothouse," *The Futurist* (January–February 2001), pp. 22–29. Reprinted by permission of the World Future Society.

Key Terms

absorptive capacity (p. 303)

best practice (p. 312)

corporate entrepreneurship (p. 306)

house of quality (p. 310)

index of R&D effectiveness (p. 311)

intellectual property (p. 301)

lead user (p. 296)

market research (p. 297)

orchestrator (p. 306)

process innovation (p. 299)

product champion (p. 306)

product innovation (p. 299)

product/market evolution matrix (p. 305)

R&D intensity (p. 298)

sponsor (p. 306)

stage-gate process (p. 309)

stage of new product development (p. 305)

strategic R&D alliance (p. 301)

technological competence (p. 303)

technology sourcing (p. 300)

time to market (p. 299)

CHAPTER 13
Strategic Issues in Entrepreneurial Ventures and Small Businesses

Learning Objectives

After reading this chapter, you should be able to:

- Differentiate between an entrepreneurial venture and a small business
- Use the strategic decision-making process to form a new venture
- Differentiate between an idea and an opportunity
- Identify sources of innovative concepts
- List the characteristics of the typical entrepreneur
- Understand the importance of moving through the substages of small-business development
- Avoid pitfalls in assessing the financial statements of a small, privately owned company

ONE NIGHT WHILE ATTENDING A PROFESSIONAL BASKETBALL GAME, VINCENT NORMENT noticed a problem on the court. As the game progressed, sweat-soaked headbands kept creeping down into the players' eyes. The athletes seemed to be constantly adjusting their headbands and were distracted from playing their best. Norment concluded that all that was needed to solve the problem was to put a thick strap across the top of the headband. The strap could be made of the same super-absorbent material as the rest of the headband. With this strap, a headband would not only absorb more of the athlete's sweat but also stay in place. With a background in sports-related products, Norment suggested his idea to headband manufacturers. "They looked at the product and said it wouldn't work," reported Norment.

When a patent search found nothing similar on the market, Norment patented his idea for DBands and planned to sell them through his own company, DApparel, Inc. Knowing that the key to success was getting the product used by athletes, Norment promoted DBands at the three-point shooting contest of the 2003 March Madness collegiate basketball playoffs. He asked players for their opinions and persuaded one player to wear the headband on ESPN. Thanks to the exposure, Norment got endorsements from Ron Artest of the Indiana Pacers and Brad Miller of the Sacramento Kings, among others. Now that DBands was starting to get the attention of the market, the next step was securing distribution.

DBands arrived in sporting goods stores such as The Athlete's Foot and Foot Locker in spring 2005, priced between $9.99 and $14.99. Norment expected to sell 50,000 to 100,000 DBands by December 2005. His goal was to make the DApparel brand a household name, one head at a time.[1]

13.1 | Importance of Small Business and Entrepreneurial Ventures

Strategic management as a field of study typically deals with large, established business corporations. However, small business cannot be ignored. There are approximately 23 million small businesses—over 99% of all businesses—in the United States. They generate 60% to 80% of net new jobs annually and produce almost 30% of known export value. Studies by the Global Entrepreneurship Monitor have found a strong correlation between national economic growth and the level of entrepreneurial activity in prior years.[2] Research reveals that not only do small firms spend almost twice as much of their R&D budget on fundamental research as do large firms, but also, small companies are roughly 13 times more innovative per employee than large firms.[3] The National Science Foundation estimates that 98% of "radical" product developments result from the research done in the labs of small companies.[4] Nevertheless, not every country is as supportive of new ventures as is the United States. See the GLOBAL ISSUE feature to learn how different countries support entrepreneurship.

Despite the overall success of small businesses, however, every year tens of thousands of small companies fail. Figures from the U.S. Small Business Administration indicate that 50%

GL🌐BAL ISSUE

Entrepreneurship: Some Countries Are More Supportive Than Others

Entrepreneurship is becoming increasingly important throughout the world. True to economist Joseph Schumpeter's view of entrepreneurship as "creative destruction," much of the world from Eastern Europe to South America to Asia envisions entrepreneurial ventures as the means to build successful free market economies. New entrepreneurial ventures are emerging daily in these countries. Unfortunately, not every country makes it easy to start a new business.

According to the World Bank, countries range from easy to difficult in terms of starting an entrepreneurial venture. The amount of difficulty is usually a function of government requirements and paperwork and can be measured in the number of days it takes to start a new venture. The *quickest* in days are Australia (2), Canada (3), New Zealand (3), Denmark (4), the United States (4), Puerto Rico (6), Singapore (8), Hong Kong (11), Latvia (11), and the Netherlands (11). The *slowest* in days are Zaire (215), Haiti (203), Laos (198), Indonesia (168), Mozambique (153), Brazil (152), Angola (146), Burkina Faso (136), Zimbabwe (122), and Venezuela (119). Not surprisingly, the World Bank analysis of 130 countries concludes that onerous regulation retards economic growth.

Even though entrepreneurship is more difficult in many other parts of the world than in the United States, the situation is changing. For example, investors are flocking to young, fast-growing companies in Europe. Politicians are beginning to see entrepreneurs as part of a solution to unemployment rather than as grasping exploiters. Venture capital is becoming more available. The EASDAQ, founded in 1996, is Europe's version of the NASDAQ. Companies can be listed on the EASDAQ regardless of size or history, so long as they agree to international accounting standards and U.S.-style financial reporting.

There is still an ingrained cultural aversion to the risk-taking so necessary to entrepreneurship. The contradiction between the Marxist ideology and private ownership in China means that business entrepreneurs are not perceived as legitimate. The social stigma attached to business failure is deeply entrenched in many countries. According to Christophe Sapet, the French founder of a computer game company called Infogrames, "When you earn money, (French) people are jealous. They think you have done something wrong."

Sources: "Down to Business," *The Economist* (October 11, 2003), p. 9; J. Kahn, "Suddenly, Startups Are Chic," *Fortune* (February 15, 1999), p. 110; "Financial Indicators," *The Economist* (October 16, 1999), p. 109; "Emerging-Market Indicators," *The Economist* (September 23, 2000), p. 128; E. W. K. Tsang, "In Search of Legitimacy: The Private Entrepreneur in China," *Entrepreneurship Theory and Practice* (Fall 1996), pp. 21–30.

of businesses founded in any one year are not in business four years later.[5] Similar rates occur in the United Kingdom, the Netherlands, Japan, Taiwan, and Hong Kong.[6] Although an increasing number of studies are more positive regarding the survival rate of new entrepreneurial ventures, new businesses are definitely considered risky.[7] The causes of small-business failure (depending on the study cited) range from inadequate accounting systems to inability to cope with growth. The underlying problem appears to be an overall lack of strategic management—beginning with an inability to plan a strategy to reach the customer and ending with a failure to develop a system of controls to keep track of performance.[8]

Definition of Small-Business Firms and Entrepreneurial Ventures

The most commonly accepted definition of a small-business firm in the United States is one that employs fewer than 500 people and that generates sales of less than $20 million annually.

Although the meanings of the terms *small business* and *entrepreneurship* overlap considerably, the concepts are different. A **small-business firm** is independently owned and operated, is not dominant in its field, and does not engage in innovative practices. An **entrepreneurial venture**, in contrast, is any business whose primary goals are profitability and growth and that can be characterized by innovative strategic practices.[9] The basic difference between a small-business firm and an entrepreneurial venture, therefore, lies not in the type of goods or services provided, but in their fundamental views on growth and innovation. According to Donald Sexton, an authority on entrepreneurship, this explains why strategic planning is more likely to be present in an entrepreneurial venture than in a typical small-business firm:

> *Most firms start with just a single product. Those oriented toward growth immediately start looking for another one. It's that planning approach that separates the entrepreneur from the small-business owner.*[10]

The Entrepreneur as Strategist

Often defined as a person who organizes and manages a business undertaking and who assumes risk for the sake of a profit, an **entrepreneur** is the ultimate strategist. He or she makes all the strategic as well as operational decisions. All three levels of strategy—corporate, business, and functional—are the concerns of this founder and owner–manager of a company. This is typical of a new venture, which is usually a Stage I company (discussed in **Chapter 9**, in the stages of corporate development section). As one entrepreneur puts it: "Entrepreneurs are strategic planners without realizing it."

The development of DBands described earlier captures the key elements of an entrepreneurial venture: a basic business idea that has not yet been successfully tried and a gutsy entrepreneur who, while working on borrowed capital and a shoestring budget, creates a new business through a lot of trial and error and persistent hard work. Similar stories can be told of other people, such as Debbie Fields, who created Mrs. Fields Cookies, and Will Parish, who founded National Energy Associates. Both were ridiculed at one time or another for their desire to start businesses. Friends and family members told Fields that starting a business to sell chocolate chip cookies "was a stupid idea." Will Parish, who built a power plant in California's Imperial Valley that burns "pasture patties," was called an "entre-manure." Every day the plant burned 900 tons of manure collected from nearby feedlots to generate 15 megawatts of electricity—enough to light 20,000 homes. The power was sold to Southern California Edison. Parish got the idea from a trip to India, where the fuel used to heat a meal was cow dung. Once the plant was earning a profit, Parish planned to build a larger plant nearby that would burn wheat straw and other crop wastes. The plants provide an environmentally sound as well as profitable way to dispose of waste. Very interested in conservation, Parish says, "I wanted to combine doing well with doing good."[11]

13.2 | Use of Strategic Planning and Strategic Management

Research shows that strategic planning is strongly related to small-business financial performance.[12] A survey of the high-growth *Inc. 500* firms revealed that 86% performed strategic planning. Of those performing strategic planning, 94% reported improved profits.[13] Nevertheless, many small companies still do not use the process.[14] A study of 131 firms filing for bankruptcy revealed that 72% lacked mission statements and objectives for their businesses.[15] Around 40% of existing small family-owned businesses do not have written strategic plans.[16] The reasons often cited for the apparent lack of strategic planning practices in many small-business firms are fourfold:

- **Not enough time:** Day-to-day operating problems take up the time necessary for long-term planning. It's relatively easy to justify avoiding strategic planning on the basis of day-to-day crisis management. Some will ask: "How can I be expected to do strategic planning when I don't know if I'm going to be in business next week?"

- **Unfamiliar with strategic planning:** A small-business CEO may be unaware of strategic planning or may view it as irrelevant to the small-business situation. Planning may be viewed as a straitjacket that limits flexibility.

- **Lack of skills:** Small-business managers often lack the skills necessary to begin strategic planning and do not have or want to spend the money necessary to import trained consultants. Future uncertainty may be used to justify a lack of planning. One entrepreneur admits, "Deep down, I know I should plan. But I don't know what to do. I'm the leader, but I don't know how to lead the planning process."

- **Lack of trust and openness:** Many small-business owner–managers are very sensitive regarding key information about the business and are thus unwilling to share strategic planning with employees or outsiders. For this reason, boards of directors are often composed only of close friends and relatives of the owner–manager—people unlikely to provide an objective viewpoint or professional advice.

Degree of Formality

Research generally concludes that the strategic planning process can be far more informal in small companies than it is in large corporations.[17] Some studies have even found that too much formalization of the strategic planning process may actually result in reduced performance.[18] Strategic planning is often forced on an entrepreneur by banks and venture capitalists when the entrepreneur is searching for capital to launch or expand the new venture. It is possible that a heavy emphasis on structured, written plans can be dysfunctional to the small entrepreneurial firm because it detracts from the very flexibility that is a benefit of small size. The process of strategic planning, not the plan itself, is probably the key to improving business performance. Research does show, however, that as an entrepreneurial firm matures, its strategic planning process tends to become more formal.[19]

These observations suggest that new entrepreneurial ventures begin life in Mintzberg's *entrepreneurial mode* of strategic planning (explained in **Chapter 1**) and move toward the *planning mode* as the company becomes established and wants to continue its strong growth. If, after becoming successfully established, the entrepreneur instead chooses stability over growth, the venture moves more toward the *adaptive mode* so common to many small businesses.

Usefulness of the Strategic Management Model

The model of strategic management (presented in **Figure 1–2** in **Chapter 1**) is also relevant to entrepreneurial ventures and small businesses. This basic model holds for both an established small company and a new entrepreneurial venture. As the research mentioned earlier concluded, small and developing companies increase their chances of success if they make a serious attempt to work through the strategic issues embedded in the strategic management model. The key is to focus on what's important—the set of managerial decisions and actions that determines the long-run performance of the company. The list of informal questions presented in **Table 13–1** may be more useful to a small entrepreneurial company than their more formal counterparts used by large, established corporations.

Usefulness of the Strategic Decision-Making Process

As mentioned in **Chapter 1**, one way in which the strategic management model can be made action oriented is to follow the strategic decision-making model presented in **Figure 1–5**. The eight steps presented in that model are just as appropriate for small companies as they are for large corporations. Unfortunately, the process does not fit new entrepreneurial

Formal	Informal
Define mission	What do we stand for?
Set objectives	What are we trying to achieve?
Formulate strategy	How are we going to get there? How can we beat the competition?
Determine policies	What sort of ground rules should we all be following to get the job done right?
Establish programs	How should we organize this operation to get what we want done as cheaply as possible with the highest quality possible?
Prepare pro forma budgets	How much is it going to cost us and where can we get the cash?
Specify procedures	In how much detail do we have to lay things out, so that everybody knows what to do?
Determine performance measures	What are those few key things that will determine whether we can make it? How can we keep track of them?

ventures. Such a company must develop a new mission and new objectives, strategies, and policies out of a comparison of its external opportunities and threats to its potential strengths and weaknesses. Consequently, we propose in **Figure 13–1** a modified version of the strategic decision-making process; this version more closely suits a new entrepreneurial venture.

The proposed **strategic decision-making process for entrepreneurial ventures** is composed of the following eight interrelated steps:

1. **Develop the basic business idea—a product and/or service that has target customers and/or markets:** An **idea** is a concept for a product or service that currently doesn't exist or is not currently available in a market niche. It may be a brand-new concept (radical innovation) or an improvement to a current product or service (incremental innovation). The idea can be developed from a person's experience or generated in a moment of creative insight. For example, Vincent Norment conceived of a headband with a stay-on strap while attending a basketball game.

2. **Scan and assess the external environment to locate factors in the societal and task environments that pose opportunities and threats:** The scanning should focus particularly on market potential and resource accessibility.

3. **Scan and assess the internal factors relevant to the new business:** The entrepreneur should objectively consider personal assets, areas of expertise, abilities, and experience, all in terms of the organizational needs of the new venture.

4. **Analyze the strategic factors in light of the current situation, using SWOT:** The venture's potential strengths and weaknesses must be evaluated in light of opportunities and threats. This analysis can be done with a SFAS Matrix (see **Figure 6–1**) of the strategic factors.

5. **Decide go or no go:** If the basic business idea appears to be a feasible business opportunity, the process should be continued. An **opportunity** is an idea for a new product or service with a market that is willing to pay for that product or service so that it can form the basis of a profitable business. Otherwise, further development of the idea should be canceled unless the strategic factors change.

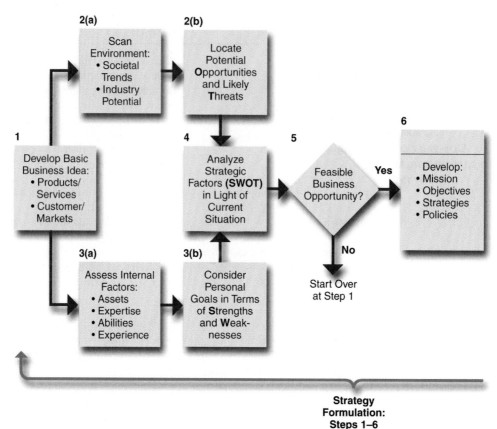

Figure 13–1
Strategic Decision-Making Process for New Ventures

Strategy Formulation: Steps 1–6

6. **Generate a business plan that specifies how the opportunity will be transformed into reality:** See **Table 13–2** for the suggested contents of a strategic **business plan**. The proposed venture's mission, objectives, strategies, and policies, as well as its likely board of directors (if a corporation) and key managers should be developed. Key internal factors should be specified and performance projections generated. The business plan serves as a vehicle through which financial support is obtained from potential investors and creditors. It increases a new venture's probability of survival and facilitates new product develop-

TABLE 13–2
CONTENTS OF A STRATEGIC BUSINESS PLAN FOR AN ENTREPRENEURIAL VENTURE

I. Table of Contents	X. Human Resources Plan
II. Executive Summary	XI. Ownership
III. Nature of the Business	XII. Risk Analysis
IV. Strategy Formulation	XIII. Timetables and Milestones
V. Market Analysis	XIV. Strategy Implementation—Action Plans
VI. Marketing Plan	XV. Evaluation and Control
VII. Operational Plans—Service/Product	XVI. Summary
VIII. Financial Plans	XVII. Appendixes
IX. Organization and Management	

Note: The Strategic Audit in Appendix 1.A can be used to develop a business plan. It provides detailed questions to serve as a checklist.

Source: Thomas L. Wheelen, "Contents of a Strategic Business Plan for an Entrepreneurial Venture." Copyright © 1988 and 2005 by Thomas L. Wheelen. Reprinted by permission.

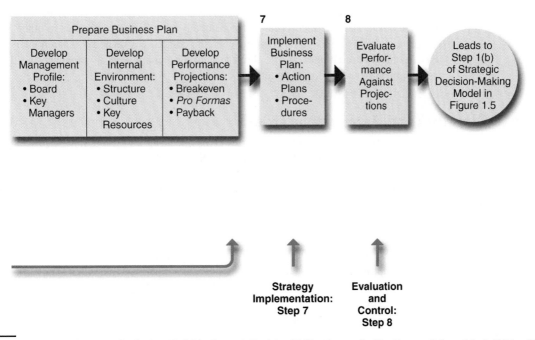

Source: T. L. Wheelen and C. E. Michaels, Jr., "Model for Strategic Decision-Making Process for New Ventures." Copyright © 1987 and 2005 by T. L. Wheelen. Reprinted by permission.

ment.[20] Firms using business plans tend to have higher revenue and sales growth than do those without them.[21] Starting a business without a business plan is the quickest way to kill a new venture.[22] For example, one study of 270 clothing retailers found that 80% of the successful stores had written business plans, whereas 65% of the failed businesses had not.[23]

A strategic audit (see **Appendix 1.A** at the end of **Chapter 1**) can be used to develop a formal business plan. The audit's sections and subsections, along with the questions within them, can be re-aligned to fit the model depicted in **Figure 13–1**. Instead of analyzing the historical events of an existing company, one can use the questions to project the proposed company's future. The questions can be reoriented to follow the outline in **Appendix 1.A**. A crucial building block of a sound business plan is the construction of realistic scenarios for the pro forma financials. The pro formas must reflect the impact of seasonality on the cash flows of the proposed new venture.

7. **Implement the business plan:** Do this through the use of action plans and procedures.

8. **Evaluate the implemented business plan through comparison of actual performance against projected performance results:** This step leads to step 1(b) of the strategic decision-making process shown in **Figure 1–5**. To the extent that actual results are less than or much greater than the anticipated results, the entrepreneur needs to reconsider the company's current mission, objectives, strategies, policies, and programs, and possibly make changes to the original business plan.

13.3 | Issues in Corporate Governance

Corporate governance is much simpler in small entrepreneurial ventures than in large, established corporations. For one thing, the owners and the managers are usually the same people—the company founders (or their close relatives). If a venture is not incorporated, there is no need for a board of directors. It may be a sole proprietorship or a simple partnership. Those entrepreneurial ventures wishing to grow quickly or to limit the liability of the owners often incorporate the business. Once incorporated, the company can sell shares of stock to others (such as venture capitalists) to finance its growth. When the company is owned by shareholders (even if the shareholders are composed of only the founding owners who also manage the firm), the company must have a board of directors.

Boards of Directors and Advisory Boards

The boards of directors of entrepreneurial firms are likely to be either very passive or very active. Passive boards exist when the stock is closely held by the founding owners (and their immediate families) who manage the company on a day-to-day basis. As the only stockholders, they elect themselves to board offices and call meetings only when the law requires it—usually as a social occasion. There is no need for an active board since there are no other stockholders and thus no agency problems. The board typically has few or no external directors.[24] In most instances, the primary role of the board is simply to be a figurehead to satisfy the law. This places it on the far left end of the board of directors' continuum shown in Chapter 2's **Figure 2–1**.

Entrepreneurial ventures financed by venture capitalists typically have very active boards of directors. The venture capitalists expect to obtain seats on the board in exchange for their investment.[25] Once on the board, venture capitalists tend to be very powerful members of the board and are highly involved in strategic management.[26] The boards of directors of fast-growth entrepreneurial firms have around five directors, of whom about three are external. Almost 80% of them have written strategic plans with a time horizon of 12 to 24 months.[27] Venture capitalists usually require three years or more of pro forma financial statements broken out on a monthly cash flow basis for the first two years and on a quarterly basis thereafter.

Since closely held entrepreneurial ventures and small businesses tend to have relatively passive boards composed primarily of insiders, this type of business should use an advisory board to provide advice to the owner–managers. An **advisory board** is a group of external business people who voluntarily meet periodically with the owner–managers of the firm to discuss strategic and other issues. The members are usually invited to join the board by the president of the company. The advisory board has no official capacity but is expected to provide management with useful suggestions and act as a sounding board. Since the members typically receive no compensation for serving, quarterly business meetings are often followed by cocktails and dinner at a nearby country club, hotel, or prestigious restaurant. It is important to staff the advisory board with knowledgeable people who have significant business experience or skills who can complement the background and skills of the company's owner–managers. Using an advisory board is an easy way to obtain free professional consulting advice. Research indicates that advisory boards improve the performance of small businesses.[28]

Impact of the Sarbanes-Oxley Act

Complying with the Sarbanes-Oxley Act is becoming a cost burden for small publicly held U.S. companies. Companies face higher audit and legal fees, new internal control systems, and higher directors' and officers' liability insurance premiums, among other expenses.

Compliance costs are estimated at $500,000 for a small firm and in the millions for a large one.[29] As a result, 198 firms "went dark" in 2003 by delisting their stock from stock exchanges. By only trading via "pink sheets" in over-the-counter stocks, these firms do not have to comply with the act's minimum requirements, and they do not have to file with the Securities and Exchange Commission (SEC). Under SEC rules, a company may choose to terminate its registration if the corporation's securities have fewer than 300 holders of record or if there are fewer than 500 holders of record and the company's total assets don't exceed $10 million. A research study of firms going dark indicated that the firms delist their stock not only to avoid compliance costs but also to evade the outside monitoring and additional scrutiny required by Sarbanes-Oxley. According to Christian Leuz, co-author of the study: "We basically find that going dark can serve as a way to conserve cash, but it may also be exploited by insiders trying to avoid the scrutiny of the market. Whether insiders succeed, and whether the decision to go dark is a good or bad one therefore depends on the governance in place."[30]

13.4 | Issues in Environmental Scanning and Strategy Formulation

Environmental scanning in small businesses is much less sophisticated than it is in large corporations. The business is usually too small to justify hiring someone to do only environmental scanning or strategic planning. Top managers, especially if they are the founders, tend to believe that they know the business and can follow it better than anyone else. A study of 220 small rapid-growth companies revealed that the majority of CEOs were actively and personally involved in all phases of the planning process, especially in the setting of objectives. Only 15% of the companies used a planning officer or formed a planning group to assist in the planning process. In the rest of the firms, operating managers who participated in strategic planning provided input only to the CEO, who then formulated the plan.[31] Unfortunately, the literature suggests that most small business owner–managers rely more on internal as opposed to external sources of information.[32] Conducting a periodic industry analysis using Porter's forces is just as important for a small business as for a large one. Nevertheless, few small businesses do much competitor analysis. If they do analyze competition, typical small business owners often only look locally, without considering competitors across town or in a nearby city.

A fundamental reason for differences in strategy formulation between large and small entrepreneurial companies lies in the relationship between owners and managers. The CEO of a large corporation has to consider and balance the varied needs of the corporation's many stakeholders. The CEO of a small business, however, is very likely also to be the owner—the company's primary stakeholder. Personal and family needs can thus strongly affect a small business's mission and objectives and can overrule other considerations.[33]

Size can affect the selection of an appropriate corporate strategy. Large corporations often choose growth strategies for their many side benefits for management as well as for shareholders. A small company may, however, choose a stability strategy because the entrepreneur is interested mostly in (1) generating employment for family members, (2) providing the family a "decent living," and (3) being the "boss" of a firm small enough that he or she can manage it comfortably. Some business owners don't pursue a growth strategy because they do not want the loss of control that results from bank debt or the sale of stock to outsiders. Some may even fear that growth will attract attention from larger competitors that might want to take over the company or drive it out of business.[34] Thus the goals of a small business are likely to be the same as the goals of the owner–manager.

Basic SWOT analysis is just as relevant to new entrepreneurial businesses as it is to established large ones. Both the greatest strength and the greatest weakness of a small firm, at least in the beginning, rest with the entrepreneur—the owner–manager of the business. The entrepreneur is the manager, the source of product/market strategy, and the dynamo who energizes the company. That is why the internal assessment of a new venture's strengths and weaknesses focuses in **Figure 13–1** on the founder's personal characteristics—his or her assets, expertise, abilities, and experience. Research reveals that founder competencies, motivations, and connections plus the firm's competitive strategies are direct predictors of new venture growth and success.[35] Intangible assets, such as leadership, strategy, and human and intellectual capital, were found to be more important than traditional financial measures for a venture's success in going public through an IPO.[36]

Just as an entrepreneur's strengths can be the key to company success, personal weaknesses can be a primary cause of failure. For example, the study of clothing retailers mentioned earlier showed that the owner–managers of 85% of the failed stores had no prior retailing experience.

Sources of Innovation

Peter Drucker, in his book *Innovation and Entrepreneurship*, proposes seven sources for innovative opportunity that should be monitored by those interested in starting an entrepreneurial venture, either within an established company or as an independent small business.[37] The first four **sources of innovation** lie within the industry itself; the last three arise in the societal environment. These seven sources are:

1. **The Unexpected:** An unexpected success, an unexpected failure, or an unexpected outside event can be a symptom of a unique opportunity. When Don Cullen of Transmet Corporation spilled a box of very fine aluminum flakes onto his company's parking lot, he discovered that their presence in the asphalt prevented it from turning sticky in high temperatures. His company now produces aluminum chips for use in roofing. Sales have doubled every year since the product's introduction, and Cullen's company will soon dominate the business.

2. **The Incongruity:** A discrepancy between reality and what everyone assumes it to be, or between what is and what ought to be, can create an opportunity for innovation. For example, a side effect of retailing via the Internet is the increasing number of packages being delivered to homes. Since neither FedEx nor UPS can leave a package unless someone is home to sign for it, many deliveries are delayed. Tony Paikeday founded zBox Company to make and sell a hard plastic container that would receive deliveries from any delivery service and would be accessible only by the owner and the delivery services. "We're amazed that it doesn't exist yet," says Paikeday.[38]

3. **Innovation Based on Process Need:** When a weak link is evident in a particular process but people work around it instead of doing something about it, an opportunity is present for the person or company willing to forge a stronger one. Tired of having to strain to use a too-small keyboard on his personal computer, David Levy invented a keyboard with 64 normal-sized keys cleverly put into an area the size of a credit card.[39]

4. **Changes in Industry or Market Structure:** A business is ready for an innovative product, service, or approach to the business when the underlying foundation of the industry or market shifts. Black Entertainment Television, Inc. (BET), was born when Robert Johnson noticed that no television programmer was targeting the increasing number of black viewers. The BET brand has expanded into magazines and is now known by more than 90% of African-Americans.[40]

5. **Demographics:** Changes in the population's size, age structure, composition, employment, level of education, and income can create opportunities for innovation. For exam-

ple, Pam Henderson started a company called Kids Kab to shuttle children and teenagers to private schools, doctor and dentist appointments, lessons, and extracurricular activities. With the trend to dual careers, parents were no longer always available to provide personal transportation for their own children and needed such a service.

6. **Changes in Perception, Mood, and Meaning:** Opportunities for innovation can develop when a society's general assumptions, attitudes, and beliefs change. For example, the increasing dominance of a few national brewers have caused beer drinkers to look for alternatives to the same old national brands. By positioning Yuengling, a local Pennsylvania beer, as a full-flavored beer and providing it with an artsy, nostalgic-looking label, the small company was able to catch the fancy of young, trendy consumers who viewed it as Pennsylvania's version of Anchor Steam, the successful San Francisco beer.

7. **New Knowledge:** Advances in scientific and nonscientific knowledge can create new products and new markets. Advances in two different areas can sometimes be integrated to form the basis of a new product. For example, Medical Foods was formed to make foods that act like medicine to treat conditions from diabetes to arthritis. Its first product, NiteBite, is a chocolate-flavored snack bar designed to help diabetics manage nocturnal hypoglycemia, caused by low blood sugar. NiteBite gradually releases glucose into the bloodstream, where it lasts for six hours or more.[41]

Factors Affecting a New Venture's Success

According to Hofer and Sandberg, three factors have a substantial impact on a new venture's performance. In order of importance, these **factors affecting new venture success** are (1) the structure of the industry entered, (2) the new venture's business strategy, and (3) behavioral characteristics of the entrepreneur.[42]

Industry Structure

Research shows that the chances for success are greater for entrepreneurial ventures that enter rapidly changing industries than for those that enter stable industries. In addition, prospects are better in industries that are in the early, high-growth stages of development.[43] Competition is often less intense. Fast market growth also allows new ventures to make some mistakes without serious penalty. New ventures also increase their chances of success when they enter markets in which they can erect entry barriers to keep out competitors.

Contrary to popular wisdom, however, patents may not always provide competitive advantage, especially for new ventures in a high-tech or hypercompetitive industry. A well-financed competitor could examine a newly filed application for a patent, work around the patent, and beat the pioneering firm to market with a similar product. In addition, the time and cost of filing and defending a patent may not be worth the effort. According to Connie Bagley, author of *The Entrepreneur's Guide to Business Law*:

> *It might take 18 months to get a patent on a product that has a 12-month life cycle. By the time you finally get the damn thing litigated, it's meaningless. So people are focusing less on proprietary assurance and more on first-mover advantage. . . . The law is just too slow for this high-speed economy.*[44]

Most new ventures enter industries that have a low degree of industry concentration (that is, no dominant competitors).[45] Industry concentration is not necessarily bad. It may create market niches being ignored by large firms.[46] Hofer and Sandberg found that a new venture is more likely to be successful entering an industry in which one dominant competitor has a 50% or more market share than entering an industry in which the largest competitor has less than a 25% market share. To explain this phenomenon, Hofer and Sandberg point out that when an industry has one dominant firm, the remaining competitors are relatively weak and are easy prey for an aggressive entrepreneur. To avoid direct competition with a major rival, the new venture can focus on a market segment that is being ignored.

Industry product characteristics also have a significant impact on a new venture's success. First, a new venture is more likely to be successful when it enters an industry with heterogeneous (different) products than when it enters one with homogeneous (similar) products. In a heterogeneous industry, a new venture can differentiate itself from competitors with a unique product; or, by focusing on the unique needs of a market segment, it can find a market niche. Second, a new venture is, according to research data, more likely to be successful if the product is relatively unimportant to the customer's total purchasing needs than if it is important. Customers are more likely to experiment with a new product if its cost is low and product failure will not create a problem.

Business Strategy

According to Hofer and Sandberg, the keys to success for most new ventures are (1) to differentiate the product from those of other competitors in the areas of quality and service and (2) to focus the product on customer needs in a segment of the market in order to achieve a dominant share of that part of the market. Adopting guerrilla-warfare tactics, these companies go after opportunities in market niches too small or too localized to justify retaliation from the market leaders.[47] It is crucial, however, that a new venture analyze its competitors to assess their likely response to the company's entry into the market.

To continue its growth once it has found a niche, an entrepreneurial firm can emphasize continued innovation and pursue natural growth in its current markets. The firm can also expand into related markets in which the company's core skills, resources, and facilities offer the keys to further success. It can leverage its resources by engaging in strategic alliances with other firms. Sixty-three percent of U.S. small business owners report that they are involved in strategic alliances, especially in marketing and distribution. Of those using strategic alliances, half maintain three or more.[48]

Some studies do indicate, however, that new ventures can also be successful following strategies other than going after an undefended niche with a focus strategy. A narrow-market approach may leave the new firm vulnerable and preordained to only limited sales. One possible approach would be to offer products that are substitutable to, but differentiated from, those offered by bigger firms.[49] For some practical suggestions for locating an opportunity and formulating a business strategy, see **STRATEGY HIGHLIGHT 13.1**.

Entrepreneurial Characteristics

Four **entrepreneurial characteristics** are key to a new venture's success. Successful entrepreneurs have:

1. **The ability to identify potential venture opportunities better than most people:** Entrepreneurs focus on opportunities—not on problems—and try to learn from failure. Entrepreneurs are goal oriented and have a strong impact on the emerging culture of an organization. They are able to envision where the company is going and are thus able to provide a strong overall sense of strategic direction. As a result, their firms have a strong entrepreneurial orientation (EO)—that is, are innovative, proactive, and willing to take risks.[50]

2. **A sense of urgency that makes them action oriented:** They have a high need for achievement, which motivates them to put their ideas into action. They tend to have an internal locus of control that leads them to believe that they can determine their own fate through their own behavior. They also have a significantly greater capacity to tolerate

STRATEGY HIGHLIGHT 13.1

Suggestions for Locating an Opportunity and Formulating a Business Strategy

Given that differentiation and focus are the most popular and effective competitive strategies for a new venture, what are some of the ways to identify a new opportunity in which these strategies can be used? *Entrepreneur* magazine provides four interesting approaches:

1. **Tap the countertrend:** For every trend, there is likely to be a potentially lucrative countertrend waiting to be discovered. When a trend is hot, look for its opposite in a small but potentially growing market niche. Note how Hardee's successfully responded to the trend to low-fat and low-carb diets with it own monster-size bacon cheeseburger with more calories, carbs, and fat than its competitors. Because the idea was so outrageous, the Hardee's product received free coverage in newspapers and on television.

2. **Eat off the established company's plate:** Trendwatching.com coined the term "feeder business" for companies that feed off giants such as Amazon or eBay. When Eric Cohen and Joyce Shulman noticed that the typical blank pizza box was 16 inches of available advertising space, they decided to partner with the box makers to print paid advertisements on them for pizzerias. They then branched out into coffee cups and ice bags.

3. **Switch the niche:** A company may be able to identify a successful product or service that caters to a particular market and tailor it to fit a different market niche. For example, when Una Cassidy encountered numerous women looking for beauty products for use during pregnancy, she founded Selph. Cassidy removed all the usual ingredients found in beauty products that would be harmful to a fetus during pregnancy and replaced them with superior products that were gentle on the skin.

4. **Borrow a business model:** Netflix developed a novel business model (discussed in **Chapter 1**) in which members are charged a set monthly fee to borrow an unlimited number of DVDs by mail. This model was picked up quickly by other entrepreneurs such as GameFly, which rents video games by mail, Booksfree.com, which rents paperbacks by mail, and Bag Borrow Or Steal, which rents designer purses by mail.

Sources: K. Axelton, "Fever Pitch," *Entrepreneur* (December 2004), p. 74; N. L. Torres, "Think Outside the Box," *Entrepreneur* (February 2004), pp. 108–111; A. Pennington, "Una Cassidy," *Entrepreneur* (November 2003), p. 24.

ambiguity and stress than do many in established organizations.[51] They also have a strong need for control and may even be viewed as "misfits who need to create their own environment." They tend to distrust others and often have a need "to show others that they amount to something, that they cannot be ignored."[52]

3. **A detailed knowledge of the keys to success in the industry and the physical stamina to make their work their lives:** Successful entrepreneurs have better-than-average education and significant work experience in the industry in which they start their businesses. They often work with partners to form a new venture. (Seventy percent of new high-tech ventures are started by more than one founder.[53]) More than half of all entrepreneurs work at least 60 hours per week in the startup year, according to a National Federation of Independent Business study.[54]

4. **Access to outside help to supplement their skills, knowledge, and abilities:** Over time, entrepreneurs develop a network of people who have key skills and knowledge, whom the entrepreneurs can call on for support. Through their enthusiasm, these entrepreneurs are able to attract key investors, partners, creditors, and employees. For example, the founders of eBay did not hesitate to bring in Meg Whitman as CEO because Whitman had the managerial skills that eBay needed to expand.

In summarizing their conclusions regarding factors affecting the success of entrepreneurial ventures, Hofer and Sandberg propose the guidelines presented in **Table 13–3**.

TABLE 13–3
**SOME GUIDELINES
FOR NEW
VENTURE SUCCESS**

- Focus on industries facing substantial technological or regulatory changes, especially those with recent exits by established competitors.
- Seek industries whose smaller firms have relatively weak competitive positions.
- Seek industries that are in early, high-growth stages of evolution.
- Seek industries in which it is possible to create high barriers to subsequent entry.
- Seek industries with heterogeneous products that are relatively unimportant to the customer's overall success.
- Seek to differentiate your products from those of your competitors in ways that are meaningful to your customers.
- Focus such differentiation efforts on product quality, marketing approaches, and customer service—and charge enough to cover the costs of doing so.
- Seek to dominate the market segments in which you compete. If necessary, either segment the market differently or change the nature and focus of your differentiation efforts to increase your domination of the segments you serve.
- Stress innovation, especially new product innovation, that is built on existing organizational capabilities.
- Seek natural, organic growth through flexibility and opportunism that builds on existing organizational strengths.

Source: C. W. Hofer and W. R. Sandberg, "Improving New Venture Performance: Some Guidelines for Success," *American Journal of Small Business* (Summer 1987), pp. 17, 19. Copyright © 1987 by C. W. Hofer and W. R. Sandberg. Reprinted from *Entrepreneurship Theory & Practice* by permission of Baylor University. All rights reserved.

13.5 | Issues in Strategy Implementation

Two key implementation issues in a small company are organizing and staffing the growing company and transferring ownership of the company to the next generation.

Substages of Small Business Development

The implementation problems of a small business change as the company grows and develops over time. Just as the decision-making process for entrepreneurial ventures is different from that of established businesses, the managerial systems in small companies often vary from those of large corporations. Those variations are based on their stage of development. The stages of corporate growth and development discussed in **Chapter 9** suggest that all small businesses are either in Stage I or trying to move into Stage II. These models imply that all successful new ventures eventually become Stage II, functionally organized, companies. This is not always true, however. In attempting to show clearly how small businesses develop, Churchill and Lewis propose five **substages of small business development**: (a) existence, (b) survival, (c) success, (d) take-off, and (e) resource maturity.[55] A review of these small-business substages shows in more detail how a company can move through the entrepreneurial Stage I into a functionally oriented, professionally managed Stage II.

Stage A: Existence
At this point, an entrepreneurial venture faces the problems of obtaining customers and delivering the promised product or service. The organizational structure is simple. The entrepreneur does everything and directly supervises subordinates. Systems are minimal. The owner is the business.

Stage B: Survival

Those ventures able to satisfy a sufficient number of customers enter this stage; the rest close when their owners run out of startup capital. Those reaching the survival stage are concerned about generating the cash flow needed to repair and replace capital assets as they wear out and to finance the growth to continue satisfying the market segment they have found.

At this stage, the organizational structure is still simple, but it probably has a sales manager or general supervisor to carry out the owner's well-defined orders. A major problem of many small businesses at this stage is finding a person who is qualified to supervise the business when the owner can't be present but who is still willing to work for a very modest salary. An entrepreneur usually tries to use a family member rather than hire an outsider who lacks the entrepreneur's dedication to the business and (in the words of one owner–manager) "steals them blind." A company that remains in this stage for a long time is often called a "mom and pop" firm. It earns marginal returns on invested time and capital (with lots of psychic income!) and eventually goes out of business when "mom and pop" give up or retire. This type of small business is viewed more as a **lifestyle company** in which the firm is purely an extension of the owner's lifestyle. More than 94% of small private companies are in this category.[56]

Stage C: Success

By this point, the company's sales have reached a level where the firm is not only profitable but has sufficient cash flow to reinvest in itself. The key issue at this stage is whether the company should be used as a platform for growth or as a means of support for the owners as they completely or partially disengage from the company. The company is transforming into a functionally structured organization, but it still relies on the entrepreneur for all key decisions. The two options are disengagement and growth.

Stage C(1): Disengagement. The company can now successfully follow a stability strategy and remain at this stage almost indefinitely—provided that environmental change does not destroy its niche or poor management reduce its competitive abilities. By now functional managers have taken over some of the entrepreneur's duties. The company at this stage may be incorporated, but it is still primarily owned by the founder or the founder's family. Consequently, the board of directors is either a rubber stamp for the entrepreneur or a forum for family squabbles. Growth strategies are not pursued because either the market niche will not allow growth or the owner is content with the company at a size he or she can still manage comfortably. Strategic decisions make limited use of objective information and tend to be intuitive—based on personal desires and the founder's background.[57]

Stage C(2): Growth. The entrepreneur risks all available cash and the established borrowing power of the company in financing further growth. Strategic and operational planning are extensive and deeply involve the owner. Managers with an eye to the company's future rather than for its current situation are hired. This is an entrepreneurial high-growth firm aiming to be included in the *Inc. 500*. The emphasis now is on teamwork rather than on the entrepreneur's personal actions and energy. The personal values and philosophy of the founder are slowly transferred into a developing corporate culture.

Stage D: Take-Off

The key problems in this stage are how to grow rapidly and how to finance that growth. By now the firm is incorporated and has sold or is planning to sell stock in its company via an initial public offering (IPO) or via a direct public offering (DPO).[58] The entrepreneur must learn to delegate to specialized professional managers or to a team of managers who now form the top management of the company.[59] Delegation is a key issue for a company at this stage of development. A functional structure of the organization should now be solidly in place. Operational and strategic planning greatly involve the hired managers, but the company is still dominated by the entrepreneur's presence and stock control. Vertical and horizontal growth strategies are being seriously considered as the firm's management debates when and how to grow. The company is now included in the *Inc. 500* select group of firms.

At this point, the entrepreneur either is able to manage the transition from a small to a large company or recognizes personal limitations, sells his or her stock for a profit, and leaves the firm. The composition of the board of directors changes from dominance by friends and relatives of the owner to a large percentage of outsiders with managerial experience who can help the owner during the transition to a professionally managed company. The biggest danger facing the firm in this stage is the owner's desire to remain in total control (not willing to delegate) as if it were still a small entrepreneurial venture, even though he or she lacks the managerial skills necessary to run an established corporation. One study of small businesses found that fewer than one-third had written succession plans to replace the current owners.[60]

Stage E: Resource Maturity

It is at this point that the small company has adopted most of the characteristics of an established, large company. It may still be a small- or medium-sized company, but it is recognized as an important force in the industry and a possible candidate for the *Fortune 500* someday. The greatest concerns of a company at this stage are controlling the financial gains brought on by rapid growth and retaining its flexibility and entrepreneurial spirit. In terms of the stages of organizational growth and development discussed in **Chapter 9**, the company has become a full-fledged Stage II functional corporation.

Transfer of Power and Wealth in Family Businesses

Small businesses are often **family businesses**. Within the United States, family businesses account for approximately 80% of the total 15 million businesses.[61] It is estimated that over one-third of the U.S. *Fortune 500* companies are either family owned or dominated. Of the world's largest firms, the proportion is over one-half.[62] Some of the world's largest family-owned or controlled firms are Wal-Mart, Ford Motor, Samsung, LG Group, Carrefour Group, Fiat Group, IFI, PSA Peugeot Citroen, Cargill, and BMW.[63] Interestingly, the 177 family companies in the 2003 *S&P 500* financially outperformed non-family companies over the previous 10 year period.[64]

Even though the founders of the companies are the primary forces in starting the entrepreneurial ventures, their needs for business support and financial assistance cause them to turn to family members, who can be trusted, over unknown outsiders of questionable integrity who may demand more salary than the enterprise can afford. Sooner or later, the founder's spouse and children are drafted into business operations either because the family standard of living is directly tied to the business or the entrepreneur desperately needs help just to staff the operation. The children are guaranteed summer jobs, and the business changes from dad's or mom's company to "our" company. The family members are extremely valuable assets to the entrepreneur because they are often also willing to put in long hours at low pay to help the business succeed. Even though the spouse and children might have no official stock in the company, they know that they will somehow share in its future and perhaps even inherit the business. The problem is that only 30% of family firms survive to the second generation, and just 15% survive to the third generation.[65] A common saying among European family businesses is: "The first generation creates, the second inherits, and the third destroys."[66] This saying is supported by research indicating that firm performance declines when descendents take over management of a firm.[67]

TABLE 13–4

TRANSFER OF POWER IN A FAMILY BUSINESS

Phase 1	**Owner-Managed Business:** Phase 1 begins at startup and continues until the entrance of another family member into the business on a full-time basis. Family considerations influence but are not yet a directing part of the firm. At this point, the founder (entrepreneur) and the business are one.
Phase 2	**Training and Development of New Generation:** The children begin to learn the business at the dining room table during early childhood and then through part-time and vacation employment. The family and the business become one. Just as the entrepreneur identified with the business earlier, the family now begins to identify itself with the business.
Phase 3	**Partnership Between Generations:** At this point, a son or daughter of the founder has acquired sufficient business and managerial competence so that he or she can be involved in key decisions for at least a part of the company. The entrepreneur's offspring, however, has to first gain respect from the firm's employees and other managers and show that he or she can do the job right. Another issue is the lack of willingness of the founder to share authority with the son or daughter. Consequently, a common tactic taken by sons and daughters in family businesses is to take a job in a large, established corporation where they can gain valuable experience and respect for their skills.
Phase 4	**Transfer of Power:** Instead of being forced to sell the company when he or she can no longer manage the business, the founder has the option in a family business of turning it over to the next generation as part of their inheritance. Often the founder moves to the position of Chairman of the Board and promotes one of the children to the position of CEO. Unfortunately, some founders cannot resist meddling in operating affairs and unintentionally undermine the leadership position of the son or daughter. To avoid this problem, the founder should sell his or her stock (probably through a leveraged buyout to the children) and physically leave the company and allow the next generation the freedom it needs to adapt to changing conditions.

Source: N. C. Churchill and K. J. Hatten, "Non-Market-Based Transfer of Wealth and Power: A Research Framework for Family Businesses," *American Journal of Small Business* (Winter 1987), pp. 51–64. Reprinted from *Entrepreneurship Theory & Practice* by permission of Baylor University. All rights reserved.

Churchill and Hatten propose that family businesses go through four sequential phases from the time in which the venture is strictly managed by the founder to the time in which the next generation takes charge.[68] These phases are detailed in **Table 13–4**. Each of these phases must be well managed if the company is to survive past the third generation. Some of the reasons family businesses may fail to successfully transfer ownership to the next generation are (1) inherited wealth destroys entrepreneurial drive, (2) the entrepreneur doesn't allow for a changing firm, (3) emphasis on business means the family is neglected, (4) the business' financial growth can't keep up with rising family lifestyles, (5) family members are not prepared to run a business, and (6) the business becomes an arena for family conflicts.[69] In addition, succession planning may be ignored because of the founder's or family's refusal to think about the founder's death, the founder's unwillingness to let go of the firm, the fear of sibling rivalry, or intergenerational envy.

According to Joe Astachan of the Cox Family Enterprise Center at Kennesaw State University, families whose businesses survive over time tend to operate on a set of agreed principles that pass from one generation to another. These include the creation of an active board of directors, a process of strategic planning that allows everyone to debate and agree upon the company's direction, and two to four family meetings a year. The surviving businesses tend to have strong boards that usually include a significant proportion of outsiders.[70]

.6 | **Issues in Evaluation and Control**

As a means by which a corporation's implementation of strategy can be evaluated, the control systems of large corporations have evolved over a long period of time in response to pressures from the environment (particularly the government). Conversely, an entrepreneur creates what is needed as the business grows. Because of his or her personal involvement in decision making, the entrepreneur managing a small business has little need for a formal, detailed reporting system. Thus a founder who has little understanding of accounting and a shortage of cash might employ a bookkeeper instead of an accountant. A formal personnel function might never appear because the entrepreneur lumps it in with simple bookkeeping and uses a secretary to handle personnel files. As an entrepreneurial venture becomes more established, it develops more complex evaluation and control systems, but they are often not the kind used in large corporations and are probably used for different purposes.

Financial statements, in particular, tell only half the story in small, privately owned companies. The formality of the financial reporting system in such a company is usually a result of pressures from government tax agencies, not from management's desire for an objective evaluation and control system. For example, the absence of taxes in Bermuda has been given as the reason why business owners keep little documentation—thus finding it nearly impossible to keep track of inventory, monitor sales, or calculate how much they are owed.[71]

Because balance sheets and income statements do not always give an accurate picture, standard ratios such as return on assets and debt–equity are unreliable. Research reveals systematic differences among liquidity and solvency measures for small compared to large companies. The mean averages of both the current ratio and the debt ratio are systematically larger for the small companies.[72] Cash flow is widely regarded as more important for an entrepreneurial business than is the traditional balance sheet or income statement. Even though a small business may be profitable in the accounting sense, a negative cash flow could bankrupt the company. Levin and Travis provide five reasons why owners, operators, and outside observers should be wary of using standard financial methods to indicate the health of a small, privately owned company[73]:

- **The line between debt and equity is blurred:** In some instances, what appears as a loan is really an easy-to-retrieve equity investment. The entrepreneur in this instance doesn't want to lose his or her investment if the company fails. Another condition is that retained earnings seldom reflect the amount of internal financing needed for the company's growth. This account may merely be a place in which cash is left so that the owner can avoid double taxation. To avoid other taxes, owner–managers may own fixed assets that they lease to the corporation. The equity that was used to buy those assets is really the company's equity, but it doesn't appear on the books.

- **Lifestyle is a part of financial statements:** The lifestyle of the owner and the owner's family is often reflected in the balance sheet. The assets of some firms include beach cottages, mountain chalets, and automobiles. In others, plants and warehouses that are used for company operations are not shown because they are held separately by the family. Income statements may not reflect how well the company is operating. Profitability is not as important in decision making in small, private companies as it is in large, publicly held corporations. For example, spending for recreation or transportation and paying rents or salaries above market rates to relatives put artificially high costs on the books of small firms. The business might appear to be poorly managed to an outsider, but the owner is acting rationally. The owner–manager wants dependable income or its equivalent with the least painful tax consequences. Because the standard profitability measures such as ROI are not useful in the evaluation of such a firm, Levin and Travis recommend return on current assets as a better measure of corporate productivity.

- **Standard financial formulas don't always apply:** Following practices that are in contrast to standard financial recommendations, small companies often use short-term debt to finance fixed assets. The absence of well-organized capital markets for small businesses, along with the typical banker's resistance to making loans without personal guarantees, leaves the private owner little choice. Although a large amount of long-term debt is considered to be a good use of financial leverage by a large publicly held firm, it can drive a smaller firm into bankruptcy by raising its break-even point.

- **Personal preference determines financial policies:** Because the owner is often the manager of the small firm, dividend policy is largely irrelevant. Dividend decisions are based not on stock price (which is usually unknown because the stock is not traded) but on the owner's lifestyle and the tradeoff between taking wealth from the corporation and double taxation.

- **Banks combine personal and business wealth:** Because of the large percentage of small businesses that go bankrupt every year, bank loan officers are reluctant to lend money to a small business unless the owner also provides some personal guarantees for the loan. In some instances, part of the loan may be composed of a second mortgage on the owner's house. If the owner does not want to succumb to this pressure by lenders to include the owner's personal assets as part of the collateral, the owner–manager must be willing to pay high interest rates for a loan that does not put the family's assets at risk.

13.7 | Conclusion

Why is it that some entrepreneurial ventures are successful almost immediately and others fail to even reach breakeven? For some, it may be just "dumb luck" or serendipity. For others, it may be a matter of thinking through the idea before taking action. The underlying reason for new venture failure appears to be an overall lack of strategic management—beginning with an inability to plan a strategy to reach the customer and ending with a failure to develop a system of controls to keep track of performance. Many people new to entrepreneurship naively think that all that is needed to start a business is a good idea. Wrong!

An idea is *not* the same as an opportunity. An idea is a concept for a product or service that doesn't exist or is not currently available in a market niche. It may be a brand-new concept or an improvement of a current product or service. The idea can be developed from a person's experience or generated in a moment of creative insight. In contrast, an opportunity is an idea for a new product or service with a market that is willing to pay for that product or service so that it can form the basis of a profitable business.

Research indicates that writing a business plan (an entrepreneur's version of a strategic plan) improves the chances for success. A business plan is the test to see whether an idea is really an opportunity. Research also suggests that differentiation and focus are the competitive strategies that are most likely to lead to success, at least in the startup stage of development. Beyond these suggestions, it is up to the entrepreneur to find the right opportunity that fits the environment and his or her strengths and weaknesses.

One reason a new venture may not get immediate results with a new product or service is because not enough people are willing to try a new product until a sufficient number of others do so. They may be waiting for the tipping point. In epidemiology, the tipping point in an epidemic is the point at which there are enough carriers of a disease to allow an explosion that will infect a large number of people. Malcolm Gladwell proposes that a **tipping point** is also the point in which a situation that may have seemed stable or only very slowly changing suddenly goes through a massive, rapid shift. "It's the boiling point. It's the moment when the line starts to shoot straight upwards," explains Gladwell.[74] Until a product reaches the tipping point, sales may be very slow to develop and usually only to the few people who like to experiment with innovative products or services. The key is to be patient and to cultivate those customers who may influence the larger market that prefers to wait until a new product is perfected or accepted as the standard.[75] This is what happened to the company Research In Motion when it introduced its wireless e-mail gadget, called Blackberry, in 1999. The company hired "evangelists" to lend the devices to executives on Wall Street. Four years later, Blackberry arrived on Oprah Winfrey's "favorite things of 2003" and became an industry wireless standard.[76]

Strategy Bits

- Nations scoring highest on an innovation index measuring human resource skills, market incentive structures, and interaction between business and scientific sectors are the United States, Taiwan, Finland, Sweden, Japan, Israel, Switzerland, Canada, Australia, and Germany.[77]

- Regions in the United States scoring highest on a creativity index measuring technology, talent, and tolerance are Austin (TX), San Francisco (CA), Seattle (WA), Burlington (VT), Boston (MA), Raleigh-Durham-Chapel Hill (NC), Portland (OR), Madison (WI), Boise (ID), and Minneapolis (MN).[78]

Discussion Questions

1. In terms of strategic management, how does a new venture's situation differ from that of an ongoing small company?

2. How should a small entrepreneurial company engage in environmental scanning? To what aspects of the environment should management pay most attention?

3. What are the characteristics of an attractive industry from an entrepreneur's point of view? What role does innovation play?

4. What considerations should small-business entrepreneurs keep in mind when they are deciding whether a company should follow a growth or a stability strategy?

5. How does being family owned (as compared to being publicly owned) affect a firm's strategic management?

Strategic Practice Exercise

Read STRATEGY HIGHLIGHT 13.1, "Suggestions for Locating an Opportunity and Formulating a Business Strategy." Your strategy instructor may form multiple groups of five people each in your strategy class. Each group may be assigned one of the four approaches to identifying some ideas that could be opportunities for an entrepreneurial venture:

1. Tap the countertrend.

2. Eat off the established company's plate.

3. Switch the niche.

4. Borrow a business model.

When your group meets, discuss your assigned approach and identify one or more ideas that could be opportunities.

Remember that an idea is a concept for a product or service that doesn't exist or is not currently available in a market niche. An opportunity is an idea for a new product or service with a market that is willing to pay for that product or service so that it can form the basis of a profitable business. This means that the idea has to have the potential to be profitable. Bring your ideas to class and see what your instructor and others in the class think of your ideas. Once all the ideas have been presented, take a vote on which of the ideas have the most likelihood of being opportunities.

(If this concept is not used as a class exercise, you may choose to meet informally with several members of your class over coffee. See if you can come up with an idea for each of the four approaches. Are any of them opportunities?)

Key Terms

advisory board (p. 324)

business plan (p. 322)

entrepreneur (p. 319)

entrepreneurial characteristic (p. 328)

entrepreneurial venture (p. 318)

factor affecting new venture success (p. 327)

family business (p. 332)

idea (p. 321)

lifestyle company (p. 331)

opportunity (p. 321)

small-business firm (p. 318)

source of innovation (p. 326)

strategic decision-making process for entrepreneurial venture (p. 321)

substage of small business development (p. 330)

tipping point (p. 335)

CHAPTER 14
Strategic Issues in Not-for-Profit Organizations

Learning Objectives

After reading this chapter, you should be able to:

- Identify the types of not-for-profit organizations
- Explain how sources of revenue influence not-for-profit strategic decision making
- Compare and contrast the strategic management of profit-making with not-for-profit organizations
- Discuss popular strategies being used by not-for-profit organizations

EIGHT TIMES A DAY, THE REVEREND BERNARD MCCOY SOLEMNLY CHANTS PRAYER IN Latin in the monastery chapel. He then goes back to his computer and telephone to manage LaserMonks. McCoy and four other monks at The Cistercian Abbey of Our Lady of Spring Bank in Sparta, Wisconsin, sell refilled inkjet and laser printer cartridges from their Internet site and telephone mail order center. LaserMonks offers the refills at prices 30% to 90% lower than offered at retail stores. Says McCoy, "You get quality products at great savings. We do good work with the extra income. Plus, the monks pray for you. I don't think Staples ever offered to do that."

Sales increased from $2,000 during their first year of business in 2002 to $500,000 in 2003, with a profit of $30,000. After expenses are paid for the business and the monastery, the money pays for everything from a defibrillator for the local fire department to providing free computer training for orphans in Vietnam. Worried about the monastery's not-for-profit status, LaserMonks was established as a profit-making corporation owned by the abbey. According to McCoy, "through charitable, legal means, we channel money to the abbey, which is how we don't jeopardize our tax-exempt status. . . . We pay business taxes like everybody else." Responding to the concern that a monastery should not be involved in business activities, McCoy states, "We're not selling God; we're selling black dust and ink so we can give our profits away to good causes. But you do have to walk a fine line in your marketing and not be offensive to God, yourself, or any other groups that have various relations to divine things."[1]

LaserMonks is an example of *strategic piggybacking*, a not-for-profit strategy that is as old as Girl Scout cookies and museum gift shops. Today's not-for-profits are using profit-making ventures as a way to diversify their revenue streams in tight financial times.[2] Piggybacking is a way for not-for-profits to earn money in a secondary business activity to support their primary mission, which may be raising orphans or providing a free educational experience.

By the mid-1990s, most not-for-profit organizations were turning to strategic management and other concepts from business to ensure their survival. According to Cynthia Massarsky, Deputy Director of the Yale School of Management—The Goldman Sachs Foundation Partnership on Nonprofit Ventures, "Nonprofits are looking to be more efficient in the way they do things. By taking a few lessons from the business world, perhaps they've learned how to operate a little more efficiently."[3] This is a significant change from past attitudes because most not-for-profit managers have traditionally felt that business concepts were not relevant to their situation. According to Peter Drucker:

> Twenty years ago, management was a dirty word for those involved in nonprofit organizations. It meant business, and nonprofits prided themselves on being free of the taint of commercialism and above such sordid considerations as the bottom line. Now most of them have learned that nonprofits need management even more than business does, precisely because they lack the discipline of the bottom line.[4]

A knowledge of not-for-profit organizations is important if only because they account for an average of 1 in every 20 jobs in nations throughout the world. A study by the Johns Hopkins University Institute for Policy Studies found that in nine countries between 1990 and 1995, nonprofit jobs grew by 23% compared to 6.2% for the whole economy.[5] Not-for-profits employ over 25% of the U.S. workforce and own approximately 15% of the nation's private wealth.[6] In the United States alone, in addition to various federal, state, and local government agencies, there are about 10,000 not-for-profit hospitals and nursing homes (84% of all hospitals), 4,600 colleges and universities, more than 100,000 private and public elementary and secondary schools, and almost 350,000 churches and synagogues, plus many thousands of charities and service organizations.[7]

Typically, **not-for-profit organizations (NFP)** include **private nonprofit corporations** (such as hospitals, institutes, private colleges, and organized charities) as well as **public governmental units or agencies** (such as welfare departments, prisons, and state universities). Traditionally, studies in strategic management have dealt with profit-making firms to the exclusion of nonprofit or governmental organizations. This, however, is changing. Increasing numbers of not-for-profit organizations are adopting strategic management.

Scholars and practitioners are concluding that many strategic management concepts and techniques can be successfully adapted for not-for-profit organizations.[8] Although the evidence is not yet conclusive, there appears to be an association between strategic planning efforts and performance measures such as growth.[9] The purpose of this chapter is, therefore, to highlight briefly the major differences between profit-making and not-for-profit organizations, so that the effects of their differences on the strategic management process can be understood.

14.1 | Why Not-for-Profit?

The not-for-profit sector of an economy is important for several reasons. First, society desires certain goods and services that profit-making firms cannot or will not provide. These are referred to as **public or collective goods** because people who might not have paid for the goods receive benefits from them. Paved roads, police protection, museums, and schools are examples of public goods. A person cannot use a private good unless he or she pays for it. Generally, once a public good is provided, however, anyone can use or enjoy it.

Certain aspects of life do not appear to be served appropriately by profit-making business firms yet are often crucial to the well-being of society. These aspects include areas in which society as a whole benefits from a particular service but in which a particular individual benefits only indirectly. It is in these areas that not-for-profit organizations have traditionally been most effective. Libraries and museums are examples. Although most people do not visit libraries or museums very often, they are usually willing to pay taxes and/or donate funds to support their existence. They do so because they believe that these organizations act to uplift the culture and quality of life of the region. To fulfill their mission, entrance fees (if any) must be set low enough to allow everyone admission. These fees, however, are not profitable—they rarely even cover the costs of the service. The same is true of animal shelters managed by the Humane Society. Although few people want abandoned pets running wild through city streets, fees charged for the adoption of these animals cannot alone pay the costs of finding and caring for them. Additional revenue is needed—in the form of either donations or public taxation. Such public or collective services cannot generate a profit, yet they are necessary for any successful civilization. Which aspects of society are most suited to being served by not-for-profit organizations rather than by profit-making business organizations? This is an issue that governments face when they privatize what has previously been provided by the state. See the GLOBAL ISSUE feature to learn more about this development.

A second reason why the not-for-profit sector is important is that a private nonprofit organization tends to receive benefits from society that a private profit-making firm cannot obtain. Preferred tax status to nonstock corporations is given in section 501(c)(3) of the U.S. Internal Revenue Service code in the form of exemptions from corporate income taxes. Private non-

GL🌐BAL ISSUE

Which Is Best for Society: Business or Not-For-Profit?

Many nations throughout the world are attempting to privatize state-owned enterprises to balance their budgets. **Privatization** is (1) the selling of state-owned enterprises to private individuals or corporations or (2) the hiring of a private business to provide services previously offered by a state agency. The British government, for example, sold British Airways, its state-owned airline, to private investors. In the United States, many city governments now allow private companies to collect and dispose of trash—something that had previously been done by the city.

Problems can result, however, if privatization goes too far. For example, in converting from a communist-oriented, centrally managed economy to a more democratic, free-market economy, Eastern European countries are finding that profit-making business firms are unable to satisfy all of society's needs. What used to be provided by the state free of charge (but tax-supported) in Russia and other countries may now be provided only for the rich or not at all. The same problem is evident in the United States in the controversies over the provision of health care, retirement benefits, and private versus public education.

Some of the aspects of life that cannot easily be privatized and are often better managed by not-for-profit organizations are as follows:

- Religion
- Education
- Charities
- Clubs, interest groups, and unions
- Health care
- Government

The privatization of state-owned business enterprises is likely to continue globally because most of these enterprises must expand internationally in order to survive in the increasingly global environment. They cannot compete successfully if they are forced to follow inefficient, socially oriented policies and regulations (emphasizing employment over efficiency) rather than economically oriented, international practices (emphasizing efficiency over employment). The global trend toward privatization will probably continue until each country reaches the point where the efficiency of business is counterbalanced by the effectiveness of the not-for-profit sector of the economy. As political motives overcome economic ones, government will likely intervene in that decision.

profit firms also enjoy exemptions from various other state, local, and federal taxes. Under certain conditions, these firms also benefit from the tax deductibility of donors' contributions and membership dues. In addition, they qualify for special reduced-cost mailing privileges.[10] These benefits are allowed because private nonprofit organizations are typically service organizations, which are expected to use any excess of revenue over costs and expenses (a surplus rather than a profit) either to improve service or to reduce the price of their service. This service orientation is reflected in the fact that not-for-profit organizations do not use the term *customer* to refer to the recipient of the service. The recipient is typically referred to as a *patient, student, client, case*, or simply *the public*.

14.2 | Importance of Revenue Source

The feature that best differentiates not-for-profit organizations from each other as well as from profit-making corporations is their source of revenue.[11] A **profit-making firm** depends on revenues obtained from the sale of its goods and services to customers, who typically pay for the costs and expenses of providing the product or service plus a profit. A not-for-profit organization, in contrast, depends heavily on dues, assessments, or donations from its membership, or on funding from a sponsoring agency, such as the United Way or the federal government, to pay for much of its costs and expenses.

Sources of Not-for-Profit Revenue

Revenue is generated from a variety of sources—not just from clients receiving the product or service from the not-for-profit. It can come from people who do not even receive the services they are subsidizing. One study of Minnesota nonprofits found that donations accounted for almost 40%, government grants for around 25%, and program service fees for about 35% of total revenues.[12] In other types of not-for-profit organizations—such as unions and voluntary medical plans—revenue comes mostly from the members, the people who receive the service. Nevertheless, the members typically pay dues in advance and must accept later whatever service is provided, whether they choose it or not and whether it is what they expected or not. The service is often received long after the dues are paid.

In profit-making corporations, there is typically a simple and direct connection between the customer or client and the organization. The organization tends to be totally dependent on sales of its products or services to the customer for revenue and is therefore extremely interested in pleasing the customer. As shown in **Figure 14–1**, a profit-making organization (organization A) tries to influence the customer (through advertising and promotion) to continue to buy and use its services. Either by buying or not buying the item offered, the customer, in turn, directly influences the organization's decision-making process. The business is thus market-oriented.

In the case of a typical not-for-profit organization, however, there is likely to be a very different sort of relationship between the organization providing and the person receiving the

Figure 14–1
The Effects of Sources of Revenue on Patterns of Client–Organization Influence

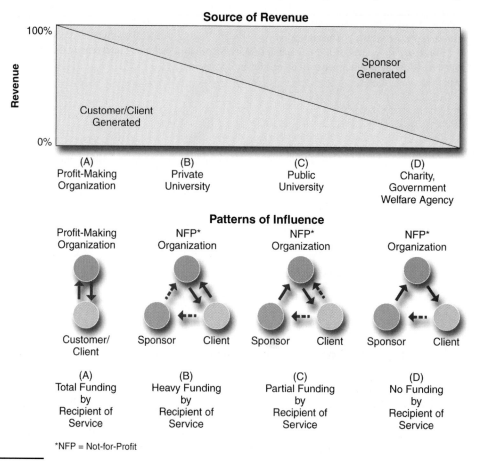

Source: Thomas L. Wheelen and J. David Hunger, "The Effect of Revenue Upon Patterns of Client–Organization Influence." Copyright © 1982 by Wheelen and Hunger Associates. Revised 1991. Reprinted by permission.

service. Because the recipient of the service typically does not pay the entire cost of the service, outside sponsors are required. In most instances, the sponsors receive none of the service but provide partial to total funding for the needed revenues. As indicated earlier, these sponsors can be the government (using taxpayers' money) or charitable organizations, such as the United Way (using voluntary donations). As shown in **Figure 14–1**, a not-for-profit organization can be partially dependent on sponsors for funding (*organizations B and C*) or totally dependent on the sponsors (*organization D*). The less money it receives from clients receiving the service or product, the less market-oriented is a not-for-profit organization.

Patterns of Influence on Strategic Decision Making

The **pattern of influence** on an organization's strategic decision making derives from its sources of revenue.[13] As shown in **Figure 14–1**, a private university (organization B) is heavily dependent on student tuition and other client-generated funds for about 70% of its revenue. Therefore, the students' desires are likely to have a stronger influence (as shown by an unbroken line) on the university's decision making than are the desires of the various sponsors such as alumni and private foundations. The sponsors' relatively marginal influence on the organization is reflected by a broken line. In contrast, a public university (organization C) is more heavily dependent on outside sponsors such as a state legislature for revenue funding. Student tuition and other client-generated funds form a small percentage (often less than 40%) of total revenue. Therefore, the university's decision making is heavily influenced by the sponsors (unbroken line) and only marginally influenced directly by the students (broken line).

In the case of organization D, however, the client has no direct influence on the organization because the client pays nothing for the services received. In this situation, the organization tends to measure its effectiveness in terms of sponsor satisfaction. It has no real measure of its efficiency other than its ability to carry out its mission and achieve its objectives within the dollar contributions it has received from its sponsors. In contrast to other organizations in which the client contributes a significant proportion of the needed revenue, organization D actually might be able to increase its revenue by heavily lobbying its sponsors while reducing the level of its service to its clients!

Regardless of the percentage of total funding that a client generates, the client may attempt to indirectly influence a not-for-profit organization through the sponsors. This is depicted by the broken lines connecting the client and the sponsor in organizations B, C, and D in **Figure 14–1**. Welfare clients or prison inmates, for example, may be able to indirectly improve the services they receive if they pressure government officials by writing to legislators or even by rioting. Students at public universities can lobby state officials for student representation on governing boards.

The key to understanding the management of a not-for-profit organization is thus learning who pays for the delivered services. If the recipients of the service pay only a small proportion of the total cost of the service, strategic managers are likely to be more concerned with satisfying the needs and desires of the funding sponsors or agency than those of the people receiving the service. The acquisition of resources can become an end in itself.

Usefulness of Strategic Management Concepts and Techniques

Some strategic management concepts can be equally applied to business and not-for-profit organizations, whereas others cannot. The marketplace orientation underlying portfolio analysis, for example, does not translate into situations in which client satisfaction and revenue are only indirectly linked. Industry analysis and competitive strategy are primarily relevant to not-for-profits that obtain most of their revenue from user fees rather than from donors or taxpayers. For example, as hospitals find themselves relying increasingly on patient fees for their revenue, they use competitive strategy to gain advantage versus other hospitals. Smaller not-for-profit hospitals stress the "high touch" of their staff over the "high tech" of competitors that have better diagnostic machinery. The concept of competitive advantage is less useful to a typical not-for-profit than the related concept of institutional advantage, which sets aside the profit-making objective of competitive advantage. A not-for-profit can be said to have **institutional advantage** when it performs its tasks more effectively than other comparable organizations.[14]

SWOT analysis, mission statements, stakeholder analysis, and corporate governance are, however, just as relevant to a not-for-profit as they are to a profit-making organization.[15] Portfolio analysis can be very helpful but is used very differently in not-for-profits than in business firms. (See the section on strategic piggybacking later in the chapter.) As with any corporation, nonprofits usually have boards of directors whose job is to ensure that the paid executive director and staff work to fulfill the organization's mission and objectives. Unlike the boards of most business firms, nonprofit boards are often required, however, to take primary responsibility for strategic planning and fund-raising. Many nonprofits find that a well-crafted mission statement not only helps in finding donors but also in attracting volunteers. Take the example of the mission statement of a local animal shelter:

> To shelter and care for stray, lost, or abandoned animals and to responsibly place animals in new homes and enforce animal laws. We are also here to better educate people in ways to be solutions to animal problems, not causes.[16]

Strategic management is difficult to apply when an organization's output is difficult to measure objectively, as is the case with most not-for-profit organizations. Thus it is very likely that many not-for-profit organizations have not used strategic management because its concepts, techniques, and prescriptions do not lend themselves to situations where sponsors, rather than the marketplace, determine revenue. The situation, however, is changing. The trend toward privatizing public organizations, such as converting subsidized community hospitals to independent (nonsubsidized) status, usually means that the clients/patients pay a larger percentage of the costs. As these not-for-profits become more market oriented (and thus client oriented), strategic management becomes more applicable and more increasingly used.[17] Nevertheless, various constraints on not-for-profits mean that strategic management concepts and techniques must be modified to be effective.

14.3 | **Impact of Constraints on Strategic Management**

Several characteristics peculiar to a not-for-profit organization constrain its behavior and affect its strategic management. Newman and Wallender list the following five **constraints on strategic management**:

1. **Service is often intangible and hard to measure.** This difficulty is typically compounded by the existence of multiple service objectives developed to satisfy multiple sponsors.
2. **Client influence may be weak.** Often the organization has a local monopoly, and clients' payments may be a very small source of funds.
3. **Strong employee commitments to professions or to a cause may undermine allegiance** to the organization employing them.
4. **Resource contributors may intrude on the organization's internal management.** Such contributors include fund contributors and government.
5. **Restraints on the use of rewards and punishments** may result from constraints 1, 3, and 4.[18]

It is true that several of these characteristics can be found in profit-making as well as in not-for-profit organizations. Nevertheless, as Newman and Wallender state, the "frequency of strong impact is much higher in not-for-profit enterprises."[19]

Impact on Strategy Formulation

The long-range planning and decision making affected by the listed constraints serve to add at least four **complications to strategy formulation**:

1. **Goal conflicts interfere with rational planning:** Because a not-for-profit organization typically lacks a single clear-cut performance criterion (such as profits), divergent goals and objectives are likely, especially with multiple sponsors. Differences in the concerns of various important sponsors can prevent management from stating the organization's mission in anything but very broad terms, if they fear that a sponsor who disagrees with a particular, narrow definition of mission might cancel its funding. For example, a study of 227 public Canadian hospitals found that more than half had very general, ambiguous, and unquantified objectives.[20] According to Heffron, an authority in public administration, "The greater openness within which they are compelled to operate—the fishbowl atmosphere—impedes thorough discussion of issues and discourages long-range plans that might alienate stakeholders."[21] In such organizations, it is the reduced influence of the clients that permits this diversity of values and goals to occur without a clear market check. For example, when a city council considers changing zoning to implement a strategic plan for the city, all sorts of people (including the press) will demand to be heard. A decision might be made based on pressure from a few stakeholders (who make significant contributions or who threaten to stir up trouble) to the detriment of the community as a whole.

2. **An integrated planning focus tends to shift from results to resources:** Because not-for-profit organizations tend to provide services that are hard to measure, they rarely have a net bottom line.[22] Planning, therefore, becomes more concerned with resource inputs, which can easily be measured, than with service, which cannot. Goal displacement (explained in **Chapter 11**) becomes even more likely than it is in business organizations.[23]

3. **Ambiguous operating objectives create opportunities for internal politics and goal displacement:** The combination of vague objectives and a heavy concern with resources allows managers considerable leeway in their activities. Such leeway makes possible political maneuvering for personal ends. In addition, because the effectiveness of a not-for-profit organization hinges on the satisfaction of the sponsoring group, management tends to ignore the needs of the client while focusing on the desires of a powerful sponsor. University administrators commonly say that people will donate money for a new building (which will carry the donor's name) but not for other more pressing needs, such as the maintenance of existing buildings. In this situation, powerful department heads might wine and dine the donor, hoping to get the money for their pet projects. This problem is compounded by the common practice of selecting people to boards of trustees/directors not on the basis of their managerial experience but on the basis of their ability to contribute money, raise funds, and work with politicians. (A major role of a not-for-profit board is to ensure adequate resources—usually translated to mean fund-raising.[24]) Directors usually receive no compensation for serving on the board. Their lack of interest in overseeing management is reflected in an overall not-for-profit board-meeting attendance rate of only 50%, compared with 90% for boards of directors of business corporations. This is one reason why boards of not-for-profits tend to be larger than are boards of business corporations. Eckerd College, for example, has a 52-member, extremely passive board of directors.[25] Board members of not-for-profit organizations tend to ignore the task of determining strategies and policies—often leaving that to the paid (or sometimes unpaid)

executive director. The larger the board, the less likely it is to exercise control over top management.[26]

4. **Professionalization simplifies detailed planning but adds rigidity:** In not-for-profit organizations in which professionals play important roles (as in hospitals or colleges), professional values and traditions can prevent the organization from changing its conventional behavior patterns to fit new service missions tuned to changing social needs. This rigidity, of course, can occur in any organization that hires professionals. The strong service orientation of most not-for-profit organizations, however, tends to encourage the development of static professional norms and attitudes. As not-for-profits attempt to become more business-like, this may be changing. One study of Minnesota nonprofits revealed that 29% of the program directors and 15% of the staff had degrees or experience in business administration.[27]

Impact on Strategy Implementation

The five constraining characteristics also affect how a not-for-profit organization is organized in both its structure and job design. Three **complications to strategy implementation** in particular can be highlighted:

1. **Decentralization is complicated:** The difficulty of setting objectives for an intangible, hard-to-measure service mission complicates the delegation of decision-making authority. Because of the heavy dependence on sponsors for revenue support, the top management of a not-for-profit organization must be always alert to the sponsors' view of an organizational activity. This necessary caution leads to **defensive centralization**, in which top management retains all decision-making authority so that low-level managers cannot take any actions to which the sponsors may object.

2. **Linking pins for external–internal integration become important:** Because of the heavy dependence on outside sponsors, a special need arises for people in buffer roles to relate to both inside and outside groups. This role is especially necessary when the sponsors are diverse (revenue comes from donations, membership fees, and federal funds) and the service is intangible (for instance, a "good" education) with a broad mission and multiple shifting objectives. The job of a *Dean for External Affairs*, for example, consists primarily of working with the school's alumnae and raising funds.

3. **Job enlargement and executive development can be restrained by professionalism:** In organizations that employ a large number of professionals, managers must design jobs that appeal to prevailing professional norms. Professionals have rather clear ideas about which activities are, and which are not, within their province. Enriching a nurse's job by expanding his or her decision-making authority for drug dosage, for example, can cause conflict with medical doctors who believe that such authority is theirs alone. Because a professional often views managerial jobs as nonprofessional and merely supportive, promotion into a management position is not always viewed positively.

Impact on Evaluation and Control

Special **complications to evaluation and control** arising from the constraining characteristics also affect how behavior is motivated and performance is controlled. Two problems, in particular, are often noticed:

1. **Rewards and penalties have little or no relationship to performance:** When desired results are vague and the judgment of success is subjective, predictable and impersonal feedback cannot be established. Performance is judged either intuitively ("You don't

seem to be taking your job seriously") or on the basis of whatever small aspects of a job can be measured ("You were late to work twice last month").

2. **Inputs rather than outputs are heavily controlled:** Because its inputs can be measured much more easily than outputs, a not-for-profit organization tends to focus more on the resources going into performance than on the performance itself.[28] The emphasis is thus on setting maximum limits for costs and expenses. Because there is little to no reward for staying under these limits, people usually respond negatively to such controls.

Because of these and other complications, not-for-profits can waste money in many ways, especially on administrative costs and expenses. Because of this, it is becoming increasingly common to calculate ratios comparing total support and revenue with the amounts spent on specific service activities. For example, analysts become concerned when the total spent on the mission of the organization (e.g., community service) is less than 50% of total income received from sponsors and activities. Other rules of thumb are that a not-for-profit should not spend more than 35% on administrative expenses and that the costs of fund-raising should not account for more than 15% of total income.[29]

14.4 | Not-for-Profit Strategies

One of the issues in the strategic management of not-for-profit organizations is the tendency of nonprofits to make program decisions based on a mission rather than on a strategy. Kasturi Rangan points out that many nonprofits don't have a strategy at all; instead, they rally under a particular cause, such as "Fight homelessness" or "Save the children."[30] Because that cause is so worthwhile, nonprofits tend to support any program that's even slightly related to the mission, so long as there is money available (at least in the beginning) to support the new program. Without a clear long-term strategy, this will eventually stretch the not-for-profit's core capabilities into unintended directions and create a budget with more expenses than revenues. The need to attract additional donors forces not-for-profits to go after grants or donations that fit within their broadly defined mission but only slightly fit their existing capabilities. The problem is that such a grant usually contains restrictions that the funding be spent on a particular program or initiative. Starved for money, not-for-profits accept these restrictions in order to obtain the funding. Because the funds barely cover the direct costs of the additional activity, unanticipated indirect costs force the not-for-profit to look for more funding, each time as a larger, less focused, and more cash-starved organization. The result is an organization with large bureaucratic overhead but not enough professionals to carry out all its programs effectively. This leads to increasing pressure to reduce costs and to use more volunteers—both of which may reduce the quality of service to clients. Professional employees become demoralized because of increasing service demands, less support, and marginal pay raises.

The organization's executive director is usually too busy administering a convoluted bureaucracy, dealing with bickering professional employees, and fund-raising to do any serious strategic planning. It is therefore usually left to the board of directors to call a stop to this *activity trap*. The board must define achievable objectives and propose a strategy to make them happen. It must decide not only what the organization will do but also what it will not do. Given that the primary mission is sacrosanct, the board should develop a narrow operational mission with measurable objectives and a strategy to go with them.[31] Once this is done, the organization is free to decide which programs to support and which to curtail.

If a not-for-profit organization has established an operational mission and measurable service objectives, it can consider various ways to support its priority programs without having to accept mission-extending donor requirements. Increasingly, not-for-profits are choosing the strategies of strategic piggybacking, mergers, and strategic alliances.

Strategic Piggybacking

Coined by Nielsen, the term **strategic piggybacking** refers to the development of a new activity for a not-for-profit organization that would generate the funds needed to make up the difference between revenues and expenses.[32] The new activity is typically related in some manner to the not-for-profit's mission, but its purpose is to help subsidize the primary service programs. It appears to be a form of concentric diversification, but it is engaged in not as part of the mission but only for its money-generating value. In an inverted use of portfolio analysis, the organization invests in new, safe cash cows to fund its current cash-hungry question marks and dogs. It is a type of **social entrepreneurship**, in which a not-for-profit organization starts a new venture to achieve social goals.

Although strategic piggybacking is not new, it has recently become very popular. As early as 1874, for example, the Metropolitan Museum of Art retained a professional to photograph its collections and to sell copies of the prints. Profits were used to defray the museum's operating costs. More recently, various income-generating ventures have appeared under various auspices, from the Girl Scouts to UNICEF, and in numerous forms, from cookies and small gift shops to vast real estate developments. A study by the U.S. General Accounting Office revealed that the amount of funds resulting from income-producing activities of not-for-profits has significantly increased since the 1970s. Hospitals are offering wellness programs, ranging from meditation classes to aerobics. Some 70% of colleges and universities now offer "auxiliary" services, such as bookstores, conference rooms, and computer centers, as sources of income.[33] The American Cancer Society earns millions annually by allowing its name to appear on products sold by private drug companies, such as GlaxoSmithKline's Nicorette chewing gum. The Metropolitan Museum of Art now has 16 stores outside the main museum and a fast-growing web site—all of which generate money. The Baptist Hospital of Nashville, Tennessee, built and operates a $15 million, 18-acre office and training-field complex, which it rents to Nashville's professional football team.

The U.S. Small Business Administration, however, views this money-making activity as "unfair competition." The U.S. Internal Revenue Service (IRS) advises that a not-for-profit that engages in a business "not substantially related" to the organization's exempt purposes may jeopardize its tax-exempt status, particularly if the income from the business exceeds approximately 20% of total organizational revenues. The IRS requires not-for-profits to pay an unrelated business income tax on commercial activities that don't relate to the organization's central mission. So far, not-for-profits are still considered tax exempt if their businesses are staffed by volunteers or if almost all their merchandise is donated. According to Marcus Owens, Director of Tax-Exempt Organizations for the IRS, "The ultimate question is should these institutions continue as tax-exempt entities. And it's being raised more than ever before."[34] This has caused many not-for-profits such as The Cistercian Abbey mentioned earlier to establish two separate entities. "Doing all the separate bookkeeping, accounting, and cost allocations can be a bit burdensome, time-consuming and distracting," says Jeffrey Tanenbaum, a lawyer specializing in representing nonprofits.[35]

Although strategic piggybacks can help not-for-profit organizations self-subsidize their primary missions and better use their resources, according to Nielsen, there are several potential drawbacks.[36] First, the revenue-generating venture could actually lose money, especially in the short run. Second, the venture could subvert, interfere with, or even take over the primary mission. Third, the public, as well as the sponsors, could reduce their contributions because of negative responses to such "money-grubbing activities" or because of a mistaken belief that the organization is becoming self-supporting. Fourth, the venture could interfere with the internal operations of the not-for-profit organization. To avoid these drawbacks, a not-for-profit should carefully evaluate its resources before choosing this strategy. See STRATEGY HIGHLIGHT 14.1 to see the resources needed for a piggyback.

STRATEGY HIGHLIGHT 14.1

Resources Needed for Successful Strategic Piggybacking

Based on his experience as a consultant to not-for-profit organizations, Edward Skloot suggests that a not-for-profit should have five resources before engaging in strategic piggybacking:

1. **Something to sell:** The organization should assess its resources to see if people might be willing to pay for goods or services closely related to the organization's primary activity. Repackaging the Boston Symphony into the less formal Boston Pops Orchestra created a way to subsidize the deficit-creating symphony and provide year-round work for the musicians.

2. **Critical mass of management talent:** Enough people must be available to nurture and sustain an income venture over the long haul. This can be very difficult, given that the most competent not-for-profit professionals often don't want to be managers.

3. **Trustee support:** If the trustees have strong feelings against earned-income ventures, they could actively or passively resist commercial involvement. When the Children's Television Workshop began licensing its Sesame Street characters to toy companies and theme parks, many people criticized it for joining business in selling more things to children.

4. **Entrepreneurial attitude:** Management must be able to combine an interest in innovative ideas with business-like practicality.

5. **Venture capital:** Because it often takes money to make money, engaging in a joint venture with a business corporation can provide the necessary startup funds as well as the marketing and management support. For example, Massachusetts General Hospital received $50 million from Hoechst, the German chemical company, for biological research in exchange for exclusive licenses to develop commercial products from particular research discoveries.

Source: Reprinted by permission of the *Harvard Business Review.* From "Should Not-for-Profits Go into Business?" by E. Skloot, January–February 1983. Copyright © 1983 by the Harvard Business School Publishing Corporation; all rights reserved.

The U.S. National Association of College and University Business Officers predicts that within a few years, more than 90% of colleges and universities in the United States will be using strategic piggybacks.[37] A similar trend is expected for other not-for-profits that heavily rely on donations and taxpayer support for their revenue.

Mergers

Dwindling resources are leading an increasing number of not-for-profits to consider mergers as a way of reducing costs through economies of scope and reducing program duplication and raising prices because of increased market power.[38] For example, the merger of Baptist Health Systems and Research Health Services created Health Midwest in Kansas City. The New York Hospital–Cornell Medical Center and Columbia–Presbyterian Medical Center combined to form the New York and Presbyterian Hospitals Health Care System. Since 1990, more than 45% of U.S. hospitals have been involved in mergers and acquisitions.[39]

Strategic Alliances

Strategic alliances involve developing cooperative ties with other organizations. Not-for-profit organizations often use alliances as a way to enhance their capacity to serve clients or to acquire resources while still enabling them to keep their identities.[40] Services can be purchased and provided more efficiently through cooperation with other organizations than if they were done alone. For example, four Ohio universities agreed to create and jointly operate a new school of international business. Alone, none of the business schools could afford the $30 million to build the school. The Collaborative Ventures Program of the Teagle Foundation has given more than $4 million in grants to help colleges set up money-saving collaborations. While only a handful of consortia existed in 1995, by 1998 there were at least 21, representing 125 colleges and universities.[41]

Strategic alliances and mergers are becoming commonplace among not-for-profit organizations. The next logical step is strategic alliances between business firms and not-for-profits. Already, business corporations are forming alliances with universities to fund university research in exchange for options on the results of that research. Business firms find it cheaper to pay universities to do basic research than to do it themselves. Universities are in need of research funds to attract top professors and to maintain expensive labs. Such alliances of convenience are being criticized, but they are likely to continue.

14.5 | Conclusion

Not-for-profit organizations are an important part of society. Understanding their reasons for existence and their differences from profit-making corporations is therefore important. The lack of profit motive often results in vague statements of mission and unmeasurable objectives. Coupled with a concern for maintaining funding from sponsors, these factors can cause a lack of consideration for the very clients the organization was designed to serve. Programs that have little or no connection with the organization's mission may develop. Nevertheless, not-for-profit organizations are usually established to provide goods and services judged valuable by society that profit-making firms cannot or will not provide. Judging their performance simply on the basis of economic considerations is dangerous because they are designed to deal with conditions under which profit-making corporations could not easily survive.

Strategy Bits

- Countries with the highest number of people in prison per 100,000 population are the United States (707), Russia (638), Belarus (554), Kazakhstan (522), Turkmenistan (489), Bermuda (447), Suriname (437), Bahamas (416), Ukraine (416), and South Africa (404).[42]

- Countries with the most hospital beds per 1,000 population are Japan (17.0), Norway (14.0), Russia (13.1), Moldova (12.9), Estonia (12.0), Belarus (11.8), the Netherlands (11.5), Martinique (10.7), Georgia (10.5), and Kirgizstan (10.4).[43]

Discussion Questions

1. Are not-for-profit organizations less efficient than profit-making organizations? Why or why not?

2. How does the lack of a clear-cut performance measure, such as profits, affect the strategic management of a not-for-profit organization?

3. What are the pros and cons of strategic piggybacking? In what way is it "unfair competition" for not-for-profits to engage in revenue generating activity?

4. What are the pros and cons of mergers and strategic alliances? Should not-for-profits engage in alliances with business firms?

5. A number of not-for-profit organizations in the United States have been converting to profit making. Why would a not-for-profit organization want to change its status to profit making? What are the pros and cons of doing so?

Strategic Practice Exercises

1. Read the GLOBAL ISSUE feature in this chapter. It lists six aspects of society that it proposes are better managed by not-for-profit organizations than by profit-making organizations. Do you agree with this list? Should some aspects be deleted from the list? Should other aspects be added?

2. Examine a local college or university—perhaps the one you may be currently attending. What strategic issues is it facing? Develop a SFAS Matrix (see **Figure 6–1**) of strategic factors. Is it attempting to use any strategic management concepts? If so, which ones? What sorts of strategies should it consider for contin-

ued survival and future growth? Is it currently using strategic piggybacks to obtain additional funding? What sorts of additional piggybacks should it consider? Are strategic alliances with another college or university or business firm a possibility?

Key Terms

complication to evaluation and control (p. 346)

complication to strategy formulation (p. 345)

complication to strategy implementation (p. 346)

constraint on strategic management (p. 344)

defensive centralization (p. 346)

institutional advantage (p. 344)

not-for-profit organization (p. 340)

pattern of influence (p. 343)

private nonprofit corporation (p. 340)

privatization (p. 341)

profit-making firm (p. 341)

public governmental unit or agency (p. 340)

public or collective good (p. 340)

social entrepreneurship (p. 348)

strategic piggybacking (p. 348)

CHAPTER 15
Suggestions for Case Analysis

Learning Objectives

After reading this chapter, you should be able to:

- Research the case situation as needed
- Analyze financial statements by using ratios and common-size statements
- Use the strategic audit as a method of organizing and analyzing case information

HOWARD SCHILIT, FOUNDER OF THE CENTER FOR FINANCIAL RESEARCH & ANALYSIS (CFRA), works with a staff of 15 analysts to screen financial databases and analyze public financial filings of 3,600 companies, looking for inconsistencies and aggressive accounting methods. Schilit calls this search for hidden weaknesses in a company's performance *forensic accounting*. "I'm like an investigative reporter," explains Schilit. "I'm interested in finding companies where the conventional wisdom is that they're very healthy, but if you dig a bit deeper, you find the emperor is not wearing the clothes you thought."[1] He advises anyone interested in analyzing a company to look deeply into its financial statements. For example, when the CFRA noticed that Kraft Foods made $122 million in acquisitions in 2002 but claimed $539 million as "goodwill" assets related to the purchases, it concluded that Kraft was padding its earnings with one-time gains. According to Schilit, unusually high goodwill gains related to recent acquisitions is a **red flag** that suggests an underlying problem.[2]

Schilit proposes a short checklist of items to examine for red flags:

- **Cash flow from operations should exceed net income:** If cash flow from operations drops below net income, it could mean that the company is propping up its earnings by selling assets, borrowing cash, or shuffling numbers. Says Schilit, "You could have spotted the problems at Enron by just doing this."[3]

- **Accounts receivable should not grow faster than sales:** A firm facing slowing sales can make itself look better by inflating accounts receivable with expected future sales and by making sales to customers who are not credit worthy. "It's like mailing a contract to a dead person and then counting it as a sale," says Schilit.[4]

- **Gross margins should not fluctuate over time:** A change in gross margins of more than 2% in either direction from year to year is worth a close look. It could mean that the company is using other revenue, such as sales of assets or write-offs, to boost profits. Sunbeam reported an increase of 10% in gross margins just before it was investigated by the SEC.

- **Information about top management and the board should be examined carefully:** In 1994, when Schilit learned that the Chairman of Checkers Restaurants had put his two young sons on the board, he warned investors of nepotism. Two years later, Checkers' huge debt caused its stock to fall 85%, and all three family members were forced out of the company.

- **The footnotes are important:** When companies change their accounting assumptions to make the statements more attractive, they often bury their rationale in the footnotes. Schilit dislikes companies that extend the depreciable life of their assets. "There's only one reason to do that—to add a penny or two to earnings—and it makes me very mistrustful of management."[5]

Schilit makes his living analyzing companies and selling his reports to investors. Annual reports and financial statements provide a lot of information about a company's health, but it's hard to find problem areas when management is massaging the numbers to make the company appear more attractive than it is. This type of in-depth, investigative analysis is a key part of analyzing strategy cases. This chapter provides various analytical techniques and suggestions for conducting this kind of case analysis.

15.1 | The Case Method

The analysis and discussion of case problems has been the most popular method of teaching strategy and policy for many years. The case method provides the opportunity to move from a narrow, specialized view that emphasizes functional techniques to a broader, less precise analysis of the overall corporation. Cases present actual business situations and enable you to examine both successful and unsuccessful corporations. In case analysis, you might be asked to critically analyze a situation in which a manager had to make a decision of long-term corporate importance. This approach gives you a feel for what it is like to face making and implementing strategic decisions.

15.2 | Researching the Case Situation

You should not restrict yourself only to the information written in the case unless your instructor states otherwise. You should, if possible, undertake outside research about the environmental setting. Check the decision date of each case (typically the latest date mentioned in the case) to find out when the situation occurred and then screen the business periodicals for that time period. An understanding of the economy during that period will help you avoid making a serious error in your analysis—for example, suggesting a sale of stock when the stock market is at an all-time low or taking on more debt when the prime interest rate is over 15%. Information about the industry will provide insights into its competitive activities. *Important Note: Don't go beyond the decision date of the case in your research unless directed to do so by your instructor.*

Use computerized company and industry information services such as Compustat, Compact Disclosure, and CD/International, available on CD-ROM or online at the library. On the Internet, Hoover's Online Corporate Directory (www.hoovers.com) and the Security and Exchange Commission's Edgar database (www.sec.gov) provide access to corporate annual reports and 10-K forms. This background will give you an appreciation for the situation as it was experienced by the participants in the case. Use a search engine such as Google or Alta Vista to find additional information about the industry and the company.

A company's **annual report** and **SEC 10-K, 10-Q**, and **14-A forms** from the year of the case can be very helpful. According to the Yankelovich Partners survey firm, 8 out of 10 portfolio managers and 75% of security analysts use annual reports when making decisions.[6] They contain not only the usual income statements and balance sheets but also cash flow statements and notes to the financial statements, indicating why certain actions were taken. 10-K forms include detailed information not usually available in an annual report. 10-Q forms include quarterly financial reports. 14-A forms include detailed information on members of a company's board of directors and proxy statements for annual meetings. Some resources available for research into the economy and a corporation's industry are suggested in **Appendix 15.A**.

A caveat: Before obtaining additional information about the company profiled in a particular case, ask your instructor if doing so is appropriate for your class assignment. Your strategy instructor may want you to stay within the confines of the case information such as the decision date, provided in the book. In this case, it is usually acceptable to at least learn more about the societal environment at the time of the case.

15.3 | Financial Analysis: A Place to Begin

Once you have read a case, a good place to begin your analysis is with the financial statements. **Ratio analysis** is the calculation of ratios from data in these statements. It is done to identify possible financial strengths or weaknesses. Thus it is a valuable part of SWOT analysis. A review of key financial ratios can help you assess a company's overall situation and pinpoint some problem areas. Ratios are useful, regardless of firm size, and they enable you to compare a company's ratios with industry averages. **Table 15–1** lists some of the most important financial ratios, which are (1) **liquidity ratios**, (2) **profitability ratios**, (3) **activity ratios**, and (4) **leverage ratios**.

Analyzing Financial Statements

In your analysis, do not simply make an exhibit that includes all the ratios (unless your instructor requires you to do so), but select and discuss only those ratios that have an impact on the company's problems. For instance, accounts receivable and inventory may provide a source of funds. If receivables and inventories are double the industry average, reducing them may provide needed cash. In this situation, the case report should include not only sources of funds but also the number of dollars freed for use. Compare these ratios with industry averages to discover whether the company is out of line with others in the industry. Annual and quarterly industry ratios can be found in the library or on the Internet. (See the resources for case research in **Appendix 15.A**.)

A typical financial analysis of a firm would include a study of the operating statements for five or so years, including a trend analysis of sales, profits, earnings per share, debt-to-equity ratio, return on investment, and so on, plus a ratio study comparing the firm under study with industry standards. As a minimum, undertake the following five steps in basic financial analysis.

1. Scrutinize historical income statements and balance sheets. These two basic statements provide most of the data needed for analysis. Statements of cash flow may also be useful.

2. Compare historical statements over time if a series of statements is available.

3. Calculate changes that occur in individual categories from year to year, as well as the cumulative total change.

4. Determine the change as a percentage as well as an absolute amount.

5. Adjust for inflation if that was a significant factor.

Examination of this information may reveal developing trends. Compare trends in one category with trends in related categories. For example, an increase in sales of 15% over three years may appear to be satisfactory until you note an increase of 20% in the cost of goods sold during the same period. The outcome of this comparison might suggest that further investigation into the manufacturing process is necessary. If a company is reporting strong net income growth but negative cash flow, this would suggest that the company is relying on something other than operations for earnings growth. Is it selling off assets or cutting R&D? If accounts receivable are growing faster than are sales revenues, the company is not getting paid for the products or services it is counting as sold. Is the company dumping product on its distributors at the end of the year to boost its reported annual sales? If so, expect the distributors to return the unordered product the next month, thus drastically cutting the next year's reported sales.

Other "tricks of the trade" need to be examined. Until June 2000, firms growing through acquisition were allowed to account for the cost of the purchased company through the pool-

TABLE 15–1 FINANCIAL RATIO ANALYSIS

	Formula	How Expressed	Meaning
1. Liquidity Ratios			
Current ratio	$\dfrac{\text{Current assets}}{\text{Current liabilities}}$	Decimal	A short-term indicator of the company's ability to pay its short-term liabilities from short-term assets; how much of current assets are available to cover each dollar of current liabilities.
Quick (acid test) ratio	$\dfrac{\text{Current assets} - \text{Inventory}}{\text{Current liabilities}}$	Decimal	Measures the company's ability to pay off its short-term obligations from current assets, excluding inventories.
Inventory to net working capital	$\dfrac{\text{Inventory}}{\text{Current assets} - \text{Current liabilities}}$	Decimal	A measure of inventory balance; measures the extent to which the cushion of excess current assets over current liabilities may be threatened by unfavorable changes in inventory.
Cash ratio	$\dfrac{\text{Cash} + \text{Cash equivalents}}{\text{Current liabilities}}$	Decimal	Measures the extent to which the company's capital is in cash or cash equivalents; shows how much of the current obligations can be paid from cash or near-cash assets.
2. Profitability Ratios			
Net profit margin	$\dfrac{\text{Net profit after taxes}}{\text{Net sales}}$	Percentage	Shows how much after-tax profits are generated by each dollar of sales.
Gross profit margin	$\dfrac{\text{Sales} - \text{Cost of goods sold}}{\text{Net sales}}$	Percentage	Indicates the total margin available to cover other expenses beyond cost of goods sold and still yield a profit.
Return on investment (ROI)	$\dfrac{\text{Net profit after taxes}}{\text{Total assets}}$	Percentage	Measures the rate of return on the total assets utilized in the company; a measure of management's efficiency, it shows the return on all the assets under its control, regardless of source of financing.
Return on equity (ROE)	$\dfrac{\text{Net profit after taxes}}{\text{Shareholders' equity}}$	Percentage	Measures the rate of return on the book value of shareholders' total investment in the company.
Earnings per share (EPS)	$\dfrac{\text{Net profit after taxes} - \text{Preferred stock dividends}}{\text{Average number of common shares}}$	Dollars per share	Shows the after-tax earnings generated for each share of common stock.
3. Activity Ratios			
Inventory turnover	$\dfrac{\text{Net sales}}{\text{Inventory}}$	Decimal	Measures the number of times that average inventory of finished goods was turned over or sold during a period of time, usually a year.
Days of inventory	$\dfrac{\text{Inventory}}{\text{Cost of goods sold} \div 365}$	Days	Measures the number of one day's worth of inventory that a company has on hand at any given time.
Net working capital turnover	$\dfrac{\text{Net sales}}{\text{Net working capital}}$	Decimal	Measures how effectively the net working capital is used to generate sales.
Asset turnover	$\dfrac{\text{Sales}}{\text{Total assets}}$	Decimal	Measures the utilization of all the company's assets; measures how many sales are generated by each dollar of assets.

TABLE 15–1 (CONTINUED)

	Formula	How Expressed	Meaning
Fixed asset turnover	$\dfrac{\text{Sales}}{\text{Fixed assets}}$	Decimal	Measures the utilization of the company's fixed assets (i.e., plant and equipment); measures how many sales are generated by each dollar of fixed assets.
Average collection period	$\dfrac{\text{Accounts receivable}}{\text{Sales for year} \div 365}$	Days	Indicates the average length of time in days that a company must wait to collect a sale after making it; may be compared to the credit terms offered by the company to its customers.
Accounts receivable turnover	$\dfrac{\text{Annual credit sales}}{\text{Accounts receivable}}$	Decimal	Indicates the number of times that accounts receivable are cycled during the period (usually a year).
Accounts payable period	$\dfrac{\text{Accounts payable}}{\text{Purchases for year} \div 365}$	Days	Indicates the average length of time in days that the company takes to pay its credit purchases.
Days of cash	$\dfrac{\text{Cash}}{\text{Net sales for year} \div 365}$	Days	Indicates the number of days of cash on hand, at present sales levels.

4. Leverage Ratios

	Formula	How Expressed	Meaning
Debt to asset ratio	$\dfrac{\text{Total debt}}{\text{Total assets}}$	Percentage	Measures the extent to which borrowed funds have been used to finance the company's assets.
Debt to equity ratio	$\dfrac{\text{Total debt}}{\text{Shareholders' equity}}$	Percentage	Measures the funds provided by creditors versus the funds provided by owners.
Long-term debt to capital structure	$\dfrac{\text{Long-term debt}}{\text{Shareholders' equity}}$	Percentage	Measures the long-term component of capital structure.
Times interest earned	$\dfrac{\text{Profit before taxes} + \text{Interest charges}}{\text{Interest charges}}$	Decimal	Indicates the ability of the company to meet its annual interest costs.
Coverage of fixed charges	$\dfrac{\text{Profit before taxes} + \text{Interest charges} + \text{Lease charges}}{\text{Interest charges} + \text{Lease obligations}}$	Decimal	A measure of the company's ability to meet all of its fixed-charge obligations.
Current liabilities to equity	$\dfrac{\text{Current liabilities}}{\text{Shareholders' equity}}$	Percentage	Measures the short-term financing portion versus that provided by owners.

5. Other Ratios

	Formula	How Expressed	Meaning
Price/earnings ratio	$\dfrac{\text{Market price per share}}{\text{Earnings per share}}$	Decimal	Shows the current market's evaluation of a stock, based on its earnings; shows how much the investor is willing to pay for each dollar of earnings.
Divided payout ratio	$\dfrac{\text{Annual dividends per share}}{\text{Annual earnings per share}}$	Percentage	Indicates the percentage of profit that is paid out as dividends.
Dividend yield on common stock	$\dfrac{\text{Annual dividends per share}}{\text{Current market price per share}}$	Percentage	Indicates the dividend rate of return to common shareholders at the current market price.

Note: In using ratios for analysis, calculate ratios for the corporation and compare them to the average and quartile ratios for the particular industry. Refer to Standard & Poor's and Robert Morris Associates for average industry data. Special thanks to Dr. Moustafa H. Abdelsamad, Dean, Business School, Texas A&M University–Corpus Christi, Corpus Christi, Texas, for his definitions of these ratios.

GL🌐BAL ISSUE

Financial Statements of Multinational Corporations: Not Always What They Seem

A multinational corporation follows the accounting rules for its home country. As a result, its financial statements may be somewhat difficult to understand or to use for comparisons with competitors from other countries. For example, British firms such as British Petroleum and The Body Shop use the term *turnover* rather than *sales revenue*. In the case of AB Electrolux of Sweden, a footnote to an annual report indicates that the consolidated accounts have been prepared in accordance with Swedish accounting standards, which differ in certain significant respects from U.S. generally accepted accounting principles (U.S. GAAP). For one year, net income of 4,830m SEK (Swedish kronor) approximated 5,655m SEK according to U.S. GAAP. Total assets for the same period were 84,183m SEK according to Swedish principles, but 86,658m SEK according to U.S. GAAP.

ing of both companies' stock. This approach was used in 40% of the value of mergers between 1997 and 1999. The pooling method enabled the acquiring company to disregard the premium it paid for the other firm (the amount above the fair market value of the purchased company, often called "goodwill"). Thus, when PepsiCo agreed to purchase Quaker Oats for $13.4 billion in PepsiCo stock, the $13.4 billion was not found on PepsiCo's balance sheet. As of June 2000, merging firms must use the "purchase" accounting rules, in which the true purchase price is reflected in the financial statements.[7]

The analysis of a multinational corporation's financial statements can get very complicated, especially if its headquarters is in another country that uses different accounting standards. See the GLOBAL ISSUE for why financial analysis can get tricky at times.

Common-Size Statements

Common-size statements are income statements and balance sheets in which the dollar figures have been converted into percentages. These statements are used to identify trends in each of the categories, such as cost of goods sold as a percentage of sales (sales is the denominator). For the income statement, net sales represent 100%: You calculate the percentage for each category so that the categories sum to the net sales percentage (100%). For the balance sheet, you give the total assets a value of 100% and calculate other asset and liability categories as percentages of the total assets with total assets as the denominator. (Individual asset and liability items, such as accounts receivable and accounts payable, can also be calculated as a percentage of net sales.)

When you convert statements to this form, it is relatively easy to note the percentage that each category represents of the total. Look for trends in specific items, such as cost of goods sold, when compared to the company's historical figures. To get a proper picture, however, you need to make comparisons with industry data, if available, to see whether fluctuations are merely reflecting industrywide trends. If a firm's trends are generally in line with those of the rest of the industry, problems are less likely than if the firm's trends are worse than industry averages. If ratios are not available for the industry, calculate the ratios for the industry's best and worst firms and compare them to the firm you are analyzing. Common-size statements are especially helpful in developing scenarios and pro forma statements because they provide a series of historical relationships (for example, cost of goods sold to sales, interest to sales, and inventories as a percentage of assets) from which you can estimate the future with your scenario assumptions for each year.

Z-Value, Index of Sustainable Growth, and Free Cash Flow

If a corporation being studied appears to be in poor financial condition, use **Altman's Bankruptcy Formula** to calculate its **Z-value**. The Z-value formula combines five ratios by weighting them according to their importance to a corporation's financial strength. The formula is:

$$Z = 1.2x_1 + 1.4x_2 + 3.3x_3 + 0.6x_4 + 1.0x_5$$

where:

x_1 = Working capital/Total assets (%)
x_2 = Retained earnings/Total assets (%)
x_3 = Earnings before interest and taxes/Total assets (%)
x_4 = Market value of equity/Total liabilities (%)
x_5 = Sales/Total assets (number of times)

A score below 1.81 indicates significant credit problems, whereas a score above 3.0 indicates a healthy firm. Scores between 1.81 and 3.0 indicate question marks.[8]

The **index of sustainable growth** is useful to learn whether a company embarking on a growth strategy will need to take on debt to fund this growth. The index indicates how much of the growth rate of sales can be sustained by internally generated funds. The formula is:

$$g^* = \frac{[P(1 - D)(1 + L)]}{[T - P(1 - D)(1 + L)]}$$

where:

P = (Net profit before tax/Net sales) × 100
D = Target dividends/Profit after tax
L = Total liabilities/Net worth
T = (Total assets/Net sales) × 100

If the planned growth rate calls for a growth rate higher than its g*, external capital will be needed to fund the growth unless management is able to find efficiencies, decrease dividends, increase the debt–equity ratio, or reduce assets through renting or leasing arrangements.[9]

Useful Economic Measures

If you are analyzing a company over many years, you may want to adjust sales and net income for inflation to arrive at "true" financial performance in constant dollars. **Constant dollars** are dollars adjusted for inflation to make them comparable over various years. One way to adjust for inflation in the United States is to use the Consumer Price Index (CPI), as given in **Table 15–2**. Dividing sales and net income by the CPI factor for that year will change the figures to 1982–1984 constant dollars (when the CPI was 1.0).

Another helpful analytical aid provided in **Table 15–2** is the **prime interest rate**, the rate of interest banks charge on their lowest-risk loans. For better assessments of strategic decisions, it can be useful to note the level of the prime interest rate at the time of the case. A decision to borrow money to build a new plant would have been a good one in 2003 at 4.12% but less practical in 2000, when the average rate reached 9.23%.

In preparing a scenario for your pro forma financial statements, you may want to use the **gross domestic product (GDP)** from **Table 15–2**. GDP is used worldwide and measures the total output of goods and services within a country's borders. The amount of change from one year to the next indicates how much that country's economy is growing. Remember that scenarios have to be adjusted for a country's specific conditions. For other economic information, see the resources for case research in **Appendix 15.A**.

TABLE 15–2
**U.S. ECONOMIC
INDICATORS***

Year	GDP (in $ billions) Gross Domestic Product	CPI (for all items) Consumer Price Index	PIR (in %) Prime Interest Rate
1985	4,180.7	1.076	9.93
1986	4,422.2	1.096	8.33
1987	4,693.3	1.136	8.21
1988	5,049.6	1.183	9.32
1989	5,483.7	1.240	10.87
1990	5,743.8	1.307	10.01
1991	5,916.7	1.362	8.46
1992	6,244.4	1.403	6.25
1993	6,553.0	1.445	6.00
1994	6,935.7	1.482	7.15
1995	7,253.8	1.524	8.83
1996	7,661.6	1.569	8.27
1997	8,318.4	1.605	8.44
1998	8,790.2	1.630	8.35
1999	9,268.4	1.666	7.99
2000	9,817.0	1.722	9.23
2001	10,128.8	1.771	6.92
2002	10,487.0	1.799	4.68
2003	11,004.0	1.840	4.12
2004	11,733.5	1.889	4.27

*Note: Gross Domestic Product (GDP) in billions of dollars; Consumer Price Index (CPI) for all items (1982–1984 = 1.0); Prime Interest Rate (PIR) in percentages.

Sources:

1. Gross Domestic Product (GDP) from *Survey of Current Business* (October 2004), Vol. 84, No. 10, Table 1.1.5, p. D-3, and (March 2005), Vol. 85, No. 3, Table 1.1.5, p. D-3.

2. Consumer Price Index (CPI) from U.S. Bureau of Labor Statistics, *Monthly Labor Review*, Vol. 128, No. 2 (February 2005), Table 37, p. 127.

3. Prime Interest Rate (PIR) from *Survey of Current Business*, Vol. 85, No. 1 (January 2005), Table D.1 (Domestic Perspectives), p. D-52.

15.4 | **Format for Case Analysis: The Strategic Audit**

There is no one best way to analyze or present a case report. Each instructor has personal preferences for format and approach. Nevertheless, in **Appendix 15.B** we suggest an approach for both written and oral reports that provides a systematic method for successfully attacking a case. This approach is based on the strategic audit, which is presented at the end of **Chapter 1** in **Appendix 1.A**. We find that this approach provides structure and is very

Figure 15–1
Strategic Audit
Worksheet

Strategic Audit Heading	Analysis		Comments
	(+) Factors	(−) Factors	
I. Current Situation			
A. Past Corporate Performance Indexes			

B. Strategic Posture:
    Current Mission
    Current Objectives
    Current Strategies
    Current Policies			

SWOT Analysis Begins:			
II. Corporate Governance			
A. Board of Directors			
B. Top Management			
III. External Environment (EFAS): **Opportunities and Threats (SWOT)**			
A. Societal Environment			
B. Task Environment (Industry Analysis)			
IV. Internal Environment (IFAS): **Strengths and Weaknesses (SWOT)**			
A. Corporate Structure			
B. Corporate Culture			
C. Corporate Resources			
1. Marketing			
2. Finance			
3. Research and Development			
4. Operations and Logistics			
5. Human Resources			
6. Information Systems			
V. Analysis of Strategic Factors (SFAS)			
A. Key Internal and External Strategic Factors (SWOT)			
B. Review of Mission and Objectives			
SWOT Analysis Ends. Recommendation Begins:			
VI. Alternatives and Recommendations			
A. Strategic Alternatives—pros and cons			
B. Recommended Strategy			
VII. Implementation			
VIII. Evaluation and Control			

Note: See the complete Strategic Audit on pages 26–33. It lists the pages in the book that discuss each of the eight headings.

Source: T. L. Wheelen and J. D. Hunger, "Strategic Audit Worksheet." Copyright © 1985, 1986, 1987, 1988, 1989, and 2005 by T. L. Wheelen. Copyright © 1989 and 2005 by Wheelen and Hunger Associates. Revised 1991, 1994, and 1997. Reprined by permission. Additional copies available for classroom use in Part D of *Case Instructors Manual* and on the Prentice Hall Web site (www.prenhall.com/wheelen).

helpful for the typical student who may be a relative novice in case analysis. Regardless of the format chosen, be careful to include a complete analysis of key environmental variables—especially of trends in the industry and of the competition. Look at international developments as well.

If you choose to use the strategic audit as a guide to the analysis of complex strategy cases, you may want to use the **strategic audit worksheet** in **Figure 15–1**. See **Appendix 15.C** for an example of a completed student-written analysis of a 1993 Maytag Corporation case (not the more recent 2002 version) done in an outline form, using the strategic audit format. This is one example of what a case analysis in outline form may look like.

Case discussion focuses on critical analysis and logical development of thought. A solution is satisfactory if it resolves important problems and is likely to be implemented successfully. How the corporation actually dealt with the case problems has no real bearing on the analysis because management might have analyzed its problems incorrectly or implemented a series of flawed solutions.

15.5 | Conclusion

Using case analysis is one of the best ways to understand and remember the strategic management process. By applying to cases the concepts and techniques you have learned, you will be able to remember them long past the time when you have forgotten other memorized bits of information. The use of cases to examine actual situations brings alive the field of strategic management and helps build your analytic and decision-making skills. These are just some of the reasons why the use of cases in disciplines from agribusiness to health care is increasing throughout the world.

Strategy Bits

- Zimbabwe had the highest rate of inflation during 2003, with consumer prices rising annually 385%.

- Hong Kong had the least inflation. Its consumer prices declined during 2003 by 2.6%.[10]

Discussion Questions

1. Why should you begin a case analysis with a financial analysis? When are other approaches appropriate?

2. What are common-size financial statements? What is their value to case analysis? How are they calculated?

3. When should you gather information outside a case by going to the library or using the Internet? What should you look for?

4. When is inflation an important issue in conducting case analysis? Why bother?

5. How can you learn what date a case took place?

Strategic Practice Exercise

Convert the following two years of income statements from the Maytag Corporation into common-size statements. The dollar figures are in thousands. What does converting to a common size reveal?

Consolidated Statements of Income: Maytag Corporation

	1992	%	1991	%
Net sales	$3,041,223	100	$2,970,626	100
Cost of sales	2,339,406	___	2,254,221	___
Gross profits	701,817	___	716,405	___
Selling, general, & admin. expenses	528,250	___	524,898	___
Reorganization expenses	95,000	___	0	___
Operating income	78,567	___	191,507	___
Interest expense	(75,004)	___	(75,159)	___
Other—net	3,983	___	7,069	___
Income before taxes and accounting changes	7,546	___	123,417	___
Income taxes	(15,900)	___	(44,400)	___
Income before accounting changes	(8,354)	___	79,017	___
Effects of accounting changes for postretirement benefits	(307,000)	___	0	___
Net income (loss)	$(315,354)	___	$79,017	___

Key Terms

activity ratio (p. 356)

Altman's Bankruptcy Formula (p. 360)

annual report (p. 355)

common-size statement (p. 359)

constant dollars (p. 360)

gross domestic product (p. 360)

index of sustainable growth (p. 360)

leverage ratio (p. 356)

liquidity ratio (p. 356)

prime interest rate (p. 360)

profitability ratio (p. 356)

ratio analysis (p. 356)

red flag (p. 354)

SEC 10-K form (p. 355)

SEC 10-Q form (p. 355)

SEC 14-A form (p. 355)

strategic audit worksheet (p. 363)

Z-value (p. 360)

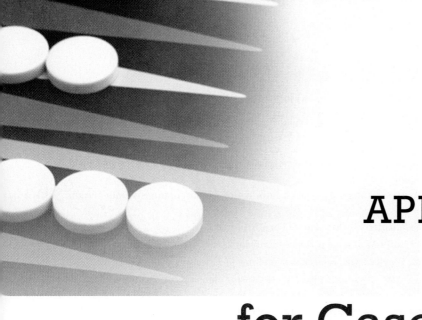

APPENDIX 15.A
Resources for Case Research

Company Information

1. Annual reports
2. Moody's *Manuals on Investment* (a listing of companies within certain industries that contains a brief history and a five-year financial statement of each company)
3. Securities and Exchange Commission Report Forms 10-K (annually) and 10-Q (quarterly)
4. Standard & Poor's *Register of Corporations*, Directors, and Executives
5. Value Line's *Investment Survey*
6. Findex's *Directory of Market Research Reports*, Studies and Surveys (a listing by Market Research.com of more than 11,000 studies conducted by leading research firms)
7. Compustat, Compact Disclosure, CD/International, and Hoover's Online Corporate Directory (computerized operating and financial information on thousands of publicly held corporations)
8. Shareholders meeting notices in SEC Form 14-A (proxy notices)

Economic Information

1. Regional statistics and local forecasts from large banks
2. *Business Cycle Development* (Department of Commerce)
3. Chase Econometric Associates' publications
4. U.S. Census Bureau publications on population, transportation, and housing
5. *Current Business Reports* (U.S. Department of Commerce)
6. *Economic Indicators* (U.S. Joint Economic Committee)
7. *Economic Report of the President to Congress*
8. *Long-Term Economic Growth* (U.S. Department of Commerce)
9. *Monthly Labor Review* (U.S. Department of Labor)
10. *Monthly Bulletin of Statistics* (United Nations)
11. *Statistical Abstract of the United States* (U.S. Department of Commerce)
12. *Statistical Yearbook* (United Nations)
13. *Survey of Current Business* (U.S. Department of Commerce)
14. *U.S. Industrial Outlook* (U.S. Department of Defense)

15. *World Trade Annual* (United Nations)
16. *Overseas Business Reports* (by country, published by the U.S. Department of Commerce)

Industry Information

1. Analyses of companies and industries by investment brokerage firms
2. *Business Week* (provides weekly economic and business information, as well as quarterly profit and sales rankings of corporations)
3. *Fortune* (each April publishes listings of financial information on corporations within certain industries)
4. *Industry Survey* (published quarterly by Standard & Poor's)
5. *Industry Week* (late March/early April issue provides information on 14 industry groups)
6. *Forbes* (mid-January issue provides performance data on firms in various industries)
7. *Inc.* (May and December issues give information on fast-growing entrepreneurial companies)

Directory and Index Information on Companies and Industries

1. *Business Periodical Index* (on computers in many libraries)
2. *Directory of National Trade Associations*
3. *Encyclopedia of Associations*
4. Funk and Scott's *Index of Corporations and Industries*
5. Thomas' *Register of American Manufacturers*
6. *Wall Street Journal Index*

Ratio Analysis Information

1. *Almanac of Business and Industrial Financial Ratios* (Prentice Hall)
2. *Annual Statement Studies* (Risk Management Associates; also Robert Morris Associates)
3. *Dun's Review* (Dun & Bradstreet; published annually in September–December issues)
4. *Industry Norms and Key Business Ratios* (Dun & Bradstreet)

Online Information

1. Hoover's Online—financial statements and profiles of public companies (www.hoovers.com)
2. U.S. Securities and Exchange Commission—official filings of public companies in Edgar database (www.sec.gov)
3. Fortune 500—statistics for largest U.S. corporations (www.fortune500.com)
4. Dun & Bradstreet's Online—short reports on 10 million public and private U.S. companies (smallbusiness.dnb.com)
5. Ecola's 24-Hour Newsstand—links to web sites of 2,000 newspapers, journals, and magazines (www.ecola.com)
6. Competitive Intelligence Guide—information on company resources (www.fuld.com)
7. Society of Competitive Intelligence Professionals (www.scip.org)
8. *The Economist*—provides international information and surveys (www.economist.com)
9. Web 100—information on 100 largest U.S. and international companies (www.w100.com).
10. Bloomberg—information on interest rates, stock prices, currency conversion rates, and other general financial information (www.bloomberg.com)
11. Annual Report Gallery (www.reportgallery.com)
12. CEOExpress—links to many valuable sources of business information (www.ceoexpress.com)
13. *Wall Street Journal*—business news (www.wsj.com)
14. CorporateInformation.com—subscription service for company profiles (www.corporate information.com)
15. Kompass International—industry information (www.kompass.com)

16. CorpTech—database of technology companies (www.corptech.com)
17. ZDNet—information technology industry (www.zdnet.com)
18. The Scannery—information on international companies (www.thescannery.com)
19. Guide to Financials—information on how to read a financial statement (www.ibm.com/investor/financialguide)
20. *CIA World Fact Book*—international information by country (www.cia.gov/cia/publications/factbook/index.html)

APPENDIX 15.B
Suggested Case Analysis Methodology Using the Strategic Audit

1. READ CASE

First Reading of the Case

- Develop a general overview of the company and its external environment.
- Begin a list of the possible strategic factors facing the company at this time.
- List the research information you may need on the economy, industry, and competitors.

2. READ THE CASE WITH THE STRATEGIC AUDIT

Second Reading of the Case

- Read the case a second time, using the strategic audit as a framework for in-depth analysis. (See **Appendix 1.A** on pages 26–33.) You may want to make a copy of the strategic audit worksheet (**Figure 15–1**) to use to keep track of your comments as you read the case.
- The questions in the strategic audit parallel the strategic decision-making process shown in **Figure 1–5** (pages 22–23).
- The audit provides you with a conceptual framework to examine the company's mission, objectives, strategies, and policies as well as problems, symptoms, facts, opinions, and issues.
- Perform a financial analysis of the company, using ratio analysis (see **Table 15–1**), and do the calculations necessary to convert key parts of the financial statements to a common-size basis.

3. DO OUTSIDE RESEARCH

Library and Online Computer Services

- Each case has a decision date indicating when the case actually took place. Your research should be based on the time period for the case.
- See **Appendix 15.A** for resources for case research. Your research should include information about the environment at the time of the case. Find average industry ratios. You may also want to obtain further information regarding competitors and the company itself (10-K forms and annual reports).

This information should help you conduct an industry analysis. *Check with your instructor to see what kind of outside research is appropriate for your assignment.*

■ Don't try to learn what actually happened to the company discussed in the case. What management actually decided may not be the best solution. It will certainly bias your analysis and will probably cause your recommendation to lack proper justification.

4. BEGIN SWOT ANALYSIS

External Environmental Analysis: EFAS

■ Analyze the four societal forces to see what trends are likely to affect the industry(s) in which the company is operating.

■ Conduct an industry analysis using Porter's competitive forces from **Chapter 4**. Develop an Industry Matrix (**Table 4–3** on page 78).

■ Generate 8 to 10 external factors. These should be the *most important* opportunities and threats facing the company at the time of the case.

■ Develop an EFAS Table, as shown in **Table 4–5** (page 98), for your list of external strategic factors.

■ **Suggestion:** Rank the 8 to 10 factors from most to least important. Start by grouping the 3 top factors and then the 3 bottom factors.

Internal Organizational Analysis: IFAS

■ Generate 8 to 10 internal factors. These should be the *most important* strengths and weaknesses of the company at the time of the case.

■ Develop an IFAS Table, as shown in **Table 5–2** (page 130), for your list of internal strategic factors.

■ **Suggestion:** Rank the 8 to 10 factors from most to least important. Start by grouping the 3 top factors and then the 3 bottom factors.

5. WRITE YOUR STRATEGIC AUDIT: PARTS I TO IV

First Draft of Your Strategic Audit

■ Review the student-written audit of an old Maytag case in **Appendix 15.C** for an example.

■ Write Parts I to IV of the strategic audit. Remember to include the factors from your EFAS and IFAS Tables in your audit.

6. WRITE YOUR STRATEGIC AUDIT: PART V

Strategic Factor Analysis Summary: SFAS

■ **Condense the list of factors from the 16 to 20 identified in your EFAS and IFAS Tables to only the 8 to 10 most important factors.**

■ Select the most important EFAS and IFAS factors. Recalculate the weights of each. The weights still need to add to 1.0.

■ Develop a SFAS Matrix, as shown in **Figure 6–1** (page 141), for your final list of strategic factors. Although the weights (indicating the importance of each factor) will probably change from the EFAS and IFAS Tables, the numeric rating (1 to 5) of each factor should remain the same. These ratings are your assessment of management's performance on each factor.

■ This is a good time to reexamine what you wrote earlier in Parts I to IV. You may want to add to or delete some of what you wrote. Ensure that each one of the strategic factors you have included in your SFAS Matrix is discussed in the appropriate place in Parts I to IV. Part V of the audit is *not* the place to mention a strategic factor for the first time.

■ Write Part V of your strategic audit. This completes your SWOT analysis.

■ This is the place to suggest a revised mission statement and a better set of objectives for the company. The SWOT analysis coupled with revised mission and objectives for the company set the stage for the generation of strategic alternatives.

7. WRITE YOUR STRATEGIC AUDIT: PART VI

Strategic Alternatives and Recommendation

A. Alternatives

■ Develop around three mutually exclusive strategic alternatives. If appropriate to the case you are analyzing, you might propose one alternative for growth, one for stability, and one for retrenchment. Within each corporate strategy, you should probably propose an appropriate business/competitive strategy. You may also want to include some functional strategies where appropriate.

■ Construct a corporate scenario for each alternative. Use the data from your outside research to project general societal trends (GDP, inflation, etc.) and industry trends. Use these as the basis of your assumptions to write pro forma financial statements (particularly income statements) for each strategic alternative for the next five years.

■ List **pros** and **cons** for each alternative based on your scenarios.

B. Recommendation

■ Specify which one of your alternative strategies you recommend. Justify your choice in terms of dealing with the strategic factors you listed in Part V of the strategic audit.

■ Develop policies to help implement your strategies.

8. WRITE YOUR STRATEGIC AUDIT: PART VII

Implementation

■ Develop programs to implement your recommended strategy.

■ Specify who is to be responsible for implementing each program and how long each program will take to complete.

■ Refer to the pro forma financial statements you developed earlier for your recommended strategy. Use common-size historical income statements as the basis for the pro forma statement. Do the numbers still make sense? If not, this may be a good time to rethink the budget numbers to reflect your recommended programs.

9. WRITE YOUR STRATEGIC AUDIT: PART VIII

Evaluation and Control

■ Specify the type of evaluation and controls that you need to ensure that your recommendation is carried out successfully. Specify who is responsible for monitoring these controls.

■ Indicate whether sufficient information is available to monitor how the strategy is being implemented. If not, suggest a change to the information system.

10. PROOF AND FINE-TUNE YOUR AUDIT

Final Draft of Your Strategic Audit

■ Check to ensure that your audit is within the page limits of your professor. You may need to cut some parts and expand others.

■ Make sure that your recommendation clearly deals with the strategic factors.

■ **Attach your EFAS and IFAS Tables, and SFAS Matrix**, plus your ratio analysis and pro forma statements. Label them as numbered exhibits and refer to each of them within the body of the audit.

■ Proof your work for errors. If on a computer, use a spell checker.

Special Note: Depending on your assignment, it is relatively easy to use the strategic audit you have just developed to write a written case analysis in essay form or to make an oral presentation. The strategic audit is just a detailed case analysis in an outline form and can be used as the basic framework for any sort of case analysis and presentation.

APPENDIX 15.C
Example of a Student-Written Strategic Audit

(For the <u>1993</u> Maytag Corporation Case)

I. CURRENT SITUATION

A. Current Performance

Poor financials, high debt load, first losses since 1920s, price/earnings ratio negative.

- First loss since 1920s.
- Laid off 4,500 employees at Magic Chef.
- Hoover Europe still showing losses.

B. Strategic Posture

1. **Mission**

   - Developed in 1989 for the Maytag Company: "To provide our customers with products of unsurpassed performance that last longer, need fewer repairs, and are produced at the lowest possible cost."
   - Updated in 1991: "Our collective mission is world class quality." Expands Maytag's belief in product quality to all aspects of operations.

2. **Objectives**

   - "To be profitability leader in industry for every product line Maytag manufactures." Selected profitability rather than market share.
   - "To be number one in total customer satisfaction." Doesn't say how to measure satisfaction.
   - "To grow the North American appliance business and become the third largest appliance manufacturer (in unit sales) in North America."
   - To increase profitable market share growth in North American appliance and floor care business, 6.5% return on sales, 10% return on assets, 20% return on equity, beat competition in satisfying customers, dealer, builder and endorser, move into third place in total units shipped per year. Nicely quantified objectives.

3. **Strategies**
   - Global growth through acquisition, and alliance with Bosch-Siemens.
   - Differentiate brand names for competitive advantage.
   - Create synergy between companies, product improvement, investment in plant and equipment.

4. **Policies**
   - Cost reduction is secondary to high quality.
   - Promotion from within.
   - Slow but sure R&D: Maytag slow to respond to changes in market

II. STRATEGIC MANAGERS

A. Board of Directors

1. Fourteen members—eleven are outsiders.
2. Well-respected Americans, most on board since 1986 or earlier.
3. No international or marketing backgrounds.
4. Time for a change?

B. Top Management

1. Top management promoted from within Maytag Company. Too inbred?
2. Very experienced in the industry.
3. Responsible for current situation.
4. May be too parochial for global industry. May need new blood.

III. EXTERNAL ENVIRONMENT (EFAS Table; see Exhibit 1)

A. Societal Environment

1. **Economic**
   a. Unstable economy but recession ending, consumer confidence growing—could increase spending for big-ticket items like houses, cars, and appliances. **(O)**
   b. Individual economies becoming interconnected into a world economy. **(O)**

2. **Technological**
   a. Fuzzy logic technology being applied to sense and measure activities. **(O)**
   b. Computers and information technology increasingly important. **(O)**

3. **Political–Legal**
   a. NAFTA, European Union, other regional trade pacts opening doors to markets in Europe, Asia, and Latin America that offer enormous potential. **(O)**
   b. Breakdown of communism means less chance of world war. **(O)**
   c. Environmentalism being reflected in laws on pollution and energy usage. **(T)**

4. **Sociocultural**
   a. Developing nations desire goods seen on TV. **(O)**
   b. Middle-aged baby boomers want attractive, high-quality products, like BMWs and Maytag. **(O)**
   c. Dual-career couples increases need for labor-saving appliances, second cars, and day care. **(O)**
   d. Divorce and career mobility means need for more houses and goods to fill them. **(O)**

B. Task Environment

1. North American market mature and extremely competitive—vigilant consumers demand high quality with low price in safe, environmentally sound products. **(T)**

2. Industry going global as North American and European firms expand internationally. **(T)**

3. European design popular and consumer desire for technologically advanced appliances. **(O)**

4. **Rivalry Among Existing Firms: High.** Whirlpool, AB Electrolux, GE have enormous resources and developing global presence. **(T)**

5. **Bargaining Power of Buyers: Low.** Technology and materials can be sourced worldwide. **(O)**

6. **Power of Other Stakeholders: Medium.** Quality, safety, environmental regulations increasing. **(T)**

7. **Bargaining Power of Supplying Distributors' Power: High.** Super retailers more important; mom and pop dealers less. **(T)**

8. **Threat of Substitutes: Low. (O)**

9. **Threat of New Entrants: High.** New entrants unlikely except for large international firms. **(T)**

IV. INTERNAL ENVIRONMENT (IFAS Table; see Exhibit 2)

A. Corporate Structure

1. Divisional structure: appliance manufacturing and vending machines. Floor care managed separately. **(S)**

2. Centralized major decisions by Newton corporate staff, with a time line of about three years. **(S)**

B. Corporate Culture

1. Quality key ingredient—commitment to quality shared by executives and workers. **(S)**

2. Much of corporate culture is based on founder F. L. Maytag's personal philosophy, including concern for quality, employees, local community, innovation, and performance. **(S)**

3. Acquired companies, except for European, seem to accept dominance of Maytag culture. **(S)**

C. Corporate Resources

1. **Marketing**

   a. Maytag brand lonely repairman advertising successful but dated. **(W)**

   b. Efforts focus on distribution—combining three sales forces into two, concentrating on major retailers. (Cost $95 million for this reconstructing.) **(S)**

   c. Hoover's well-publicized marketing fiasco involving airline tickets. **(W)**

2. **Finance** (see **Exhibits 3 and 4**)

   a. Revenues are up slightly; operating income is down significantly. **(W)**

   b. Some key ratios are troubling, such as a 57% debt/asset ratio, 132% long-term debt/equity ratio. No room for more debt to grow company. **(W)**

   c. Net income is 400% less than 1988, based on common-size income statements. **(W)**

3. **R&D**

   a. Process-oriented with focus on manufacturing process and durability. **(S)**

   b. Maytag becoming a technology follower, taking too long to get product innovations to market (competitors put out more in last 6 months than prior 2 years combined) lagging in fuzzy logic and other technological areas. **(W)**

4. **Operations**

   a. Maytag's core competence. Continual improvement process kept it dominant in the U.S. market for many years. **(S)**

   b. Plants aging and may be losing competitiveness as rivals upgrade facilities. Quality no longer distinctive competence? **(W)**

5. **Human Resources**

    a. Traditionally very good relations with unions and employees. **(S)**

    b. Labor relations increasingly strained, with two salary raise delays, and layoffs of 4500 employees at Magic Chef. **(W)**

    c. Unions express concern at new, more distant tone from Maytag Corporation. **(W)**

6. **Information Systems**

    a. Not mentioned in case. Hoover fiasco in Europe suggests information systems need significant upgrading. **(W)**

    b. Critical area where Maytag may be unwilling or unable to commit resources needed to stay competitive. **(W)**

V. ANALYSIS OF STRATEGIC FACTORS

A. Situational Analysis (See SFAS Matrix in Exhibit 5)

B. Review of Current Mission and Objectives

1. Current mission appears appropriate.

2. Some of the objectives are really goals and need to be quantified and given time horizons.

VI. STRATEGIC ALTERNATIVES AND RECOMMENDED STRATEGY

A. Strategic Alternatives

1. *Growth Through Concentric Diversification:* Acquire a company in a related industry like commercial appliances.

    a. [*Pros*] Product/market synergy created by acquisition of related company.

    b. [*Cons*] Maytag does not have the financial resources to play this game.

2. *Pause Strategy:* Consolidate various acquisitions to find economies and to encourage innovation among the business units.

    a. [*Pros*] Maytag needs to get its financial house in order and get administrative control over its recent acquisitions.

    b. [*Cons*] Unless it can grow through a stronger alliance with Bosch-Siemens or some other backer, Maytag is a prime candidate for takeover because of its poor financial performance in recent years, and it is suffering from the initial reduction in efficiency inherent in acquisition strategy.

3. *Retrenchment:* Sell Hoover's foreign major home appliance businesses (Australia and UK) to emphasize increasing market share in North America.

    a. [*Pros*] Divesting Hoover improves bottom line and enables Maytag Corp. to focus on North America while Whirlpool, Electrolux, and GE are battling elsewhere.

    b. [*Cons*] Maytag may be giving up its only opportunity to become a player in the coming global appliance industry.

B. Recommended Strategy

1. Recommend pause strategy, at least for a year, so Maytag can get a grip on its European operation and consolidate its companies in a more synergistic way.

2. Maytag quality must be maintained, and continued shortage of operating capital will take its toll, so investment must be made in R&D.

3. Maytag may be able to make the Hoover UK investment work better since the recession is ending and the EU countries are closer to integrating than ever before.

4. Because it is only an average competitor, Maytag needs the Hoover link to Europe to provide a jumping-off place for negotiations with Bosch-Siemens that could strengthen their alliance.

VII. IMPLEMENTATION

A. The only way to increase profitability in North America is to further involve Maytag with the superstore retailers; sure to anger the independent dealers, but necessary for Maytag to compete.

B. Board members with more global business experience should be recruited, with an eye toward the future, especially with expertise in Asia and Latin America.

C. R&D needs to be improved, as does marketing, to get new products online quickly.

VIII. EVALUATION AND CONTROL

A. MIS needs to be developed for speedier evaluation and control. While the question of control vs. autonomy is "under review," another Hoover fiasco may be brewing.

B. The acquired companies do not all share the Midwestern work ethic or the Maytag Corporation culture, and Maytag's managers must inculcate these values into the employees of all acquired companies.

C. Systems should be developed to decide if the size and location of Maytag manufacturing plants is still correct and to plan for the future. Industry analysis indicates that smaller automated plants may be more efficient now than in the past.

Note: The following exhibits were originally attached in their entirety to this strategic audit, but for reasons of space, only their titles are listed here:

Exhibit 1: EFAS Table
Exhibit 2: IFAS Table
Exhibit 3: Ratio Analysis for 5 Years
Exhibit 4: Common-Size Income Statements
Exhibit 5: SFAS Matrix

Notes

Chapter 1

1. S. Holmes and M. Arndt, "A Plane That Could Change the Game," *Business Week* (August 9, 2004), p. 33; D. Carpenter and A. Linn, "Hoping for a Lift," *The (Ames, IA) Tribune* (May 22, 2004), p. C7; S. Holmes, "Will This Idea Really Fly?" *Business Week* (June 23, 2003), pp. 34–35; C. Matlack and S. Holmes, "Mega Plane," *Business Week* (November 10, 2003), pp. 88–92; S. Holmes, "Boeing: What Really Happened," *Business Week* (December 15, 2003), pp. 33–38; H. Jung, "Boeing Must Build 7E7 or Lose Credibility," *Des Moines Register* (December 9, 2003), p. 3D; "Where's Boeing Going?" *Economist* (November 29, 2003), pp. 57–58; B. Acohido, "Boeing Hopes to Reclaim Glory with 7E7," *USA Today* (December 17, 2003), p. 3B; B. Acohido, "Boeing Rips a Page out of Airbus' Book," *USA Today* (October 22, 2003), p. 3B; S. Holmes, "The Battle over a Radical New Plane," *Business Week* (November 25, 2002), pp. 106–108; R. C. Scamehorn, "The Boeing Commercial Airplanes Group: Decision 2001" in T. Wheelen and J. D. Hunger, *Strategic Management and Business Policy*, 9th edition, Upper Saddle River, NJ: Prentice Hall, 2004, pp. 32.1—32.17.
2. F. W. Gluck, S. P. Kaufman, and A. S. Walleck, "The Four Phases of Strategic Management," *Journal of Business Strategy* (Winter 1982), pp. 9–21.
3. M. R. Vaghefi and A. B Huellmantel, "Strategic Leadership at General Electric," *Long Range Planning* (April 1998), pp. 280–294.
4. T. J. Andersen, "Strategic Planning, Autonomous Actions and Corporate Performance," *Long Range Planning* (April 2000), pp. 184–200; C. C. Miller and L. B. Cardinal, "Strategic Planning and Firm Performance: A Synthesis of More Than Two Decades of Research," *Academy of Management Journal* (December 1994), pp. 1649–1665; P. Pekar, Jr., and S. Abraham, "Is Strategic Management Living Up to Its Promise?" *Long Range Planning* (October 1995), pp. 32–44; W. E. Hopkins and S. A. Hopkins, "Strategic Planning—Financial Performance Relationship in Banks: A Causal Examination," *Strategic Management Journal* (September 1997), pp. 635–652; N. O'Regan and A. Ghobadian, "Refocusing Performance: A Strategy-Centered Approach," paper presented at *Academy of Management* (Seattle, WA, 2003).
5. E. J. Zajac, M. S. Kraatz, and R. F. Bresser, "Modeling the Dynamics of Strategic Fit: A Normative Approach to Strategic Change," *Strategic Management Journal* (April 2000), pp. 429–453.
6. K. G. Smith and C. M. Grimm, "Environmental Variation, Strategic Change and Firm Performance: A Study of Railroad Deregulation," *Strategic Management Journal* (July–August 1987), pp. 363–376; J. A. Nickerson and B. S. Silverman, "Why Firms Want to Organize Efficiently and What Keeps Them from Doing So: Inappropriate Governance, Performance, and Adaptation in a Deregulated Industry," *Administrative Science Quarterly* (September 2003), pp. 433–465.
7. I. Wilson, "Strategic Planning Isn't Dead—It Changed," *Long Range Planning* (August 1994), p. 20.
8. D. Rigby, "Management Tools Survey 2003: Usage Up as Companies Strive to Make Headway in Tough Times," *Strategy & Leadership*, Vol. 31, No. 5 (2003), pp. 4–11.
9. R. M. Grant, "Strategic Planning in a Turbulent Environment: Evidence from the Oil Majors," *Strategic Management Journal* (June 2003), pp. 491–517.
10. M. J. Peel and J. Bridge, "How Planning and Capital Budgeting Improve SME Performance," *Long Range Planning* (December 1998), pp. 848–856; L. W. Rue and N. A. Ibrahim, "The Relationship Between Planning Sophistication and Performance in Small Businesses," *Journal of Small Business Management* (October 1998), pp. 24–32; J. C. Carland and J. W. Carland, "A Model of Entrepreneurial Planning and Its Effect on Performance," paper presented to *Association for Small Business and Entrepreneurship* (Houston, TX, 2003).
11. R. M. Grant, "Strategic Planning in a Turbulent Environment: Evidence from the Oil Majors," *Strategic Management Journal* (June 2003), pp. 491–517.
12. Quoted in "Companies that Expand Abroad: 'Knowledge Seekers' vs. Conquerors," *Knowledge@Wharton* (March 24, 2004), p. 1.
13. C. V. Callahan and B. A. Pasternack, "Corporate Strategy in the Digital Age," *Strategy & Business*, Issue 15 (2nd Quarter 1999), p. 3.
14. J. J. Ballow, R. Burgman, and M. J. Molnar, "Managing for Shareholder Value: Intangibles, Future Value and Investment Decisions," *Journal of Business Strategy*, Vol. 25, No. 3 (2004), pp. 26–34.
15. J. A. C. Baum, "Organizational Ecology," in *Handbook of Organization Studies*, edited by S. R. Clegg, C. Handy, and W. Nord (London: Sage, 1996), pp. 77–114.
16. B. M. Staw and L. D. Epstein, "What Bandwagons Bring: Effects of Popular Management Techniques on Corporate Performance, Reputation, and CEO Pay," *Administrative Science Quarterly* (September 2000), pp. 523–556.
17. T. W. Ruefli and R. R. Wiggins, "Industry, Corporate, and Segment Effects and Business Performance: A Non-Parametric Approach," *Strategic Management Journal* (September 2003), pp. 861–879; Y. E. Spanos, G. Zaralis, and S. Lioukas, "Strategy and Industry Effects on Profitability: Evidence from Greece," *Strategic Management Journal* (February 2004), pp. 139–165; E. H. Bowman and C. E. Helfat, "Does Corporate Strategy Matter?" *Strategic Management Journal* (January 2001), pp. 1–23; T. H. Brush, P. Bromiley, and M. Hendrickx, "The Relative Influence of Industry and Corporation on Business Segment Performance: An Alternative Estimate," *Strategic*

Management Journal (June 1999), pp. 519–547; K. M. Gilley, B. A. Walters, and B. J. Olson, "Top Management Team Risk Taking Propensities and Firm Performance: Direct and Moderating Effects," *Journal of Business Strategies* (Fall 2002), pp. 95–114.

18. For more information on these theories, see A. Y. Lewin and H. W. Voloberda, "Prolegomena on Coevolution: A Framework for Research on Strategy and New Organizational Forms," *Organization Science* (October 1999), pp. 519–534, and H. Aldrich, *Organizations Evolving* (London: Sage, 1999), pp. 43–74.

19. C. Gebelein, "Strategic Planning: The Engine of Change," *Planning Review* (September/October 1993), pp. 17–19.

20. R. A. D'Aveni, *Hypercompetition* (New York: The Free Press, 1994). Hypercompetition is discussed in more detail in Chapter 3.

21. R. S. M. Lau, "Strategic Flexibility: A New Reality for World-Class Manufacturing," *SAM Advanced Management Journal* (Spring 1996), pp. 11–15.

22. M. A. Hitt, B. W. Keats, and S. M. DeMarie, "Navigating in the New Competitive Landscape: Building Strategic Flexibility and Competitive Advantage in the 21st Century," *Academy of Management Executive* (November 1998), pp. 22–42.

23. D. Lei, J. W. Slocum, and R. A. Pitts, "Designing Organizations for Competitive Advantage: The Power of Unlearning and Learning," *Organizational Dynamics* (Winter 1999), pp. 24–38.

24. D. A. Garvin, "Building a Learning Organization," *Harvard Business Review* (July/August 1993), p. 80. See also P. M. Senge, *The Fifth Discipline: The Art and Practice of the Learning Organization* (New York: Doubleday, 1990).

25. A. D. Chandler, *Inventing the Electronic Century* (New York: The Free Press, 2001).

26. T. T. Baldwin, C. Danielson, and W. Wiggenhorn, "The Evolution of Learning Strategies in Organizations: From Employee Development to Business Redefinition," *Academy of Management Executive* (November 1997), pp. 47–58.

27. N. Collier, F. Fishwick, and S. W. Floyd, "Managerial Involvement and Perceptions of Strategy Process," *Long Range Planning* (February 2004), pp. 67–83; J. A. Parnell, S. Carraher, and K. Holt, "Participative Management's Influence on Effective Strategic Planning," *Journal of Business Strategies* (Fall 2002), pp. 161–179.

28. E. W. K. Tsang, "Internationalization as a Learning Process: Singapore MNCs in China," *Academy of Management Executive* (February 1999), pp. 91–101; J. M. Shaver, W. Mitchell, and B. Yeung, "The Effect of Own-Firm and Other Firm Experience on Foreign Direct Investment Survival in the U.S., 1987–92," *Strategic Management Journal* (November 1997), pp. 811–824.

29. W. Mitchell, J. M. Shaver, and B. Yeung, "Getting There in a Global Industry: Impacts on Performance of Changing International Presence," *Strategic Management Journal* (September 1992), pp. 419–432.

30. Research supports the use of this model in examining firm strategies. See J. A. Smith, "Strategies for Start-Ups," *Long Range Planning* (December 1998), pp. 857–872.

31. See A. Campbell and S. Yeung, "Brief Case: Mission, Vision, and Strategic Intent," *Long Range Planning* (August 1991), pp. 145–147, and S. Cummings and J. Davies, "Mission, Vision, Fusion," *Long Range Planning* (December 1994), pp. 147–150.

32. J. Cosco, "Down to the Sea in Ships," *Journal of Business Strategy* (November/December 1995), p. 48.

33. J. S. Sidhu, E. J. Nijssen, and H. R. Commandeur, "Business Domain Definition Practice: Does It Affect Organizational Performance?" *Long Range Planning* (June 2000), pp. 376–401.

34. W. C. Symonds, "Thinking Outside the Big Box," *Business Week* (August 4, 2003), pp. 62–63.

35. W. C. Symonds, "Thinking Outside the Big Box," *Business Week* (August 4, 2003), pp. 62–63.

36. K. M. Eisenhardt and D. N. Sull, "Strategy as Simple Rules," *Harvard Business Review* (January 2001), p. 110.

37. N. Nohria, W. Joyce, and B. Roberson, "What Really Works," *Harvard Business Review* (July 2003), p. 46.

38. D. Welch, "Cadillac Hits the Gas," *Business Week* (September 4, 2000), p. 50.

39. S. Holmes, "GE: Little Engines That Could," *Business Week* (January 20, 2003), pp. 62–63.

40. H. A. Simon, *Administrative Behavior*, 2nd edition (New York: The Free Press, 1957), p. 231.

41. M. Useem, "Lenovo Chairman Liu Chuanzhi: 'We Have Decided to Refocus on the PC Business,'" *Knowledge @ Wharton* (25 August–7 September, 2004).

42. H. Mintzberg, "Planning on the Left Side and Managing on the Right," *Harvard Business Review* (July–August 1976), p. 56.

43. See E. Romanelli and M. L. Tushman, "Organizational Transformation as Punctuated Equilibrium: An Empirical Test," *Academy of Management Journal* (October 1994), pp. 1141–1166.

44. S. S. Gordon, W. H. Stewart, Jr., R. Sweo, and W. A. Luker, "Convergence Versus Strategic Reorientation: The Antecedents of Fast-Paced Organizational Change," *Journal of Management*, Vol. 26, No. 5 (2000), pp. 911–945.

45. Speech to the 1998 Academy of Management, reported by S. M. Puffer, "Global Executive: Intel's Andrew Grove on Competitiveness," *Academy of Management Executive* (February 1999), pp. 15–24.

46. D. J. Hickson, R. J. Butler, D. Cray, G. R. Mallory, and D. C. Wilson, *Top Decisions: Strategic Decision-Making in Organizations* (San Francisco: Jossey-Bass, 1986), pp. 26–42.

47. T. A. Fogarty, "Keeping Zippo's Flame Eternal," *USA Today* (June 24, 2003), p. 3B.

48. H. Mintzberg, "Strategy-Making in Three Modes," *California Management Review* (Winter 1973), pp. 44–53.

49. F. Vogelstein, "Mighty Amazon," *Fortune* (May 26, 2003), pp. 60–74.

50. M. Wong, "Once-Prized Encyclopedias Fall into Disuse," *Des Moines Register* (March 9, 2004), p. 3D.

51. L. V. Gerstner, *Who Says Elephants Can't Dance?* (New York: HarperCollins, 2002).

52. J. B. Quinn, *Strategies for Change: Logical Incrementalism* (Homewood, IL: Irwin, 1980), p. 58.

53. R. M. Grant, "Strategic Planning in a Turbulent Environment: Evidence from the Oil Majors," *Strategic Management Journal* (June 2003), pp. 491–517.

54. P. J. Brews and M. R. Hunt, "Learning to Plan and Planning to Learn: Resolving the Planning School/Learning School Debate," *Strategic Management Journal* (October 1999), pp. 889–913; I. Gold and A. M. A. Rasheed, "Rational Decision-Making and Firm Performance: The Moderating Role of the Environment," *Strategic Management Journal* (August 1997), pp. 583–591; R. L. Priem, A. M. A. Rasheed, and A. G. Kotulic, "Rationality in Strategic Decision Processes, Environmental Dynamism and Firm Performance," *Journal of*

Management, Vol. 21, No. 5 (1995), pp. 913–929; J. W. Dean, Jr., and M. P. Sharfman, "Does Decision Process Matter? A Study of Strategic Decision-Making Effectiveness," *Academy of Management Journal* (April 1996), pp. 368–396.

55. T. L. Wheelen and J. D. Hunger, "Using the Strategic Audit," *SAM Advanced Management Journal* (Winter 1987), pp. 4–12; G. Donaldson, "A New Tool for Boards: The Strategic Audit," *Harvard Business Review* (July–August 1995), pp. 99–107.

56. D. C. Hambrick and J. W. Fredrickson, "Are You Sure You Have a Strategy?" *Academy of Management Executive* (November 2001), pp. 48–59.

57. Hambrick and Fredrickson, p. 49.

58. "Free Trade on Trial," *Economist* (January 3, 2004), pp. 13–16; "A Club in Need of a New Vision," *Economist* (May 1, 2004), pp. 25–27; *World in Figures, 2004 Edition*, published by *The Economist* in association with Profile Books (2003), p. 14.

59. P. Jones and L. Kahaner, *Say It & Live It: 50 Corporate Mission Statements That Hit the Mark* (New York: Currency Doubleday, 1995), p. 53.

Chapter 2

1. N. Byrnes and W. C. Symonds, "Is the Avalanche Headed for PriceWaterhouse?" *Business Week* (October 14, 2002), pp. 45–46; W. C. Symonds, "Tyco: How Did They Miss a Scam So Big?" *Business Week* (September 30, 2002), pp. 40–42; H. R. Weber, "Questions Arise about Board Reviewing Tyco's Finances," *The (Ames, IA) Tribune* (July 6, 2002), p. C8; N. Varchaver, "The Big Kozlowski," *Fortune* (November 18, 2002), pp. 123–126; H. R. Weber, "The King Is Gone," *Des Moines Register* (September 18, 2002), p. D1; "Tyco Settles," *Des Moines Register* (October 24, 2002), p. 3D; H. Bray, "Tyco's Walsh Agrees to Pay Back $20 Million," *Des Moines Register* (December 18, 2002), p. 3D; P. N. Levenson, "Tyco's Betrayal of Board Governance," *Directors & Boards* (Summer 2002), pp. 35–38.

2. A. G. Monks and N. Minow, *Corporate Governance* (Cambridge, MA: Blackwell Business, 1995), pp. 8–32.

3. Ibid., p. 1.

4. W. Symonds, "Tyco: The Vise Grows Ever-Tighter," *Business Week* (October 7, 2002), pp. 48–49.

5. A. Demb and F. F. Neubauer, "The Corporate Board: Confronting the Paradoxes," *Long Range Planning* (June 1992), p. 13. These results are supported by a 1995 Korn/Ferry International survey in which chairs and directors agreed that strategy and management succession, in that order, are the most important issues the board expects to face.

6. Reported by E. L. Biggs in "CEO Succession Planning: An Emerging Challenge for Boards of Directors," *Academy of Management Executive* (February 2004), pp. 105–107.

7. A. Borrus, "Less Laissez-Faire in Delaware?" *Business Week* (March 22, 2004), pp. 80–82.

8. L. Light, "Why Outside Directors Have Nightmares," *Business Week* (October 23, 1996), p. 6.

9. "Where's All the Fun Gone?" *Economist* (March 20, 2004), p. 76.

10. *Directors' Compensation and Board Practices in 2003*, Research Report R-1339-03-RR (New York: Conference Board, 2003), p. 35.

11. Nadler proposes a similar five-step continuum for board involvement ranging from the least involved "passive board" to the most involved "operating board," plus a form for measuring board involvement in D. A. Nadler, "Building Better Boards," *Harvard Business Review* (May 2004), pp. 102–111.

12. H. Ashbaugh, D. W. Collins, and R. LaFond, "The Effects of Corporate Governance on Firms' Credit Ratings," unpublished paper (March 2004); W. Q. Judge, Jr., and C. P. Zeithaml, "Institutional and Strategic Choice Perspectives on Board Involvement in the Strategic Choice Process," *Academy of Management Journal* (October 1992), pp. 766–794; J. A. Pearce II and S. A. Zahra, "Effective Power-Sharing Between the Board of Directors and the CEO," *Handbook of Business Strategy*, 1992/93 Yearbook (Boston: Warren, Gorham, and Lamont, 1992), pp. 1.1–1.16.

13. *26th Annual Board of Directors Study* (New York: Korn/Ferry International, 1999), p. 7.

14. The 2003 percentages for Asian Pacific and UK boards are 69% and 84%, respectively. See *30th Annual Board of Directors Study* (New York: Korn/Ferry International, 2003), p. 6.

15. *Current Board Practices,* American Society of Corporate Secretaries, 2002, as reported by B. Atkins in "Directors Don't Deserve Such a Punitive Policy," *Directors & Boards* (Summer 2002), p. 23.

16. D. A. Nadler, "Building Better Boards," *Harvard Business Review* (May 2004), pp. 102–111; L. Lavelle, "The Best and Worst Boards," *Business Week* (October 7, 2002), pp. 104–114.

17. Nadler, p. 109.

18. A. L. Ranft and H. M. O'Neill, "Board Composition and High-Flying Founders: Hints of Trouble to Come?" *Academy of Management Executive* (February 2001), pp. 126–138.

19. D. F. Larcher, S. A. Richardson, and I. Tuna, "Does Corporate Governance Really Matter?" *Knowledge @ Wharton* (September 8–21, 2004); J. Merritt and L. Lavelle, "A Different Kind of Governance Guru," *Business Week* (August 9, 2004), pp. 46–47; A. Dehaene, V. DeVuyst, and H. Ooghe, "Corporate Performance and Board Structure in Belgian Companies," *Long Range Planning* (June 2001), pp. 383–398; M. W. Peng, "Outside Directors and Firm Performance During Institutional Transitions," *Strategic Management Journal* (May 2004), pp. 453–471.

20. *30th Annual Board of Directors Study Supplement: Governance Trends of the Fortune 1000* (New York: Korn/Ferry International, 2004), p. 3.

21. L. L. Carr, "Strategic Determinants of Executive Compensation in Small Publicly Traded Firms," *Journal of Small Business Management* (April 1997), pp. 1–12.

22. *30th Annual Board of Directors Study* (New York: Korn/Ferry International, 2003).

23. W. S. Schulze, M. H. Lubatkin, R. N. Dino, and A. K. Buchholtz, "Agency Relationships in Family Firms: Theory and Evidence," *Organization Science* (March–April 2001), pp. 99–116.

24. J. P. Katz and B. P. Niehoff, "How Owners Influence Strategy—A Comparison of Owner-Controlled and Manager-Controlled Firms," *Long Range Planning* (October 1998), pp. 755–761; M. Kroll, P. Wright, L. Toombs, and H. Leavell, "Form of Control: A Critical Determinant of Acquisition Performance and CEO Rewards," *Strategic Management Journal* (February 1997), pp. 85–96.

25. L. Tihanyi, R. A. Johnson, R. E. Hoskisson, and M. A. Hitt, "Institutional Ownership Differences and International Diversification: The Effects of Boards of Directors and Technological Opportunity," *Academy of Management Journal*

(April 2003), pp. 195–211; A. E. Ellstrand, L. Tihanyi, and J. L. Johnson, "Board Structure and International Political Risk," *Academy of Management Journal* (August 2002), pp. 769–777; S. A. Zahra, D. O. Neubaum, and M. Huse, "Entrepreneurship in Medium-Size Companies: Exploring the Effects of Ownership and Governance Systems," *Journal of Management*, Vol. 26, No. 5 (2000), pp. 947–976.

26. G. Kassinis and N. Vafeas, "Corporate Boards and Outside Stakeholders as Determinants of Environmental Litigation," *Strategic Management Journal* (May 2002), pp. 399–415; P. Dunn, "The Impact of Insider Power on Fraudulent Financial Reporting," *Journal of Management*, Vol. 30, No. 3 (2004), pp. 397–412.

27. W. S. Schulze, M. H. Lubatkin, R. N. Dino, and A. K. Buckholtz, "Agency Relationships in Family Firms: Theory and Evidence," *Organization Science* (March–April 2001), pp. 99–116.

28. M. N. Young, A. K. Bushholtz, and D. Ahlstrom, "How Can Board Members Be Empowered if They Are Spread Too Thin?" *SAM Advanced Management Journal* (Autumn 2003), pp. 4–11.

29. *Directors' Compensation and Board Practices in 2003*, Research Report R-1339-03-RR (New York: Conference Board, 2003), Table 49, p. 38.

30. C. M. Daily and D. R. Dalton, "The Endangered Director," *Journal of Business Strategy*, Vol. 25, No. 3 (2004), pp. 8–9.

31. I. Sager, "The Boardroom: New Rules, New Loopholes," *Business Week* (November 29, 2004), p. 13.

32. *Directors' Compensation and Board Practices in 2003*, Research Report R-1339-03-RR (New York: Conference Board, 2003), Table 49, p. 38.

33. See S. Finkelstein and D. C. Hambrick, *Strategic Leadership: Top Executives and Their Impact on Organizations* (St. Paul, MN: West, 1996), p. 213.

34. R. A. G. Monks, "What Will Be the Impact of Acting Shareholders? A Practical Recipe for Constructive Change," *Long Range Planning* (February 1999), p. 20.

35. "TIAA-CREF's Role in Corporate Governance," *Investment Forum* (June 2003), p. 13.

36. *30th Annual Board of Directors Study Supplement: Governance Trends of the Fortune 1000* (New York: Korn/Ferry International, 2004), pp. 3–4; K. Weisul, "Make Way for the Madame Director," *Business Week* (December 22, 2003), p. 57.

37. J. Daum, "Portrait of Boards on the Cusp of Historic Change," *Directors & Boards* (Winter 2003), p. 56; J. Daum, "SSBI: Audit Committees Are Leading the Change," *Directors & Boards* (Winter 2004), p. 59.

38. *30th Annual Board of Directors Study* (New York: Korn/Ferry International, 2003), p. 38.

39. *Globalizing the Board of Directors: Trends and Strategies* (New York: The Conference Board, 1999).

40. *30th Annual Board of Directors Study Supplement: Governance Trends of the Fortune 1000* (New York: Korn/Ferry International, 2004), pp. 7–11; *Directors' Compensation and Board Practices in 2003*, Research Report R-1339-03-RR (New York: Conference Board, 2003), p. 10.

41. R. W. Pouder and R. S. Cantrell, "Corporate Governance Reform: Influence on Shareholder Wealth," *Journal of Business Strategies* (Spring 1999), pp. 48–66.

42. M. L. Gerlach, "The Japanese Corporate Network: A Blockmodel Analysis," *Administrative Science Quarterly* (March 1992), pp. 105–139.

43. J. D. Westphal, M. L. Seidel, and K. J. Stewart, "Second-Order Imitation: Uncovering Latent Effects of Board Network Ties," *Administrative Science Quarterly* (December 2001), pp. 717–747; M. A. Geletkanycz, B. K. Boyd, and S. Finkelstein, "The Strategic Value of CEO External Directorate Networks: Implications for CEO Compensation," *Strategic Management Journal* (September 2001), pp. 889–898; M.A. Carpenter and J. D. Westphal, "The Strategic Context of External Network Ties: Examining the Impact of Director Appointments on Board Involvement in Strategic Decision Making," *Academy of Management Journal* (August 2001), pp. 639–660.

44. M. Warner, "Inside the Silicon Valley Money Machine," *Fortune* (October 26, 1998), pp. 128–140.

45. D. Jones and B. Hansen, "Chairmen Still Doing Do-Si-Do," *USA Today* (November 5, 2003), p. 3B; J. H. Daum and T. J. Neff, "SSBI: Audit Committees Are Leading the Charge," *Directors & Boards* (Winter 2003), p. 59.

46. J. A. C. Baum and C. Oliver, "Institutional Linkages and Organizational Mortality," *Administrative Science Quarterly* (June 1991), pp. 187–218; J. P. Sheppard, "Strategy and Bankruptcy: An Exploration into Organizational Death," *Journal of Management* (Winter 1994), pp. 795–833.

47. *Directors' Compensation and Board Practices in 2003*, Research Report R-1339-03-RR (New York: Conference Board, 2003), Table 49, p. 38.

48. J. Canavan, B. Jones, and M. J. Potter, "Board Tenure: How Long Is Too Long?" *Boards & Directors* (Winter 2004), pp. 39–42.

49. *30th Annual Board of Directors Study Supplement: Governance Trends of the Fortune 1000* (New York: Korn/Ferry International, 2004), p. 5.

50. D. F. Larcker and S. A. Richardson, "Does Governance Really Matter?" *Knowledge @ Wharton* (September 8–21, 2004).

51. *26th Annual Board of Directors Study* (New York: Korn/Ferry International, 1999), p. 30.

52. *30th Annual Board of Directors Study* (New York: Korn/Ferry International, 2003), pp. 8, 31, 44.

53. *Directors' Compensation and Board Practices in 2003*, Research Report R-1339-03-RR (New York: Conference Board, 2003), p. 37; H. Sherman, Review of "The Recurrent Crisis in Corporate Governance" by MacAvoy and Millstein, *Directors & Boards* (Spring 2004), p. 15.

54. A. Desai, M. Kroll, and P. Wright, "CEO Duality, Board Monitoring, and Acquisition Performance," *Journal of Business Strategies* (Fall 2003), pp. 147–156; D. Harris and C. E. Helfat, "CEO Duality, Succession, Capabilities and Agency Theory: Commentary and Research Agenda," *Strategic Management Journal* (September 1998), pp. 901–904; C. M. Daily and D. R. Dalton, "CEO and Board Chair Roles Held Jointly or Separately: Much Ado About Nothing," *Academy of Management Executive* (August 1997), pp. 11–20; D. L. Worrell, C. Nemec, and W. N. Davidson III, "One Hat Too Many: Key Executive Plurality and Shareholder Wealth," *Strategic Management Journal* (June 1997), pp. 499–507; J. W. Coles and W. S. Hesterly, "Independence of the Chairman and Board Composition: Firm Choices and Shareholder Value," *Journal of Management*, Vol. 26, No. 2 (2000), pp. 195–214; H. Ashbaugh, D. W. Collins, and R. LaFond, "The Effects of Corporate Governance on Firms' Credit Ratings," unpublished paper, March 2004.

55. N. R. Augustine, "How Leading a Role for the Lead Director?" *Directors & Boards* (Winter 2004), pp. 20–23.

56. *30th Annual Board of Directors Study Supplement: Governance Trends of the Fortune 1000* (New York: Korn/Ferry International, 2004), p. 5.

57. *30th Annual Board of Directors Study* (New York: Korn/Ferry International, 2003), p. 5.

58. H. Bray, "Tyco's Walsh Agrees to Pay Back $20 Million," *Des Moines Register* (December 18, 2002), p. 3D.

59. J. D. Westphal, "Board Games: How CEOs Adapt to Increases in Structural Board Independence from Management," *Administrative Science Quarterly* (September 1998), pp. 511–537; J. D. Westphal and P. Khanna, "Keeping Directors in Line: Social Distancing as a Control Mechanism in the Corporate Elite," *Administrative Science Quarterly* (September 2003), pp. 361–398.

60. H. L. Tosi, W. Shen, and R. J. Gentry, "Why Outsiders on Boards Can't Solve the Corporate Governance Problem," *Organizational Dynamics*, Vol. 32, No. 2 (2003), pp. 180–192.

61. *30th Annual Board of Directors Study Supplement: Governance Trends of the Fortune 1000* (New York: Korn/Ferry International, 2004), p. 5. Other committees are succession planning (32%), directors' compensation (31%), finance (30%), corporate responsibility (19%), and investment (16%).

62. Perhaps because of their potential to usurp the power of the board, executive committees are being used less often.

63. "Re-examining the Role of the Chairman of the Board," *Knowledge @ Wharton* (May 20, 2004). Summary of an article originally published December 18, 2002.

64. *30th Annual Board of Directors Study Supplement: Governance Trends of the Fortune 1000* (New York: Korn/Ferry International, 2004), p. 5.

65. "Where's All the Fun Gone?" *Economist* (March 20, 2004), pp. 75–77.

66. J. H. Daum and T. J. Neff, "SSBI: Audit Committees Are Leading the Charge," *Directors & Boards* (Winter 2002), p. 58.

67. *30th Annual Board of Directors Study* (New York: Korn/Ferry International, 2003), p. 25.

68. J. Sonnenfeld, "Good Governance and the Misleading Myths of Bad Metrics" *Academy of Management Executive* (February 2004), pp. 108–113.

69. H. Ashbaugh, D. W. Collins, and R. LaFond, "The Effects of Corporate Governance on Firms' Credit Ratings," unpublished paper (March 2002).

70. *30th Annual Board of Directors Study* (New York: Korn/Ferry International, 2003), pp. 7, 22, 27, 37, 52.

71. I. Sager, "Access Denied: A Private Matter," *Business Week* (January 26, 2004), p. 13; J. Weber, "One Share, Many Votes," *Business Week* (March 29, 2004), pp. 94–95.

72. E. Thorton, "Corporate Control Freaks," *Business Week* (May 31, 2004), p. 86.

73. D. R. Dalton, C. M. Daily, A. E. Ellstrand, and J. L. Johnson, "Meta-Analytic Reviews of Board Composition, Leadership Structure, and Financial Performance," *Strategic Management Journal* (March 1998), pp. 269–290; G. Beaver, "Competitive Advantage and Corporate Governance—Shop Soiled and Needing Attention!" *Strategic Change* (September–October 1999), p. 330.

74. For governance trends in Europe, see A. Cadbury, "What Are the Trends in Corporate Governance? How Will They Impact Your Company?" *Long Range Planning* (February 1999), pp. 12–19.

75. A. Backover, "Sprint to Pay $50M, Alter Board Procedures," *USA Today* (March 20, 2003), p. 5B.

76. A. Borrus and L. Young, "Nothing Like a Little Exposure," *Business Week* (September 13, 2004), p. 92.

77. L. He and M. J. Conyon, "The Role of Compensation Committees in CEO and Committee Compensation Decisions," paper presented to *Academy of Management* (Seattle, WA, 2003).

78. L. Lavelle, "A Fighting Chance for Boardroom Democracy," *Business Week* (June 9, 2003), p. 50; L. Lavelle, "So That's Why Boards Are Waking Up," *Business Week* (January 19, 2004), pp. 72–73.

79. S. Finkelstein and D. C. Hambrick, *Strategic Leadership: Top Executives and Their Impact on Organizations* (St. Louis: West, 1996).

80. D. C. Hambrick, T. S. Cho, and M-J Chen, "The Influence of Top Management Team Heterogeneity on Firms' Competitive Moves," *Administrative Science Quarterly* (December 1996), pp. 659–684.

81. P. Pitcher and A. D. Smith, "Top Management Heterogeneity: Personality, Power, and Proxies," *Organization Science* (January–February 2001), pp. 1–18; M. A. Carpenter and J. W. Fredrickson, "Top Management Teams, Global Strategic Posture, and the Moderating Role of Uncertainty," *Academy of Management Journal* (June 2001), pp. 533–545; M. A. Carpenter, "The Implications of Strategy and Social Context for the Relationship Between Top Management Team Heterogeneity and Firm Performance," *Strategic Management Journal* (March 2002), pp. 275–284; L. Tihanyi, A. E. Ellstrand, C. M. Daily, and D. R. Dalton, "Composition of the Top Management Team and Firm International Expansion," *Journal of Management*, Vol. 26, No. 6 (2000), pp. 1157–1177.

82. "One on One with Steve Reinemund," *Business Week* (December 17, 2001), special advertising insert on leadership by Heidrick & Struggles, executive search firm.

83. D. A. Waldman, G. G. Ramirez, R. J. House, and P. Puranam, "Does Leadership Matter? CEO Leadership Attributes and Profitability Under Conditions of Perceived Environmental Uncertainty," *Academy of Management Journal* (February 2001), pp. 134–143; F. J. Flynn and B. M. Staw, "Lend Me Your Wallets: The Effect of Charismatic Leadership on External Support for an Organization," *Strategic Management Journal* (April 2004), pp. 309–330.

84. J. Burns, *Leadership* (New York: HarperCollins, 1978); B. Bass, "From Transactional to Transformational Leadership: Learning to Share the Vision," *Organizational Dynamics*, Vol. 18 (1990), pp. 19–31; W. Bennis and B. Nanus, *Leaders: Strategies for Taking Charge* (New York: HarperCollins, 1997).

85. L. V. Gerstner, Jr., *Who Says Elephants Can't Dance?* (New York: HarperCollins, 2002), p. 124.

86. M. Lipton, "Demystifying the Development of an Organizational Vision," *Sloan Management Review* (Summer 1996), p. 84.

87. S. Hahn, "Why High Tech Has to Stay Humble," *Business Week* (January 19, 2004), pp. 76–77.

88. J. H. David, F. D. Schoorman, R. Mayer, and H. H. Tan, "The Trusted General Manager and Business Unit Performance: Empirical Evidence of a Competitive Advantage," *Strategic Management Journal* (May 2000), pp. 563–576.

89. D. B. McNatt and T. A. Judge, "Boundary Conditions of the Galatea Effect: A Field Experiment and Constructive Replication," *Academy of Management Journal* (August 2004), pp. 550–565.

90. J. E. Bono and T. A. Judge, "Self-Concordance at Work: Toward Understanding the Motivational Effects of Transformational Leaders," *Academy of Management Journal* (October 2003), pp. 554–571.

91. T. Lowry, R. O. Crockett, and I. M. Kunii, "Verizon's Gutsy Bet," *Business Week* (August 4, 2003), pp. 52–62.

92. G. Tate and U. Malmendier, "Who Makes Acquisitions? CEO Overconfidence and the Market's Reaction," summarized by *Knowledge @ Wharton* (February 25, 2004).

93. M. S. Chae and J. S. Hill, "The Hazards of Strategic Planning for Global Markets," *Long Range Planning* (December 1996), pp. 880–891.

94. T. R. Eisenmann and J. L. Bower, "The Entrepreneurial M-Form: Strategic Integration in Global Media Firms," *Organization Science* (May–June 2000), pp. 348–355.

95. For an in-depth guide to conducting the strategic planning process, see C. D. Fogg, *Team-Based Strategic Planning* (New York: AMACOM, 1994).

96. M. Wiersema, "Holes at the Top: Why CEO Firings Backfire," *Harvard Business Review* (December 2002), pp. 70–77.

97. L. Greiner, T. Cummings, and A. Bhambri, "When New CEOs Succeed and Fail: 4-D Theory of Strategic Transformation," *Organizational Dynamics*, Vol. 32, No. 1 (2003), pp. 1–16.

98. G. Strauss, "Board Pay Gets Fatter as Job Gets Harrier," *USA Today* (March 7, 2005), p. 1B.

Chapter 3

1. M. Conlin, J. Hempel, J. Tanzer, and D. Poole, "The Corporate Donors," *Business Week* (December 1, 2003), pp. 92–96; I. Sager, "The List: Angels in the Boardroom," *Business Week* (July 7, 2003), p. 12.

2. M. Friedman, "The Social Responsibility of Business Is to Increase Its Profits," *New York Times Magazine* (September 13, 1970), pp. 30, 126–127; M. Freidman, *Capitalism and Freedom* (Chicago: University of Chicago Press, 1963), p. 133.

3. W. J. Byron, *Old Ethical Principles for the New Corporate Culture*, presentation to the College of Business, Iowa State University, Ames, Iowa (March 31, 2003).

4. A. B. Carroll, "A Three-Dimensional Conceptual Model of Corporate Performance," *Academy of Management Review* (October 1979), pp. 497–505. This model of business responsibilities was reaffirmed in A. B. Carroll, "Managing Ethically with Global Stakeholders: A Present and Future Challenge," *Academy of Management Executive* (May 2004), pp. 114–120.

5. Carroll refers to discretionary responsibilities as philanthropic responsibilities in A. B. Carroll, "The Pyramid of Corporate Social Responsibility: Toward the Moral Management of Organizational Stakeholders," *Business Horizons* (July–August 1991), pp. 39–48.

6. M. S. Baucus and D. A. Baucus, "Paying the Piper: An Empirical Examination of Longer-Term Financial Consequences of Illegal Corporate Behavior," *Academy of Management Journal* (February 1997), pp. 129–151.

7. J. Oleck, "Pink Slips with a Silver Lining," *Business Week* (June 4, 2001), p. 14.

8. A. McWilliams and D. Siegel, "Corporate Social Responsibility and Financial Performance: Correlation or Misspecification?" *Strategic Management Journal* (May 2000), pp. 603–609; P. Rechner and K. Roth, "Social Responsibility and Financial Performance: A Structural Equation Methodology," *International Journal of Management* (December 1990), pp. 382–391; K. E. Aupperle, A. B. Carroll, and J. D. Hatfield, "An Empirical Examination of the Relationship Between Corporate Social Responsibility and Profitability," *Academy of Management Journal* (June 1985), p. 459.

9. M. M. Arthur, "Share Price Reactions to Work-Family Initiatives: An Institutional Perspective," *Academy of Management Journal* (April 2003), pp. 497–505; S. A. Waddock and S. B. Graves, "The Corporate Social Performance—Financial Performance Link," *Strategic Management Journal* (April 1997), pp. 303–319; M.V. Russo and P. A. Fouts, "Resource-Based Perspective on Corporate Environmental Performance and Profitability," *Academy of Management Journal* (July 1997), pp. 534–559; H. Meyer, "The Greening of Corporate America," *Journal of Business Strategy* (January/February 2000), pp. 38–43.

10. J. D. Margolis and J. P. Walsh, "Misery Loves Companies: Rethinking Social Initiatives by Business," *Administrative Science Quarterly* (June 2003), pp. 268–305.

11. M. F. L. Orlitzky, F. L. Schmidt, and S. L. Rynes, "Corporate Social and Financial Performance: A Meta Analysis," *Organization Studies*, Vol. 24 (2003), pp. 403–441.

12. M. Porter and M. R. Kramer, "The Competitive Advantage of Corporate Philanthropy," *Harvard Business Review* (December 2002), p. 59.

13. P. S. Adler and S. W. Kwon, "Social Capital: Prospects for a New Concept," *Academy of Management Journal* (January 2002), pp. 17–40.

14. L. Gard, "We're Good Guys, Buy from Us," *Business Week* (November 22, 2004), pp. 72–74.

15. S. A. Muirhead, C. J. Bennett, R. E. Berenbeim, A. Kao, and D. J. Vidal, *Corporate Citizenship in the New Century* (New York: The Conference Board, 2002), p. 6.

16. *2002 Sustainability Survey Report*, PricewaterhouseCoopers, reported in "Corporate America's Social Conscience," Special Advertising Section, *Fortune* (May 26, 2003), pp. 149–157.

17. C. L. Harman and E. R. Stafford, "Green Alliances: Building New Business with Environmental Groups," *Long Range Planning* (April 1997), pp. 184–196.

18. D. B. Turner and D. W. Greening, "Corporate Social Performance and Organizational Attractiveness to Prospective Employees," *Academy of Management Journal* (July 1997), pp. 658–672; S. Preece, C. Fleisher, and J. Toccacelli, "Building a Reputation Along the Value Chain at Levi Strauss," *Long Range Planning* (December 1995), pp. 88–98; J. B. Barney and M. H. Hansen, "Trustworthiness as a Source of Competitive Advantage," *Strategic Management Journal* (Special Winter Issue, 1994), pp. 175–190.

19. R. E. Freeman and D. R. Gilbert, *Corporate Strategy and the Search for Ethics* (Upper Saddle River, NJ: Prentice Hall, 1988), p. 6.

20. M. Arndt, W. Zellner, and P. Coy, "Too Much Corporate Power?" *Business Week* (September 11, 2000), pp. 144–158.

21. "Report: CEOs of Companies with Greatest Outsourcing Got Biggest Pay," *Des Moines Register* (August 31, 2004), p. B5.

22. "Andy Grove to Corporate Boards: It's Time to Take Charge," *Knowledge @ Wharton* (September 9—October 5, 2004).

23. "Nearly Half of Workers Take Unethical Actions—Survey," *Des Moines Register* (April 7, 1997), p. 18B.

24. J. Kurlantzick, "Liar, Liar," *Entrepreneur* (October 2003), p. 70.

25. M. Roman, "True Confessions from CFOs," *Business Week* (August 12, 2002), p. 40.

26. J. Kurlantzick, "Liar, Liar," *Entrepreneur* (October 2003), p. 71.

27. J. Hempel and L. Gard, "The Corporate Givers," *Business Week* (November 29, 2004), pp. 100–104.

28. S. Li, S. H. Park, and S. Li, "The Great Leap Forward: The Transition from Relation-Based Governance to Rule-Based Governance," *Organizational Dynamics*, Vol. 33, No. 1 (2004), pp. 63–78; M. Davids, "Global Standards, Local Problems," *Business Strategy* (January/February 1999), pp. 38–43; "The Opacity Index," *Economist* (September 18, 2004), p. 106.

29. K. Kumar, "Ethical Orientation of Future American Executives: What the Value Profiles of Business School Students Portend," *SAM Advanced Management Journal* (Autumn 1995), pp. 32–36, 47; M. Gable and P. Arlow, "A Comparative Examination of the Value Orientations of British and American Executives," *International Journal of Management* (September 1986), pp. 97–106; W. D. Guth and R. Tagiuri, "Personal Values and Corporate Strategy," *Harvard Business Review* (September–October 1965), pp. 126–127; G. W. England, "Managers and Their Value Systems: A Five Country Comparative Study," *Columbia Journal of World Business* (Summer 1978), p. 35.

30. J. F. Veiga, T. D. Golden, and K. Dechant, "Why Managers Bend Company Rules," *Academy of Management Executive* (May 2004), pp. 84–91.

31. H. Collingwood, "The Earnings Game," *Harvard Business Review* (June 2001), pp. 65–74; J. Fox, "Can We Trust Them Now?" *Fortune* (March 3, 2003), pp. 97–99.

32. S. Watkins, "Former Enron Vice President Sherron Watkins on the Enron Collapse," *Academy of Management Executive* (November 2003), p. 122.

33. L. K. Trevino, "Ethical Decision Making in Organizations: A Person–Situation Interactionist Model," *Academy of Management Review* (July 1986), pp. 601–617.

34. L. Kohlberg, "Moral Stage and Moralization: The Cognitive-Development Approach," in *Moral Development and Behavior*, edited by T. Lickona (New York: Holt, Rinehart & Winston, 1976).

35. L. K. Trevino, "Ethical Decision Making in Organizations: A Person–Situation Interactionist Model," *Academy of Management Review* (July 1986), p. 606.

36. J. Keogh, ed., *Corporate Ethics: A Prime Business Asset* (New York: The Business Roundtable, 1988), p. 5.

37. G. F. Kohut and S. E. Corriher, "The Relationship of Age, Gender, Experience and Awareness of Written Ethics Policies to Business Decision Making," *SAM Advanced Management Journal* (Winter 1994), pp. 32–39; J. C. Lere and B. R. Gaumitz, "The Impact of Codes of Ethics on Decision Making: Some Insights from Information Economics," *Journal of Business Ethics*, Vol. 48 (2003), pp. 365–379.

38. *Business Roundtable Institute for Corporate Ethics Announces Key Findings from "Mapping the Terrain" Survey of CEOs*, press release (Charlottesville, VA: Business Roundtable Institute for Corporate Ethics, June 10, 2004).

39. "Reebok Finds Bad Conditions in Two Factories," *Des Moines Register* (October 19, 1999), p. 8S.

40. T. J. Von der Embse and R. A. Wagley, "Managerial Ethics: Hard Decisions on Soft Criteria," *SAM Advanced Management Journal* (Winter 1988), p. 6.

41. G. F. Cavanagh, *American Business Values*, 3rd ed. (Upper Saddle River, NJ: Prentice Hall, 1990), pp. 186–199.

42. B. R. Agle, R. K. Mitchell, and J. A. Sonnenfeld, "Who Matters Most to CEOs? An Investigation of Stakeholder Attributes and Salience, Corporate Performance, and CEO Values," *Academy of Management Journal* (October 1999), pp. 507–525.

43. G. F. Cavanagh, *American Business Values*, 3rd ed. (Upper Saddle River, NJ: Prentice Hall, 1990), pp. 195–196.

44. I. Kant, "The Foundations of the Metaphysic of Morals," in *Ethical Theory: Classical and Contemporary Readings*, 2nd ed., by L. P. Pojman (Belmont, CA: Wadsworth Publishing, 1995), pp. 255–279.

45. J. L. Badaracco, Jr., *Defining Moments* (Boston: Harvard Business School Press, 1997).

46. "Datbit," *Biz Ed* (March/April 2004).

Chapter 4

1. D. Debelak, "All Fired Up," *Entrepreneur* (July 2004), pp. 116–120.

2. J. B. Thomas, S. M. Clark, and D. A. Gioia, "Strategic Sensemaking and Organizational Performance: Linkages Among Scanning, Interpretation, Action, Outcomes," *Academy of Management Journal* (April 1993), pp. 239–270; J. A. Smith, "Strategies for Start-ups," *Long Range Planning* (December 1998), pp. 857–872.

3. V. K. Garg, B. A. Walters, and R. L. Priem, "Chief Executive Scanning Emphases, Environmental Dynamism, and Manufacturing Performance," *Strategic Management Journal* (August 2003), pp. 725–744.

4. P. Lasserre and J. Probert, "Competing on the Pacific Rim: High Risks and High Returns," *Long Range Planning* (April 1994), pp. 12–35.

5. M. J. Cetron, "Economics: Prospects for the 'Dragon' and the 'Tiger,'" *Futurist* (July–August 2004), pp. 10–11.

6. W. E. Halal, "The Top 10 Emerging Technologies," *Special Report* (World Future Society, 2000).

7. F. Dobbin and T. J. Dowd, "How Policy Shapes Competition: Early Railroad Foundings in Massachusetts," *Administrative Science Quarterly* (September 1997), pp. 501–529.

8. A. Shleifer and R. W. Viskny, "Takeovers in the 1960s and the 1980s: Evidence and Implications," in *Fundamental Issues in Strategy: A Research Agenda*, edited by R. P. Rumelt, D. E. Schendel, and D. J. Teece (Boston: Harvard Business School Press, 1994), pp. 403–418.

9. "Europe's Workplace Revolution," *Economist* (July 31, 2004), pp. 51–52.

10. "Old Europe," *Economist* (October 2, 2004), pp. 49–50.

11. "The Incredible Shrinking Country," *Economist* (November 13, 2004), pp. 45–46.

12. J. Wyatt, "Playing the Woofie Card," *Fortune* (February 6, 1995), pp. 130–132.

13. D. Carpenter, "Walgreen Pursues 12,000 Corners of Market," *Des Moines Register* (May 9, 2004), pp. 1D, 5D.

14. D. Pitt, "Winnebago Industries Benefits from Motor Home Boom," *The (Ames, IA) Tribune* (August 30, 2004), p. B5.

15. M. Arndt, "Zimmer: Growing Older Gracefully," *Business Week* (June 9, 2003), pp. 82–84.

16. H. Yen, "Empty Nesters Push Growth of Pet Health Care Businesses," *The (Ames, IA) Tribune* (September 27, 2003), p. C8.

17. A. Bianco, "The Vanishing Mass Market," *Business Week* (July 12, 2004), pp. 61–68.

18. M. Conlin, "UnMarried America," *Business Week* (October 20, 2003), pp. 106–116.

19. N. Irvin II, "The Arrival of the Thrivals," *Futurist* (March–April 2004), pp. 16–23.

20. G. Smith and C. Lindblad, "Mexico: Was NAFTA Worth It?" *Business Week* (December 22, 2003), pp. 66–72.

21. "Multicultural Retailing," *Arizona Republic* (October 10, 2004), p. D4.

22. "Islamic Finance: West Meets East," *Economist* (October 25, 2003), p. 69.

23. J. Naisbitt, *Megatrends Asia* (New York: Simon & Schuster, 1996), p. 79.

24. K. Ohmae, "The Triad World View," *Journal of Business Strategy* (Spring 1987), pp. 8–19.

25. A. Menon and A. Tomkins, "Learning About the Market's Periphery: IBM's WebFountain," *Long Range Planning* (April 2004), pp. 153–162.

26. I. M. Cockburn, R. M. Henderson, and S. Stern, "Untangling the Origins of Competitive Advantage," *Strategic Management Journal* (October–November 2000), Special Issue, pp. 1123–1145.

27. L. Fuld, "Be Prepared," *Harvard Business Review* (November 2003), pp. 20–21.

28. H. Wissema, "Driving Through Red Lights," *Long Range Planning* (October 2002), pp. 521–539; B. K. Boyd and J. Fulk, "Executive Scanning and Perceived Uncertainty: A Multidimensional Model," *Journal of Management*, Vol. 22, No. 1 (1996), pp. 1–21.

29. P. G. Audia, E. A. Locke, and K. G. Smith, "The Paradox of Success: An Archival and a Laboratory Study of Strategic Persistence Following Radical Environmental Change," *Academy of Management Journal* (October 2000), pp. 837–853; M. L. McDonald and J. D. Westphal, "Getting By with the Advice of Their Friends: CEOs Advice Networks and Firms' Strategic Responses to Poor Performance," *Administrative Science Quarterly* (March 2003), pp. 1–32; R. A. Bettis and C. K. Prahalad, "The Dominant Logic: Retrospective and Extension," *Strategic Management Journal* (January 1995), pp. 5–14; J. M. Stofford and C. W. F. Baden-Fuller, "Creating Corporate Entrepreneurship," *Strategic Management Journal* (September 1994), pp. 521–536; J. M. Beyer, P. Chattopadhyay, E. George, W. H. Glick, and D. Pugliese, "The Selective Perception of Managers Revisited," *Academy of Management Journal* (June 1997), pp. 716–737.

30. H. I. Ansoff, "Strategic Management in a Historical Perspective," in *International Review of Strategic Management*, Vol. 2, No. 1 (1991), edited by D. E. Hussey (Chichester, England: Wiley, 1991), p. 61.

31. M. E. Porter, *Competitive Strategy* (New York: The Free Press, 1980), p. 3.

32. This summary of the forces driving competitive strategy is taken from Ibid., pp. 7–29.

33. M. McCarthy, "Rivals Scramble to Topple Nike's Sneaker Supremacy," *USA Today* (April 3, 2003), pp. B1–B2.

34. M. E. Porter, *Competitive Strategy* (New York: The Free Press, 1980), p. 23.

35. A. S. Grove, "Surviving a 10x Force," *Strategy & Leadership* (January/February 1997), pp. 35–37.

36. A fragmented industry is defined as one whose market share for the leading four firms is equal to or less than 40% of total industry sales. See M. J. Dollinger, "The Evolution of Collective Strategies in Fragmented Industries," *Academy of Management Review* (April 1990), pp. 266–285.

37. M. E. Porter, "Changing Patterns of International Competition," *California Management Review* (Winter 1986), pp. 9–40.

38. T. N. Gladwin, "Assessing the Multinational Environment for Corporate Opportunity," in *Handbook of Business Strategy*, edited by W. D. Guth (Boston: Warren, Gorham and Lamont, 1985), pp. 7.28–7.41.

39. K. J. Hatten and M. L. Hatten, "Strategic Groups, Asymmetrical Mobility Barriers, and Contestability," *Strategic Management Journal* (July–August 1987), p. 329.

40. J. D. Osborne, C. I. Stubbart, and A. Ramaprasad, "Strategic Groups and Competitive Enactment: A Study of Dynamic Relationships Between Mental Models and Performance," *Strategic Management Journal* (May 2001), pp. 435–454; A. Fiegenbaum and H. Thomas, "Strategic Groups as Reference Groups: Theory, Modeling and Empirical Examination of Industry and Competitive Strategy," *Strategic Management Journal* (September 1995), pp. 461–476; H. R. Greve, "Managerial Cognition and the Mimities Adoption of Market Positions: What You See Is What You Do," *Strategic Management Journal* (October 1998), pp. 967–988.

41. C. C. Pegels, Y. I. Song, and B. Yang, "Management Heterogeneity, Competitive Interaction Groups, and Firm Performance," *Strategic Management Journal* (September 2000), pp. 911–923.

42. R. E. Miles and C. C. Snow, *Organizational Strategy, Structure, and Process* (New York: McGraw-Hill, 1978). See also D. J. Ketchen, Jr., "An Interview with Raymond E. Miles and Charles C. Snow," *Academy of Management Executive* (November 2003), pp. 97–104.

43. R. A. D'Aveni, *Hypercompetition* (New York: The Free Press, 1994), pp. xiii–xiv.

44. C. W. Hofer and D. Schendel, *Strategy Formulation: Analytical Concepts* (St. Paul: West Publishing Co., 1978), p. 77.

45. "Information Overload," *Journal of Business Strategy* (January–February 1998), p. 4.

46. E. Von Hipple, *Sources of Innovation* (New York: Oxford University Press, 1988), p. 4.

47. "CI of 'Singular Importance,' Says Procter & Gamble's Chairman," *Competitive Intelligence Magazine* (July–September 1999), p. 5.

48. R. G. Vedder, "CEO and CIO Attitudes about Competitive Intelligence," *Competitive Intelligence Magazine* (October–December 1999), pp. 39–41.

49. J. Schlosser, "Looking for Intelligence in Ice Cream," *Fortune* (March 17, 2003), pp. 114–120.

50. S. H. Miller, "Beware Rival's Web Site Subterfuge," *Competitive Intelligence Magazine* (January–March 2000), p. 8.

51. E. Iwata, "More U.S. Trade Secrets Walk Out Door with Foreign Spies," *USA Today* (February 13, 2003), pp. B1, B2.

52. "Twenty-nine Percent Spy on Co-Workers," *USA Today* (August 19, 2003), p. B1.

53. B. Flora, "Ethical Business Intelligence is NOT Mission Impossible," *Strategy & Leadership* (January/February 1998), pp. 40–41.

54. A. L. Penenberg and M. Berry, *Spooked: Espionage in Corporate America* (Cambridge, MA: Perseus Publishing, 2000).

55. T. Kendrick and J. Blackmore, "Ten Things You Really Need to Know About Competitors," *Competitive Intelligence Magazine* (September–October 2001), pp. 12–15.

56. "CI at Avnet: A Bottom-Line Impact," *Competitive Intelligence Magazine* (July–September 2000), p. 5. For further information on competitive intelligence, see C. S. Fleisher and D. L. Blenkhorn, *Controversies in Competitive Intelligence: The Enduring Issues* (Westport, CT: Praeger Publishers, 2003); C. Vibert, *Competitive Intelligence: A Framework for Web-Based Analysis and Decision Making* (Mason, OH: Thomson/Southwestern, 2004); and C. S. Fleisher and B. E. Bensoussan, *Strategic and Competitive Analysis* (Upper Saddle River, NJ: Prentice Hall, 2003).

57. L. M. Grossman, "Families Have Changed But Tupperware Keeps Holding Its Parties," *Wall Street Journal* (July 21, 1992), pp. A1, A13.

58. H. E. Klein and R. E. Linneman, "Environmental Assessment: An International Study of Corporate Practices," *Journal of Business Strategy* (Summer 1984), p. 72.

59. See L. E. Schlange and U. Juttner, "Helping Managers to Identify the Key Strategic Issues," *Long Range Planning* (October 1997), pp. 777–786, for an explanation and application of the cross-impact matrix.

60. This process of scenario development is adapted from M. E. Porter, *Competitive Advantage* (New York: The Free Press, 1985), pp. 448–470.

61. H. C. Sashittal and A. R. Jassawalla, "Learning from Wayne Gretzky," *Organizational Dynamics* (Spring 2002), pp. 341–355.

62. "Fast Food and Strong Currency" *Economist* (June 11, 2005), p. 70.

63. M. E. Porter, *Competitive Strategy: Techniques for Analyzing Industries and Competitors* (New York: The Free Press, 1980), pp. 47–75.

64. M. Treacy and F. Wiersema, *The Discipline of Market Leaders* (Reading, MA: Addison-Wesley, 1995).

65. Presentation by W. A. Rosenkrans, Jr., to the Iowa Chapter of the Society of Competitive Intelligence Professionals, Des Moines, IA (August 5, 2004).

66. B. Gilad, *Early Warning* (New York: AMACOM, 2004), pp. 97–103. Also see C. S. Fleisher and B. E. Bensoussan, *Strategic and Competitive Analysis* (Upper Saddle River, NJ: Prentice Hall, 2003), pp. 122–143.

67. Presentation by W. A. Rosenkrans, Jr., to the Iowa Chapter of the Society of Competitive Intelligence Professionals, Des Moines, IA (August 5, 2004).

68. L. Fahey, "Invented Competitors: A New Competitor Analysis Methodology," *Strategy & Leadership*, Vol. 30, No. 6 (2002), pp. 5–12.

Chapter 5

1. A. Park and L. Young, "Dell Outfoxes Its Rivals," *Business Week* (September 6, 2004), p. 54.

2. A. Serwer, "Dell Does Domination," *Fortune* (January 21, 2002), p. 71.

3. A. Park and P. Burrows, "What You Don't Know About Dell," *Business Week* (November 3, 2003), pp. 77–84.

4. K. Maney, "Dell Business Model Turns to Muscle as Rivals Struggle," *USA Today* (January 20, 2003), pp. 1B–2B.

5. Ibid., p. 2B.

6. M. Javidan, "Core Competence: What Does It Mean in Practice?" *Long Range Planning* (February 1998), pp. 60–71.

7. M. A. Hitt, B. W. Keats, and S. M. DeMarie, "Navigating in the New Competitive Landscape: Building Strategic Flexibility and Competitive Advantage in the 21st Century," *Academy of Management Executive* (November 1998), pp. 22–42; C. E. Helfat and M. A. Peteraf, "The Dynamic Resources-Based View: Capability Life Cycles," *Strategic Management Journal* (October 2003), pp. 997–1010.

8. D. Brady and K. Capell, "GE Breaks the Mold to Spur Innovation," *Business Week* (April 26, 2004), pp. 88–89.

9. J. B. Barney, *Gaining and Sustaining Competitive Advantage*, 2nd edition (Upper Saddle River, NJ: Prentice Hall, 2003), pp. 159–172. Barney's VRIO questions are very similar to those proposed by G. Hamel and S. K. Prahalad in their book *Competing for the Future* (Boston: Harvard Business School Press, 1994) on pages 202–207, in which they state that to be distinctive, a competency must (a) provide customer value, (b) be competitor unique, and (c) be extendable to develop new products and/or markets.

10. Barney, p. 161.

11. R. M. Grant, "The Resource-Based Theory of Competitive Advantage: Implications for Strategy Formulation," *California Management Review* (Spring 1991), pp. 114–135.

12. P. J. Verdin and P. J. Williamson, "Core Competencies, Competitive Advantage and Market Analysis: Forging the Links," in *Competence-Based Competition*, edited by G. Hamel and A. Heene (New York: John Wiley & Sons, 1994), pp. 83–84.

13. M. E. Porter, "Clusters and the New Economics of Competition," *Harvard Business Review* (November–December 1998), pp. 77–90.

14. J. M. Shaver and F. Flyer, "Agglomeration Economies, Firm Heterogeneity, and Foreign Direct Investment in the United States," *Strategic Management Journal* (December 2000), pp. 1175–1193; W. Chung and A. Kalnins, "Agglomeration Effects and Performance: A Test of the Texas Lodging Industry," *Strategic Management Journal* (October 2001), pp. 969–988.

15. J. E. McGee and L. G. Love, "Sources of Competitive Advantage for Small Independent Retailers: Lessons from the Neighborhood Drugstore," *Association for Small Business & Entrepreneurship*, Houston, TX (March 10–13, 1999), p. 2.

16. M. Polanyi, *The Tacit Dimension* (Garden City, NY: Doubleday, 1966).

17. S. K. McEvily and B. Chakravarthy, "The Persistence of Knowledge-Based Advantage: An Empirical Test for Product Performance and Technological Knowledge," *Strategic Management Journal* (April 2002), pp. 285–305.

18. P. E. Bierly III, "Development of a Generic Knowledge Strategy Typology," *Journal of Business Strategies* (Spring 1999), p. 3.

19. S. Abraham, "Experiencing Strategic Conversations about the Central Forces of our Time," *Strategy & Leadership*, Vol. 31, No. 2 (2003), pp. 61–62.

20. C. A. de Kluyver and J. A. Pearce II, *Strategy: A View from the Top* (Upper Saddle River, NJ: Prentice Hall, 2003), pp. 63–66.

21. O. Gadiesh and J. L. Gilbert, "Profit Pools: A Fresh Look at Strategy," *Harvard Business Review* (May–June 1998), pp. 139–147.

22. J. R. Galbraith, "Strategy and Organization Planning," in *The Strategy Process: Concepts, Contexts, and Cases*, 2nd ed., edited by H. Mintzberg and J. B. Quinn (Upper Saddle River, NJ: Prentice Hall, 1991), pp. 315–324.

23. M. Porter, *Competitive Advantage: Creating and Sustaining Superior Performance* (New York: The Free Press, 1985), p. 36.

24. M. Leontiades, "A Diagnostic Framework for Planning," *Strategic Management Journal* (January–March 1983), p. 14.

25. E. H. Schein, *The Corporate Culture Survival Guide* (San Francisco: Jossey-Bass, 1999), p. 12; L. C. Harris and E. Ogbonna, "The Strategic Legacy of Company Founders," *Long Range Planning* (June 1999), pp. 333–343.

26. D. M. Rousseau, "Assessing Organizational Culture: The Case for Multiple Methods," in *Organizational Climate and Culture*, edited by B. Schneider (San Francisco: Jossey-Bass, 1990), pp. 153–192.

27. L. Smircich, "Concepts of Culture and Organizational Analysis," *Administrative Science Quarterly* (September 1983), pp. 345–346.

28. J. B. Sorensen, "The Strength of Corporate Culture and the Reliability of Firm Performance," *Administrative Science Quarterly* (March 2002), pp. 70–91.

29. K. E. Aupperle, "Spontaneous Organizational Reconfiguration: A Historical Example Based on Xenophon's Anabasis," *Organization Science* (July–August 1996), pp. 445–460.

30. J. B. Barney, *Gaining and Sustaining Competitive Advantage* (Reading, MA: Addison-Wesley, 1997), p. 155.

31. D. Brady, R. D. Hof, A. Reinhardt, M. Ihlwan, S. Holmes, and K. Capell, "Cult Brands," *Business Week* (August 2, 2004), pp. 64–69.

32. R. T. Wilcox, "The Hidden Potential of Powerful Brands," *Batten Briefings* (Summer 2003), pp. 1, 4–5.

33. C. Fombrun and C. Van Riel, "The Reputational Landscape," *Corporate Reputation Review*, Vol. 1, Nos. 1 & 2 (1997), pp. 5–13.

34. P. W. Roberts and G. R. Dowling, "Corporate Reputation and Sustained Financial Performance," *Strategic Management Journal* (December 2002), pp. 1077–1093; J. Shamsie, "The Context of Dominance: An Industry-Driven Framework for Exploiting Reputation," *Strategic Management Journal* (March 2003), pp. 199–215; M. D. Michalisin, D. M. Kline, and R. D. Smith, "Intangible Strategic Assets and Firm Performance: A Multi-Industry Study of the Resource-Based View," *Journal of Business Strategies* (Fall 2000), pp. 91–117; S. S. Standifird, "Reputation and E-Commerce: eBay Auctions and the Asymmetrical Impact of Positive and Negative Ratings," *Journal of Management*, Vol. 27, No. 3 (2001), pp. 279–295.

35. R. L. Simerly and M. Li, "Environmental Dynamism, Capital Structure and Performance: A Theoretical Integration and an Empirical Test," *Strategic Management Journal* (January 2000), pp. 31–49.

36. Ibid.; A. Heisz and S. LaRochelle-Cote, "Corporate Financial Leverage in Canadian Manufacturing: Consequences for Employment and Inventories," *Canadian Journal of Administrative Science* (June 2004), pp. 111–128.

37. J. M. Poterba and L. H. Summers, "A CEO Survey of U.S. Companies' Time Horizons and Hurdle Rates," *Sloan Management Review* (Fall 1995), pp. 43–53.

38. "R&D Scoreboard," *Business Week* (June 27, 1994), pp. 81–103.

39. B. O'Reilly, "The Secrets of America's Most Admired Corporations: New Ideas and New Products," *Fortune* (March 3, 1997), p. 62.

40. P. Pascarella, "Are You Investing in the Wrong Technology?" *Industry Week* (July 25, 1983), p. 37.

41. D. J. Yang, "Leaving Moore's Law in the Dust," *U.S. News & World Report* (July 10, 2000), pp. 37–38; R. Fishburne and M. Malone, "Laying Down the Laws: Gordon Moore and Bob Metcalfe in Conversation," *Forbes ASAP* (February 21, 2000), pp. 97–100.

42. P. Pascarella, "Are You Investing in the Wrong Technology?" *Industry Week* (July 25, 1983), p. 38.

43. C. M. Christensen, *The Innovator's Dilemma* (Boston: Harvard Business School Press, 1997).

44. B. J. Pine, *Mass Customization: The New Frontier in Business Competition* (Boston: Harvard Business School Press, 1993).

45. S. L Rynes, K. G. Brown, and A. E. Colbert, "Seven Common Misconceptions About Human Resource Practices: Research Findings Versus Practitioner Belief," *Academy of Management Executives* (August 2002), pp. 92–103.

46. E. E. Lawler, S. A. Mohrman, and G. E. Ledford, Jr., *Creating High Performance Organizations* (San Francisco: Jossey-Bass, 1995), p. 29.

47. A. Versteeg, "Self-Directed Work Teams Yield Long-Term Benefits," *Journal of Business Strategy* (November/December 1990), pp. 9–12.

48. R. Sanchez, "Strategic Flexibility in Product Competition," *Strategic Management Journal* (Summer 1995), p. 147.

49. A. R. Jassawalla and H. C. Sashittal, "Building Collaborative Cross-Functional New Product Teams," *Academy of Management Executives* (August 1999), pp. 50–63.

50. A. M. Townsend, S. M. DeMarie, and A. R. Hendrickson, "Virtual Teams: Technology and the Workplace of the Future," *Academy of Management Executives* (August 1998), pp. 17–29.

51. S. A. Furst, M. Reeves, B. Rosen, and R. S. Blackburn, "Managing the Life Cycle of Virtual Teams," *Academy of Management Executives* (May 2004), pp. 6–20; L. L. Martins, L. L. Gilson, and M. T. Maynard, "Virtual Teams: What Do We Know and Where Do We Go From Here?" *Journal of Management*, Vol. 30, No. 6 (2004), pp. 805–835.

52. A. M. Townsend, S. M. DeMarie, and A. R. Hendrickson, "Virtual Teams: Technology and the Workplace of the Future," *Academy of Management Executives* (August 1998), p. 18.

53. A. Bernstein, "Can This Man Save Labor?" *Business Week* (September 13, 2004), pp. 80–88.

54. D. Welsh, "What Goodyear Got from its Union," *Business Week* (October 20, 2003), pp. 148–149.

55. S. F. Matusik and C. W. L. Hill, "The Utilization of Contingent Work, Knowledge Creation, and Competitive Advantage," *Academy of Management Executives* (October 1998), pp. 680–697.

56. "Part-Time Workers," *Economist* (July 24, 2004), p. 90.

57. A. Bernstein, "At UPS, Part-Time Work Is a Full-Time Issue," *Business Week* (June 16, 1997), pp. 88–90.

58. J. Muller, "A Ford Redesign," *Business Week* (November 13, 2000), Special Report.

59. G. Colvin, "The 50 Best Companies for Asians, Blacks, and Hispanics," *Fortune* (July 19, 1999), pp. 53–58.

60. V. Singh and S. Point, "Strategic Responses by European Companies to the Diversity Challenge: An Online Comparison," *Long Range Planning* (August 2004), pp. 295–318.

61. Ibid., p. 310.

62. J. Bachman, "Coke to Pay $192.5 Million to Settle Lawsuit," *The (Ames, IA) Tribune* (November 20, 2000), p. D4.

63. J. Lee and D. Miller, "People Matter: Commitment to Employees, Strategy, and Performance in Korean Firms," *Strategic Management Journal* (June 1999), pp. 579–593.

64. A. Cortese, "Here Comes the Intranet," *Business Week* (February 26, 1996), p. 76.

65. D. Bartholomew, "Blue-Collar Computing," *InformationWeek* (June 19, 1995), pp. 34–43.

66. C. C. Poirier, *Advanced Supply Chain Management* (San Francisco: Berrett-Koehler Publishers, 1999), p. 2.

67. M. Cook and R. Hagey, "Why Companies Flunk Supply-Chain 101: Only 33 Percent Correctly Measure Supply-Chain Performance; Few Use the Right Incentives," *Journal of Business Strategy*, Vol. 24, No. 4 (2003), pp. 35–42.

68. C. C. Poirier, *Advanced Supply Chain Management* (San Francisco: Berrett-Kohler Publishers, 1999), pp. 3–5.

69. B. Horowitz, "KFC Roast Line Flops After 3 Months," *USA Today* (July 16, 2004), p. 6D.

70. *Economist Pocket World in Figures, 2004 Edition* (London: Profile Books, 2003), p. 54.

Chapter 6

1. A. Fitzgerald, "Cedar Rapids Export Company Serves Muslims Worldwide," *Des Moines Register* (October 26, 2003), pp. 1M–2M.

2. K. W. Glaister and J. R. Falshaw, "Strategic Planning: Still Going Strong?" *Long Range Planning* (February 1999), pp. 107–116.

3. T. Brown, "The Essence of Strategy," *Management Review* (April 1997), pp. 8–13.

4. T. Hill and R. Westbrook, "SWOT Analysis: It's Time for a Product Recall," *Long Range Planning* (February 1997), pp. 46–52.

5. W. H. Newman, "Shaping the Master Strategy of Your Firm," *California Management Review*, Vol. 9, No. 3 (1967), pp. 77–88.

6. "A Teaching Tool Outlining a Special Day with Howard Shultz," Videotaped Interview, Lloyd Greif Center for Entrepreneurial Studies, University of Southern California (2004).

7. M. E. Porter, *Competitive Strategy* (New York: The Free Press, 1980), pp. 34–41, as revised in M. E. Porter, *The Competitive Advantage of Nations* (New York: The Free Press, 1990), pp. 37–40.

8. J. O. DeCastro and J. J. Chrisman, "Narrow-Scope Strategies and Firm Performance: An Empirical Investigation," *Journal of Business Strategies* (Spring 1998), pp. 1–16; T. M. Stearns, N. M. Carter, P. D. Reynolds, and M. L. Williams, "New Firm Survival: Industry, Strategy, and Location," *Journal of Business Venturing* (January 1995), pp. 23–42.

9. M. E. Porter, *Competitive Strategy* (New York: The Free Press, 1980), p. 35.

10. R. E. Caves and P. Ghemawat, "Identifying Mobility Barriers," *Strategic Management Journal* (January 1992), pp. 1–12.

11. N. K. Geranios, "Potlach Aims to Squeeze Toilet Tissue Leaders," *Des Moines Register* (October 22, 2003), p. 3D.

12. "Hewlett-Packard: Losing the HP Way," *Economist* (August 21, 2004), pp. 49–50.

13. C. Campbell-Hunt, "What Have We Learned About Generic Competitive Strategy? A Meta Analysis," *Strategic Management Journal* (February 2000), pp. 127–154.

14. M. Kroll, P. Wright, and R. A. Heiens, "The Contribution of Product Quality to Competitive Advantage: Impacts on Systematic Variance and Unexplained Variance in Returns," *Strategic Management Journal* (April 1999), pp. 375–384.

15. R. M. Hodgetts, "A Conversation with Michael E. Porter: A 'Significant Extension' Toward Operational Improvement and Positioning," *Organizational Dynamics* (Summer 1999), pp. 24–33.

16. N. Brodsky, "Size Matters," *INC.* (September 1998), pp. 31–32.

17. M. Rushlo, "P.F. Chang's Plans Succeed Where Others Have Failed," *Des Moines Register* (May 18, 2004), pp. 1D, 6D.

18. P. F. Kocourek, S. Y. Chung, and M. G. McKenna, "Strategic Rollups: Overhauling the Multi-Merger Machine," *Strategy + Business* (2nd Quarter 2000), pp. 45–53.

19. J. A. Tannenbaum, "Acquisitive Companies Set Out to 'Roll Up' Fragmented Industries," *Wall Street Journal* (March 3, 1997), pp. A1, A6; VCA Antech, Inc., 10Q Statement, June 30, 2004.

20. R. A. D'Aveni, *Hypercompetition* (New York: The Free Press, 1994), pp. xiii–xiv.

21. P. C. Nutt, "Surprising but True: Half the Decisions in Organizations Fail," *Academy of Management Executive* (November 1999), pp. 75–90.

22. Some refer to this as the economic concept of "increasing returns." Instead of the curve leveling off when the company reaches a point of diminishing returns when a product saturates a market, the curve continues to go up as the company takes advantage of setting the standard to spin off new products that use the new standard to achieve higher performance than competitors. See J. Alley, "The Theory That Made Microsoft," *Fortune* (April 29, 1996), pp. 65–66.

23. H. Lee, K. G. Smith, C. M. Grimm, and A. Schomburg, "Timing, Order and Durability of New Product Advantages with Imitation," *Strategic Management Journal* (January 2000), pp. 23 30; Y. Pan and P. C. K. Chi, "Financial Performance and Survival of Multinational Corporations in China," *Strategic Management Journal* (April 1999), pp. 359–374; R. Makadok, "Can First-Mover and Early-Mover Advantages Be Sustained in an Industry with Low Barriers to Entry/Imitation?" *Strategic Management Journal* (July 1998), pp. 683–696; B. Mascarenhas, "The Order and Size of Entry into International Markets," *Journal of Business Venturing* (July 1997), pp. 287–299.

24. At these respective points, cost disadvantages vis-à-vis later entrants fully eroded the earlier returns to first movers. See W. Boulding and M. Christen, "Idea—First Mover Disadvantage," *Harvard Business Review*, Vol. 79, No. 9 (2001), pp. 20–21, as reported by D. J. Ketchen, Jr., C. C. Snow, and V. L. Hoover, "Research on Competitive Dynamics: Recent Accomplishments and Future Challenges," *Journal of Management*, Vol. 30, No. 6 (2004), pp. 779–804.

25. M. B. Lieberman and D. B. Montgomery, "First-Mover (Dis) Advantages: Retrospective and Link with the Resource-Based View," *Strategic Management Journal* (December, 1998), pp. 1111–1125; G. J. Tellis and P. N. Golder, "First to Market, First to Fail? Real Causes of Enduring Market Leadership," *Sloan Management Review* (Winter 1996), pp. 65–75.

26. J. Pope, "Schick Entry May Work Industry into a Lather," *Des Moines Register* (May 15, 2003), p. 6D.

27. For an in-depth discussion of first- and late-mover advantages and disadvantages, see D. S. Cho, D. J. Kim, and D. K. Rhee, "Latecomer Strategies: Evidence from the Semiconductor Industry in Japan and Korea," *Organization Science* (July–August 1998), pp. 489–505.

28. J. Shamsie, C. Phelps, and J. Kuperman, "Better Late Than Never: A Study of Late Entrants in Household Electrical Equipment," *Strategic Management Journal* (January 2004), pp. 69–84.

29. T. S. Schoenecker and A. C. Cooper, "The Role of Firm Resources and Organizational Attributes in Determining Entry

Timing: A Cross-Industry Study," *Strategic Management Journal* (December 1998), pp. 1127–1143.

30. Summarized from various articles by L. Fahey in *The Strategic Management Reader*, edited by L. Fahey (Upper Saddle River, NJ: Prentice Hall, 1989), pp. 178–205.

31. M. Boyle, "Dueling Diapers," *Fortune* (February 17, 2003), pp. 115–116.

32. P. Burrows, "Show Time," *Business Week* (February 2, 2004), pp. 56–64.

33. A. Serwer, "Happy Birthday, Steinway," *Fortune* (March 17, 2003), pp. 94–97.

34. This information on defensive tactics is summarized from M. E. Porter, *Competitive Advantage* (New York: The Free Press, 1985), pp. 482–512.

35. H. D. Hopkins, "The Response Strategies of Dominant U.S. Firms to Japanese Challengers," *Journal of Management*, Vol. 29, No. 1 (2003), pp. 5–25.

36. T. M. Burton, "Archer-Daniels Faces a Potential Blow As Three Firms Admit Price-Fixing Plot," *Wall Street Journal* (August 28, 1996), pp. A3, A6; R. Henkoff, "The ADM Tale Gets Even Stranger," *Fortune* (May 13, 1996), pp. 113–120.

37. B. Gordon, "Qwest Defends Pacts with Competitors," *Des Moines Register* (April 30, 2002), p. 1D.

38. Much of the content on cooperative strategies was summarized from J. B. Barney, *Gaining and Sustaining Competitive Advantage* (Reading, MA: Addison-Wesley, 1997), pp. 255–278.

39. E. A. Murray, Jr., and J. F. Mahon, "Strategic Alliances: Gateway to the New Europe?" *Long Range Planning* (August 1993), p. 103.

40. R. D. Ireland, M. A. Hitt, and D. Vaidyanath, "Alliance Management as a Source of Competitive Advantage," *Journal of Management*, Vol. 28, No. 3 (2002), pp. 413–446.

41. P. Anslinger and J. Jenk, "Creating Successful Alliances," *Journal of Business Strategy*, Vol. 25, No. 2 (2004), pp. 18–22.

42. S. H. Park and G. R. Ungson, "Interfirm Rivalry and Managerial Complexity: A Conceptual Framework of Alliance Failure," *Organization Science* (January–February 2001), pp. 37–53; D. C. Hambrick, J. Li, K. Xin, and A. S. Tsui, "Compositional Gaps and Downward Spirals in International Joint Venture Management Groups," *Strategic Management Journal* (November 2001), pp. 1033–1053; T. K. Das and B. S. Teng, "Instabilities of Strategic Alliances: An Internal Tensions Perspective," *Organization Science* (January–February 2000), pp. 77–101; J. F. Hennart, D. J. Kim, and M. Zeng, "The Impact of Joint Venture Status on the Longevity of Japanese Stakes in U.S. Manufacturing Affiliates," *Organization Science* (May–June 1998), pp. 382–395.

43. N. K. Park, J. M. Mezias, and J. Song, "A Resource-Based View of Strategic Alliances and Firm Value in the Electronic Marketplace," *Journal of Management*, Vol. 30, No. 1 (2004), pp. 7–27; T. Khanna and J. W. Rivkin, "Estimating the Performance Effects of Business Groups in Emerging Markets," *Strategic Management Journal* (January 2001), pp. 45–74; G. Garai, "Leveraging the Rewards of Strategic Alliances," *Journal of Business Strategy* (March–April 1999), pp. 40–43.

44. L. Segil, "Strategic Alliances for the 21st Century," *Strategy & Leadership* (September/October 1998), pp. 12–16.

45. J. Draulans, A. P. deMan, and H. W. Volberda, "Building Alliance Capability: Management Techniques for Superior Alliance Performance," *Long Range Planning* (April 2003),

pp. 151–166; P. Kale, J. H. Dyer, and H. Singh, "Alliance Capability, Stock Market Response, and Long-Term Alliance Success: The Role of the Alliance Function," *Strategic Management Journal* (August 2002), pp. 747–767.

46. M. M. Bear, "How Japanese Partners Help U.S. Manufacturers to Raise Productivity," *Long Range Planning* (December 1998), pp. 919–926.

47. P. Anslinger and J. Jenk, "Creating Successful Alliances," *Journal of Business Strategy*, Vol. 25, No. 2 (2004), p. 18.

48. J. W. Lu and P. W. Beamish, "The Internationalization and Performance of SMEs," *Strategic Management Journal* (June–July 2001), pp. 565–586.

49. C. Sheehan, "Brewery Bottles a Cool Idea," *Des Moines Register* (August 26, 2004), p. 6D.

50. R. M. Kanter, "Collaborative Advantage: The Art of Alliances," *Harvard Business Review* (July–August 1994), pp. 96–108.

51. B. Bremner, Z. Schiller, T. Smart, and W. J. Holstein, "Keiretsu Connections," *Business Week* (July 22, 1996), pp. 52–54.

52. R. P. Lynch, *The Practical Guide to Joint Ventures and Corporate Alliances* (New York: John Wiley & Sons, 1989), p. 7.

53. H. Green, "Double Play," *Business Week E-Biz* (October 23, 2000), pp. EB-42–EB-46.

54. L. L. Blodgett, "Factors in the Instability of International Joint Ventures: An Event History Analysis," *Strategic Management Journal* (September 1992), pp. 475–481; J. Bleeke and D. Ernst, "The Way to Win in Cross-Border Alliances," *Harvard Business Review* (November–December 1991), pp. 127–135; J. M. Geringer, "Partner Selection Criteria for Developed Country Joint Ventures," in *International Management Behavior*, 2nd ed., edited by H. W. Lane and J. J. DiStephano (Boston: PWS-Kent, 1992), pp. 206–216.

55. B. Horovitz, "New Coffee Maker May Jolt Industry," *USA Today* (February 18, 2004), pp. 1E–2E.

56. K. Z. Andrews, "Manufacturer/Supplier Relationships: The Supplier Payoff," *Harvard Business Review* (September–October 1995), pp. 14–15.

57. P. Lorange, "Black-Box Protection of Your Core Competencies in Strategic Alliances," in *Cooperative Strategies: European Perspectives*, edited by P. W. Beamish and J. P. Killing (San Francisco: The New Lexington Press, 1997), pp. 59–99.

58. E. P. Gee, "Co-opetition: The New Market Milieu," *Journal of Healthcare Management*, Vol. 45 (2000), pp. 359–363.

59. D. J. Ketchen, Jr., C. C. Snow, and V. L. Hoover, "Research on Competitive Dynamics: Recent Accomplishments and Future Challenges," *Journal of Management*, Vol. 30, No. 6 (2004), pp. 779–804.

60. "Growth Competitiveness," *Economist* (October 16, 2004), p. 98.

61. *Economist Pocket World in Figures, 2004 Edition* (London: Profile Books, 2003) p. 60.

62. R. Beck, "Kmart + Sears = Success?" *The (Ames, IA) Tribune* (November 20, 2004), p. C8.

Chapter 7

1. C. Zook and J. Allen, "Growth Outside the Core," *Harvard Business Review* (December 2003), pp. 66–73.

2. Ibid., p. 67.

3. R. P. Rumelt, D. E. Schendel, and D. J. Teece, "Fundamental Issues in Strategy," in *Fundamental Issues in Strategy: A Research Agenda*, edited by R. P. Rumelt, D. E. Schendel, and D. J. Teece (Boston: HBS Press, 1994), p. 42.

4. This analogy of corporate parent and business unit children was initially proposed by A. Campbell, M. Goold, and M. Alexander. See "Corporate Strategy: The Quest for Parenting Advantage," *Harvard Business Review* (March–April, 1995), pp. 120–132.

5. M. E. Porter, "From Competitive Strategy to Corporate Strategy," *in International Review of Strategic Management*, Vol. 1, edited by D. E. Husey (Chicester, UK: John Wiley & Sons, 1990), p. 29.

6. This is in agreement with Toyohiro Kono, who proposes that corporate headquarters has three main functions: formulate corporate strategy, identify and develop the company's core competencies, and provide central resources. See T. Kono, "A Strong Head Office Makes a Strong Company," *Long Range Planning* (April 1999), pp. 225–236.

7. "Larry Ups the Ante," *Economist* (February 7, 2004), pp. 59–60.

8. "Cisco Buys Wireless Chip-Set Maker," *The (Ames, IA) Tribune* (November 11, 2000), p. B7.

9. J. Perkins, "It's a Hog Predicament," *Des Moines Register* (April 11, 1999), pp. J1–J2.

10. C. Woodyard, "FedEx Ponies Up $2.4B for Kinko's," *USA Today* (December 31, 2003), p. B1.

11. J. W. Slocum, Jr., M. McGill, and D. T. Lei, "The New Learning Strategy: Anytime, Anything, Anywhere," *Organizational Dynamics* (Autumn 1994), p. 36.

12. M. J. Leiblein, J. J. Reuer, and F. Dalsace, "Do Make or Buy Decisions Matter? The Influence of Organizational Governance on Technological Performance," *Strategic Management Journal* (September 2002), pp. 817–833.

13. K. R. Harrigan, *Strategies for Vertical Integration* (Lexington, MA: Lexington Books, 1983), pp. 16–21.

14. H. Norr, "Apple Opening 25 Stores to Showcase Products," *The (Ames, IA) Tribune* (May 4, 2001), p. B7.

15. L. Grant, "Partners in Profit," *U. S. News & World Report* (September 20, 1993), pp. 65–66.

16. For a discussion of the pros and cons of contracting versus vertical integration, see J. T. Mahoney, "The Choice of Organizational Form: Vertical Financial Ownership Versus Other Methods of Vertical Integration," *Strategic Management Journal* (November 1992), pp. 559–584.

17. D. Welch, D. Roberts, and G. Edmondson, "GM: Gunning It in China," *Business Week* (June 21, 2004), pp. 112–115.

18. C. Zook, "Increasing the Odds of Successful Growth: The Critical Prelude to Moving 'Beyond the Core.'" *Strategy & Leadership*, Vol. 32, No. 4 (2004), pp. 17–23.

19. A. Y. Ilinich and C. P. Zeithaml, "Operationalizing and Testing Galbraith's Center of Gravity Theory," *Strategic Management Journal* (June 1995), pp. 401–410.

20. "Flying into Battle," *Economist* (May 8, 2004), p. 60.

21. R. F. Bruner, "Corporation Diversification May Be Okay After All," *Batten Briefings* (Spring 2003), pp. 2–3, 12.

22. A. Delios and P. W. Beamish, "Geographic Scope, Product Diversification, and the Corporate Performance of Japanese Firms," *Strategic Management Journal* (August 1999), pp. 711–727.

23. E. Elango and V. H. Fried, "Franchising Research: A Literature Review and Synthesis," *Journal of Small Business Management* (July 1997), pp. 68–81.

24. T. Thilgen, "Corporate Clout Replaces 'Small Is Beautiful,' " *Wall Street Journal* (March 27, 1997), p. B14.

25. J. E. McCann III, "The Growth of Acquisitions in Services," *Long Range Planning* (December 1996), pp. 835–841.

26. P. Gogoi and G. Smith, "The Way to Run a Railroad," *Business Week* (October 23, 2000), pp. 106–110.

27. J. Ewing and J. Weber, "Brewers: The Beer Wars Come to a Head," *Business Week* (May 24, 2004), p. 68.

28. B. Voss, "Strategic Federations Frequently Falter in Far East," *Journal of Business Strategy* (July/August 1993), p. 6; S. Douma, "Success and Failure in New Ventures," *Long Range Planning* (April 1991), pp. 54–60.

29. A. Delios and P. W. Beamish, "Ownership Strategy of Japanese Firms: Transactional, Institutional, and Experience Approaches," *Strategic Management Journal* (October 1999), pp. 915–933.

30. A. Seth, K. P. Song, and R. R. Pettit, "Value Creation and Destruction in Cross-Border Acquisitions: An Empirical Analysis of Foreign Acquisitions of U.S. Firms," *Strategic Management Journal* (October 2002), pp. 921–940.

31. K. D. Brouthers and L. E. Brouthers, "Acquisition or Greenfield Start-up? Institutional, Cultural, and Transaction Cost Influences," *Strategic Management Journal* (January 2000), pp. 89–97.

32. J. Naisbitt, *Megatrends Asia* (New York: Simon & Schuster, 1996), p. 143.

33. K. Carow, R. Heron, and T. Saxton, "Do Early Birds Get the Returns? An Empirical Investigation of Early-Mover Advantages in Acquisitions," *Strategic Management Journal* (June 2004), pp. 563–585; K. Ramaswamy, "The Performance Impact of Strategic Similarity in Horizontal Mergers: Evidence from the U.S. Banking Industry," *Academy of Management Journal* (July 1997), pp. 697–715; D. J. Flanagan, "Announcements of Purely Related and Purely Unrelated Mergers and Shareholder Returns: Reconciling the Relatedness Paradox," *Journal of Management*, Vol. 22, No. 6 (1996), pp. 823–835; D. D. Bergh, "Predicting Diversification of Unrelated Acquisitions: An Integrated Model of Ex Ante Conditions," *Strategic Management Journal* (October 1997), pp. 715–731.

34. J. M. Pennings, H. Barkema, and S. Douma, "Organizational Learning and Diversification," *Academy of Management Journal* (June 1994), pp. 608–640.

35. L. E. Palich, L. B. Cardinal, and C. C. Miller, "Curvilinearity in the Diversification-Performance Linkage: An Examination of over Three Decades of Research," *Strategic Management Journal* (February 2000), pp. 155–174.

36. "The Great Merger Wave Breaks," *The Economist* (January 27, 2001), pp. 59–60.

37. D. R. King, D. R. Dalton, C. M. Daily, and J. G. Covin, "Meta-Analyses of Post-Acquisition Performance: Indications of Unidentified Moderators," *Strategic Management Journal* (February 2004), pp. 187–200; W. B. Carper, "Corporate Acquisitions and Shareholder Wealth: A Review and Exploratory Analysis" *Journal of Management* (December 1990), pp. 807–823; P. G. Simmonds, "Using Diversification as a Tool for Effective Performance," *Handbook of Business Strategy, 1992/93 Yearbook*, edited by H. E. Glass and M. A. Hovde (Boston: Warren, Gorham & Lamont, 1992), pp. 3.1–3.7; B. T. Lamont and C. A. Anderson, "Mode of Corporate Diversification and Economic Performance," *Academy of Management Journal* (December 1985), pp. 926–936.

38. "The HP–Compaq Merger Two Years Out: Still Waiting for the Upside," *Knowledge@Wharton* (October 6–19, 2004).

39. D. J. Miller, "Firms' Technological Resources and the Performance Effects of Diversification: A Longitudinal Study," *Strategic Management Journal* (November 2004), pp. 1097–1119.

40. R. Langford and C. Brown III, "Making M&A Pay: Lessons from the World's Most Successful Acquirers," *Strategy & Leadership*, Vol. 32, No. 1 (2004), pp. 5–14; J. G. Lynch and B. Lind, "Escaping Merger and Acquisition Madness," *Strategy & Leadership*, Vol. 30, No. 2 (2002), pp. 5–12; M. L. Sirower, *The Synergy Trap* (New York: The Free Press, 1997); B. Jensen, "Make It Simple! How Simplicity Could Become Your Ultimate Strategy," *Strategy & Leadership* (March/April 1997), p. 35.

41. E. Thornton, "Why Consumers Hate Mergers," *Business Week* (December 6, 2004), pp. 58–64.

42. J. M. Pennings, H. Barkema, and S. Douma, "Organizational Learning and Diversification," *Academy of Management Journal* (June 1994), pp. 608–640.

43. L. Selden and G. Colvin, "M&A Needn't Be a Loser's Game," *Harvard Business Review* (June 2003), pp. 70–79; E. C. Busija, H. M. O'Neill, and C. P. Zeithaml, "Diversification Strategy, Entry Mode, and Performance: Evidence of Choice and Constraints," *Strategic Management Journal* (April 1997), pp. 321–327; A. Sharma, "Mode of Entry and Ex-Post Performance," *Strategic Management Journal* (September 1998), pp. 879–900.

44. S. Rovitt, D. Harding, and C. Lemire, "A Simple M&A Model for All Seasons," *Strategy & Leadership*, Vol. 32, No. 5 (2004), pp. 18–24.

45. P. Porrini, "Can a Previous Alliance Between an Acquirer and a Target Affect Acquisition Performance?" *Journal of Management*, Vol. 30, No. 4 (2004), pp. 545–562.

46. F. Vermeulen, "Controlling International Expansion," *Business Strategy Review* (September 2001), pp. 29–36.

47. A. Inkpen and N. Choudhury, "The Seeking of Strategy Where It Is Not: Towards a Theory of Strategy Absence," *Strategic Management Journal* (May 1995), pp. 313–323.

48. P. Burrows and S. Anderson, "Dell Computer Goes into the Shop," *Business Week* (July 12, 1993), pp. 138–140.

49. J. L. Morrow, Jr., R. A. Johnson, and L. W. Busenitz, "The Effects of Cost and Asset Retrenchment on Firm Performance: The Overlooked Role of a Firm's Competitive Environment," *Journal of Management*, Vol. 30, No. 2 (2004), pp. 189–208.

50. J. A. Pearce II and D. K. Robbins, "Retrenchment Remains the Foundation of Business Turnaround," *Strategic Management Journal* (June 1994), pp. 407–417.

51. C. Chadwick, L. W. Hunter, and S. L. Walston, "Effects of Downsizing Practices on the Performance of Hospitals," *Strategic Management Journal* (May 2004), pp. 405–427; J. R. Morris, W. F. Cascio, and C. E. Young, "Downsizing After All These Years," *Organizational Dynamics* (Winter 1999), pp. 78–87; P. H. Mirvis, "Human Resource Management: Leaders, Laggards, and Followers," *Academy of Management Executive* (May 1997), pp. 43–56; J. K. DeDee and D. W. Vorhies, "Retrenchment Activities of Small Firms During Economic Downturn: An Empirical Investigation," *Journal of Small Business Management* (July 1998), pp. 46–61.

52. C. Chadwick, L. W. Hunter, and S. L. Walston, "Effects of Downsizing Practices on the Performance of Hospitals," *Strategic Management Journal* (May 2004), pp. 405–427.

53. J. B. Treece, "U.S. Parts Makers Just Won't Say 'Uncle,' " *Business Week* (August 10, 1987), pp. 76–77.

54. "Quaker Oats Gives Up on Snapple, Sells It at a $1.4 Billion Loss," *Des Moines Register* (March 28, 1997), p. 8S.

55. B. Grow, "Can Wonder Bread Rise Again?" *Business Week* (October 18, 2004), pp. 108–110.

56. D. D. Dawley, J. J. Hoffman, and B. T. Lamont, "Choice Situation, Refocusing, and Post-Bankruptcy Performance," *Journal of Management*, Vol. 28, No. 5 (2002), pp. 695–717.

57. R. M. Kanter, "Leadership and the Psychology of Turnarounds," *Harvard Business Review* (June 2003), pp. 58–67.

58. B. C. Reimann and A. Reichert, "Portfolio Planning Methods for Strategic Capital Allocation: A Survey of Fortune 500 Firms," *International Journal of Management* (March 1996), pp. 84–93; D. K. Sinha, "Strategic Planning in the Fortune 500," *Handbook of Business Strategy, 1991/92 Yearbook*, edited by H. E. Glass and M. A. Hovde (Boston: Warren, Gorham & Lamont, 1991), p. 9.6.

59. L. Dranikoff, T. Koller, and A. Schneider, "Divestiture: Strategy's Missing Link," *Harvard Business Review* (May 2002), pp. 74–83.

60. B. Hedley, "Strategy and the Business Portfolio," *Long Range Planning* (February 1977), p. 9.

61. B. Elgin, "Can HP's Printer Biz Keep Printing Money?" *Business Week* (July 14, 2003), pp. 68–70.

62. A. Fitzgerald, "Going Global," *Des Moines Register* (March 14, 2004), pp. 1M, 3M.

63. C. Anterasian, J. L. Graham, and R. B. Money, "Are U.S. Managers Superstitious About Market Share?" *Sloan Management Review* (Summer 1996), pp. 67–77.

64. D. Rosenblum, D. Tomlinson, and L. Scott, "Bottom-Feeding for Blockbuster Businesses," *Harvard Business Review* (March 2003), pp. 52–59.

65. R. G. Hamermesh, *Making Strategy Work* (New York: John Wiley & Sons, 1986), p. 14.

66. J. J. Curran, "Companies That Rob the Future," *Fortune* (July 4, 1988), p. 84.

67. A. Campbell, M. Goold, and M. Alexander, *Corporate-Level Strategy: Creating Value in the Multibusiness Company* (New York: John Wiley & Sons, 1994). See also M. Goold, A. Campbell, and M. Alexander, "Corporate Strategy and Parenting Theory," *Long Range Planning* (April 1998), pp. 308–318, and M. Goold and A. Campbell, "Parenting in Complex Structures," *Long Range Planning* (June 2002), pp. 219–243.

68. A. Campbell, M. Goold, and M. Alexander, "Corporate Strategy: The Quest for Parenting Advantage," *Harvard Business Review* (March–April 1995), p. 121.

69. Ibid., p. 122.

70. A. van Oijen and S. Douma, "Diversification Strategy and the Roles of the Centre," *Long Range Planning* (August 2000), pp. 560–578.

71. "Jack's Gamble," *The Economist* (October 28, 2000), pp. 13–14.

72. D. J. Collis, "Corporate Strategy in Multibusiness Firms," *Long Range Planning* (June 1996), pp. 416–418; D. Lei, M. A. Hitt, and R. Bettis, "Dynamic Core Competencies Through Meta-Learning and Strategic Context," *Journal of Management*, Vol. 22, No. 4 (1996), pp. 549–569.

73. D. J. Teece, "Strategies for Managing Knowledge Assets: The Role of Firm Structure and Industrial Context," *Long Range Planning* (February 2000), pp. 35–54.

74. R. S. Kaplan and D. P. Norton, "The Strategy Map: Guide to Aligning Intangible Assets," *Strategy & Leadership*, Vol. 32, No. 5 (2004), pp. 10–17; L. Edvinsson, "The New Knowledge Economics," *Business Strategy Review* (September 2002), pp. 72–76; C. Havens and E. Knapp, "Easing into Knowledge Management," *Strategy & Leadership* (March/April 1999), pp. 4–9.

75. T. S. Frost, J. M. Birkinshaw, and P. C. Ensign, "Centers of Excellence in Multinational Corporations," *Strategic Management Journal* (November 2002), pp. 997–1018.

76. M. E. Porter, *Competitive Advantage* (New York: The Free Press, 1985), pp. 317–382.

77. J. Gimeno, "Reciprocal Threats in Multimarket Rivalry: Staking Out 'Spheres of Influence' in the U.S. Airline Industry," *Strategic Management Journal* (February 1999), pp. 101–128; J. Baum and H. J. Korn, "Dynamics of Dyadic Competitive Interaction," *Strategic Management Journal* (March 1999), pp. 251–278; J. Gimeno and C. Y. Woo, "Hypercompetition in a Multimarket Environment: The Role of Strategic Similarity and Multimarket Contact in Competitive De-escalation," *Organization Science* (May/June 1996), pp. 322–341.

78. W. Boeker, J. Goodstein, J. Stephan, and J. P. Murmann, "Competition in a Multimarket Environment: The Case of Market Exit," *Organization Science* (March/April 1997), pp. 126–142.

79. J. Gimeno and C. Y. Woo, "Multimarket Contact, Economies of Scope, and Firm Performance," *Academy of Management Journal* (June 1999), pp. 239–259.

80. D. Little, "Emerson Electric Jump-Starts Itself," *Business Week* (July 24, 2000), pp. 78–80.

81. From *Corruption Perceptions Index 2004*, as reported in "Countries Rated for Corruption," *Des Moines Register* (October 21, 2004), p. 2D.

82. Ibid.

83. "Learning to E-Read," *The Economist Survey E-Entertainment* (October 7, 2000), p. 22.

Chapter 8

1. Arm & Hammer is a registered trademark of Church & Dwight Company, Inc.

2. S. F. Slater and E. M. Olson, "Marketing's Contribution to the Implementation of Business Strategy: An Empirical Analysis," *Strategic Management Journal* (November 2001), pp. 1055–1067; B. C. Skaggs and T. R. Huffman, "A Customer Interaction Approach to Strategy and Production Complexity Alignment in Service Firms," *Academy of Management Journal* (December 2003), pp. 775–786.

3. S. M. Oster, *Modern Competitive Analysis*, 2nd ed. (New York: Oxford University Press, 1994), p. 93.

4. M. Springer, "Plowed Under," *Forbes* (February 21, 2000), p. 56.

5. W. Redmond, "The Strategic Pricing of Innovative Products," *Handbook of Business Strategy, 1992/1993 Yearbook*, edited by H. E. Glass and M. A. Hovde (Boston: Warren, Gorham & Lamont, 1992), pp. 16.1–16.13.

6. A. Kambil, H. J. Wilson III, and V. Agrawal, "Are You Leaving Money on the Table?" *Journal of Business Strategy* (January/February 2002), pp. 40–43.

7. A. Safieddine and S. Titman in April 1999 *Journal of Finance,* as summarized by D. Champion, "The Joy of Leverage," *Harvard Business Review* (July–August 1999), pp. 19–22.

8. R. Kochhar and M. A. Hitt, "Linking Corporate Strategy to Capital Structure: Diversification Strategy, Type and Source of Financing," *Strategic Management Journal* (June 1998), pp. 601–610.

9. A. Rappaport and M. L. Sirower, "Stock or Cash?" *Harvard Business Review* (November–December 1999), pp. 147–158.

10. D. Angwin and I. Contardo, "Unleashing Cerberus: Don't Let Your MBOs Turn on Themselves," *Long Range Planning* (October 1999), pp. 494–504.

11. For information on different types of LBOs, see M. Wright, R. E. Hoskisson, and L. W. Busenitz, "Firm Rebirth: Buyouts as Facilitators of Strategic Growth and Entrepreneurship," *Academy of Management Executive* (February 2001), pp. 111–125.

12. B. Deener, "Back Up and Look at Reasons for Reverse Stock Split," *The (St. Petersburg, FL) Times* (December 29, 2002), p. 3H.

13. S. Scherreik, "Tread Carefully When You Buy Tracking Stocks," *Business Week* (March 6, 2000), pp. 182–184.

14. T. Due, "Dean Foods Thrives on Regional Off-Brand Products," *Wall Street Journal* (September 17, 1987), p. A6.

15. S. Stevens, "Speeding the Signals of Change," *Appliance* (February 1995), p. 7.

16. H. W. Chesbrough, "A Better Way to Innovate," *Harvard Business Review* (July 2003), pp. 12–13.

17. J. Greene, J. Carey, M. Arndt, and O. Port, "Reinventing Corporate R&D," *Business Week* (September 22, 2003), pp. 74–76.

18. G. Dushnitsky and M. J. Lenox, "When Do Firms Undertake R&D by Investing in New Ventures?" Paper presented to annual meeting of the *Academy of Management*, Seattle, WA (August 2003).

19. A. Aston and M. Arndt, "The Flexible Factory," *Business Week* (May 5, 2003), pp. 90–91.

20. J. R. Williams and R. S. Novak, "Aligning CIM Strategies to Different Markets," *Long Range Planning* (February 1990), pp. 126–135.

21. J. Wheatley, "Super Factory—or Super Headache," *Business Week* (July 31, 2000), p. 66.

22. M. Tayles and C. Drury, "Moving from Make/Buy to Strategic Sourcing: The Outsource Decision Process," *Long Range Planning* (October 2001), pp. 605–622.

23. F. R. Bleakley, "Some Companies Let Supplier Work on Site and Even Place Orders," *Wall Street Journal* (January 13, 1995), pp. A1, A6.

24. J. Richardson, "Parallel Sourcing and Supplier Performance in the Japanese Automobile Industry," *Strategic Management Journal* (July 1993), pp. 339–350.

25. S. Roberts-Witt, "Procurement: The HP Way," *PC Magazine* (November 21, 2000), pp. 21–22.

26. J. Bigness, "In Today's Economy, There Is Big Money to Be Made in Logistics," *Wall Street Journal* (September 6, 1995), pp. A1, A9.

27. F. Keenan, "Logistics Gets a Little Respect," *Business Week* (November 20, 2000), pp. 112–116.

28. B. L. Kirkman and Debra L. Shapiro, "The Impact of Cultural Values on Employee Resistance to Teams: Toward a Model of Globalized Self-Managing Work Team Effectiveness," *Academy of Management Review* (July 1997), pp. 730–757.

29. R. D. Banker, J. M. Field, R. G. Schroeder, and K. K. Sinha, "Impact of Work Teams on Manufacturing Performance: A Longitudinal Field Study," *Academy of Management Journal* (August 1996), pp. 867–890; B. L. Kirkman and B. Rosen, "Beyond Self-Management: Antecedents and Consequences of Team Empowerment," *Academy of Management Journal* (February 1999), pp. 58–74.

30. V. Y. Haines III, S. St. Onge, and A. Marcoux, "Performance Management Design and Effectiveness in Quality-Driven Organizations," *Canadian Journal of Administrative Sciences* (June 2004), pp. 146–160.

31. A. S. DeNisi and A. N. Kluger, "Feedback Effectiveness: Can 360-Degree Appraisals Be Improved?" *Academy of Management Executive* (February 2000), pp. 129–139; G. Toegel and J. A. Conger, "360-Degree Assessment: Time for Reinvention," *Academy of Management Learning and Education* (September 2003), pp. 297–311.

32. O. C. Richard, "Racial Diversity, Business Strategy, and Firm Performance: A Resource-Based View," *Academy of Management Journal* (April 2000), pp. 164–177.

33. G. Robinson and K. Dechant, "Building a Business Case for Diversity," *Academy of Management Executive* (August 1997), pp. 21–31.

34. K. Labich, "Making Diversity Pay," *Fortune* (September 9, 1996), pp. 177–180.

35. N. G. Carr, "IT Doesn't Matter," *Harvard Business Review* (May 2003), pp. 41–50.

36. J. Greco, "Good Day Sunshine," *Journal of Business Strategy* (July/August 1998), pp. 4–5.

37. W. Howard, "Translate Now," *PC Magazine* (September 19, 2000), p. 81.

38. H. Green, "The Web Smart 50," *Business Week* (November 24, 2003), p. 84.

39. T. Smart, "Jack Welch's Cyber-Czar," *Business Week* (August 5, 1996), p. 83.

40. B. Kelley, "Outsourcing Marches On," *Journal of Business Strategy* (July/August 1995), p. 40.

41. S. Holmes and M. Arndt, "A Plane That Could Change the Game," *Business Week* (August 9, 2004), p. 33.

42. J. Greco, "Outsourcing: The New Partnership," *Journal of Business Strategy* (July/August 1997), pp. 48–54.

43. "Out of Captivity," *Economist* (November 13, 2004), p. 68.

44. "IBM's Plan to Buy India Firm Points to Demand for Outsourcing," *Des Moines Register* (April 11, 2004), p. 2D.

45. A. Castro, "Complaints Push Dell to Use U.S. Call Centers," *Des Moines Register* (November 25, 2003), p. 1D.

46. J. A. Byrne, "Has Outsourcing Gone Too Far?" *Business Week* (April 1, 1996), pp. 26–28.

47. R. C. Insinga and M. J. Werle, "Linking Outsourcing to Business Strategy," *Academy of Management Executive* (November 2000), pp. 58–70; D. Lei and M. A. Hitt, "Strategic Restructuring and Outsourcing: The Effect of Mergers and Acquisitions and LBOs on Building Firm Skills and Capabilities," *Journal of Management*, Vol. 21, No. 5 (1995), pp. 835–859.

48. S. E. Ante, "Shifting Work Offshore? Outsourcer Beware," *Business Week* (January 12, 2004), pp. 36–37.

49. J. Barthelemy, "The Seven Deadly Sins of Outsourcing," *Academy of Management Executive* (May 2003), pp. 87–98.

50. A. Takeishi, "Bridging Inter- and Intra-Firm Boundaries: Management of Supplier Involvement in Automobile Product Development," *Strategic Management Journal* (May 2001), pp. 403–433.

51. J. B. Quinn, "The Intelligent Enterprise: A New Paradigm," *Academy of Management Executive* (November 1992), pp. 48–63.

52. M. J. Leiblein and D. J. Miller, "An Empirical Examination of Transaction and Firm-Level Influences on the Vertical Boundaries of the Firm," *Strategic Management Journal* (September 2003), pp. 839–859.

53. S. Hamm, "Is Outsourcing on the Outs?" *Business Week* (October 4, 2004), p. 42.

54. R. Grover and D. Polek, "Millionaire Buys Disney Time," *Business Week* (June 26, 2000), pp. 141–144.

55. D. K. Sinha, "Strategic Planning in the Fortune 500," *Handbook of Business Strategy, 1991/1992 Yearbook*, edited by H. E. Glass and M. A. Hovde (Boston: Warren, Gorham and Lamont, 1991), pp. 9.6–9.8.

56. N. Checa, J. Maguire, and J. Berry, "The New World Disorder," *Harvard Business Review* (August 2003), pp. 70–79.

57. T. B. Palmer and R. M. Wiseman, "Decoupling Risk Taking from Income Stream Uncertainty: A Holistic Model of Risk," *Strategic Management Journal* (November 1999), pp. 1037–1062.

58. D. Clark, "All the Chips: A Big Bet Made Intel What It Is Today; Now It Wagers Again," *Wall Street Journal* (June 6, 1995), pp. A1, A5.

59. L. W. Busenitz and J. B. Barney, "Differences Between Entrepreneurs and Managers in Large Organizations: Biases and Heuristics in Strategic Decision-Making," *Journal of Business Venturing* (January 1997), pp. 9–30.

60. T. Copeland and P. Tufano, "A Real-World Way to Manage Real Options," *Harvard Business Review* (March 2004), pp. 90–99.

61. J. Rosenberger and K. Eisenhardt, "What Are Real Options: A Review of Empirical Research," Paper presented to annual meeting of the *Academy of Management*, Seattle, WA (August 2003).

62. P. Coy, "Exploiting Uncertainty," *Business Week* (June 7, 1999), pp. 118–124. For further information on real options, see M. Amram and N. Kulatilaka, *Real Options* (Boston: Harvard University Press, 1999). For a simpler summary, see R. M. Grant, *Contemporary Strategy Analysis*, 5th edition (Malden, MA: Blackwell Publishing, 2005), pp. 48–50.

63. C. Anderson, "Values-Based Management," *Academy of Management Executive* (November 1997), pp. 25–46.

64. H. M. O'Neill, R. W. Pouder, and A. K. Buchholtz, "Patterns in the Diffusion of Strategies Across Organizations: Insights from the Innovation Diffusion Literature," *Academy of Management Executive* (January 1998), pp. 98–114.

65. B. B. Tyler and H. K. Steensma, "Evaluating Technological Collaborative Opportunities: A Cognitive Modeling Perspective," *Strategic Management Journal* (Summer 1995), pp. 43–70; D. Duchan, D. P. Ashman, and M. Nathan, "Mavericks, Visionaries, Protestors, and Sages: Toward a Typology of Cognitive Structures for Decision Making in Organizations," *Journal of Business Strategies* (Fall 1997), pp. 106–125; P. Chattopadhyay, W. H. Glick, C. C. Miller, and G. P. Huber, "Determinants of Executive Beliefs: Comparing Functional Conditioning and Social Influence," *Strategic Management Journal* (August 1999), pp. 763–789; B. Katey and G. G. Meredith, "Relationship Among Owner/Manager Personal Values, Business Strategies, and Enterprise Performance," *Journal of Small Business Management* (April 1997), pp. 37–64.

66. C. S. Galbraith and G. B. Merrill, "The Politics of Forecasting: Managing the Truth," *California Management Review* (Winter 1996), pp. 29–43.

67. M. A. Geletkanycz and D. C. Hambrick, "The External Ties of Top Executives: Implications for Strategic Choice and Performance," *Administrative Science Quarterly* (December 1997), pp. 654–681.

68. M. Song, R. J. Calantone, and C. A. Di Benedetto, "Competitive Forces and Strategic Choice Decisions: An Experimental Investigation in the United States and Japan," *Strategic Management Journal* (October 2002), pp. 969–978.

69. M. A. Hitt, M. T. Dacin, B. B. Tyler, and D. Park, "Understanding the Differences in Korean and U.S. Executives' Strategic Orientation," *Strategic Management Journal* (February 1997), pp. 159–167; L. G. Thomas III and G. Waring, "Competing Capitalisms: Capital Investment in American, German, and Japanese Firms," *Strategic Management Journal* (August 1999), pp. 729–748.

70. J. A. Wagner III and R. Z. Gooding, "Equivocal Information and Attribution: An Investigation of Patterns of Managerial Sensemaking," *Strategic Management Journal* (April 1997), pp. 275–286.

71. J. Ross and B. M. Staw, "Organizational Escalation and Exit: Lessons from the Shoreham Nuclear Power Plant," *Academy of Management Journal* (August 1993), pp. 701–732; P. W. Mulvey, J. F. Veiga, and P. M. Elsass, "When Teammates Raise a White Flag," *Academy of Management Executive* (February 1996), pp. 40–49.

72. R. A. Cosier, and C. R. Schwenk, "Agreement and Thinking Alike: Ingredients for Poor Decisions," *Academy of Management Executive* (February 1990), p. 69.

73. G. P. West III and G. D. Meyer, "To Agree or Not to Agree? Consensus and Performance in New Ventures," *Journal of Business Venturing* (September 1998), pp. 395–422; L. Markoczy, "Consensus Formation During Strategic Change," *Strategic Management Journal* (November 2001), pp. 1013–1031.

74. A. C. Amason, "Distinguishing the Effects of Functional and Dysfunctional Conflict on Strategic Decision Making: Resolving a Paradox for Top Management Teams," *Academy of Management Journal* (February 1996), pp. 123–148; A. C. Amason and H. J. Sapienza, "The Effects of Top Management Team Size and Interaction Norms on Cognitive and Affective Conflict," *Journal of Management*, Vol. 23, No. 4 (1997), pp. 495–516.

75. D. M. Schweiger, W. R. Sandberg, and P. L. Rechner, "Experiential Effects of Dialectical Inquiry, Devil's Advocacy, and Consensus Approaches to Strategic Decision Making," *Academy of Management Journal* (December 1989), pp. 745–772; G. Whyte, "Decision Failures: Why They Occur and How to Prevent Them," *Academy of Management Executive* (August 1991), pp. 23–31; R. L. Priem, D. A. Harrison, and N. K. Muir, "Structured Conflict and Consensus Outcomes in Group Decision Making," *Journal of Management*, Vol. 21, No. 4 (1995), pp. 691–710.

76. S. C. Abraham, "Using Bundles to Find the Best Strategy," *Strategy & Leadership* (July/August/September 1999), pp. 53–55.

77. O. Gadiesh and J. L Gilbert, "Transforming Corner-Office Strategy into Frontline Action," *Harvard Business Review* (May 2001), pp. 73–79.

78. A. M. Hayashi, "When to Trust Your Gut," *Harvard Business Review* (February 2001), pp. 59–65.

79. Ibid., pp. 59–60.

80. D. Kirkpatrick, "The Net Makes It All Easier—Including Exporting U.S. Jobs," *Fortune* (May 26, 2003), p. 146.

81. C. Matlack, M. Kripalani, D. Fairlamb, S. Reed, G. Edmundson, and A. Reinhardt, "Job Exports: Europe's Turn," *Business Week* (April 19, 2004), pp. 50–51.

82. T. A. Badger, "Levi's Factories Fade Away," *Des Moines Register* (January 9, 2004), pp. 1D–2D; L. Lee, "Jean Therapy, $23 a Pop," *Business Week* (June 28, 2004), pp. 91–93.

Chapter 9

1. A. Barrett, "Staying on Top," *Business Week* (May 5, 2003), pp. 60–68.

2. J. W. Gadella, "Avoiding Expensive Mistakes in Capital Investment," *Long Range Planning* (April 1994), pp. 103–110; B. Voss, "World Market Is Not for Everyone," *Journal of Business Strategy* (July/August 1993), p. 4.

3. A. Bert, T. MacDonald, and T. Herd, "Two Merger Integration Imperatives: Urgency and Execution," *Strategy & Leadership*, Vol. 31, No. 3 (2003), pp. 42–49.

4. L. D. Alexander, "Strategy Implementation: Nature of the Problem," *International Review of Strategic Management*, Vol. 2, No. 1, edited by D. E. Hussey (New York: John Wiley & Sons, 1991), pp. 73–113.

5. F. Arner and A. Aston, "How Xerox Got Up to Speed," *Business Week* (May 3, 2004), pp. 103–104.

6. E. Brynjolfsson, A. A. Renshaw, and M. Van Alstyne, "The Matrix of Change," *Sloan Management Review* (Winter 1997), pp. 37–54.

7. M. S. Feldman and B. T. Pentland, "Reconceptualizing Organizational Routines as a Source of Flexibility and Change," *Administrative Science Quarterly* (March 2003), pp. 94–118.

8. S. F. Slater and E. M. Olson, "Strategy Type and Performance: The Influence of Sales Force Management," *Strategic Management Journal* (August 2000), pp. 813–829.

9. B. Grow, "Thinking Outside the Box," *Business Week* (October 25, 2004), pp. 70–72.

10. M. Goold and A. Campbell, "Desperately Seeking Synergy," *Harvard Business Review* (September–October 1998), pp. 131–143.

11. A. D. Chandler, *Strategy and Structure* (Cambridge, MA: MIT Press, 1962).

12. A. P. Sloan, Jr., *My Years with General Motors* (Garden City, NY: Doubleday, 1964).

13. T. L. Amburgey and T. Dacin, "As the Left Foot Follows the Right? The Dynamics of Strategic and Structural Change," *Academy of Management Journal* (December 1994), pp. 1427–1452; M. Ollinger, "The Limits of Growth of the Multidivisional Firm: A Case Study of the U.S. Oil Industry from 1930–90," *Strategic Management Journal* (September 1994), pp. 503–520.

14. D. F. Jennings and S. L. Seaman, "High and Low Levels of Organizational Adaptation: An Empirical Analysis of Strategy, Structure, and Performance," *Strategic Management Journal* (July 1994), pp. 459–475; L. Donaldson, "The Normal Science of Structured Contingency Theory," in *Handbook of Organization Studies*, edited by S. R. Clegg, C. Hardy, and W. R. Nord (London: Sage Publications, 1996), pp. 57–76.

15. A. K. Gupta, "SBU Strategies, Corporate–SBU Relations, and SBU Effectiveness in Strategy Implementation," *Academy of Management Journal* (September 1987), pp. 477–500.

16. L. E. Greiner, "Evolution and Revolution As Organizations Grow," *Harvard Business Review* (May–June 1998), pp. 55–67. This is an updated version of Greiner's classic 1972 article.

17. Ibid., p. 64. Although Greiner simply labeled this as the *"?"* crisis, the term *pressure-cooker* seems apt.

18. J. Hamm, "Why Entrepreneurs Don't Scale," *Harvard Business Review* (December 2002), pp. 110–115.

19. W. P. Barnett, "The Dynamics of Competitive Intensity," *Administrative Science Quarterly* (March 1997), pp. 128–160; D. Miller, *The Icarus Paradox: How Exceptional Companies Bring About Their Own Downfall* (New York: Harper Business, 1990).

20. D. Miller and P. H. Friesen, "A Longitudinal Study of the Corporate Life Cycle," *Management Science* (October 1984), pp. 1161–1183.

21. J. Green, "The Toy-Train Company That Thinks It Can," *Business Week* (December 4, 2000), pp. 64–69.

22. G. David, F. Garcia, and I. Gashurov, "Welcome to the Valley of the Damned.Com," *Fortune* (January 22, 2001), p. 52.

23. R. Berner, "Turning Kmart into a Cash Cow," *Business Week* (July 12, 2004), p. 81.

24. H. Tavakolian, "Bankruptcy: An Emerging Corporate Strategy," *SAM Advanced Management Journal* (Spring 1995), p. 19.

25. L. G. Hrebiniak and W. F. Joyce, *Implementing Strategy* (New York: Macmillan, 1984), pp. 85–86.

26. S. M. Davis and P. R. Lawrence, *Matrix* (Reading, MA: Addison-Wesley, 1977), pp. 11–24.

27. J. G. March, "The Future Disposable Organizations and the Rigidities of Imagination," *Organization* (August/November 1995), p. 434.

28. M. A. Schilling and H. K. Steensma, "The Use of Modular Organizational Forms: An Industry-Level Analysis," *Academy of Management Journal* (December 2001), pp. 1149–1168.

29. M. P. Koza and A. Y. Lewin, "Coevolution of Network Alliances: A Longitudinal Analysis of an International Professional Service Network," *Organization Science* (September/October, 1999), pp. 638–653.

30. For more information on managing a network organization, see G. Lorenzoni and C. Baden-Fuller, "Creating a Strategic Center to Manage a Web of Partners," *California Management Review* (Spring 1995), pp. 146–163.

31. R. E. Miles, C. C. Snow, J. A. Mathews, G. Miles, and H. J. Coleman, Jr., "Organizing in the Knowledge Age: Anticipating the Cellular Form," *Academy of Management Executive* (November 1997), pp. 7–24.

32. J. Naylor and M. Lewis, "Internal Alliances: Using Joint Ventures in a Diversified Company," *Long Range Planning* (October 1997), pp. 678–688.

33. Summarized from M. Hammer, "Reengineering Work: Don't Automate, Obliterate," *Harvard Business Review* (July–August 1990), pp. 104–112.

34. D. Paper, "BPR: Creating the Conditions for Success," *Long Range Planning* (June 1998), pp. 426–435.

35. S. Drew, "BPR in Financial Services: Factors for Success," *Long Range Planning* (October 1994), pp. 25–41.

36. "Do As I Say, Not As I Do," *Journal of Business Strategy* (May/June 1997), pp. 3–4.

37. L. Raymond and S. Rivard, "Determinants of Business Process Reengineering Success in Small and Large Enterprises: An Empirical Study in the Canadian Context," *Journal of Small Business Management* (January 1998), pp. 72–85.

38. K. Grint, "Reengineering History: Social Resonances and Business Process Reengineering," *Organization* (July 1994), pp. 179–201; A. Kleiner, "Revisiting Reengineering," *Strategy + Business* (3rd Quarter 2000), pp. 27–31.

39. M. Arndt, "Quality Isn't Just for Widgets," *Business Week* (July 22, 2002), pp. 72–73.

40. Ibid., p. 73.

41. F. Arner and A. Aston, "How Xerox Got Up to Speed," *Business Week* (May 3, 2004), pp. 103–104.

42. J. Hoerr, "Sharpening Minds for a Competitive Edge," *Business Week* (December 17, 1990), pp. 72–78.

43. S. X. Li and T. J. Rowley, "Inertia and Evaluation Mechanisms in Interorganizational Partner Selection: Syndicate Formation Among U.S. Investment Banks," *Academy of Management Journal* (December 2002), pp. 1104–1119.

44. M. U. Douma, J. Bilderbeek, P. J. Idenburg, and J. K. Loise, "Strategic Alliances: Managing the Dynamics of Fit," *Long Range Planning* (August 2000), pp. 579–598; W. Hoffmann and R. Schlosser, "Success Factors of Strategic Alliances in Small and Medum-Sized Enterprises—An Empirical Survey," *Long Range Planning* (June 2001), pp. 357–381.

45. J. H. Taggart, "Strategy Shifts in MNC Subsidiaries," *Strategic Management Journal* (July 1998), pp. 663–681.

46. C. A. Bartlett and S. Ghoshal, "Beyond the M-Form: Toward a Managerial Theory of the Firm," *Strategic Management Journal* (Winter 1993), pp. 23–46.

47. C. Matlack, "Nestlé Is Starting to Slim Down at Last," *Business Week* (October 27, 2003), pp. 56–57; "Daring, Defying, to Grow," *Economist* (August 7, 2004), pp. 55–58.

48. J. Sterling, "Translating Strategy into Effective Implementation: Dispelling the Myths and Highlighting What Works," *Strategy & Leadership*, Vol. 31, No. 3 (2003), pp. 27–34.

49. R. O. Crockett, "Reinventing Motorola," *Business Week* (August 2, 2004), pp. 82–83.

50. S. Miller, D. Wilson, and D. Hickson, "Beyond Planning: Strategies for Successfully Implementing Strategic Decisions," *Long Range Planning* (June 2004), pp. 201–218.

51. J. Darragh and A. Campbell, "Why Corporate Initiatives Get Stuck?" *Long Range Planning* (February 2001), pp. 33–52.

Chapter 10

1. B. O'Reilly, "The Rent-A-Car Jocks Who Made Enterprise #1," *Fortune* (October 28, 1996), pp. 125–128; J. Schlereth, "Putting People First," an interview with Andrew Taylor, *BizEd* (July/August 2003), pp. 16–20.

2. The numbers are approximate averages from three separate studies of top management turnover after mergers. See M. Lubatkin, D. Schweiger, and Y. Weber, "Top Management Turnover in Related M&Ss: An Additional Test of the Theory of Relative Standing," *Journal of Management*, Vol. 25, No. 1 (1999), pp. 55–73.

3. J. A. Krug, "Executive Turnover in Acquired Firms: A Longitudinal Analysis of Long-Term Interaction Effects," paper presented to annual meeting of *Academy of Management*, Seattle, WA (2003).

4. J. A. Krug and W. H. Hegarty, "Post-Acquisition Turnover Among U.S. Top Management Teams: An Analysis of the Effects of Foreign vs. Domestic Acquisitions of U.S. Targets," *Strategic Management Journal* (September 1997), pp. 667–675; J. A. Krug and W. H. Hegarty, "Predicting Who Stays and Leaves After an Acquisition: A Study of Top Managers in Multinational Firms," *Strategic Management Journal* (February 2001), pp. 185–196.

5. A. Hinterhuber, "Making M&A Work," *Business Strategy Review* (September 2002), pp. 7–9.

6. R. N. Ashkenas and S. C. Francis, "Integration Managers: Special Leaders for Special Times," *Harvard Business Review* (November–December 2000), pp. 108–116.

7. J. Hoerr, "Sharpening Minds for a Competitive Edge," *Business Week* (December 17, 1990), pp. 72–78.

8. "Training and Human Resources," *Business Strategy News Review* (July 2000), p. 6.

9. *High Performance Work Practices and Firm Performance* (Washington, DC: U.S. Department of Labor, Office of the American Workplace, 1993), pp. i, 4.

10. T. T. Baldwin, C. Danielson, and W. Wiggenhorn, "The Evolution of Learning Strategies in Organizations: From Employee Development to Business Redefinition," *Academy of Management Executive* (November 1997), pp. 47–58; K. Kelly, "Motorola: Training for the Millennium," *Business Week* (March 28, 1996), pp. 158–161.

11. R. Henkoff, "Companies That Train Best," *Fortune* (March 22, 1993), pp. 62–75.

12. D. Miller and J. Shamsie, "Learning Across the Life Cycle: Experimentation and Performance Among the Hollywood Studio Heads," *Strategic Management Journal* (August 2001), pp. 725–745.

13. B. Grow, "Fat's in the Fire for This Burger King," *Business Week* (November 8, 2004), pp. 69–70.

14. D. K. Datta and N. Rajagopalan, "Industry Structure and CEO Characteristics: An Empirical Study of Succession Events," *Strategic Management Journal* (September 1998), pp. 833–852; A. S. Thomas and K. Ramaswamy, "Environmental Change and Management Staffing: A Comment," *Journal of Management* (Winter 1993), pp. 877–887; J. P. Guthrie, C. M. Grimm, and K. G. Smith, "Environmental Change and Management Staffing: An Empirical Study," *Journal of Management* (December 1991), pp. 735–748.

15. J. Greco, "The Search Goes On," *Journal of Business Strategy* (September/October 1997), pp. 22–25; W. Ocasio and H. Kim, "The Circulation of Corporate Control: Selection of Functional Backgrounds on New CEOs in Large U.S. Manufacturing Firms, 1981–1992," *Administrative Science Quarterly* (September 1999), pp. 532–562.

16. R. Drazin and R. K. Kazanjian, "Applying the Del Technique to the Analysis of Cross-Classification Data: A Test of CEO Succession and Top Management Team Development," *Academy of Management Journal* (December 1993), pp. 1374–1399; W. E. Rothschild, "A Portfolio of Strategic Leaders," *Planning Review* (January/February 1996), pp. 16–19.

17. R. Subramanian and C. M. Sanchez, "Environmental Change and Management Staffing: An Empirical Examination of the Electric Utilities Industry," *Journal of Business Strategies* (Spring 1998), pp. 17–34.

18. M. A. Carpenter and B. R. Golden, "Perceived Managerial Discretion: A Study of Cause and Effect," *Strategic Management Journal* (March 1997), pp. 187–206.

19. J. A. Parnell, "Functional Background and Business Strategy: The Impact of Executive–Strategy Fit on Performance," *Journal of Business Strategies* (Spring 1994), pp. 49–62.

20. M. Smith and M. C. White, "Strategy, CEO Specialization, and Succession," *Administrative Science Quarterly* (June 1987), pp. 263–280.

21. "Making Companies Work," *Economist* (October 25, 2003), p. 14.

22. A. Bianco, L. Lavelle, J. Merrit, and A. Barrett, "The CEO Trap," *Business Week* (December 11, 2000), pp. 86–92.

23. Y. Zhang and N. Rajagopalan, "When the Known Devil Is Better Than an Unknown God: An Empirical Study of the Antecedents and Consequences of Relay CEO Succession," *Academy of Management Journal* (August 2004), pp. 483–500; W. Shen and A. A. Cannella, Jr., "Will Succession Planning Increase Shareholder Wealth? Evidence from Investor Reactions to Relay CEO Successions," *Strategic Management Journal* (February 2003), pp. 191–198.

24. G. A. Bigley and M. F. Wiersema, "New CEOs and Corporate Strategic Refocusing: How Experience As Heir Apparent Influences the Use of Power," *Administrative Science Quarterly* (December 2002), pp. 707–727.

25. "Coming and Going," Survey of Corporate Leadership, *Economist* (October 25, 2003), pp. 12–14.

26. D. C. Carey and D. Ogden, *CEO Succession: A Window on How Boards Do It Right When Choosing a New Chief Executive* (New York: Oxford University Press, 2000).

27. "Coming and Going," Survey of Corporate Leadership, *Economist* (October 25, 2003), pp. 12–14.

28. "The King Lear Syndrome," *Economist* (December 13, 2003), p. 65.

29. "Coming and Going," Survey of Corporate Leadership, *Economist* (October 25, 2003), pp. 12–14.

30. M. S. Kraatz and J. H. Moore, "Executive Migration and Institutional Change," *Academy of Management Journal* (February 2002), pp. 120–143; Y. Zhang and N. Rajagopalan, "When the Known Devil Is Better Than an Unknown God: An Empirical Study of the Antecedents and Consequences of Relay CEO Succession," *Academy of Management Journal* (August 2004), pp. 483–500; W. Shen and A. A. Cannella, Jr., "Revisiting the Performance Consequences of CEO Succession: The Impacts of Successor Type, Post-Succession Senior Executive Turnover, and Departing CEO Tenure," *Academy of Management Journal* (August 2002), pp. 717–733.

31. C. Lucier and J. Dyer, "Hiring an Outside CEO: A Board's Best Moves," *Directors & Boards* (Winter 2004), pp. 36–38.

32. Q. Yue, "Antecedents of Top Management Successor Origin in China," paper presented to the annual meeting of the *Academy of Management*, Seattle, WA (2003); A. A. Buchko and D. DiVerde, "Antecedents, Moderators, and Consequences of CEO Turnover: A Review and Reconceptualization," paper presented to *Midwest Academy of Management* (Lincoln, NE: 1997), p. 10; W. Ocasio, "Institutionalized Action and Corporate Governance: The Reliance on Rules of CEO Succession," *Administrative Science Quarterly* (June 1999), pp. 384–416.

33. C. Gopinath, "Turnaround: Recognizing Decline and Initiating Intervention," *Long Range Planning* (December 1991), pp. 96–101.

34. K. B. Schwartz and K. Menon, "Executive Succession in Failing Firms," *Academy of Management Journal* (September 1985), pp. 680–686; A. A. Cannella, Jr., and M. Lubatkin, "Succession as a Sociopolitical Process: Internal Impediments to Outsider Selection," *Academy of Management Journal* (August 1993), pp. 763–793; W. Boeker and J. Goodstein, "Performance and Succession Choice: The Moderating Effects of Governance and Ownership," *Academy of Management Journal* (February 1993), pp. 172–186.

35. W. Boeker, "Executive Migration and Strategic Change: The Effect of Top Manager Movement on Product-Market Entry," *Administrative Science Quarterly* (June 1997), pp. 213–236.

36. E. Brockmann, J. J. Hoffman, and D. Dawley, "A Contingency Theory of CEO Successor Choice and Post-Bankruptcy Strategic Change," paper presented to annual meeting of *Academy of Management*, Seattle, WA (2003).

37. P. Lorange and D. Murphy, "Bringing Human Resources into Strategic Planning: System Design Characteristics," in *Strategic Human Resource Management*, edited by C. J. Fombrun, N. M. Tichy, and M. A. Devanna (New York: John Wiley & Sons, 1984), pp. 281–283.

38. M. Leuchter, "Management Farm Teams," *Journal of Business Strategy* (May/June 1998), pp. 29–32.

39. S. Armour, "Playing the Succession Game," *USA Today* (November 24, 2003), p. 3B.

40. R. Sharpe, "As Leaders, Women Rule," *Business Week* (November 20, 2000), pp. 75–84.

41. D. A. Waldman and T. Korbar, "Student Assessment Center Performance in the Prediction of Early Career Success," *Academy of Management Learning and Education* (June 2004), pp. 151–167.

42. "Coming and Going," Survey of Corporate Leadership, *Economist* (October 25, 2003), pp. 12–14.

43. R. A. Pitts, "Strategies and Structures for Diversification," *Academy of Management Journal* (June 1997), pp. 197–208.

44. K. E. Mishra, G. M. Spreitzer, and A. K. Mishra, "Preserving Employee Morale During Downsizing," *Sloan Management Review* (Winter 1998), pp. 83–95.

45. B. O'Reilly, "Is Your Company Asking Too Much?" *Fortune* (March 12, 1990), p. 41. For more information on the emotional reactions of survivors of downsizing, see C. R. Stoner and R. I. Hartman, "Organizational Therapy: Building Survivor Health & Competitiveness," *SAM Advanced Management Journal* (Summer 1997), pp. 15–31, 41.

46. S. R. Fisher and M. A. White, "Downsizing in a Learning Organization: Are There Hidden Costs?" *Academy of Management Review* (January 2000), pp. 244–251.

47. T. M. Amabile and R. Conti, "Changes in the Work Environment for Creativity During Downsizing," *Academy of Management Journal* (December 1999), pp. 630–640; A. G. Bedeian and A. A. Armenakis, "The Cesspool Syndrome: How Dreck Floats to the Top of Declining Organizations," *Academy of Management Executive* (February 1998), pp. 58–67.

48. *Wall Street Journal* (December 22, 1992), p. B1.

49. R. D. Nixon, M. A. Hitt, H. Lee, and E. Jeong, "Market Reactions to Announcements of Corporate Downsizing Actions and Implementation Strategies," *Strategic Management Journal* (November 2004), pp. 1121–1129; G. D. Bruton, J. K. Keels, and C. L. Shook, "Downsizing the Firm: Answering the Strategic Questions," *Academy of Management Executive* (May 1996), pp. 38–45.

50. M. A. Hitt, B. W. Keats, H. F. Harback, and R. D. Nixon, "Rightsizing: Building and Maintaining Strategic Leadership and Long-Term Competitiveness," *Organizational Dynamics* (Autumn 1994), pp. 18–32. For additional suggestions, see W. F. Cascio, "Strategies for Responsible Restructuring," *Academy of Management Executive* (August 2002), pp. 80–91, and T. Mroczkowski and M. Hanaoka, "Effective Rightsizing Strategies in Japan and America: Is There a Convergence of Employment Practices?" *Academy of Management Executive* (May 1997), pp. 57–67.

51. J. S. Black and H. B. Gregersen, "The Right Way to Manage Expats," *Harvard Business Review* (March–April 1999), pp. 52–61.

52. *Ibid.*, p. 54.

53. J. I. Sanchez, P. E. Spector, and C. L. Cooper, "Adapting to a Boundaryless World: A Developmental Expatriate Model," *Academy of Management Executive* (May 2000), pp. 96–106.

54. R. L. Tung, *The New Expatriates* (Cambridge, MA: Ballinger, 1988); J. S. Black, M. Mendenhall, and G. Oddou, "Toward a Comprehensive Model of International Adjustment: An Integration of Multiple Theoretical Perspectives," *Academy of Management Review* (April 1991), pp. 291–317.

55. M. A. Carpenter, W. G. Sanders, and H. B. Gregersen, "Bundling Human Capital with Organizational Context: The Impact of International Assignment Experience on Multinational Firm Performance and CEO Pay," *Academy of Management Journal* (June 2001), pp. 493–511.

56. M. A. Shaffer, D. A. Harrison, K. M. Gilley, and D. M. Luk, "Struggling for Balance Amid Turbulence on International Assignments: Work–Family Conflict, Support, and Commitment," *Journal of Management*, Vol. 27, No. 1 (2001), pp. 99–121.

57. J. S. Black and H. B. Gregersen, "The Right Way to Manage Expats," *Harvard Business Review* (March–April 1999), p. 54.

58. G. Stern, "GM Executive's Ties to Native Country Help Auto Maker Clinch Deal in China," *Wall Street Journal* (November 2, 1995), p. B7.

59. K. Roth, "Managing International Interdependence: CEO Characteristics in a Resource-Based Framework," *Academy of Management Journal* (February 1995), pp. 200–231.

60. M. Subramaniam and N. Venkatraman, "Determinants of Transnational New Product Development Capability: Testing the Influence of Transferring and Deploying Tacit Overseas Knowledge," *Strategic Management Journal* (April 2001), pp. 359–378.

61. J. S. Lublin, "An Overseas Stint Can Be a Ticket to the Top," *Wall Street Journal* (January 29, 1996), pp. B1, B2.

62. P. Elstrom and S. V. Brull, "Mitsubishi's Morass," *Business Week* (June 3, 1996), p. 35.

63. L. G. Love, R. L. Priem, and G. T. Lumpkin, "Explicitly Articulated Strategy and Firm Performance Under Alternative Levels of Centralization," *Journal of Management*, Vol. 28, No. 5 (2002), pp. 611–627.

64. G. G. Gordon, "The Relationship of Corporate Culture to Industry Sector and Corporate Performance," in *Gaining Control of the Corporate Culture*, edited by R. H. Kilmann, M. J. Saxton, R. Serpa, and Associates (San Francisco: Jossey-Bass, 1985), p. 123; T. Kono, "Corporate Culture and Long-Range Planning," *Long Range Planning* (August 1990), pp. 9–19.

65. B. Mike and J. W. Slocum, Jr., "Changing Culture at Pizza Hut and Yum! Brands," *Organizational Dynamics*, Vol. 32, No. 4 (2003), pp. 319–330.

66. T. J. Tetenbaum, "Seven Key Practices That Improve the Chance for Expected Integration and Synergies," *Organizational Dynamics* (Autumn 1999), pp. 22–35.

67. B. Bremner and G. Edmondson, "Japan: A Tale of Two Mergers," *Business Week* (May 10, 2004), p. 42.

68. P. Very, M. Lubatkin, R. Calori, and J. Veiga, "Relative Standing and the Performance of Recently Acquired European Firms," *Strategic Management Journal* (September 1997), pp. 593–614.

69. A. R. Malekzadeh and A. Nahavandi, "Making Mergers Work by Managing Cultures," *Journal of Business Strategy* (May/June 1990), pp. 53–57; A. Nahavandi and A. R. Malekzadeh,

"Acculturation in Mergers and Acquisitions," *Academy of Management Review* (January 1988), pp. 79–90.

70. C. Ghosn, "Saving the Business Without Losing the Company," *Harvard Business Review* (January 2002), pp. 37–45; B. Bremner, G. Edmondson, C. Dawson, D. Welch, and K. Kerwin, "Nissan's Boss," *Business Week* (October 4, 2004), pp. 50–60.

71. M. Lubatkin, D. Schweiger, and Y. Weber, "Top Management Turnover in Related M&Ss: An Additional Test of the Theory of Relative Standing," *Journal of Management*, Vol. 25, No. 1 (1999), pp. 55–73.

72. J. J. Keller, "Why AT&T Takeover of NCR Hasn't Been a Real Bell Ringer," *Wall Street Journal* (September 19, 1995), pp. A1, A5.

73. J. W. Gibson and D. V. Tesone, "Management Fads: Emergence, Evolution, and Implications for Managers," *Academy of Management Executive* (November 2001), pp. 122–133.

74. For additional information, see S. J. Carroll, Jr., and M. L. Tosi, Jr., *Management by Objectives: Applications and Research* (New York: Macmillan, 1973), and A. P. Raia, *Managing by Objectives* (Glenview, IL: Scott, Foresman, and Company, 1974).

75. J. W. Gibson, D. V. Tesone, and C. W. Blackwell, "Management Fads: Here Yesterday, Gone Today?" *SAM Advanced Management Journal* (Autumn 2003), pp. 12–17.

76. J. W. Gibson and D. V. Tesone, "Management Fads: Emergence, Evolution, and Implications for Managers," *Academy of Management Executive* (November 2001), p. 125.

77. S. S. Masterson and M. S. Taylor, "Total Quality Management and Performance Appraisal: An Integrative Perspective," *Journal of Quality Management*, Vol. 1, No. 1 (1996), pp. 67–89.

78. T. J. Douglas and W. Q. Judge, Jr., "Total Quality Management Implementation and Competitive Advantage: The Role of Structural Control and Exploration," *Academy of Management Journal* (February 2001), pp. 158–169.

79. T. Y. Choi and O. C. Behling, "Top Managers and TQM Success: One More Look After All These Years," *Academy of Management Executive* (February 1997), pp. 37–47.

80. R. J. Schonberger, "Total Quality Management Cuts a Broad Swath—Through Manufacturing and Beyond," *Organizational Dynamics* (Spring 1992), pp. 16–28.

81. T. C. Powell, "Total Quality Management as Competitive Advantage: A Review and Empirical Study," *Strategic Management Journal* (January 1995), pp. 15–37.

82. G. Hofstede, "Culture's Recent Consequences: Using Dimensional Scores in Theory and Research," *International Journal of Cross Cultural Management*, Vol. 1, No. 1 (2001), pp. 11–17; G. Hofstede, *Cultures and Organizations: Software of the Mind* (London: McGraw-Hill, 1991); G. Hofstede and M. H. Bond, "The Confucius Connection: From Cultural Roots to Economic Growth," *Organizational Dynamics* (Spring 1988), pp. 5–21; R. Hodgetts, "A Conversation with Geert Hofstede," *Organizational Dynamics* (Spring 1993), pp. 53–61.

83. M. Javidan and R. J. House, "Cultural Acumen for the Global Manager: Lessons from Project GLOBE," *Organizational Dynamics*, Vol. 29, No. 4 (2001), pp. 289–305.

84. Ibid., p. 303.

85. See G. Hofstede and M. H. Bond, "The Confucius Connection: From Cultural Roots to Economic Growth," *Organizational Dynamics* (Spring 1988), pp. 12–13.

86. H. K. Steensma, L. Marino, K. M. Weaver, and P. H. Dickson, "The Influence of National Culture on the Formation of Technology Alliances by Entrepreneurial Firms," *Academy of Management Journal* (October 2000), pp. 951–973.

87. "Emerging-Market Indicators," *The Economist* (October 7, 2000), p. 124.

88. T. T. Herbert, "Multinational Strategic Planning: Matching Central Expectations to Local Realities," *Long Range Planning* (February 1999), pp. 81–87.

89. M. A. Geletkancz, "The Salience of 'Culture's Consequences': The Effects of Cultural Values on Top Executive Commitment to the Status Quo," *Strategic Management Journal* (September 1997), pp. 615–634.

90. G. Hofstede and M. H. Bond, "The Confucius Connection: From Cultural Roots to Economic Growth," *Organizational Dynamics* (Spring 1988), p. 20.

91. B. Groysberg, A. Nanda, and N. Nohria, "The Risky Business of Hiring Stars," *Harvard Business Review* (May 2004), pp. 92–100.

92. D. Jones, "Employers Learning That 'B Players' Hold the Cards," *USA Today* (September 9, 2003), pp. 1B–2B.

93. From a study by the British Council reported in "Studying Abroad," *Futurist* (November–December 2004), p. 2.

94. D. Keirsey, *Please Understand Me II* (Del Mar, CA: Prometheus Nemesis Book Co., 1998).

Chapter 11

1. K. F. Iverson with T. Varian, "Plain Talk," *Inc.* (October 1997), p. 81. Excerpted from Iverson's book, *Plain Talk: Lessons from a Business Maverick* (New York: John Wiley & Sons, 1997).

2. R. Barker, "A Surprise in Office Depot's In-Box," *Business Week* (October 25, 2004), p. 122.

3. R. Muralidharan and R. D. Hamilton III, "Aligning Multinational Control Systems," *Long Range Planning* (June 1999), pp. 352–361. These types are based on W. G. Ouchi, "The Relationship Between Organizational Structure and Organizational Control," *Administrative Science Quarterly*, Vol. 20 (1977), pp. 95–113, and W. G. Ouchi, "A Conceptual Framework for the Design of Organizational Control Mechanisms," *Management Science*, Vol. 25 (1979), pp. 833–848. Muralidhara and Hamilton refer to Ouchi's clan control as input control.

4. W. G. Rowe and P. M. Wright, "Related and Unrelated Diversification and Their Effect on Human Resource Management Controls," *Strategic Management Journal* (April 1997), pp. 329–338.

5. R. Muralidharan and R. D. Hamilton III, "Aligning Multinational Control Systems," *Long Range Planning* (June 1999), pp. 356–359.

6. F. C. Barnes, "ISO 9000 Myth and Reality: A Reasonable Approach to ISO 9000," *SAM Advanced Management Journal* (Spring 1998), pp. 23–30.

7. M. Henricks, "A New Standard," *Entrepreneur* (October 2002), pp. 83–84.

8. M. V. Uzumeri, "ISO 9000 and Other Metastandards: Principles for Management Practice?" *Academy of Management Executive* (February 1997), pp. 21–36.

9. A. M. Hormozi, "Understanding and Implementing ISO 9000: A Manager's Guide," *SAM Advanced Management Journal* (Autumn 1995), pp. 4–11.

10. M. Henricks, "A New Standard," *Entrepreneur* (October 2002), p. 84.

11. L. Armstrong, "Someone to Watch Over You," *Business Week* (July 10, 2000), pp. 189–190.

12. J. K. Shank and V. Govindarajan, *Strategic Cost Management* (New York: The Free Press, 1993).

13. S. S. Rao, "ABCs of Cost Control," *Inc. Technology*, No. 2 (1997), pp. 79–81.

14. R. Gruber, "Why You Should Consider Activity-Based Costing," *Small Business Forum* (Spring 1994), pp. 20–36.

15. "Easier Than ABC," *Economist* (October 25, 2003), p. 56.

16. T. P. Pare, "A New Tool for Managing Costs," *Fortune* (June 14, 1993), pp. 124–129.

17. K. Hopkins, "The Risk Agenda," *Business Week*, Special Advertising Section (November 22, 2004), pp. 166–170.

18. T. L. Barton, W. G. Shenkir, and P. L. Walker, "Managing Risk: An Enterprise-wide Approach," *Financial Executive* (March/April 2001), p. 51.

19. T. L. Barton, W. G. Shenkir, and P. L. Walker, "Managing Risk: An Enterprise-wide Approach," *Financial Executive* (March/April 2001), pp. 48–51; P. L. Walker, W. G. Shenkir, and T. L. Barton, "Enterprise Risk Management: Putting It All Together," *Internal Auditor* (August 2003), pp. 50–55.

20. C. K. Brancato, *New Corporate Performance Measures* (New York: Conference Board, 1995); C. D. Ittner, D. F. Larcker, and M. V. Rajan, "The Choice of Performance Measures in Annual Bonus Contracts," working paper reported by K. Z. Andrews in "Executive Bonuses," *Harvard Business Review* (January–February 1996), pp. 8–9; J. Low and T. Siesfeld, "Measures That Matter: Wall Street Considers Non-Financial Performance More Than You Think," *Strategy & Leadership* (March/April 1998), pp. 24–30.

21. A similar measure, EBITDA (Earnings Before Interest, Taxes, Depreciation, and Amortization), is sometimes used but is *not* determined in accordance with generally accepted accounting principles and is thus subject to varying calculations.

22. J. M. Laderman, "Earnings, Schmernings: Look at the Cash," *Business Week* (July 24, 1989), pp. 56–57.

23. H. Greenberg, "Don't Count on Cash Flow," *Fortune* (May 13, 2002), p. 176; A. Tergesen, "Cash-Flow Hocus-Pocus," *Business Week* (July 15, 2002), pp. 130–132.

24. E. H. Hall, Jr., and J. Lee, "Diversification Strategies: Creating Value or Generating Profits?" paper presented to the annual meeting of the *Decision Sciences Institute*, Orlando, FL (November 18–21, 2000).

25. S. Tully, "America's Best Wealth Creators," *Fortune* (November 28, 1994), p. 143.

26. P. C. Brewer, G. Chandra, and C. A. Hock, "Economic Value Added (EVA): Its Uses and Limitations," *SAM Advanced Management Journal* (Spring 1999), pp. 4–11.

27. D. J. Skyrme and D. M. Amidon, "New Measures of Success," *Journal of Business Strategy* (January/February 1998), p. 23.

28. G. B. Stewart III, "EVA Works—But Not if You Make These Common Mistakes," *Fortune* (May 1, 1995), pp. 117–118.

29. S. Tully, "The Real Key to Creating Wealth," *Fortune* (September 20, 1993), p. 38.

30. A. Ehrbar, "Using EVA to Measure Performance and Assess Strategy," *Strategy & Leadership* (May/June 1999), pp. 20–24.

31. P. C. Brewer, G. Chandra, and C. A. Hock, "Economic Value Added (EVA): Its Uses and Limitations," *Advanced Management Journal* (Spring 1999), pp. 7–9.

32. Pro: K. Lehn and A. K. Makhija, "EVA & MVA As Performance Measures and Signals for Strategic Change," *Strategy & Leadership* (May/June 1996), pp. 34–38. Con: D. I. Goldberg, "Shareholder Value Debunked," *Strategy & Leadership* (January/February 2000), pp. 30–36.

33. A. Ehrbar, "Using EVA to Measure Performance and Assess Strategy," *Strategy & Leadership* (May/June 1999), p. 21.

34. S. Tully, "America's Wealth Creators," *Fortune* (November 22, 1999), pp. 275–284; A. B. Fisher, "Creating Stockholder Wealth: Market Value Added," *Fortune* (December 11, 1995), pp. 105–116.

35. A. B. Fisher, "Creating Stockholder Wealth: Market Value Added," *Fortune* (December 11, 1995), pp. 105–116.

36. K. Lehn and A. K. Makhija, "EVA & MVA As Performance Measures and Signals for Strategic Change," *Strategy & Leadership* (May/June 1996), p. 37.

37. R. S. Kaplan and D. P. Norton, "Using the Balanced Scorecard as a Strategic Management System," *Harvard Business Review* (January–February 1996), pp. 75–85; R. S. Kaplan and D. P. Norton, "The Balanced Scorecard—Measures That Drive Performance," *Harvard Business Review* (January–February, 1992), pp. 71–79.

38. D. I. Goldenberg, "Shareholder Value Debunked," *Strategy & Leadership* (January/February 2000), p. 34.

39. C. K. Brancato, *New Performance Measures* (New York: Conference Board, 1995).

40. A. Gumpus and B. Lyons, "The Balanced Scorecard at Philips Electronics," *Strategic Finance*, Vol. 84 (2002), pp. 92–101.

41. P. D. Heaney, "Can Performance Be Measured?" *Progressive Grocer*, Vol. 82 (2003), pp. 11–13.

42. B. P. Stivers and T. Joyce, "Building a Balanced Performance Management System," *SAM Advanced Management Journal* (Spring 2000), pp. 22–29.

43. D. J. Skyrme and D. M. Amidon, "New Measures of Success," *Journal of Business Strategy* (January/February 1998), p. 22.

44. G. J. M. Braam and E. Nijssen, "Performance Effects of Using the Balanced Scorecard: A Note on the Dutch Experience," *Long Range Planning* (August 2004), pp. 335–349; H. Ahn, "Applying the Balanced Scorecard Concept: An Experience Report," *Long Range Planning* (August 2001), pp. 441–461.

45. J. M. Ivancevich, T. N. Duening, J. A. Gilbert, and R. Konopaske, "Deterring White-Collar Crime," *Academy of Management Executive* (May 2003), pp. 114–127.

46. R. Charan, *Boards at Work* (San Francisco: Jossey-Bass, 1998), pp. 176–177.

47. T. D. Schellhardt, "Directors Get Tough: Inside a CEO Performance Review," *Wall Street Journal Interactive Edition* (April 27, 1998).

48. T. L. Wheelen and J. D. Hunger, "Using the Strategic Audit," *SAM Advanced Management Journal* (Winter 1987), pp. 4–12; G. Donaldson, "A New Tool for Boards: The Strategic Audit," *Harvard Business Review* (July–August 1995), pp. 99–107.

49. H. Threat, "Measurement Is Free," *Strategy & Leadership* (May/June 1999), pp. 16–19.

50. Z. U. Khan, S. K. Chawla, M. F. Smith, and M. F. Sharif, "Transfer Pricing Policy Issues in Europe 1992," *International Journal of Management* (September 1992), pp. 230–241.

51. H. Rothman, "You Need Not Be Big to Benchmark," *Nation's Business* (December 1992), p. 64.

52. C. W. Von Bergen and B. Soper, "A Problem with Benchmarking: Using Shaping as a Solution," *SAM Advanced Management Journal* (Autumn 1995), pp. 16–19.

53. "Tool Usage Rates," *Journal of Business Strategy* (March/April 1995), p. 12.

54. R. J. Kennedy, "Benchmarking and Its Myths," *Competitive Intelligence Magazine* (April–June 2000), pp. 28–33.

55. "Just the Facts: Numbers Runners," *Journal of Business Strategy* (July/August 2002), p. 3; L. Mann, D. Samson, and D. Dow, "A Field Experiment on the Effects of Benchmarking & Goal Setting on Company Sales Performance," *Journal of Management*, Vol. 24, No. 1 (1998), pp. 73–96.

56. S. A. W. Drew, "From Knowledge to Action: The Impact of Benchmarking on Organizational Performance," *Long Range Planning* (June 1997), pp. 427–441.

57. S. M. Robbins and R. B. Stobaugh, "The Bent Measuring Stick for Foreign Subsidiaries," *Harvard Business Review* (September–October 1973), p. 82.

58. J. D. Daniels and L. H. Radebaugh, *International Business*, 5th ed. (Reading, MA: Addison-Wesley, 1989), pp. 673–674.

59. W. A. Johnson and R. J. Kirsch, "International Transfer Pricing and Decision Making in United States Multinationals," *International Journal of Management* (June 1991), pp. 554–561.

60. "Global Economy Makes Taxing Harder," *The Futurist* (March–April 2000), p. 11; "Financial Indicators," *The Economist* (August 26, 2000), p. 89.

61. "Fixing the Bottom Line," *Time* (November 23, 1992), p. 20.

62. T. A. Stewart, "The New Face of American Power," *Fortune* (July 26, 1993), p. 72; G. P. Zachary, "Behind Stocks' Surge Is an Economy in Which Big U.S. Firms Thrive," *Wall Street Journal* (November 22, 1995), pp. A1, A5.

63. J. M. L. Poon, R. Ainuddin, and H. Affrim, "Management Policies and Practices of American, British, European, and Japanese Subsidiaries in Malaysia: A Comparative Study," *International Journal of Management* (December 1990), pp. 467–474.

64. M. Egan, "Setting Standards: Strategic Advantages in International Trade," *Business Strategy Review*, Vol. 13, No. 1 (2002), pp. 51–64; L. Swatkowski, "Building Towards International Standards," *Appliance* (December 1999), p. 30.

65. C. W. L. Hill, P. Hwang, and W. C. Kim, "An Eclectic Theory of the Choice of International Entry Mode," *Strategic Management Journal* (February 1990), pp. 117–128; D. Lei, J. W. Slocum, Jr., and R. W. Slater, "Global Strategy and Reward Systems: The Key Roles of Management Development and Corporate Culture," *Organizational Dynamics* (Autumn 1990), pp. 27–41; W. R. Fannin and A. F. Rodriques, "National or Global?—Control vs. Flexibility," *Long Range Planning* (October 1986), pp. 84–188.

66. A. V. Phatak, *International Dimensions of Management*, 2nd ed. (Boston: Kent, 1989), pp. 155–157.

67. S. McAlary, "Three Pitfalls in ERP Implementation," *Strategy & Leadership* (October/November/December 1999), pp. 49–50.

68. J. B. White, D. Clark, and S. Ascarelli, "This German Software Is Complex, Expensive—And Wildly Popular," *Wall Street Journal* (March 14, 1997), pp. A1, A8; D. Ward, "Whirlpool Takes a Dive with Software Snarl," *Des Moines Register* (April 29, 2000), p. 8D.

69. A. Lashinsky, "Meg and the Machine," *Fortune* (September 1, 2003), pp. 68–78.

70. R. M. Hodgetts and M. S. Wortman, *Administrative Policy*, 2nd ed. (New York: John Wiley & Sons, 1980), p. 128.

71. J. R. Wooldridge and C. C. Snow, "Stock Market Reaction to Strategic Investment Decisions," *Strategic Management Journal* (September 1990), pp. 353–363.

72. M. C. Jensen, "Corporate Budgeting Is Broken—Let's Fix It," *Harvard Business Review* (November 2001), pp. 94–101.

73. D. Henry, "Fuzzy Numbers," *Business Week* (October 4, 2004), pp. 79–88.

74. D. R. Schmidt and K. L. Fowler, "Post-Acquisition Financial Performance and Executive Compensation," *Strategic Management Journal* (November–December 1990), pp. 559–569.

75. H. L. Tosi, S. Werner, J. P. Katz, and L. R. Gomez-Mejia, "How Much Does Performance Matter? A Meta-Analysis of CEO Pay Studies," *Journal of Management*, Vol. 26, No. 2 (2000), pp. 301–339; P. Wright, M. Kroll, and D. Elenkov, "Acquisition Returns, Increase in Firm Size, and Chief Executive Officer Compensation: The Moderating Role of Monitoring," *Academy of Management Journal* (June 2002), pp. 599–608.

76. D. Jones, "Bad News Can Enrich Executives," *Des Moines Register* (November 26, 1999), p. 8S.

77. J. F. Porac, J. B. Wade, and T. G. Pollock, "Industry Categories and the Politics of the Comparable Firm in CEO Compensation," *Administrative Science Quarterly* (March 1999), pp. 112–144.

78. C. D. Ittner and D. F. Larcker, "Coming Up Short," *Harvard Business Review* (November 2003), pp. 88–95.

79. See the classic article by S. Kerr, "On the Folly of Rewarding A, While Hoping for B," *Academy of Management Journal*, Vol. 18 (December 1975), pp. 769–783.

80. W. Zellner, E. Schine, and G. Smith, "Trickle-Down Is Trickling Down at Work," *Business Week* (March 18, 1996), p. 34.

81. T. J. Peters and R. H. Waterman, *In Search of Excellence* (New York: HarperCollins, 1982), pp. 75–76.

82. T. Aeppel, "Not All Workers Find Idea of Empowerment as Neat as It Sounds," *Wall Street Journal* (September 8, 1997), pp. A1, A13.

83. R. S. Allen and M. M. Helms, "Employee Perceptions of the Relationship Between Strategy, Rewards, and Organizational Performance," *Journal of Business Strategies* (Fall 2002), pp. 115–140; M. A. Carpenter, "The Price of Change: The Role of CEO Compensation in Strategic Variation and Deviation from Industry Strategy Norms," *Journal of Management*, Vol. 26, No. 6 (2000), pp. 1179–1198; M. A. Carpenter and W. G. Sanders, "The Effects of Top Management Team Pay and Firm Internationalization on MNC Performance," *Journal of Management*, Vol. 30, No. 4 (2004), pp. 509–528; J. D. Shaw, N. Gupta, and J. E. Delery, "Congruence Between Technology and Compensation Systems: Implications for Strategy Implementation," *Strategic Management Journal* (April 2001), pp. 379–386; E. F. Montemazon, "Congruence Between Pay Policy and Competitive Strategy in High-Performing Organizations," *Journal of Management*, Vol. 22, No. 6 (1996), pp. 889–908.

84. D. B. Balkin and L. R. Gomez-Mejia, "Matching Compensation and Organizational Strategies," *Strategic Management Journal* (February 1990), pp. 153–169.

85. C. S. Galbraith, "The Effect of Compensation Programs and Structure on SBU Competitive Strategy: A Study of Technology-Intensive Firms," *Strategic Management Journal* (July 1991), pp. 353–370.

86. T. A. Stewart, "CEO Pay: Mom Wouldn't Approve," *Fortune* (March 31, 1997), pp. 119–120.

87. P. J. Stonich, "The Performance Measurement and Reward System: Critical to Strategic Management," *Organizational Dynamics* (Winter 1984), pp. 45–57.

88. A. Rappaport, "New Thinking on How to Link Executive Pay with Performance," *Harvard Business Review* (March–April 1999), pp. 91–101.

89. Motley Fool, "Fool's School: Hooray for GE," *The (Ames, IA) Tribune* (October 27, 2003), p. 1D.

90. E. Iwata and B. Hansen, "Pay, Performance Don't Always Add Up," *USA Today* (April 30, 2004), pp. 1B–2B; W. Grossman and R. E. Hoskisson, "CEO Pay at the Crossroads of Wall Street and Main: Toward the Strategic Design of Executive Compensation," *Academy of Management Executive* (February 1998), pp. 43–57.

91. *Pocket World in Figures 2004* (London: The Economist and Profile Books, 2003), p. 70.

92. Ibid., p. 67.

93. A. Harrington, "America's Most Admired Companies," *Fortune* (March 8, 2004), pp. 80–81.

94. J. Useem, "Should We Admire Wal-Mart?" *Fortune* (March 8, 2004), p. 118.

Chapter 12

1. D. Brady, "A Thousand and One Noshes," *Business Week* (June 14, 2004), pp. 54–56.

2. "Don't Laugh at Gilded Butterflies," *Economist* (April 24, 2004), pp. 71–73

3. R. Jonash and T. Sommerlatte, *The Innovation Premium* (Perseus Books, 1999).

4. G. Getz and C. Christensen, "Should You Fear Disruptive Technology?" *Fortune* (April 3, 2000), pp. 249–250.

5. E. Berggen and T. Nacher, "Introducing New Products Can Be Hazardous to Your Company: Use the Right New-Solutions Delivery Tools," *Academy of Management Executive* (August 2001), pp. 92–101.

6. "Fear of the Unknown," *The Economist* (December 4, 1999), pp. 61–62.

7. M. S. Malone, "Which Are the Most Valuable Companies in the New Economy?" *Forbes ASAP* (May 29, 2000), pp. 212–214.

8. F. T. Rothaermel, "Incumbent's Advantage Through Exploiting Complementary Assets via Interfirm Cooperation," *Strategic Management Journal* (June–July 2001), pp. 687–699.

9. S. J. Towner, "Four Ways to Accelerate New Product Development," *Long Range Planning* (April 1994), p. 57.

10. R. Garud and P. R. Nayyar, "Transformative Capacity: Continual Structuring by Intertemporal Technology Transfer," *Strategic Management Journal* (June 1994), p. 379.

11. J. P. Andrew and H. L. Sirkin, "Innovating for Cash," *Harvard Business Review* (September 2003), pp. 76–83.

12. R. D. Hof, P. Burrows, S. Hamm, D. Brady, and I. Rowley, "Building an Idea Factory," *Business Week* (October 22, 2004), pp. 194–200.

13. M. A. Schilling and C. W. L. Hill, "Managing the New Product Development Process: Strategic Imperatives," *Academy of Management Executive* (August 1998), pp. 67–81.

14. C. Power, K. Kerwin, R. Grover, K. Alexander, and R. D. Hof, "Flops," *Business Week* (August 16, 1993), pp. 76–82.

15. "Expect the Unexpected," *Economist* (September 6, 2003), p. 5. This article summarizes research reported in *Why Innovation Fails* by Carl Franklin (London: Spiro Press, 2003).

16. R. D. Hof, P. Burrows, S. Hamm, D. Brady, and I. Rowley, "Building an Idea Factory," *Business Week* (October 22, 2004), p. 196.

17. L. Rosenkopf and A. Nerkar, "Beyond Local Search: Boundary-Spanning, Exploration, and Impact in the Optical Disk Industry," *Strategic Management Journal* (April 2001), pp. 287–306.

18. G. C. Hill and K. Yamada, "Motorola Illustrates How an Aged Giant Can Remain Vibrant," *Wall Street Journal* (December 9, 1992), pp. A1, A14.

19. L. Huston, "Mining the Periphery for New Products," *Long Range Planning* (April 2004), pp. 191–196; N. Snyder, "Environmental Volatility, Scanning Intensity and Organizational Performance," *Journal of Contemporary Business* (September 1981), p. 16.

20. R. Nobel and J. Birkinshaw, "Innovations in MNCs: Control and Communication Patterns in International R&D Operations," *Strategic Management Journal* (May 1998), pp. 479–496.

21. J. Kerstetter, "An Old Hotbed with New Crops," *Business Week* (October 11, 2004), pp. 164–170; P. Almeida, "Knowledge Sourcing by Foreign Multinationals: Patent Citation Analysis in the U.S. Semiconductor Industry," *Strategic Management Journal* (December 1996), pp. 155–165.

22. E. Von Hippel, *The Sources of Innovation* (Oxford, UK: Oxford University Press, 1988), p. 4. See also S. Thomke and E. Von Hippel, "Customers As Innovators: A New Way to Create Value," *Harvard Business Review* (April 2002), pp. 74–81.

23. M. R. Neale and D. R. Corkindale, "Co-Developing Products: Involving Customer Earlier and More Deeply," *Long Range Planning* (June 1998), pp. 418–425.

24. E. Von Hippel, *The Sources of Innovation* (Oxford, UK: Oxford University Press, 1988), p. 107; E. Von Hippel, S. Thomke, and M. Sonnack, "Creating Breakthroughs at 3M," *Harvard Business Review* (September–October 1999), p. 48.

25. L. Lavelle, "Inventing to Order," *Business Week* (July 5, 2004), pp. 84–85.

26. E. Von Hippel, S. Thomke, and M. Sonnack, "Creating Breakthroughs at 3M," *Harvard Business Review* (September–October 1999), p. 52.

27. G. Hamel and C. K. Prahalad, "Seeing the Future First," *Fortune* (September 5, 1995), p. 70.

28. C. M. Christensen, *The Innovator's Dilemma* (Boston: HBS Press, 1997); J. Wade, "A Community-Level Analysis of Sources and Rates of Technological Variation in the Microprocessor Market," *Academy of Management Journal* (October 1996), pp. 1218–1244.

29. C. M. Christensen and J. L. Bower, "Customer Power, Strategic Investment, and the Failure of Leading Firms," *Strategic Management Journal* (March 1996), pp. 197–218.

30. G. S. Lynn, J. G. Morone, and A. S. Paulson, "Marketing and Discontinuous Innovation: The Probe and Learn Process," *California Management Review* (Spring 1996), pp. 8–37.

31. W. I. Zangwill, "When Customer Research Is a Lousy Idea," *Wall Street Journal* (March 8, 1993), p. A10.

32. S. Baker, "What Every Business Should Learn from Microsoft," *Journal of Business Strategy* (September/October 1998), pp. 36–41.

33. "Don't Laugh at Gilded Butterflies," *Economist* (April 24, 2004), pp. 71–73.

34. D. F. Kuratko, J. S. Hornsby, D. W. Naffziger, and R. V. Montagno, "Implement Entrepreneurial Thinking in Established Organizations," *SAM Advanced Management Journal* (Winter 1993), p. 29.

35. "Business Bulletin," *Wall Street Journal* (May 1, 1997), p. A1. The number improved from 58 ideas in 1967 to 11 in 1990, to 7 in 1995.

36. L. G. Franko, "Global Corporate Competition: Who's Winning, Who's Losing, and the R&D Factor as One Reason Why," *Strategic Management Journal* (September–October 1989), pp. 449–474; See also P. S. Chan, E. J. Flynn, and R. Chinta, "The Strategies of Growing and Turnaround Firms: A Multiple Discriminant Analysis," *International Journal of Management* (September 1991), pp. 669–675.

37. M. J. Chussil, "How Much to Spend on R&D?" *The PIMS-letter of Business Strategy*, No. 13 (Cambridge, MA: The Strategic Planning Institute, 1978), p. 5.

38. J. S. Harrison, E. H. Hall, Jr., and R. Nargundkar, "Resource Allocation as an Outcropping of Strategic Consistency: Performance Implications," *Academy of Management Journal* (October 1993), pp. 1026–1051.

39. S. B. Graves and N. S. Langowitz, "Innovative Productivity and Returns to Scale in the Pharmaceutical Industry," *Strategic Management Journal* (November 1993), pp. 593–605; A. Brady, "Small Is As Small Does," *Journal of Business Strategy* (March/April 1995), pp. 44–52.

40. "Small Firms Make More Than Their Share of Big Inventions," *The Small Business Advocate* (March 2003), pp. 1, 4.

41. J. B. Sorensen and T. E. Stuart, "Aging, Obsolescence, and Organizational Innovation," *Administrative Science Quarterly* (March 2000), pp. 81–112.

42. D. H. Freedman, "Through the Looking Glass," in "The State of Small Business," *Inc.* (May 21, 1996), pp. 48–54.

43. N. Nohria and R. Gulati, "Is Slack Good or Bad for Innovation?" *Academy of Management Journal* (October 1996), pp. 1245–1264.

44. M. A. Hitt, R. E. Hoskisson, and J. S. Harrison, "Strategic Competitiveness in the 1990s: Challenges and Opportunities for U.S. Executives," *Academy of Management Executive* (May 1991), p. 13.

45. T. F. O'Boyle, "Steel's Management Has Itself to Blame," *Wall Street Journal* (May 17, 1983), p. 32.

46. M. Silva and B. Sjogren, *Europe 1992 and the New World Power Game* (New York: John Wiley & Sons, 1990), p. 231.

47. E. Mansfield, M. Schwartz, and S. Wagner, "Imitation Costs and Patents: An Empirical Study," *Economic Journal* (December 1981), pp. 907–918.

48. G. Stalk, Jr., and A. M. Webber, "Japan's Dark Side of Time," *Harvard Business Review* (July–August 1993), p. 99.

49. M. Robert, "Market Fragmentation versus Market Segmentation," *Journal of Business Strategy* (September/October 1992), p. 52.

50. M. J. Benner and M. Tushman, "Process Management and Technological Innovation: A Longitudinal Study of the Photography and Paint Industries," *Administrative Science Quarterly* (December 2002), pp. 676–706.

51. W. T. Robinson and J. Chiang, "Product Development Strategies for Established Market Pioneers, Early Followers, and Late Entrants," *Strategic Management Journal* (September 2002), pp. 855–866.

52. C. L. Nicholls-Nixon and C. Y. Woo, "Technology Sourcing and Output of Established Firms in a Regime of Encompassing Technological Change," *Strategic Management Journal* (July 2003), pp. 651–666.

53. "Business Briefcase," *Des Moines Register* (November 17, 2004), p. 3D.

54. M. Silva and B. Sjogren, *Europe 1992 and the New World Power Game* (New York: John Wiley & Sons), pp. 239–241. See also P. Nueno and J. Oosterveld, "Managing Technology Alliances," *Long Range Planning* (June 1988), pp. 11–17.

55. M. Krantz, "Amgen Thinks Small to Grow," *USA Today* (October 23, 2003), p. 3B.

56. P. R. Nayak, "Should You Outsource Product Development?" *Journal of Business Strategy* (May/June 1993), pp. 44–45.

57. C. W. L. Hill, "Establishing a Standard: Competitive Strategy and Technological Standards in Winner-Take-All Industries," *Academy of Management Executive* (May 1997), pp. 7–25.

58. M. H. Roy and S. S. Dugal, "The Effect of Technological Environment and Competitive Strategy on Licensing Decisions," *American Business Review* (June 1999), pp. 112–118.

59. T. M. Apke, "International Licensing of Technology: Protecting Your Interests," paper presented to the annual meeting of the *Western Decision Sciences Institute* (Honolulu, HI, April 15–19, 2003).

60. "The Cost of Ideas," *Economist* (November 13, 2004), p. 71; "Patent Wars," *Economist* (April 8, 2000), pp. 75–78.

61. "The Right to Good Ideas," *Economist* (June 23, 2001), pp. 21–23.

62. M. A. Hitt, R. E. Hoskisson, R. A. Johnson, and D. D. Moesel, "The Market for Corporate Control and Firm Innovation," *Academy of Management Journal* (October 1996), pp. 1084–1119.

63. W. M. Cohen and D. A. Levinthal, "Absorptive Capacity: A New Perspective on Learning and Innovation," *Administrative Science Quarterly* (March 1990), pp. 128–152.

64. P. J. Lane and M. Lubatkin, "Absorptive Capacity and Interorganizational Learning," *Strategic Management Journal* (May 1998), pp. 461–477.

65. M. B. Heeley, "Appropriating Rents from External Knowledge: The Impact of Absorptive Capacity on Firm Sales Growth and Research Productivity," paper presented to *Babson Entrepreneurship Research Conference* (Wellesley, MA, 1997).

66. S. A. Zahra and G. George, "Absorptive Capacity: A Review, Reconceptualization, and Extension," *Academy of Management Review* (April 2002), pp. 185–203.

67. "The Impact of Industrial Robotics on the World of Work," *International Labour Review*, Vol. 125, No. 1 (1986). Summarized in "The Risks of Robotization," *The Futurist* (May–June 1987), p. 56.

68. M. A. Hitt, R. E. Hoskisson, and J. S. Harrison, "Strategic Competitiveness in the 1990s: Challenges and Opportunities for U.S. Executives," *Academy of Management Executive* (May 1991), p. 9.

69. C. Hickman and C. Raia, "Incubating Innovation," *Journal of Business Strategy* (May/June 2002), pp. 14–18.

70. D. Dougherty and C. Hardy, "Sustained Product Innovation in Large, Mature Organizations: Overcoming Innovation-to-Organization Problems," *Academy of Management* (October 1996), pp. 1120–1153.

71. C. A. O'Reilly III and M. L. Tushman, "The Ambidextrous Organization," *Harvard Business Review* (April 2004), pp. 74–81.

72. E. M. Rogers, *Diffusion of Innovations*, 4th edition (New York: The Free Press, 1995).

73. C. A. Lengnick-Hall, "Innovation and Competitive Advantage: What We Know and What We Need to Know," *Journal of Management* (June 1992), pp. 399–429.

74. J. R. Galbraith, "Designing the Innovative Organization," *Organizational Dynamics* (Winter 1982), pp. 5–25.

75. P. R. Nayak, "Product Innovation Practices in Europe, Japan, and the U.S.," *Journal of Business Strategy* (May/June 1992), pp. 62–63.

76. E. M. Olson, O. C. Walker, Jr., and R. W. Ruekert, "Organizing for Effective New Product Development: The Moderating Role of Product Innovativeness," *Journal of Marketing* (January 1995), pp. 48–62.

77. D. Rowe, "Up and Running," *Journal of Business Strategy* (May/June 1993), pp. 48–50.

78. N. Freundlich and M. Schroeder, "Getting Everybody Into the Act," *Business Week* (Quality 1991 edition), p. 152.

79. W. D. Guth and A. Ginsberg, "Corporate Entrepreneurship," *Strategic Management Journal* (Summer 1990), p. 5.

80. S. A. Zahra and J. G. Covin, "Contextual Measures on the Corporate Entrepreneurship–Performance Relationship: A Longitudinal Analysis," *Journal of Business Venturing*, Vol. 10 (1995), pp. 43–58.

81. R. A. Burgelman, "Designs for Corporate Entrepreneurship," *California Management Review* (Spring 1984), pp. 154–166; R. A. Burgelman and L. R. Sayles, *Inside Corporate Innovation* (New York: The Free Press, 1986).

82. W. J. Holstein, "Remaking Motorola Isn't Easy," *U.S. News & World Report* (October 23, 2000), p. 52; R. O. Crockett, "A New Company Called Motorola," *Business Week* (April 17, 2000), pp. 86–92.

83. T. A. Stewart, "How Teradyne Solved the Innovator's Dilemma," *Fortune* (June 10, 2000), pp. 188–190.

84. J. Carey, "An Ivory Tower That Spins Pure Gold," *Business Week* (April 19, 1999), pp. 167–170.

85. S. K. Yoder, "How H-P Used Tactics of the Japanese to Beat Them at Their Game," *Wall Street Journal* (September 8, 1994), pp. A1, A6.

86. C. Y. Woo, G. E. Willard, and S. M. Beckstead, "Spin-Offs: What Are the Gains?" *Journal of Business Strategy* (March–April 1989), pp. 29–32.

87. M. A. Schilling and C. W. L. Hill, "Managing the New Product Development Process: Strategic Imperatives," *Academy of Management Executive* (August 1998), pp. 67–81.

88. J. R. Hauser and D. Clausing, "The House of Quality," *Harvard Business Review* (May–June 1988), pp. 63–73.

89. E. H. Kessler, P. E. Bierly III, and S. Gopalakrishnan, "Vasa Syndrome: Insights from a 17th-Century New-Product Disaster," *Academy of Management Executive* (August 2001), pp. 80–91.

90. M. A. Schilling and C. W. L. Hill, "Managing the New Product Development Process: Strategic Imperatives," *Academy of Management Executive* (August 1998), pp. 67–81.

91. J. B. Levin and R. D. Hof, "Has Philips Found Its Wizard?" *Business Week* (September 6, 1993), pp. 82–84.

92. O. Port, "Rating R&D: How Companies Get the Biggest Bang for the Buck," *Business Week* (July 5, 1993), p. 98.

93. I. Krause and J. Liu, "Benchmarking R&D Productivity," *Planning Review* (January/February 1993), pp. 16–21, 52–53.

94. L. Valikangas and P. Merlyn, "How Market-Based Organization Sustains Organic Innovation," *Business Strategy Review* (September 2002), pp. 3–6.

95. Ibid., p. 4.

96. M. Stepanek, "Using the Net for Brainstorming," *Business Week E.Biz* (December 13, 1999), p. EB55. (See note 28 for *The Innovator's Dilemma*.)

97. Ibid., pp. EB55–EB59.

98. "Robots," *Economist* (October 18, 2003), p. 98.

99. J. Fowler, "Vacuums Lead Surge in Household Robots," *Des Moines Register* (October 21, 2004), p. 3D.

100. Ibid., p. 30.

Chapter 13

1. Summarized from N. L. Torres, "No Sweat," *Entrepreneur* (December 2004), p. 126.

2. "Small Business Resources for Faculty, Students, and Researchers: Answers to Frequently Asked Questions," *Small Business Advocate* (May 2004), p. 5.

3. W. J. Baumol, "Entrepreneurial Cultures and Countercultures," *Academy of Management Learning and Education* (September 2004), pp. 316–326; *The State of Small Business: A Report to the President* (Washington, DC: U.S. Government Printing Office, 1987), p. 117.

4. J. Castro, J. McDowell, and W. McWhirter, "Big vs. Small," *Time* (September 5, 1988), p. 49. This is supported by a 2003 study by the U.S. Small Business Administration which found that a small-firm patent is more likely than a large-firm patent to be among the top 1% of most frequently cited patents.

5. B. Headd, "Redefining Business Success: Distinguishing Between Closure and Failure," *Small Business Economics* (August 2003), as reported in "Frequency of Small Business Failure Reassessed by Advocacy Economist," *Small Business Advocate* (October 2003), p. 2.

6. M. J. Foster, "Scenario Planning for Small Businesses," *Long Range Planning* (February 1993), p. 123; M. S. S. El-Namacki, "Small Business—The Myth and the Reality," *Long Range Planning* (August 1990), p. 79.

7. J. Hopkins, "Study: New Company Failure Rate Not So High," *USA Today* (February 18, 2003), p. 1B. This article summarizes Brian Headd's 2003 study for the Small Business Administration. It revealed that after four years, the 50% that had closed included 33% that were considered unsuccessful. The remaining 17% were sold or closed but were considered successful by their founders. According to a study by Dun & Bradstreet of 800,000 small U.S. businesses started in 1985, 70% were still in business in March 1994. Contrary to other studies, this study counted firms as failures only if they owed money at the time of their demise. Also see J. Aley, "Debunking the Failure Fallacy," *Fortune* (September 6, 1993), p. 21.

8. R. N. Lussier, "Startup Business Advice from Business Owners to Would-Be Entrepreneurs," *SAM Advanced Management Journal* (Winter 1995), pp. 10–13.

9. J. W. Carland, F. Hoy, W. R. Boulton, and J. A. C. Carland, "Differentiating Entrepreneurs from Small Business Owners: A Conceptualization," *Academy of Management Review* (April 1984), p. 358; J. W. Carland, J. C. Carland, F. Hoy, and W. R. Boulton, "Distinctions Between Entrepreneurial and Small Business Ventures," *International Journal of Management* (March 1988), pp. 98–103.

10. S. P. Galante, "Counting on a Narrow Market Can Cloud Company's Future," *Wall Street Journal* (January 20, 1986), p. 17. Sexton's statement that entrepreneurial firms engage in more sophisticated strategic planning than do small businesses is supported by C. H. Matthews and S. G. Scott, "Uncertainty and Planning in Small Entrepreneurial Firms: An Empirical Assessment," *Journal of Small Business Management* (October 1995), pp. 34–52. See also W. H. Stewart, Jr., W. E. Watson,

NOTES

J. C. Carland, and J. W. Carland, "A Proclivity for Entrepreneurship: A Comparison of Entrepreneurs, Small Business Owners, and Corporate Managers," *Journal of Business Venturing* (March 1999), pp. 189–214.

11. D. Fields, "Mrs. Fields' Weekends," *USA Weekend* (February 3–5, 1989), p. 16; M. Alpert, "In the Chips," *Fortune* (July 17, 1989), pp. 115–116.

12. J. S. Bracker, B. W. Keats, and J. N. Pearson, "Planning and Financial Performance Among Small Firms in a Growth Industry," *Strategic Management Journal* (November–December 1988), pp. 591–603; J. Kargar and J. A. Parnell, "Strategic Planning Emphasis and Planning Satisfaction in Small Firms: An Empirical Investigation," *Journal of Business Strategies* (Spring 1996), pp. 1–20; C. R. Schwenk and C. B. Shrader, "Effects of Formal Strategic Planning on Financial Performance in Small Firms: A Meta-Analysis," *Entrepreneurship Theory & Performance* (Spring 1993), pp. 53–64; L. W. Rue and N. A. Ibrahim, "The Relationship Between Planning Sophistication and Performance in Small Businesses," *Journal of Small Business Management* (October 1998), pp. 24–32.

13. W. H. Baker, H. Lon, and B. Davis, "Business Planning in Successful Small Firms," *Long Range Planning* (December 1993), pp. 82–88. Another study of 184 owner–managers of small businesses in the U.S. Midwest found that they were using strategic planning by formally documenting their mission (99%), objectives (95%), and strategies (93%). See D. F. Kuratko, J. C. Goodale, and J. S. Hornsby, "Quality Practices for a Competitive Advantage in Smaller Firms," *Journal of Small Business Management* (October 2001), pp. 293–311.

14. S. C. Perry, "The Relationship Between Written Business Plans and the Failure of Small Businesses in the U.S.," *Journal of Small Business Management* (July 2001), pp. 201–208.

15. D. B. Bradley III, "The Importance of Marketing Planning to Prevent Small Business Failure," paper presented to annual meeting of the Small Business Institute Directors Association (SBIDA) (San Diego, CA, February 7–9, 2002).

16. L. W. Rue and N. A. Ibrahim, "The Status of Planning in Smaller Family-Owned Businesses," *Family Business Review* (Spring 1996), pp. 29–43.

17. A. Thomas, "Less Is More: How Less Formal Planning Can Be Best," in *The Strategic Planning Management Reader*, edited by L. Fahey (Upper Saddle River, NJ: Prentice Hall, 1989), pp. 331–336; C. B. Shrader, C. L. Mulford, and V. L. Blackburn, "Strategic and Operational Planning, Uncertainty, and Performance in Small Firms," *Journal of Small Business Management* (October 1989), pp. 45–60.

18. R. B. Robinson, Jr., and J. A. Pearce II, "The Impact of Formalized Strategic Planning on Financial Performance in Small Organizations," *Strategic Management Journal* (July–September 1983), pp. 197–207; R. Ackelsberg and P. Arlow, "Small Businesses Do Plan and It Pays Off," *Long Range Planning* (October 1985), pp. 61–67.

19. M. Berry, "Strategic Planning in Small High-Tech Companies," *Long Range Planning* (June 1998), pp. 455–466.

20. F. Delmar and S. Shane, "Does Business Planning Facilitate the Development of New Ventures?" *Strategic Management Journal* (December 2003), pp. 1165–1185; S. Shane and F. Delmar, "Planning for the Market: Business Planning Before Marketing and the Continuation of Organizing Efforts," *Journal of Business Venturing* (November 2004), pp. 767–785.

21. T. Mazzarol, "Do Formal Business Plans Really Matter? A Survey of Small Business Owners in Australia," paper presented to the 45th International Conference on Small Business (ICSB) World Conference 2000 (Brisbane, Australia, June 7–10, 2000).

22. S. C. Perry, "The Relationship Between Written Business Plans and the Failure of Small Businesses in the U.S.," *Journal of Small Business Management* (July 2001), pp. 201–208.

23. V. Fowler, "Business Study Focuses on Failures," *Des Moines Register* (August 9, 1992), p. G1. For information on preparing a business plan, see R. Hisrich and M. Peters, *Entrepreneurship*, 6th ed. (New York: Irwin/McGraw-Hill, 2004).

24. M. K. Fiegener, B. M. Brown, D. R. Dreux IV, and W. J. Dennis, Jr., "CEO Stakes and Board Composition in Small Private Firms," *Entrepreneurship Theory & Practice* (Summer 2000), pp. 5–24.

25. L. W. Busenitz, D. D. Moesel, J. O. Fiet, and J. B. Barney, "The Framing of Perceptions of Fairness in the Relationship Between Venture Capitalists and New Venture Teams," *Entrepreneurship Theory & Practice* (Spring 1997), pp. 5–21.

26. V. H. Fried, G. D. Bruton, and R. D. Hisrich, "Strategy and the Board of Directors in Venture Capital–Backed Firms," *Journal of Business Venturing* (November 1999), pp. 493–503.

27. D. L. Sexton and F. I. Steele, *Leading Practices of Fast Growth Entrepreneurs* (Kansas City, MO: National Center for Entrepreneurship Research, 1997).

28. D. J. Garsombke and T. W. Garsombke, "An Empirical Investigation of the Utilization of External and Internal Boards of Directors and Management Advisory Assistance on the Performance of Small Businesses," *Journal of Business Strategies* (Fall 1996), pp. 167–184.

29. "Does Sarbanes-Oxley Hurt Shareholders and Hide Poor Management?" *Knowledge@Wharton* (November 17–30, 2004).

30. *Ibid.*

31. J. C. Shuman and J. A. Seeger, "The Theory and Practice of Strategic Management in Smaller Rapid Growth Firms," *American Journal of Small Business* (Summer 1986), p. 14.

32. R. C. Pineda, L. D. Lerner, M. C. Miller, and S. J. Phillips, "An Investigation of Factors Affecting the Information-Search Activities of Small Business Managers," *Journal of Small Business Management* (January 1998), pp. 60–71.

33. S. Birley and P. Westhead, "Growth and Performance Contrasts Between 'Types' of Small Firms," *Strategic Management Journal* (November–December 1990), pp. 535–557; J. L. Ward and C. E. Aronloff, "How Family Affects Strategy," *Small Business Forum* (Fall 1994), pp. 85–90.

34. P. Westhead, "Company Performance and Objectives Reported by First and Multi-Generation Family Companies: A Research Note," *Journal of Small Business and Enterprise Development*, Vol. 10, No. 1 (2003), pp. 93–105; J. Wiklund, P. Davidsson, and F. Delmar, "What Do They Think and Feel About Growth? An Expectancy-Value Approach to Small Business Managers' Attitudes Toward Growth," *Entrepreneurship Theory & Practice* (Spring 2003), pp. 247–270; A. Morrison, J. Breen, and S. Ali, "Small Business Growth: Intention, Ability, and Opportunity," *Journal of Small Business Management* (October 2003), pp. 417–425.

35. J. R. Baum, E. A. Locke, and K. G. Smith, "A Multidimensional Model of Venture Growth," *Academy of Management Journal* (April 2001), pp. 292–303; J. Florin, M. Lubatkin, and W. Schulze, "A Social Capital Model of High-Growth Ventures," *Academy of Management Journal* (June 2003), pp. 374–384.

36. J. Low and P. C. Kalafut, *Invisible Advantage: How Intangibles Are Driving Business Performance* (New York: Perseus Publishing, 2002), as reported in "Counting Intangible Assets," *Futurist* (September–October 2003), pp. 12–13.

37. P. F. Drucker, *Innovation and Entrepreneurship* (New York: HarperCollins, 1985), pp. 30–129.

38. F. Donnely, "Let zBox Accept Deliveries," *Des Moines Register* (October 31, 2000), p. TW1.

39. D. Stipp, "Inventor on the Verge of a Nervous Breakthrough," *Fortune* (March 29, 1999), pp. 104–117.

40. D. Whitford, "Taking BET Back from the Street," *Fortune* (November 9, 1998), pp. 167–170.

41. A. Bianchi, "Medical-Food Start-up Offers Tasty Treatments," *Inc.* (January 1997), p. 15.

42. C. W. Hofer and W. R. Sandberg, "Improving New Venture Performance: Some Guidelines for Success," *American Journal of Small Business* (Summer 1987), pp. 12–23. See also J. J. Chrisman and A. Bauerschmidt, "New Venture Performance: Some Critical Extensions to the Model," paper presented to the State-of-the-Art Symposium on Entrepreneurship (Ames: Iowa State University, April 12–14, 1992).

43. K. C. Robinson, "An Examination of the Influence of Industry Structure on Eight Alternative Measures of New Venture Performance for High Potential Independent New Ventures," *Journal of Business Venturing* (March 1999), pp. 165–187.

44. Interview with C. Bagley by J. Useem, "Forget Patents, Says Stanford Prof," *Inc.* (October 1996), p. 23.

45. K. C. Robinson, "An Examination of the Influence of Industry Structure on Eight Alternative Measures of New Venture Performance for High Potential Independent New Ventures," *Journal of Business Venturing* (March 1999), pp. 165–187.

46. J. Wade, "A Community-Level Analysis of Sources and Rates of Technological Variation in the Microprocessor Market," *Academy of Management Journal* (October 1996), pp. 1218–1244.

47. Supported by R. C. Shrader and M. Simon, "Corporate Versus Independent New Ventures: Resources, Strategy, and Performance Differences," *Journal of Business Venturing* (January 1997), pp. 47–66; R. Tonge, P. C. Larsen, and M. Ito, "Strategic Leadership in Super-Growth Companies—A Reappraisal," *Long Range Planning* (December 1998), pp. 838–847; G. Qian and L. Li, "Profitability of Small- and Medium-Sized Enterprises in High-Tech Industries: The Case of the Biotechnology Industry," *Strategic Management Journal* (September 2003), pp. 881–887.

48. K. M. Weaver and P. Dickson, "Strategic Alliances," *NFIB National Small Business Poll*, Vol. 4, Issue 4 (2004).

49. J. R. Baum, E. A. Locke, and K. G. Smith, "A Multidimensional Model of Venture Growth," *Academy of Management Journal* (April 2001), pp. 292–303; A. C. Cooper, G. E. Willard, and C. Y. Woo, "A Reexamination of the Niche Concept," in *The Strategy Process: Concepts, Contexts, and Cases*, 2nd ed., edited by H. Mintzberg and J. B. Quinn (Upper Saddle River, NJ: Prentice Hall, 1991), pp. 619–628; P. P. McDougal, J. G. Covin, R. B. Robinson, Jr., and L. Herron, "The Effects of Industry Growth and Strategic Breadth on New Venture Performance and Strategy Content," *Strategic Management Journal* (September 1994), pp. 537–554; C. E. Bamford, T. J. Dean, and P. P. McDougall, "Initial Strategies and New Venture Growth: An Examination of the Effectiveness of Broad vs. Narrow Breadth Strategies," in *Frontiers of Entrepreneurial Research*, edited by P. D. Reynolds, et al. (Babson Park, MA: Babson College, 1997), pp. 375–389; G. H. Lim, K. S. Lee, and S. J. Tan, "SMEs' Market Entry Strategy: Substitution Instead of Niching," paper presented to the International Council for Small Business Conference (Naples, Italy, June 1999).

50. J. Wiklund and D. Shepherd, "Knowledge-Based Resources, Entrepreneurial Orientation, and the Performance of Small and Medium-Sized Businesses," *Strategic Management Journal* (December 2003), pp. 1307–1314; J. Kickul and L. K. Gundry, "Prospecting for Strategic Advantage: The Proactive Entrepreneurial Personality and Small Firm Innovation," *Journal of Small Business Management* (April 2002), pp. 85–97.

51. H. P. Welsch, "Entrepreneurs' Personal Characteristics: Causal Models," paper presented at the State-of-the-Art Symposium on Entrepreneurship (Ames: Iowa State University, April 12–14, 1992); A. Rahim, "Stress, Strain, and Their Moderators: An Empirical Comparison of Entrepreneurs and Managers," *Journal of Small Business Management* (January 1996), pp. 46–58; C. Korunka, H. Frank, M. Lueger, and J. Mugler, "The Entrepreneurial Personality in the Context of Resources, Environment, and the Startup Process—A Configurational Approach," *Entrepreneurship Theory & Practice* (Fall 2003), pp. 23–42.

52. M. Kets de Vries, "The Dark Side of Entrepreneurship," *Harvard Business Review* (November–December 1985), pp. 160–167.

53. A. C. Cooper, F. J. Gimeno-Gascon, and C. Y. Woo, "Initial Human and Financial Capital as Predictors of New Venture Performance," *Journal of Business Venturing* (Volume 9, 1994), pp. 371–395; H. R. Feeser and G. E. Willard, "Founding Strategies and Performance in High-Tech Firms," in *Handbook of Business Strategy, 1991/92 Yearbook*, edited by H. E. Glass and M. A. Hovde (Boston: Warren, Gorham & Lamont, 1991), pp. 2.1–2.18.

54. R. Ricklefs and U. Gupta, "Traumas of a New Entrepreneur," *Wall Street Journal* (May 10, 1989), p. B1.

55. N. C. Churchill and V. L. Lewis, "The Five Stages of Small Business Growth," *Harvard Business Review* (May–June 1983), pp. 30–50. The life cycle concept is supported by research by M. Beverland, "Organizational Life Cycles in Small Enterprises," paper presented to the 45th International Conference on Small Business (ICSB) World Conference (Brisbane, Australia, June 7–10, 2000).

56. J. W. Petty and W. D. Bygrave, "What Does Finance Have to Say to the Entrepreneur?" *Journal of Small Business Finance* (Spring 1993), pp. 125–137.

57. K. D. Brouthers, F. Andriessen, and J. Nicolaes, "Driving Blind: Strategic Decision-Making in Small Companies," *Long Range Planning* (February 1998), pp. 130–138.

58. See C. Farrell, K. Rebello, R. D. Hof, and M. Maremont, "The Boom in IPOs," *Business Week* (December 18, 1995), pp. 64–72, and S. Gruner, "When Mom & Pop Go Public," *Inc.* (December 1996), pp. 66–73.

59. A. Caruana, M. H. Morris, and A. J. Vella, "The Effect of Centralization and Formalization on Entrepreneurship in Export Firms," *Journal of Small Business Management* (January 1998), pp. 16–29.

60. F. David, D. Kelley, and F. David, "Small Business Owner Succession Planning: An Empirical Study," *Management in Practice*, Society for the Advancement of Management, No. 1 (2002), p. 3.

61. M. C. Sonfield, R. N. Lussier, S. Pfeifer, S. Manikutty, L. Maherault, and L. Verdier, "A Cross-National Investigation of First-Generation and Subsequent-Generation Family Members," paper presented to the Small Business Institute Conference (Clearwater, FL, February 12–14, 2004).

62. J. Magretta, "Governing the Family-Owned Enterprise: An Interview with Finland's Krister Ahlstrom," *Harvard Business Review* (January–February 1998), pp. 113–123.

63. "Passing on the Crown," *Economist* (November 6, 2004), pp. 69–71.

64. M. K. Allio, "Family Businesses: Their Virtues, Vices, and Strategic Path," *Strategy & Leadership*, Vol. 32, No. 4 (2004), pp. 24–33; J. Weber, L. Lavelle, T. Lowry, W. Zellner, and A. Barrett, "Family, Inc.," *Business Week* (November 10, 2003), pp. 100–114.

65. S. Birley, D. Ng, and A. Godfrey, "The Family and the Business," *Long Range Planning* (December 1999), pp. 598–608; "Passing on the Crown," *Economist* (November 6, 2004), pp. 69–71.

66. J. Magretta, "Governing the Family-Owned Enterprise: An Interview with Finland's Krister Ahlstrom," *Harvard Business Review* (January–February 1998), p. 119.

67. "Family Business: Why Firms Do Well When Founders Are at the Helm?" *Knowledge @ Wharton* (October 20–November 2, 2004).

68. N. C. Churchill and K. J. Hatten, "Non-Market-Based Transfers of Wealth and Power: A Research Framework for Family Businesses," *American Journal of Small Business* (Winter 1987), pp. 51–64.

69. J. L. Ward and C. E. Aronoff, "Shirt Sleeves to Shirt Sleeves," *Nation's Business* (September 1992), pp. 62–63.

70. "Passing on the Crown," *Economist* (November 6, 2004), pp. 69–71.

71. J. Applegate, "Business People in Bermuda Get Sloppy Without Taxes," *Des Moines Register* (July 6, 1992), p. 8B.

72. P. L. Huff, R. M. Harper, Jr., and A. E. Eikner, "Are There Differences in Liquidity and Solvency Measures Based on Company Size?" *American Business Review* (June 1999), pp. 96–106.

73. R. I. Levin and V. R. Travis, "Small Company Finance: What the Books Don't Say," *Harvard Business Review* (November–December 1987), pp. 30–32.

74. M. Gladwell, *The Tipping Point* (New York: Little, Brown and Co., 2000).

75. M. Henricks, "Big Tippers," *Entrepreneur* (December 2000), pp. 95–96.

76. D. Brady, "The Brains Behind Blackberry," *Business Week* (April 19, 2004), pp. 55–56.

77. *Pocket World in Figures 2004* (London: Economist and Profile Books, 2003), p. 58.

78. R. Florida, "Breakthrough Ideas for 2004: No Monopoly on Creativity," *Harvard Business Review* (February 2004), pp. 14–15.

Chapter 14

1. R. Imrie, "Ink Venture Reaps Profits for High-Tech Monks," *Des Moines Register* (February 27, 2004), p. 3D; G. Williams, "Charity Begins at Work," *Entrepreneur* (December 2005), p. 40.

2. C. Penttila, "Heart of Gold," *Entrepreneur* (September 2004), pp. 19–22.

3. *Ibid.*, p. 22.

4. P. F. Drucker, "What Business Can Learn from Nonprofits," *Harvard Business Review* (July–August 1989), p. 89.

5. "The Non-Profit Sector: Love or Money," *The Economist* (November 14, 1998), pp. 68–73.

6. G. Rudney, "The Scope and Dimensions of Nonprofit Activity," in *The Nonprofit Sector: A Research Handbook*, edited by W. W. Powell (New Haven, CT: Yale University Press, 1987), p. 56; C. P. McLaughlin, *The Management of Nonprofit Organizations* (New York: John Wiley & Sons, 1986), p. 4.

7. M. O'Neill, *The Third America* (San Francisco: Jossey-Bass, 1989).

8. K. Ascher and B. Nare, "Strategic Planning in the Public Sector," *International Review of Strategic Management*, Vol. 1, edited by D. E. Hussey (New York: John Wiley & Sons, 1990), pp. 297–315; I. Unterman and R. H. Davis, *Strategic Management of Not-for-Profit Organizations* (New York: Praeger Press, 1984), p. 2.

9. P. V. Jenster and G. A. Overstreet, "Planning for a Non-Profit Service: A Study of U.S. Credit Unions," *Long Range Planning* (April 1990), pp. 103–111; G. J. Medley, "Strategic Planning for the World Wildlife Fund," *Long Range Planning* (February 1988), pp. 46–54.

10. J. G. Simon, "The Tax Treatment of Nonprofit Organizations: A Review of Federal and State Policies," in *The Nonprofit Sector: A Research Handbook*, edited by W. W. Powell (New Haven, CT: Yale University Press, 1987), pp. 67–98.

11. B. P. Keating and M. O. Keating, *Not-for-Profit* (Glen Ridge, NJ: Thomas Horton & Daughters, 1980), p. 21.

12. K. A. Froelich, "Business Management in Nonprofit Organizations," paper presented to the Midwest Management Society (Chicago, 1995).

13. J. D. Hunger and T. L. Wheelen, "Is Strategic Management Appropriate for Not-for-Profit Organizations?" in *Handbook of Business Strategy, 1989/90 Yearbook*, edited by H. E. Glass (Boston: Warren, Gorham & Lamont, 1989), pp. 3.1–3.8. The contention that the pattern of environmental influence on the organization's strategic decision making derives from the organization's source(s) of income agrees with the authorities in the field. See R. E. Emerson, "Power-Dependence Relations," *American Sociological Review* (February 1962), pp. 31–41; J. D. Thompson, *Organizations in Action* (New York: McGraw-Hill, 1967), pp. 30–31, and J. Pfeffer and G. R. Salancik, *The External Control of Organizations: A Resource Dependence Perspective* (New York: HarperCollins, 1978), p. 44.

14. M. Goold, "Institutional Advantage: A Way into Strategic Management in Not-for-Profit Organizations," *Long Range Planning* (April 1997), pp. 291–293.

15. K. Ascher and B. Nare, "Strategic Planning in the Public Sector," *International Review of Strategic Management*, Vol. 1, edited by D. E. Hussey (New York: John Wiley & Sons, 1990), pp. 297–315; R. McGill, "Planning for Strategic Performance in Local Government," *Long Range Planning* (October 1988), pp. 77–84.

16. Lorna Lavender, Supervisor of Ames (Iowa) Animal Shelter, quoted by K. Petty, "Animal Shelter Cares for Homeless," *ISU Daily* (July 25, 1996), p. 3.

17. E. Ferlie, "The Creation and Evolution of Quasi Markets in the Public Sector: A Problem for Strategic Management," *Strategic Management Journal* (Winter 1992), pp. 79–97. Research has found that profit-making hospitals have more mission statement components dealing with principal services, target customers, and geographic domain than do not-for-profit hospitals. See R. Subramanian, K. Kumar, and C. C. Yauger, "Mission Statements of Hospitals: An Empirical Analysis of Their Contents and Their Relationship to Organizational Factors," *Journal of Business Strategies* (Spring 1993), pp. 63–78.

18. W. H. Newman and H. W. Wallender III, "Managing Not-for-Profit Enterprises," *Academy of Management Review* (January 1978), p. 26.

19. *Ibid.*, p. 27. The following discussion of the effects of these constraining characteristics is taken from pp. 27–31.

20. J. Denis, A. Langley, and D. Lozeau, "Formal Strategy in Public Hospitals," *Long Range Planning* (February 1991), pp. 71–82.

21. F. Heffron, *Organization Theory and Public Administration* (Upper Saddle River, NJ: Prentice Hall, 1989), p. 132.

22. V. K. Rangan, "Lofty Missions, Down-to-Earth Plans," *Harvard Business Review* (March 2004), pp. 112–119.

23. F. Heffron, *Organization Theory and Public Administration* (Upper Saddle River, NJ: Prentice Hall, 1989), pp. 103–115.

24. R. T. Ingram, *Ten Basic Responsibilities of Nonprofit Boards*, 2nd ed. (Washington, DC: National Center for Nonprofit Boards, 1997), pp. 9–10.

25. A. C. Smith, "Endowment Use Overlooked," *St. Petersburg Times* (June 23, 2000), p. 3B. Eckerd's board was strongly criticized because it had tolerated improper financial practices on the part of the president and had allowed the college's endowment to dissipate.

26. I. Unterman and R. H. Davis, *Strategic Management of Not-for-Profit Organizations* (New York: Praeger Press, 1984), p. 174; J. A. Alexander, M. L. Fennell, and M. T. Halpern, "Leadership Instability in Hospitals: The Influence of Board–CEO Relations and Organizational Growth and Decline," *Administrative Science Quarterly* (March 1993), pp. 74–99.

27. K. A. Froelich, "Business Management in Nonprofit Organizations," paper presented to the Midwest Management Society (Chicago, 1995), p. 9.

28. R. M. Kanter and D. V. Summers, "Doing Well While Doing Good: Dilemmas of Performance Measurement in Nonprofit Organizations and the Need for a Multiple-Constituency Approach," in *The Nonprofit Sector: A Research Handbook*, edited by W. W. Powell (New Haven, CT: Yale University Press, 1987), p. 163.

29. J. P. Dalsimer, *Understanding Nonprofit Financial Statement: A Primer for Board Members*, 2nd ed. (Washington, DC: National Center for Nonprofit Boards, 1997), p. 17.

30. V. K. Rangan, "Loft Missions: Down-to-Earth Plans," *Harvard Business Review* (March 2004), pp. 112–119.

31. *Ibid.*, p. 115.

32. R. P. Nielsen, "SMR Forum: Strategic Piggybacking—A Self-Subsidizing Strategy for Nonprofit Institutions," *Sloan Management Review* (Summer 1982), pp. 65–69; R. P. Nielsen, "Piggybacking for Business and Nonprofits: A Strategy for Hard Times," *Long Range Planning* (April 1984), pp. 96–102.

33. D. C. Bacon, "Nonprofit Groups: An Unfair Edge?" *Nation's Business* (April 1989), pp. 33–34; "Universities Push Auxiliary Services to Generate More Revenue," *Wall Street Journal* (April 27, 1995), p. A1.

34. M. Langley, "Nonprofit Hospitals Sometimes Are That in Little but Name," *Wall Street Journal* (July 14, 1997), p. A1. See also D. Brady, "When Nonprofits Go After Profits," *Business Week* (June 26, 2000), pp. 173–178; E. Skloot, "Should Not-for-Profits Go into Business?" *Harvard Business Review* (January–February 1983), p. 21; E. Felsenthal, "As Nonprofits Add Sidelines, IRS Takes Aim," *Wall Street Journal* (May 3, 1996), p. B1.

35. C. Penttila, "Heart of Gold," *Entrepreneur* (September 2004), p. 22.

36. R. P. Nielsen, "Piggybacking Strategies for Nonprofits: A Shared Costs Approach," *Strategic Management Journal* (May–June 1986), pp. 209–211.

37. "Universities Push Auxiliary Services to Generate More Revenue" (Business Bulletin), *Wall Street Journal* (April 27, 1995), p. A1.

38. R. A. Krishnan, S. Joshi, and H. Krishnan, "The Influence of Mergers on Firms' Product-Mix Strategies," *Strategic Management Journal* (June 2004), pp. 587–611.

39. *Ibid.*

40. K. G. Provan, "Interorganizational Cooperation and Decision Making Autonomy in a Consortium Multihospital System," *Academy of Management Review* (July 1984), pp. 494–504; R. D. Luke, J. W. Begun, and D. D. Pointer, "Quasi-Firms: Strategic Interorganizational Forms in the Health Care Industry," *Academy of Management Review* (January 1989), pp. 9–19.

41. "More Colleges Are Opting for Mergers," *The (Ames, IA) Daily Tribune* (August 12, 1998), p. B3.

42. *Pocket World in Figures 2004* (London: Economist and Profile Books, 2003), p. 95.

43. *Ibid.*, p. 83.

Chapter 15

1. M. Heimer, "Wall Street Sherlock," *Smart Money* (July 2003), pp. 103–107.

2. *Ibid.*, p. 107.

3. *Ibid.*, p. 105.

4. *Ibid.*, p. 105.

5. *Ibid.*, p. 105.

6. M. Vanac, "What's a Novice Investor to Do?" *Des Moines Register* (November 30, 1997), p. 3G.

7. A. R. Sorking, "New Path on Mergers Could Contain Loopholes," *The (Ames, IA) Daily Tribune* (January 9, 2001), p. B7; "Firms Resist Effort to Unveil True Costs of Doing Business," *USA Today* (July 3, 2000), p. 10A.

8. M. S. Fridson, *Financial Statement Analysis* (New York: John Wiley & Sons, 1991), pp. 192–194.

9. D. H. Bangs, *Managing by the Numbers* (Dover, NH: Upstart Publications, 1992), pp. 106–107.

10. "Consumer Prices," *Economist* (May 8, 2004), p. 98.

Glossary

10-K form An SEC form containing income statements, balance sheets, cash flow statements, and information not usually available in an annual report. p. 355

10-Q form An SEC form containing quarterly financial reports. p. 355

360-degree performance appraisal An evaluation technique in which input is gathered from multiple sources. p. 197

Absorptive capacity A firm's ability to value, assimilate, and utilize new external knowledge. p. 303

Acquisition The purchase of a company that is completely absorbed by the acquiring corporation. p. 166

Action plan A plan that states what actions are going to be taken, by whom, during what time frame, and with what expected results. p. 253

Activity ratios Ratios that indicate how well a corporation is managing its operations. p. 356

Activity-based costing (ABC) An accounting method for allocating indirect and fixed costs to individual products or product lines based on the value-added activities going into that product. p. 266

Adaptive mode A decision-making mode characterized by reactive solutions to existing problems, rather than a proactive search for new opportunities. p. 21

Advisory board A group of external business people who voluntarily meet periodically with the owners/managers of the firm to discuss strategic and other issues. p. 324

Affiliated directors Directors who, though not really employed by the corporation, handle the legal or insurance work for the company or are important suppliers. p. 40

Agency theory A theory that states that problems arise in corporations because the agents (top management) are not willing to bear responsibility for their decisions unless they own a substantial amount of stock in the corporation. p. 39

Altman's Bankruptcy Formula A formula used to estimate how close a company is to declaring bankruptcy. p. 360

Analytical portfolio manager A type of general manager needed to execute a diversification strategy. p. 241

Annual report A document published each year by a company to show its financial condition and products. p. 355

Assessment centers An approach to evaluating the suitability of a person for a position. p. 244

Assimilation A strategy which involves the domination of one corporate culture over another. p. 252

Association of South East Asian Nations (ASEAN) A regional trade association composed of Asian countries of Brunei, Indonesia, Malaysia, the Philippines, Singapore, Thailand, and Vietnam. p. 7

Autonomous (self-managing) work teams A group of people who work together without a supervisor to plan, coordinate, and evaluate their own work. p. 125

Backward integration Assuming a function previously provided by a supplier. p. 167

Balanced scorecard Combines financial measures with operational measures on customer satisfaction, internal processes, and the corporation's innovation and improvement activities. p. 272

Bankruptcy A retrenchment strategy which forfeits management of the firm to the courts in return for some settlement of the corporation's obligations. p. 178

Basic R&D Research and development that is conducted by scientists in well-equipped laboratories where the focus is on theoretical problem areas. p. 121

BCG (Boston Consulting Group) Growth-Share Matrix A simple way to portray a corporation's portfolio of products or divisions. p. 179

Behavior control A control that specifies how something is to be done through policies, rules, standard operating procedures, and orders from a superior. p. 265

Behavior substitution A phenomenon that occurs when people substitute activities that do not lead to goal accomplishment for activities that do lead to goal accomplishment because the wrong activities are being rewarded. p. 281

Benchmarking The process of measuring products, services, and practices against those of competitors or companies recognized as industry leaders. p. 275

Best practice A procedure that is followed by successful companies. p. 311

Board of director responsibilities Commonly agreed obligations of directors include: setting corporate strategy, overall direction, mission or vision; hiring and firing the CEO and top management; controlling, monitoring, or supervising top management; reviewing and approving the use of resources; and caring for shareholder interest. p. 36

Board of directors continuum A range of the possible degree of involvement by the Board of Directors (from low to high) in the strategic management process. p. 37

BOT (build-operate-transfer) concept A type of international entry option for a company. After building a facility, the company operates the facility for a fixed period of time during which it earns back its investment, plus a profit. p. 174

Brainstorming The process of proposing ideas in a group without first mentally screening them. p. 96

Brand A name that identifies a particular company's product in the mind of the consumer. p. 118

Budget A statement of a corporation's programs in terms of money required. p. 17

Business model The mix of activities a company performs to earn a profit. p. 110

Business plan A written strategic plan for a new entrepreneurial venture. p. 322

Business policy A previous name for strategic management; it has a general management orientation and tends to look inward with concern for integrating the corporation's many functional activities. p. 3

Business strategy Competitive and cooperative strategies that emphasize improvement of the competitive position of a corporation's products or services in a specific industry or market segment. p. 15

Cannibalize To replace popular products before they reach the end of their life cycle. p. 90

Capability A corporation's ability to exploit its resources. p. 106

Capital budgeting The process of analyzing and ranking possible investments in terms of the additional outlays and additional receipts that will result from each investment. p. 120

Captive company strategy Dedicating a firm's productive capacity as primary supplier to another company in exchange for a long-term contract. p. 177

Cash cow A product that brings in far more money than is needed to maintain its market share. p. 180

Categorical imperatives Kant's two principles to guide actions: A person's action is ethical only if that person is willing for that same action to be taken by everyone who is in a similar situation and a person should never treat another human being simply as a means but always as an end. p. 67

Cautious profit planner The type of leader needed for a corporation choosing to follow a stability strategy. p. 241

Cellular organization A structure composed of cells (self-managing teams, autonomous business units, etc.) that can operate alone but can interact with other cells to produce a more potent and competent business mechanism. p. 229

Center of excellence A designated area in which a company has a capability or a core competence. p. 184

Center of gravity The part of the industry value chain that is most important to the company and the point where the company's greatest expertise and capabilities lay. p. 112

Central American Free Trade Agreement (CAFTA) A regional trade association composed of El Salvador, Guatemala, Nicaragua, Costa Rica, the United States, and the Dominican Republic. p. 7

Clusters Geographic concentrations of interconnected companies and industries. p. 107

Codes of ethics A code that specifies how an organization expects its employees to behave while on the job. p. 66

Codetermination The inclusion of a corporation's workers on its board of directors. p. 42

Collusion The active cooperation of firms within an industry to reduce output and raise prices in order to get around the normal economic law of supply and demand. This practice is usually illegal. p. 157

Commodity A product whose characteristics are the same regardless of who sells it. p. 84

Common-size statements Income statements and balance sheets in which the dollar figures have been converted into percentages. p. 359

Competency A cross-functional integration and coordination of capabilities. p. 106

Competitive intelligence A formal program of gathering information about a company's competitors. p. 92

Competitive scope The breadth of a company's or a business unit's target market. p. 147

Competitive strategy A strategy that states how a company or a business unit will compete in an industry. p. 145

Competitors The companies that offer the same products or services as the subject company. p. 94

Complementor A company or an industry whose product works well with another industry's or firm's product and without which a product would lose much of its value. p. 86

Complication to evaluation and control Constraints in not-for-profit organizations that make it difficult to properly evaluate and control performance. p. 346

Complication to strategy formulation Constraints in not-for-profit organizations that make it difficult to formulate a new strategy. p. 345

Complication to strategy implementation Constraints in not-for-profit organizations that make it difficult to implement a new strategy. p. 346

Concentration A corporate growth strategy which concentrates a corporation's resources on competing in one industry. p. 166

Concentric diversification A diversification growth strategy in which a firm uses its current strengths to diversify into related products in another industry. p. 170

Concurrent engineering A process in which specialists from various functional areas work side-by-side rather than sequentially in an effort to design new products. p. 125

Conglomerate diversification A diversification growth strategy that involves a move into another industry to provide products unrelated to its current products. p. 170

Conglomerate structure An assemblage of legally independent firms (subsidiaries) operating under one corporate umbrella but controlled through the subsidiaries' boards of directors. p. 115

Connected line batch flow A part of a corporation's manufacturing strategy in which components are standardized and each machine functions like a job shop but is positioned in the same order as the parts are processed. p. 194

Consensus A situation in which all parties agree to one alternative. p. 207

Consolidated industry An industry in which a few large companies dominate. p. 86

Consolidation The second phase of a turnaround strategy that implements a program to stabilize the corporation. p. 177

Constant dollar Dollars adjusted for inflation. p. 360

Constraint on strategic management A characteristic peculiar to a not-for-profit organization that constrains its behavior and affects its strategic management. p. 344

Continuous improvement A system developed by Japanese firms in which teams strive constantly to improve manufacturing processes. p. 195

Continuous systems Production organized in lines on which products can be continuously assembled or processed. p. 124

Continuum of sustainability A representation which indicates how durable and imitable an organization's resources and capabilities are. p. 109

Contraction The first phase of a turnaround strategy which includes a general across-the-board cutback in size and costs. p. 177

Cooperative strategies Strategies that involve working with other firms to gain competitive advantage within an industry. p. 157

Co-opetition A term used to describe simultaneous competition and cooperation among firms. p. 161

Core competency A collection of corporate capabilities that cross divisional borders and are wide spread within a corporation, and is something that a corporation can do exceedingly well. p. 106

Corporate brand A type of brand in which the company's name serves as the brand name. p. 119

Corporate capabilities See capability. p. 106

Corporate culture A collection of beliefs, expectations, and values learned and shared by a corporation's members and transmitted from one generation of employees to another. p. 116

Corporate culture pressure A force from existing corporate culture against the implementation of a new strategy. p. 206

Corporate entrepreneurship Also called intrapreneurship, the creation of a new business within an existing organization. p. 306

Corporate governance The relationship among the board of directors, top management, and shareholders in determining the direction and performance of a corporation. p. 36

Corporate parenting A view that considers the corporation in terms of resources and capabilities that can be used to build business unit value as well as generate synergies across business units. p. 183

Corporate reputation A widely held perception of a company by the general public. p. 119

Corporate scenario Pro forma balance sheets and income statements that forecast the effect that each alternative strategy will likely have on return on investment. p. 202

Corporate stakeholders Groups that affect or are affected by the achievement of a firm's objectives. p. 59

Corporate strategy A strategy that states a company's overall direction in terms of its general attitude toward growth and the management of its various business and product lines. p. 164

Corporation A mechanism legally established to allow different parties to contribute capital, expertise, and labor for their mutual benefit. p. 36

Cost focus A low-cost competitive strategy that concentrates on a particular buyer group or geographic market and attempts to serve only that niche. p. 149

Cost leadership A low-cost competitive strategy that aims at the broad mass market. p. 148

Cost proximity A process that involves keeping the higher price a company charges for higher quality close enough to that of the competition so that customers will see the extra quality as being worth the extra cost. p. 149

Crisis of autonomy A time when people managing diversified product lines need more decision-making freedom than top management is willing to delegate to them. p. 222

Crisis of control A time when business units act to optimize their own sales and profits without regard to the overall corporation. p. 222 See also *suboptimization*.

Crisis of leadership A time when an entrepreneur is personally unable to manage a growing company. p. 222

Cross-functional work teams A work team composed of people from multiple functions. p. 214

Cultural integration The extent to which units throughout an organization share a common culture. p. 116

Cultural intensity The degree to which members of an organizational unit accept the norms, values, or other culture content associated with the unit. p. 116

Deculturation The disintegration of one company's culture resulting from unwanted and extreme pressure from another to impose its culture and practices. p. 252

Dedicated transfer line A highly automated assembly line making one mass-produced product using little human labor. p. 194

Defensive centralization A process in which top management of a not-for-profit retains all decision-making authority so that lower-level managers cannot take any actions to which the sponsors may object. p. 346

Defensive tactic A tactic in which a company defends its current market. p. 155

Delphi technique A forecasting technique in which experts independently assess the probabilities of specified events. These assessments are combined and sent back to each expert for fine-tuning until agreement is reached. p. 96

Devil's advocate An individual or a group assigned to identify the potential pitfalls and problems of a proposal. p. 207

Dialectical inquiry A decision-making technique that requires that two proposals using different assumptions be generated for consideration. p. 208

Differentiation A competitive strategy that is aimed at the broad mass market and that involves the creation of a product or service that is perceived throughout its industry as unique. p. 147

Differentiation focus A differentiation competitive strategy that concentrates on a particular buyer group, product line segment, or geographic market. p. 149

Differentiation strategy See differentiation. p. 147

Dimensions of national culture A set of five dimensions by which each nation's unique culture can be identified. p. 256

Directional strategy A strategy that is composed of three general orientations: growth, stability, and retrenchment. p. 165

Distinctive competencies A firm's core competencies which are superior to those of competitors. p. 106

Diversification A basic growth strategy that implements the expansion of product lines or expanding into another industry. p. 170

Divestment A sell-out strategy that refers to selling off a division of a corporation with low growth potential. p. 178

Divisional structure An organizational structure in which employees tend to be functional specialists organized according to product/market distinctions. p. 115

Downsizing Planned elimination of positions or jobs. p. 245

Due care The obligation of board members to closely monitor and evaluate top management. p. 37

Durability The rate at which a firm's underlying resources and capabilities depreciate or become obsolete. p. 109

Dynamic industry expert A leader with a great deal of experience in a particular industry appropriate for executing a concentration strategy. p. 241

Dynamic pricing A marketing practice in which different customers pay different prices for the same product or service. p. 191

Earnings per share (EPS) A calculation that is determined by dividing net earnings by the number of shares of common stock issued. p. 268

Economic value added (EVA) A shareholder value method of measuring corporate and divisional performance. Measures after-tax operating income minus the total annual cost of capital. p. 270

Economies of scale A process in which unit costs are reduced by making large numbers of the same product. p. 125

Economies of scope A process in which unit costs are reduced when the value chains of two separate products or services share activities, such as the same marketing channels or manufacturing facilities. p. 125

EFAS (External Factor Analysis Summary) Table A table that organizes external factors into opportunities and threats and how well management is responding to these specific factors. p. 97

80/20 rule Rule stating that one should monitor those 20% of the factors that determine 80% of the results. p. 282

Electronic commerce The use of the Internet to conduct business transactions. p. 7

Engineering (or process) R&D R&D concentrating on quality control and the development of design specifications and improved production equipment. p. 121

Enterprise resource planning (ERP) software Software that unites all of a company's major business activities, from order processing to production, within a single family of software modules. p. 278

Enterprise risk management (ERM) A corporate-wide, integrated process to manage the uncertainties that could negatively or positively influence the achievement of the corporation's objectives. p. 267

Entrepreneur A person who initiates and manages a business undertaking and who assumes risk for the sake of a profit. p. 319

Entrepreneurial characteristics Traits of an entrepreneur which lead to a new venture's success. p. 328

Entrepreneurial mode Strategic decision making by one powerful individual in which the focus is on opportunities; problems are secondary. p. 20

Entrepreneurial venture Any new business whose primary goals are profitability and growth and that can be characterized by innovative strategic practices. p. 318

Entry barriers An obstruction that makes it difficult for a company to enter an industry. p. 83

Environmental scanning The monitoring, evaluation, and dissemination of information from the external and internal environments to key people within the corporation. p. 73

Environmental uncertainty The degree of complexity plus the degree of change existing in an organization's external environment. p. 72

Ethics The consensually accepted standards of behavior for an occupation, trade, or profession. p. 66

European Union (EU) A regional trade association composed of 25 European countries. p. 7

Evaluation and control A process in which corporate activities and performance results are monitored so that actual performance can be compared with desired performance. p. 262

Evaluation and control information Information to use in the evaluation and control of performance. p. 263

Evaluation and control process A process in which corporate activities and performance results are monitored so that actual performance can be compared with desired performance. p. 262

Executive leadership The directing of activities toward the accomplishment of corporate objectives. p. 49

Executive succession The process of grooming and replacing a key top manager. p. 243

Executive type An individual with a particular mix of skills and experiences. p. 241

Exit barrier An obstruction that keeps a company from leaving an industry. p. 84

Expense center A business unit that uses money but contributes to revenues only indirectly. p. 274

Experience curve A conceptual framework which states that unit production costs decline by some fixed percentage each time the total accumulated volume of production in units doubles. p. 181

Expert opinion A nonquantitative forecasting technique in which authorities in a particular area attempt to forecast likely developments. p. 96

Explicit knowledge Knowledge that can be easily articulated and communicated. p. 109

Exporting Shipping goods produced in a company's home country to other countries for marketing. p. 171

External environment Forces outside an organization that are not typically within the short-run control of top management. p. 11

External strategic factor Environmental trend with both high probability of occurrence and high probability of impact on the corporation. p. 82

Extranet An information network within an organization that is available to key suppliers and customers. p. 128

Extrapolation A form of forecasting which extends present trends into the future. p. 96

Factor affecting new venture success An issue that has a substantial impact on a new venture's performance. p. 327

Family business A company that is either owned or dominated by relatives. p. 332

Family directors Board members who are relatives of the founder and own significant blocks of stock. p. 40

Financial leverage The ratio of total debt to total assets. p. 120

Financial strategy A functional strategy to make the best use of corporate monetary assets. p. 191

First mover The first company to manufacture and sell a new product or service. p. 154

Flexible manufacturing A type of manufacturing that permits the low-volume output of custom-tailored products at relatively low unit costs through economies of scope. p. 125

Forward integration Assuming a function previously provided by a distributor. p. 167

14-A form An SEC form containing proxy statements and information on a company's board of directors. p. 355

Fragmented industry An industry in which no firm has large market share and each firm serves only a small piece of the total market. p. 86

Franchising An international entry strategy in which a firm grants rights to another company/individual to open a retail store using the franchiser's name and operating system. p. 173

Free cash flow The amount of money a new owner can take out of a firm without harming the business. p. 269

Full vertical integration A growth strategy under which a firm makes 100% of its key supplies internally and completely controls its distributors. p. 167

Functional strategy An approach taken by a functional area to achieve corporate and business unit objectives and strategies by maximizing resource productivity. p. 189

Functional structure An organizational structure in which employees tend to be specialists in the business functions important to that industry, such as manufacturing, sales, or finance. p. 114

GE Business Screen A portfolio analysis matrix developed by General Electric, with the assistance of the Mc Kinsey and Company consulting firm. p. 181

Geographic-area structure A structure that allows a multinational corporation to tailor products to regional differences and to achieve regional coordination. p. 235

Global industry An industry in which a company manufactures and sells the same products, with only minor adjustments for individual countries around the world. p. 87

Globalization The internationalization of markets and corporations. p. 6

Goal displacement Confusion of means with ends, which occurs when activities originally intended to help managers attain corporate objectives become ends in themselves or are adapted to meet ends other than those for which they were intended. p. 280

Goals An open-ended statement of what one wants to accomplish, with no quantification of what is to be achieved and no time criteria for completion. p. 14

Green-field development An international entry option to build a company's manufacturing plant and distribution system in another country. p. 173

Gross domestic product (GDP) A measure of the total output of goods and services within a country's borders. p. 360

Growth strategies A directional strategy that expands a company's current activities p. 165

Hierarchy of strategy A nesting of strategies by level from corporate to business to functional, so that they complement and support one another. p. 15

Horizontal growth A corporate growth concentration strategy that involves expanding the firm's products into other geographic locations and/or increasing the range of products and services offered to current markets. p. 169

Horizontal integration The degree to which a firm operates in multiple geographic locations at the same point in an industry's value chain. p. 169

Horizontal strategy A corporate parenting strategy that cuts across business unit boundaries to build synergy across business units and to improve the competitive position of one or more business units. p. 185

House of quality A method of managing new product development to help project teams make important design decisions by getting them to think about what users want and how to get it to them most effectively. p. 310

Human resource management (HRM) strategy A functional strategy that makes the best use of corporate human assets. p. 197

Human diversity A mix of people from different races, cultures, and backgrounds in the workplace. p. 127

Hypercompetition An industry situation in which the frequency, boldness, and aggressiveness of dynamic movement by the players accelerates to create a condition of constant disequilibrium and change. p. 90

Idea A concept for a new product or service. p. 321

IFAS (Internal Factor Analysis Summary) Table A table that organizes internal factors into strengths and weaknesses and how well management is responding to these specific factors. p. 129

Imitability The rate at which a firm's underlying resources and capabilities can be duplicated by others. p. 108

Index of R&D effectiveness An index that is calculated by dividing the percentage of total revenue spent on research and development into new product profitability. p. 311

Index of sustainable growth A calculation that shows how much of the growth rate of sales can be sustained by internally generated funds. p. 360

Individual rights approach An ethics behavior guideline that proposes that human beings have certain fundamental rights that should be respected in all decisions. p. 67

Individualism-collectivism (IC) The extent to which a society values individual freedom and independence of action compared with a tight social framework and loyalty to the group. p. 256

Industry A group of firms producing a similar product or service. p. 11

Industry analysis An in-depth examination of key factors within a corporation's task environment. p. 73

Industry matrix A chart that summarizes the key success factors within a particular industry. p. 91

Industry scenario A forecasted description of an industry's likely future. p. 96

Information technology strategy A functional strategy that uses information systems technology to provide competitive advantage. p. 198

Input control A control that specifies resources, such as knowledge, skills, abilities, values, and motives of employees. p. 265

Inside directors An officer or executive employed by a corporation who serves on that company's board of directors; also called management directors. p. 39

Institution theory A concept of organizational adaptation that proposes that organizations can and do adapt to changing conditions by imitating other successful organizations. p. 9

Institutional advantage A benefit for a not-for-profit organization when it performs its tasks more effectively than other comparable organizations. p. 344

Integration A process that involves a relatively balanced give-and-take of cultural and managerial practices between merger partners, with no strong imposition of cultural change on either company. p. 251

Intellectual property Special knowledge used in a new product or process developed by a company for its own use and is usually protected by a patent, copyright, trademark, or trade secret. p. 301

Interlocking directorate A condition that occurs when two firms share a director or when an executive of one firm sits on the board of a second firm. p. 43

Intermittent system A method of manufacturing in which an item is normally processed sequentially, but the work and the sequence of the processes vary. p. 123

Internal environment Variables within the organization not usually within the short run control of top management. p. 11

Internal strategic factors Strengths (core competencies) and weaknesses that are likely to determine whether a firm will be able take advantage of opportunities while avoiding threats. p. 106

International transfer pricing A pricing method used to minimize the effect of taxes on the measurement of performance across international markets. p. 276

Intranet An information network within an organization that also has access to the Internet. p. 128

Investment center A unit in which performance is measured in terms of the difference between the units resources and its services or products. p. 275

ISO 9000 Standards Series An internationally accepted way of objectively documenting a company's high level of quality operations. p. 265

ISO 14000 Standards Series An internationally accepted way to document a company's impact on the environment. p. 265

Issues priority matrix A chart that ranks the probability of occurrence versus the probable impact on the corporation of developments in the external environment. p. 81

Job characteristics model An approach to job design that is based on the belief that tasks can be described in terms of certain objective characteristics and that those characteristics affect employee motivation. p. 231

Job design The design of individual tasks in an attempt to make them more relevant to the company and to the employee. p. 231

Job enlargement Combining tasks to give a worker more of the same type of duties to perform. p. 231

Job enrichment Altering jobs by giving the worker more autonomy and control over activities. p. 231

Job rotation Moving workers through several jobs to increase variety. p. 231

Job shop One-of-a-kind production using skilled labor. p. 194

Joint venture An independent business entity created by two or more companies in a strategic alliance. p. 159

Justice approach An ethical approach which proposes that decision makers be equitable, fair, and impartial in the distribution of costs and benefits. p. 67

Just-In-Time A purchasing concept in which parts arrive at the plant just when they are needed rather than being kept in inventories. p. 196

Key performance measures Essential measures for achieving a desired strategic option—used in the balanced scorecard. p. 272

Key success factors Variables that significantly affect the overall competitive position of a company within a particular industry. p. 91

Late movers Companies that enter a new market only after other companies have done so. p. 154

Law A formal code that permits or forbids certain behaviors. p. 66

Lead director An outside director who calls meetings of the outside board members and coordinates the annual evaluation of the CEO. p. 45

Lead user A customer who is ahead of market trends and has needs that go beyond those of the average user. p. 296

Leading Providing direction to employees to use their abilities and skills most effectively and efficiently to achieve organizational objectives. p. 240

Lean Six Sigma A program developed to identify and improve a poorly performing process. p. 231

Learning organization An organization that is skilled at creating, acquiring, and transferring knowledge and at modifying its behavior to reflect new knowledge and insights. p. 9

Levels of moral development Kohlberg proposed three levels of moral development: preconventional, conventional, and principled. p. 65

Leverage ratio An evaluation of how effectively a company utilizes its resources to generate revenues. p. 356

Leveraged buy-out An acquisition in which a company is acquired in a transaction financed largely by debt—usually obtained from a third party, such as an insurance company or an investment banker. p. 191

Licensing arrangement An agreement in which the licensing firm grants rights to another firm in another country or market to produce and/or sell a branded product. p. 159

Lifestyle company A small business in which the firm is purely an extension of the owner's lifestyle. p. 331

Line extension Using a successful brand name on additional products, such as Arm & Hammer's brand first on baking soda, then on laundry detergents, toothpaste, and deodorants. p. 189

Linkage The connection between the way one value activity (for example, marketing) is performed and the cost of performance of another activity (for example, quality control). p. 113

Liquidation The termination of a firm in which all its assets are sold. p. 178

Liquidity ratio The percentage showing to what degree a company can cover its current liabilities with its current assets. p. 356

Logical incrementalism A decision-making mode, that can be viewed as a synthesis of planning, adaptive, and entrepreneurial modes. p. 21

Logistics strategy A functional strategy that deals with the flow of products into and out of the manufacturing process. p. 196

Long-term contract Agreements between two separate firms to provide agreed-upon goods and services to each other for a specified period of time. p. 169

Long-term evaluation method A method in which managers are compensated for achieving objectives set over a multiyear period. p. 283

Long-term orientation (LT) The extent to which society is oriented toward the long term versus the short term. p. 257

Lower cost strategy A strategy in which a company or business unit designs, produces, and markets a comparable product more efficiently than its competitors. p. 147

Management audit A technique used to evaluate corporate activities. p. 273

Management By Objectives (MBO) An organization wide approach ensuring purposeful action toward desired objectives. p. 254

Management contract Agreements through which a corporation uses some of its personnel to assist a firm in another country for a specified fee and period of time. p. 174

Market development A marketing functional strategy in which a company or business unit captures a larger share of an existing market for current products through market penetration or develops new markets for current products. p. 190

Market location tactics Tactics that determine where a company or business unit will compete. p. 155

Market position Refers to the selection of specific areas for marketing concentration and can be expressed in terms of market, product, and geographical locations. p. 118

Market research A means of obtaining new product ideas by surveying current or potential users regarding what they would like in a new product. p. 297

Market segmentation The division of a market into segments to identify available niches. p. 118

Market value added (MVA) The difference between the market value of a corporation and the capital contributed by shareholders and lenders. p. 271

Marketing mix The particular combination of key variables (product, place, promotion, and price) that can be used to affect demand and to gain competitive advantage. p. 118

Marketing strategy A functional strategy that deals with pricing, selling, and distributing a product. p. 190

Masculinity-femininity (MF) The extent to which society is oriented toward money and things. p. 256

Mass customization The low-cost production of individually customized goods and services. p. 125

Mass production A system in which employees work on narrowly defined, repetitive tasks under close supervision in a bureaucratic and hierarchical structure to produce a large amount of low-cost, standard goods and services. p. 194

Matrix of change A chart that compares target practices (new programs) with existing practices (current activities). p. 216

Matrix structure A structure in which functional and product forms are combined simultaneously at the same level of the organization. p. 226

Mercosur/Mercosul South American free-trade area including Argentina, Brazil, Uruguay, and Paraguay. p. 7

Merger A transaction in which two or more corporations exchange stock, but from which only one corporation survives. p. 166

Mission The purpose or reason for an organization's existence. p. 12

Modular manufacturing A system in which pre-assembled subassemblies are delivered as they are needed to a company's assembly-line workers who quickly piece the modules together into finished products. p. 195

Moral relativism A theory which proposes that morality is relative to some personal, social, or cultural standard, and that there is

no method for deciding whether one decision is better than another. p. 65

Morality Precepts of personal behavior that are based on religious or philosophical grounds. p. 66

Multidomestic industry An industry in which companies tailor their products to the specific needs of consumers in a particular country. p. 87

Multinational corporation (MNC) A company that has significant assets and activities in multiple countries. p. 78

Multiple sourcing A purchasing strategy in which a company orders a particular part from several vendors. p. 195

Multipoint competition A rivalry in which a large multi-business corporation competes against other large multi-business firms in a number of markets. p. 185

Mutual service consortium A partnership of similar companies in similar industries that pool their resources to gain a benefit that is too expensive to develop alone. p. 158

Net present value (NPV) A calculation of the value of a project that is made by predicting the project's payouts, adjusting them for risk, and subtracting the amount invested. p. 205

Network structure An organization (virtual organization)that outsources most of its business functions. p. 228

New entrants Businesses entering an industry that typically bring new capacity to an industry, a desire to gain market share, and substantial resources. p. 83

New product experimentation A method of test marketing the potential of innovative ideas by developing products, probing potential markets with early versions of the products, learning from the probes and probing again. p. 297

No-change strategy A decision to do nothing new; to continue current operations and policies for the foreseeable future. p. 176

North American Free Trade Agreement (NAFTA) Regional free trade agreement between Canada, the United States, and Mexico. p. 7

Not-for-profit organization Private nonprofit corporations and public governmental units or agencies. p. 340

Objectives The end result of planned activity stating what is to be accomplished by when and quantified if possible. p. 14

Offensive tactic A tactic that calls for competing in an established competitor's current market location. p. 155

Open innovation A new approach to R&D in which a firm uses alliances and connections with corporate, government, and academic labs to learn about new developments. p. 193

Operating budget A budget for a business unit that is approved by top management during strategy formulation and implementation. p. 274

Operating cash flow The amount of money generated by a company before the costs of financing and taxes are subtracted. p. 269

Operating leverage The impact of a specific change in sales volume on net operating income. p. 124

Operations strategy A functional strategy that determines how and where a product or service is to be manufactured, the level of vertical integration in the production process, and the deployment of physical resources. p. 193

Opportunity A strategic factor considered using the SWOT analysis. p. 321

Orchestrator A top manager who articulates the need for innovation, provides funding for innovating activities, creates incentives for middle managers to sponsor new ideas, and protects idea/product champions from suspicious or jealous executives. p. 306

Organization slack Unused resources within an organization. p. 166

Organizational analysis Internal scanning concerned with identifying an organization's strengths and weaknesses. p. 106

Organizational learning theory A theory proposing that an organization adjusts to changes in the environment through the learning of its employees. p. 9

Organizational life cycle How organizations grow, develop, and eventually decline. p. 224

Organizational structure The formal setup of a business corporation's value chain components in terms of work flow, communication channels, and hierarchy. p. 114

Output control A control that specifies what is to be accomplished by focusing on the end result of the behaviors through the use of objectives and performance targets. p. 265

Outside directors Members of a board of directors who are not employees of the board's corporation; also called non-management directors. p. 39

Outsourcing A process in which resources are purchased from others through long-term contracts instead of being made within the company. p. 169

Parallel sourcing A process in which two suppliers are the sole suppliers of two different parts, but they are also backup suppliers for each other's parts. p. 196

Pattern of influence A concept stating that influence in strategic management derives from a not-for-profit organization's sources of revenue. p. 343

Pause/proceed with caution strategy A corporate strategy in which nothing new is attempted; an opportunity to rest before continuing a growth or retrenchment strategy. p. 175

Penetration pricing A marketing pricing strategy to obtain dominant market share by using low price. p. 191

Performance The end result of activities, actual outcomes of a strategic management process. p. 18

Performance appraisal system A system to systematically evaluate employee performance and promotion potential. p. 244

Performance gap A performance gap exists when performance does not meet expectations. p. 19

Periodic statistical report Reports summarizing data on key factors such as the number of new customer contracts, volume of received orders, and productivity figures. p. 274

Phases of strategic management Four levels of development through which a firm generally evolves into strategic management. p. 4

Piracy The making and selling counterfeit copies of well-known name-brand products. p. 277

Planning mode A decision-making mode that involves the systematic gathering of appropriate information for situation analysis, the generation of feasible alternative strategies, and the rational selection of the most appropriate strategy. p. 21

Policy A broad guideline for decision making that links the formulation of strategy with its implementation. p. 15

Political strategy A strategy to influence a corporation's stakeholders. p. 205

Population ecology A theory which proposes that once an organization is successfully established in a particular environmental niche, it is unable to adapt to changing conditions. p. 8

Portfolio analysis An approach to corporate strategy in which top management views its product lines and business units as a series of investments from which it expects a profitable return. p. 179

Power distance (PD) The extent to which a society accepts an unequal distribution of influence in organizations. p. 256

Pressure-cooker crisis A situation that exists when employees in collaborative organizations eventually grow emotionally and physically exhausted from the intensity of teamwork and the heavy pressure for innovative solutions. p. 223

Primary activity A manufacturing firm's corporate value chain including inbound logistics, operations process, outbound

logistics, marketing and sales, and service. p. 113

Primary stakeholders A high priority group which affects or is affected by the achievement of a firm's objectives. p. 60

Prime interest rate The rate of interest banks charge on their lowest-risk loans. p. 360

Private nonprofit corporation A non-governmental not-for-profit organization. p. 340

Privatization The selling of state-owned enterprises to private individuals. Also the hiring of a private business to provide services previously offered by a state agency. p. 341

Procedures A list of sequential steps that describe in detail how a particular task or job is to be done. p. 17

Process innovation Improvement to the making and selling of current products. p. 299

Product champion A person who generates a new idea and supports it through many organizational obstacles. p. 306

Product development A marketing strategy in which a company or unit develops new products for existing markets or develops new products for new markets. p. 189

Product innovation The development of a new product or the improvement of an existing product's performance. p. 299

Product life cycle A graph showing time plotted against sales of a product as it moves from introduction through growth and maturity to decline. p. 118

Product R&D Research and development concerned with product or product-packaging improvements. p. 121

Product/market evolution matrix A chart depicting products in terms of their competitive positions and their stages of product/market evolution. p. 305

Product-group structure A structure of a multinational corporation that enables the company to introduce and manage a similar line of products around the world. p. 235

Production sharing The process of combining the higher labor skills and technology available in developed countries with the lower-cost labor available in developing countries. p. 174

Professional liquidator An individual called on by a bankruptcy court to close a firm and sell off its assets. p. 242

Profit center A unit's performance, measured in terms of the difference between revenues and expenditures. p. 274

Profit strategy A strategy that artificially supports profits by reducing investment and short-term discretionary expenditures. p. 176

Profitability ratios Ratios evaluating a company over a period of time. p. 356

Profit-making firm A firm depending on revenues obtained from the sale of its goods and services to customers, who typically pay for the costs and expenses of providing the product or service plus a profit. p. 341

Program A statement of the activities or steps needed to accomplish a single-use plan in strategy implementation. p. 16

Propitious niche A portion of a market that is so well suited to a firm's internal and external environment that other corporations are not likely to challenge or dislodge it. p. 142

Public governmental unit or agency A kind of not-for-profit organization that is established by government or governmental agencies (such as welfare departments, prisons, and state universities). p. 340

Public or collective good Goods that are freely available to all in a society. p. 340

Pull strategy A marketing strategy in which advertising pulls the products through the distribution channels. p. 190

Punctuated equilibrium A point at which a corporation makes a major change in its strategy after evolving slowly through a long period of stability. p. 18

Purchasing power parity (PPP) A measure of the cost, in dollars, of the U.S.-produced equivalent volume of goods that another nation's economy produces. p. 79

Purchasing strategy A functional strategy that deals with obtaining the raw materials, parts and supplies needed to perform the operations functions. p. 195

Push strategy A marketing strategy in which a large amount of money is spent on trade promotion in order to gain or hold shelf space in retail outlets. p. 190

Quality of work life A concept that emphasizes improving the human dimension of work to improve employee satisfaction and union relations. p. 127

Quasi-integration A type of vertical growth/integration in which a company does not make any of its key supplies but purchases most of its requirements from outside suppliers that are under its partial control. p. 169

Question marks New products that have potential for success and need a lot of cash for development. p. 180

R&D intensity A company's spending on research and development as a percentage of sales revenue. p. 120

R&D mix The balance of basic, product, and process research and development. p. 121

R&D strategy A functional strategy that deals with product and process innovation. p. 192

Ratio analysis The calculation of ratios from data in financial statements to identify possible strengths or weaknesses. p. 356

Real options approach An approach to new project investment when the future is highly uncertain. p. 205

Red tape crisis A crisis that occurs when a corporation has grown too large and complex to be managed through formal programs. p. 223

Reengineering The radical redesign of business processes to achieve major gains in cost, service, or time. p. 229

Relationship-based governance A government system perceived to be less transparent and have a higher degree of corruption. p. 64

Repatriation of profits The transfer of profits from a foreign subsidiary to a corporation's headquarters. p. 74

Replicability The ability of competitors to duplicate resources and imitate another firm's success. p. 108

Resources A company's physical, human, and organizational assets that serve as the building blocks of a corporation. p. 106

Responsibility center A unit that is isolated so that it can be evaluated separately from the rest of the corporation. p. 274

Retired executive directors Past leaders of a company kept on the board of directors after leaving the company. p. 40

Retrenchment strategy Corporate strategy to reduce a company's level of activities and to return it to profitability. p. 176

Return on equity (ROE) A measure of performance that is calculated by dividing net income by total equity. p. 268

Return on investment (ROI) A measure of performance that is calculated by dividing net income before taxes by total assets. p. 268

Revenue center A responsibility center in which production, usually in terms of unit or dollar sales, is measured without consideration of resource costs. p. 274

Reverse engineering Taking apart a competitor's product in order to find out how it works. p. 108

Reverse stock split A stock split in which an investor's shares are reduced for the same total amount of money. p. 192

Risk A measure of the probability that one strategy will be effective, the amount of assets the corporation must allocate to that strategy, and the length of time the assets will be unavailable. p. 204

Role of the board of directors in strategic management Three basic tasks (monitor, evaluate and influence, initiate and determine) that are carried out by the board of directors. p. 37

Rule-based governance A governance system based on clearly-stated rules and procedures. p. 64

Sarbanes-Oxley Act Legislation passed by the U.S. Congress in 2002 to promote and formalize greater board independence and oversight. p. 46

Scenario writing A forecasting technique in which focused descriptions of different likely futures are presented in a narrative fashion. p. 96

Secondary stakeholders Lower priority groups which affect or are affected by the achievement of a firm's objectives. p. 60

Sell-out strategy A retrenchment option used when a company has a weak competitive position resulting in poor performance. p. 178

Separation A method of managing the culture of an acquired firm in which the two companies are structurally divided, without cultural exchange. p. 252

SFAS (Strategic Factors Analysis Summary) Matrix A chart that summarizes an organization's strategic factors by combining the external factors from an EFAS table with the internal factors from an IFAS table. p. 139

Shareholder value The present value of the anticipated future stream of cash flows from a business plus the value of the company if it were liquidated. p. 269

Short-term orientation The tendency of managers to consider only current tactical or operational issues and ignore strategic ones. p. 279

Simple structure A structure for new entrepreneurial firms in which the employees tend to be generalists and jacks-of-all-trades. p. 114

Six Sigma A program developed to identify and improve a poorly performing process. p. 230

Skim pricing A marketing strategy in which a company charges a high price while a product is novel and competitors are few. p. 191

Small-business firm An independently owned and operated business that is not dominant in its field and that does not engage in innovative practices. p. 312

SO, ST, WO, WT Strategies A series of possible business approaches based on combinations of opportunities, threats, strengths, and weaknesses. p. 145

Social capital The goodwill of key stakeholders, which can be used for competitive advantage. p. 59

Social entrepreneurship A business in which a not-for-profit organization starts a new venture to achieve social goals. p. 348

Social responsibility The ethical and discretionary responsibilities a corporation owes its stakeholders. p. 56

Societal environment Economic, technological, political-legal, and sociocultural environmental forces that do not directly touch on the short run activities of an organization but influence its long-run decisions. p. 73

Sole sourcing Relying on only one supplier for a particular part. p. 195

Sources of innovation Drucker's proposed seven sources of new ideas that should be monitored by those interested in starting entrepreneurial ventures. p. 326

Sponsor A department manager who recognizes the value of a new idea, helps obtain funding to develop the innovation, and facilitates the implementation of the innovation. p. 306

Stability strategy Corporate strategies to make no change to the company's current direction or activities. p. 175

Staffing Human resource management priorities and use of personnel. p. 240

Stages of corporate development A pattern of structural development that corporations follow as they grow and expand. p. 220

Stages of international development The stages through which international corporations evolve in their relationships with widely dispersed geographic markets and the manner in which they structure their operations and programs. p. 233

Stages of new product development The stages of getting a new innovation into the marketplace. p. 305

Stage-gate process A method of managing new product development to increase the likelihood of launching new products quickly and successfully. The process is a series of steps to move products through the six stages of new product development. p. 309

Staggered board A board on which directors serve terms of more than 1 year so that only a portion of the board of directors stands for election each year. p. 44

Stakeholder analysis The identification and evaluation of corporate stakeholders. p. 60

Stakeholder measure A method of keeping track of stakeholder concerns. p. 269

Stakeholder priority matrix A chart that categorizes stakeholders in terms of their interest in a corporation's activities and their relative power to influence the corporation's activities. p. 205

Standard cost center A responsibility center that is primarily used to evaluate the performance of manufacturing facilities. p. 274

Standard operating procedures Plans that detail the various activities that must be

carried out to complete a corporation's programs. p. 218

Star Market leader that is able to generate enough cash to maintain its high market share. p. 180

Statistical modeling A quantitative technique that attempts to discover causal or explanatory factors that link two or more time series together. p. 96

Steering control Measures of variables that influence future profitability. p. 264

Stewardship theory A theory proposing that executives tend to be more motivated to act in the best interests of the corporation than in their own self-interests. p. 40

Strategic alliance A partnership of two or more corporations or business units to achieve strategically significant objectives that are mutually beneficial. p. 157

Strategic audit A checklist of questions by area or issue that enables a systematic analysis of various corporate functions and activities. p. 23

Strategic audit worksheet A tool used to analyze a case. p. 362

Strategic business unit (SBU) A division or group of divisions composed of independent product-market segments that are given primary authority for the management of their own functions. p. 115

Strategic choice The evaluation of strategies and selection of the best alternative. p. 207

Strategic choice perspective A theory which proposes that organizations adapt to a changing environment and have the opportunity and power to reshape their environment. p. 9

Strategic decision-making process An eight-step process that improves strategic decision making. p. 21

Strategic decision-making process for entrepreneurial venture A set of eight interrelated steps through which strategic decision making is applied to form entrepreneurial ventures. p. 321

Strategic decisions Decisions that deal with the long-run future of an entire organization and are rare, consequential, and directive. p. 20

Strategic factors External and internal factors that determine the future of a corporation. p. 10

Strategic group A set of business units or firms that pursue similar strategies and have similar resources. p. 88

Strategic management A set of managerial decisions and actions that determine the long-run performance of a corporation. p. 3

Strategic myopia The willingness to reject unfamiliar as well as negative information. p. 81

Strategic piggybacking The development of a new activity for a not-for-profit organization that would generate the funds needed to make up the difference between revenues and expenses. p. 348

Strategic planning staff A group of people charged with supporting both top management and business units in the strategic planning process. p. 52

Strategic R&D alliance A coalition through which a firm coordinates its research and development with another firm(s) to offset the huge costs of developing new technology. p. 301

Strategic rollup A means of consolidating a fragmented industry in which an entrepreneur acquires hundreds of owner-operated small businesses resulting in a large firm with economies of scale. p. 152

Strategic type A category of firms based on a common strategic orientation and a combination of structure, culture, and processes that are consistent with that strategy. p. 88

Strategic vision A description of what the company is capable of becoming. p. 49

Strategic window A unique market opportunity that is available only for a limited time. p. 142

Strategic-funds method An evaluation method that encourages executives to look at development expenses as being different from expenses required for current operations. p. 284

Strategies to avoid Strategies sometimes followed by managers who have made a poor analysis or lack creativity. p. 201

Strategy A comprehensive plan that states how a corporation will achieve its mission and objectives. p. 14

Strategy formulation Development of long-range plans for the effective management of environmental opportunities and threats in light of corporate strengths and weaknesses. p. 138

Strategy implementation A process by which strategies and policies are put into action through the development of programs, budgets, and procedures. p. 214

Strategy-culture compatibility The match between existing corporate culture and a new strategy to be implemented. p. 249

Structure follows strategy The process through which changes in corporate strategy normally lead to changes in organizational structure. p. 219

Stuck in the middle A situation in which a company or business unit has not achieved a generic competitive strategy and has no competitive advantage. p. 150

Suboptimization A phenomenon in which a unit optimizes its goal accomplishment to the detriment of the organization as a whole. p. 281

Sub-stages of small business development A set of five levels through which new ventures often develop. p. 330

Substitute products Products that appear to be different but can satisfy the same need as other products. p. 85

Supply-chain management The formation of networks for sourcing raw materials, manufacturing products or creating services, storing and distributing goods, and delivering goods or services to customers and consumers. p. 128

Support activity An activity which ensures that the primary value-chain activities operate effectively and efficiently. p. 113

SWOT analysis Identification of strengths, weaknesses, opportunities, and threats that may be strategic factors for a specific company. p. 138

Synergy A concept which states that the whole is greater than the sum of its parts; that two units will achieve more together than they could separately. p. 170

Tacit knowledge Knowledge that is not easily communicated because it is deeply rooted in employee experience or in a corporation's culture. p. 109

Tactic A short-term operating plan detailing how a strategy is to be implemented. p. 153

Taper integration A type of vertical integration in which a firm internally produces less than half of its own requirements and buys the rest from outside suppliers. p. 168

Task environment The part of the business environment that includes the elements or groups that directly affect the corporation and, in turn, are affected by it. p. 73

Technological competence A corporation's proficiency in managing research personnel and integrating their innovations into its day-to-day operations. p. 121

Technological discontinuity The displacement of one technology by another. p. 122

Technological follower A company that imitates the products of competitors. p. 192

Technological leader A company that pioneers an innovation. p. 192

Technology sourcing A make-or-buy decision that can be important in a firm's R&D strategy. p. 300

Technology transfer The process of taking a new technology from the laboratory to the marketplace. p. 121

Time to market The time from inception to profitability of a new product. p. 289

Timing tactics Tactics that determines when a business will enter a market with a new product. p. 154

Tipping point The point at which a slowly changing situation goes through a massive, rapid change. p. 335

Top management responsibilities Leadership tasks which involve getting things accomplished through and with others in order to meet the corporate objectives. p. 48

Total Quality Management (TQM) An operational philosophy that is committed to customer satisfaction and continuous improvement. p. 255

TOWS Matrix A chart that illustrates how the external opportunities and threats facing a particular corporation can be matched with that company's internal strengths and weaknesses to result in four sets of strategic alternatives. p. 144

Tracking stock A type of common stock that is tied to one portion of a corporation's business. p. 192

Transaction cost economics A theory which proposes that vertical integration is more efficient than contracting for goods and services in the marketplace when the transaction costs of buying goods on the open market become too great. p. 167

Transfer price A practice in which one unit can charge a transfer price for each product it sells to a different unit within a company. p. 275

Transferability The ability of competitors to gather the resources and capabilities necessary to support a competitive challenge. p. 108

Transformational leader A leader who causes change and movement in an organization by providing a strategic vision. p. 49

Transparent The speed with which other firms can understand the relationship of resources and capabilities supporting a successful firm's strategy. p. 108

Trends in governance Current developments in corporate governance. p. 47

Triad The three developed markets of Japan, North America, and Western Europe forming a single market with common needs. p. 79

Triggering event Something that acts as a stimulus for a change in strategy. p. 19

Turnaround specialist A manager who is brought into a weak company to salvage that

company in a relatively attractive industry. p. 242

Turnaround strategy A plan that emphasizes the improvement of operational efficiency when a corporation's problems are pervasive but not yet critical. p. 176

Turnkey operation Contracts for the construction of operating facilities in exchange for a fee. p. 174

Uncertainty avoidance (UA) The extent to which a society feels threatened by uncertain and ambiguous situations. p. 256

Utilitarian approach A theory which proposes that actions and plans should be judged by their consequences. p. 67

Value chain A linked set of value-creating activities that begins with basic raw materials coming from suppliers and ends with distributors getting the final goods into the hands of the ultimate consumer. p. 111

Value-chain partnership A strategic alliance in which one company or unit forms a long-term arrangement with a key supplier or distributor for mutual advantage. p. 159

Vertical growth A corporate growth strategy in which a firm takes over a function previously provided by a supplier or distributor. p. 167

Vertical integration The degree to which a firm operates in multiple locations on an industry's value chain from extracting raw materials to retailing. p. 167

Virtual organization An organizational structure that is composed of a series of project groups or collaborations linked by changing nonhierarchical, cobweb-like networks. p. 228

Virtual team A group of geographically and/or organizationally dispersed coworkers that are assembled using a combination of telecommunications and information technologies to accomplish an organizational task. p. 126

VRIO framework Barney's proposed analysis to evaluate a firm's key resources in terms of value, rareness, imitability, and organization. p. 106

Weighted-factor method A method that is appropriate for measuring and rewarding the performance of top SBU managers and group-level executives when performance factors and their importance vary from one SBU to another. p. 283

Z-value A formula that combines five ratios by weighting them according to their importance to a corporation's financial strength to predict the likelihood of bankruptcy. p. 360

Name Index

Subject Index